Encyclopedia
of Weird War Stories

ALSO BY PAUL GREEN AND FROM MCFARLAND

Encyclopedia of Weird Westerns: Supernatural and Science Fiction Elements in Novels, Pulps, Comics, Films, Television and Games, 2d ed. (2016)

Pete Duel: A Biography, 2d ed. (2015)

Jeffrey Hunter: The Film, Television, Radio and Stage Performances (2014)

Roy Huggins: Creator of Maverick, 77 Sunset Strip, The Fugitive *and* The Rockford Files (2014)

Jennifer Jones: The Life and Films (2011)

A History of Television's The Virginian, *1962–1971* (2006; softcover 2010)

Encyclopedia of Weird War Stories

Supernatural and Science Fiction Elements in Novels, Pulps, Comics, Film, Television, Games and Other Media

Paul Green

McFarland & Company, Inc., Publishers
Jefferson, North Carolina

LIBRARY OF CONGRESS CATALOGUING-IN-PUBLICATION DATA

Names: Green, Paul, 1955– author.
Title: Encyclopedia of weird war stories : supernatural and science fiction elements in novels, pulps, comics, film, television, games and other media / Paul Green.
Other titles: Weird war stories
Description: Jefferson, North Carolina : McFarland & Company, Inc., Publishers, 2017 | Includes bibliographical references and index.
Identifiers: LCCN 2017016900 | ISBN 9781476666723 (softcover : acid free paper) ∞
Subjects: LCSH: War films—Encyclopedias. | War stories—Encyclopedias. | War—Comic books, strips, etc.—Encyclopedias. | War in mass media—Encyclopedias.
Classification: LCC PN1995.9.W3 G74 2017 | DDC 791.43/658—dc23
LC record available at https://lccn.loc.gov/2017016900

BRITISH LIBRARY CATALOGUING DATA ARE AVAILABLE

ISBN (print) 978-1-4766-6672-3
ISBN (ebook) 978-1-4766-2874-5

© 2017 Paul Green. All rights reserved

No part of this book may be reproduced or transmitted in any form or by any means, electronic or mechanical, including photocopying or recording, or by any information storage and retrieval system, without permission in writing from the publisher.

Front cover: *Yankee Doodle Dandy* © 2017 kreicher/iStock; airplanes © 2017 narvikk/iStock

Printed in the United States of America

McFarland & Company, Inc., Publishers
Box 611¡, Jefferson, North Carolina 28640
www.mcfarlandpub.com

To all who have sacrificed their lives
in the service of their country

Table of Contents

Preface 1

Introduction 3

THE ENCYCLOPEDIA 7

Appendix: Weird War Stories by Medium 215

Bibliography 223

Index 225

Preface

The Weird War genre opens up a new world of imagination for both the scholar and casual reader. I explore the many faces of the Weird War genre in films, television, novels, pulps, comic books, animation and games.

The supernatural, science fiction, and fantasy themes are primarily concentrated within a framework of historical wars, with subjects that include the Trojan War, Crusades, English Civil War, American Revolutionary War, Napoleonic Wars, American Civil War, World War I and II, Spanish Civil War, Korean War, Vietnam War and the wars in Iraq and Afghanistan. The nature of the genre lends itself to works that might be offensive to some.

My task is not to control or censor the material published or released, but to document it. Language and images we now consider racist were in common use in past wars. Racial stereotyping was incorporated for propaganda purposes in an effort to dehumanize the enemy. Their inclusion in this book is a historical record of the political and social environment of the time.

My intention is to inform, first and also entertain the reader in the hope of stimulating further interest in the genre. The main body of this book incorporates an A–Z encyclopedia format. Entries are divided into sub-genres that define the Weird War subject according to content. Subjects that appear as entries themselves are featured in **bold type**. An appendix lists the individual entries under their respective subheadings. My choices for inclusion are based on my own research and criteria. I have divided subjects into the following categories.

Weird War [WW]

A war story that includes horror, supernatural or fantasy elements. Themes include: angels, apparitions, astral projection, demons, enchantment, faeries, ghosts, goblins, hexes and curses, magic, mediums, mummies, the occult, possession, shape-shifters, sirens, spirit guides, telekinesis, telepathy, vampires, visions, werewolves, witchcraft and zombies.

Alternative History War [AHW]

A "what if" scenario that speculates an alternative history to various historical wars. This category is only included if the alternate history setting contains supernatural, science fiction or super-hero elements. Alternate history in itself is speculative fiction rather than weird.

Mythological Weird War [MWW]

Stories where mythological gods intervene in historical wars. Usually confined to ancient wars such as the Trojan War, gods also feature in tales of modern warfare.

Science Fiction War [SFW]

Stories involving war and the military may include extraterrestrial intervention in historical wars on Earth, time travel, future technology, medical experimentation and mutants. This category often merges with Alternative History War [AHW] where time travel and future technology introduced into the past can change the outcome of a war.

Super-Hero War [SHW]

Stories, usually in the form of comic books, strips or graphic novels based around super-heroes or villains in a historical war setting. These include heroes or villains with various powers including, flight, invulnerability, x-ray vision, heat vision, telescopic vision, flame-throwing, super-cold breath, super-speed, super-strength, super-lungs, invisibility, mind control, occult powers, stretchable limbs and shape-shifting.

Introduction

The Weird War story has always been with us, beginning with the exploits of mythological gods and their interaction with mankind in the epic poems of the ancient world. Homer's *The Iliad* (760–710 BC) takes place against the backdrop of the Trojan War. The gods Athena and Hera aid the Greeks (Achaeans), while Zeus, Poseidon and Apollo favor the Trojans. With the Trojans gaining the upper hand the reluctant Achilles joins the battle and slays Hector outside the walls of Troy. Achilles accepts a ransom to return Hector's body to the Trojans where Hector receives a hero's funeral.

Homer's influence ensured the Trojan War continued to be a popular subject for ancient poets and playwrights. The celebrated Roman poet Virgil tells the story of Aeneas, a Trojan warrior blessed by the gods, who survives the fall of Troy. *The Aeneid* (29–19 BC) recalls the story of the Trojan wooden horse and the sack of Troy. Aeneas and fellow surviving Trojans journey to Italy, encountering numerous ordeals that include plagues and part female-part bird creatures known as Harpies. Finally Aeneas descends into the underworld to visit his dead father, guided by Sibyl of Cumae. Here Aeneas is shown the future glory of Rome. But on his return from the underworld more trials await in the form of a new enemy named Turnus. Another war begins, but out of the carnage the ancestor of the Romans will triumph.

In Elizabethan England playwright William Shakespeare employed ghosts for dramatic effect in *Richard III*, *Hamlet*, *Macbeth* and *Julius Caesar*. Richard III is visited by the spirits of his victims in his tent before the Battle of Bosworth Field, while the ghost of the murdered Julius Caesar appears to Brutus on the eve of the Battle of Philippi. The supernatural lends itself to the subject of violent, premature death. Ghosts, whether real, imagined or the result of nightmares, are a natural outlet for the horrors of war. It is a time when horror and sadism comes to the surface and all manner of atrocities are allowed. Tales of ghostly apparitions are frequent in the Weird War genre. In war there is no place for appeasement of the enemy. When your life and those of your colleagues are in mortal danger you aim to strike first. Stories of great courage are tempered with accounts of cowardice in battle. This is where we enter the world of trapped souls and haunted battlefields. The American Civil War, in particular, is a favorite of haunted battlefields. These battlefields often lead to unsolved murder mysteries and ghosts seeking a resolution to conflicts that stopped them from crossing over after death.

Sometimes fiction proves more powerful than fact and the lines become blurred. Inspired by the retreat of British forces at Mons, France in August 1914, Arthur Machen's story "The Bowmen," first published in *The Evening News* (London, September 29, 1914) was never meant to be read as a factual account. In his short story St. George and an army of medieval Agincourt bowmen cover the retreat of British armed forces on the battlefield at Mons during World War I. The fictional story perpetuated the legend of the "Angels of Mons" where soldiers claimed this was a real-life event. Such is the power of words that touch a patriotic nerve.

In contrast World War II lends itself to subjects that include medical experimentations

Introduction

that produce super-soldiers or mutants, super-weapons, Nazis meddling in the occult, vampires or zombie armies, and military bases on the moon or Mars. It is the point where the supernatural and science fiction cross paths and the genre broadens its horizon.

In the years between the two World Wars the pulp magazines became a popular medium for fantastic adventures, ranging from detective fiction, to Westerns, to science fiction and the paranormal. Adolf Hitler's advance through Europe offered the American pulp magazine editors a new focus with the introduction of stories featuring Nazis. After the attack on Pearl Harbor in December 1942 science fiction pulp magazines such as *Amazing Stories* extended their reach to Japanese forces with stories involving aliens, time travel, super-weapons, ancient curses and apparitions.

Charles Dana Gibson's cartoon commentary on World War I for *Life* (1916).

As the pulps reached their peak of popularity they morphed into the comic book. We all need heroes, whether earth bound or paranormal. Individuals willing to place others above themselves. And every hero needs a villain to conquer. During times of war, heroes and villains come to the forefront of public consciousness. The comic book industry wasted no time in exploiting their young reader's desire for heroes with the creation of patriotic super-heroes such as *Captain America*. Editors for smaller publishers seized on the opportunity to expand their readership by creating an assortment of lesser known patriotic super-heroes that included, *Captain Battle* and *Captain Fearless*. Their time in the spotlight was often brief before they disappeared into oblivion when World War II ended. With the Axis powers defeated even war heroes such as *Captain America* found it hard to justify their existence and were forced into early retirement. Popular heroes such as *Superman*, *Batman* and *Wonder Woman* survived because their reason for existing wasn't tied to the war.

As a new generation who never experienced World War II began reading comics for the first time the war comic book made a comeback. Most publications included standard World War II stories featuring a heroic figure leading his army, naval or air force unit into battle. But a few strips, such as *Haunted Tank* and *The War That Time Forgot*, ventured into the supernatural and science fiction genres. Then along came Stan Lee, Jack Kirby and the "Marvel Age" where they revived the Timely war heroes *Captain America*, *Sub-Mariner* and *Human Torch* (now in human form and no relation to his World War II counterpart). But as the 1960s came to an end and the war in Vietnam continued to cost young lives super-heroes such as *Captain America* were subject to self doubt. The world was a more complex place than the 1940s and war wasn't always seen as heroic by an anti–Vietnam War youth culture. In this social context the Weird War tale resurfaced in late 1971 with DC Comics' *Weird War Tales*, exclusively dedicated to the supernatural and science fiction war story. The relaxation of guidelines by the Comics Code Authority once again allowed for supernatural subject matter and the use of the word "Weird" in comic book titles. Publisher James Warren had avoided the censorship of the CCA in the 1960s by publishing horror and fantasy comic books in a black-and-white magazine format. His titles, *Creepy* and *Eerie* featured the occasional Weird War strips.

Stories aimed at the juvenile market haven't been confined to comic books or graphic novels. Weird War literature, in the form of novels or illustrated story books, has mainly concentrated on ghost stories, where soldiers seek resolution for their untimely deaths, and time travel, where youngsters find themselves experiencing life during various wars in history. In *Charlotte Sometimes* by Penelope Farmer (Harcourt, Brace & World, 1969), Charlotte Makepeace is still adapting to her new boarding school when she finds herself thrown back in time to 1918 with a new identity. And in 1918 Clare Moby is thrust forward in time to exchange identities with Charlotte. Each girl is living the life of the other displaced in time. In *Rebel Spirits* by Lois Ruby (Point, 2013), Lori Chase moves with her parents to Coolspring Inn in Gettysburg, Pennsylvania. She discovers its reputation for being haunted is deserved when she meets handsome but deceased Civil War Union soldier Nathaniel Pierce in her bedroom. Lori has three days to discover the truth behind his death and charges of treason before he disappears forever.

Meanwhile, old war movies turn up on television where viewers can meet the spirit of *A Guy Named Joe* (1944) and became witness to the strange afterlife of a lovesick bomber pilot played by David Niven in *A Matter of Life and Death* (1946). These films originally acted as tranquilizers to comfort the nerves and point to a deeper meaning behind the deaths of loved ones during World War II. The television anthology shows *One Step Beyond* and Rod Serling's *The Twilight Zone* introduced audiences to many Weird War tales in the late 1950s and early 1960s. Producer Irwin Allen continued the trend in the mid–1960s with various episodes of his action-packed TV series *Voyage to the Bottom of the Sea* and *The Time Tunnel*. The original *Star Trek* series also featured two Weird War episodes from the same period.

In the post–9/11 world, terrorists groups such as Al-Qaeda and ISIS strike a raw nerve and are still being assimilated by the general public. Fiction from this period is grim and based on actual events rather than the paranormal, although this area is gradually being explored. In the film *Djinns* (2010) French soldiers investigating a military plane crash in Algeria are attacked by local Mujahideen fighters. They take cover in a village but cannot find shelter from the evil supernatural enemy that attacks their minds and souls. In *Neither Heaven or Earth* (2015) French soldiers, on a mission in Afghanistan, begin to disappear from their posts. Captain Antares Bonassieu investigates by talking to local villagers, but supernatural forces may be at work. *Camel Spiders* (2011) begins in Afghanistan where the Taliban are attacked by giant spiders known by locals as "Devils of the Sand." Despite initial cynicism U.S. soldiers soon find themselves under attack. The spiders crawl inside the body bag of Corporal Schwalb and on arrival in the U.S. make their exit into the desert of the Southwest where they attack and kill anyone who crosses their path.

Modern warfare is increasingly complex. The wars in Vietnam, Afghanistan, Iraq and Syria have created heated debate. The nature of warfare itself is evolving and expanding to domestic terrorism. It is understandable that so much Weird War fiction is concentrated within the two World Wars where the Nazis and the Japanese were identifiable enemies and events such as Pearl Harbor and D-Day have become ingrained in the public psyche. Winston Churchill's famous speech to the House of Commons in 1940 where he tells the British people, "We shall fight on the beaches, we shall fight on the landing grounds, we shall fight in the fields, and in the streets, we shall fight in the hills; we shall never surrender…" exemplifies the unified spirit of a nation fighting the Nazi enemy. Nobody questions or doubts the evil nature of Adolf Hitler and the Gestapo. The fact the Nazis lost the war in real life gives the reader more room to enjoy alternative history, science fiction and horror scenarios in Weird War fiction, games or films. Present day warfare doesn't offer the same comfort of victory or the distance of time to heal emotional wounds.

Given the seriousness of war some may comment the Weird War genre is a triviality that reduces war to entertainment. That heroes are nothing more than a device to manipulate the readers or audiences into patriotic fervor. Complex because simple. Shades of gray become black-and-white. The truth is the Weird War genre covers a broad spectrum. From the juvenile heroics found in war-time comic books or pulp fiction, to films, television, videogames and novels that either exploit war in simplistic terms or incorporate the supernatural or science fiction as a means to social commentary. In the acclaimed graphic novels *Maus: A Survivor's Tale* and *Maus II: And Here My Troubles Began* by Art Spiegelman (Random House, 1986, 1991), mice represent the Jews and cats represent the evil, sadistic Nazis, in a moving tale of the horrors of the Holocaust. At the opposite end of the spectrum the novel *Mr. Limpet* by Theodore Pratt (Alfred A. Knopf, 1942) features a man who transforms into a talking fish to help the U.S. Navy destroy U-boats in World War II. The story was later adapted into the film *The Incredible Mr. Limpet* (1964) starring Don Knotts. The target audience must always be taken into account when reading through the entries that form the main body of this encyclopedia.

The Encyclopedia

Abe Lincoln at Last! (*Magic Tree House* #47) [Juvenile book; WW]
Author: Mary Pope Osborne; Illustrator: Sal Murocca; First publication: New York: Random House, 2000.

In Frog Creek, Pennsylvania, eight-year-old Jack and his seven-year-old sister Annie come across a magical tree house filled with books that can take them to any time and place in history. Those books belong to Morgan le Fay, magical librarian at King Arthur's court in Camelot. Young enchanter Teddy has accidentally placed a spell turning Merlin's beloved penguin into a statue. To reverse the spell Jack and Annie must collect four special items from different places and times in history.

In Washington, D.C., 1861 that special item is a feather. But President Abraham Lincoln has more important concerns on his mind, primarily the Civil War between the States. The young time travelers try to comfort President Lincoln with a special handwritten note. "Never lose hope. This land will live peacefully as one nation one day, with freedom for everyone. We give you our word."—Jack and Annie.

See: ***Civil War on Sunday***

Abraham Lincoln, Vampire Hunter [Novel, Film; WW]

1. Author: Seth Grahame-Smith; First publication: New York: Grand Central, 2010.

Following the tragic death of his mother from a vampire attack, Abraham Lincoln records his thoughts in his secret journal. "Henceforth my life shall be one of rigorous study and devotion. I shall become a great warrior.... My life shall have but one purpose. That purpose is to kill as many vampires as I can."

The young Lincoln learns to be deadly with his ax as he wreaks his vengeance on the vampire menace. Joining him in his fight against the undead is author Edgar Allan Poe. Lincoln's time in the White House is dominated by a bloody Civil War as soldier turns upon soldier and slaves turn on their vampire captors. In a letter to his bride, Union private Andrew Merrow describes the gruesome events at the First Battle of Bull Run.

"The rebels smashed into our ranks and tore men apart in front of my eyes. I do not mean to suggest that they ran them through with bayonets, or fired on them with revolvers. I mean to say these rebels—these thirty unarmed men—tore one hundred men to pieces with nothing more than their bare hands."

Amidst the carnage of war Lincoln becomes increasingly paranoiac about being assassinated. His fears are justified as vampire John Wilkes Booth awaits.

Speaking to Liane Hansen on *NPR Weekend Edition* (March 20, 2010), author Seth Grahame-Smith commented on the link between slavery and vampirism in his novel. "I see them as sort of one and the same. Both creatures, basically slaveholders and vampires, steal lives—take the blood of others—to enrich themselves."

2. Premiere: June 22, 2012; Main Cast: Benjamin Walker as Abraham Lincoln, Dominic Cooper as Henry Sturges, Anthony Mackie as Will Johnson, Mary Elizabeth Winstead as Mary Todd Lincoln, Rufus Sewell as Adam, Jimmi Simpson as Joshua Speed, Erin Wasson as Vadoma, Robin McLeavy as Nancy Lincoln, Joseph Mawle as Thomas Lincoln; Executive producers: Seth Grahame-Smith, John J. Kelly, Simon Kinberg, Michele Wolkoff; Screenplay: Seth Grahame-Smith, based on his novel; Director: Timur Bekmambetov; 105 min.; Tim Burton Productions, 20th Century–Fox; 3-D; Color.

Abraham

Pigeon Creek, Indiana, 1818. Following an altercation with plantation owner and vampire slave trader Jack Barts young Abraham Lincoln witnesses an attack on his mother that leads to her death. Nine years later Henry Sturges teaches Lincoln about the reality of vampires and how to hunt them. Lincoln, a former rail splitter, chooses an ax with a silver plated blade as the weapon of his choice as he seeks revenge for his mother's death. Lincoln eventually tires of hunting vampires and decides to enter law and politics where he fights "with words and ideals before the ax."

Abraham Lincoln vs. Zombies (2012) starring Bill Oberst, Jr., as Abraham Lincoln (The Asylum).

Lincoln wants freedom for the negro from their vampire slave owners. But vampire leader Adam has other ideas and arms the Confederate troops with vampires. When Lincoln's young son is attacked by the vampire Vadoma he decides to tackle the problem head-on by melting all the silver and turning it into ammunition for the Union army. Adam learns of the plan through an informant but he is purposely given the wrong information and led into a trap while attacking the train to Gettysburg.

With the vampire problem defeated for now Lincoln heads for a relaxing night at the theater with his wife Mary.

Peter Bradshaw of *The Guardian* (June 21, 2012) commented that the film is "Cheerfully subversive post-steam punk fantasy.... It's a joke which some will find in sacrilegious bad taste. For me, the self-aware craziness is the whole point."

The film underperformed at the box-office with an opening weekend of $16,306,974 against an estimated budget of $69 million.

Abraham Lincoln vs. Zombies (2012)
[Film; WW]

Premiere: May 29, 2012; Main Cast: Bill Oberst, Jr., as Abraham Lincoln, Kent Igleheart as Thomas Lincoln, Rhianna Van Helton as Nancy Lincoln, Brennen Harper as Young Abe Lincoln, Debra Crittenden as Mary Todd Lincoln, Bernie Askas Edwin Stanton, Joshua Sinyard as Aide, Chris Hlozek as Major John McGill, Richard Schenkman as Dr. Malinoff, Jim E. Chandler as Eckert; Executive producer: David Rimawi; Screenplay: Richard Schenkman; Story: Karl T. Hirsch, J. Lauren Proctor; Director: Richard Schenkman; 96 min.; The Asylum; Color.

Cover of *Abraham Lincoln Vampire Hunter* by Seth Grahame-Smith (2010).

Perry County, Indiana 1818. Young Abe Lincoln has to decapitate his parents after they are attacked and infected by zombies. Decades later President Lincoln is on a mission to destroy the Confederate walking dead.

A low budget direct-to-video "mockbuster" production released to coincide with the publicity generated by *Abraham Lincoln, Vampire Hunter*.

Achilles [Novel; MWW]

Author: Elizabeth Cook; First publication: London: Methuen, 2001.

Born of a union between the sea nymph Thetis and the mortal King Peleus, Achilles is dipped into the river Styx by Thetis and granted invulnerability, except for a vulnerable spot on his heel where his mother held him. In an attempt to escape his fate Thetis hides her son from the world under the cover of a girl. This story of the Greek's greatest warrior at Troy includes the slaying of Trojan champion Hector and the public parade of his corpse, Achilles' encounter with Odysseus in Hades, Helen of Troy, Amazon Queen Penthiseleia, the centaur Chiron, and poet John Keats' meditations and affinity to Achilles.

Achtung! Cthulhu [RPG; UK; WW]

First publication: 2012; Publisher: London: Modiphius.

The secret history of World War II where an alliance of science and the occult sees Cthulhu's minions and Nazis threatening to take over the world. Players take part in campaigns that see their characters unite against the dark powers that threaten civilization. The following RPG Weird War books in the *Achtung! Cthulhu* universe have been published by Modiphius.

Achtung! Cthulhu: Dark Tales from the Secret War

First publication: December 2015; Story: John Houlihan; Art: Dim Martin, Thomas Shook.

Thirteen stories from the *Achtung! Cthulhu* universe. A mix of H.P. Lovecraft and World War II featuring demonic Nazis, occult secret ceremonies, monstrous creatures and Allied heroes.

Achtung! Cthulhu: Elder Godlike

First publication: January 2016; Story: Greg Stolze, Dennis Detwiller, Allan Gooda II, Shane Ivey, Dave Blewer.

Crossover roleplaying game combines the superhuman *Elder Godlike* with *Achtung! Cthulhu* in the Secret War. Talented Allied commandos confront super powered Nazi Ubermenschen and the Black Sun.

Achtung! Cthulhu: Heroes of the Sea

First publication: October 2012; Setting: *Call of Cthulu*; Story: Sarah Newton; Art: Dim Martin, Michael E. Cross.

At the Battle of Dunkirk a menacing conspiracy threatens Allied forces. The second standalone adventure supplement in the *Zero Point* campaign.

Achtung! Cthulhu: Interface 19.40

First publication: January 2015; Setting: *Call of Cthulu—Savage Worlds*; Story: Lynne Hardy, Dave Blewerr, Jason Brick, Josh Vogt; Art: Emilien Francois, Sam Manley, Michael E. Cross.

A crossover setting for *Achtung! Cthulhu* and *Interface Zero 2.0: Full Metal Cyberpunk*. 1941—an alternate history war featuring enhanced cybersoldiers and technology, the occult and a society where humanity is on the brink.

Achtung! Cthulhu: Kontamination

First publication: April 2014; Setting: *Call of Cthulu—Savage Worlds*; Story: Matthew Pook, Sam Richards, Dave Blewer, Lynne Hardy, Bill Bodden; Art: Dim Martin, Michael E. Cross.

In late 1944 the Allies advance toward the German border but have to overcome diabolical Nazis and their war machines.

Achtung! Cthulhu: Secrets of the Dust

First publication: February 2016; Story: Chris Lites, Brad Bell, Bill Boden, T.R. Knight, Benjamin Wenham.

A cross-over roleplaying game featuring the *Achtung! Cthulhu* world and the *Dust* universe. VK technology and walking tanks from *Dust* merge with the World War II alliance of science and the occult in *Achtung! Cthulhu*.

Achtung! Cthulhu: Shadows of Atlantis

First publication: September 2015; Setting: *Call of Cthulu—Savage Worlds*; Story: John Lynne Hardy, Dave Blewer, Jonathan M. Thompson; Art: Dim Martin, Michael E. Cross.

Discover the lost story of Atlantis as players search for a powerful ancient artefact and race against the occult forces of the German High Command in the first major wartime campaign for the *Secret War*.

Achtung! Cthulhu: Terrors of the Secret War

First publication: December 2014; Setting: *Call of Cthulu—Savage Worlds*; Story: Dave Blewer, Lynne

Hardy, Jesse Hawkins, Joshua O'Connor, Reuben Sanders; Art: Dim Martin, Ian Schofield, Giorgio Baroni, Michael E. Cross.

Combat the terrors of the Mythos: The Great Old Ones, the Outer Gods and their servitors and cultists as mankind fights to survive.

Achtung! Cthulu: The Crystal Void—The Seraph Chronicles Book Two

First publication: 2015; Author: John Houlihan.

The Napoleonic Wars, 1810. British ally Major Seraph comes to the aid of French Hussar Gaston d'Bois to rescue Gaston's true love Odette from her abductor Marquis Da Foz. But within the ancient fortress of Da Foz lies fearful underwater allies and the foreboding Crystal Void that must never be opened.

Achtung! Cthulhu: Three Kings

First publication: May 2012; PDF; Setting: *Call of Cthulu—Savage Worlds*; Story: Sarah Newton; Art: Dim Martin; Publisher: Modiphius.

On the eve of World War II, soldiers, agents and partisans in occupied Czechoslovakia discover the terrifying horrors of Castle Karlstein. The first standalone adventure supplement in the *Zero Point* campaign.

Achtung! Cthulu: Tomb of the Aeons— The Seraph Chronicles Book Three

First publication: 2015; Author: John Houlihan.

1941. The crew of the panzer Ingrid are ambushed as they pursue a British tank across the desert wastelands. When the surviving crew awake they become lost in a sand storm and come across a strange temple where they discover a unit of dead Black Sun SS. As they wander deeper into the ziggurats they approach a horror waiting for them at the center of the tomb of aeons.

Achtung! Cthulhu: Trellborg Monstrosities

First publication: June 2013; Setting: *Call of Cthulu—Savage Worlds*; Story: John Houlihan; Art: Michael E. Cross, Gregor Kari, MK Ultra Studios.

1943. Resistance partisans and British special forces go deep into enemy territory entering the village of Trellborg on the snow-covered Finnish-Norwegian border. Monstrosities await them. Based on the first of the Seraph novellas by John Houlihan.

"Adam Link Fights a War" [Pulp fiction; SFW]

Author: Eando Binder (pen-name of Earl and Otto Binder); First publication: *Amazing Stories* (Vol. 14 #12; December 1940); Publisher: Ziff-Davis Publishing Company.

"Adam Link constructed his robots for peace, to prove their worth in Man's world. But when the crushing Panzer blitzkrieg surged over the Mexican border, he had to lead them to war!"

Adam Link is an intelligent, self aware "human" robot who can feel emotions and empathize with humans even if he doesn't understand them.

"Adam Link Saves the World" [Pulp fiction; SFW]

Author: Eando Binder; First publication: *Amazing Stories* (Vol. 16 #4; April 1942); Publisher: Ziff-Davis Publishing Company.

"America is invaded by a great power. Can it be Nazi Germany? And, if so, can Adam Link solve the menace of it's incredible science?"

Adventure Comics [Comic book]

Title featuring **Superboy** and the *Legion of Super-Heroes*.

"Benjamin Franklin's Super-Reporter" [SHW]

First publication: #296 (May 1962); Art: Al Plastino; Publisher: National Periodical Publications, Inc. (DC Comics).

Superboy and the Kent family travel back in time to the Revolutionary War where they meet Benjamin Franklin, Paul Revere and George Washington.

Adventures into Darkness [Comic book]

Supernatural and fantasy anthology title.

"The Ghost That Warned a King" [WW]

First publication: #7 (December 1952); Art: Vince Colletta; Publisher: Visual Editions.

King James IV of Scotland prepares to lead an expedition against England but is warned by an old man, "If you go, you will not prosper!" King James has never seen the man before but is told by the Bishop, "He is well known to me. He was laid in his grave some years ago." King James ignores the message of the ghost and is killed in the Battle of Flodden Field.

Adventures into the Unknown [Comic book]

This anthology comic book title, published by American Comics Group, featured supernatural stories covering all genres, including Weird War stories.

"The Ghostly Goths" [WW]
First publication: #15 (January 1951); Art: Edvard Moritz.

Dr. Charles Wentworth and his wife join Professor Thorvaldsen and his team in Denmark to decipher ancient runes on a monument found in the Torsbjaerg bog lands. The runes date back to the 4th century from the "magical period." Disturbed by the message on the runes that warns of death to anyone who defiles the monument, the Wentworths listen to a record to relax. But a ghostly voice comes from the speaker followed by the spirit of a Goth who wants vengeance on the person who looted the gold and diamonds from the monument. That person now lives in exile in the Andes. Summoning a ghostly army of Goths, they confront Adolf Hitler and the Nazis in exile and exact their revenge.

"Medal of Honor" [WW]
First publication: #149 (June–July 1964); Story: Shane O'Shea (Richard Hughes); Art: Chic Stone.

"Why did ghosts snatch away his decoration for valor?"

"Shall I tell him Sarge? Tell him why I'm a ghost and you're getting a medal?"

"The Werewolf Strikes" [WW]
First publication: #14 (December 1950–January 1951); Story: Charles Spain Verral; Art: Bill Ely.

At U.S. Zone occupied Germany Counter Intelligence headquarters Captain Dixon states "I know about a band of die-hard Nazis who called themselves "The Werewolf Underground" and who pledged themselves to last ditch resistance, even after the war was over!"

The Werewolf Underground disbanded, but their leader was never caught, and now, the Nazis are terrorizing all Germans who co-operated with the Allies. In the Black Forest anti–Nazi lecturer Hans Castorp presents a lecture renouncing the Nazi philosophy and is later found with his throat cut and a wolf running from the scene. Further down the road two soldiers come across a fraulein named Marlene Lupus who claims her arm was scratched on thorn bushes. But when one of the soldiers is murdered his friend suspects the girl and decides to use himself as bait. As they embrace Marlene turns into a werewolf, revealing herself as the head of the Nazi resistant movement.

The Adventures of Bob Hope [Comic book]
Title based on the wise-cracking film, radio and stand-up comedian.

"A Comedy of Eras"—"Aviator Bob, the Chicken Eagle" [SFW]
First publication: #89 (October–November 1964); Two-part story; Art: Mort Drucker; Publisher: National Periodical Publications (DC Comics).

Bob Hope is asked to retrieve Tuesday Wednesday's Golden Gazelle statuette which contains a valuable treasure map. Hope travels back in time in the Professor's time machine, to visit the statuette's previous owner, Tuesday's great-great grandfather Captain Wednesday. But as Hope emerges into the past he joins the Captain at the moment he is about to engage the enemy in aerial combat during World War I. Hope's search for the statuette and the treasure map eventually takes him to December 26, 1776, and George Washington crossing the Delaware.

Adventures of the Outsiders [Comic book]
Title featuring a metahuman superhero team from war-torn Markovia.

"A Tiny Deadly War"—"Against All Odds"—"Sympathy for the Fuhrer" [SHW]
First publication: Adventures of the Outsiders #33–35 (May–July 1986); Three-issue story; Story: Mike W. Barr; Art: Alan Davis, Paul Neary; Publisher: DC Comics.

In the European kingdom of Markovia the *Outsiders* are captured by the Masters of Disaster. Baron Bedlam reveals his secret weapon, an Adolf Hitler clone as Madame Ovary attempts to restore Hitler's memories.

The Aeneid [Epic poem; MWW]
Composed by the acclaimed Roman poet Virgil (Publius Vergilius Maro) between 29–19 BC, the *Aeneid* is a poem that glorifies the founding and rise of Rome. Its hero, the Trojan Aeneas recalls the story of the wooden horse and the sack of Troy, after a ten-year siege. Hector appears to Aeneas in a dream, telling him to flee the burning Troy and take the surviving Trojans with him to form a new homeland. Aeneas takes heed of Hector's warning and carries his father Anchises on his shoulder to safety while taking his son Ascanius by the hand. His wife Cruesa follows behind

but is lost in the confusion. Desperate to find his wife, Aeneas returns to the burning city, and meets her ghost. She tells him his fate is a long exile, but he will eventually find a new home for his people and marry a queen.

Aeneas and the surviving Trojans continue on to Italy following the advice of the oracle of Apollo. On the Ionian Strophades islands they encounter part female-part bird creatures known as Harpies who seize their food. Finding harbor in Sicily, Aeneas and his men flee the harbor when they spot the Cyclops Polyphemus on a mountaintop. In Drepanum tragedy strikes when Aeneas' father Anchises dies.

Finally arriving at Cumae in Italy Aeneas consults the Sibyl at the temple of Apollo. The Sibyl warns him of a future war that he must face with heroic courage. Aeneas requests to descend into the underworld to visit his dead father. But first he must travel across the River Styx to enter the land of Hades and witness the punishment of the evil souls in Tartarus. The Sibyl finally guides Aeneas to the Elysian Fields where righteous souls dwell, including his father. He tells Aeneas of the future glory of Rome, but before that happens there will be much bloodshed.

On his return from the underworld more trials await Aeneas and the Trojans in the form of a new enemy named Turnus. The god Juno summons the Fury Allecto from Hades who visits Turnus in the form of an old woman. She creates a lust for war in his soul and sets Latins against Trojans. War begins with the opening of the gates of Janus, but out of the carnage the ancestor of the Romans will triumph. Turnus is defeated and the Latins and Trojans make peace under one condition that the god Jupiter grants to Juno. The Trojans must adopt the language of the Latins.

Aeneas is also mentioned in Book XX of Homer's *Iliad*. The gods save him for his future destiny by removing Aeneas from the battlefield and combat with Achilles.

After Dachau: A Novel [Novel; AHW]

Author: Daniel Quinn; First publication: New York: Context Books, 2001.

College graduate Jason Tull, Jr., works for the "We Live Again" foundation that investigates reported cases of reincarnation. But when he discovers artist Gloria MacArthur now occupies the body of deaf mute Mallory Hastings events take a dark turn. Tull lives in a world where Hitler defeated the Allies and achieved his ideal of an Aryan world. The black person no longer exists. But Gloria MacArthur was a black woman who lived through World War II and who now sees a world she no longer recognizes. AD no longer represents *Anno Domini* but *After Dachau*.

After the Downfall [Novel; WW]

Author: Harry Turtledove; First publication: San Francisco: Nightshade Books, 2008.

Wehrmacht officer Hasso Pemsel flees a sniper's bullet and falls into a magical world as Russian troops move through the ruins of Berlin. He rescues the beautiful blonde goddess Velona, who seduces him. Velona tells Pemsel about the blond Lenelli invaders who rule over the dark, barbaric Grenye. Pemsel recognizes his Third Reich ideals in the Lenelli and supports their cause until he is captured by the Grenye. The high priestess Drepteaza enlightens him about the true nature of the Lenelli and he changes sides after Velona tries to terminate him.

Against the Tide of Years [Novel; SFW]

Author: S.M. Stirling; First publication: New York: Roc, 1999.

The island of Nantucket has been swept back through time to the Bronze Age and the year 1250 BC Renegade coastguard officer William Walker, now allied with Agamemnon and Odysseus from the Trojan War, has to deal with the effects of modern technology being introduced into Bronze Age Greece, Phoenicia and Babylonia.

This sequel to *Island in the Sea of Time* (Nantucket: Book One; 1998) is concluded in *On the Oceans of Eternity* (Nantucket: Book Three; 2000).

Age of Bronze: The Story of the Trojan War [Comic book; MWW]

First publication: November 1998; Story-Art: Eric Shanower; Publisher: Image Comics.

A thirty-three-issue comic book version of the Trojan War based on classical sources, including Homer's **Iliad**.

Airboy [Comic book character; Comic book; SFW]

1. First publication: *Air Fighters Comics* #2 (November 1942); Creators: Charles Biro, Dick Wood, Al Camy; Publisher: Hillman Periodicals.

"We are now going to that 'Last Landing Field' where Amelia Earhart, Billy Mitchell, Wiley Post and the Wright Brothers are welcoming a newcomer, Colin P. Kelly."

The departed air aces of the past watch over a young orphan boy being instructed in a California monastery by Padre Martier. The Padre has studied Cellini and his "wings that flapped like a bird." Now he has applied Cellini's invention to a plane with wings like a bat. But his invention attracts unwelcome attention and on his test flight the "Batplane" is sabotaged and Padre Martier perishes in the crash landing. The young orphan vows to continue his work as Airboy, but now the Japanese want the plane so they can build their own fleet. Airboy meets their challenge with the defiant words "We'll show 'em what we Americans are made of...."

Although Airboy possessed no super-powers his "Batplane" that later went by the affectionate name of "Birdie" fits into the weird category. The pressure applied to the press of a button allowed the wings to flap slower or faster. The design of the tail and the wings also enabled Airboy to stop "Birdie" instantly and turn around. The ability to hover, takeoff vertically and be flown by remote control by Airboy added to the mystique of the heavily-armed fighter plane.

Airboy graduated to his own title in December 1945, but the post-war years saw a gradual decline in sales as his wartime adventures were replaced by more traditional crime-fighting adventures. He finally retired in May 1953.

2. First publication: June 2015: Story: James Robinson; Art: Greg Hinkle; Publisher: Image Comics.

Comics author James Robinson is reluctant when asked to reboot the 1940s flying ace character Airboy. But a night of drink and drugs with artist Greg Hinkle leads them to a personal meeting with Airboy during World War II.

Airboy 1942: Best of Enemies [Comic book; SFW]

First publication: 2009; Story: Chuck Dixon; Art: Todd Fox, Lito Fernandez; Publisher: Moonstone.

In December 1942 Airboy meets femme-fatale Valkyrie for the first time.

Alfred Hitchcock Presents (1955) [TV series]

Anthology series hosted by film director Alfred Hitchcock.

"AN OCCURRENCE AT OWL CREEK BRIDGE" (5:13) [WW]

First broadcast: December 20, 1959; Main Cast: Ronald Howard as Peyton Farquhar, James Coburn as Union Sergeant, Kenneth Tobey as Jeff, Juano Hernandez as Josh, Douglas Kennedy as Union Officer; Teleplay: Harold Swanton, based on the short story by Ambrose Bierce; Director: Robert Stevenson; 30 min.; Shamley Productions, Revue Studios; B/W.

Adaptation of the American Civil War story by Ambrose Bierce.

See: *An Occurrence at Owl Creek*

All Clear [Novel: SFW]

Author: Connie Willis; First publication: Spectra Ballantine Books, 2010.

In the second volume of the story that began with *Blackout* the three Oxford time traveling historians from 2060 find themselves trapped in 1940 London during the Blitz. But history has become warped and finding Michael, Merope and Polly won't be

The first appearance of Airboy in *Air Fighters Comics* #2 (November 1942). Cover art by Charles Biro. Published by Hillman Periodicals.

an easy task for 17-year-old Colin Templer. their supervisor in 2060.

All Evil Shed Away [Novel; SFW]
Author: Archie Edmiston Roy; First publication: London: Long, 1970.

British scientist David Hamilton's mundane life under Nazi rule in Glasgow, Scotland is enlivened by his involvement in a secret research project on the island of St. Kilda. When he learns the project is the development of time travel Hamilton grasps his chance to change history and reverse all the evil in the world.

All-Star Squadron [Comic book; SHW]
First appearance: *Justice League of America* #193 (August 1981); Creators: **Roy Thomas**, Rich Buckler, Jerry Ordway; Publisher: DC Comics.

Following the attack by the Japanese air force at Pearl Harbor, President Franklin D. Roosevelt forms the *All-Star Squadron* to oppose the Axis menace. Comprised of the **Justice Society of America** and members of the Seven Soldiers of Victory, **Freedom Fighters** and solo super-heroes, the newly formed team answers directly to the President and the War Department. The members include, **Commander Steel**, **Liberty Belle**, Robotman, **Amazing-Man**, **Firebrand**, Tarantula, Johnny Quick, Hawkman, Hawkgirl, Green Lantern, Hourman, Plastic Man, Dr. Fate, The Guardian, **Shining Knight** and Atom.

All-Winners Squad [Comic book characters; SHW]
First appearance: *All-Winners Comics* #19 (Fall 1946); Creator: Bill Finger; Publisher: Timely Comics.

Consisting of **Captain America** and Bucky, the **Human Torch** and Toro, **Sub-Mariner**, the **Whizzer** and **Miss America**, the All Winners Squad fights the Axis powers during World War II.

Amazing Adult Fantasy [Comic book]
Supernatural and fantasy anthology title.

"Where Walks the Ghost?" [WW]
First publication: #11 (April 1962); Story: **Stan Lee**; Art: Steve Ditko; Publisher: Marvel Comics Group.

A "ghost" soldier from the American Civil War believes he's been killed in battle but his parents are the ones who are dead and he is still among the living.

The Amazing Adventures of Kavalier and Clay [Novel; WW]
Author: Michael Chabon; First publication: New York: Random House, 2000.

1939. Joe Kavalier has escaped Nazi-occupied Poland using his Houdini-like skills to join Sammy Clay in New York City. Together, the two Jewish cousins create the superhero **The Escapist**. Inspired by the free spirited and beautiful Rosa Saks the two cousins create the mistress of the night, Luna Moth. But unknown to Kavalier, Rosa carries his child as he abruptly abandons his comic book career to join the navy.

Amazing Man [Comic book character; SHW]
1. First appearance: *Amazing Man Comics* #5 (Fall 1939); Creator: **Bill Everett**; Publisher: Centaur Publications.

In the mountains of Tibet, the Council of Seven select an orphan to be trained in the qualities of great strength, knowledge and courage. His friend Nika enables him the power to make himself invisible in a cloud of green vapor. But before being sent to America John Amon undergoes a series of grueling physical feats of strength in preparation for fighting evil arch-criminal the Great Question (known as the Great Que).

During World War II Amazing Man is joined by sidekick, Tommy, the Amazing Kid as they fight with the allies against their enemies.

2. First appearance; *All-Star Squadron* #23; Creators: Roy Thomas, Jerry Ordway; Publisher: DC Comics.

African American athlete Will Everett enters the 1936 Berlin Olympics and wins gold medals alongside Jessie Owens. Back in America he is kidnapped and subjected to an experiment with an electro-generator which explodes. Now Everett can absorb organic material and transform himself into a living copy of that material.

During World War II he becomes a member of the ***All-Star Squadron***.

Amazing Stories (1985) [TV series]
Steven Spielberg returned to television in this weekly anthology series featuring assorted tales of fantasy and the supernatural and the occasional Weird War tale; 43 × 25, 2 × 46; Amblin Entertainment, Universal Television; National Broadcasting System (NBC); Color.

"Alamo Jobe" (1:03) [WW]

Air date: October 20, 1985; Main Cast: Kelly Reno as Alamo Jobe, William Boyett as Colonel Travis, Richard Young as Davy Crockett, Lurene Tuttle as Harriet Wendse; Teleplay: John Falsey; Director: Michael Moore; 25 min.

A young man fighting in the battle of the Alamo suddenly finds himself in San Antonio, Texas, in 1985.

"The Mission" (1:05) [WW]

Air date: November 3, 1985; Main Cast: Kevin Costner as The Captain, Kiefer Sutherland as Static, Casey Siemaszko as Jonathan; Teleplay: Menno Meyjes; Director: Steven Spielberg; 46 min.

When a B-17 bomber is damaged by shrapnel from a Messerschmitt ME-101 the gunner Jonathan puts his cartoonist training to dramatic use.

"No Day at the Beach" (1:14) [WW]

Air date: January 12, 1986; Main Cast: Charlie Sheen as Casey, Larry Spinak as Arnold Skamp, Ralph Seymour as Ira, Philip McKeon as Stick; Teleplay: Mick Garris; Director: Lesli Linka Glatter; 24 min.

Treated as an outcast by his fellow poker playing soldiers Arnold Skamp becomes a hero when he miraculously saves their lives.

The American Crusader [Comic book character; SHW]

First appearance: *America's Best Comics* #6 (July 1943); Creator: Alex Schomburg; Publisher: Nedor/Better/Standard Publications.

"Exposed to the rays of a giant atom-smasher, Professor Archibald Masters develops super-human strength. As the American Crusader he wages war against the Axis tyrants in conquered Europe."

The American Eagle [Comic book character; SHW]

First appearance: *America's Best Comics* #2 (September 1942); Creators: Richard Hughes, Kin Platt; Publisher: Nedor/Better/Standard Publications.

In a remote mountain laboratory Dr. Wolfe is paid a visit. "The Fatherland has need of your services Herr Doktor." Meanwhile his assistant Tom Standish accidentally drops a test tube that imparts a strange light to a cathode tube. Placing the tube in a giant projector Standish is immersed in a weird, black ray. Overhearing Dr. Wolfe planning to poison the American water supply Standish is knocked unconscious by Nazi spies and thrown over a cliff to his certain death. But he survives ... and discovers he can smash rocks with his bare hands! "Good heavens, the black ray has given me the power of Hercules!" And the flight of an eagle as he "bounds and catapults" up the cliff face.

With his new costume and super powers Tom Standish becomes the American Eagle and sets about stopping the poisoning of Mansfield Reservoir and a bombing attack on the Governor by Dr. Wolfe and his Nazi cohorts.

Joining him in his adventures is young Bud Pierce who Standish adopts after saving his life. Bud becomes Eaglet after the black rays also give him the powers of an eagle.

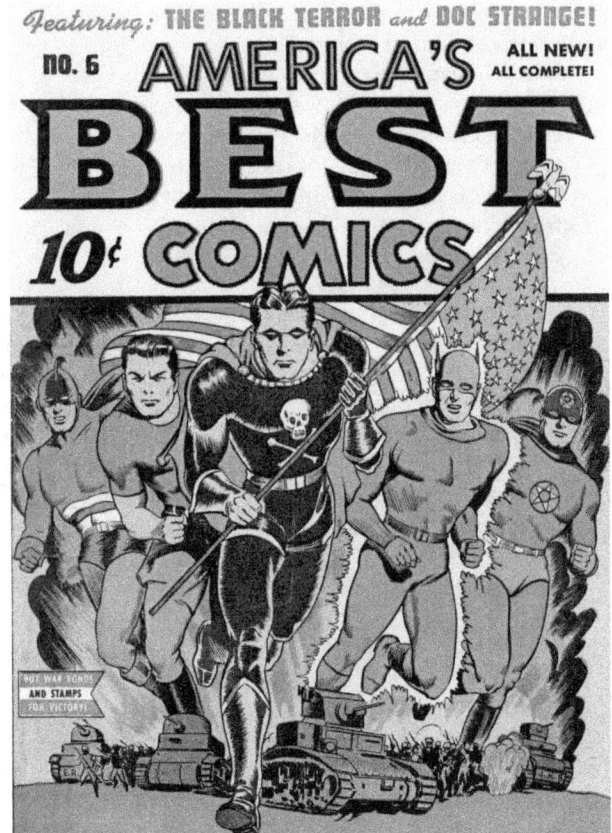

The American Eagle featured in *America's Best Comics*. The cover for issue #6 includes (left to right) American Crusader, Doc Strange, Black Terror, Pyroman and American Eagle. Cover art by Alex Schomburg. Published by Nedor Publications.

American Vampire [Comic book]

"Ghost War" [WW]

First publication: #13 (May 2011); Six-part story; Story: Scott Snyder; Art: Rafael Albuquerque; Publisher: DC Comics.

At the dawn of the 20th century a new kind of vampire named Skinner Sweet is born in the American West. In 1925 he creates a second American Vampire—actress Pearl Jones. Pearl goes her own way and leaves Hollywood with a human musician named Henry Preston. In hiding, until 1936, they are located in northern California. Unknown to Pearl, Preston reaches a deal with the Vassals of the Morning Star in return for protection. He discloses the American vampire's weakness—vulnerability to gold.

1943. Taipan, off the coast of Japan. Henry Preston joins a unique military team formed by the Vassals of the Morning Star, dedicated to protecting American troops in World War II from vampires. But on their mission into vampire infested Taipan they are taken prisoner by the Japanese Imperial Army. Now they must plan their escape and protect themselves from the savage, feral vampires long enough for the Allied bombers to reach the island. Meanwhile Pearl receives a letter from Skinner Sweet telling her of Henry Preston's deception.

Andersonville [Novel; WW]

Author: Edward M. Erdelac; First publication: New York: Hydra, 2015.

Posing as a Union officer Barclay Lourdes is on a mission. Incarcerating oneself in the Civil War's darkest, cruelest prison camp demands a grim dedication. First he must survive the sadistic fury of Captain Wirz and Sergeant Turner. But even their cruelty doesn't prepare him for the evil forces of the supernatural at work in the camp.

Andie and the Alien [Graphic novel; AHW]

First publication: July 2011; Story: Brian Phillipson, Phil Phillipson; Art: Alex Nino; Publisher: Bliss on Tap Publishing.

Five-hundred years in the past, a spacecraft piloted by an alien on his first observation mission to Earth, crashes into the Americas. The friendly alien is rescued by a young, female native American who returns her kindness by placing a forcefield over the Americas to repel any future invaders. But in a distant land, almost five-hundred years later the Nazis win World War II and capture a spaceship and its alien occupant. The Nazis plan to attack the Americas with the help of the alien and genius scientist Albert Einstein. But Einstein and the alien have plans of their own that involve destroying the Third Reich forever with nuclear power.

Angel (1999) [TV series]

A vampire cursed with a soul, Angel helps fight the supernatural in modern day Los Angeles while seeking redemption for the evil deeds of his past.

Main Cast: David Boreanaz as Angel, James Marsters as Spike, J. August Richards as Charles Gunn, Amy Acker as Winifred "Fred" Burkle.

"Why We Fight" (5:13) [WW]

Premiere: February 18, 2004; Guest Cast: Eyal Podell as Sam Lawson, Lindsay Ginter as Commander Petrie, Camden Troy as Prince of Lies, Bart McCarthy as Nostroyev; Producers: Steven S. DeKnight, Kelly A. Manners; Story: Drew Goddard, Steven S. DeKnight; Director: Terrence O'Hara; 42 min.; Mutant Enemy, Kuzui Enterprises, Sandollar Television, WB Television Network; Color.

Wes, "Fred" and Gunn are taken hostage by a person from Angel's past, Sam Lawson, who is seeking revenge. In a flashback to 1943 a German U–Boat commandeered by the U.S. military has a secret cargo of three kidnapped vampires. Angel must recover the U-boat at the directive of the Demon Research Initiative. Lawson blames Angel for turning him into a vampire to save the submarine and the rest of the crew.

An Angel for May [Juvenile book; Telefilm; UK; SFW]

1. Author: Melvin Burgess; First publication: London: Andersen Press, 1992.

Depressed by his parent's divorce, Tam Sams takes refuge in a derelict farmhouse. Making friends with homeless Rosey, Tam is playing with her dog Winnie when he is pushed through the farmhouse fireplace into another time. The farm is full of life with farmer Mr. Sam Nutter in charge. Tam meets May, a mentally challenged girl traumatized by the German bombing raids over England. It is World War II. Gradually Tam and May become good friends and she wants him to stay on the farm. But Tam knows his place is in his own time and he begins to fear remaining out-of-time forever. When he eventually returns to his present

Tam discovers how the past and present are linked in mysterious and surprising ways.

2. Air date: December 23, 2002; Main Cast: Tom Wilkinson as Sam Wheeler, Charlotte Wakefield as Young May, Matthew Beard as Tom Collins, Hugo Speer as Bob Harris, Michael McNulty as Sniffer, Anna Massey as Rosie, Julie Cox as Alison Wheeler, Angeline Ball as Barbara Collins; Dora Bryan as Evelyn, Richard Fleeshman as School Team Captain; Executive Producers: Tim Buxton, Keith Evans, Emma Hayter, Anna Home, Alex Marshall, Screenplay: Peter Milligan; Based on the book by Melvin Burgess; Director: Harley Cokeliss; 95 min.; Portman Films, Children's Film and Television Foundation (CFTV), Barzo Productions, Gentian Productions, Spice Factory, Yorkshire Media Production Agency (YMPA), Studio of the North; Independent Television (ITV); Color.

Adaptation of the book by Melvin Burgess.

Anthem [Comic book; AHW]

First publication: March 2006; Five-issue mini-series; Story: Roy Thomas, Billy Tucci, Denis Mallonee; Art: Daniel Acuna, Jorge Santamaria Garcia, Benito Gallego, Mark Beachum, Billy Tucci; Publisher: Heroic Publishing.

In an alternate World War II universe Japan launches an attack on America's West Coast, headed by a gigantic monster. Meanwhile the East Coast is invaded by Nazi troops and military flying saucers. In desperation the U.S. survivors form a team of super-heroes under Project Anthem. Native American female archer Stars and Stripes, twins Rockets and Redglare, human rocket BombBurst, Liberty, an incarnation of the destroyed Statue of Liberty, living rock Stonewall Jackson and their leader Agent 76. But Adolf Hitler has his own Aryan supermen ready for action.

Anthem also features Billy Tucci's World War II adventures of *Liberty Girl*.

Are You Afraid of the Dark? (1990) [TV series; Canada]

Anthology series featuring a group of youngsters who tell ghost stories around a camp fire. First broadcast: August 15, 1990; Main Cast: Jason Alisharan as Frank, Daniel DeSanto as Tucker, Joanna Garcia as Sam, Ross Hull as Gary, Raine Pare-Coull as Betty Ann, Jodie Resther as Kiki; Creator: D.J. MacHale; Executive Producer: Ronald A. Weinberg; 91 × 22 min.; CINAR, YTV, Nickelodeon Network; Color.

"The Tale of the Long Ago Locket" (4:02) [SFW]

Air date: October 8, 1994; Guest Cast: Will Freddie as Jimmy Armstrong, Paul Hopkins as Lieutenant William, Peter Colvey as Redcoat Captain, Kim Johnson as April, Joel Gordon as Josh, Victor Knight as Mr. Olshak, Rachelle Glait as Mrs. Ritter; Story: Gerald Wexler; Director: David Winning.

A soldier in the Revolutionary War is visited by a boy from the future who helps him reunite with his girlfriend before she marries another man.

"The Tale of the Room for Rent" (4:08) [WW]

Air date: November 19, 1994; Guest Cast: Alison Hildreth as Jessie Dixon, Melissa Altro as Alex, Walter Massey as Grandpa Samuel, Andreas Apergis as Spirit Man, Sheena Larkin as Sara Simpson; Story: Lucy Falcone; Director: Will Dixon.

A World War II pilot haunts the man he believed killed him in combat and then stole his girlfriend.

Are You Afraid of the Dark?—The Tale of the Zero Hero [Juvenile book; WW]

Author: John Peel; First publication: New York: Pocket Books-Aladdin, 1997.

Simon's family has always believed his great-grandfather was a coward during World War I. But Simon discovers the truth when his great-grandfather's ghosts takes him back in time to experience what really happened in the war.

Army of Frankensteins (2013) [Film; SFW]

Premiere: November 10, 2013; Main Cast: Jordan Farris as Alan Jones, Christian Bellgardt as Igor, John Ferguson as Dr. tanner Finski, Eric Gesecus as Frankenstein, Rett Terrell as Solomon Jones; Executive Producer: Amy Bellgardt; Story: Ryan Bellgardt, Josh McKamie, Andy Swanson; Director: Ryan Bellgardt; 108 min.; Six Stitches Entertainment, Boiling Point Media; Scream Factory; Color.

A series of grisly experiments to reanimate a Frankenstein leads to a hole in time and space through which an Army of Frankensteins from parallel universes manifest during the American Civil War.

Arnim Zola [Comic book character; SHW]

First appearance: *Captain America and the Falcon* #208 (April 1977); Creator: **Jack Kirby**; Publisher: Marvel Comics.

Former Nazi geneticist who served the **Red Skull** during World War II as his "master of science." After the end of the war Zola transferred his consciousness to a robot body and later to a digitized brain within a computer. In the modern age he has re-united with a revived Red Skull to once again defeat **Captain America**.

Arrowsmith [Comic book; AHW]

First publication: September 2003; Six-issue miniseries; Story: Kurt Busiek; Art: Carlos Pacheco, Jesus Merino; Publisher: Wildstorm Comics—Cliffhanger.

World War I re-imagined with magic, dragons, vampires and sorcery as mystical aviator Fletcher Arrowsmith joins the Allies to fight the Prussians.

Assassin's Creed (2007) [Videogame; Canada; AHW]

Release date: November 2007; Voice Cast: Kristen Bell as Lucy Stillman, Philip Shahbaz as Altair, Nolan North as Desmond Miles/Abbas, Phil Proctor as Warren Vidic, Peter Renaday as Al Mualim, Haaz Sleiman as Malik A-Sayf; Producer: Jade Raymond; Story: Corey May, M. Dooma Wendschuh; Director: Patrice Desilets; Single-player; Original platforms: Xbox 360, PlayStation 3; Developer: Ubisoft Montreal; Publisher: Ubisoft.

This action-adventure video game takes place during the Third Crusade in 1191. In the present day bartender Desmond Miles is captured by scientists and placed in a machine called Animus to relive his ancestor's past as assassin Altair. In the Holy Land the Secret Order of Assassins and the Knights Templar are in conflict over an ancient artifact used to control minds.

At the Firefly Gate [Juvenile book; WW]

Author: Linda Newbery; First publication: London: Orion Publishing Group, 2004.

Young Henry moves with his parents to a Suffolk village, located near a former World War II airfield. He quickly makes friends with his neighbor's great-aunt Dottie. Her fiancé, also named Henry, was a Royal Air Force navigator who never returned from his last bombing mission. The young Henry feels a strange affinity with the RAF navigator and has vivid dreams where he is the pilot on one of the bombing missions. A shadowy figure standing by the orchard gate in Henry's garden and the sound of war planes flying overhead add to his spooky experiences as he gradually learns more about Henry and his heroic final mission.

Athena Voltaire [Comic book character; WW]

First appearance: *Modern Tales* (2002); Creators: Steve Bryant, Paul Daly; Publishers: Speakeasy Comics, Ape Entertainment, Dark Horse Comics.

Athena Voltaire is a globetrotting aviatrix for hire who battles Nazis, the occult and mythical creatures in exotic locales of the 1930s. Partly based on the real-life aviatrix adventuress Pancho Barnes.

In "Flight of the Falcon" (August 2006) Athena Voltaire is hired to transport an ancient artifact, a golden falcon statue, to the United States. But the statue is coveted by Adolf Hitler for the occult power it possesses. It is said to unlock the doorway to the hollow earth and control a lost race of super mortals who live within the earth. S.S. Aviatrix Hannah von Helm leads the Nazi occultists in pursuit of Athena and the golden falcon statue.

The aviatrix ventures to South America in "Athena Voltaire and the Feathered Serpent" (July 2014) where she attempts to stop the Third Reich from obtaining an artifact to summon the legendary feathered serpent.

Atomic Knight [Comic book character; SHW]

First appearance: *Strange Adventures* #117 (June 1960); Creators: John Broome, Murphy Anderson; Publisher: DC Comics.

Army sergeant Gardner Grayle is an average soldier selected by S.T.A.R. Labs to test his response to nuclear war and its aftermath. Placed in a sensory deprivation tank, Gayle is able to control the computer that regulates the tank with his subconscious and enter a virtual reality world. In this world Grayle believes he is part of a group of Atomic Knights restoring order after World War III.

When Grayle is finally freed from the virtual world he remains true to his knight persona wearing radiation proof armor designed for soldiers in a post-nuclear America and becomes the second **Shining Knight**.

Atomic Robo and the Dogs of War [Comic book; SFW]

First publication: August 2008; 5-issue mini-series; Story: Brian Clevinger; Art: Scott Wegener; Publisher: Red 5 Comics.

Atomic Robo is a self-aware robot with "automatic intelligence" built by Nikola Tesla in 1923. In June 1943 Nazi "weird war" super mechs threaten the Allied invasion of Sicily. Atomic Robo teams up with British spy Sparrow and confronts Hitler's personal commando, Otto Skorzeny and his "walking" German tanks known as Laufpanzers.

"The Avengers" [Pulp fiction; SFW]

Author: William P. McGivern; Illustrator: Ned Hadley; First publication: *Amazing Stories* (Vol. 16 #6; June 1942); Publisher: Ziff-Davis Publishing Company.

"Even though Hitler has been dead for four years and his armies smashed to bits, it's still hard to realize it's all over and done with."—Dirk Masters, Chief Engineer of the Standard Broadcasting System.

"It's all over though. Or after today it will be forever. When we send all the armaments of the earth to the bottom of the Atlantic, we'll be putting an end to war for all time."—Larry Winters, Standard's top-notch announcer.

Among the weapons to be sunk is the American "Death Ray," capable of destroying all forms of life by splitting the atomic structure of the cell into myriad organisms. Sealed in a leaden casket, along with the formula for its discovery and operation, the Death Ray is towed out to sea and sunk by radio-controlled planes. But the sense of optimism is premature as the nations of the world face a new enemy in the skies and on the sea.

AWOL in North Africa (*Ghosts of War* #3) [Juvenile book; WW]

Author: Steve Watkins; First publication: New York: Scholastic, Inc., 2016.

Once again Anderson and his friends Greg and Julie are tempted to look inside the mysterious trunk in Anderson's family basement. This time they discover an old medic's bag from World War II, followed by the obligatory ghost—an army medic who tended wounded soldiers in North Africa. The three youngsters aren't aware of any fighting in North Africa during World War II, but when they investigate the ghost they receive a history lesson in desert warfare.

See: **Fallen in Fredericksburg**

"Baby Face" [Pulp fiction; WW]

Author: Henry Kuttner: Illustrator: Virgil Finlay; First publication: *Thrilling Wonder Stories* (Vol. 27 #1; Spring 1945); Publisher: Standard Magazines, Inc.

Sergeant Jerry Cassidy of the U.S. Marines becomes involved in a "Thought-Matrix-Transfer" when he takes a baby to the doctor. Temporarily switching minds will help the doctor diagnose the baby's symptoms. But the transfer is interrupted by Nazis who want the mind transfer helmet for their own nefarious reasons. With Sgt. Cassidy's mind trapped in the baby's body, the doctor must recover the helmet. They locate the Nazis and helmet at a circus where Cassidy accidentally transfers his mind into a gorilla. After dispatching the Nazis as the gorilla Cassidy finally returns to his own body.

Back to the Future (1991) [Animated TV series]

The animated adventures of "Marty" McFly and Dr. Emmett Brown as they travel through time.

"Brothers" (1:01) [SFW]

Air date: September 14, 1991; Voice Cast: David Kaufman as Martin "Marty" McFly, Dan Castellaneta as Dr. Emmet Brown, Joshua Wiener as Jules Erastosthenes Brown, Troy Davidson as Verne Newton Brown, Cathy Cavadini as Jennifer Parker, Hal Rayle as General Beauregard Tannen; Executive Producers: Japhet Asher, Bob Gale, Steven Spielberg; 25 min.; Universal Cartoon Studios, Amblin Television; Color.

Marty, Doc Brown and Jules travel back in time to rescue Verne Newton Brown, but find themselves in the middle of an American Civil War battle.

Backtrack: Nazi Vengeance (2014) [Film; UK; WW]

Premiere: March 3, 2014; Main Cast: Mark Drake as Ralph Lowe, Sophie Barker as Andrea Carver, Rosie Ackerman as Claudia Werner, Miles Jovian as Lucas Burke, Julian Glover as Old Man, Callie Moore as Gloria, Rene Zimmerman as Senior SS Officer; Executive Producer—Story: Mick Sands; Director: Tom Sands; 97 min.; Substantial Films, The Road to Ashvem Productions; Kaleidoscope Home Entertainment (UK), Midnight Releasing (U.S.); Color.

When journalist Ralph Lowe undergoes past life regression by his psychic friend Claudia

Werner he relives his life as a Nazi Commando in 1940. Back in the present day Ralph finds himself and his friends stalked by the Nazi from his past life.

The Backyard Ghost [Juvenile book; WW]

Author: Lynn Cullen; First publication: New York: Clarion Books, 1993.

When seventh-grader Eleanor is transferred across town to Sagamore School she finds it difficult to make friends with the popular girls. But she has a trick up her sleeve in the form of Joseph, a young Civil War ghost who haunts her backyard. Soon she is part of the "in crowd" but her new found popularity isn't all she hoped for.

Baffling Mysteries [Comic book]

Anthology title.

"APPOINTMENT IN HADES" [WW]

First publication: #11 (November 1952); Art: Gene Colan; Publisher: Periodical House (Ace Magazines).

A soldier drowns after deserting his fellow soldiers and leaving them to die while fighting on a beachhead. But his cowardice comes at an eternal price when the ghosts of his fallen unit drag him into the bowels of hell.

"BAFFLING MYSTERIES #31" [WW]

First publication: #19 (January 1954); Art: Sy Grudko; Publisher: Periodical House (Ace Magazines).

A French hero under Napoleon disappears in action during a campaign in 1812, without a trace of him or his sword ever being found. In 1914 the great grandson of the French soldier serves France in World War I as a Lieutenant.

Surrounded by the Huns the Lieutenant orders a retreat from a strategic outpost. Suddenly the ghost of his great-grandfather appears before him.

"Take heart lad. You are no coward. Here, take my sword and lead your men bravely."

The Lieutenant rallies his soldiers to the offensive and wins the battle, but dies clutching the sword. That sword now hangs in a Paris museum "to testify to the weird powers of the strange and the supernatural."

Baltimore, or, The Steadfast Tin Soldier and the Vampire [Novel; WW]

Authors-Illustrators: Mike Mignola, Christopher Golden; First publication: New York: Bantam Spectra, 2007.

November 1914, Ardennes Forest, France. Captain Henry Baltimore sees his battalion under Hessian attack and decimated. Baltimore survives and awakens to the nightmare vision of seeing his dead men being eaten by giant bat creatures. Baltimore's leg becomes infected when he attempts to defend himself and has to be amputated. Recovering in hospital Baltimore receives a visitor. Baltimore recognizes him from a battle when he cut into his face. Now that same man declares a war between vampires and humans.

The Bargain [Novel; WW]

Author: Jon Ruddy; First publication: New York: Knightsbridge Publishing, 1990.

Count Dracula confronts invading Nazis and village elders who have betrayed his trust in Arefu, Romania. Eventually the vampire hordes reach Adolf Hitler and threaten the world with a new breed of undead immortals.

Baron Blitzkrieg [Comic book character; SHW]

First appearance: *World's Finest Comics* #246 (September 1977); Creators: Gerry Conway, Don Heck; Publisher: DC Comics.

A Nazi concentration camp commandant and favorite of Adolf Hitler is attacked by an inmate with a vial of acid that destroys his face. Hitler's scientists transform the commandant into a superhuman known as Baron Blitzkrieg. His powers include psychic control over his physical functions and metabolism, including super-strength and heat beams from his eyes. His foes include the **All-Star Squadron** and **Wonder Woman**.

Baron Blood [Comic book character; SHW]

First appearance: *Invaders* #7 (July 1976); Creators: Roy Thomas, Frank Robbins; Publisher: Marvel Comics.

England, 1942. English aristocrat John Falsworth journeys to Transylvania where he is attacked by Dracula. Following his transformation into a vampire Falsworth allies with Germany during World War I and attacks his brother (Union Jack). During World War II he aids the Nazis and stays at his family home Falsworth Manor. Posing as his own son his latest target is his niece Jaqueline who survives his bloodlust but is transformed into **Spitfire** following a life saving blood transfusion by the **Human Torch**.

After the **Sub-Mariner** slays the Baron with a

stake through his heart he is revived in the modern era where he once again pursues the Falsworth family. But **Captain America** puts an end to his vampirism when he decapitates him with his shield.

Baron Heinrich Zemo [Comic book character; SHW]

First appearance: The Avengers #4 (March 1964); Creators: **Stan Lee**, **Jack Kirby**; Publisher: Marvel Comics.

During World War II Heinrich Zemo is one of Adolf Hitler's top scientists. His most lethal inventions include a death ray and invulnerable androids capable of super-strength. But when Zemo becomes a reviled figure after turning the death ray on his fellow civilians he has to hide his face behind a hood to continue his work for the Nazi Party. The hood becomes a permanent feature when **Captain America** destroys his new invention Adhesive X. The super glue formula covers his hood, bonding it permanently to Zemo's face. Zemo vows revenge and finally succeeds in killing Bucky Jones and sending Captain America to a watery grave. But when Captain America is revived from his deep freeze in 1964 Baron Heinrich Zemo resurfaces from his South American domain. He finally meets his end after he kidnaps Captain America's new partner Rick Jones and is killed in an avalanche during Captain America's rescue of his partner.

Batman

1. [Comic book character]

First appearance: *Detective Comics* #27 (May 1939); Creators: Bob Kane, Bill Finger; Publisher: National Periodical Publications, Inc. (DC).

Batman and Robin the Boy Wonder gradually entered World War II with stories concentrating on fifth columnist enemy agents and spies. They would be best utilized on the home front defending America from the Axis powers. Most were standard crime-fighting adventures with no weird aspect to the stories. But even the dynamic duo encountered the occasional weird adventure as featured in the following stories.

"Atlantis Goes to War" [SFW]

First publication: *Batman* #118 (October–November 1943); Story: Don Cameron; Art: Dick Sprang.

U.S. merchant vessels are being torpedoed by vanishing Nazi submarines. Batman and Robin try to locate the elusive Nazi naval base in their batplane. Over the Atlantic they find themselves sucked into a tidal whirlpool that emerges into a blaze of light and "a great city of marble and metal." The German secret base is the fabled city of Atlantis! Kano, high priest of Atlantis informs Batman and Robin that the Nazis are their friends who love peace and justice. The Nazis have been telling the Atlanteans that America "wishes to enslave the world." Batman and Robin are sentenced to death for fear of bringing war to Atlantis if they are set free. But Robin has other plans. Imitating the brother of the young Empress Lanya the Atlanteans finally see through the Nazi charade when they threaten the lookalike Emperor with death if he doesn't order the death of Batman and Robin. Meanwhile Robin has fallen for the Empress and on his return to the surface is dejected that he will probably never see her again.

"The Year 3000" [SFW]

First publication: *Batman* #26 (December 1944– March 1945); Story: Joe Greene; Art: Dick Sprang.

In the year 3000 the warlord Fura from Saturn rules an enslaved Earth. One fateful evening Brane and young Ricky find a time capsule at the bottom of an atomic bomb crater. Shaped like a torpedo the inscription reads, "New York World's Fair 1939 Time Capsule." Opening the torpedo they find microfilm and instructions for building a machine to show the film. It is a history lesson about the birth of America with newsreel footage of two masked heroes named Batman and Robin.

Inspired by the film Brane and Ricky decide to become Batman and Robin in the year 3000, freeing political prisoners from concentration camps. The two-man army read up on "Commando Battle Tactics" from the Museum of Ancient History and become leaders of the resistance against the invaders from Saturn. The invading army are exposed as nothing more than robots and Earth is free again thanks to Batman and Robin of the future. In the final panels of the story Brane is revealed to be the twentieth direct descendant of.... Bruce Wayne!

2. *Batman* (1943) [Film serial; SFW]

Premiere: July 16, 1943; Main Cast: Lewis Wilson as Batman/Bruce Wayne, Douglas Croft as Robin/Dick Grayson, J. Carroll Naish as Dr. Daka, Shirley Patterson as Linda Page; Producer: Rudolph C. Flothow; Screenplay: Victor McLeod, Leslie Swabacker, Harry Fraser; Based on comic book characters created by Bob Kane and Bill Finger; Director:

The Batman (1943), a film serial starring Lewis Wilson as Batman/Bruce Wayne, Douglas Croft as Robin/Dick Grayson, J. Carroll Naish as Dr. Daka, and Shirley Patterson as Linda Page (Columbia Pictures).

Lambert Hillyer; 260 min. × 15 episodes; Columbia Pictures; B/W.

This fifteen-part serial saw the first appearance of Batman and Robin, the Boy Wonder on screen. J. Carrol Naish played the "Nipponese" spy attempting to turn Americans into zombies under his control. His sentiments echoed the real-life threat of Japanese forces in World War II.

"I am Doctor Daka, humble servant of his majesty Hirohito, heavenly ruler as prince of the rising sun. By divine destiny my country shall destroy the democratic forces of evil in the United States to make way for the new order. An order that will bring about the liberation of the enslaved people of America."

Chapter titles: 1. *The Electrical Brain*; 2. *The Bat's Cave*; 3. *The Mark of the Zombies*; 4. *Slaves of the Rising Sun*; 5. *The Living Corpse*; 6. *Poison Peril*; 7. *The Phony Doctor*; 8. *Lured by Radium*; 9. *The Sign of the Sphinx*; 10. *Flying Spies*; 11. *The Nipponese Trap*; 12. *Embers of Evil*; 13; *Eight Steps Down*; 14. *The Executioner Strikes*; 15. *Doom of the Rising Sun*.

Battle Hymn [Comic book; SHW]

First publication: January 2005; Five-issue miniseries; Story: B. Clay Moore; Art: Jeremy Haun; Publisher: Image Comics.

The final year of World War II sees the emergence of a new breed of super-humans, beginning with the Artificial Man. The U.S. government has its own agenda for these five powerful beings they call heroes, but the heroes have been kept in the dark about the government's true motives.

"The Battle of Manetong" [Pulp fiction; SFW]

Author: William P. McGivern; Illustrator: Robert Fuqua; First publication: *Fantastic Adventures* (Vol. 4 #6; June 1942); Publisher: Ziff-Davis Publishing Company.

A young German officer delivers a radio message to Captain Hohffer, ordering him to break camp immediately. The Nazi's new mission is to blow up a bridge and destroy a British truck column and their caravan escort of wounded colonials and Egyptian natives. But when the time to attack arrives the German soldiers become confused and "act like they've gone sun daffy."

The Germans have accidentally built an artillery structure on the foundation of the Tower of Babel and have been struck with the curse of many tongues.

Battler Britton [Comic book character; UK]

First appearance: *Knockout* (June 25, 1960); Publisher: Fleetway (Five-Star Weekly).

Wing Commander Robert Hereward "Battler" Britton of the Royal Air Force, battles the Axis powers during World War II. The majority of his stories are standard military heroics, but on occasion he battled a Weird War menace.

"Battler Britton and the Menace of the 'M' Men" [SFW]

First publication: *Knockout* (November 10, 1962).

The German Mechanic Men storm across the

British airfield, destroying everything in its path, including Battler Britton's fighting squadron. The Nazi robots continue on their destructive path, overrunning the British front line troops in France. As tanks cross a vital bridge it comes crashing down, destroyed by the mechanical army. Battler Britton rescues the Brigadier from drowning in the river and sets about stopping the Nazi robots with direct hits from tank shells. But his plan only has limited results....

Bedknobs and Broomsticks (1971) [Film; WW]

Premiere: December 13, 1971; Main Cast: Angela Lansbury as Miss Eglantine Price, David Tomlinson as Professor Emelius Brown, Roddy McDowall as Mr. Jelk, Sam Jaffe as Bookman, Roy Snart as Paul Rawlins, Ian Weighill as Charlie, Cindy O'Callaghan as Carrie; Producer: Robert Walsh; Screenplay: Bill Walsh, Don DaGradi; Animation Story: Ralph Wright, Ted Berman; Director: Robert Stevenson; 117 min.; Walt Disney Productions; Buena Vista Distribution Co.; Color.

August 1940. During World War II three cockney orphans are evacuated to the country village of Pepperinge Eye, England where they live with apprentice witch Miss Eglantine Price. The children uncover Miss Price's secret when they discover her witchcraft correspondence course. Flying on a magic bed with the aid of a magic bedknob Miss Price and the children travel to London to meet Professor Emelius Brown, headmaster of the Correspondence College of Witchcraft. Miss Price is searching for the elusive spell known as Substituary Locomotion that animates inanimate objects. They must locate the other half of the magic book "The Spells of Astoroth" in the hope of casting a spell to fight the invading Germans with a magical army.

Behemoth [Novel; SFW]

Author: Scott Westerfeld; Art: Keith Thompson; First publication: New York: Simon Pulse, 2010.

The British Darwinists and the Clanker Powers are at war in this sequel to **Leviathan**. Teenage female Darwinist Deryn Sharp is posing as an airman in order to serve in the British Air Service and her newfound friend Clanker Prince Aleksander is posing as a commoner. Their hopes of ending the war are frustrated when they find themselves hunted in enemy territory.

Meanwhile the British Navy has a new biological weapon that can swallow enemy battleships with one bite—the behemoth.

See: **Goliath**

Behind the Red Mist [Short story anthology; Vietnam; WW]

Author: Ho Anh Thai; First publication [U.S.]: Willimantic, CT; Curbstone Press, 1998.

A collection of ten short stories on the theme of patriotism versus the harsh reality of postwar life, by noted Vietnamese author Ho Anh Thai. In the title novella, after a young man from Hanoi receives an electric shock in his apartment he finds himself a part of his own past during the height of the Vietnam War in 1967. Meeting his parents before he was born, the young man discovers his parent's generation differs from the version he has been told.

Below (2002) [Film; WW]

Premiere: October 18, 2002; Main Cast: Matt Davis as Odell, Bruce Greenwood as Brice, Holt McCallany as Loomis, Dexter Fletcher as Kingsley, Olivia Williams as Claire; Executive Producers; Andrew Rona, Bob Weinstein, Harvey Weinstein; Story: Lucas Sussman, Darren Aronofsky, David Twohy; Director: David Twohy; 105 min.; Protozoa Pictures, Dimension Films; Miramax; Color.

On a routine mission during World War II, the crew of the submarine U.S.S. Tiger Shark encounter their deepest fears after taking on board two men and a woman after their boat is attacked. "Their senses betray them. Their minds deceive them. Their fear surrounds them."

Bernice Summerfield: Just War [Audio drama; UK; SFW]

Release date: August 1999; Main Cast: Lisa Bowerman as Bernice Summerfield, Stephen Fewell as Jason Kane, Michael Wade as Oberst Oskar Steinmann, Mark Gatiss as Standardtenfuhrer Joachim Wolff, Maggis Stables as Ma Doras, Nicky Golding as Nurse Rosa Kitzel; Adapted for audio by Jaqueline Rayner; Based on the novel by Lance Parkin; Director: Gary Russell; 115 min.; Publisher: Big Finish Productions.

Set in the Nazi-occupied island of Guernsey in 1941, British citizens are being deported to concentration camps or executed if they don't comply. Bernice Summerfield is stranded in time and must stop the creation of a new Nazi secret weapon that could alter history. This audio drama is an adaptation of the novel by Lance Parkin.

See: **Doctor Who: Just War**

Bernice Summerfield: Secret Origins [Audio drama; UK; SFW]

Release date: September 2009; Voice Cast: Lisa Bowerman as Bernice Summerfield, Donna Berlin as Robyn, Doug Bradley as Frost, Thomas Grant as Peter Summerfield, Duncan Wisbey as Agent Green/Captain Strasser/Lambton/Sebastian; 60 min.; Publisher: Big Finish Productions.

At a hospital in the ruined city of Buenos Aires a recuperating Bernice Summerfield alternates between memories of past and present. But she begins to doubt if her memories, that include Nazis attempting to create a race of super soldiers, are real.

Bernice Summerfield: The Oracle of Delphi [Audio drama; UK; SFW]

Release date: November 2006; Voice Cast: Lisa Bowerman as Bernice Summerfield, Stephen Fewell as Jason Kane, Paul Shelley as Socrates, Brigid Zengeni as Megaira, Scott Handcock as Plato; Story: Scott Handcock; Director: Edward Salt; 72 min.; Publisher: Big Finish Productions.

Greece, 430 BCE. Athens is at war with the Spartans. Amidst the chaos, time-traveling Bernice "Benny" Summerfield is searching for her husband Jason. Enlisting the help of Socrates in locating Jason, Bernice must also contend with the ancient powers of the Oracle of Delphi.

Beware of the Haunted Toilet [Juvenile book; SFW]

Author: Elaine Moore; First publication: Mahwah, N.J.: Troll Communications, 1998.

Crossfield Elementary School, Virginia. Friends Danny, Bill and Megan are beginning their sixth grade in a new school wing, built during the summer break. Now the toilet in the bathroom at the back of the class is acting strangely. Every time the topic of the American Civil War is discussed in class the toilet flushes by itself. When Danny and Mega investigate the mysterious toilet after school hours they meet the ghost of Joshua, a boy who was killed near the school during the Civil War. His reason for haunting the bathroom is simple— he wants the education he never had during his brief life.

The Beyond [Comic book]

Supernatural anthology title.

"CURSE OF THE MIDNIGHT PIPER" [WW]
First publication; #16 (October 1952); Art: Lou Cameron; Publisher: Ace Magazines.

Jean MacNorn inherits the ancestral MacNorn Castle in Scotland. Together with her cousin Duncan they explore the castle where they meet Scottish historian Bruce Glowry who tells them of its history.

"Many years ago the castle which originally belonged to the clan Glowry was besieged by the Black Duke, Angus MacNorn and his clansmen. After a bloody battle the MacNorns butchered the surviving Glowrys. Only Malcolm Glowry remained and he was entombed in the castle tower alive. With his last breath he cursed the clan Mac-Norn."

Duncan breaks into the sealed tower to see if the story is true and inadvertently releases Glowry's ghost. The ghost wastes no time in summoning the dead Glowry clan back to life. The undead army goes through the nearby village seeking out the MacNorn clan. Only light can defeat them.

Big X [Manga; Japan; SFW]

1. First publication: "Shonen Book" (November 1963); Creator: Tezuka Osamu; Publisher: Shueisha, Inc., Tokyo, Japan.

In the latter days of World War II Japanese Dr. Asagumo and German Dr. Engel work on a secret formula named Big X that will enable men to transform into giant super-soldiers. But when the Nazis are defeated in 1945 Dr. Asagumo passes on the Big X formula to his son Shigeru, before the Nazis kill him.

Twenty years later Shigeru is murdered by the newly formed Nazi Alliance who find the formula in his possession. Shigeru's son Asagumo Akira recovers Big X from the Nazis and continues the fight to defeat them with the help of telepathic Nina Burton.

2. **Big X** (1964) [Animated TV series; Japan]
First broadcast: August 3, 1964; Main Characters; Asagumo Akira, Big X, Nina, Dr. Hanamaru, Hans Engel; Executive Producer: Inada Nobuo; Animation: Eiji Suzuki, Renzo Kinoshita; Story: Jiro Kadota, Mami Murano, Tadashi Hirose, Yamamoto Group; Directors: Mitsuteru Okamoto, Osamu Dezaki; 30 × 59 min.; Tezuka Productions, Tokyo Movie, TBS; B/W.

Animated adaptation of the original manga by Tezuka Osamu.

Biggles: Adventures In Time (1986) [Film; UK; SFW]

Premiere: May 30, 1986 (UK); Main Cast: Neil Dickson as James "Biggles" Bigglesworth, Peter Cushing as Air Commodore Colonel William Raymond, Alex-Hyde-White as Jim Ferguson, Fiona Hutchison as Debbie Stephens, Marcus Gilbert as Eric Von Stalhein; Executive Producer: Adrian Scope; Screenplay: John Groves, Kent Walwin; Based on characters created by Captain W.E. Johns; Director: John Hough; 108 min.; Tambarle, Compact Yellowbill; Image Entertainment; Color.

Modern day New York advertising executive Jim Ferguson finds himself transported to 1917, flying a bi-plane during World War I. He has entered the body of his time-twin, ace pilot "Biggles." Together they must attempt to stop the Germans from using a new super-weapon that could turn the tide of the war.

Bitter Seeds [Novel; WW]

Author: Ian Tregillis; First publication: New York: Tor, 2010.

During the Spanish Civil War British secret agent Raybould Marsh sees a German woman with wires growing out of her head. In World War II he sees the same woman plus many other mutants being utilized by the Nazis. He decides to counter the German menace with his own secret occult army of warlocks and demons.

The Black Beetle [Comic book character; WW]

First publication: *Dark Horse Presents* #11 (April 2012); Creator: Francesco Francavilla; Publisher: Dark Horse Comics.

The mysterious vigilante Black Beetle fights crime in Colt City in the 1940s. In *The Black Beetle: Night Shift* #0 (December 2012)—a collection of his first three stories—Adolf Hitler sends his Werwolf Korps to steal a totem of dark magic on display in Colt City's Natural History Museum. But first they have to get past the city's protector, the Black Beetle.

Black Dahlia (1998) [Videogame; WW]

Released: February 28, 1998; Main Cast (live-action scenes): Dennis Hopper as Walter Pensky, Hillary Morris as Elizabeth Short, Teri Garr as Madame Cassandra, Darren Eliker as Jim Pearson, Rick Applegate as Wilhelm von Hess, John Hall as Eliot Ness; Story: Patrick Freeman, Steve Glasstetter; Directors: Eric Trow, Lance Laspina; Platform: Microsoft Windows; First-person shooter; Developer: Take2 Interactive Software; Publisher: Interplay Entertainment.

In this point-and-click puzzle solving adventure intercut with live-action scenes the player is in control of special government agent Jim Pearson as he uncovers the occult Nazi Thule Society and its link to ritualistic murders. Elizabeth Short possesses a gemstone with supernatural powers known as the Black Dahlia. When she is found brutally murdered and the gemstone missing Pearson delves ever deeper into the secrets of the evil Nazi society in his search for the missing Black Dahlia.

Black Max [Comic book character; UK; WW]

First appearance: *Thunder* #1 (October 17, 1970); Art: Alfonso Font; Publisher: IPC Magazines.

World War I flying ace, Baron Maximilien Von Klorr, found an ancient potion that transformed his pet bat into a giant Kingbat. Known by the Allied forces as Black Max, the Bat Master he believes he is a descendant of the Bat People. Able to communicate telepathically over vast distances his main foe is Lieutenant Tim Wilson of the Royal Flying Corps.

The Black Terror [Comic book character; SHW]

First appearance: *Exciting Comics* #9 (May 1942); Creators: Richard E. Hughes, David Gabrielsen; Publisher: Standard Comics.

After ingesting "formic ethers" pharmacist Bob Benton gains super-strength and invulnerability. *The Black Terror* strikes fear into foes such as the Nazis and Japanese with his black and gold trim costume with a large skull and crossbones emblem on the chest. Joining him in his wartime adventures was young assistant Tim Roland with mayor's secretary Jean Starr providing the romantic interest.

Blackadder Back & Forth (1999) [Film short; UK; SFW]

Premiere: December 6, 1999; Main Cast: Rowan Atkinson as Blackadders, Tony Robinson as Baldricks, Stephen Fry as Melchetts, Tim McInnerny as Darlings, Miranda Richardson as Elizabeths, Hugh Laurie as Viscount George Bufton-Tufton/Georgius, Simon Russell Beale as Napoleon, Rik Mayall as Robin Hood, Kate Moss as Maid Marian, Crispin Harris as Friar Tuck, Colin Firth as William Shakespeare; Executive Producers: Peter Bennett-Jones, Geoffrey Perkins; Story: Richard Curtis, Ben Elton; Director: Paul Weiland; 33 min.; New Millennium Experience Company, Sky, Tiger Aspect Productions; BBC Enterprises; Color.

When Baldrick devises a plan to build a fake time machine to make Edmund Blackadder's friends part with their money they are amazed when it actually works. The pair are whisked to various eras in time where they meet Robin Hood, William Shakespeare and Napoleon at the Battle of Waterloo.

The Blackhawks [Comic book characters]

First appearance: *Military Comics* #1 (August 1941); Creator: Charles "Chuck" Cuidera; Publisher: Quality Comics.

"Over land, over sea,
We fight to make men free,
We're Blackhawks!"

The freedom fighters originally consisted of their expatriate American leader Blackhawk, Andre, a ladies man from France, physically imposing Stanislaus from Poland, weapons expert and anti–Nazi Hendrickson from Germany, Swedish gymnast Olaf and the comical Chinaman Chop-Chop and his meat cleaver. Boris and Zeg were replaced by Chuck, a young communications specialist from America after the first year of adventures.

With Blackhawk Island as their secret airbase of operations the Blackhawks tackled the Axis powers during the war years but shifted to more weird premises in the 1950s.

"Breaking Through the Time Barrier" [WW]

First publication: *Blackhawk* #93 (October 1955); Story: Dick Wood; Art: Dick Dillin, Chuck Cuidera; Publisher: Quality Comics.

The bewildered Blackhawks find themselves in the midst of the Saratoga Campaign in the American Revolution. It is 1777. Three thousand Hessian troops under British command are about to attack a small Colonial force near Fort Ticonderoga.

Blackout [Novel: SFW]

Author: Connie Willis; First publication: Spectra Ballantine Books, 2010.

Oxford, England, 2060. The time-travel lab is cancelling assignments and rearranging schedules. Time traveling historians Michael Davies, Merope Ward and Polly Churchill find history taking strange turns as they journey to 1940 London during the London Blitz. Their belief that the past cannot be changed is put to the test when the war and the fabric of British society seems to be spinning out of control.

See: ***All Clear***

Blazing Glory [Comic book character; SHW]

First publication: *Heavy Metal Magazine* Vol. 259 #201211 (November 2012); Creator: David Elliott; Publisher: Titan Comics.

Blackhawk #93 (October 1955), "Breaking Through the Time Barrier," page 1. Art by Dick Dillin, Chuck Cuidera. Published by Quality Comics.

Cover of *Blackout* by Connie Willis (2010).

Sergeant Jason Wilson vows to take revenge on Adolf Hitler after his father dies during the attack on Pearl Harbor and his severely depressed mother drowns herself. Biology professor Abednego Danner, the brother of his grandmother subjects Jason Wilson to a series of experiments in 1942 and creates immortal super warrior *Blazing Glory*. Wilson alias *Blazing Glory* survives into the present day without aging, becoming a General in the Iraq War.

"Blitz Against Japan" [Pulp fiction; SFW]

Author: Robert Moore Williams; Illustrator: Robert Fuqua; First publication: *Amazing Stories* (Vol. 16 #9; September 1942); Publisher: Ziff-Davis Publishing Company.

When Japanese forces attack and land ashore in California it is time to use the secret weapon. A torpedo shaped "rocket ship" that projects a beam of radiation. Reimann, inventor of the weapon stated, "When this beam strikes a metallic object, the effect is to accelerate the action of the forces normally present in the metal that cause it to disintegrate."

Blitzed [Juvenile book; SFW]

Author: Robert E. Swindells; First publication: London: Doubleday, 2002.

Teenager George finds life in Witchfield dreary and boring and takes out his frustrations on his sister and the old lady who lives across the street. Going on a field trip with his school to the World War II museum, Eden Camp lifts his spirits. It is a subject that fascinates him. When he sees a hand sticking out through some fake rubble he can't resist touching it. But when he grasps the hand George finds himself slipping back through time to 1940s London and the Blitz. Now the war is a reality and George must learn to survive by joining a gang of homeless children who live through German air raids and track a German spy in their midst.

"Blitzkrieg in the Past" [Pulp fiction; SFW]

Author: John York Cabot; First publication: *Amazing Stories* (Vol. 16 #7; July 1942); Publisher: Ziff-Davis Publishing Company.

"The United States Tank division found itself facing something more terrible than Japs—across a million years of time…. The Tank Corps faced formidable foes in the jungles of Earth's youth. Lunging down on the surprised men was a huge nine-legged frog creature!"

Blood Creek (2009) [Film; WW]

Premiere; January 27, 2009; Main Cast: Henry Cavill as Evan Marshall, Dominic Purcell as Victor Alan Marshall, Emma Booth as Liese Wollner, Laszlo Matray as Karl Wollner, Joy McBrinn as Mrs. Wollner, Michael Fassbinder as Richard Wirth; Executive Producers: Scott Niemeyer, Eli Richbourg, Norm Waitt; Story: David Kajganich; Director: Joel Schumacher; 90 min.; Gold Circle Films, Lionsgate; Color.

An occult experiment conducted in 1936 by the Third Reich on the German Wollner family living in West Virginia has modern day repercussions. In 2007 paramedic Evan Marshall's missing brother suddenly turns up after two years claiming he escaped his captors on Wollner's farm. The Marshall's seek revenge but find evil in return.

Blood Red Roses [Novel; WW]

Author: Russell James; First publication: Cincinnati, OH; Samhain Publishing, 2014.

Ramses is the sadistic overseer of Beechwood plantation, Mississippi. Slave boys are vanishing from the plantation in the final days of the Civil War. Indentured slave Jebediah Abernathy will discover the ghastly truth behind those disappearances through the intervention of the ghost of his father and an escaped slave who also happens to be a sorceress.

BloodRayne [Videogame; WW]

Release Date: October 2002; Voice Cast: Laura Bailey as Rayne, Dameon Clarke as Hedrox, Josh Ashworth, Holt Boggs, Mary Beth Brooks, Bob Hess, Carolyn McCormick; Multiple Platforms; Developer: Terminal Reality; Publisher: Majesco Games; Distributor: Universal Interactive Studios.

Rayne, a half-vampire or Dhampir is recruited by the Brimstone Society as she continues the search for her father. In Argentina Rayne infiltrates a Nazi base and attempts to prevent Jurgen Wolf, leader of the Gengenheist Gruppe a.k.a. Counter-Ghost Group (G.G.G.) from obtaining an occult artefact that transfers supernatural powers to the owner. Her mission then takes BloodRayne to Nazi Germany and Castle Gaustadt where she must destroy the G.G.G. and Wolf.

BloodRayne: The Third Reich (2011) [Film; WW]

Premiere: June 10, 2011; Main cast: Natassia Malthe as Rayne, Brendan Fletcher as Nathaniel Gregor, Michael Pare as Commandant Ekart Brand, Annett Culp as Magda Markovic, William Belli as Vasyl Tishenko, Clint Howard as Doctor Mangler; Executive Producers: Wolfgang Herold, Jonathan Shore; Story: Michael C. Nachoff; Director: Uwe Boll; 79 min.; Herold Productions, Brightlight Pictures; Phase 4 Films; Color.

When Rayne's blood enables Commandant Ekart Brand to turn into a vampire Rayne must stop Doctor Mangler from using her blood to transform Adolf Hitler into an immortal dhampir.

Bloody Awful [Novel: WW]

Author: Georgia Evans (Rosemary Laurey); First publication: Kensington Books 2009.

The second book in the World War II paranormal trilogy. Gloria Prewiit has a secret. By day she is your friendly district nurse—but when the moon appears over the English country village of Brytewood, Gloria turns into a werefox. Now she has a new enemy to fight in the form of Nazi saboteur and vampire William Block who plans to complete the destruction of the munitions plant. But will Gloria's budding romance with Andrew Barron, manager of the munitions plant, compromise her mission?

Book Two in the World War II paranormal trilogy.

See: *Bloody Right*

Bloody Good a.k.a. Super Natural Acts [Novel: WW]

Author: Georgia Evans (Rosemary Laurey); First publication: Kensington Books 2009.

World War II, 1940. When country doctor Alice Doyle discovers corpses drained of blood she seeks the help of fellow Brytewood villagers in solving the mystery. But these villagers are far from average. Alice Doyle and her grandmother Helena are Devonshire Pixies, the police sergeant is a shape-shifting dragon, Old Mother Longhurst is a witch, the grocer is an elf, and Gloria Prewitt, the district nurse, is a werefox. But can they defeat the Nazi vampire Gerhardt Eiche, intent on blowing up the secret munitions plant?

Book One in the World War II paranormal trilogy.

See: *Bloody Awful*

The Bloody Red Baron [Novel; WW]

Author: Kim Newman; First publication: New York: Carroll & Graf, 1995.

Vampires take over the skies during World War I as shape-shifting Manfred von Richthofen, the Red Baron fights British vampire pilots. British Lieutenant Edwin Winthrop leads his squadron of Sopwith Camels into battle against winged vampires before he becomes a vampire himself.

Bloody Right [Novel: WW]

Author: Georgia Evans (Rosemary Laurey); First publication: Kensington Books 2009.

Battle scarred Gryffyth Pendragon has returned from the war in Norway minus a leg. The son of the village police sergeant who is also a shape shifting dragon, Gryffyth falls in love with school teacher Mary LaPrioux, a water sprite. Will the combined efforts of the "Others" in the form shape-shifting dragons, a were fox, a witch, Devonshire Pixies and a water sprite be enough to defeat the two Nazi vampires, Weiss and Schmidt, who plan to assassinate Winston Churchill when he visits Brytewood?

Book Three in the World War II paranormal trilogy.

Blubberella (2011) [Film; Germany-Canada; WW]

Premiere: July 29, 2011; Main Cast: Lindsay Hollister as Blubberella, Brendan Fletcher as Nathaniel Gregor, Michael Pare as Commandant Ekart Brand, Annett Culp as Magda Markovic, William Belli as Vasyl Tishenko, Clint Howard as Doctor Mangler; Executive Producers: Sandra Basso, Jonathan Shore; Story: Uwe Boll, Michael Christopher; Director: Uwe Boll; 87 min.; Event Film Distribution; Color.

Half vampire Blubberella has two loves in life. Killing Nazis and food. But when Blubberella exchanges bodily fluids with Commandant Ekart Brand he becomes a vampire. Blubberella has more troubles ahead as she faces a horde of undead Nazi soldiers.

This comedy film from Uwe Boll was filmed back-to-back *BloodRayne: The Third Reich* (2011) with has the same supporting cast.

Blue Devil Island [Novel; SFW]

Author: Stephen Mark Rainey; First publication: Waterville, ME: Five Star, 2007.

October 1943. The naval fighting squadron, the Blue Devils, commanded by Lieutenant Commander Drew McLachlan are based on the remote Conquest Island in the Pacific. Soon it becomes apparent that the Japanese aren't their only enemy when members of the Blue Devils team are found mutilated. A giant, half-invisible shape leads the men to the caves scattered among the mountain landscape and the discovery of an extraterrestrial menace.

The Blue Diamond [Comic book character; SHW]

First appearance: *Daring Mystery Comics* #7 (April 1941); Creator: Ben Thompson; Publisher: Timely Comics.

Professor Elton Morrow uncovers a gigantic blue diamond on an Antarctic expedition. On the journey home Morrow's ship is sunk by a Nazi U-boat, resulting in diamond particles penetrating Morrow's brain. The only survivor from the sunken ship, Morrow now finds the properties of the blue diamond have transformed his body. "I feel as solid as a granite cliff!"

During World War II Morrow battles Nazi spies as the Blue Diamond where he is affiliated with the **Liberty Legion**, *New Invaders* and *Crazy Sues*.

The Blue Tracer [Comic book character; SFW]

First appearance: *Military Comics* #1 (August 1941); Creator: Fred Guardineer; Publisher: Quality Comic Group.

"Somewhere in the jungles of Ethiopia the remains of an ambushed British scouting division lies under the merciless sun. All are apparently dead. At last one figure moves—It is Captain Bill Dunn, an American engineer sent out with the expedition."

Bill Dunn is nursed back to health in a native village where he meets Australian Boomerang Jones, the only survivor of the 25th Anzacs who were attacked and killed by super beings named M'Bujies. From their impregnable fortress city base they are making plans to rule the world.

Dunn decides to counter their threat by building a super-weapon "that will fly like an airplane, dive like a submarine and smash into obstacles like a tank. From its bullet-like nose cannons and machine guns belch death and destruction. Seen only as a streak of blue this newest and most formidable of all modern engines of war zooms away like a tracer bullet fired from a gigantic cannon—the Blue Tracer is born!"

Captain Dunn and Boomerang Jones encountered undead Nazis in issue #15 of *Military Comics* (January 1943). "Chaos stalks the Eastern Front as Allied forces fall back before a hideous German army—for the Nazi legions are rising from the dead to fight again, sweeping onward to certain victory!"

Their limbs regenerated instantly by a radio electric compound directed on a radio beam, the Nazis are electrified. The Blue Tracer tracks the beam to a radio tower and destroys it as, "The oncoming Nazis, the deathless dead, stagger and fall."

Bombshell—Son of War [Comic book character; MWW]

First appearance: *Boy Comics* #3 (April 1942); Creator: Dick Wood, "Michael"; Publisher: Lev Gleason Publications.

"On the battlefields of warring nations, a brazen young figure alights to single-handedly combat the blood-crazed war lords ... ripping through their ranks with sword and shield, Bombshell, endowed with the mystic gifts of Mars himself, blasts a path of peace over the world...."

Mars, the god of war, is disgusted with Hitler.

"War was never meant to be turned into reckless slaughter ... for selfish greed. He must be stopped!" As Mars and his two fellow gods discuss the war a monstrous beast named Koro prepares to attack them. Mars' youthful son Bombshell slays the beast before he can pounce.

Mars makes a fateful decision. "Bombshell shall go to Earth and fight against the barbaric wars of civilization. He shall have a costume that denotes his power and a sword to destroy the machines of war, but which, cannot take human life."

And so Bombshell, son of war, enters World War II to defeat the Nazis and preserve the peace.

El Bosc a.k.a. ***The Wood*** (2012)
[Film; Spain; SFW]
Premiere: December 14, 2012 (Spain); Main Cast: Maria Mollins as Dora, Tom Sizemore as Pickett, Pere Ponce as Coixo, Alex Brendemuhl as Ramon, Josep Maria Domenech as Fusteret; Executive Producer: Ramon Vidal; Story: Albert Sanchez Pinol; Director: Oscar Albar; 94 min.; Audiovisual Aval SGR; Savor; Color.

The Spanish Civil War in 1936. Strange lights are seen twice a year in the woods surrounding the farmhouse of Ramon and his wife Dora. Legend says the lights lead to a portal to another world. When an anarchist from the militia occupying the Lower Aragon falls in love with Dora the legend is put to the test.

"The Bowmen" [Short story; WW]
First publication: *The Evening News* (London September 29, 1914); Author: Arthur Machen.

Overwhelmed by German artillery on the battlefield during World War I a British soldier suddenly recalls the motto he has seen inscribed on dinner plates in a London restaurant and utters the prayer "Adsit Anglis Sanctus Georgius—May St. George be a present help to the English" Suddenly he hears a thundering voice cry, "Array, array, array!" as the shining spirits of English bowmen "let fly a cloud of arrows at the advancing Germans, who fall dead in their thousands."

Inspired by the retreat of British forces at Mons, France a few weeks earlier in August 1914, Arthur Machen's story was never meant to be read as a factual account. Instead it perpetuated the legend of the "Angels of Mons." In his introduction to the short story collection *The Bowmen and Other Legends of the War* (Reynolds & Charlton, 1915) Machen explained the truth behind the story and the reasons for the misunderstanding.

"In THE BOWMEN my imagined soldier saw 'a long line of shapes, with a shining about them.' And Mr. A.P. Sinnett, writing in the May issue of THE OCCULT REVIEW, reporting what he had heard, states that "those who could see said they saw 'a row of shining beings' between the two armies." Now I conjecture that the word "shining" is the link between my tale and the derivative

The Bowmen and Other Legends of the War by Arthur Machen. Published by Simpkin, Marshall, Hamilton, Kent & Co., London, 1915.

from it. In the popular view shining and benevolent supernatural beings are angels, and so, I believe, the Bowmen of my story have become "the Angels of Mons." In this shape they have been received with respect and credence everywhere, or almost everywhere.

"And here, I conjecture, we have the key to the large popularity of the delusion—as I think it. We have long ceased in England to take much interest in saints, and in the recent revival of the cultus of St. George, the saint is little more than a patriotic figurehead. And the appeal of the saints to succour us is certainly not a common English practice; it is held Popish by most of our countrymen. But angels, with certain reservations, have retained their popularity, and so, when it was settled that the English army in its dire peril was delivered by angelic aid, the way was clear for general belief, and for the enthusiasms of the religion of the man in the street. And so soon as the legend got the title 'The Angels of Mons' it became impossible to avoid it."

Despite Machen's assertion that the Angel of Mons legend originated with his story, others remained cynical. Officers on the front-line gave first hand testimony based on what they considered to be actual events. "They heard the German cavalry coming after them ... turned and faced the enemy, expecting nothing but instant death, when to their wonder they saw, between them and the enemy, a whole troop of angels. The German horses turned round terrified and regularly stampeded. The men tugged at their bridles, while the poor beasts tore away in every direction" (*All Saints Parish Magazine*. Clifton: May 1915).

The London Times Literary Supplement (August 19, 1915) stated: "Long after the war is over, and the facts have been recorded in histories, one of the most widely known events will be the appearance of St. George and his angel-warriors in the defence of the British during the retreat from Mons. We say 'known,' because posterity will 'know' that the Saint came down. People 'know' it already. The papers are full of the occurrence, and the testimony pours from all sides. And here is Arthur Machen roundly declaring that none of the testimony yet given is worth a rap: that the whole thing arose out of a story which he himself made up out of his head, in church, and sent to the Evening News."

See: **Weird Horrors**.

Boy Commandos [Comic book characters]

A motley group of orphaned kids fight the Germans during World War II. Although the characters don't possess any super-powers or weird qualities they are introduced to readers with a Weird War tale.

"Nostradamus Predicts" [WW]

First publication: *Detective Comics* #65 (July 1942); Story: **Jack Kirby**; Art: **Joe Simon**; Publisher: National Periodical Publications (DC).

"To most of us a book of history is dull ... far from interesting. This is a tale from history, past and present—of those who wrote it and those who live it ... it is not dull."

16th century prophet Nostradamus is summoned to the court of Catherine, Queen of France. She is curious about the future. Nostradamus tells her of a dark leader who will conquer France and shows her a sketch of Adolf Hitler. But he assures the queen that he too will be conquered and driven from France. "There will be child warriors among them, innocents of great courage, who led by a soldier from the new world across the sea, will write a glorious chapter in the annals of free men! They will come to France in armored ships ... they will land in monstrous firespewing machines ... even drop from the skies!"

His vision of future events becomes a reality as Commandos parachute from the sky into enemy territory and we are introduced to Rip Carter training the Boy Commandos in England.

The Boys from Brazil (1978) [Film; UK-USA; SFW]

Premiere: October 6, 1978; Main Cast: Gregory Peck as Dr. Josef Mengele, Laurence Olivier as Ezra Lieberman, James Mason as Eduard Seibert, Lilli Palmer as Esther Lieberman, Uta Hagen as Drieda Maloney, Steven Guttenberg as Barry Kohler, Denholm Elliott as Sidney Beynon; Executive Producer: Robert Fryer; Screenplay Heywood Gould. Based on the novel by Ira Levin; Director: Franklin J. Schaffner; 125 min.; Producer's Circle, ITC, Lew Grade; Twentieth Century–Fox; Color.

Nazi Dr. Josef Mengele, now living in Paraguay, clones 95 youngsters from Adolf Hitler. Nazi hunter Ezra Lieberman tracks Mengele to the home of one of the Hitler clones who takes sides with Lieberman and sets his dogs on Mengele. Lieberman must decide whether to hunt the remaining young Hitler clones and kill them or to show them mercy.

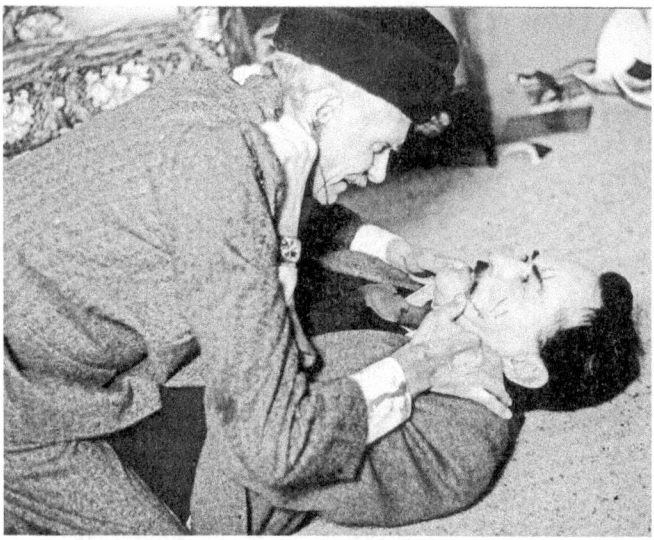

The Boys from Brazil (1978), starring (from left) Laurence Olivier as Nazi hunter Ezra Lieberman and Gregory Peck as infamous Nazi geneticist Dr. Josef Mengele (Twentieth Century–Fox).

Braddock [Comic book character; UK]
First appearance: *Rover* #1414 (August 2, 1952); Publisher: D.C. Thomson.

Sergeant Matt Braddock V.C. D.F.M. was Britain's greatest pilot during World War II. His adventures were initially chronicled by his navigator Sergeant George Bourne in the text story series, *I Flew With Braddock*. His adventures concentrated on standard war heroics, but he wasn't immune to weird stories.

"Braddock Fought the Flying Saucers" [SFW]
First publication: *Rover and Wizard* #270–#289 (March 19, 1966–August 22, 1966).

The final story of Braddock's original run in *Rover and Wizard* sees him encountering Unidentified Flying Objects.

Brainiape [Comic book character; SFW]
First appearance: *Savage Dragon* #23 (October 1995); Story-Art: Erik Larsen; Publisher: Image Comics.

Adolf Hitler survived World War II with a double dying in the Berlin bunker in 1945. But in 1952 as he plans to resurrect the Nazi party in Romania Hitler is defeated by paranormal investigator **Hellboy**. With his body destroyed Hitler's brain is salvaged by Nazi scientists and stored in a dome on top of a large gorilla. In 1966 the gorilla breaks free and continues to emulate Hitler's brutal, dictatorial personality despite having no memory of him. When his memory returns in 1996 he is killed but once again his brain survives. It is recovered by long-time Nazi follower **Baron Blitzkrieg** who fits Hitler with a new robotic body.

Breath of Bones: A Tale of the Golem [Comic book; WW]
First Publication: June 2013; Story: Steve Niles, Matt Santoro; Art: Dave Wachter; Publisher: Dark Horse Comics.

World War II. After a young boy and his grandfather witness a British plane crash into a field they give shelter to the badly injured pilot. But when German soldiers come to the village in search of the pilot they are ambushed and killed. Sensing serious trouble ahead the grandfather gives his grandson a family heirloom—a small figure of a golem. "Because sometimes it takes monsters to stop monsters."

The grandfather, grandson and children of the village proceed to create a huge golem out of clay. At the orders of the grandson the golem comes to life as his grandfather passes away. When German tanks and soldiers return to the village in force the golem awaits to fight and destroy them.

Bride of the Night [Novel: WW]
Author: Heather Graham; First publication: Don Mills, Ontario: HQN, 2011.

Pinkerton detective Finn Dunne captures Confederate spy Tara Fox aboard a ship, thinking she's part of a conspiracy to kill President Lincoln. But the beautiful vampire Tara wants to protect Lincoln from harm. Together they must keep the President safe, despite Dunne's misgivings.

Bring the Jubilee [Novel; SFW]
Author: Ward Moore; First publication: *The Magazine of Fantasy and Science Fiction* (November 1952).

The victory of the Confederate States of America at the Battle of Gettysburg has plunged the United States into poverty and violence. Industrial and technological progress has been stifled and the horse drawn carriage and gaslight remains in use into the early 1950s. Now a new war is threatened between the Confederacy and the German Union.

Historian Hodgins McCormick Backmaker wants to escape the present day and the clutches of the Grand Army. But when his wishes come true and he travels back in time to the Battle of Gettysburg he inadvertently changes the outcome of the battle and becomes trapped in the past.

Originally published as a novella in 1952, author Ward Moore expanded his alternate history science fiction story for publication by New York publisher Farrar, Straus & Young in 1953.

Bring the Thunder [Comic book; SHW]
First publication: December 2010; Four-issue miniseries; Story: Jai Nitz, Alex Ross; Art: Wilson Tortosa; Publisher: Dynamite Entertainment.

Following a deadly mission elite U.S. Air Force para-rescue jumper Wayne Russell is declared dead in Afghanistan. But one year later he finds himself alive in Chicago with superhuman sonic powers. Meanwhile back in Afghanistan, an Afghan sniper named Fariad has developed the same powers. He must return to Afghanistan to face Fariad in a showdown to the death.

B.R.P.D.: 1946 [Comic book; WW]
First publication: January 2008; Five-issue miniseries; Story: Mike Mignola, Joshua Dysart; Art: Paul Azaceta; Publisher: Dark Horse Comics.

Amid the ruins of post World War II Berlin, occult investigator Professor Trevor Bruttenholm, and his demon guardian **Hellboy**, form the Bureau for Paranormal Research and Defense. It's first mission to investigate the Nazi Occult Bureau's, Project Vampir Sturm.

Followed by *B.R.P.D.: 1947* (November 2009) and *B.R.P.D.: 1948* (October 2012).

Bulletman [Comic book character]
First appearance: *Nickle Comics* #1 (May 1940); Creator: Jon Small; Publisher: Fawcett Publications.

Orphan Jim Barr vows to find a cure for crime after his father, a police sergeant is killed by gangsters. After he fails the physical to follow his father's profession the 97-pound weakling creates a serum that gives him super-strength and vastly increased brain power. He then creates a bullet shaped "gravity regulating helmet" that gives him the power of flight.

Over time he is joined by police chief's daughter Susan Kent alias *Bulletgirl*. Although their adventures mainly center on tackling crime they do help out in the war effort.

The *Bulletman* comic book included the feature "Ghost Stories" by writer and artist Dave Berg. Issue #8 (October 1942) was a Weird War tale.

When a sadistic Nazi Lieutenant, identified as "V-31" by the marking on his collar, shoots American concentration camp victim Sam Schwartz, he vows with his final breath to return from the grave. Fearing for his life the Lieutenant changes uniforms with Karl in the hope of misleading the ghost of Schwartz.

Meanwhile the ghost leads the living concentration camp prisoners in an escape attempt. Karl is killed as the Lieutenant warns the other German officers of the escape. But the Lieutenant, now wearing Private Karl's uniform, is mocked by the guards who refuse to listen to him and is gunned down by a ghostly machine-gunner. Sam Schwartz's revenge is complete.

Bulletproof Monk [Comic Book; Film; WW]

1. First publication: 1998; 3-Issue Mini-Series; Story: R.A. Jones. Brett Lewis; Art: Michael Avon Oeming, Jason Baumgartner; Publisher: Image Comics.

2. Premiere: April 16, 2003; Main Cast: Chow Yun-Fat as Monk With No Name, Sean William Scott as Kar, Jamie King as Jade, Karel Roden as Struker, Victoria Smurfit as Nina, Marcus Jean Pirae as Mr. Funkastic, Roger Yuan as Master Monk; Executive Producers: Michael Yanover, Kelly Smith-Waite, Gotham Chopra, Caroline Macauley; Story: Ethan Reiff, Cyrus Voris; Director: Paul Hunter; 103 min.; Metro-Goldwyn Mayer Pictures (MGM); Color.

The "Monk With No Name" has protected a Tibetan scroll called "The Scroll of the Ultimate" for 60 years. He was first given the task in 1943 during World War II and has spent those 60 years being hunted across the world by Nazis who want the supernatural power the scroll grants. Now it is time to name a successor. Street-wise Kar, who works at a decrepit Kung Fu cinema, is chosen. Together with a Russian mob princess named Jade the threesome must save the world from the scroll reaching the Nazi enemy.

The Bunker (2001) [Film; UK; WW]
Premiere: June 8, 2004; Main Cast: Jason Flemyng as Cpt. Baumann; Andrew Tiernan as Lt. Cpl. Schenke, Christopher Fairbank as Sgt. Heydrich, Simon Kunz as Lt. Krupp, Andrew Lee Potts as Pvt. Newman; Executive Producer: George Marshall; Story: Clive Dawson; Director: Rob Green; 95 min.; Millennium Pictures; High Point Film and Television; Color.

When a group of German soldiers find themselves trapped in a bunker following an attack by U.S. troops they decide to explore its tunnels in the hope of finding an escape route. But they only find an escape into the supernatural.

Burgos, Carl (1917–1984) [Comic book artist-writer]

Born Max Finkelstein, April 18, 1916, in New York City. After a short stint at the Harry "A" Chesler studio, Burgos worked for Lloyd Jacquet's Funnies, Inc., studio that supplied strips for Timely Comics. October 1939 saw the introduction of Burgos' **Human Torch** in *Marvel Comics* #1. The following year the Human Torch graduated to his own title, becoming one of Timely's most successful wartime characters. In 1942 Burgos left comics to serve in the Air Force and Signal Corps. Never an outstanding artist, Burgos' postwar comic book work was sparse, although he did resurface briefly in 1964–65 for Marvel Comics, contributing to *Giant-Man* and the new, revised *Human Torch* in *Strange Tales* # 123 (August 1964).

A disillusioned Burgos failed in his attempt to gain the rights to the Human Torch in the 1960s and discarded his Golden Age comic book collection in 1966. In later years Burgos served as editor for the black-and-white horror comics of Eerie Publications.

He died March 1, 1984, age 67.

The Burning Zone (1996) [TV series]

Main Cast: Michael Harris as Dr. Daniel Cassian, Jeffrey Dean Morgan as Dr. Edward Marcase, Tamlyn Tomita as Dr. Kimberly Shiroma, James Black as Agent Michael Hailey; Creator; Coleman Luck.

A top-secret federal biological task force investigates potential disasters and "The Dawn" whose aim is to destroy the human race.

MIDNIGHT CARRIER (1:11) [WW]

Air date: January 7, 1997; Guest Cast: Tim O'Connor as William Heldermann/ Erhardt Boem, Tim Ryan as Robert Stennis, Wolf Muser as Nazi Doctor; Executive Producers: Coleman Luck, James D. McAdams; Story: Carleton Eastlake; Director: Janet Greek; 44 min.; Universal Television, Sandstar Productions; United Paramount Network (UPN); Color.

A capsule recovered from the head of an old man is linked to occultism in the Third Reich.

Bury the Dead (1936) [Stage play; WW]

Premiere: April 18, 1936, Ethel Barrymore Theater, New York, NY; Originally published in *New Theatre Magazine* (April 1936); Playwright: Irwin Shaw; Original Cast: Robert Thomsen as "Blinky," Private Driscoll, Frank Twedell as "Basket," Private Schelling, Will Geer as "Poppy," Reporter, David Sands as Private Morgan, Douglass Parkhurst as Private Dean, James Shelburne as Private Webster, Bertram Thorn as Private Levy, Edwin Cooper as Priest, Samson Gordon as Rabbi, Jay Adler as Charlie, Paula Bauersmith as Martha Webster, Norma Chambers as Katherine Driscoll, Kathryn Grill as Bess Schelling, Mary Perry as Mrs. Dean, Rose Keane as Joan, Leslie Stafford as Julia Blake; Alex Yokel presents The Actors' Repertory Company, Directors: Worthington Minor, Walter Hart.

Six dead American soldiers refuse to be buried as an anti-war protest. They don't want to become a party to the military narrative that glorifies the death and sacrifice of soldiers.

By the Blood of Heroes: The Great Undead War (Book 1) [Novel; WW]

Author: Joseph Nassise; First publication: New York: HarperCollins, 2012.

In the killing fields of France during World War I the Germans have created an undead army with a deadly new weapon capable of restoring life to the dead, T-Leiche—"Corpse Gas." When air ace Major Jack Freeman is shot down and captured Captain Michael "Madman" Burke assembles a team including an expert on the supernatural to rescue Freeman from behind enemy lines.

See: **On Her Majesty's Behalf: The Great Undead War**

"Cain's Atonement" [Short story; WW]

Author: Algernon Blackwood; First publication: *Land and Water* Vol. 66 #2793 (November 20, 1915).

Two cousins named Jones and Smith find their paths crossing at regular intervals throughout their young lives. Jones leads a charmed life while the dice are always loaded against Smith. He can't shake the feeling he is "paying off a debt." World War I breaks out and the cousins' friendship deepens. Smith is wounded by a bullet in the chest protecting Jones from a bomb. In his hospital bed Smith is overcome with a strange feeling.

"All of this had happened before. He had already, somewhere, somehow seen death descending upon his cousin from the air. Yet with a difference."

True to form Jones is decorated for bravery and Smith's heroic actions are ignored by the military. But Smith isn't bitter because he feels he owes it to Jones. As he continues to recover from his bullet wound Smith encounters, "flashes of another kind of consciousness ... bathed in a high, soft light, he was aware of things he could not quite account for." To Smith "it was absolutely real."

Smith finds himself in a land of wooded hills on the edge of a riverbank with his twin brother at his side. His brother holds a bloody spear in his hand from hunting a wild beast that has been destroying their flock. But Smith has hate in his heart for his brother over their love for the same woman. As they cross the stream a wounded beast lunges at his brother from above. Smith hesitates in killing the beast with his spear and his brother dies. Smith is grief stricken, blaming his hesitation for his brother's death. Now back in the present in his hospital bed Smith knows the reason he needs to pay off a debt.

Call of Cthulhu: The Wasted Land [Video game; WW]

Release date: January 30, 2012; Platforms: iOS, Microsoft Windows, Android; Designer: Tomas Rawlings; Developer-Publisher: Red Wasp Design-Chaosium.

The tactical role-playing game takes place during World War I and centers around a secret cult headed by Doctor Kaul who is creating an undead army from the war dead using a mixture of magic and stolen re-animation technology. His ultimate aim is a new hybrid species, part human, part Star Spawn of Cthulhu. Professor Brightmeer and British Army officer Captain Hill must go behind enemy lines and stop Kraul from summoning a Star Spawn.

Based on the Cthulhu mythos originally created by author H. P. Lovecraft.

Call of Duty: World at War: Zombies [Video game; WW]

Release date: November 16, 2009; Platform: iOS; Developer: Ideaworks Game Studio; Publisher: Activision.

This first-person shooter game takes place from the perspective of a U.S. Marine in a German bunker during World War II. Players must defend themselves in the bunker from the ever increasing threat of Nazi zombie soldiers.

Camel Spiders (2011) [Telefilm; WW]

Premiere: March 4, 2011; Main Cast: Brian Krause as Capt. Mike Sturges, C. Thomas Howell as Sheriff Ken Beaumont, Rocky DeMarco (Melissa Brasselle) as Sgt. Shelley Underwood, Frankie Cullen as Cpl. Schwalb; Executive Producer: Roger Corman; Story: J. Brad Wilke, Jay Andrews; Director: Jay Andrews (Jim Wynorski); 80 min.; Anchor Bay Entertainment, New Horizons; Syfy; Color.

While fighting in Afghanistan the Taliban are attacked by giant spiders known by locals as, "Devils of the Sand." Despite initial cynicism U.S. soldiers soon find themselves under attack. The spiders crawl inside the body bag of Corporal Schwalb and on arrival in the U.S. make their exit into the desert of the Southwest where they attack and kill anyone who crosses their path.

Cannibal Apocalypse (1980) [Film; Italy-Spain; WW]

Premiere: August 4, 1980 (Italy); Main Cast: John Saxon as Norman Hopper, Elizabeth Turner as Jane Hopper, John Morghen as Charlie Bukowski, Cindy Hamilton as Mary, Tony King as Tom Thompson; Producers: Edmondo Amati, Maurizio Armati, Sandro Amati; Screenplay: Anthony M. Dawson, Jimmy Gould; Director: Anthony M. Dawson; 96 min.; Jose Frade, New Fida, Edmondo Amati; Almi Cinema 5; Color.

In Vietnam Norman Hopper is bitten by infected prisoner-of-war Charlie Bukowski. Back in America Bukowski is now a cannibal with those he infected, including Hopper, joining him in his bloody pursuit of human flesh.

English credit pseudonyms were adopted by Antonio Margheriti (Anthony M. Dawson), Dardano Sacchetti (Jimmy Gould), Giovanni Lombardo Radice (John Morghen) and Cinzia De Carolis (Cindy Hamilton).

Captain America [Comic book character; SHW]

1. First appearance: *Captain America* #1 (March 1941); Creators: Joe Simon, Jack Kirby; Publisher: Timely.

On December 20, 1940, Captain America was introduced to his readers striking Adolf Hitler with a right-handed fist to his face, and deflecting Nazi bullets with his shield which proudly displayed an abbreviated version of the stars and stripes of the American flag. **Joe Simon** and **Jack Kirby**'s creation was a patriotic super-hero with a specific mission—to defeat the Axis enemies—personified in his greatest foe, the **Red Skull**.

Captain America began life as puny 4-F Steve Rogers, a volunteer for a secret government program to test a serum aimed at creating "the first of a corps of super-agents whose mental and physical ability will make them a terror to spies and saboteurs!" But after Rogers was injected a Nazi spy, intent on stealing the serum, opened fire, killing Professor Reinstein and others in the room. Meanwhile, the effects of the serum had transformed Rogers into a muscle-bound dynamo. But as he tackled the Nazi spy the serum was destroyed and the infiltrator electrocuted. Rogers was now accepted into the U.S. Army but needed to protect his super-soldier status. Captain America was born, complete with star-spangled costume and shield, that transformed in shape from triangular in *Captain America* # 1 (March 1941) to round in *Captain America* # 2 (April 1941). Soon he was joined by young sidekick Bucky Barnes, who had discovered Private Steve Rogers' secret identity at Camp Lehigh where they were both stationed.

During the war years Cap and Bucky encountered numerous weird foes including Nazi agents Dr. Creeper (posing as a fake medium), the Creeper and the Reaper. Outlandish plots featured invaders from Mars armed with German Lugar guns, the Sea People under the command of a Nazi known as the Hooded Horror, the brain of Olaf Olsen transferred into the body of a living dinosaur in order to destroy an American munitions plant and Man-Monster Fungi, created by Hitler's scientists to ruin crops in America and a Nazi mole-man targeting London with a series of bombs.

After World War II ended Captain America suffered declining sales and was relaunched as *Captain America's Weird Tales* with #74 in October 1949. Captain America battled his old war nemesis the Red Skull yet again, but this time he had to journey to his new residence in Hell to fight him. Time was up for Captain America. This would be his final appearance in his own title until 1954 when his new enemy was "The Betrayers!— Communism was spreading its ugly, grasping tentacles all over the world!" But the readers showed little interest in Captain America fighting the Communist menace and he disappeared from the newsstands for the next decade.

Stan Lee, editor of Marvel Comics, resurrected Captain America in *The Avengers* #4 (March 1964). While attempting to stop an explosive-filled drone plane Steve Rogers and Bucky Barnes discover it is booby-trapped. Bucky dies in the explosion and Rogers plummets into the ocean where he survives in a frozen state of suspended animation until he is discovered by the **Sub-Mariner** and thawed in warmer waters. But a revived Captain America still has a World War II mindset. He is a man out of time obsessed with the death of Bucky and the desire to seek revenge on those responsible.

Stan Lee stated, "He's the ultimate patriot in our country. He wasn't just a guy fighting bad guys."

Captain America [Animated TV series; SHW]

2. Premiere: September 1, 1966; Voice Cast: Sandy Becker as Captain America/Steve Rogers, Carl Banas as Bucky, Paul Kligman as Red Skull; Story: **Stan Lee**; Key Art: **Jack Kirby**, Don Heck; Directors: Clyde Geronimi, Sid Marcus; 13x22 min.; Gantray-Lawrence Animation, Superhero Productions, Inc.; Saban Entertainment; Color.

Limited animation series featuring three seven-minute chapters per episode. Adapted from Marvel comic book stories, incorporating Jack Kirby and Don Heck's original artwork. Episodes include the origin of **Captain America**, his return from suspended animation and his battles with **Red Skull** and **Baron Zemo**. The *Captain America* episodes were part of a rotating format featuring Iron Man, Thor and **Sub-Mariner** on *The Marvel Super-Heroes* animated series.

Season One

1:01—*The Origin of Captain America*—*Wreckers Among Us*—*Enter Red Skull*; 1:02—*The Sentinel and the Spy*—*The Fantastic Origin of the Red Skull*—*Lest Tyranny Triumph*; 1:03—*Midnight at Greymore Castle*—*This Be Treason*—*When You Lie Down with Dogs*; 1:04—*The Revenge of Captain America*—*The Trap Is Sprung*—*So Dies a Villain*; 1:05—*The Return of Captain America*—*The Search*—*To Live Again*; 1:06—*Zemo and His Masters of Evil*—*Zemo Strikes*—*The Fury of Zemo*; 1:07—*Let the Past Be Gone*—*The Adaptoid*—*The Super Adaptoid*; 1:08—*Coming of the Swordsman*—*Vengeance Is Ours*—*Emissary of Destruction*; 1:09—*Bitter Taste*—*Sorcery Triumph*—*The Road Back*; 1:10—*When the Commisar Commands*—*Doorway to Doom*—*Duel or Die*; 1:11—*The Sleeper Shall Awake*—*Where Walks the Sleeper*—*The Final Sleep*; 1:12—*The Girl from Cap's Past*—*The Stage Is Set*—*Thirty Minutes to Live*; 1:13—*The Red Skull Lives*—*He Who Holds the Cosmic Tube*—*The Red Skull Supreme*.

Captain America (1990) [Film; SHW]

3. Premiere: July 22, 1992; Main Cast: Matt Salinger as Captain America/Steve Rogers. Scott Paulin as

Red Skull, Ronny Cox as Tom Kimball, Ned Beatty as Sam Kolawetz, Darren McGavin as General Fleming, Carla Cassola as Dr. Maria Vaselli, Bill Mumy as Young General Fleming, Kim Gillingham as Bernice Stewart/Sharon, Melinda Dillon as Mrs. Rogers; Producer: Menaheim Golan; Story: Stephen Tolkin, Lawrence J. Block. Based on characters created by Joe Simon, Jack Kirby; Director: Albert Pyun; 97 min.; 21st Century Film Corp,. Marvel Enterprises, Jadran Film; Color.

This live-action adaptation of *Captain America* begins in Mussolini's Italy. Italian scientist Dr. Maria Vaselli has developed a new drug that enhances physical and mental capabilities. But the scientist's good intentions are perverted by Mussolini's storm troopers, who inject an abducted boy genius with the drug in "Project Rebirth." He emerges with super-strength, but a scarred and deformed red skull-face.

Meanwhile Dr. Vaselli has fled to America and offered her drug to the U.S. government where weak Steve Rogers is a willing test subject. Now outfitted in his patriotic red, white and blue costume, Captain America fights the Red Skull. At the end of the war Captain America finds himself fastened to a flying bomb headed for the White House. The Red Skull awaits its destruction, but Captain America diverts the bomb off course to Alaska where he remains in deep freeze until early 1990s.

Captain America is restored from deep freeze only to find his old World War II enemy Red Skull still alive. U.S. President Tom Kimball has been kidnapped by the Red Skull's henchmen and now Captain America must rescue the President in Italy before they place a mind control implant in his brain.

Captain America: Super Soldier [Video game; SHW]

Release date: July 19, 2011; Voice Cast: Chris Evans as Captain America/Steve Rogers, Hayley Atwell as Peggy Carter, Sebastian Stan as Bucky Barnes, Keith Ferguson as Red Skull, Steve Blum as Baron Heinrich Zemo, Liam O'Brien as Howard Stark; Story: Christos N. Gage; Third person single-player perspective; Platforms: Nintendo DS & 3DS, PlayStation 3, Xbox 360, Wii; Developer: Next Level Games; Publisher: Sega Games.

The player controls Captain America as he explores HYDRA's castle and battles Iron Cross, Red Skull, Amim Zola and various agents of HYDRA. The game is based on events that take place during *Captain America: The First Avenger* (2011).

Captain America: The First Avenger (2011) [Film; SHW]

Premiere: July 22, 2011; Main Cast: Chris Evans as Captain America/Steve Rogers, Hayley Atwell as Peggy Carter, Sebastian Stan as James Buchanan/Bucky Barnes, Tommy Lee Jones as Colonel Chester Phillips, Hugo Weaving as John Schmidt/Red Skull, Dominic Cooper as Howard Stark, Samuel L. Jackson as Nick Fury, Stanley Tucci as Dr. Abraham Erskine, Richard Armitage as Heinz Kruger, Toby Jones as Dr. Amim Zola; Producer: Kevin Feige; Screenplay: Christopher Markus, Stephen McFeely; Based on characters created by Joe Simon, Jack Kirby; Director: Joe Johnston; 124 min.; Marvel Entertainment, Marvel Studios, Paramount Pictures; 3D; Color.

A physically weak Steve Rogers is offered a back door into the U.S. Army after he is repeatedly rejected for military service during World War II. Dr. Abraham Erskine transforms Rogers physically using his super-soldier serum. But when Erskine is murdered by a Nazi agent of HYDRA, Steve Rogers begins his crusade against the HYDRA and its leader Red Skull.

When co-creator **Joe Simon** watched *Captain America: The First Avenger* he told his granddaugh-

***Captain America: The First Avenger* (2011), starring (from left) Chris Evans as Steve Rogers/Captain America, Hayley Atwell as Peggy Carter (Paramount Pictures/Marvel Entertainment).**

ter, "Man I wish Kirby was around to see this." A tearful Neal Kirby, son of the late **Jack Kirby** commented, "I think he would have loved the movies. It's really a shame he didn't get to see them."

Captain Battle [Comic book character; SHW]

First publication: *Silver Streak Comics* #10 (May 1941); Creators: Carl Formes, Jack Binder; Publisher: Comic House Publications.

"Captain Battle, who lost his eye in the World War in which he was the youngest combatant, has given his life to the scientific perfection of inventions which he uses to overcome evil."

His Curvoscope allows Captain Battle to see anywhere on Earth with lenses that follow the curvature of the Earth. The Luceflyer allows him to streak through the air at near to the speed of light and his Dissolvo is a color-concentrate, whose vibrations melt down nerve and bone tissue into a gelatinous mass.

In *Silver Streak Comics* #13 (August 1941) Captain Battle is joined by Captain Battle, Jr., alias youngster Hale Battle, after Captain Battle rescues Hale from a mysterious priesthood about to sacrifice him to their pagan god. Their first task—to tackle a Nazi submarine in the Yangtse River. In subsequent adventures the pair defeat various Nazi spies and saboteurs, including Herr Skull, Herr Death, Dr. Dracula and his Nazi vampires, Sir Satan and his Devil worshippers and Baron Doom.

Captain Battle: Legacy War (2013) [Film; SHW]

Premiere: February 2013; Main cast: Cuyle Carvin as Sam Battle/Captain Battle, Andrew McGuiness as Brendan Storm, Marlene McCohen as Jane Storm, Todd James Jackson as Heinrich Himmler, Jenny Allford as The Necromancer; Producer: Donald S. Sterling; Story: Keith Parker, Danny White; Director: David Palmieri; 90 min.; Sterling Entertainment, Saint James Films, TomCat Films; Color.

During a tour of duty in the Gulf War Sam Battle is critically injured. Scientist Brandon Storm saves Battle's life with a secret serum. When Battle returns to the U.S. the side-effects of the serum give him super-strength and increased energy. He learns he is carrying on the tradition of his grandfather who adopted a crime fighting alter ego during World War II. Wearing his grandfather's costume Sam Battle is now Captain Battle and is soon ready for action. The man who saved his life in Iraq, Brandon Storm has been kidnapped by a Neo-Nazi sorceress known as the Necromancer. He is forced to bring Heinrich Himmler cloned body back to life. Her future plans include Brandon raising Hitler's cloned body and restoring the Third Reich.

Captain Confederacy [Comic book; SHW]

First publication: 1986; Creators: Will Shetterly, Vince Stone; Publishers: Steeldragon Press, Epic Comics (Marvel).

An unemployed actor agrees to become part of a propaganda program to create real-life superheroes for the Confederate States of America. But when his African American friend refuses to continue in his role as the super-villain Blacksnake he is murdered. Captain Confederacy is outraged and turns on his own country. But he has another struggle ahead of him. The procedure that granted him super powers has resulted in drug addiction for both himself and his female partner Miss Dixie.

Captain Fearless [Comic book; SHW]

First publication: August 1941; Art: Charles Quinlan; Publisher: Helnit-Holyoke Publishing.

1773. The Old Owl's Head Inn, Boston. Young patriot John Fearless objects to paying higher taxes for tea. Disguised as Indians the young colonists dump the tea into Boston harbor. But Fearless dies later in battle, cut down by British troops.

One hundred-and-sixty-years later a young cadet walks through Boston's military cemetery and finds the grave of his ancestor, John Fearless. Before the headstone he vows to "devote my life to the protection of the sacred American ideals of life, liberty and pursuit of happiness." Suddenly the ghost of Fearless appears before the cadet and tells him of his other fighting ancestors. Now he must continue their legacy and fight Hitler's fifth columnists. The ghost disappears and a small package remains containing a buckskin uniform and horn that he must only blow when in great danger. Captain Fearless is born.

Captain Hurricane [Comic book character; SHW]

First appearance: *Valiant* #1 (October 6, 1962); Publisher: Fleetway.

Captain Hercules Hurricane, "The Toughest Fighting Man of World War II" leads his unit of Royal Marine Commandos and his pint-sized batman, Maggot Malone, into battle against the Nazis.

Valiant Annual **1972** featuring Captain Hurricane of the Royal Marine Commandos. Published by IPC Magazines Ltd., UK.

When Captain Hurricane loses his temper his face flushes at "the onset of an earth-shaking ragin' fury" shouting, "Great blistering barnacles!" The rage gives him almost super-human strength as he tosses heavy metal objects and weapons aside and confronts the Nazis. "I've seen enough bits o' machinery dreamed up by Kraut crackpots to last me a flippin' lifetime. But if you're so flamin' keen to have 'em back—here they are!"

Captain Marvel [Comic book character]

First appearance: *Whiz Comics* #2 (February 1940); Creators: Bill Parker, Charles Clarence Beck; Publisher: Fawcett Publications.

Young Billy Batson has been cheated out of his inheritance and driven from his home by a wicked uncle. Selling newspapers in a rain-soaked street, Batson is approached by a mysterious stranger who leads him to a strange driverless subway train. At the end of the line they step onto a platform resembling "the mouth of a weird, subterranean cavern" and enter an ancient underground hall. Carved figures on the wall highlight the "seven deadly enemies of man."

At the end of the hall an old man seated on a marble throne greets Batson and announces, "I know everything, I am Shazam!" The 3,000-year-old sorcerer tells Batson, "All my life I have fought injustice and cruelty. But I am old now—my time is almost up. You shall be my successor. Merely by speaking my name you can become the strongest and mightiest man in the world—Captain Marvel."

During World War II Captain Marvel fights Adolf Hitler, **Captain Nazi**, Nippo the Nipponese, Mr. Mind, Dr. Sivana and the Axis powers.

Captain Marvel, Jr. [Comic book character]

First appearance: *Whiz Comics* #25 (December 1941); Creators: Ed Herron, Mac Raboy; Publisher: Fawcett Publications.

Knocked out of his airplane cockpit by **Captain Marvel**, **Captain Nazi** lands in the waters below where young Freddy Freeman and his grandfather are fishing in their small boat. As they rescue the drowning man he returns their favor by killing the grandfather and badly injuring Freddy. The crippled young boy is rescued by Captain Marvel but only given hours to live. Billy Batson takes Freddy to the ancient underground temple and awakens Shazam from his "thousand years of sleep." Batson is told only he can save Freddy by becoming Captain Marvel. As Batson is transformed Freddy awakens and speaks the words "Captain Marvel." Suddenly he stands before Marvel as a healthy, strong teenage boy who will be known as Captain Marvel, Jr.

Captain Marvel, Jr., fights Captain Nazi, Captain Nippon and the Axis powers during World War II, enhanced by the polished artwork of Mac Raboy.

Captain Midnight [Comic book character; SFW]

First appearance: *The Funnies* #47 (July 1941); Voice Cast: Creators: Willfred G. Moore, Robert M. Burit; Publisher: Dell.

Based on the radio show that debuted on regional stations in 1939, Captain Midnight was loosely based on the World War I adventures of co-creator Robert Burit, who served with the Lafayette Escadrille.

When Captain Midnight migrated to comic books he initially remained close to his radio persona. Aviator Captain Albright was assisted by the Secret Squadron in his missions to defeat the Nazi enemy. Fawcett acquired Captain Midnight from Dell, gave him his own comic book and transformed him from an aviator wearing a brown leather jacket and matching helmet with goggles into a crimson and blue costumed hero, complete with sci-fi gadgetry under the guidance of the Otto Binder studio. The Doom-Beam torch emitted infra-red rays that branded his enemies. The Swing Spring was a stronger than steel line and the Gliderchute enabled Captain Midnight to glide in mid-air thanks to super-strength silk stretched between his extended arms and body.

"Captain Midnight and the Silent Wings of Destruction" (June 1943) is an example of a typical comic book story from World War II. A defense plant on the East Coast is bombed by the Nazis. Captain Jim Albright, alias Captain Midnight, listens to President Roosevelt's appeal for help over the radio and together with sidekick Icky they investigate the mystery of the bombs that appeared to drop out of thin air.

Scanning the sky in the Grumman Avenger Captain Midnight spots a camouflaged black-jet glider bomber with the help of his infra-red Doom-Beam. Following the Nazi plane with the aid of his Gliderchute Captain Midnight sees it land on a giant flying aircraft carrier.

Posing as a Nazi officer, Midnight discovers the wings are fueled with hydrogen to give it extra lift and rescues captured American sailors who are being tortured.

Like many characters defined by World War II Captain Midnight struggled in the post-war years and finally folded with #67 in September 1947. The Mutual radio show lasted until December 15, 1949. A Columbia movie serial (1942) and television series in the 1950s featured standard spy stories with no Weird War elements.

Captain Nazi [Comic book character; SHW]

First appearance: *Master Comics* #21 (December 1941); Creators: William Woolfolk, Mac Raboy; Publisher: Fawcett Publications, DC Comics.

Albrecht Krieger is raised on a diet of "Miracle Food" that gives him super-strength, stamina and intelligence. When Adolf Hitler is introduced to Krieger he sees him as a perfect example of the superiority of the Aryan race and tells him to rid America of "those weaklings called 'Heroes!'"

Captain Nazi swoops through the crowds at Times Square as they scatter and proudly states, "Bring on your Bulletman—bring them all on. Captain Nazi challenges them all!"

Bulletman and **Captain Marvel** meet his challenge but Captain Nazi shows how evil he is by throwing a young boy off a cliff before he is rescued from death by Captain Marvel.

His evil nature is demonstrated once again when he plunges into the sea after failing to force a crash landing of a fighter plane. An old man rescues him in his small boat only to be killed by the Nazi. When the old man's young grandson puts up a fight Captain Nazi breaks the boy's back with an oar, leaving him for dead in the sea.

Captain Marvel once again comes to the rescue and takes pity on the disabled boy by asking Shazam to grant him some of his powers. **Captain Marvel, Jr.**, is born. Captain Nazi has helped give birth to one of his greatest foes.

DC Comics revived Captain Nazi in *Shazam!* #34 (March–April 1978). He entered the modern era in *The Power of Shazam!* (1995) as yet another World War II character revived from suspended animation.

See: **Monster Society of Evil**

Captain Wonder [Comic book character: SHW]

First appearance: *Kid Comics* #1 (February 1943); Creators: Otto Binder, Frank Giacoia; Publisher: Timely Comics.

Youngster Tim Mulrooney saves the life of Professor Jeff Jordan following an accident in Jordan's laboratory. In the accident a vial of a drug that gives a person the strength of twelve men smashes on the floor. When the Professor awakens he discovers the fumes from the drug have taken effect and he now possesses superhuman strength. With young Tim as his sidekick Professor Jordan decides to fight the Nazis as Captain Wonder.

A Carol for Another Christmas (1964) [TV Movie; WW]

First broadcast: December 1964; Main Cast: Sterling Hayden as Daniel Grudge, Ben Gazzara as Fred,

Peter Sellars as "The Imperial Me," Eva Marie Saint as Lt. Gibson, Percy Rodriguez as Charles, Barbara Ann Teer as Ruby, James Shigeta as Doctor, Britt Ekland as Mother, Steve Lawrence as Ghost of Christmas Past, Pat Hingle as Ghost of Christmas Present, Robert Shaw as Ghost of Christmas Future; Executive producer: Edgar Rosenberg; Writer: Rod Serling; Producer-Director: Joseph L. Mankiewicz; Michael Myerburg Studios, New York; Telsun Foundation, Inc.; B/W.

Embittered by the death of his son who was killed in action on Christmas Eve, ex–Commander Daniel Drudge sees visions of his dead son and finds himself in conversation with the Ghost of Christmas Past on a ship containing the coffins of fallen soldiers.

"Hey wouldn't you think sport, with all the brains we got on this earth ... wouldn't you think we could come up with something that would keep a kid from getting killed at the age of 18?," asks the ghost in the form of a soldier.

Drudge is then transported to Hiroshima, Japan, September 1945 where he sees himself and Lt. Gibson visiting schoolgirls affected by the atom bomb. The instantaneous thermal radiation has destroyed the girls' faces. Among the rubble a young boy searches for his sisters who were killed when their school was incinerated. A sudden crack of thunder sends a shudder through the boy, traumatized by the bomb.

Drudge now finds himself watching the Ghost of Christmas Present feasting at a table while starving, displaced and dispossessed people walk aimlessly behind a barbed wire fence. Drudge doesn't want to face the reality of their suffering and his selective morality and runs from the scene into the Ghost of Christmas Future.

People are sparse following Doomsday and the town he lived in has been destroyed. The ghost states, "What you see before you Mr. Drudge is a tiny part of a big, round radioactive mud burying ground."

The few survivors gather before their leader. "The Imperial Me" addresses the "Non-government of the Me people." Drudge thinks the leader insane but on closer inspection his views actually reflect his own. A lone voice of reason in the crowd is mocked and greeted with laughter and charged with treason of involvement and the subversion of "the individual Me."

The "traitor" is shot dead by a boy in a cowboy suit. The leader then calls upon everyone to kill each other so there remains a perfect civilization of "the individual I."

Drudge is relieved of the nightmare future when he once again finds himself in the present, a changed man, his mind open to involvement with the realization that "no man is an island."

Rod Serling's reworking of Charles Dickens' *A Christmas Carol* is at its strongest in the Hiroshima and the bleak Christmas Future segments. Peter Sellars is very effective as the egotistical maniac with an ultimate lust for power, able to brainwash the crowd with the chilling effect of a cult leader.

The Case of the Soldier's Ghost (*Museum Mysteries*) [Juvenile book; WW]

Author: Steven Brezenoff; Illustrator: Lisa K. Weber; First publication: North Mankato, MN: Stone Arch Books, 2017.

A new exhibit on the Vietnam War, at the American History Museum at Capitol City, has angered a spirit. Now Raining Sam and his friends must find out what has made the ghost so angry before further damage can be done.

The Castle in the Forest [Novel; WW]

Author: Norman Mailer; First publication: New York: Random House, 2007.

Norman Mailer's final novel is a fictional biography of the early life of Adolf Hitler, narrated by a demon named Dieter, under orders from the Maestro (Satan).

The *Booklist* reviewer, Brad Hooper, noted: "Many readers will find the Satan-and-his-army-of-devils conceit a gimmick, perhaps even an offensive one, in trying to reach an understanding of evil."

Catch Me Once, Catch Me Twice [Novel; WW]

Author: Janet McNaughton; First publication: Toronto, Canada: Stoddart, 1994.

World War II, 1942. Twelve-year-old Evelyn McCallum moves to St. John's, Newfoundland with her pregnant mother, after her father is posted overseas in the army. When he's declared missing-in-action Evelyn feels lost until she makes friends with Peter, a disabled boy in her class at school. Together the explore St. John's and encounter fairies. The fairies renew Evelyn's spirit and make her feel confident she can locate her missing father.

A sequel, *Make or Break Spring*, taking place in

post-war Newfoundland, was released by Tuckamore Books in 1998.

"Cave City of Hel" [Pulp fiction; SFW]

Author: Richard S. Shaver; Illustration: Brady; First publication: *Amazing Stories* (Vol. 19 #3; September 1945); Publisher: Ziff-Davis Publishing Company.

Two Norwegians escape from their Nazi prison and take cover in a cave located deep within a snow-covered forest. Within the cave is a labyrinth of tunnels that descend deep into the bowels of the Earth. Suddenly they see a light ahead and "a mighty rock doorway flanked by ice-covered beasts...."

Above the door are three letters HEL. The Norwegians wonder if this is the same Hel of the Gods spoken of in ancient legend. Opening the door they enter hallways and come across frozen giants feasting in a banquet room. The ancient legend of Hel is real and its inhabitants have a plan to defeat the Nazis. "We do not make war—we cure it."

Chamber of Chills [Comic book]

Horror and fantasy anthology title.

"THE SKEPTIC" [WW]

First publication: #22 (March 1954); Art: Joe Certa; Publisher: Harvey Comics.

World War II. Three soldiers attempt to take a highly strategic house on a hill, located in the heart of enemy territory. Despite constant gunfire from the Germans the soldiers make it into the house. But once inside, the house gives them the creeps—with good cause. Their Sergeant has been dead from the moment he stepped into the house. So who have the two remaining soldiers been talking to?

"Change for the Bitter" [Pulp fiction; WW]

Author: Lee Francis; Illustrator: Margaret Brundage; First publication: *Fantastic Adventures* (Vol. 7 #2; April 1945); Publisher: Ziff-Davis Publishing Company.

A Voice pits Göring and Hirohito against each other to vanquish both. "You are destined to be earth's true superman," the Voice said. "But you must slay the one called Hirohito. He dreams of having all the power."

To Hirohito the Voice said, " Your future plans depend on his death. You must kill the pig Göring if your plans are to be successful."

Charlotte Sometimes [Juvenile book; WW]

Authors: Penelope Farmer, Chris Connor; First publication: New York: Harcourt, Brace & World, 1969.

Charlotte Makepeace is still adapting to her new boarding school when she finds herself thrown back in time to 1918 with a new identity. And in 1918 Clare Moby is thrust forward in time to exchange identities with Charlotte. Each girl is living the life of each other displaced in time. Those around them initially see no difference until Clare's sister Emily senses Clare is not the same sister she knows. When Charlotte explains what has happened to Emily they attempt to discover the reason behind the change in identities. Meanwhile in the present Charlotte alias Clare has confided in room mate Elizabeth.

Charlotte has to face the reality of World War I as she tries to come to terms with her new life as Clare Moby. But when she learns Clare is to leave the boarding school Charlotte fears the link will be broken and she will be stranded in the past permanently.

Chrononauts [Comic book; SFW]

First publication: March 2015; Story: Mark Millar; Art: Sean Gordon Murphy, Matt Hollingsworth; Publisher: Image Comics.

Artifacts are being displaced in time. In southeast Turkey an archeological expedition uncovers an ancient temple that has been built around a missing F-14 Tomcat from the Vietnam war. To tackle the mystery a prototype time machine-satellite named Mark Twain-One has been transmitting live footage from actual events, including the Battle of Gettysburg, on television screens across the nation. The next step is first-hand accounts of the past with a team of time traveling Chrononauts.

Chronos Commandos [Comic book; SFW]

First publication: July 2013; Story-Art: Stuart Jennett; Publisher: Titan Comics.

World War II history is in danger of being changed due to dinosaurs from the Cretaceous Period traveling through time. The Chronos Commandos must save the future by defeating creatures from the past.

Circle of Fear (1972) [TV series]

Supernatural anthology series.

"BAD CONNECTION" (1:04) [WW]

Air date: October 6, 1972; Main Cast: Sebastian Cabot as Winston Essex, Karen Black as Barbara

Sanders, Michael Tolan as Keith Newton, Kaz Garas as Phil Briggs, Skip Homeier as Steve; Producer: Joel Rogosin; Story: John McGreevey; Director: Walter Doniger; 50 min.; William Castle Productions, Screen Gems Television; National Broadcasting Company (NBC); Color.

A young widow receives phone calls from a man who sounds like her late husband who was killed in action in Vietnam.

Civil War on Sunday (*Magic Tree House* #21) [Juvenile book; WW]
Author: Mary Pope Osborne; Illustrator: Sal Murocca; First publication: New York: Random House–Stepping Stone, 2000.

In Frog Creek, Pennsylvania, eight-year-old Jack and his seven-year-old sister Annie come across a magical tree house filled with books. Those books belong to Morgan le Fay, magical librarian at King Arthur's court in Camelot. The children are given the task of finding four special kind of writings to save Camelot. "Something to follow, Something to send, Something to learn and Something to lend."

The tree sends Jack and Annie back in time to the American Civil War, near Richmond, Virginia. Here they help wounded soldiers alongside Clara Barton, the "Angel of the Battlefield." One of the wounded on the battlefield is Jack and Annie's great-great-great-grandfather.

See: ***Revolutionary War on Wednesday***

The Claw [Comic book character; SHW]
First appearance: *Silver Streak Comics* #1 (December 1939); Creator: Jack Cole; Publisher: Your Guide Publications (Lev Gleason).

The mid–Pacific island of Ricca is home to the yellow-skinned Oriental figure known as "The Claw." "A mammoth creature of supernatural powers who keeps a constant reign of terror over the island's 10,000 inhabitants."

In *Silver Streak Comics* #2 the Claw offers his services to Adolf Hitler in return for "half of Europe." A fearful Hitler accepts his terms as the Claw sets his military operation in motion. As the full moon rises the Claw rises from the sea, assuming gigantic proportions and creating a vortex that pulls ships off-course. A huge mobile undersea fortress and railroad transports the sunken battleships back to his base in Ricca. But when the younger brother of Jerry Morris is lost at sea he vows revenge on the Claw.

See: ***Daredevil Battles Hitler***

Clive Barker's Jericho [Video game; WW]
Release date: October 2007; Single-player; Platforms: Microsoft Windows, PlayStation 3, Xbox 360; Story: Clive Barker; Designers: Clive Barker, Joe Falke; Developers: MercurySteam, Alchemic Productions; Publisher: Codemasters.

The Firstborn, imprisoned by God in the reality known as the Box, has been released by a renegade member of The Department of Occult Warfare (DOW). A seven-man Special Forces Jericho team are assigned to seal the breach in the Box and prevent former General Arnold Leach from releasing the Firstborn yet again.

The Jericho team must confront the evil souls from the past who have breached the Box, including Nazis who experimented with the paranormal during World War II.

Code Red (2013) [Film; SFW]
Premiere: December 20, 2013 (Japan); Main Cast: Julian Kostov as Harold Miller, Paul Logan as Capt. John McGahey, Manal El-Feitury as Anna Bennett; Executive Producers: Paul Hudson, Stefan Ivanov, Atanas Krustanoff, Dilian Pavlov, Aleksander Zdravkov; Story: Valeri Milev, Matthew Waynee; Director: Valeri Malev; 91 min.; Indi Films, eOne Television, Amarath Arc; Outrider Pictures; Color.

In modern day Bulgaria the local populace have been infected with a biochemical agent first developed by Stalin during World War II. Now the locals have become mutants and the dead are returning to life. U.S. Special Forces Captain John McGahey must save the day.

Cold City [RPG; Sourcebook; WW]
Release date: 2007; Story: Malcolm Craig; Art: Stuart Beel; Publisher: Contested Ground Studios.

In post-war Berlin the Underground War is fought in ruined bunkers, dark tunnels and bombed apartment blocks. Players adopt the roles of members of the multinational and secretive Reserve Police Agency (RPA). Their mission, to track down and destroy monsters created by Nazi scientists during World War II, that now hide in the darkness.

A Coming Evil [Juvenile book; WW]
Author: Vivian Vande Velde; First publication: Boston, MA: Houghton Mifflin, 1998.

Reluctant thirteen-year-old Lisette Beaucaire is staying at Aunt Josephine's farm in the Dordogne Valley to escape German-occupied Paris. Although she misses her friends and life in Paris, an unusual new friend piques Lisette's interest. Gerard is the ghost of a Templar knight who was murdered by King Phillip IV in 1314. As time passes Gerard transforms from a spirit to a solid human being. When Lisette learns her aunt is hiding Jewish and Gypsy orphans at her farmhouse Gerard's story of his persecution in medieval times makes Lisette understand the dangers of the Nazi persecution of Jews and Gypsies in present day 1940.

Command & Conquer: Red Alert
[Videogame; AHW]

Release date: October 1996; Main Cast: Arthur Roberts as General Gunter von Esling, Barry Kramer as General Nikos Stavros, John Milford as Professor Albert Einstein, Lynne Litteer as Tanya Adams; Executive Producer: Brett W. Sperry; Story: Ron Smith, Ed Del Castillo; Screenplay: John Scott Lewinski, Adam Isgreen; Director: Joseph D. Kucan; Original platforms: MS-DOS, Windows 95; Developer: Westwood Studios; Publisher: Virgin Interactive Entertainment.

In an alternate 1946 Albert Einstein creates a Chronosphere time machine that takes him to December 20, 1924, where he meets Adolf Hitler after he's released from Landsberg Prison. By shaking Hitler's hand Einstein removes him from history. With Hitler eliminated the Nazis fail to rise to power. The Soviet Union under Stalin fills the vacuum as they invade Eastern Europe and seize land from China. A European Alliance is formed to defeat the Soviet advance. Players choose between the Alliance or Soviets as they battle to control the European mainland.

Command & Conquer: Red Alert 2
[Videogame; AHW]

Release date: October 2000; Main cast: Athena Massey as Lt. Eva Lee, Udo Kier as Yuri, Aleksandra Kaniak as Lt. Zofia, Kari Wuhrer as Special Agent Tanya Adams, Barry Corbin as General Ben Carville, Nicholas Worth as Premier Alexander Romanov, Ray Wise as President Michael Dugan, Larry Gelman as Albert Einstein, Adam Gregor as General Vladimir; Executive Producer: Michael Skaggs; Story: John Hight, Jason Henderson; Director: Joseph D. Kucan; Original platform: Microsoft Windows; Developer: Westwood Studios; Publisher: Electronic Arts.

The Soviet Union, under the leadership of Premier Romanov, launches an attack on both coasts of the United States by land, sea and air. Yuri, leader of the Soviet Psychic Corps, deflects a U.S. nuclear response using mind control. Soon Yuri plans his own world domination using his Psychic Dominator. The game divides into Soviet and Allied campaigns.

Command & Conquer: Red Alert 3
[Videogame; AHW]

Release date: October 2008; Main Cast: Jonathan Pryce as Field Marshall Robert Bingham, Peter Stormare as Dr. Gregor Zelinsky, George Takei as Emperor Yoshiro, J.K. Simmons as President Howard T. Ackerman, Ivana Milicevic as Lt. Dasha Fedorovich, Ron Yuan as Crown Prince Tatsu, Jenny McCarthy as Special Agent Tanya Adams, Andrew Divoff as General Nocolai Krukov; Producer: Nina Dobner; Story: Haris Orkin, Micai Pedriana; Director: Richard Taylor; Original platform: Microsoft Windows; Developer–Publisher: Electronic Arts.

Using a time machine Albert Einstein is eliminated by the Soviet General Krukov and Colonel Cherdenko in 1927. The Soviets hope his death will turn the tide of the war in the present. It backfires when the Empire of the Rising Sun declares war on the Soviet Union and the Allies. With Einstein gone nuclear weapons were never invented. A new World War begins.

Command & Conquer: Red Alert 3: Uprising [Videogame; AHW]

Release date: March 2009; Main Cast: Ivana Milicevic as Lt. Dasha Fedorovich, Malcolm McDowell as EU President Rupert Thornley, Greg Ellis as Cmdr. Giles Price, Ron Yuan as Crown Prince Tatsu, Moaran Atias as Cmdr. Vera Belova, Jamie Chung as Cmdr. Takara Sato, Jodi Lyn O'Keefe as Kelly Weaver; Ric Flair as Cmdr. Douglas Hill, Dimitri Diatchenko as Cmdr. Oleg Vodnik, Bruce Locke as Cmdr. Shinzo Nagama, Gene Farber as Cmdr. Nikolai Moskvin, Jack Yang as Cmdr. Kenji Tenzai, Louise Griffiths as Cmdr. Lydia Winters, Holly Valance as Brenda Snow; Producers: Nina Dobner, Micai Pedriana; Story: Haris Orkin, Micai Pedriana; Director: Richard Taylor; Original platform: Microsoft Windows; Developer: EA Los Angeles; Publisher: Electronic Arts.

President of the European Union Rupert Thornley is forming an army with his "FutureTech" technology while the Soviet Union and the Empire of the Rising Sun are planning an uprising.

Command & Conquer: Yuri's Revenge
[Videogame; AHW]

Release date: October 15, 2001; Main cast: Athena Massey as Lt. Eva Lee, Udo Kier as Yuri, Aleksandra

Kaniak as Lt. Zofia, Kari Wuhrer as Special Agent Tanya Adams, Barry Corbin as General Ben Carville, Nicholas Worth as Premier Alexander Romanov, Ray Wise as President Michael Dugan, Larry Gelman as Albert Einstein; Producer: Donny Miele; Story: John Hight; Screenplay: Wynne McLaughlin; Director: Joseph D. Kucan; Original platform: Microsoft Windows; Developer: Westwood Pacific; Publisher: EA Games.

In the *Red Alert 2* Expansion. While the Allies have been dealing with a Russian uprising mad scientist and psychic Yuri has been finalizing his to take over Earth using mind control weapons. Albert Einstein hopes to stop his plans by helping his U.S. allies to travel back in time. The player takes up arms against Yuri on either the Soviet or Allied side.

Commander Steel [Comic book character; SHW]

First appearance: *Steel: The Indestructible Man* #1 (September 1977); Creators; Gerry Conway, Don Heck; Publisher: DC Comics.

Henry Heywood of the United States Marines Corps. undergoes surgery after he's severely injured during an attack by saboteurs on his base. Dr. Gilbert Giles rebuilds Heywood with steel alloy tubing replacing shattered bones, a metal casing to protect his skull and new flesh thanks to Giles' special bioretardant formula. He is reborn as an indestructible cyborg with superhuman strength and speed, ready to fight the Nazi's and kidnap Adolf Hitler. But even his new powers can't stop him from being captured by **Baron Blitzkrieg** and brainwashed to assassinate Winston Churchill.

Commander Steel joins the **All-Star Squadron** for a brief time before returning to duty behind enemy lines.

Common Foe [Comic book; WW]

First publication: May 2005; Story: Keith Giffen, Shannon Eric Denton; Art: Jean-Jaques Dzialowski; Publisher: Desperado Publishing.

At the Battle of the Bulge U.S. and German troops form an alliance to fight a monstrous foe intent on their destruction.

Confederates Don't Wear Couture [Juvenile book; WW]

Author: Stephanie Kate Strohm; First publication: Boston: Houghton Mifflin Harcourt, 2013.

Teenager and secret history nerd Libby Kelting joins her fashion designer friend Dev in Alabama modeling and selling period gowns to the wives and girlfriends of Civil War re-enactors. Libby takes a shine to handsome re-enactor Corporal Beau Anderson while a vengeful ghost haunts the battlegrounds.

The Conqueror [Comic book character; SHW]

First appearance: *Victory Comics* #1 (August 1941); Creators: **Bill Everett**, Gilbert James; Publisher: Hillman Periodicals.

While attempting to travel from California to New York by plane pilot Daniel Lyons runs into a storm over the Rockies.

"I was high over the Rockies when it happened. Lightning crashed once, twice. The plane shuddered, came to a dead halt. For what seemed hours we hung there, as though suspended by some supernatural thread. Then the thread snapped, and we plunged into the black abyss beneath."

Lyons is hurled through a door as the plane crash lands in a tree. Dazed and wandering by foot a stunned and bleeding Lyons collapses as he enters the laboratory of scientist Professor James Norton.

Norton restores him to health with his Cosmic Ray Lamp which also dramatically enhances Lyons' mental and physical abilities. With personal blessings from the President Lyons travels to Europe to confront the enemy.

"I am going after the one man in this world who is responsible for all of its present troubles. Professor, I am going to rid the world of Adolf Hitler!"

To strike fear into the Axis powers Lyons adopts a new persona complete with patriotic uniform. His final decision is his name.

"Something that would describe my very purpose in life. And what better title could I have than—the Conqueror?"

Corydon and the Siege of Troy [Juvenile book; MWW]

Author: Tobias Druitt; First publication: Alfred A. Knopf, 2009.

Corydon, a son of the god Pan, is a goat-footed misfit, rejected and outcast by his mother. After the fall of Atlantis Corydon is keeping a distance from his friends in a self-imposed exile. In the final book in the Corydon trilogy Troy is under siege and the gods want him to defend Troy and rescue his friends trapped inside the walled city. Reuniting with two Gorgons and the Minotaur they attempt to help Sikandar, Prince of Troy, fight against the invaders. But Corydon also has the mighty Zeus to contend with.

Countdown [Comic book; UK]

The weekly UK comic book from Polystyle Publications featured a ***Doctor Who*** comic strip. The strip also featured Weird War adventures in ***TV Action*** and ***TV Comic***.

"Timebenders" [SFW]

First publication: *Countdown* #6–13; (March 27–May 22, 1971); Story: Dennis Hopper; Art: Harry Lindfield.

Following a chance encounter with World War II Nazi soldiers on Dartmoor the Doctor finds himself in Nazi occupied France. Professor Vedrun has been reluctantly aiding the Nazi war effort building a transporter that can move matter through time and space. German Commander Spiegal wants to travel through time to secure advanced weaponry to win the war.

The Creature Commandos [Comic book characters; SHW]

First appearance: *Weird War Tales* #93 (November 1980); Creators: Jim De Matteis, Pat Broderick: Publisher: DC Comics.

Psychological warfare takes the form of the Creature Commandos in World War II. "Project M" transforms three volunteers into copies of feared creatures. Warren Griffith, a 4F farm boy becomes a werewolf. Sgt. Vincent Velcro is a vampire who can morph into a bat. Marine Private Elliot "Lucky" Taylor was in bad shape when he stepped on a landmine, but surgeons have kept him alive as an eight-foot Frankenstein type monster. Leading the outfit is U.S. Army Intelligence officer Lt. Matthew Shrieve. Plastic surgeon Myrna Rhodes, alias Dr. Medusa, whose hair became writhing snakes after attending an injured Lt. Shrieve and inhaling chemical fumes, is the latest member of the Creature Commandos.

Creature with the Atom Brain (1955) [Film; SFW]

Premiere: July 1955; Main Cast: Richard Denning as Dr. Chet Walker, Angela Stevens as Joyce Walker, Linda Bennett as Penny Walker, Michael Granger as Frank Buchanan, Gregory Gay as Dr. Wilheim Steigg; Executive Producer: Sam Katzman; Story" Curt Siodmak; Director: Edward L. Cahn; 69 min.; Clover Productions; Columbia Pictures; B/W.

Exiled gangster Frank Buchanan teams up with Nazi scientist Wilheim Steigg in Europe. Steigg can restore dead people to life and command them to do his wishes. Buchanan decides to take revenge on his enemies with Steigg's undead creatures.

Creepy [Comic book]

Horror anthology title. Originally published by Warren Publishing from 1964–1983, the title was revived by Dark Horse Comics in 2010.

"Angel of Jaipur" [WW]

First publication: *Creepy* #89 (June 1977); Story: Bill DuBay; Art: John Severin; Publisher: Warren Publishing.

Jaipur, India, 1857. Natives turn on the British colonists in the Bengal Revolt after a mixture of beef and pork is used to grease the cartridges of the Enfield rifles. It is anathema to Hindus and Muslims alike.

Only two British Lancers remain guarding a garrison of women and children. Suddenly out of a mysterious fog emerges a British Bristol Bullet World War I bi-plane that repels the Indians, forcing them to retreat. In World War I a Bristol Bullet piloted by the son of one of the Lancers is found riddled with Enfield shot.

"Army of the Walking Dead" [WW]

First publication: *Creepy* #35 (September 1970); Story: R. Michael Rosen; Art: Syd Shores; Publisher: Warren Publishing.

Nazi scientist Major Sporich has perfected a regenerating process that gives zombies the strength of ten men. Unable to die, they respond only to Sporich's voice. All the scientist requires is a steady supply of fallen German soldiers.

At the front lines the zombie soldiers are given the order to "destroy all soldiers and weapons in their path." Hitler is ecstatic at the news of the undead army. But a fog has descended over the battlefield and the zombies become disorientated and turn in the opposite direction, killing all German soldiers "in their path."

In an unusual move, the President of Warren Publishing, James Warren wrote a full-page editorial in this issue addressed to, "The President of the United States and all the Members of Congress—on behalf of our readers." His editorial carried a strong anti–Vietnam War message.

"Most of our readers are under 21. We can't vote—yet. But we don't have to be 21 to die in a war that was a mistake to begin with. We've tried to tell you this in our demonstrations. We tried to tell you this at Kent state. Were you listening? Before another human life is wasted—give us PEACE NOW!"

"Blood Brothers" [WW]
First publication: *Creepy* #89 (June 1977); Story: Bruce Jones; Art: Jose Ortiz; Publisher: Warren Publishing.

When his platoon comes under attack during World War II PFC Ted Mears searches for survivors. He encounters a soldier he doesn't recognize who calls himself Volper. Mears views Volper with greater suspicion after a bullet apparently passes through him, leaving him unharmed. When Volper disappears out of view Mears believes himself to be surrounded by German infantry. But what is real and what is illusion?

"The Red Badge of Terror" [WW]
First publication: *Creepy* #57 (November 1973); Story: Doug Moench; Art: Jose Bea; Publisher: Warren Publishing.

Pursuing a Confederate dispatch courier, Union cavalrymen Frank Hawkins and Ben Stark come across a plantation house. Upon entering they discover a coffin with nothing inside except for dirt. The courier is found upstairs, his back broken "like a dry-twig." Turning, the two soldiers come face-to-face with a vampire. Meanwhile Confederate troops are looking forward to resting at the plantation house as the vampires await them.

"Warrior on the Edge of Forever" [WW]
First publication: *Creepy* #90 (July 1977); Story: Bill DuBay; Art: Jose Ortiz; Publisher: Warren Publishing.

Fedor and Erik have memories of past lives fighting in wars throughout the centuries. From Roman wars to the Crusades to the Indian rebellion against the British in 1858 to the two World Wars of the 20th century—and to their final battle in World War III.

"X-Change" [WW]
First publication: *Creepy* #3 (May 2010); Story: Dan Braun, Craig Haffner; Art: Dennis Calero; Publisher: Dark Horse Comics.

In this two-part story a German woman's horrific activities during World War II are slowly exposed by federal agents.

Crusade (*Destroyermen*, Book 2) [Novel; AHW]
Author: Taylor Anderson; First publication: New York: Roc, 2008.

Lieutenant Commander Matthew Reddy finally tracks down the destroyer that went through the space and time rift with the U.S.S. Walker. The combined crew of Walker and U.S.S. Mahan prepare the pacifist Lemurians for battle against the Grand Swarm of the reptilian Grik. But the Grik have a new ally in the form of the Japanese forces who also came through the rift on the battleship Amagi.

See: **Maelstrom**

Crusade in Jeans (2006) [Film; SFW]
Premiere: November 15, 2006; Main Cast: Joe Flynn as Dolf Vega, Emily Watson as Mary Vega, Robert Timmins as Nicholas, Michael Culkin as Anselmus, Stephanie Leonidas as Jenne, Jake Kedge as Carolus; Executive Producers: Carlo Dusi, H. Michael Heuser, Marc Noyons; Story: Bill Haney; Based on the novel *Kruistocht in Spijkerbroek* by Thea Beckman; Director: Ben Sombogaart; 125 min.; Focusfilm KFT, Marmont Film Productions, Intuit Pictures, De Lux Productions, Kasander Film Company; Allumination Filmworks; Color.

Teenager Dolf Vega uses his mother's time machine to go back one day to replay the outcome of a soccer game that he blames himself for losing. But when security guards spot him Dolf panics and he accidentally finds himself back in 1212. He joins the 8.000 strong Children's Crusade traveling from Germany to Jerusalem to free the city from Muslim rule by non-violent action. Dolf applies his knowledge of modern medicine and technology to save many lives.

Cry Havoc [Comic book; WW]
First publication: January 2016; Six-issue miniseries; Story: Simon Spurrier; Art: Ryan Kelly; Publisher: Image Comics.

After street musician Lou is attacked by a wolf and infected with a virus she becomes part of a were-beasts Special Ops unit in Afghanistan.

"The Curse of El Dorado" [Pulp fiction; WW]
Author: P.F. Costello; First publication: *Fantastic Adventures* (Vol. 6 #3; April 1944); Publisher: Ziff-Davis Publishing Company.

"A falling plane brought two Americans to a forgotten race, a group of Nazis, and the curse of a golden idol. At first it was the girl who was the greatest enemy. The Nazi greed for gold changed all that."

Cybersix [Comic book; Argentina; SFW]
1. First publication: *Skorpio* (May 1992); Creators: Carlos Meglia, Carlos Trillo; Publisher: Eura Editorale.

During World War II Nazi scientist Dr. Von Reichter experiments with cybernetic implants on dead prisoners in an attempt to restore them to life to serve in Hitler's army. After the defeat of the Nazis Reichter flees to South America and works on perfecting artificial humans with superhuman abilities. But Reichter's Cyber creations possess free will and rebel against their creator. Only one female Cyber survives Reichter's destruction of his own creations. Cybersix lives undercover in the town of Meridiana, adopting the male identity of librarian Adrian Seidelman by day and fights Reichter's various fiendish creations by night. Cybersix is pursued by Jose, a child clone of Reichter and his team of mutants whose green blood-like sustenance Cybersix must drink to stay alive. Meanwhile Cybersix, in her male identity, is the object of affection of schoolgirl Lori and Cybersix in her female identity, is desired by Adrian's co-worker Lucas.

2. [TV series; Argentina]
First broadcast: March 15, 1995; Main Cast: Carolina Peleritti as Cybersix, Rodrigo de la Serna as Jose, Mario Moscoso as Doguyy; Executive Producer: Fernando Rascovsky; Story: Ricardo Rodriguez, Carlos Meglia, Carlos Trillo; 60 min.; Patagonik TV Group, Television Federal (Telefe); Color.

This campy live-action adaptation of the comic book character *Cybersix* featured former fashion model Carolina Peleritti in the lead role. It failed to gain an audience and was canceled after one month.

3. [Animated TV series]
First broadcast: September 6, 1999; Main Voice Cast: Cathy Weseluck as Cybersix-Adrian, Michael Dobson as Lucas Amato, Terry Klassen as Von Reichter, Andrew Francis as Julian, Alex Doduk as Jose, Janyse Jaud as Lori Anderson, L. Harvey Gold as Terra; Animation: Tokyo Movie Shinsha, NOA; Producers: Herve Bedard, Toshihiko Masuda, Koji Takeuchi; Story: Catherine Girczyc, Carlos Meglia, Carlos Trillo; Directors: Hiroyuki Aoyama, Toshihiko Masuda, Atsuko Tanaka, Nobuo Tomizawa, Kazuhide Tomonaga; 13 × 25 min.; Canada, Argentina, Japan co-production; Color.

This animated series, which aired on Fox Kids in the U.S.A. lasted one season.

Dagon [Pulp fiction; WW]
Author: H. P. Lovecraft; First publication: *The Vagrant* #11 (November 1919).

During World War I an American sailor and his crew are taken prisoner of the Hun in the Pacific. Escaping capture he drifts in a small boat until he reaches land. Setting ashore the American spots a "Cyclopean monolith" with bas-reliefs depicting grotesque creatures.

"The suddenly I saw it. With only a slight churning to mark its rise to the surface, the thing slid into view above the dark waters. Vast, Polyphemus-like, and loathsome, it darted like a stupendous monster of nightmares...."

The man awakes in a hospital in San Francisco after being picked up by an American ship. But by now he is mentally unhinged and upon hearing noises outside his room is convinced the fish-god Dagon has followed him with evil intentions.

Danger 5 (2011) [TV series; Australia; WW]
First broadcast: February 24, 2011; Main Cast: David Ashby as Jackson, Sean James Murphy as Tucker, Natasa Ristic as Llsa, Amanda Simons as Claire, Pacharo Mzembe as Pierre, Carmine Russo/Andreas Sobik as Adolf Hitler, Dario Russo as Bormann; Executive Producers: Vincent Beasley, Caterina De Nave; Story: David Ashby, Dario Russo; Director: Dario Russo; 24 min.; Hedone Productions, Dinosaur; Special Broadcasting Service (SBS); Color.

An action-comedy series set in a bizarre 1960s inspired version of World War II. A team of five spies are on a mission to kill Adolf Hitler.

Danger in the Darkest Hour (*Magic Tree House Super Edition* #1) [Juvenile book; WW]
Author: Mary Pope Osborne; Illustrator: Sal Murocca; First publication: New York: Random House, 2015.

In Frog Creek, Pennsylvania, eight-year-old Jack and his seven-year-old sister Annie come across a magical tree house filled with books that can take them to any time and place in history. Those books belong to Morgan le Fay, magical librarian at King Arthur's court in Camelot. Young enchanter Kathleen is working for the French Resistance during World War II. Jack and Annie travel back in time, parachuting behind enemy lines into Normandy. It is June 5, 1944, and they must locate Kathleen.

Daredevil Battles Hitler [Comic book; WW]
First publication: July 1941; Story-Art: Charles Biro; Publisher: Young Guide Publications (Lev Gleason).

With Hitler planning to invade England, British Prime Minister Winston Churchill assigns Daredevil and Silver Streak to watch a mysterious cottage south of London. Silver Streak discovers the cottage is being used by double agents to send messages to Hitler by carrier pigeon. A game of bluff and counter-bluff follows before Hitler orders a blitzkrieg of London. A fierce naval battle ensues with Daredevil and **Silver Streak** in the thick of the action.

In the issue's second strip "The Claw Double Crosses Hitler" (Story: Charles Biro; Art: Jack Cole), Hitler asks the villainous Claw for help in destroying the British in Singapore. In return Hitler promises to give the Claw Upper Mongolia, together with millions of native slaves. Daredevil poses as a Lieutenant of the Claw and advises him to destroy a fleet of British submarines and destroyers. But Daredevil has tricked the Claw into destroying Japanese submarines and ships.

Charles Biro's *Daredevil* has no super-powers beyond great athleticism but the supporting cast of this issue, Silver Streak and the Claw qualify this as a Weird War title.

See: **The Claw**; **Silver Streak**

Dark Axis—Secret Battles of World War II: Rise of the Overmen [Comic book; AHW]

First publication: 2011; 4-issue mini-series; Story: Greg McLean; Art: Xavier Irvine; Publisher: Ape Entertainment.

Promoted as a cross between "Saving Private Ryan" and "Evil Dead" this World War II alternate history takes place in occupied Germany. Sgt. Bill Bryce and his squad encounter an enemy creating super weapons that could change the course of the war in favor of the Axis powers.

Dark Mysteries [Comic book]

Anthology title.

"THE LIVING-DEAD" [SFW]

First publication: #20 (October 1954); Art: Jon D'Agostino; Publisher: Story Comics.

Lost in the snow-covered Black Forest, Ivor Blau comes across a lone house in a clearing. A beautiful young woman named Vania greets him, but Ivor can't shake a feeling of unease and his discovery of a room full of sleeping women only serves to increase his anxiety.

Ivor confides to Vania that he is the son of Nazi Scientist Dr. Klaus Blau. Vania knows of the Nazi doctor and shocks Ivor when she tells him his father used him in an experiment. Klaus Blau would draw blood from living subjects injected with his secret formula—including a young Ivor—and inject concentration camp survivors to be used as guinea pigs. When news reached Dr. Blau that the war was coming to a close with defeat for the Nazis he abandoned his experiments, leaving his subjects hovering between life and death, needing blood injected with the secret formula to release them. Back in the present day, Vania and the young women who have now raised from their sleep as rotting skeletons need the blood of Ivor to survive.

Dark Shadows [Comic book]

Based on the popular television series featuring vampire Barnabas Collins.

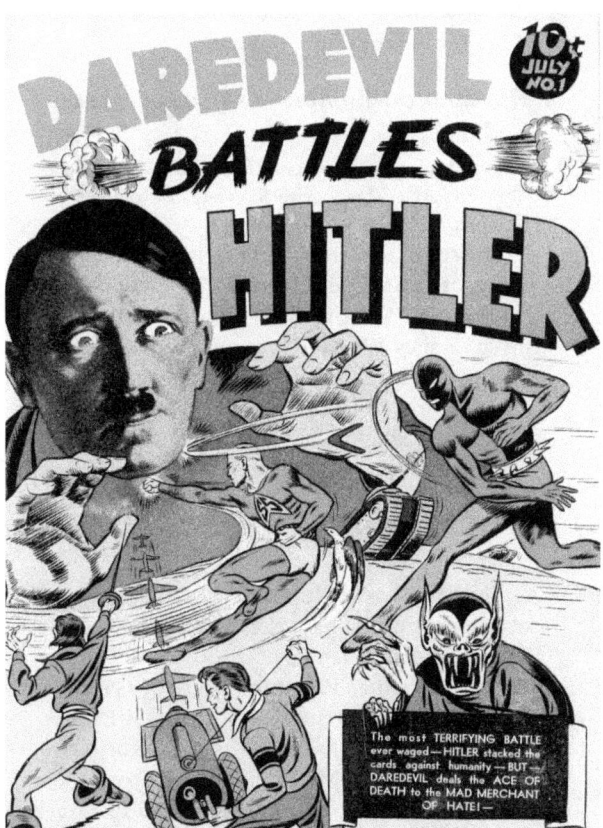

Daredevil Battles Hitler a.k.a. *Daredevil* #1 (July 1941). Cover art by Charles Biro under the pen-name "Woodro." Published by Young Guide Publications (Lev Gleason).

"The Year Is 1940" [WW]
First publication: *Dark Shadows* #21 (October 2013); Story: Mike Raicht; Art: Nacho Tenorio; Publisher: Dynamite Entertainment.

The vampire origins of Grace Baker during World War II. Grace is the sole survivor on her street of the London blitz. Discovered by vampire Ephraim Grace is "brought into the world of immortals." Together Grace and Ephraim prey and feed on the dying in the rubble of London.

Dark Victory [Novel; WW]
Author: Michele Lang; First publication: New York: Tor, 2012.

Descended from the witch of Ein Dor, the beautiful Jewish woman Magda Lazarus has inherited her family's ability to summon spirits. Now, as Nazis prepare to invade Poland, Magda Lazarus and the fallen angel, Raziel, gather a supernatural army to battle Hitler's human and demonic forces.

See: ***Rebel Angels***

Darkroom (1981) [TV series]
Short-lived horror anthology series, starring James Coburn as the host. Executive Producer: Peter S. Fischer; 7 × 60 min. (16 episode titles); Universal Television, American Broadcasting Company (ABC), Studios USA Television; Color.

"Siege of 31 August" (1:06) [WW]
Air date: December 11, 1981; Guest Cast: Ronny Cox as Neil, the Farmer, Gail Strickland as Helen, Hank Brandt as Colonel Brandt, Patrick Brennan as Ben, Pat Corley as Colonel/Sheriff; Story: Davis Grubb; Director: Peter Crane.

Vietnam veteran Neil, now a farmer, buys his son a toy soldier play set and is amazed to find the number of soldiers increasing with a purpose. To recreate the massacre he was a part of in Vietnam.

"Stay Tuned, We'll Be Right Back" (1:02) [WW]
Air date: November 27, 1981; Guest Cast: Lawrence Pressman as Charlie Miller, Bert Freed as Charlie Miller's Father, Shane Butterworth as Kenny, Joanna Miles as Janet Miller, Robert Gray as Nazi; Story: Simon Muntner; Director: Paul Lynch.

While listening to his crystal radio Charlie Miller contacts the German U-boat that sunk his father's ship in 1942. Should he change history and save his father's life?

Darkwitch Rising [Novel; WW]
Author: Sara Douglass; First publication: New York: Tor, 2006.

Brutus, last of the Trojan kings and seductive sorceress Genvissa are thwarted by Brutus' wife Cornelia, in their attempt to create a magical Labyrinth to rival the power of the gods. As a result of Cornelia's actions they are trapped in an endless cycle of birth and rebirth and find themselves reborn in war-torn seventeenth-century England. Brutus is a courtier to King Charles II, Cornelia a young woman named Noah, and Genvissa is an abused prostitute and sex slave to Weyland Orr, the reborn Asterion the Minotaur.

See: ***Druid's Sword***

"The Daughter of Thor" [Pulp fiction; MWW]
Author: Edmond Hamilton; Illustrator: Malcolm Smith; First publication: *Fantastic Adventures* (Vol. 4 #2; August 1942); Publisher: Ziff-Davis Publishing Company.

"With the coming of the Nazi invaders, war came once again to the gods; who loved to fight. But how could they know which was the right side? Should they fight Nazis?"

DC Comics: Bombshells [Comic book; SHW]
First publication: October 2015; Story: Marguerite Bennett; Art: Marguerite Sauvage; Publisher: DC Comics.

The super powered Bombshells are called into action as World War II increases in ferocity across Europe. Kate Kane, alias Batwoman, Diana of Themyscira alias **Wonder Woman**, Supergirl, StarGirl, Zatanna, Mera, royal daughter of Atlantis and defenders of Mother Russia, Kara Starikov and Kortni Duginovna join the Allied forces.

Based on the popular DC Collectibles figures.

DC's Legends of Tomorrow (2016) [TV series]
The adventures of **Rip Hunter** and his entourage of heroes and villains as they travel through time. First broadcast: January 21, 2016; Main Cast: Arthur Darvill as Rip Hunter, Victor Garber as Dr. Martin Stein, Brandon Routh as Ray Palmer/The Atom, Dominic Purcell as Mick Rory/Heat Wave, Wentworth Miller as Leonard Snart, Caity Lotz as Sara Lance/White Canary, Franz Drameh as Jefferson Jackson/Firestorm, Ciara Renee as Kendra Saunders/Hawkgirl, Falk Hentschel as Carter Hall/Hawkman, Amy Pemberton as Gideon (voice); Executive Producers: Gerg Berlanti, Chris

Fedak, Phil Klemmer, Andrew Kreisberg, Sarah Scechter; 42 min.; Berlanti Productions, DC Entertainment. Warner Bros. Television: The CW Television Network; Color.

"Abominations" (2:04) [SHW]
Air date: November 3, 2016; Guest Cast: Warren Belle as Henry Scott, Joshua Hinkson as Plantation Hand, Tintswalo Khumbuza as Mary, Lex Lang as Uber Nazi; Story: Marc Guggenheim. Ray Utarnachitt; Director: Michael A. Allowitz.

The Legends fight for survival against Confederate zombie soldiers in the American Civil War.

"Legendary" (1:15) [SHW]
Air date: May 19, 2016; Guest Cast: Casper Crump as Vandal Savage, Isabella Hoffman as Clarissa Stein, Patrick J. Adams as Rex Tyler/Hourman, Art Kitching as Nazi Commandant, Keifer O'Reilly as Jonas, Shane Leydon as Carmine Broome, Alex Duncan as Mother; Story: Greg Berlanti, Chris Ferdak; Teleplay: Phil Klemmer, Mark Guggenheim; Director: Dermott Downs.

In France, 1944 **Vandal Savage** seeks a meteorite—one of three that he intends to detonate simultaneously in different time periods to create a temporal paradox, resulting in a time quake. Kendra and Carter Hall, held prisoner in Nazi Germany are vital to Vandal Savage's plans as their blood is to be incorporated in a ritual that will erase time and return it to 1700 BC in Ancient Egypt.

"The Justice Society of America" (2:02) [SHW]
Air date: October 20, 2016; Guest Cast: Nick Zano as Dr. Nate Heywood, Patrick J. Adams as Rex Tyler/Hourman, Maisie Richardson-Sellers as Amaya Jiwe/Vixen, Kwes Ameyaw as Dr. Mid-Nite, Sarah Grey as Stargirl, Matthew MacCaull as Commander Steel; Andre Eriksen as Baron Krieger, Matt Letscher as Eobard Thawne/Reverse-Flash; Story: Chris Fedak, Sarah Nicole Jones; Director: Michael Grossman.

Rex Tyler of the **Justice Society of America** warns the Legends not to return to 1942 or "the consequences will be catastrophic." But the Legends ignore his warning to in order stop Baron Krieger destroying the JSA, along with Dr. Heywood's grandfather, Commander Steel. The Legends and JSA intercept a Nazi convoy carrying the occult Askaran Amulet, but encounter a super-serum, physically enhanced Krieger. Without the absent Rip Hunter, the Legends need a new leader to co-ordinate a plan of attack to rescue Ray Palmer and Vixen from their Nazi captors and defeat Von Krieger.

"Out of Time" (2:01) [SHW]
Air date: October 13, 2016; Guest Cast: Nick Zano as Dr. Nate Heywood, Neal McDonough as Damien Darhk, Stephen Amell as Oliver Queen, John Rubinstein as Albert Einstein, Christina Jastrzembska As Mileva Maric, Matthew MacCaull as Commander Steel, Kwesi Ameyaw as Dr. Mid-Nite; Story: Greg Berlanti, Chris Ferdak; Teleplay: Marc Guggenheim, Phil Klemmer; Director: Dermott Downs.

Dr. Nate Heywood and Oliver Queen locate the Legends so they can go back to 1942 to stop the Nazis from blowing up New York City with an atomic bomb. First they must kidnap Albert Einstein before the Nazis get to him, but unknown to the Legends, Einstein's former wife Mileva has already been kidnapped and is helping the Nazis. Damien Dahrk, who killed Sarah Lance's sister, has been supplying the Nazis with uranium. Tracking the uranium signature with the Atom's suit, the Legends locate the U-boat carrying the atomic bomb and stop the threat.

Dead Birds (2004) [Film; WW]

Premiere: September 13, 2004; Main Cast: Henry Thomas as William, Patrick Gugit as Sam, Nicki Aycox as Annabelle, Michael Shannon as Clyde, Marke Boone Junior as Joseph; Executive Producers: Barry Brooker, Sundip Shah; Story: Simon Barrett; Director: Alex Turner; 91 min.; Dead Bird Films, Silver Nurse Pictures; Sony Pictures Home Entertainment; Color.

Fairhope, Alabama, 1863. A group of former Confederate soldiers rob a bank of Confederate gold, leaving dead bodies in their path. Plans at fleeing to Mexico are put on hold by a fierce storm that sees them spending the night in an isolated house. But unknown to them the house belonged to a dead soldier from their Confederate unit and the house is infested with demons.

Dead of Night a.k.a. *Deathdream* (1974) [Film; UK-Canada; WW]

Premiere: August 29, 1974; Main Cast: John Marley as Charles Brooks, Lynn Carlin as Christine Brooks, Richard Backus as Andy Brooks; Executive Producers: Gerard Flint-Shipman, Geoffrey Nethercott; Screenplay: Alan Ormsby; Director: Bob Clark; 88 min.; Quadrant Films, Impact Films; Entertainment International Pictures; Color.

Andy Brooks is killed in action in Vietnam but miraculously returns home to his family in America, apparently alive but not entirely well. Soon he is connected to two local murders and his true undead state is revealed.

Dead Snow (2009) [Film; Norway; WW]

Premiere: January 9, 2009; Main Cast: Vegar Hoel as Martin, Stig Frode Henriksen as Roy, Charlotte Frogner as Hanna, Lasse Valdal as Vegard, Evy Kasseth Rosten as Liv, Orjan Gamst as Oberst Herzog; Executive Producers: Magne Ek, Espen Horn, Kjetil Omberg, Harald Zwart; Story: Tommy Wirkola, Stig Frode Henriksen; Director: Tommy Wirkola; 90 min.; Barentsfilm AS; Eurofia Film; IFC Films; Color.

Nazi zombies from World War II attack a group of medical students on vacation in modern-day Norway. The majority of the occupying German soldiers were killed by locals near the end of the war but some escaped into the mountains where they froze to death. But now to the horror of the students they survive as zombies with Standartenfuhrer Herzog leading them.

Dead Snow 2: Red vs. Dead (2014) [Film; Norway-Iceland-USA: WW]

Premiere: January 19, 2014; Main Cast: Vegar Hoel as Martin, Stig Frode Henriksen as Glenn Kenneth, Charlotte Frogner as Hanna, Orjan Gamst as Oberst Herzog, Martin Starr as Daniel, Jocelyn DeBoer as Monica, Ingrid Haas as Blake; Executive Producers: Kjetil Omberg, Terje Stroemstad; Story: Tommy Wirkola, Stig Frode Henriksen, Vegar Hoel; Director: Tommy Wirkola; 100 min.; Barentsfilm AS; Eurofia Film; IFC Films; Color.

American zombie experts help fight against Nazi zombies with an army of their own making.

Dead Soldier [Comic book; WW]

First publication: September 2010; Four-issue miniseries; Story: John Moore, Richie Smyth; Art: Dean Ruben Hyrapiet; Publisher: Liquid Comics.

In the final days of World War I American Colonel John Donner a.k.a. John Doe is the only survivor from a German offensive. As he wanders through the battlefields, lost and shell-shocked he is transformed into a brutish creature of abnormal strength, vowing revenge.

Dead Walkers: Rise of the 4th Reich (2013) [Film; UK-U.S.; WW]

Premiere: July 31, 2013; Main Cast: Philip Berzamanis, Jane Haslehurst as Pvt. Anael Sraosha, Bob Lee as Dr. Gavreel, Nathan Head as Professor Mastema, Melissa Hollett as Major Adler, Rudy Barrow as Alpha Five; Executive Producer: Warren Coyle; Story-Director: Philip Gardiner; 79 min.; Sector 5 Films; Chemical Burn Entertainment; Color.

The Nazi Occult continues after the end of World War II and the 4th Reich is ready to rule. Only this time the Nazi army will come from the pits of hell itself.

Death of a Shadow (2012) [Short film; Belgium-France; WW]

Premiere: June 4, 2012 (France); Main Cast: Matthias Schoenaerts as Nathan Rijckx, Laura Verlinden as Sarah Winters, Peter Van Den Eede as Collector of Shadows, Benjamin Ramon as Daniel Hainaut; Producer: Ellen De Waele; Story-Director: Tom Van Avermaet; 20 min.; Serendipity Films; Color.

This award winning short film centers around soldier Nathan Rijckx, now in limbo following his death. Before he died Nathan fell in love with a girl he desperately wants to meet again. Now that girl is in love with another man. But that doesn't stop the soldier in his quest to return to the living.

Death Ship (1980) [Film; Canada-UK; WW]

Premiere: March 7, 1980; Main Cast: George Kennedy as Captain Ashland, Richard Crenna as Trevor Marshall, Nick Mancuso as Nick, Sally Ann Howes as Margaret Marshall; Producers; Derek Gibson, Harold Greenberg; Screenplay: John Robins; Story: Jack Hill, David P. Lewis; Director; Alvin Rakoff; 91 min.; Bloodstar Productions, Lamitas, Astral Belle vue Pathe; AVCO Embassy Pictures; Color.

Rescued passengers from a doomed ship find themselves aboard a strange ship that has sailed the ocean for decades. The crew are Nazis who lure people to a tortuous death.

Deathwatch (2002) [Film; UK-Germany; WW]

Premiere: June 22, 2004; Main Cast: Jamie Bell as Pfc. Charlie Shakespeare, Mike Downey as Martin Plummer, Ruaidhri Conroy as Pvt. Colin Chevasse, Laurence Fox as Capt. Bramwell Jennings; Executive Producers: Caroline Hewitt, Sam Lavender, Dan Maag; Story-Director: Michael J. Bassett; 94 min.; Bavaria Film, ApolloMedia Distribution; Lion Gate Films; Color.

World War I in 1917. British Infantry Company Y hold a German trench after killing all the remaining soldiers except for one. The captured

German soldier warns the British of a supernatural force at work that will turn the soldiers to kill each other.

Declare [Novel; WW]
Author: Tim Powers; First publication: New York: William Morrow, 2001.

During World War II, 18-year-old Andrew Hale is recruited to a secret British spy organization with a mission that culminates on Mount Ararat in 1948. The mountain that many believe to be the resting place of Noah's Ark is also home to supernatural entities known as djinns. Now that power is protecting the Soviet Union in the form of an old woman. Hale fails in his mission to destroy the djinn and now, fifteen years later, he must complete Operation Declare. Opposing Hale is real-life British traitor Kim Philby, who seeks control of the djinns for the Soviets.

The Deepest Night [Juvenile book; WW]
Author: Shana Abe; First publication: New York: Bantam Books, 2013.

Sixteen-year-old Lora Jones is an enchanted being with magical powers, serving as a nurse at the home of Armand Louis, recently converted to a military hospital for wounded soldiers during World War I. Armand's brother Aubrey is being held in a German prison. Now Lora and Armand cross enemy lines to rescue him and in the process learn more about her powers and their connection to Armand and his brother.

"Delenda Est" [Short story; SFW]
Author: Poul Anderson; First publication: *The Magazine of Fantasy and Science Fiction* (December 1955).

Time patrol agent Manse Everard finds himself in a new timeline after renegade time travelers change the outcome of the Second Punic War and the Battle of Ticinus in 218 BC Now he lives in a world changed by Hannibal's destruction of Rome in 210 BC and must decide whether to change the timeline to its original history and therefore wipe out all the people who are alive in his alternate timeline.

The Demon [Comic book]
"Haunted Glory" [WW]
First publication: #46 (April 1994); Three-issue story; Story: Garth Ennis; Art: John McCrea, Wayne Faucher; Publisher: DC Comics.

The aged **Haunted Tank** crew are hired by the Demon Etrigan and Jason Blood when General Von Raddel awakens German soldiers from their graves to seize a U.S. army base.

The Demon Assassin [Juvenile book; WW]
Author: Alan Gibbons; First publication: London: Orion, 2008.

Teenager Paul Rector is the latest inheritor of an evil family curse. Like his brother John and great uncle Harry, he is part human, part demon. Paul takes Hell's Underground back to the Blitz in World War II London where he must stop Harry Rector from assassinating Prime Minister Winston Churchill.

"La Dernière Mobilization" [Short story; WW]
Author: W.A. Dwiggins; First publication: *The Fabulist* (1915).

"The leaders advance into the moonlight…. The uniforms of the men—of various sorts, indicating that they are from many commands—are in shreds and spotted with stains of mold and earth; their heads are bound in cloths so that their faces are covered…. Slowly the head of the line advances to the shadow of the wood, touches it and is swallowed. The leaders, the bare-flag staff, the drummer disappear; but still from the shade is heard the muffled sound of the drum.

Still the column comes out of the mist, still it climbs the hill and passes with its endless articulated burden. At last the rearmost couple disengages itself from the mist, ascends, and is swallowed by the shadow. There remain only the moonlight and the dusty hedgerow.

From the left the road runs from Belgium, to the right it crosses into France.

The dead were leaving their resting places in that lost land."

Designated Targets [Novel; SFW]
Author: John Birmingham; First publication: New York: Del Rey-Ballantine Books, 2005.

In the second book of the *Axis of Time* trilogy the U.S., Great Britain and the Axis powers all compete to get their hands on 21st century weapons of warfare. The world will never be the same with an apocalyptic outcome entirely possible.

See: ***Final Impact***

Dessous: La Montagne des Morts [Comic book; France; WW]
First publication: April 2016; Story-Art: Bones; Publisher: Sandawe.

During the Great War French troops launch an assault on German positions on the hill of Vauquois. To the amazement of the soldiers the German held trenches and bunkers have been deserted. Signs of desperate fighting are soon discovered in the enemy galleries when badly mutilated bodies are found. Later they find vats containing what once had been men. A guttural moan escapes as the bowels of the Earth are exposed and a nightmare vision awaits the French soldiers.

The Destroyer [Comic book character]
1. First publication: *Mystic Comics* #6 (October 1941); Creators: **Stan Lee**, Jack Binder; Publisher: Timely Comics.

American reporter Keen Marlow is imprisoned in a concentration camp by the Third Reich. While in the camp he takes a super-soldier formula perfected by fellow prisoner Professor Eric Schmitt. Now he is "a mighty avenging figure ... who has sworn not to rest until he has destroyed the Nazi hordes." Dressed in red and black striped tights and a gray tunic with a skull motif emblazoned on it, the pale-blue faced Destroyer strikes fear into the Nazis.

2. First appearance: *The Invaders* #18 (March 1977); Story: Roy Thomas; Art: Frank Robbins; Publisher: Marvel Comics Group.

The re-imagined *Destroyer* is now Brian Falsworth, son of World War I British hero Lord Falsworth, alias *Union Jack*. And brother of **Spitfire** from **The Invaders.** Falsworth later retires as the Destroyer and becomes the second *Union Jack*. Falsworth's good friend Roger Aubrey, previously known as Dyna-Mite, now calls himself the *Mighty Destroyer*.

The Devil with Hitler (1942) [Short film; WW]
Premiere: October 22, 1942; Main Cast: Alan Mowbray as Gesatan, Bobby Watson as Adolf Hitler, Joe Devlin as Benito Mussolini, George E. Stone as Suki Yaki, Marjorie Woodworth as Linda Kraus, Douglas Fowley as Walter Beeter; Producer: Glenn Tryon; Screenplay: Al Martin; Adaptation: Cortland Fitzsimmons; Director: Gordon Douglas; 44 min.; Hal Roach Studios; United Artists; B/W.

The Board of Directors of Hell ask for the resignation of the Devil claiming, "Adolf Hitler is the perfect man for your job." The Devil vows to find Hitler's soft spot within 48 hours and have him perform a good deed thus proving he isn't a suitable candidate for his job.

Hitler is portrayed as an idiotic maniac who is joined by Mussolini and Suki Yaki in various slapstick routines.

The Devil's Arithmetic (1999) [Telefilm; WW]
Premiere: March 28, 1999; Main Cast: Kirsten Dunst as Hannah Stern, Brittany Murphy as Rivkah, Paul Freeman as Rabbi, Mimi Rogers as Leonore Stern, Louise Fletcher as Aunt Eva; Executive Producers: Chris Ciaffa, Jay Cohen, Dustin Hoffman, Mimi Rogers; Teleplay: Robert J. Avrech. Based on the novel by Jane Yolen; Director; Donna Deitch; 95 min.; Millbrook Farm Productions, Punch Productions, Lietuvos Kinostudija; Showtime Networks; Color.

Teenager Hannah Stern opens a door in the present and finds herself back in World War II where she experiences all the horrors of being a prisoner in a German death camp.

The Devil's Backbone (2001) [Film; Spain-Mexico-France; WW]
Premiere: September 2, 2001; Main Cast: Marisa Paredes as Carmen, Eduardo Noriega as Jacinto, Federico Luppi as Dr. Casares, Inigo Garces as Jaime, Irene Visedo as Conchita, Fernando Tielve as Carlos, Berta Ojea as Alma; Executive Producers: Pedro Almodovar, Guillermo del Toro; Story: Guillermo del Toro, Antonio Trashorras, David Munoz: Director: Guillermo del Toro; 106 min.; Canal+Espana, Sogepaq, El Deseo; Sony Pictures Classics; Color.

1939. The Spanish Civil War. The ghost of a boy named Santi, who was killed in the bombing of an orphanage courtyard by General Franco's Fascists haunts 12-year-old Carlos, a newcomer to the orphanage-boarding school. But an unexploded bomb still remains in the courtyard and Santi warns Carlos of death in the near future.

The *New York Times* (November 21, 2001) praised the film. "Mr. del Toro takes an almost sensuous delight in weaving aural and visual textures of fear; water droplets and heartbeats echo in the stillness, and the camera replicates that primal childhood state of being poised between curiosity and dread. Is it worse to hide under the covers, where whatever it is might come and find you, or to seek it out in the murky darkness?"

See: *El espinazo del Diablo*

Devils of D-Day [Novel; WW]
Author: Graham Masterton; First publication: New York: Pinnacle Books, 1978.

American surveyor and cartographer Dan McCook discovers a mysterious black tank with its hatch sealed on the outskirts of the French village of Le Vey. Unknown to McCook the tank was one of thirteen involved in the slaughter of German soldiers. Black tanks under demonic forces—and now McCook is about to unleash one of those demons into the world again when he breaks the seal on the hatch.

Devils of War (2013) [Film; WW]

Premiere: April 15, 2013; Main Cast: Lawrence Anthony as Adam Wall, Jerry L. Buxbaum as William Baldy, Jamin Watson as Herman "Black Hercules" Jackson, Jeremiah Grace as Jasper Linnerooth, Jeff Richardson as Thorn, Carly Kingston as Claudia Klum; Story-Director: Eli Dorsey; 74 min.; Signature Entertainment, Automatic Entertainment; Color.

U.S. Special Forces soldiers carry out a top secret mission against Nazi super-soldiers and the occult in Poland, 1944.

The Devil's Rock (2011) [Film; New Zealand; WW]

Premiere; May 13, 2011; Main Cast: Craig Hall as Cpt. Ben Grogan, Matthew Sunderland as Colonel Klaus Meyer, Gina Varela as Helena—Demon, Karlos Drinkwater as Sgt. Joe Tane; Executive Producer: Paul Campion; Screenplay: Paul Finch, Paul Campion, Brett Ihaka; Director: Paul Campion; 83 min.; Severe Features, Chameleon Pictures; Entertainment One; Color.

June 1944 on the eve of D-Day New Zealand commandos Captain Ben Grogan and Sergeant Joseph Tane are ordered to create a diversion from the Normandy landings by exploding a military installation on a German occupied Channel Island. But they uncover a den of occult activity and demonic forces that the Nazis intend to use to defeat the Allies.

The Devil's Tomb (2009) [Film; WW]

Premiere: May 26, 2009; Main Cast: Cuba Gooding, Jr., as Mack, Taryn Manning as Doc, Ron Perlman as Wesley, Ray Winstone as Blakeley, Henry Rollins as Fulton; Producers: Steve B. Harris, Bill Sheinberg, Jonathan Sheinberg, Sid Sheinberg; Story: Keith Kjomes; Director: Jason Connery; 90 min.; Ice Cold Productions, Empyreal Entertainment, Ringleader Studios, The Bubble Factory; Voltage Pictures; Sony Pictures Home Entertainment; Color.

A CIA agent enlists the help of an elite group of soldiers to locate and rescue her father, working on an archaeological dig in the Middle East. But when they arrive at the underground laboratory the soldiers encounter deadly demonic creatures who feed on emotional vulnerabilities in the form of hallucinations.

"Direct Wire" [Pulp fiction; SFW]

Author: Clee Garson; Illustrator: Robert Fuqua; First publication: *Amazing Stories* (Vol. 17 #1; January 1943); Publisher: Ziff-Davis Publishing Company.

The sign over an empty cigar store reads: "Closed for the Duration, due to our having entered the Armed Forces of the U.S. God Bless America. Mort & Mike." The sign puzzles their customers because they know Mort Robbins and Mike Harrigan have never been the patriotic type.

A few days earlier Mike is troubled with news that the State Attorney's office is investigating the lists of the telephone company to link businesses to bookmakers. Mike knows their cigar store is basically a front for illegal gambling. When they receive a phone call asking to speak to Hitler and Mussolini they ignore it as a prank call. Maybe it's a ruse by the State Attorney's office to obtain information. The calls continue every twenty minutes with the same request. "Please fetch Hitler and Mussolini to the wire."

Finally the mystery caller identifies himself as the angel Gabriel calling on behalf of God. He wants to tell Hitler and Mussolini, "Enough is enough." Mort and Mike dismiss the explanation until a telephone engineer turns up to tell them their phone has been disconnected since last night.

The Discovery (Ghost Hunters book #5) [Juvenile book; WW]

Author: Marley Gibson; First publication: Boston: Graphia, 2011.

High school senior Kendall Moorehead forms a ghost hunting team after her family moves from Chicago to Radisson, Georgia. Her psychic abilities are put to the test when she encounters a doll from the American Civil War that is said to be the work of a voodoo priestess and may contain the soul of evil.

Les Divisions de Fer [Comic book; France; AHW]

First publication: September 2014; Three volumes; Story: Jean-Luc Sala; Art: Ronan Toulhoat; Publisher: Soleil.

In 1944 a new German technology appears that will change the outcome of World War II. Giant Mecha Panzers. In Moscow General Joukov forms the mechanized and armored Red Commando division to fight the new German menace. But there is conflict in the Russian camp between idealistic and high spirited pilot Nia and a devotee to the brutal Komissar. They must learn to fight side-by-side to defeat the Mecha Panzers.

Djinns a.k.a. *Stranded* (2010) [Film; France-Morocco; WW]

Premiere: July 16, 2010; Main Cast: Gregoire Leprince-Ringuet as Michel, Thierry Fremont as Vacard, Said Taghmaoui as Arout, Aurelien Wilk as Saria, Cyril Raffaelli as Louvier, Matthias Van Khache as Malovitch; Executive Producers: Benedicte Bellocq, Sovad Lamriki; Story-Directors: Sandra Martin, Hugues Martin; 103 min.; Kare Productions, Agora Films, Delante Films; Applause Entertainment; Color.

French soldiers investigating a military plane crash in Algeria are attacked by local Mujahideen fighters. They take cover in a village but cannot find shelter from the evil supernatural enemy that attacks their minds and souls.

"Dr. Loudon's Armageddon" [Pulp fiction; SFW]

Author: Alexander Blade; First publication: *Amazing Stories* (Vol. 15 #9; September 1941).

"One man's science could win the war—and this man's science was Nazi Germany's...."

Doctor Manhattan [Comic book character; SHW]

First appearance: *Watchmen* #1 (September 1986); 12-issue mini-series; Creators: Alan Moore, Dave Gibbons; Publisher: DC Comics.

Nuclear physicist Dr. Jonathan Osterman becomes "the supreme super-hero" after his body is ripped apart and vaporized during after being trapped in his intrinsic filled experiment chamber. Slowly Osterman's body is regenerated, until finally he lives again as a tall, naked, blue-skinned man with special powers. Now he can control atomic and sub-atomic particles, alter his body size and teleport himself over vast distances.

Seeing the military potential in Osterman, the U.S. government adopt his services and codename him Doctor Manhattan. Richard Nixon employs Manhattan as a super-weapon in Vietnam. Within three months the war ends with an American victory in 1971.

The Vietnam scenario features briefly in the live-action film *Watchmen* (2009), directed by Rick Snyder and featuring Billy Crudup as Dr. Jonathan Osterman/Doctor Manhattan.

Doctor Who (1963) [TV series; UK]

The adventures of a Time Lord and his companions as they travel through time and space in the TARDIS (Time and Relative Dimensions in Space) posing as a British police phone box.

"THE CRUSADE" (2:22–2:25) [SFW]

Air dates; March 27–April 17, 1965; Main Cast: William Hartnell as Dr. Who, William Russell as Ian Chesterton, Jacqueline Hill as Barbara Wright, Maureen O'Brien as Vicki, Julian Glover as Richard the Lionheart, Bernard Kay as Saladin, Walter Randall as El Akir, Roger Avon as Saphadin, Reg Pritchard as Ben Daheer, Bruce Wightman as William de Tornebu, Jean Marsh as Joanna, Robert Lankesheer as Chamberlain; Producer: Verity Lambert; Story: David Whitaker; Director: Douglas Camfield; 4 × 25 min.; B/W.

In this four-part story set in 12th century Palestine the Doctor is an advisor to Richard the Lionheart. Richard and his knights are ambushed by the Saracens and the Doctor's companion Barbara captured. The Doctor only makes the situation worse when he mistakenly reveals Richard the Lionheart's secret marriage plans.

"THE CURSE OF FENRIC" (26:08–26:11) [SFW]

Air dates: October 25–November 15, 1989; Main Cast: Sylvester McCoy as The Doctor, Sophie Aldred as Ace, Dinsdale Landen as Doctor Judson, Alfred Lynch as Commander Millington, Nicholas Parsons as Reverend Wainwright, Tomek Bork as Captain Soren, Anne Reid as Nurse Crane; Producer: John Nathan Turner; Story: Ian Briggs; Director: Nick Mallett; 4 × 25 min.; Color.

In this four-part episode the Doctor and companion Ace become involved in a World War II mystery set on a naval base. Commander Millington is obsessed with decoding a mysterious Viking inscription found in a local tomb by Doctor Judson. Meanwhile an ancient evil named Fenric causes vampiric creatures known as Heamovores to attack the base.

"THE MYTH MAKERS" (3:06–3:09) [SFW]

Air dates: October 16–November 6, 1965; Main Cast: William Hartnell as The Doctor, Maureen O'Brien as Vicki, Peter Purves as Steven Taylor,

Adrienne Hill as Katarina, Cavan Kendall as Achilles, Ivor Salter as Odysseus, Barrie Ingham as Paris, Tutte Lemkow as Cyclops, Francis de Woolf as Agamemnon, Frances White as Cassandra, James Lynn as Troilus, Jack Melford as Menelaus, Max Adrian as King Priam; Producer" John Wiles; Story: Donald Cotton; Director: Michael Leeston-Smith.

This four-part story takes place during the Trojan War where the Doctor is mistaken for a God and the Tardis is thought to be the Temple of Zeus. Companion Steven Taylor enters Troy as a prisoner in order to find fellow companion Vicki, while the Doctor suggests the idea of a Trojan Horse to rescue both of them. The Doctor gains a new companion in slave girl Katarina when Vicki decides to leave the Doctor behind after she falls in love with Troilus. 4 × 25 min.; B/W.

"The War Games" (6:35–6:44) [SFW]

Air dates: April 19–June 21, 1969; Main cast: Patrick Troughton as Dr. Who, Frazer Hines as Jamie, Wendy Padbury as Zoe, Jane Sherwin as Lady Jennifer Buckingham, David Saville as Lt. Carstairs, Noel Coleman as General Smythe, David Garfield as General Von Weich, Edward Brayshaw as War Chief, Philip Madoc as War Lord; Producer: Derrick Sherwin; Story: Terrance Dicks, Malcolm Hulke; Director: David Maloney; 10 × 25 min.; B/W.

A ten-episode story arc begins in No Man's Land during World War I. The Doctor and his companion Zoe are captured by General Smythe but manage to escape into a strange mist before being recaptured. Meanwhile companion Jamie encounters a Redcoat who tells him the year is 1745. The soldiers have in fact been taken from various wars on Earth as part of an alien war game masterminded by the War Chief.

The Doctor is arrested and put on trial by the Time Lords for "interference" by stealing the Tardis from his home planet. He is forced to regenerate and banished to Earth. Jamie and Zoe return to their own times with all memory of the Doctor and their adventures erased forever in this final episode featuring Patrick Troughton as the Doctor.

Doctor Who (2005) [TV series; UK]

The long-running series was successfully relaunched in 2005 beginning with the ninth incarnation of the Doctor and Season One.

"The Doctor, the Widow and the Wardrobe" (7:00) [SFW]

Air date: December 25, 2011; Main Cast: Matt Smith as The Doctor, Karen Gillan as Amy Pond, Arthur Darvill as Rory, Claire Skinner as Madge Arwell, Maurice Cole as Cyril Arwell, Holly Earl as Lily Arwell, Alexander Armstrong as Reg Arwell, Bill Bailey as Droxil, Sam Stockman as Co-Pilot; Producer: Marcus Wilson; Story: Steven Moffat; Director; Farren Blackburn; 60 min.; Color.

Christmas Eve, 1938. Madge Arwell is granted a wish by an injured alien angel after she comes to his aid. Christmas Eve, 1941. Madge is grieving over news of her husband being lost in battle over the English Channel. But she buries her grief to give her children Lily and Cyril a Christmas to remember as they retreat to the countryside from war torn London. They are greeted with a magical winter wonderland.

"The Empty Child" "The Doctor Dances" (1:09–1:10) [SFW]

Air date: May 5–12, 2006; Main Cast: Christopher Ecclestone as Doctor Who, Billy Piper as Rose Tyler, John Barrowman as Capt. Jack Harness, Florence Hoath as Nancy, Albert Valentine as The Child, Richard Wilson as Dr. Constantine, Joseph Tremain as Jim; Producer: Phil Collinson; Story: Steven Moffat; Director: James Hawes; 42 min.; Color.

The Tardis lands in London in the midst of the London blitz in 1941. A child wearing a gas mask repeatedly asking, "Are you my Mummy?" catches the attention of companion Rose Tyler who in her pursuit of the child ends up dangling from a barrage balloon. Fellow time traveler Captain Jack Harness rescues Rose with a tractor beam from his cloaked spaceship.

In Albion Hospital the patients have no heartbeat, are unable to die and have gas masks fused to their faces made of flesh and bone.

In the concluding episode we learn of Captain Jack Harness' connection to a battlefield ambulance that crashed to Earth with escaped nano genes able to manipulate DNA and "repair" humans. A young woman named Nancy and the mysterious child become the key players in saving London from invaders even more menacing than the German air raids over war torn London.

"Let's Kill Hitler" (6:08) [SFW]

Air date: August 27, 2011; Main Cast: Matt Smith as The Doctor, Karen Gillan as Amy Pond, Arthur Darvill as Rory, Alex Kingston as River Song, Nina Toussaint-White as Mels, Albert Welling as Adolf Hitler, Philip Rham as Eric Zimmerman; Producer: Marcus Wilson; Story: Steven Moffat; Director: Richard Senior; 48 min.; BBC Cymru Wales, BBC; Color.

Berlin, 1938. Nazi officer Eric Zimmerman is replaced by a shape-shifting robot that assumes his identity. The robot's mission is to kill Adolf Hitler. The landing of the Tardis interrupts the mission and accidentally saves Hitler's life. Rory locks Hitler in a cupboard to keep him quiet. The time traveling Justice Department Agency hunts war criminals with the help of their shape-shifting technology and now has Melody Pond in their sights as "the woman who kills the Doctor." Amy Pond is confused as her best friend Mels is revealed to be her future daughter Melody Pond who in turn is River Song.

"Victory of the Daleks" (5:03) [SFW]
Air date: April 17, 2010; Main Cast: Matt Smith as The Doctor, Karen Gillan as Amy Pond, Ian McNeice as Winston Churchill, Bill Paterson as Bracewell, Nina De Cosimo as Blanche, Tim Wallers as Childers; Producer: Peter Bennett; Story: Mark Gatiss; Director: Andrew Gunn; 42 min.; Color.

Prime Minister Winston Churchill has a new weapon aimed at the Nazi menace that he wants to share with the Doctor. But when the Doctor and Amy Pond travel back to London during World War II they are shocked to discover Churchill's new weapon is the Daleks.

Doctor Who (Comic book)

"Sky Jacks" [SFW]

First publication: Vol. 3, #9–12 (May 2013); 4-issue story; Story: Andy Diggle, Eddie Robson; Art: Andy Kuhn; Publisher: IDW Publishing.

The eleventh Doctor and his companion Clara Oswald are trapped in a steam punk "sky" world. With the TARDIS missing the Doctor uses a retrofitted B-29 bomber from World War II to journey to the center of the strange dimension with infinite skies.

Doctor Who Adventures (Comic book; UK)

"Trust" [SFW]

First publication: #5 (August 13, 2015); Story: Jason Quinn; Art: Russ Leach; Publisher: Panini UK.

The twelfth Doctor celebrates the liberation of Paris in World War II with companion Clara. But the party turns sour when the Darapok Empire threatens to take over the city.

Doctor Who and the Crusaders [Novel; UK; SFW]

Author: David Whitaker; First publication: London: Frederick Muller, 1965.

Adaptation of the four-part **Doctor Who** TV series adventure set in 12th century Palestine where the first Doctor is an advisor to Richard the Lionheart.

Doctor Who: Atom Bomb Blues [Novel; UK; SFW]

Author: Andrew Cartmel; First publication: BBC Books, 2005.

The seventh Doctor and Ace pose as a nuclear scientist and his assistant in Los Alamos, New Mexico, 1945. The race is on the build the first atom bomb to end the Second World War. But others are showing an interest in the groundbreaking technology, including extraterrestrials and beings from another dimension.

Doctor Who: Autumn Mist [Novel; UK; SFW]

Author: David A. McIntee; First publication: BBC Books, 1999.

The eighth Doctor, Sam and Fitz land in the Ardennes in December 1944. Nazi troops are making their last offensive at the Battle of the Bulge. But corpses are disappearing and an ancient force seems to be in play.

Doctor Who: Casualties of War [Novel; UK; SFW]

Author: Steve Emmerson; First publication: London: BBC Books, 2000.

Hawkswick, North Yorkshire, 1918 during World War I. A psychiatric hospital for shell-shocked soldiers comes under suspicion when wounded soldiers with terrible wounds are seen on maneuvers in the night. But when the eighth Doctor arrives to investigate the strange happenings Constable Briggs believes him to be sent by the Ministry. The bizarre events continue to occur when one of the patients, Private Daniel Corey is found murdered in his bed and a squad of corpse soldiers wanders the grounds. The Doctor links blood sacrifices with an Offering Tree and Dark Forces.

Doctor Who: Colditz [Audio drama; UK; SFW]

Release date: October 2001; Main Cast: Sylvester McCoy as The Doctor, Sophie Aldred as Ace, Tracey Childs as Elizabeth Klein, David Tennant as Kurtz, Toby Lingworth as Hauptmann Jukius Scafer, Nichols Young as Flying Officer Bill Gower, Peter Rae as Timothy Wilkins; Story: Steve Lyons; Director:

Gary Russell; 2 × 60 min.; Publisher: Big Finish Productions.

Colditz Castle, October 1944. Time traveling intruders in the impenetrable P.O.W. camp, Colditz Castle in Germany may hold the key to victory for the Third Reich.

This audio drama marks the first performance of David Tennant in any *Doctor Who* drama. Four years later he would be cast as the tenth Doctor in the BBC-TV series.

Doctor Who: Daleks Among Us [Audio drama; UK; SFW]

Release date: September 11, 2003; Voice Cast: Sylvester McCoy as The Doctor, Tracey Childs as Dr. Elizabeth Klein/Elizabeth Volkenrath, Christian Edwards as Will Arrowsmith, Terry Malloy as Davros, Jonathan Forbes as Hinterberger, Tim Delap as Falkus, Jessica Brooks as Qaren, Nicholas Briggs as Ralf/The Daleks, Paul Chahidi as The Shepherd; Story: Alan Barnes; Director: Ken Bentley; 4 episodes × 2 CDs; Publisher: Big Finish Productions.

Azimuth, Germany, 1945. Revisionism is already taking hold with official announcements. "Azimuth Department of Re-Education. Reminder: To All Citizens: Twenty years ago the Daleks did not invade Azimuth. There was no war. There were no death camps. A man named "the Doctor" did not help liberate Azimuth. There are no such things as Daleks. They do not exist."

Doctor Who: Dark Convoy [Audio drama; UK; SFW]

Release date: July 20, 2015; Main Cast: Sophie Aldred as Narrator; Story: Mark B. Oliver; Director: Lisa Bowerman; 33 min.; Publisher: Big Finish Productions.

The seventh Doctor and his companion Ace track a British submarine in distress on the HMS Thunder submarine during World War II. But the rescue is hampered by Nazi planes flying overhead.

Doctor Who: Illegal Alien [Novel; UK; SFW]

Authors: Mike Tucker, Robert Perry; First publication: BBC Books, 1997.

The seventh Doctor and Ace are in the middle of the London blitz in November 1940. But it isn't just deadly Nazi bombs falling from the sky. A strange silver sphere has crash landed and something has emerged from within. American private eye Cody McBride has seen the sphere and its sinister occupant, but only the Doctor and Ace believe him. Now the deadly menace from the sphere is loose in London and the Doctor's old enemies the Cybermen are involved.

Doctor Who: Just War [Novel; UK; SFW]

Author: Lance Parkin; First publication: Virgin Books, 1996.

March 1941. Nazis occupy the British island of Guernsey and are building a secret weapon that will determine to outcome of the war. The seventh Doctor and his assistants must discover and neutralize the weapon before it is too late.

See: ***Bernice Summerfield: Just War***

Doctor Who Magazine (Comic book; UK)

"ME AND MY SHADOW" [SFW]

First publication: #318 (June 26, 2002); Story: Scott Gray; Publisher: Panini Comics.

The Austrian-Swiss border, 1941. British undercover agent Fey Truscott-Sade an the elderly Jacob Gansmann are being tracked by Nazi troops. Before Jacob is wounded and captured he passes on vital documents to Fey. Meanwhile the artificial being Shayde has awoken and allows Fey to use his powers to kill the Nazis. Only Colonel Kessler remains. Before his death he accuses Fey of being a witch and demon.

"MEMORIAL" [SFW]

First publication: #191 (September 30, 1992); Story: Warwick Gray; Art: John Ridgway; Publisher: Marvel Comics.

World War II veteran Simon Galway meets the seventh Doctor and Ace at the Westmouth Cenotaph in December 1995. Looking at the Cenotaph that memorializes his brother Brian, takes Galway's memory back to December 1945 when he attended the original ceremony for the war memorial. And he swears he saw a man who is a lookalike for the Doctor at that same ceremony.

Doctor Who: More Short Trips [Short story anthology; UK]

Editor: Stephen Cole; First publication: London: BBC Books, March 1999.

A collection of short stories that includes the Weird War tale, "Special Weapons" by Paul Leonard. The seventh Doctor and his companion Mel find themselves in an English village occupied by Nazis who have captured a light wanderer that feeds on solar radiation. Utilizing the powers of the strange creature the Nazis plan to create a barrier that will cut off England from the outside world, eliminating sunlight and warmth.

Doctor Who: Persuasion [Audio drama; UK; SFW]

Release date: July 10, 2013; Main Cast: Sylvester McCoy as The Doctor, Tracey Childs as Dr. Elizabeth Klein, Christian Edwards as Will Arrowsmith, David Sibley as Kurt Schalk, Jonathan Forbes as Lukas Hinterberger, Paul Cahidi as The Shepherd, Miranda Raison as The Shepherdess, Gemma Whelan as The Khlect; Story: Jonathan Barnes; Director: Ken Bentley; 2 × 60 min.; Publisher: Big Finish Productions.

The seventh Doctor recruits Elizabeth Klein, the scientific advisor for UNIT for a mission to a Nazi base in Dusseldorf, Germany in May 1945. But the base and scientist Kurt Schalk have also attracted the attention of twenty-three other species from across the Universe.

Doctor Who: Resistance [Audio drama; UK; SFW]

Release date: March 2009; Main Cast: Anneke Wills as Polly Wright, John Sackville as the Pilot; Story: Steve Lyons; Director: Lisa Bowerman; 60 min.; Publisher: Big Finnish Productions.

Vichy, France, February 1944. The second Doctor and companions Jamie and Polly land in Nazi-occupied territory, where the Gestapo is attempting to neutralize all French resistance movements. Meanwhile a British flying officer crash lands his plane in the same hostile territory and is desperate to reach safety.

The drama is seen through the eyes of the two narrators, Polly Wright and the British pilot.

Doctor Who: Short Trips: The Ghosts of Christmas [Short story anthology; UK]

Editors: Cavan Scott, Mark Wright; First publication: Berkshire, UK: Big Finish, December 2007.

This collection of short stories includes the Weird War tale, "Tell Me You Love Me" by Scott Matthewman. The first Doctor and his companions Ian, Barbara and Susan take cover in a shelter during an air raid in World War II. But strange events begin to occur when Barbara's late father appears to her. Elsewhere in the street a similar occurrence has happened to young Sarah Miller and her mother. But in reality the fathers are alien survivors of a crashed space ship who have taken their form and thrive on love.

Doctor Who: The Churchill Years: Hounded [Audio drama; UK; SFW]

Release date: January 14, 2016; Main Cast: Ian McNeice as Winston Churchill, Emily Atack as Hetty Warner, Jo Stone-Frewlings as Major Wheatley, Amerjit Deu as The Swami, Stewart Scudamore as Danvers; Story; Alan Barnes; Director: Ken Bentley; Publisher: Big Finish Productions.

London, Autumn, 1941. Winston Churchill is overcome with a darkness in his mind that he names "The Black Dog," The tenth Doctor comes to the aid of England but finds himself labeled a traitor.

Doctor Who: The Churchill Years: Living History [Audio drama; UK; SFW]

Release date: January 14, 2016; Main Cast: Ian McNeice as Winston Churchill, Danny Horn as Kazran Sardick, Alistair Petrie as Julius Caesar, Laura Rogers as Queen Tristahna, Nicholas Briggs as Dalek; Story: Justin Richards; Director: Ken Bentley; Publisher: Big Finnish Productions.

Winston Churchill takes a trip in the TARDIS to meet Julius Caesar, but becomes stranded in Ancient Britain with a young man from the future and is captured by Roman soldiers. He also learns the Ancient Britons are worshipping a Bronze God who is in reality a Dalek.

Doctor Who: The Churchill Years: The Oncoming Storm [Audio drama; UK; SFW]

Release date: January 14, 2016; Main Cast: Ian McNeice as Winston Churchill, Emily Atack as Hetty Warner, Michael Gould as Frederick Lindemann, Derek Riddell as Lt-Commander Sandy McNish, Phil Mulryne as Able Seaman Phillips; Story: Phil Mulryne; Director: Ken Bentley; Publisher: Big Finish Productions.

London, December 1939. First Lord of the Admiralty, Winston Churchill and new secretary Hetty Warner face a mysterious new menace. A "stone" has been found in the Thames' sands. Unknown to Churchill it comes from Gallifrey and a strange group of soldiers are lurking in the shadows of London streets attempting to acquire it. And the ninth Doctor is proving to be elusive.

Doctor Who: The Nemonite Invasion [Audio drama; UK; SFW]

Release date: February 12, 2009; Main Cast: Catherine Tate as Narrator; Producer: Simon Hunt; Story:

David Roden; Director: Kate Thomas; Publisher: BBC Audio.

The cliffs of Dover, England, May 1940. At the secret command center, Vice-Admiral Ramsay is finalizing Operation: Dynamo. But a mysterious sphere has crash landed nearby containing a parasite Nemonite that will place Operation Dynamo and all humanity in peril.

Catherine Tate narrates a story involving the tenth Doctor and the character she played in the BBC-TV series, Donna Noble.

Doctor Who: The Scapegoat [Audio drama; UK; SFW]

Release date: July 2009; Main Cast: Paul McGann as The Doctor, Sheridan Smith as Lucie Miller, Samantha Bond as Mother Baroque, Clifford Rose as Major Treptow, Christopher Fairbank as Doc Baroque, Paul Rhys as Max Paul, Thorston Manderlay as Lieutenant, Beth Chalmers as Helene; Story: Pat Mills; Director: Nicholas Briggs; 60 min.; Publisher: Big Finnish Productions.

Doctor Who: The Shadow in the Glass [Novel; UK; SFW]

Authors: Stephen Cole, Justin Richards; First publication: London: BBC Books, 2001.

The sixth Doctor and retired Brigadier Lethbridge-Stewart travel back in time to World War II to uncover the link between a crashed UFO over an English village and Adolf Hitler.

Doctor Who—Timewyrm: Exodus [Novel; UK; SFW]

Author: Terrance Dicks; First publication: London: Virgin Books, 1991.

London, 1951. The seventh Doctor and his companion Ace are alarmed to discover Hitler's Germany won World War II. Now they must try and restore the timeline by traveling to 1923 and 1939 where the Doctor discovers the Timewyrm is trapped within Adolf Hitler's mind. The Timewyrm has the power to replace the brain neurons of any subject she inhabits.

Doll Man (Comic book character; SHW]

First appearance: *Feature Comics* #27 (December 1939): Creators: Will Eisner (as William Erwin Maxwell); Publisher: Quality Comics.

Against Professor Roberts' advice scientist Darrel Dane drinks an experimental formula. He tells the Professor, "This liquid will shrink a human being to the size of a doll." Dane shrinks to doll size as expected but his brain becomes clouded as he attacks the Professor in a fit of rage with his new super-strength. Soon his mind clears as he wills himself back to normal size and dedicates his life to, "A crusade against crime and evil."

Originally fighting the criminal underworld Doll Man expands his operations to fighting " the foes of our democracy" during World War II. "Disguising himself as that eight inches of concentrated dynamite, Darrel Dane rips apart an Axis plot to destroy a troopship carrying thousands of Yankee boys." (*Feature Comics* #63, December 1942).

See: **Freedom Fighters**

S.S. Doomtrooper (2006) [Telefilm; SFW]

Premiere: 2006; Main Cast: Corin Nemec as Captain Malloy, Ben Cross as Professor Ullman, Marian Filali as Mariette Martinet, James Pomichter as Pvt. Parker Lewis, Kirk B.R. Woller as Lt. Reinhardt; Executive Producers: Phillip J. Roth, T.J. Sakasegawa; Story: Berkeley Anderson; Director: David Flores; 90 min; Nu Image/Millennium Films, Sc-Fi Pictures, UFO, Combat Productions; Sci-Fi Channel; Color.

In the final days of World War II Nazi scientist Professor Ullman has developed a super-soldier. U.S. Army Captain Joe Malloy gathers together a group of soldiers, including French resistance fighter Marriette Martinet, to destroy the genetically enhanced monster.

Dragon Ball Z: Fusion Reborn [Animated film; Japan; SFW]

Premiere: March 5, 1995 (Japan); Voice Cast: Bin Shimada as West Kaio/The Dictator/Romeo, Takeshi Kusao as Trunks/Gotenks; Executive Producer: Gen Fukunaga; Screenplay: Takao Koyama; Director: Shigeyasu Yamauchi; 51 min.; Bird Studios, Toei Animation, Toei Doga; Color.

In a small segment of the animated film the Dictator (a caricature of Adolf Hitler) and his undead army (swastikas have been substituted with a "x" insignia) return from hell with the intention of dominating the world. But they are defeated by Goten and Trunks.

The Dragon in the Sword [Novel; WW]

Author: Michael Moorcock; First publication: New York: Ace Fantasy Books, 1986.

The Eternal Champion incarnates across the Multiverse whenever Chaos or Law threatens to dominate the other. Unlike other Champions, average Londoner John Daker recalls all his incarnations as he is thrown from one body to another. In his latest incarnation he befriends another Eternal Champion in aristocratic German Ulrich Von Bek. Von Bek has retreated into the Middle Marches to escape the Gestapo after failing to assassinate Adolf Hitler.

The Dragon Waiting: A Masque of History [Novel: AHW]

Author: John M. Ford; First publication: New York: Timescape Books-Simon & Schuster, 1983.

Edward IV is on the throne of England following the Wars of the Roses. But medieval Europe is under a new threat from the Byzantium Empire and the Vampire Duke, Sforza plans an attack on Florence. But a Welsh Wizard and a young woman physician fleeing Florence succeed in securing the English throne for Richard, Duke of Gloucester. As Richard III he wins the Battle of Bosworth and kills the once-future king Henry Tudor.

"Dragons Behind Us" [Pulp fiction; WW]

Author: Richard Casey; Illustrator: Julian Krupa; First publication: *Fantastic Adventures* (Vol. 7 #2; April 1945); Publisher: Ziff-Davis Publishing Company.

Field Marshal Hermann Göring addresses his men, "You officers will have the honor of destroying a great force of American troops who plan to establish a beachhead near Rome."

Göring lifts morale recounting the story of Siegmund who slew a dragon and the legend of the Rhine Gold. He then pins a medal featuring the golden symbol of Siegmund's sword and dragon on each soldier.

When the soldiers reach the beach as they lay in wait for the Americans a huge fire breathing dragon appears, killing the German Lieutenant Miller in a blast of fire.

The next morning Captain Richter recalls events from his prison camp. "Göring gave us the medal of the sword and the dragon and said it would give us great power to conquer you. Göring forgot that his hero, Siegmund, wasn't trying to conquer the world. Seigmund killed a dragon while fighting for justice, not for power. He expected Seigmund; instead the dragons came!"

The Dreamthief's Daughter: A Tale of the Albino [Novel; WW]

Author: Michael Moorcock; First publication: New York: Warner Books, 2001.

Adolf Hitler is on the trail of German nobleman Count Ulric von Bek after he learns he may own a mystical sword and the elusive Holy Grail. Hitler send Major Gaynor von Minct to recover the relics. But Gaynor and Von Bek are the avatars of John Daker, the Eternal Champion, fighting the causes of Chaos and Law in a Multiverse of alternate realities.

Druid's Sword [Novel; WW]

Author: Sara Douglass; First publication: New York: Tor, 2006.

The final book in the *Troy Game* quartet centers around exiled Trojan prince and supernatural Greek Kingman Brutus reincarnated as American Major Jack Skelton in World War II London. As Hitler's Luftwaffe continues to bomb London in the Blitz Major Skelton joins his fellow immortals for one final battle to complete the magical Labyrinth and end the Troy Game.

See: **Darkwitch Rising**

Dust Adventures Core Book [RPG book; AHW]

First publication: November 2015; Creator: Paolo Parente; Story: Chris Lites, Benn Beaton, CS Barnhart; Art: Gio Baroni, Michael E. Cross, Rick Hershey; Publisher: Modiphius Entertainment.

Inspired by the ***Dust Tactics*** tactical miniatures board game, this core book features the roleplaying rules for adventures in the *Dust* universe. The year is 1947 and the Axis powers continue their fight despite the death of Adolf Hitler. The Soviet Union are allies with China and England is about to fall. Players must go behind enemy lines to tackle the Axis powers and end their plans of world domination.

Dust Adventures: Operation Apocalypse [RPG book; AHW]

First publication: November 2015; Creator: Paolo Parente; Story: Chris Lites, Benn Beaton, CS Barnhart; Art: Gio Baroni, Michael E. Cross; Publisher: Modiphius Entertainment.

An elite Allied team battles the Axis powers and a cult in search of the Seven Seals in an adventure that spans London to the Grand Canyon to the Amazonian pre–Mayan ruins.

Dust Tactics [Board game; AHW]

First publication: 2010; Creator: Paolo Parente; Designers: Paolo Parente, Ilivier Zamfirescu; Art: Karl Kopinski, Paolo Parente; Publisher: Dust Games, Fantasy Flight Games.

This tactical miniatures board game for 2–4 players is set in an alternate 1947 where World War II has spread to every continent on Earth. Alien technology has been reverse engineered from a crashed UFO discovered in Antarctica in 1938. The result is advanced war machines and a war between Axis forces and Allies as they battle to control the limitless VK source of energy and mineral deposits that are vital to the outcome of the war.

Dust Wars [Comic book; AHW]
First publication: June 2010; 3-issue mini-series; Creator: Paolo Parente; Story: Christopher "Mink" Morrison; Art: David Fabbri, Paolo Parente; Publisher: Image Comics.

Axis Commander Sigrid Von Thaler plans one final assault on Europe with her Gunther robots. Only the Russian KV-47 Squad and a motley assortment of Americans can spoil Sigrid's plans.

Dynaman [Comic book character; SHW]
First appearance: *Elseworlds: The Golden Age #1* (1993); Creators: James Robinson, Paul Martin Smith; Publisher: DC Comics.

Following a nuclear test Daniel Dunbar is transformed into super-hero *Dynaman*. But unknown to anyone the *Ultra-Humanite* has replaced Dunbar's brain with Adolf Hitler's brain. The people believe World War II hero Tex Thompson killed Hitler and survived the war. But Thompson died at the end of the war and Ultra-Humanite has taken his place. Now he plans to become president of the United States with Dynaman alias Adolf Hitler by his side. After Joan Dale, formerly **Miss America**, suspects Tex Thompson isn't the same man she once loved the truth is revealed and a showdown in Washington, D.C., with the **Justice Society of America** and *All-Star Squadron* awaits.

Eerie [comic book]

1. Horror and supernatural anthology title from Avon Periodicals

"Master of the Dead" [WW]
First publication: #14 (January–February 1954); Art: Norman Nodel, Vince Alascia.

Mad scientist and master of the occult, Pierre Jarnac is interred in an insane asylum for experimenting on corpses thinking he can bring them back to life. As time passes Jarnac is considered to be cured of his obsession with the dead and released. Jarnac takes a job as caretaker of a military cemetery near the Marne where he continues his experiments with the dead.

Using his occult powers the dead soldiers of all nations rise from their graves thinking they are on a mission of peace. But soon they turn on Jarnac after they are ordered to kill innocent civilians. "Those people we killed meant us no harm. You do! We've become an army of terror, not peace! You have lied and tricked us. You don't want to end wars. You want to create more suffering. You want boundless personal power. We will march, Pierre Jarnac—against you!"

2. Horror and supernatural anthology title from Warren Publishing

"Cave of the Druids" [WW]
First publication: #6 (November 1966); Story: Archie Goodwin; Art: Reed Crandall.

Julius Caesar's invading Roman legions have reached the British Isles in 41 A.D. Marcus Severus is warned not to venture into a forest by an ancient Celt, but ignores his warning. In the forest he finds his patrol dead with no signs of dying in battle. Suddenly the trees come to life and local druids attack. Severus survives but is intrigued by a druidstone leading to an underground altar where a priestess is working her magic with a wand of yew.

"The Covered Bridge" [WW]
First publication: #8 (March 1967); Story: Archie Goodwin; Story" Bob Jenney.

The Revolutionary War. Lieutenant Farnsworth is warned of a haunted covered bridge by a Yankee rebel as the noose is placed around his neck. Farnsworth dismisses his words as superstition. "We're supposed to be soldiers, not old wives!" But as Farnsworth and his soldiers approach the covered bridge their horses bolt. Entering on foot, two soldiers disappear into the bridge and others run away in fear. Farnsworth enters and discovers the bridge doesn't cross a river but is a bridge between the world of the living and the dead.

"The Curse of Kali" [WW]
First publication: #6 (November 1966); Story: Archie Goodwin; Art: Angelo Torres.

Queen Victoria's army in India enter a village to find a garrison of British soldiers slaughtered, with no sign of Lieutenant Smythe. Sergeant Cairn recalls the story of Smythe and his forbidden love. Smythe persists in his pursuit of the beautiful girl and saves her from becoming a blood sacrifice to the goddess Kali. But in saving her life Kali still demands blood and now Smythe will be her conduit and his garrison the blood sacrifices.

"Death Plane" [WW]

First publication: #1 (September 1965); Story: Larry Ivie; Art: George Evans.

When an unidentified plane bombs both German and Allied troops during World War I a two-day truce is agreed upon to allow both sides to shoot the mutual enemy out of the skies. But when a British pilot is hit he sees himself piloting the enemy plane. His only hope of finding peace for his soul is to replace himself with another doomed pilot.

"Experiment in Fear!" [WW]

First publication: #9 (May 1967); Story: Archie Goodwin; Art: Eugene Colan.

1943. A World War II German concentration camp is using Jews as guinea pigs in an experiment in fear. Prisoners are placed in a room expecting to be executed and left alone for hours—their fear building. Then calculated false alarms in the form of non-toxic gas, increase their fear levels even further. After all the data is received the Jews are finally executed. The Nazis claim the results prove the Jews are prone to fear more than other races. But Doctor Strasser is in for a shock when a prisoner escapes and leaves Strasser in his cell. When Strasser shows the same fear as the Jews the Nazis are left with one conclusion—Strasser must also be a Jew and join the rest of the Jewish prisoners at the camp.

"An Occurrence at Owl Creek Bridge" [WW]

First publication: #9 (May 1967); Story adapted by: Archie Goodwin; Art: Bob Jenney.

Ambrose Bierce's story of a an American Civil War soldier who believes he has escaped the noose is adapted into a six-page B/W comic strip by Archie Goodwin.

See: *An Occurrence at Owl Creek Bridge*

Elves (1989) [Film; WW]

Premiere: 1989; Main Cast: Dan Haggerty as Mike McGavin/ Santa Claus, Julie Austin as Kirsten, Deanna Lund as Kirsten's Mother, Laura Lichstein as Brooke, Stacey Dye as Amy; Executive Producers: John Fitzgerald, Jerry Graham; Story: Jeff Mandel, Mike Griffin, Bruce Taylor; Director: Jeff Mandel; 89 min.; Triangle Films, Fitzgerald Film Corp; AIP; Color.

Three girls accidentally summon an evil elf who is part of a Nazi prophecy concerning the anti–Christ. In order for the prophecy to come true Kirsten must mate with the elf. Only a store detective Santa Claus can help her resist the evil elf.

The Empty Mirror (1996) [Film; WW]

Premiere: November 1996 (UK); Main Cast: Norman Rodway as Adolf Hitler, Joel Grey as Joseph Goebbels, Camilla Soeberg as Eva Braun, Glenn Shadix as Herman Goring, Peter Michael Goetz as Sigmund Freud, Hope Allen as the Woman in Black, Lori Scott as Floating Female Spirit; Producers: Jay Roach, David D. Johnson, William Dance; Story: Barry J. Hershey, R. Buckingham; Director: Barry J. Hershey; 118 min.; Walden Woods Films; Lionsgate; Color.

A psychological study of Adolf Hitler as he dictates his memoirs and literally confronts his demons in a post-war underground bunker. The film incorporates footage from Leni Riefenstahl's *Triumph of the Will* (1935) and Eva Braun home movies.

The Enchanted Life of Adam Hope [Novel; WW]

Author: Rhonda Riley; First publication: New York: Ecco-HarperCollins, 2013.

While staying at the family farm in North Carolina during World War II, teenager Evelyn Roe discovers a half-buried, badly burned soldier. But he is no ordinary soldier as she quickly learns, when he recovers at an accelerated pace. Adam and Evelyn fall in love, despite Evelyn knowing little of his unusual origins. Adam possesses supernatural gifts which he passes to their daughters, but when tragedy strikes and Adam is forced to display his powers, his community views him with suspicion and he has to flee with his daughters to Florida. In new surroundings, Adam's family gains a new appreciation of just how different Adam is from other men.

The Enemy (2011) [Film; Serbia; WW]

Premiere: March 6, 2011; Main Cast: Aleksandar Stojkovic as Cole, Vuk Kostic as Caki, Tihomir Stanic as Daba, Ljubomir Bandovic as Sirovina, Marja Pikic as Danica; Executive Producer: Nikolina Vucetic; Story: Djordje Milosavljevic; Director: Dejan Zecevic; 108 min.; Tivoli Film Production, Balkcan film, Maxima Film; Biberche; Color.

While removing mines an engineering unit comes across a man walled up in the basement of a destroyed factory building. After he is rescued tensions increase among the minesweepers leading to fighting and death.

Escape from Ghost Hotel [Juvenile book; WW]

Author: Larry Weinberg; First publication: Mahwah, N.J.: Troll, 1997.

Twelve-year-old Anna steps into Ghost Hotel in the present but encounters the past when she finds herself in a Civil War military hospital and becomes involved in the Underground Railroad in Kentucky.

The Escapist [Comic book character; SHW]

First appearance: *The Amazing Adventures of Kavalier and Clay: A Novel* (2000); Creator: Michael Chabon; Publishers: Random House, Dark Horse Comics.

Crippled Tom Mayflower is rescued from an orphanage by escape artist Max Mayflower. When Max is fatally wounded onstage he tells Tom to carry on his legacy and hands him a golden key. The key grants Max full use of his legs and enables him to become a great escapologist. The source of Tom's powers comes from the mystic organization The League of the Golden Key, dedicated to helping those in need.

During World War II Tom, under his costumed alter-go the Escapist, becomes a Champion of Freedom, with temporary superhuman powers to fight the Axis forces.

See: *The Amazing Adventures of Kavalier and Clay*.

Everett, Bill (1917–1973) [Comic book artist-writer]

Born May 18, 1917, in Cambridge, Massachusetts, Everett created his most memorable character, the undersea anti-hero **Sub-Mariner**, while working for the Lloyd Jacquet Comic Shop in 1939. Appearing in the same issue of *Marvel Comics* #1 (October 1939) was a character who would provide Sub-Mariner with his greatest wartime battle, the **Human Torch**. In 1939 Everett also created the Weird War characters **Amazing Man** for Centaur Publications, and in 1941, **The Conqueror** for Hillman.

Everett returned to the Sub-Mariner in the 1950s for Timely-Atlas and in the 1960s and early 1970s for Marvel. Sadly his comeback was cut short by his untimely death on February 27, 1973, age 55.

Exit Humanity (2011) [Film; Canada; WW]

Premiere: September 18, 2011; Main Cast: Dee Wallace as Eve, Mark Gibson as Edward Young, Bill Moseley as General Williams, Stephen McHattie as Medic Johnson, Brian Cox as the voice of Malcolm Young; Producers: Jesse Thomas Cook, John Geddes, Matt Wiele; Story-Director: John Geddes; 114 min.; Foresight Features, Optix Digital Pictures; The Collective Studios; Color.

Six years after the end of the American Civil War Edward Young is still haunted by memories of fighting the undead. Now he must fight them again.

"Extra Men" [Short story; WW]

Author: Harrison Rhodes; First publication: *Harper's Magazine* (1918).

"With the coming of the Great War strange things are stirring in the world, and in the farthest corners of the land the earth is shaken by the tramp of new armies. In the skies by day and night there is a sign. And the things one does not believe can happen, may be happening, even in New Jersey."

Mrs. Buchan's grandson George goes to war, sailing for France, leaving the old lady to care for the little farm surrounding her old Colonial house. One night a visitor arrives on horseback at her door claiming to have lost his way. Mrs. Buchan points him in the direction of Princeton.

"Princeton, of course. That's where we fought the British and beat them. It seems strange, does it not, that we now fight with them?"

The mysterious visitor tells Mrs. Buchan he will be joining her grandson in France, despite his age. "Every one who has ever fought for America is going. There is a company of them behind me. Listen."

As Mrs. Buchan looks into the distance she sees soldiers on horses in "almost grotesquely old-fashioned clothes—in shabby blue or worn gray. She is reminded of the Civil War, but these are brothers-in-arms.

"We are extra men, supercargo. We shall cross with every boat-load of boys who sail for France—we who fought once as they must fight now…. When the shells scream out of the French sky they will not forget the many times America has fought for liberty. They will not forget those early soldiers. And they will not forget Grant and Lee and Lincoln. The American eagle, madam, has a very shrill note. I think it can be heard above the whistle of German shrapnel."

The Extraordinary Seaman (1969) [Film; WW]

Premiere: 1969; Main Cast: David Niven as Lt. Commander Finchhaven R.N., Alan Alda as Lt. J/G Morton Krim, Faye Dunaway as Jennifer Winslow, Mickey Rooney as Cook 3/C W. J. Oglethorpe, Jack Carter as Gunner's mate Orville Toole; Director: John Frankenheimer; Metro-Goldwyn-Mayer; Color.

"Show me a battle and I'll show you a Finchhaven" has become a family tradition that Lt. Commander Finchhaven R.N. (David Niven) continues during World War I when he takes command of the Royal Navy gunboat H.M.S Curmudgeon, "Guardian of the Indian Ocean." But when the womanizing Finchhaven dies drinking on the job, therefore failing to launch an attack on the German cruiser "Prince Siegfried," his enraged ancestors temporarily restore him to life, ten years later in 1924. He is doomed to serve on the H.M.S. Curmudgeon until he finally sinks a cruiser and restores the reputation of his family.

After years of idle labor on the increasingly ramshackle Curmudgeon Finchhaven sets his sights set on destroying a Japanese cruiser during World War II. Helping him in his task is an increasingly exasperated Morton Krim (Alan Alda), a cook (Mickey Rooney), a gunner's mate (Jack Carter) and an attractive female civilian (Faye Dunaway).

This offbeat war comedy from John Frankenheimer combines World War II black-and-white newsreel film footage with the fictional color antics of the cast, resulting in a film that mostly misses the mark and is more farcical than comical.

Fallen in Fredericksburg (*Ghosts of War* #4) [Juvenile book; WW]

Author: Steve Watkins; First publication: New York: Scholastic, Inc., 2016.

Band members Anderson, Greg and Julie have been free of any ghost sightings connected to the trunk in the basement for quite some time. Life has been normal, except for dogs barking nonstop the last few days. Then suddenly a ghost appears. A teenage Union soldier from the Civil War enquires about his brother, who also fought in the Union army. The trio set out on solving another wartime mystery.

See: *The Secret of Midway*

Family Guy (1999) [Animated TV series]

The animated adventures of the dysfunctional Griffin family.

"Road to Germany" (7:03) [SFW]

Air date: October 19, 2008; Voice Cast: Seth MacFarlane as Stewie Griffin/ Brian Griffin, John G. Brennan as Mort Goldman, Brian Blessed as Prince Vultan, John Viener as Hitler, Gregory Jbara as Nazi Guard/Nazi General/Priest, Steve Callaghan as German General; Story: Patrick Meighan; Directors: Greg Colton, Peter Shin; 22 min.; 20th Century-Fox Television; Color.

Stevie and Brian travel back in time to Poland under Nazi rule to rescue Mort Goldman from falling into the clutches of Adolf Hitler.

Fantastic Four [Comic book]

The adventures of Reed Richards (Mr. Fantastic), Human Torch (Johnny Storm), The Thing (Benjamin Grimm) and The Invisible Girl (Susan Storm Richards).

"And Then—the Invaders" [SFW]

First publication: Fantastic Four Annual #11 (June 1976); Story: Roy Thomas; Art: John Buscema, Sam Grainger; Publisher: Marvel Comics.

The Nazis have won World War II thanks to a canister of vibranium. The *Fantastic Four* travel back in time to 1942 to retrieve the vibranium and with the help of **The Invaders** defeat **Baron Zemo**. But after returning to the present the Thing discovers half of the vibranium is missing. He must return to World War II to find the missing vibranium and stop Germany from winning the war.

Fantastic World War II [Short story anthology; WW; SFW]

Editor: Frank McSherry Jr.; First publication: 1990.

A compilation of Weird War stories, previously published from various sources, including *Astounding Science Fiction*, *Weird Tales* and *Blue Book*.

Stories and authors include: "The Howling Man" by Charles Beaumont; "Take My Drum to England" by Nelson S. Bond; **"Vengeance in Her Bones"** by Malcolm Jameson; "Red Moon on the Flores Sea" by H. Bedford Jones; "The Devil Is Not Mocked" by Manly Wade Wellman; **"Secret Unattainable"** by A.E. Vogt; "My Name Is Legion" by Lester del Rey; "Barbarossa" by Edward Wellen; "Two Dooms" by C. M. Kornbluth; "The Last Article" by Harry Turtledove.

See: *The Twilight Zone*; *Night Gallery*

Fantasy Island (1977) [TV series]

The enigmatic host of a resort island in the Pacific helps his guests fulfill their wildest fantasies. Main Cast: Ricardo Montalban as Mr. Roarke, Herve Villechaize as Tattoo (seasons 1–6), Christopher Hewett as Lawrence (Season 7); Creator: Gene Levitt; Executive Producers: Leonard Goldberg, Aaron Spelling; 50 min.; Spelling-Goldberg Productions, Columbia Television; American Broadcasting Company (ABC).

"Flying Aces" (4:02) [WW]

Air date: November 1, 1980; Guest Cast: Sam Melville as Tony Chilton, Tom Wopat as David Chilton, Robert Mandan as Captain Rosicker, Donald Petrie as Flyer; Producer: Skip Webster; Story: Don Ingalls; Director: Earl Bellamy.

Tony Chilton is a commercial pilot who wants to fulfill his fantasy of meeting and flying with his father, David Chilton—a World War II flying ace who died during the war while searching for a missing pilot. Chilton is tempted to change his father's fate but he knows history cannot be altered without consequences.

"The Last Dogfight" (7:10) [WW]

Air date: March 10, 1984; Guest Cast: Leigh McCloskey as Paul Spenser, Leah Ayres as Lauren Spenser, Grant Goodeve as Hunter Richter; Producer: Don Ingalls; Story: Robert Sherman; Director: Jerome Courtland.

World War II veteran Paul Spenser gets his wish to fight German air ace Hunter Richter.

"The Lost Platoon" (6:06) [WW]

Air date: November 27, 1982; Guest Cast: Steve Kanaly as Ken, Tony Travis as Cimino; Producer-Story: Don Ingalls; Director: Ricardo Montalban.

A man seeks the truth behind this brother's alleged shady past and desertion by returning to Italy during World War II.

"Magnolia Blossoms" (2:03) [WW]

Air date: September 21, 1979; Guest Cast: Christopher Connelly as Captain Hampstead, Gene Evans as Confederate, Pamela Franklin as Myra Collinsky-Melody, Lisa Hartman as Gladys Boylin-Magnolia Blossoms, Dack Rambo as Captain Rawlins; Producer-Story: Arthur Rowe; Director: Earl Bellamy.

Two young women fantasize about being Southern heroines like Scarlett O'Hara. Host, Mr. Roarke tells the women, "On certain rare occasions here on Fantasy Island, a strange geomagnetic condition develops. One which allows a person to step back into another time." But the two women must return at a certain hour or remain trapped forever in Civil War Georgia.

Gladys Boylin is advised by Roarke to call herself Magnolia Blossoms, the code name of Florence Nightingale of the South. When the two women come to the aid of a wounded soldier they complain about the noise of the shooting and prefer the fictional world of *Gone With the Wind*. But love awaits them in the form of Rhett Butler and Ashley Wilkes look-a-likes.

"My Fair Pharoah" (3:22) [WW]

Air date: May 10, 1980; Guest Cast: Joan Collins as Lucy Atwell/Cleopatra, Ron Ely as Eric Williams/Mark Antony, Michael Ansara as Ptolemy, Ruth Roman as Mistress of the Harem, Brioni Farrel as Cleopatra, James Whitworth as Abdu, the Slavemaster; Teleplay: Ellen Wittman, Ray Brenner; Story: Ellen Wittman, Richard Bluel, Pat Fieldler; Director: George McCowan.

Lucy Atwell is living her fantasy of being Egyptian Queen Cleopatra in 49 BC The real Cleopatra is being held prisoner by her brother Ptolemy in order to stop a truce between Egypt and Rome. Atwell is posing as Cleopatra to welcome Mark Antony, who has never seen Cleopatra in person. But when they fall in love she confides to Antony that she isn't Cleopatra but merely a diversion to keep him occupied while the Egyptian armies are positioned for battle. Only the genuine Cleopatra can save the day for the outnumbered Roman legions by ordering an Egyptian withdrawal.

"The Red Baron" (3:06) [WW]

Air date: October 27, 1979; Guest Cast: Don Adams as Captain Wieselfarber, Ron Ely as Baron Manfred von Richthofen, Martine Beswick as Monique, Gene Scherer as Herman Goring; Producer: Arthur Rowe; Story: Sam Orr, Herman Groves; Director: Earl Bellamy.

A bumbling locksmith and Boy Scout leader from Milwaukee Wisconsin fantasizes about being a flying ace in World War I. Mr. Roarke obliges and soon Mr. Wieselfarber is engaged in aerial combat with the legendary Red Baron. He comes to realize the romance of war no longer holds any interest for him. It has been replaced with his love for the beautiful Monique, a member of the French Resistance.

"Smith's Valhalla" (3:17) [WW]
Air date: January 26, 1980; Guest Cast: Hugh O'Brian as Jason Smith, Leslie Nielsen as Emile Bouvier, Sean Garrison as Captain Buck Tanner, Charles Dierkop as Harry "Weasel" Forbes, Emily Banks as Linda Smith; Producer: Skip Webster; Story: Mike Vejar; Teleplay: Don Ingalls; Director: Mike Vejar.

Jason Smith, a rancher from Oregon, has always fantasized about being a war hero. He never saw combat with the U.S. Marine Corp in Korea and wants to see if he has what it takes to lead a group of men on a daring Commando raid. It is his last hope for becoming the type of soldier he always wanted to be. Roarke tells him his mission is to save eight lives in a hostage situation. But there is a catch. One of the hostages is his wife and her life is in mortal danger.

FDR: American Badass! (2012) [Film; AHW]

Premiere: September 24, 2012; Main Cast: Barry Bostwick as Franklin Delano Roosevelt, Lin Shaye as Eleanor Roosevelt, Ray Wise as Douglas MacArthur, Kevin Sorbo as Abraham Lincoln, Paul Ben-Victor as Mussolini, Jesse Merlin as Adolf Hitler, Jamison Yang as Emperor Hirohito, Ed Metzger as Albert Einstein, Bruce McGill as Louis, William Mapother as Dr. Ellington; Executive Producers: Marshall Plante, Kevin Sorbo, Jim Kehoe; Story: Ross Patterson; Director: Garrett Brawith; 93 min.; Street Justice Films, A Common Thread; Screen Media Films; Color.

Franklin Delano Roosevelt is attacked by the Axis of Evil under the guise of a werewolf. Despite contracting polio Roosevelt continues to run for President and declares war on the werewolves, arming his wheelchair with missiles and silver bullets.

A Field in England (2013) [Film; UK; WW]

Premiere: July 4, 2013; Main Cast: Julian Barratt as Trower, Peter Ferdinando as Jacob, Richard Glover as Friend, Ryan Pope as Cutler, Reece Shearsmith as Whitehead, Michael Smiley as O'Neil; Sara Dee as the voice of the Field; Executive Producer: Story: Amy Jump; Director: Ben Wheatley; 91 min.; Film4, Rook Films; Drafthouse Films; B/W.

A group of deserters, during the English Civil War, encounter an alchemist and necromancer in the West Country. Holding the men under his sinister control O'Neil forces his captives to search for a cache of gold buried in a field. When they decide to eat the mushrooms sprouting in the field their real nightmares begin.

Peter Bradshaw of *The Guardian* (July 4, 2013) stated: "A Field in England actually draws on a tradition that sees the English revolution as a period of visionary radicalism and insurrection, though this is here converted with cynicism and despair. All the digging and ranting is something other than utopia in view. The English revolution may be the one that isn't taught in schools, but it has provided the inspiration for a punk nightmare."

Fiends of the Eastern Front [Comic strip; UK; WW]

First publication: *2000 AD* #152 (February 1980); Creators: Gerry Finley-Day, Carlos Ezquerra; Publisher: IPC.

A diary reveals the vampire menace on the Eastern Front during World War II.

Fiends of the Eastern Front: Fiends of the Rising Sun [Novel; WW]

Author: David Bishop; Publisher: Black Flame (2007).

Japanese Prime Minister General Tojoto forms an alliance with the undead in the Pacific War. American forces must defeat not only the Japanese but a vampyr legion that only attacks under cover of night.

Fiends of the Eastern Front: Operation Vampyr [Novel; WW]

Author: David Bishop; Publisher: Black Flame (2005).

The trilogy opens in Russia in 1941. Advancing German troops are joined by a mysterious Rumanian platoon under the control of Lord Constanta. Young German soldier Hans Vollmer senses something is wrong when he realizes the Rumanian troops are only seen after twilight and the dead Russian soldiers are drained of blood.

Fiends of the Eastern Front: Stalingrad [Comic strip; UK; WW]

First publication: *Judge Dredd Magazine* #245–252 (May–December 2006); Story: David Bishop; Art: Colin MacNeil; Publisher: IPC.

The eerie encounter between Wehrmacht soldier, Hans Schmitt and Romanian Captain Constanta and his blood-sucking platoon is recalled when Schmitt's diary and corpse is discovered by a group of women in West Berlin.

Fiends of the Eastern Front: The Blood Red Army [Novel; WW]
Author: David Bishop; Publisher: Nottingham (UK): Black Flame (2006).

The second book in the *Fiends of the Eastern Front* trilogy takes place in Leningrad in the freezing winter of 1942. The city is besieged by German troops as the Russians starve to death. To make matters worse Russian soldiers are being attacked by Rumanian vampyr warriors.

Fiends of the Eastern Front: Twilight of the Dead [Novel; WW]
Author: David Bishop; Publisher: Black Flame (2006).

The final book in the *Fiends of the Eastern Front* trilogy. It is April 1945. The Red Army has the German troops on the retreat as the Rumanian vampyr troops are now fighting alongside the Russians. But Lord Constanta won't be satisfied defeating Hitler. He has plans for all mankind. Russians must join with Germans to defeat a mutual enemy.

"Fifth Column of Mars" [Pulp fiction; WW]
Author: Robert Moore Williams; First publication: *Amazing Stories* (Vol. 14 #9; September 1940); Publisher: Ziff-Davis Publishing Company.

"How could a U.S. secret service man suspect the fifth column he trailed would lead him to Mars? The fifth column of Mars and the fifth column of Earth had joined bloody hands! They were working together, the science of one aiding and supplementing the science of the other. A bomb sliding down a light ray from Mars, landing in the middle of an arsenal in the United States would explode violently. And not once, but dozens of times. Industrial plants, steel mills, factories, all subject to mysterious explosions. Within a month the country would be mad with fear. And those bombs could easily be directed at a battle fleet. The fleet would be destroyed. An invading army would land on American shores. The United States was doomed!"

The Fighting Yank [Comic book character; SHW]
First appearance: *Startling Comics* #10 (September 1941); Creators: Richard Hughes, Jon Blummer; Publisher: Better Publications (Nedor).

1776. Bruce Carter is ordered by General Washington to deliver vital dispatches through British lines. Unknown to Carter, British spies are on his trail. At a wayside inn the courier is taken by surprise and fatally wounded as the spies flee with the dispatches. But death cannot stop Carter as his spirit vows to "wander whenever my country is in danger!"

New York, 1941. Carter's ancestor is chastised by his father for wasting his life. Even his fiancée Joan Farwell is upset with Carter's attitude and bids him goodbye. But as Carter sinks into despair the spirit of his ancestor appears to give him a message. "Yours will be the mission to save your country against the forces of evil. And yours will be the great strength which only I, as a spirit, can confer! Seek out my cloak...."

Carter finds his great-great grandfather's cloak in a trunk inside a hidden chamber. As he places it around his shoulders Carter feels transformed

The Fighting Yank #7 (1943). Cover art by Alex Schomburg; Published by Nedor Publications.

with super-strength. "Oh boy! I was never more awake in my life. From now on I'll be the Fighting Yank!"

Aided by his bullet-proof cloak and the spirit of Bruce Carter the Fighting Yank fights the enemies of freedom.

The Final Countdown (1980) [Film; SFW]
Premiere: August 1, 1980; Main Cast: Kirk Douglas as Capt. Matthew Yelland, Martin Sheen as Warren Lasky, Katherine Ross as Laurel Scott, James Farentino as Cdr. Richard Owens, Charles Durning as Senator Samuel Chapman; Executive Producer: Richard R. St. Johns; Story: Thomas Hunter, Peter Powell, David Ambrose, Gerry Davis; Director: Don Taylor; 103 min.; The Bryna Company; United Artists; Color.

1980. The nuclear-powered aircraft carrier *U.S.S. Nimitz* is on routine exercises out of Pearl Harbor when a severe storm throws the ship and crew back in time to 6 December 1941. On the eve of the Japanese attack on Pearl Harbor the *Nimitz* captain decides to change history and defeat the Japanese fleet. A pair of F-14 Tomcats engage a scouting party of Japanese Zeros, but the time-travel vortex will return to favor the Japanese.

The Final Countdown (1980) starring Kirk Douglas as Capt. Matthew Yelland, Martin Sheen as Warren Lasky, Katherine Ross as Laurel Scott, James Farentino as Cdr. Richard Owens and Charles Durning as Senator Samuel Chapman (United Artists).

Final Impact [Novel; SFW]
Author: John Birmingham; First publication: New York: Del Rey-Ballantine Books, 2007.

The conclusion to the *Axis of Time* trilogy set in 1944 sees the Germans and Japanese forces on the verge of building an atom bomb as the Soviet Union advances through Europe. Admiral Kolhammer knows the historical timeline has been altered and the outcome of the war is no longer predictable.

Find Me Where the Water Ends (Book #3) [Juvenile book; SFW]
Author: Rachel Carter; First publication: New York: HarperTeen, 2014.

Lydia Bentley's quest to find the truth behind the World War II Montauk Project has taken her through time from 2012 to 1944 to 1989. Now she finds herself in a timeline where the Montauk Project never existed. Her past and present must be reconciled with a future without the Project and the possibility of losing a person she loves.

See: ***So Close to You***

Firebrand [Comic book character; SHW]
First appearance: *All-Star Squadron* #5 ( ); Creators: Roy Thomas, Rich Buckler, Jerry Ordway; Publisher: DC Comics.

The sister of millionaire playboy Rod Reilly alias the masked crime-fighter *Firebrand*. Danette Reilly assumes his name after he is critically injured while serving in the Navy at Pearl Harbor. Vulcanologist Danette gained her power over flames while escaping Per Degaton on his Hawaiian island. A green aura enveloped her after she was struck with a mystical bolt and fell into a vat of artificial lava.

Firebrand serves as a member of the ***All-Star Squadron*** during World War II.

The Firebrand [Novel; MWW]
Author: Marion Zimmer Bradley; First publication: New York: Simon & Schuster, 1987.

During the fall of Troy, King Priam's daughter Kassandra is cursed by the god Apollo. Her prophetic powers will be reduced to the ravings of a deranged woman.

First Squad: The Moment of Truth (2009) [Animated-Live Action Film; Russia-Japan-Canada; WW]
Premiere: May 13, 2009; Main Voice Cast (English): Cassandra Lee as Nadya, Dick Smallberries, Jr., as Valya, Evelyn Lantto as Zena, Phineas as Baron Von

Wolff, Tony Oliver as Marat, Joey Morris as Leo; Animation Director: Hirofumi Nakata; Producers: Eiko Tanaka, Aljosha Klimov, Misha Shprits; Screenplay: Aljosha Klimov, Misha Shprits; Director: Yoshiharu Ashino; 73 min.; Studio 4 degrees C (Japan), Molot Entertainment Film (Russia); Anchor Bay Entertainment; Color.

Winter 1941. The Soviets have a paranormal "Sixth Division" headed by gifted teenager Nadya, who confronts the Nazi occult menace attempting to raise 12th century Crusaders from the Order of the Sacred Cross to join the Nazis. This anime is mixed with live-action sequences featuring veteran soldiers recalling the supernatural events of World War II.

The Flag [Comic book character; SHW]

First appearance: *Our Flag Comics* #1 (August 1941); Creator: Harry Anderson; Publisher: Ace Magazines.

"Meet the Flag—America's answer to the threat of invading hordes from the dictator nations, and to the menace of sneaky human rodents within our borders. Watch these enemies, who seek to destroy our fair nation, run like the rats they are, when they come up against the Flag—son of 'Old Glory'"

Crippled war veteran and flag maker John Courtney takes in a baby abandoned on his doorstep. To his surprise he notices the baby has the birthmark of a the American flag on his chest. Turning to his wall calendar he also notes the date is June 14, Flag Day. The old flag maker sees the signs as fate and adopts and raises him under his adopted name Jim Courtney.

On his 21st birthday Jim has a vivid dream of George Washington and the great American Patriots. Washington touches the birthmark on Jim's chest to grant him super-powers. The strength of 100 men, the speed of the wind and immunity from weapons. All Jim has to do is touch his birthmark when he requires super-powers. When he awakes Jim discovers the dream has come true and he now possesses super-powers.

Operating to keep his real identity secret with a special patriotic costume made by his adoptive father, the Flag "goes forth to wage war against those who would seek to destroy our country."

The Flame [Comic book character; SHW]

First appearance: *Wonderworld Comics* #3 (July 1939); Creators: Basil Berold, Lou Fine; Publisher: Fox Features Syndicate.

When a torrential downpour threatens the safety of a city in China, a young boy's missionary parents place their infant in a basket. The flood sweeps the basket into Tibet where it is found by Buddhist priests. The adopted child is taught mastery over fire by the Grand High Lamas. When he reaches adulthood the Flame returns to America to fight against crime.

As World War II progresses the Flame's adventures involve the Axis powers. When fighting U-boats his ability to skim over the surface of the sea using his flame gun and to hurl his unique and lethal exploding capsules over distance help defeat the German enemy.

Flash Gordon: Zeitgeist [Comic book; SFW]

First publication: November 2011; Ten issue mini-series; Story: Eric Trautmann; Art: Daniel Lindro; Publisher: Dynamite Entertainment.

The Flag featured in *Our Flag Comics* #2 (October 1941). Cover art by Jim Mooney. Published by Ace Magazines.

Adolf Hitler joins forces with extraterrestrial invaders of Earth, led by Ming the Merciless, his daughter Princess Aura and spymaster Klytus. Meanwhile, Flash Gordon, Dale Arden and scientist Dr. Hans Zarkov find themselves far away from Earth as prisoners on the planet Mongo.

The Flesh Eaters (1964) [Film; SFW]

Premiere: March 18, 1964; Main Cast: Martin Kosleck as Professor Peter Bartell, Byron Saunders as Grant Murdoch, Barbara Wilkin as Jan Letterman, Rita Morley as Laura Winters, Ray Tudor as Omar; Producers: Jack Curtis, Arnold Drake, Terry Curtis; Screenplay: Arnold Drake; Director: Jack Curtis; 87 min.; Vulcan Productions; Cinema Distributors of America; B/W.

A former Nazi scientist continues his flesh eating experiments on a desert island where an alcoholic movie star, her assistant and the pilot of the plane have been forced to land due to a storm.

The DVD release from 2005 includes a previously deleted scene where Nazis are experimenting on women and they are forced to enter a pool of flesh eating monsters.

Flesh Feast (1970) [Film; WW]

Premiere: May 20, 1970; Main Cast: Veronica Lake as Dr. Elaine Frederick, Phil Philbin as Ed Casey, Doug Foster as Carl Schumann, Harry Kerwin as Dan Carter, Martha Mischon as Virginia Day, Heather Hughes as Kristine; Executive Producer: Veronica Lake; Screenplay: Brad F. Grinter, Thomas B. Casey; Director: Brad F. Grinter; 72 min.; Viking International Pictures; Cineworld Pictures; Color.

In this final screen appearance of former Hollywood sex symbol Veronica Lake, she plays Dr. Elaine Frederick, a former mental patient working on a fountain of youth. Unfortunately her secret to eternal youth involves flesh eating maggots. To make matters worse a disguised Adolf Hitler seeks out the maggot youth treatment.

Flight World War II (2015) [Film: SFW]

Premiere; June 2, 2015; Main Cast: Faran Tahir as William Strong, Robbie Kay as Corporal Nigel Sheffield, Aqueela Zoll as Cameron Hicks, Matias Ponce as Daniel Prentice, Adam Blake as Adam Kruger; Executive Producer: David Rimawi; Screenplay: Jacob Cooney, Bill Hanstock; Director: Emile Edwin Smith; 85 min.; The Asylum; Color.

The crew and passengers of present day Flight 42 pass through a violent storm and find themselves in the middle of a war zone in France, 1940.

"The Flying Teuton" [Short story; WW]

Author: Alice Brown; First publication: New York: *Harper's Magazine* (1916).

"I've seen things. I haven't the slightest doubt a fellow blown out of a trench into the next world meets so many of the other fellows, who were blown there before him that it gives them that look.... I'll tell you about the ship, the *Treve Konigin* and the first sailing from Bremen. She was the first after John Bull tied up their navy. I was the only American aboard."

Suddenly a great ship "struck us amidships and went through us." The following night a British liner, "...raked us and passed through us from stem to stern." Ten o'clock the next morning the freighter Marlborough runs through the German ship, "as neat as wax." But the German ship remains untouched and all calls for help to passing ships are ignored. On the approach to New York harbor the ship turns course, heading back to Germany. The ship is controlling itself, invisible to all on the sea.

"German ships were in full possession, as they had been before the war, of the freedom of the seas, except that they mysteriously could not use it. German ships took passengers as of old, and loaded themselves with merchandise. But there was not a port on the surface of the globe that could receive them."

"For the Love of Barbara Allen" [Pulp fiction; WW]

Author: Robert E. Howard; First publication: *The Magazine of Fantasy & Science Fiction* Vol. 31 #2 (August 1967).

It is love at first sight for Rachel Ormond and Joel beside the Cumberland River in Tennessee.

"When Joel saw her standin' there with the morning' sun makin' jewels out of the dew on the bushes, he stopped dead and just stared like a fool. He told me it seemed as if she was standin' in a white blaze of light."

But all too soon the Civil War separates them by distance and finally by death when Joel is killed in battle. Rachel is devastated and never looks at another man again. In her final years she awaits death surrounded by family in Texas and to her great joy finds Joel waiting to comfort her, in the body of another man and "another, different voice, whispering down the ages."

Forbidden Worlds [Comic book]

Paranormal anthology title.

"THE GHOSTLY ARMY OF BETHUNE" [WW]

First publication: #1 (July–August 1951); Art: Henry Kiefer; Publisher: American Comics Group.

This one-page "True Ghosts of History" strip tells the story of a medieval cavalry comprising of ghosts coming to the aid of British soldiers fighting the Germans near a small Belgian town in World War I.

The Forest of Time [Novella; AHW]

Author: Michael Flynn; First publication: *Analog* (June 1987).

A lost time traveler moves through an alternate history reality where the Axis powers won World War II and the Thirteen Colonies developed into hostile "pumpernickel principalities."

'48 [Novel; WW]

Author: James Herbert; First publication: New York: HarperPrism, 1997.

In a last desperate effort to win the war, Adolf Hitler initiates Blood Death. A deadly virus kills the majority of the population, including the Nazis when the wind changes direction. But a handful survive thanks to their rare AB-neg blood group giving them immunity. Now the survivors, including an American pilot, are the target of the partially immune who need their blood to survive.

Frankenstein [Comic book character; SFW]

First appearance: *Prize Comics* #7 (December 1940); Creator: Dick Briefer; Publisher: Prize Publications.

Manhattan, New York, 1940. Dr. Victor Frankenstein sees his monstrous creation turn into a vicious killer before he is captured and placed in the care of Dr. Carrol who sets out to rehabilitate him. Frankenstein then fights the Nazis during World War II.

Frankenstein's Army (2013) [Film; SFW]

Premiere: April 18, 2013; Main cast: Robert Gwilym as Novikov, Hon Ping Tang as Ivan/Ivan Zombot, Alexander Mercury as Dimitri-Wall Zombot Legs, Luke Newberry as Sacha; Executive Producers: Badie Ali, Hamza Ali, Malik B. Ali, Nate Bolotin, Nick Spicer, Aram Tertzakiam; Story: Richard Raaphorst, Miguel Tejada-Flores, Chris W. Mitchell; Director: Richard Raaphorst; 84 min.; Dark Skyfilms, Pellicola, XYZ Films, Sirena Film, MPI Media Group; Color.

Frankenstein joins the Nazis in *Prize Comics* Vol. 4 #3 (February 1944). Art by Dick Briefer. Published by Feature Publications.

Russian soldiers encounter an army of undead Frankenstein creatures created using the journals of Dr. Victor Frankenstein. They are Hitler's last stand near the end of World War II.

Freedom Fighters [Comic book characters; SHW]

First appearance: *Justice League of America* #107 (October 1973); Creators: Len Wein, Dick Dillin; Publisher: DC Comics.

In an alternate reality the Nazi's rule over Earth X. The Freedom Fighters, with the help of the **Justice Society of America** and Justice League of America overthrow the Nazi government.

Formed by **Uncle Sam** in the summer of 1941 after discovering a vortex that enabled travel to Earth X, the Freedom Fighters consisted of many members who fought the Nazi and Japanese menace in an alternate World War II that lasted twenty-five years. Key members who finally rid Earth X of Nazi rule include Uncle Sam, **Doll Man**, Black Condor, **Firebrand**, Human Bomb, The Ray and Phantom Lady.

Freedom's Five [Comic book characters; SHW]
First appearance: *The Invaders* #7 (July 1975); Creators: Roy Thomas, Frank Robbins; Publisher: Marvel Comics.

World War I heroes Freedom's Five consist of Phantom Eagle, Union Jack, **Sir Steel**, Silver Squire and the Crimson Cavalier. Fighting valiantly against the Germans and their allies, including **Baron Blood**, Freedom's Five defeat a Martian invasion of London in 1917.

Friends Forever: The Mystery Tour [Juvenile book; WW]
Author: Judi Curtin; First publication: London: Puffin, 2013.

Lauren's cat, Saturn, has the magical ability to travel back through time. Together with her friend Tilly, Lauren and Saturn find themselves in London during the Blitz in 1939. After making friends with Violet, they catch the evacuation train to the English countryside and experience life during World War II.

From a Whisper to a Scream a.k.a. *The Offspring* (1987) [Film; WW]
Premiere: September 25, 1987; Main Cast (Civil War segment): Vincent Price as Julian White, Susan Tyrrell as Beth Chandler, Cameron Mitchell as Sgt. Gallen, C. J. Fox as Pike, Ashli Bare as Amanda, Jajary Bennett as Jake, Tommy Nowell as Andrew, Sergio Aguire as Ambrose; Executive producer: David Shaheen; Story: C. Courtney Joyner, Mike Malone, Darin Scott, Jeff Burr; Director: Jeff Burr; 113 min.; Moviestone Entertainment; Color.

Separated from their unit, four Union soldiers discover the Civil War has ended after the ambush and kill a small group of Confederate soldiers. Private Pike decides it's time to leave his fellow soldiers and walk home but Sgt. Gallen (Cameron Mitchell) shoots him in the back for desertion of duty.

The three remaining Union soldiers are knocked unconscious by the blast from land mines and awaken to find themselves prisoners of children in the town of Oldfield. The children inform Gallen that their leader is "The Magistrate." A young girl named Amanda is told by the manipulative Gallen that he will adopt her if she sets him free. But he thanks her by snapping her neck. Attempting to escape, Gallen is confronted by Pike the soldier he killed and is recaptured by the children. They reveal the secret identity of The Magistrate—the remains of the children's murdered parents who still communicate with them—before burning him to death.

The Civil War horror tale is the final segment of four tales "introduced" by Vincent Price and Susan Tyrrell.

"From Out of the Dark Water" [Pulp fiction: WW]
Author: H. Bedford Jones; First publication: *Blue Book* (December 1940); Publisher: McCall.

Captain Michael Gallister invokes leprechauns to save Britain from the Nazis during World War II.

"From the House of the Rat Catcher" [Pulp fiction; WW]
Author: H. Bedford Jones; First publication: *Weird Tales* (Vol. 37 #4; March 1944); Publisher: Weird Tales.

"The airborne Yank soldiers never expected to find Carthaginian agents, envious nobles and traitor guard—all centuries old."

From Time to Time [Novel: SFW]
Author: Jack Finney; First publication: New York: Simon & Schuster, 1995.

New York advertising executive Simon Morley attempts to prevent World War I by going back in time to 1912. But the aide to President Taft who holds the documents that could prevent a war is traveling back to the United States on the Titanic's maiden voyage.

Frostbitten (2006) [Film; Sweden; SFW]
Premiere: February 24, 2006; Main Cast: Petra Nielsen as Annika Wallen, Carl-Ake Eriksson as Professor Gerhard Beckert, Grete Havneskold as Saga Wallen, Emma T. Aberg as Vega; Producers: Goran Lindstrom, Magnus Paulsson; Story: Daniel Ojaniatva, Pidde Andersson; Director: Anders Banke; 98 min.; Cinepost Studios, Fido Film AB, Filmpost Nord, Ulitka Studio, Paramount Pictures; Color.

Geneticist Gerhard Beckert is working on an experimental drug at a hospital in Sweden. His sinister work goes back to World War II and his time serving in the Waffen-SS. When interns see Beckart's vaccine as an excuse to get high they turn into vampires. Soon the town has an epidemic of vampires.

The Frozen Dead (1966) [Film: UK; SFW]
Premiere: October 1966 (UK); Main Cast: Dana Andrews as Dr. Norberg, Anna Palk as Jean Norberg, Philip Gilbert as Dr. Ted Roberts, Kathleen

Breck as Elsa Tenney, Edward Fox as Norburg's Brother; Executive Producer: Robert Goldstein; Story-Director: Herbert J. Leder; 95 min.; Gold Star Productions; Warner Bros.-Seven Arts; Color.

Mad scientist Dr. Norberg experiments on the brain of his niece's best friend Elsa Tenney to understand why his resurrected Nazi war criminals are all acting crazy.

Fubar: European Theater of Blood [Comic book; WW]

First publication: September 2010; Creator: Jeffrey W. McComsey; Publisher: Fubar Press-Alterna Comics.

The first volume in the Fubar series is a World War II zombie anthology featuring fifteen black-and-white/grayscale comic strips of Allied forces facing the walking dead across war-torn Europe.

Further volumes in the anthology series are: *Fubar: Empire of the Rising Dead* (2011); A zombie outbreak in the Pacific theater of World War II; *Fubar: American History Z* (2013); The zombie threat throughout American history; *Fubar: By the Sword* (2014); Zombies doing battle from Genghis Khan to medieval Europe; *Fubar: Declassified* (2014); From the Bay of Pigs to Afghanistan—highly classified U.S. government military missions involving the undead.

"Fugitives from Earth" [Pulp fiction; SFW]

Author: Nelson S. Bond; First publication: *Amazing Stories* (Vol. 14 #2; December 1939); Publisher: Ziff-Davis Publishing Company.

"Two pitiful spaceships flee the war-holocaust in 1939. But because enemy bombers found their hiding place the American ship had to take off too soon, and out in space she missed a rendezvous with her destination."

Fullmetal Alchemist: Conqueror of Shamballa (2005) [Animated film; Japan; WW]

Premiere: July 2005 (Japan); Voice Cast [U.S.]: Vic Mignogna as Edward Elric, Aaron Dismuke as Alphonse Elric, E. Jason Liebrecht as Alfons Heiderich, Kelly Manison as Dietlinde Eckhart, John Swasey as Karl Haushofer, Ed Blaylock as Fritz Lang, Leah Clark as Noah, Caitlin Glass as Winry Rockbell, Juli Erickson as Pinako Rockbell, Travis Willingham as Roy Mustang, Jason Douglas as Rudolf Hess; Story: Sho Aikawa; Director: Seiji Mizushima; 105 min.; Aniplex, Bones, Dentsu, Nippan, Square Enix Company, Mainichi Broadcasting System (MBS), Tokyo Broadcasting System (TBS); Shochiku Company; Color.

Fullmetal Alchemist Edward Elric has been separated in time and space from his brother Alphonse. In an alternate world Edward discovers a Nazi plot involving the Thule Society that could mean war for everyone on both sides of the gate that separates them.

Futatsu no Kurumi a.k.a. *Two Walnuts* (2007) [Animated TV Special; Japan; SFW]

Air date: August 15, 2007; Voice Cast: Eri Kitamura as Ayaka Nakanishi, Megumi Nasu as Tomoko Saitou, Mami Matsui as Toshiko, Tomoko Kaneda as Kenta, Rica Matsumoto as Shoukichi Taniguchi, Yuki Matsuoka as Rena, Ai Satou as Tomiko, Yuko Nagashima as Youko; Producers: Noboru Sugiyama, Toshihide Yamada; Screenplay: Tetsuo Yasumi; Directors: Shinji Kawaai, Minetaro Hirai, Tetsuo Yasumi; 45 min.; Shin-Ei Animation; TV Asahi; Color.

While taking her German shepherd dog Ryan for a walk, twelve-year-old Ayaka Nakanishi takes shelter from a sudden downpour in a telephone booth. When lightning strikes the booth Ayaka and Ryan are sent back in time to March 7, 1945, days before Tokyo was bombed with the loss of 100,000 people. Her grandmother's tales of World War II come to life as Ayaka struggles to come to terms with her predicament.

Futurama (1999) [Animated TV series]

A pizza delivery boy, frozen in 1999, wakes up in New York City in 2999.

"ALL THE PRESIDENT'S HEADS" (6:20) [SFW]

Air date: July 28, 2011; Guest Voices (as President's heads): Maurice LaMarche, Phil LaMarr, David Herman; Executive Producers: Matt Groening, David X Cohen, Ken Keeler; Story: Josh Weinstein; Director: Stephen Sandoval; 22 min.; The Curiosity Company, 20th Century-Fox Television (30th Century Fox Television); Color.

The outcome of the American Revolution is changed when the crew go back in time.

"THE LATE PHILIP J. FRY" (6:07) [SFW]

Air date: July 29, 2010; Voice Cast: Billy West as Philip J. Fry/ Professor Hubert Farnsworth, Katey Sagal as Turanga Leela, John DiMaggio as Bender, Tress MacNeille as Dr. Cahill; David Herman as Adolf Hitler; Story: Lewis Morton; Director: Peter Avanzino.

Trapped in 10,000 A.D. in Professor Farnsworth's time machine that only travels forward Philip Fry and his companions decide to travel further into the future until a time machine that goes back in time is invented. When they succeed Farnsworth decides to kill Adolf Hitler but accidentally kills Eleanor Roosevelt instead.

Galactica 1980 (1980) [TV series]
Main Cast: Kent McCord as Captain Troy, Barry Van Dyke as Lieutenant Dillon, Robyn Douglass as Jamie Hamilton, Lorne Greene as Commander Adama.

"GALACTICA DISCOVERS EARTH: PART 3" (1:03) [SFW]

Air date: February 10, 1980; Guest Cast: Richard Lynch as Xavier, Robert Reed as Professor Mortinson, Christopher Stone as Stockwell, Michael Strong as Resistance Leader/Old Man; Executive Producer-Story: Glen A. Larson; Director: Sidney Hayers; 60 min.; Glen A. Larson Productions; American Broadcasting Company (ABC); Color.

Troy, Dillon and Jamie Hamilton journey back in time to 1944 to stop the development of the V-2 rocket by Xavier.

"Gallery of Glacial Doom" [Pulp fiction; SFW]
Author: Frances M. Deegan; Illustrator: Robert Fuqua; First publication: *Amazing Stories* (Vol. 19 #4; December 1945); Publisher: Ziff-Davis Publishing Company.

"This was the most amazing museum imaginable—specimens of all humanity, frozen in ice. 'Put 'em on ice' is a very fine way to 'salt away' guys like Hitler (is he dead?) and a few others."

Gamma 693 a.k.a. *Night of the Zombies* (1979) [Film; SFW]
Premiere: 1979; Main Cast: Jamie Gillis as Nick Monroe, Ryan Hilliard as Dr. Clarence Proud, Ron Armstrong as Police Capt. Fleck; Producer: Lorin E. Price; Story-Director; Joel M. Reed; 88 min.; N.M.D. Film Distributing Company; Color.

During World War II mortally wounded U.S. and German soldiers are kept alive with the secret gas Gamma 693. CIA special agent Nick Monroe investigates missing soldiers who are suspected to be deserters, but uncovers a plot to take over the world with an army of undead soldiers who eat flesh to survive.

The Gate of Time [Novel; SFW]
Author: Philip Jose Farmer: First publication: New York: Belmont Books, 1966.

World War II combat pilot Roger Two Hawks, an Iroquois Indian, is shot down during a raid on Ploiesti, Romania. Parachuting over enemy territory, Two Hawks is overcome with dizziness. On landing he finds himself in an alternate Universe where the continent of America doesn't exist. Although in this reality there is another war involving an alternate Germany attempting to conquer Europe. But is Two Hawks from an alternate world himself where Kaiser Wilhelm IV is in power during World War II?

The Gay Ghost [Comic book character; WW]
First appearance: *Sensation Comics* #1 (January 1942); Creators: Gardner Fox, Howard Purcell; Publisher: All-American Publications (DC Comics).

Ireland, 1700. Keith Everet, Earl of Strathmere, is murdered as he travels to propose to his girlfriend Deborah Wallace. Everet returns to Connaught Castle as a spirit awaiting Deborah Wallace. In 1941, a descendant of Deborah visit's the castle accompanied by American playboy Charles Collins. When Collins is killed by Nazi spies Everet possesses his body, restoring him to life and rescues Deborah from the Nazis.

Alternating between his spirit body as the Gay Ghost and his physical body as Charles Collins, Deborah Wallace can see his spirit but doesn't realize he has possessed Charles Collins. As the Gay Ghost he is summoned to a council before his immortal ancestors who give him his mission to stamp out the enemies of England.

DC Comics later renamed the Gay Ghost, the *Grim Ghost*.

Gear Krieg [RPG; Tactical Wargame; Canada; AHW]
Release date: 2000; Designers: Dave Graham, Lloyd D. Jesse, Gene Marcil, Stephane I. Matis, Marc A. Vezina; Art: Jean-Francois Fortier, Pierre Ouellette, John Wu; System: Silhouette; Publisher: Dream Pod 9.

An alternate history World War II where technology is more advanced. Jetpacks, walking tanks and rocket fighters have been developed and have drastically affected famous battles and major events of the war.

Gear Krieg: African Theater [RPG; Tactical Wargame; Canada; AHW]
Release date: 2000; Designers: Dave Graham, Lloyd D. Jesse, Pat Paulsen, Alex Rhodes; Art: Jean-Francois Fortier, Pierre Ouellette, Marc Ouellette; System: Silhouette; Publisher: Dream Pod 9.

Gear Krieg expansion into North Africa.

Gene a.k.a. ***La Conspirazione del Minotauro*** [Novel; MWW]
Author: Stel Pavlou; First publication: London: Simon & Schuster, 2005.

After Greek warrior Cyclades is mortally wounded during the Trojan War, a Sybil forces him to have sex to continue his family line. He is reincarnated seven times until the present day (2004) where, as detective James North he discovers his past lives while investigating a genetic memory experiment. But North has an enemy in Athanatos, who has pursued him through multiple lives from Troy to the place of Knossos, to Byzantium, to Ancient Rome, to present day New York.

General Leonardo [Graphic novel; AHW]
First publication: 2006; Three-volumes; Creators: Erik Svane, Dan Greenberg; Publisher: Editions Pacquet: Geneva.

The renowned artist and inventor Leonardo is dismayed to learn the Holy See at the Vatican want to commandeer his unique military machines for a new Crusade. Commanded by General Scharano the Vatican forces head to Rhodes, now besieged by the Ottoman army, unaware of the seeds of betrayal in their midst.

George Washington's Socks [Juvenile book; SFW]
Author: Elvira Woodruff; First publication: New York: Scholastic, 1991.

During a campout, a rowboat transports Matthew, Quentin, Hooter, Tony, and Katie, back in time to the American Revolution and the eve of the Battle of Trenton. Encountering George Washington, Hessian soldiers and revolutionaries, the children come face-to-face with the reality of war and the founding of the United States of America.

Germania [Novel; WW]
Author: Brendan McNally; First publication: New York: Simon & Schuster, 2008.

During the closing days of the Third Reich following Hitler's suicide in a Berlin bunker Heinrich Himmler, Göring and Albert Speer all desire to be his successor. But the title of Führer goes to Grand Admiral Karl Dönitz.

A Jewish cabaret act, the Flying Magical Loerber Brothers have disbanded but the Russians want triple agent Franzi eliminated. As Himmler's personal masseur and advisor he can no longer be trusted. His three brothers use their physical and psychic skills to rescue him from harm.

Ghost Boat (2006) [Telefilm; UK; WW]
Air date: April 9, 2006; Main Cast: David Jason as Jack Hardy, Ian Puleston-Davies as Travis, Tony Haygarth as Cassidy, Julian Wadham as Capt. Byrnes, James Laurenson as Admiral Nealy, Robert Whitelock as Spender, Crispin Bonham-carter as Redding; Executive Producers: David Jason, David Reynolds; Screenplay; Guy Burt; Director: Stuart Orme; 180 min.; Yorkshire Television (YTV); Independent Television (ITV); Color.

The British submarine Scorpion, long thought lost at sea during World War II, surfaces again in 1981. They find no bodies on board and no sign that anything has been disturbed. The only survivor, marine biologist Jack Hardy, has no memory of the submarine's final days and wants to find out what happened. Together with a crew he decides to try and retrace the Scorpion's path to doom but is soon confronted with strange occurrences on board as the past breaks into the present.

The production is based on the 1976 novel by George E. Simpson and Neal R. Burger.

Ghost Cadet [Juvenile book; WW]
Author: Elaine Marie Alphin; First publication: New York: Henry Holt, 1991.

While visiting his grandmother in New Market, Virginia 12-year-old Benjy Stark encounters former Virginia Military Institute cadet Hugh McDowell, a ghost from the Civil War who wants to restore his honor. Hugh buried his family's gold watch before he died in the Battle of New Market in 1864. Now he wants Benjy's help in recovering the family heirloom.

Ghost Fever (1986) [Film; WW]
Premiere: December 12, 1986; Main Cast: Sherman Hemsley as Buford-Jethro, Luis Avalos as Benny, Jennifer Rhodes as Madame St. Esprit, Deborah Benson as Linda, Myron Healey as Andrew Lee, Joe Frazier as Terrible Tucker; Executive Producer: Kenneth Johnson; Story: Oscar Brodney; Director: Lee Madden; 86 min.; Infinite Productions; Miramax; Color.

Two policemen serving an eviction notice encounter American Civil War ghosts.

Ghost of the Great River Inn [Juvenile book; WW]
Author: Lynn Hall; First publication: Chicago: Follett Publishing, 1980.

Two school friends make a shocking discovery in Iowa after they encounter the ghost of a paymaster who was slaughtered in the American Civil War.

Ghost Patrol [Comic book characters; WW]

1. First appearance: *Flash Comics* #29 (May 1940); Story: Ted Udall, Emmanuel Demby; Art: Frank Harry; Publisher: J.R. Publishing Co. "A Superman DC Publication."

Fred, Pedro and Slim, members of the French Foreign Legion, are ordered to drop bombs on innocent villagers in North Africa by Nazi Captain Buehler. They refuse and drop the bombs harmlessly in the desert. But plane mechanic Henri has planted a bomb on board the plane to stop the bombing of the villages. When the bomb explodes Fred, Pedro and Slim should have perished but instead they find themselves still "alive" as ghosts.

Now dedicated to defeating the Nazis the threesome form the Ghost Patrol and are soon fighting Adolf Hitler. As ghosts they can walk through walls, fly and become invisible—but when they materialize in human form they can be injured like any living person.

2. First appearance: *Wings Comics* #66 (February 1946); Publisher: Fiction House Magazines.

The group of ethereal pilots and their adventures with mortals became known as *The Ghost Squadron* with issue #71.

"Revenge of the Shadow Squadron"
First publication: *Wings Comics* #66 (February 1946); Story: Captain Derek West (pen-name); Art: Rodlow Willard.

"Sky-war stories—the deeds of specter legions—the human hawks who return from Valhalla to fly and fight again."

While on a lone reconnaissance flight Bruce Barrett is attacked by, "Six Jerries out for my scalp!" To his amazement a ghost squadron of World War I Nieuports come to his rescue but can't save his plane from crash landing in enemy territory. The ghost pilots expect to recruit another dead pilot to their Ghost Patrol but Barrett survives and is nursed back to health by a doctor and his daughter, Elaine. In the tunnels beneath the old castle where Barrett is recovering Nazis are planning attacks on London and New York with atomic bombs. Barrett must stop them, but his task won't be easy.

Ghost Soldier [Juvenile book; WW]

1. Author: Elaine Marie Alphin; First publication: New York: Henry Holt, 2001.

Young Alexander Raskin reluctantly travels to North Carolina with his father to visit his father's girlfriend, Paige Hambrick, and her two children. Visiting a Civil War site Alexander's psychic gifts return when he sees the ghost of a Confederate soldier. The soldier won't leave Alexander alone until he helps him find out what became of his family after he died in the war.

2. Author: Theresa Breslin; First publication: London: Doubleday Children's, 2014.

A farming community in Scotland during World War I. When Rob and Millie's father is reported missing in action in the Battle of the Somme their mother can't handle the news. During her recovery the children take care of themselves and set about the quest of finding their fa-

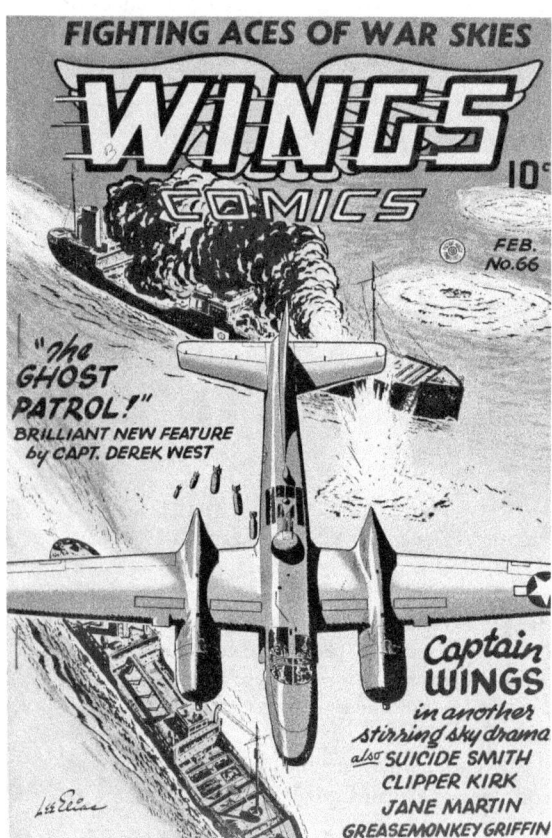

The first appearance of The Ghost Patrol in *Wings Comics* #66 (February 1946). Cover art by Lee Elias. Published by Fiction House Magazines.

ther on the hospital trains carrying wounded soldiers. One night as they wander through woods the brother and sister see a strange figure in the window of an abandoned building that is now a hospital treating soldiers with shellshock.

"As Rob helped Millie over the wall, he couldn't resist taking a final glance back at the house. Again—from the end attic window ... a flash of white. Rob's breath caught in his throat. Then he laughed at himself. It would be a gull nest on the windowsill. Not a ghost. There were no such thing as ghosts...."

Ghost Stories [Comic book]

Supernatural anthology title.

"THE DAY THE SOLDIERS RAN" [WW]
First publication: #3 (July–September 1963); Story: Carl Memling; Art: Gerald McCann; Publisher: Dell Publishing Co.

Three soldiers plead guilty to "Fear of the Unknown." Assigned to a forward post by their platoon Sergeant the soldiers are ordered to hold the post at all costs. When the post comes under heavy enemy attack they manage to hold it. But after the smoke clears they run like scared rabbits claiming the place is haunted by knights in armor on horses riding in the sky.

German soldiers tell the same story of running from an army of medieval sky soldiers. The fleeing soldiers are told a great battle was fought on the same land in medieval times and in moments of great crisis the knights reappear.

"SCRATCH ONE GHOST" [WW]
First publication: #18 (May 1967); Story: Paul S. Newman; Art: Frank Springer; Publisher: Dell Publishing Co.

An American air force base in England is haunted by a German zeppelin from World War I.

Ghost Talkers [Novel; WW]

Author: Mary Robinette Kowal; First publication: New York: Tor, 2016.

In World War I, a group of mediums work for the British Army's Spirit Corps. When a soldier dies in battle they must report to the Spirit Corps in order to pass on vital intelligence concerning troop movements. American heiress Ginger Stuyvensant is engaged to British officer Ben Harford. Ginger becomes aware of a spy in the ranks and an effort by the Germans to infiltrate the Spirit Corps. With no support from the top brass, Ginger must stop the Germans and expose the spy.

"The Ghost That Haunted Hitler" [Pulp fiction; WW]

Author: William P. McGivern; First publication: *Fantastic Adventures* (Vol. 4 #12; December 1942); Publisher: Ziff-Davis Publishing Company.

The assassination of Reinhardt Heydrich—the Hangman—is followed by the execution of three-hundred-and-fifty innocent men and women in Prague. Worries of a revolt by the Czech people are mocked by Marshal von Bock. "That is ridiculous. We can grind them to powder under our heels and they will whine for pity."

Bock receives news that the village of Lidice will be reduced to dust, the men executed, the women sent to concentration camps and the children becoming wards of the Third Reich. But Heydrich's assassin Paul Cheval has a plan to help

Fantastic Adventures (Vol.4 #12; December 1942), featuring "The Ghost That Haunted Hitler" by William P. McGivern. Cover art by Harold W. McCauley. Published by Ziff-Davis Publishing Company.

defeat the Nazis. Doctor Schultz has invented a head-piece device that can make Cheval invisible to the Gestapo.

Ghost Whisperer (2005) [TV series]

Main Cast: Jennifer Love Hewitt as Melinda Gordon, David Conrad as Jim Clancy, Aisha Tyler as Andrea Moreno, Jay Mohr as Professor Rick Payne, Camryn Manheim as Delia Banks, Jamie Kennedy as Eli James; Creator: John Gray; Executive Producers: John Gray, Kim Moses, Ian Sanders, P.K. Simonds; 45 min.; Sanders/Moses Productions, Touchstone Television, Paramount Network; Columbia Broadcasting System (CBS); Color.

Melinda Gordon runs an antiques store in Grandview. She can also see and talk to ghosts. Episodes revolve around Melinda helping ghosts to crossover into the light.

"Haunted Hero" (3:03) [WW]

Air date: October 12, 2007; Guest Cast: Matthew Marsden as Sgt. Matt Murphy, Kate Levering as Gina Prince, Dan Colman as Steve Simon, Lela Loren as Anna Sanchez; Story: Karl Schaefer; Teleplay: Breen Frazier, Karl Schaefer; Director: Eric Laneuville.

Silver Star recipient Sergeant Matt Murphy of the National Guard 1st Platoon, Bravo Company, returns home to Grandview a hero. But soon filmed footage surfaces to suggest he deserted his platoon while under enemy fire from insurgents in Iraq. Murphy is haunted by nightmares of the war and the foggy memory of the night he supposedly left his fellow soldiers to die.

"I think Matt brought the war home with him," states Melinda Gordon. "He's being haunted by his own men."

These soldiers also appear to Melinda and point her in the direction of a letter and an "engagement ring" made out of reeds. Murphy finally comes to terms with the reality of what happened on that traumatic night in Iraq.

Separated from their convoy the platoon was pinned down by an insurgent ambush. Matt Murphy made a run for the Humvee, not to desert his squad but to sacrifice his life to protect them. His men died trying to protect him when his gun jammed while shooting the insurgents.

This episode included real-life war veterans William Owen, Josh Cannon, Mike Siembruzch, Dustin Senella and Sgt. Tom Kane.

"Pilot" (1:01) WW]

Air date: September 23, 2005; Guest Cast: Wentworth Miller as Sgt. Paul Adams, Balthazar Getty as Michael Adams, Rodney Scott as Dan Clancy, Allison McDonell as Vera Adams; Story-Director: John Gray.

The ghost of Sergeant Paul Adams, missing in action in Vietnam, visits Melinda Gordon on her wedding day. When Melinda follows up on Adams' request to contact his son Michael she is met with disbelief and hostility. But when a phone call to the Pentagon confirms Melinda's leads, the remains of Sgt. Paul Adams are finally found and he enters the light.

The Ghost Wore Gray [Juvenile book; WW]

Author: Bruce Colville; First publication: New York: Bantam, 1988.

School girl Nina Tanleven and her best friend Chris are staying at a broken down inn in the Catskills that is being restored by Nina's architect father. The two girls are startled by the ghost of a young Confederate soldier and realize it's the same handsome soldier they saw in a faded photograph on their arrival at the inn. A mystery involving the Confederate soldier, treasure and the conductor of the Underground Railroad is one the girls must solve with the ghost's help.

Ghostscape [Juvenile book; SFW]

Author: Joe Layburn; Illustrator: John Williams; First publication: London: Frances Lincoln Children's Books, 2008.

Somali refugee Aisha encounters the ghost of young Richard, while hiding from a bully at her school in modern-day London. Then, to her amazement, Aisha travels through time to World War II London, where she meets Richard again. This time he is a living boy during the Blitz. Aisha comes to realize there are bullies in both the present and the past, including Adolf Hitler. As difficult as it might be, you must stand up to them and not retreat in hiding.

Ghostly Tales [Comic book]

Supernatural anthology title from Charlton Comics hosted by Mr. L. Dedd.

"Army of the Dead" [WW]

First publication: #55 (May 1966); Art: Rocco Mastroserio.

Reichsmarshal Wolfgang Von Hocksdorff of the 7th Panzer Division was once a stalwart in the Kaiser's armies on the Marne during World War I. Now, twenty years later, he recalls the day he almost died fighting a French soldier named Louis

Valjean. Now the Nazi Reichsmarshal plans another defeat for France. The spirit of Valjean decides it's time to pay Hocksdorff a visit, for in the recalling of his story he neglected to tell his fellow men that after Valjean spared his life, Hocksdorff shot Valjean in the back of his head. Now Valjean shows the Nazi his own army—of ghosts.

"Attack of the Phantom" [WW]

First publication: #68 (September 1968); Art: Pat Boyette.

Disaster strikes in the early days of World War II as 2nd Lieutenant Terry Arnold of the U.S. Air Corps crashes his plane in the Texan countryside, breaking his back. He is told by doctors he will never walk or fly again. Decades later Arnold's son follows in his father's footsteps as a pilot in the U.S. Air Force. But another war in Vietnam is his battleground and the destruction of a strategic bridge is his unit's assignment.

As Arnold tries to shake off enemy aircraft he's amazed to see his father's old World War II plane coming to his rescue as the pursuing MiG aircraft crashes in a ball of flames. Arnold is bemused. "I … I don't understand! I know I saw it…. Other pilot saw it too…. But it's gone…. There's nothing down there at all!"

"The Phantom Green Beret" [WW]

First publication: #58 (November 1966); Art: Pat Boyette.

A regiment of Green Berets stationed in Vietnam don't believe in ghosts, but events may change their minds. In his jungle fortress Ho Chu Ming prepares for an attack by the American soldiers. Unknown to them Ming has inside information on their attack plans and is ready for them. Meanwhile the Berets receive a radio message from Sergeant Douglas Roberts warning them of danger ahead. But they have no idea Sgt. Roberts was killed by Ho Chu Ming days earlier. The Berets change their plan of attack and catch Ming unawares. Their lives have been saved by a ghost they never believed in.

"A Promise Is a Promise" [WW]

First publication: #57 (September 1966); Art: Rocco Mastroserio.

Fort Hillyard. Two new inductees are given another series of inoculations as they prepare to head for war in the Pacific. The two young men, Mel Steiner and Fred Kane become good friends as Kane tries to calm Steiner's fears about the war. "If you ever have any doubts, look around. I'll be there. That's a promise!" Kane dies on the battlefield vowing to keep his promise to his friend. And true to his word, the spirit of Kane saves Steiner's life by warning him of dangers ahead.

"Superstition" [WW]

First publication: #62 (August 1967); Story: Carl Wessler; Art: Pat Boyette.

1917. Jimmy Duncan of Squadron Seven gives "Pop" credit for his reputation as an air fighter ace in World War I. "Pop" is his stuffed cloth dog, a childhood Christmas present from his mother. Newcomer Hank Flagg doesn't believe in lucky mascots and mocks Duncan's superstition. But when Flagg's plane comes under enemy fire Duncan and "Pop" save his life. And when Flagg safely lands he is shocked to be told Duncan died in battle—but "Pop" was protecting him in his cockpit—placed there by Duncan.

Ghostly Tales #68 (September 1968). **Cover art by Pat Boyette. Published by Charlton Comics.**

Ghosts

"Timeless Desert" [WW]
First publication: #62 (October 1967); Art: Charles Nicholas.

Earl Wills, lost in the Sahara desert while prospecting for oil, comes across a derelict B-52 bomber from World War II. Seeking shelter in the plane the engines come to life and the plane becomes airborne after twenty-three years of inaction. In the cockpit is a pilot and his officers, shooting down a German plane. But the B-52 has been hit and pilot and crew are bailing out. Wills takes the final parachute from a badly wounded officer, who tells him he will get his revenge for stealing his chute. Back in the present a helicopter comes across the B-52 and the body of a man with an unopened parachute. It is Earl Wills and the B-52 "B. B Gun" is the same plane he served on during World War II.

Ghosts [Comic book]

Horror anthology title from DC Comics that carried the cover blurb "If you don't believe in Ghosts we challenge you to read True Tales of the Weird and the Supernatural!"

"Conversation with a Corpse" [WW]
First publication: #27 (June 1974); Story: Leo Dorfman; Art: Bob Brown, Frank McLaughlin.

A damaged B-17 bomber limps back to England with the help of a World War I German pilot, who happens to have died long ago.

"Flight of the Last Phantom" [WW]
First publication: #28 (July 1974); Story: Leo Dorfman; Art: Don Perlin.

Twenty years after he died the ghost of Lieutenant Carver is still attempting to land on the U.S.S. Washington.

"The Ghost Battalions" [WW]
First publication: #2 (November–December 1971); Story: Leo Dorfman; Art: Sam Glanzman.

When a battalion disappears into thin air it serves as reminder of all the vanished soldiers of the past.

"Ghost in the Iron Coffin" [WW]
First publication: #1 (October 1971); Story: David George; Art: Sam Glanzman.

1942. Celebrations at the launch of the latest Nazi submarine at the Kiel shipyard are ruined by the sight of a phantom sabotaging the launch, causing the U-boat to ram a torpedo boat.

"Graveyard of Vengeance" [WW]
First publication: #18 (September 1973); Art: Alfredo Alcala.

His family slaughtered by English redcoats during the Revolutionary War, an Indian Chief vows revenge by placing a curse on all white men.

"A Phantom in Our Family" [WW]
First publication: #30 (September 1974); Story: Murray Boltinoff; Art: Lee Elias.

Has the ghost of Joey Rodriguez, who was killed-in-action in Vietnam, returned to haunt his family?

"The Specter from the Bog" [WW]
First publication: #19 (October 1973); Story: Leo Dorfman; Art: Sam Glanzman.

Two Dutch regiments are saved when a ghost rider leads the Nazis into quicksand.

"A Specter Stalks Saigon" [WW]
First publication: #10 (December 1972); Story: Leo Dorfman; Art: Gerry Talaoc, Redondo Studios.

The ghost of a soldier in Vietnam attempts to warn other soldiers to change their plans.

The Ghosts of Iron Bottom Sound [Juvenile book; WW]

Author: Sandy Nelson; First publication: Auckland, New Zealand: HarperCollins, 2010.

Eleven-year-old Paddy is passionate about a book he has borrowed from his library that recalls the Battle of Savo Island and Iron Bottom Sound, during World War II. But his passion has taken on an added dimension with the voices he hears in his head. Voices of marines who died in the Battle of Savo Island who tell him about his grandfather who served on the *HMAS Canberra* when it sank in that battle. Only Paddy's Grandfather knows why the ghosts of the past have contacted his grandson.

Ghosts of the Civil War [Juvenile book; WW]

Author-Illustrator: Cheryl Harness; First publication: New York: Simon & Schuster Books for Young Readers, 2001.

Young Lindsey begrudgingly attends a Civil War re-enactment with her parents. But her day takes a strange and unique turn when she meets the ghost of Abraham Lincoln's older son Willie. He takes Lindsey back in time as she witnesses the Civil War first hand. From the Gettysburg Address to the battle at Fort Sumter to General Lee's surrender at Appomattox to the assassination of President Lincoln.

Ghosts of Time (*Jason Thanou Time Travel* book #4) [Novel; AHW]

Author: Steve White; First publication: Riverdale, N.Y.: Baen Publishing, 2014.

Special operations officer Jason Thanou of the Temporal Regulatory Authority travels back in time with his team to the American Civil War to combat the Transhumanist underground who plan to change history. By escaping the Observer Effect that states past history cannot be changed the Transhumanists hope to transform humanity into a race of gods and monsters. Jason Thanou and his team must prevent a Transhumanist plan to change the outcome of the Fall of Richmond in the final days of the Civil War.

See: ***Sunset of the Gods***

G.I. Robot [Comic book character; SFW]

First appearance: *Star Spangled War Stories* #101 (March 1962); Creators: **Robert Kanigher**, Ross Andru; Publisher: DC Comics.

There have been a number of incarnations of G.I. Robot, beginning with his debut in "The GI Robot and the Dinosaur" (March 1962). Active during World War II, the two original robots, Mac and Joe are destroyed on missions to Dinosaur Island.

JAKE-1 (Jungle Automatic Killer Experiment) is introduced in ***Weird War Tales*** #101 (1981), followed by JAKE-2 in #113 (1982). Yet another version appears in *Frankenstein, Agent of S.H.A.D.E.* #4 where G.I. Robot J.A.K.E. (Japanese Attack Killer Elite) is being held by the Japanese to be used as a weapon. But when J.A.K.E. is released he joins the Allied Forces and reveals himself to be Joint Allied Killer Elite, teaming up with Frankenstein to prevent the annihilation of New York City.

G. I. Robot Squadron is the final incarnation to date.

G.I. Zombie [Comic book character; WW]

First appearance: *Star Spangled War Stories Featuring G.I. Zombie* #1 (March 2015); Creators: Jimmy Palmiotti, Justin Gray, Scott Hampton; Publisher: DC Comics.

Carmen King, a woman with two tours of duty and suffering with post-traumatic stress syndrome, is partnered with Jared Kabe, an undead soldier who has been fighting in wars for many years in secret. Their first mission, to infiltrate an anti-government militia that plans to destroy towns with the chemical weapon Black Ice.

Gingersnap [Juvenile book; WW]

Author: Patricia Reilly Giff; First publication: New York: Wendy Lamb Books, 2013.

Upstate New York, 1944. Jayna is an orphan whose only family is her older brother Rob, a cook for the U.S. Navy. When his ship leaves for action in the Pacific, Jayna is left in the care of her testy landlady. But tragedy strikes when Rob's ship is attacked and sunk and her brother is listed as missing in action. Now Jayna feels totally alone and longs to connect with her family roots. Her brother once told her they had a grandmother living in Brooklyn. Now she sets out to find her, accompanied by her turtle Theresa and a ghost as her guide.

Godlike: Superhero Roleplaying in a World on Fire, 1936–1946 [RPG; SHW]

Release date: 2001; System: d20; Designers: Dennis Detwiller, John Scott Tynes, Stolze; Publisher: Hawthorn Hobgoblynn Press.

In this tabletop roleplaying game it is World War II and ordinary men and women have mysteriously gained superhuman powers. Known collectively as the Talents these super-heroes still face great dangers and risks during in the battle between good and evil.

"Gods of the Jungle" [Pulp fiction; SFW]

Author: Nelson S. Bond; Illustrator: Robert Fuqua; First publication: *Amazing Stories* (Vol. 16 #6–7; June–July 1942); Publisher: Ziff-Davis Publishing Company.

"The Japs made Angkor too hot, but when Romney found himself in Angkor's past, it was a sight hotter. Deep in the ruined temple was a strange room, and when Romney came out of it, many centuries had been wiped out!"

Gojira a.k.a. ***Godzilla*** (1954) [Film; Japan: SFW]

Premiere: November 3, 1954; Main Cast: Akira Takarada as Hideto Ogata, Momoko Kochi as Emiko Yamane, Akihiko Hirati as Daisuke Serizawa-hakase, Takashi Shimura as Kyohei Yamane-hakase, Fuyuki Murakami as Professor Tanabe; Executive Producer: Iwao Mori; Story: Shigaru Kayama; Director: Ishiro Honda; 96 min.; Toho Film Co.; B/W.

Odo Island, Japan is attacked by a 164-foot-tall monster named Gojira. Its rampage soon threatens the rest of Japan.

The film is a stark reminder of the horrors of atomic warfare that traumatized the Japanese psyche with the bombings of Hiroshima and Nagasaki at the end of World War II. Gojira has been awakened by H-bomb tests and attacks the civilians of Tokyo with his fire breathing flames that disintegrate bodies in an instant. Meanwhile the radiation levels are off the chart. Even young children suffer graphic deaths in the carnage.

Director Ishiro Honda had experienced the devastation of Hiroshima first-hand. "There was a feeling that the world was already coming to an end. I took the characteristics of an atomic bomb and applied them to Gojira. Mankind had created the bomb, and now nature was going to take revenge on mankind."

The film was recut, with additional scenes shot, featuring Raymond Burr as an American reporter, for U.S. distribution in 1956. *Gojira* became *Godzilla, King of the Monsters!* Future films in the series were simple "monster movies" with Godzilla battling Mechagodzilla, Mothra and other creatures in a genre now known as Kaiju. Godzilla starred in 28 films from Toho Studios, concluding with the 50th anniversary special *Godzilla: Final Wars* in 2004. Two big budget *Godzilla* movies from Hollywood were also produced in 1998 and 2014.

Goliath [Novel; SFW]

Author: Scott Westerfeld; Art: Keith Thompson; First publication: New York: Simon Pulse, 2011.

In the final book in the trilogy Prince Aleksander set in an alternative World War I Europe Aleksandar Ferdinand reclaims his throne as Prince of Austria and falls in love with English Darwinist Deryn Sharp.

Goodnight Sweetheart (1993) [TV series; UK; SFW]

Premiere: November 18, 1993; Main Cast: Nicholas Lyndhurst as Gary Sparrow, Elizabeth Carling as Phoebe Sparrow, Emma Amos as Yvonne Sparrow, Dervla Kirwan as Phoebe, Michelle Holmes as Yvonne, Victor McGuire as Ron, Christopher Ettridge as Reg; 57 × 30 min.; Executive Producers: Claire Hinson, Allan McKeown; Alomo Productions; British Broadcasting Corporation (BBC); Color.

Unhappily married television repair man Gary Sparrow walks into the Royal Oak pub in London's East End and finds himself in wartime London in 1940. Attracted to the landlord's married daughter Phoebe, Gary Sparrow lives a double life between past and present.

Graveyard of Empires [Comic book; WW]

First publication: June 2011; Four-issue mini-series; Story: Mark Sable; Art: Paul Azaceta; Publisher: Image Comics.

U.S. Marines are forced to forge a fragile truce with the Taliban when a new enemy appears in Afghanistan—the undead.

Great American Comics Present: The Secret Voice [Comic book; WW]

First publication: 1945; Art: Ronald Marcus; Publisher: Peter George Four Star Publication; American Features Syndicate.

"What Really Happened To Hitler! America's No. 1 Secret Weapon Revealed!"

An invisible insect with a super-intellect and the ability to project his thoughts helps the Allied war effort and influences the assembly of the atomic bomb.

Grey Knight a.k.a. The Killing Box (1993) [Film; WW]

Premiere: March 7, 1993; Main Cast: Corbin Bernsen as Colonel Nehemiah Strayn, Adrian Pasdar as Capt. John Harling, Ray Wise as Colonel George Thalman, Billy Bob Thornton as Langston, Martin Sheen as General Haworth, David Arquette as Murphy, Matt LeBlanc as Terhune; Executive Producer: Fred T. Kuehnert; Story: Matt Greenberg; Director: George Hickenlooper; Motion Picture Corporation of America (MPCA); Turner Home Entertainment; Color.

The Union and Confederates join forces to face the unknown and fight an undead army after an evil entity possesses the corpses of soldiers.

Grunts [Comic book; SFW]

First publication: November 2006; Three-issue mini-series; Story: Shannon Eric Denton, Keith Giffen; Art: Matt Jacobs; Publisher: Arcana Studio.

Near the French-German border a U.S.–British force advances into German territory. But awaiting them in the woodland is a German superhuman assault squad.

Gun of the Black Sun (2011) [Film; UK-Romania; WW]

Premiere: March 4, 2011 (UK); Main Cast: Gary Douglas as Axel O'Rourke, Richard Lynch as Damian

Lupescu, Ina Wright as Duke, Mihaela Sinca as Loredana Anescu, Kitty Cepraga as Alessandra; Executive Producer: Andrew Stear; Screenplay: Peter Lee; Story: Parv Bancil, Gary Douglas, Elaine Thompson; Director: Jeff Burr; 90 min.; Silver Bullet, Max Productions, Luger the Movie; Fundamental Film; Color.

A golden Luger gun is presented as a gift from Himmler to the Romanian Iron Guard during World War II. The Iron Guard place a spell on the Luger which remains hidden until it is discovered in modern day Bucharest among the possessions of Loredana Anescu's dying grandfather. When tech mogul Damian Lupescu learns of the Luger he sets his sights on possessing it and using its mystical power to bring about the Fourth Reich in Europe.

Gunparade March [Japan; SFW]

1. [Video game]; Release date: September 28, 2000; Platform: PlayStation; Developer: Alfa System; Publisher: Sony Computer Entertainment.

2. [Manga]; Original publication: Dengeki Comics (2001); 3 vol.; Story: Rei Hiroe; Publisher: ASCII Media Works.

World War II comes to an abrupt conclusion in 1945 when hostile extraterrestrials, known as the Genjyu or Phantom Beasts, invade the Earth. In 1999, mankind is still fighting the aliens. Humanoid Walking Tanks have had limited results with too many pilots killed-in-action. Now the Japanese government is recruiting high school students to become HWT pilots. Unit 5121, consisting of drafted students of both sexes goes into action on the Japanese island of Kyushu.

Gunparade March: The New March (2003) [Animated TV series; Japan; SFW]

Premiere: February 6, 2003; Voice Cast: Akira Ishida as Atsushi Hayami, Akemi Okamura as Mai Shibamura, Akio Suyama as Yohei Takigawa, Emi Shinohara as Motoko Hara, Mayumi Yoshida as Nonomi Higashihara, Tomoe Hanba as Seika Mori, Kelichi Sonobe as Hisaomi Sakaue, Junko Noda as Matsui Kato, Chiaki Maeda as Maki Tanabe; Producers: Kazuya Furuse, Takayuki Matsunaga, Yuchi Sekido; Story: Fumihiko Takayama, Jun'ichi Shintaku, Seishi Minakami; Directors: Katsushi Sakurabi, Shuku Negao, Matsuo Asami, Yoyoi Minazuki; 12 × 25 min.; J.C. Staff, Project GPM, Rondo Robe, d-rights; Media Blasters; Chiba TV, MBS; Color.

Based on the video game and manga.

Season One

1:01—*Playback*—*The Visitor*; 1:02—*Do Whatever You Like*—*Going My Way*; 1:03—*Summer Blues*—*Fireworks*; 1:04—*Let's Have Tea Together*—*Duelist*; 1:05—*Withered Leaf*—*Thursday's Child*; 1:06—*After You Left*—*I Guess Everything Reminds You of Something*; 1:07—*A Long Night*—*In the Forests of Nights*; 1:08—*In April, She Will*—*With Your Musket, Fife and Drum*; 1:09—*You Are the One Who Makes My Heart Pound*—*A Day in the Life*; 1:10—*Hello Sadness*—*Once Upon a Dime*; 1:11—*I Couldn't Bring It Up*—*A Good Reward for Their Labor*; 1:12—*Every Time I Say Goodbye*—*Gun Parade March*

Gunparade Orchestra (2005) [Animated TV series; Japan; SFW]

Premiere: October 5, 2005; Voice Cast: Megumi Toyoguchi as Sara Ishida, Norio kakemono as Hard-Boiled Penguin, Junichi Suwabe as Michiya Noguchi; Story: Shouji Yonemura; Directors: Toshiya Shinohara, Harume Kosaka; 24 × 25 min.; Brain's Base, Bandai Visual: ABC, NBN, TV Asahi; Color.

The sequel to *Gunparade March* features the adventures of the 108th Guard Squad under new Company Commander Sara Ishida. The inexperienced young pilots, stationed in Aomori, find themselves plunged into a war with enemy armies.

The Guns of the South [Novel; AHW]

Author: Harry Turtledove; First publication: New York: Ballantine Books, 1992.

South African time traveler Andrew Rhoodie from 2014 journeys back to January 1864 to supply General Lee with AK-47 assault rifles. Rhoodie, a white supremacist, seeks a continuation of slavery into the present day. But the victorious Confederate government is divided over slavery and views Rhoodie and his armed militia from the future as enemies of freedom.

GURPS World War II: Weird War II—Secret Weapons and Twisted History [RPG sourcebook; WW]

First publication: 2003; Compiler and Editor: Kenneth Hite with Gene Seabolt; Art: Gene Seabolt; Publisher: Steve Jackson Games.

In this supplement to the *GURPS World War II* system we have World War II with a supernatural twist. Nazi mystic archmages, SS supersoldiers, secret Antarctic bases, "foo fighters," werewolves and a race for the Ark of the Covenant.

GURPS World War II: Weird War II— The Secret of the Gneisenau [RPG book (PDF); WW]

First publication: 2004; Story: Dennis Detwiller; Publisher: Steve Jackson Games.

The German battle cruiser *Gneisenau* steams toward Holland with the Allies in pursuit. The historical and fantastic are mixed as the player must save the *Gneisenau* before her luck runs out.

A Guy Named Joe (1944) [Film; WW]

Premiere: December 24, 1943; Main Cast: Spencer Tracy as Pete Sandridge, Irene Dunn as Dorinda Durston, Van Johnson as Ted Randall, Ward Bond as Al Yackey, James Gleason as "Nalls" Kilpatrick, Lionel Barrymore as The General, Esther Williams as Ellen Bright; Screenplay: Dalton Trumbo from an original story by David Boehm and Chandler Sprague; Producer: Everett Riskin; Director: Victor Fleming; 120 min.; Distribution: Loew's, Inc.; Production Company: Metro-Goldwyn-Mayer Corp; B&W.

Reckless U.S. Squadron commander Pete Sandridge, stationed at an air force base in England during World War II is transferred to a base in Scotland. Pete agrees to girlfriend Dorinda's request to return to the United States and become a flying instructor—but not before one final mission. Dorinda's sense of impending doom is confirmed when Pete Sandridge's plane is attacked. In a final heroic act the badly injured Pete crashes his plane into the German aircraft carrier.

A Guy Named Joe (1944), starring (from left) Spencer Tracy as Pete Sandridge and Irene Dunn as Dorinda Durston (Metro-Goldwyn Mayer).

The dead pilot finds himself assigned by The General as a guide and protector for new pilots on Earth still earning their wings in the combat zone of the South Pacific.

The original script and first revision were both rejected by the U.S. War Department because of the potentially harmful effects of "hovering ghosts of deceased pilots." Nominated for "Best Original Story" at the 1944 Academy Awards the film was a top ten box-office hit but received mixed reviews.

Variety (December 1943) commented: "In taking a fling at the spirit world, Metro doesn't quite succeed in reaching the nebulous but manages to turn out an entertaining and excellently performed picture. Had the fantasy been interpreted wholly in terms of the sharp wit and dry humor which Spencer Tracy, only occasionally injects, instead of investing it with spiritual counseling, the film might have attained smash proportions."

Half Past Danger [Comic book; WW]

First publication: May 2013; Six issue mini-series; Story-Art: Stephen Mooney; Publisher: IDW Publishing.

1943. Staff Sergeant Thomas Michael Flynn and his squad encounter a nightmare scenario as they come under attack from dinosaurs on a Japanese island in the South Pacific. Months later Flynn is asked to return to the island by British soldier Captain John Noble and Agent Huntingdon-Moss of British Intelligence. Their target is a Nazi base and their collection of dinosaurs, headed toward the island coast and their final destination, Adolf Hitler.

Hanussen (1988) [Film; Hungary-Germany-Austria; WW]

Premiere: May 20, 1988 (Cannes); Main Cast: Klaus Maria Brandauer as Klaus Schneider/Eric Jan Hanussen, Erland Josephson as Dr. Emil Bettelheim, Walter Schmidinger as Propaganda Chief, Idiko Bansagi as Sister Betty, Karoly Eperjes as Capt. Tibor Nowotny; Producer: Artur Brauner; Story: Peter Dobai, Paul Hengee, Gabriella Prekop, Istvan Szabo. Based on the autobiography by Erik Jan Hanussen; Director: Istvan Szabo; 140 min.; Hungarofilm, Mafilm, Mokep, Central Cinema Company Film; Columbia Pictures; Color.

Austrian Klaus Schneider is taken into the care of Dr. Emil Bettelheim following serious injuries received during World War

I. During his convalescence the doctor discovers Schneider has powers of clairvoyance. Schneider decides to put his talents to use on the Berlin stage and changes his name to Eric Jan Hanussen. Here he encounters Nazis. His visions of their rise to power and the pain and violence they will inflict fills Hanussen with dread for the future.

Hard Rock Zombies (1985) [Film; WW]
Premiere: September 1985; Main Cast: E. J. Curcio as Jessie, Jack Bliesener as Adolf Hitler, Ted Wells as Ron, Sam Mann as Bobby, Lisa Toothman as Elsa, Jennifer Coe as Cassie, Crystal Shaw as Mrs. Buff; Executive Producer: Shashi Patel; Story: David Ball, Hrishna Sha, Director: Krishna Shah; 98 min.; Patel-Shah Film Company; Cannon Film Distributors; Color.

Four members of a hard rock band travel to their latest gig in the town of Grand Guignol, little knowing it is populated by werewolves, evil dwarfs, sexual predators and Adolf Hitler. The band are murdered but not before the lead singer falls for a young groupie named Cassie. She raises the band from the dead playing one of their songs. Now they can take their revenge on Hitler and his Nazi followers and finally get to play their gig and save the town from Nazi zombies.

The Hate-Monger [Comic book character; SFW]
First appearance: *Fantastic Four* #21 (December 1963); Creators: **Stan Lee, Jack Kirby**; Publisher: Marvel Comics.

The purple-robed *Hate-Monger* is introduced to the **Fantastic Four** preaching his message of fanatical bigotry. To help him in his cause the Hate-Monger uses his "Hate Ray" gun to turn the Fantastic Four against each other. While searching for an antidote to the effects of the ray Reed Richards discovers the Hate-Monger's deadly plans to spread his hatred worldwide. With the help of Agent of S.H.I.E.L.D. Nick Fury Richards receives the antidote and learns the true identity of the Hate-Monger—Adolf Hitler!

Later additions to the Hate-Monger's origin story reveal Hitler's consciousness was transferred to a cloned brain by brilliant Nazi scientist **Armin Zola** when the original Hitler died in 1945.

The Haunted Airman (2006) [Telefilm; UK; WW]
First broadcast: October 31, 2006; Main Cast: Robert Pattinson as Toby Jugg, Rachael Stirling as Julia Jugg, Julian Sands as Dr. Hal Burns, Scott Handy as Squadron Leader Peter Enfield, Melissa Lloyd as Sister Sally Grant, Daniel Ainsleigh as Pilot Officer, Robert Whitelock as Commando; Executive Producer: Richard Fell; Story: Chris Durlacher; Based on "The Haunting of Toby Jugg" by Dennis Wheatley; Director: Chris Durlacher; 68 min.; British Broadcasting Corporation (BBC); BBC Four; Color.

RAF pilot Toby Jugg becomes a paraplegic after he is hit in the spine during a bombing raid in Germany during World War II. While recuperating in a country clinic recommended by his only relative Julia Jugg, Toby comes under the care of Dr. Hal Burns. But soon Jugg is haunted by various menacing apparitions and bug infestations that make him doubt his own sanity. Is this supernatural activity real or is there a hidden agenda at work?

See: *The Haunting of Toby Jugg*

The Haunted Tank [WW]

1. Comic book feature

First appearance: *G.I. Combat* #87 (May 1961); Creators: **Robert Kanigher, Russ Heath**; Publisher: DC Comics.

Following his death in the Battle of Richmond in 1864 the ghost of Confederate General James Ewell Brown (J.E.B) Stuart is summoned by Alexander the Great to act as guardian for Sergeant Jeb Stuart and his Stuart M3 tank. Tank commander Stuart is the only person who can see the General. Stuart's crew have great respect for him but don't believe his stories about seeing JEB Stuart. The ghost can warn Stuart of dangers ahead but only in an obscure manner. Stuart has to make sense of the warnings for himself resulting in loss of life among his crew when he fails to decipher the ghostly messages.

There have been many guest appearances of The Haunted Tank crew, in various DC Comics titles, since the end of its original run in *G.I. Combat* with issue #288 (March 1987).

2. Comic book (1).

First publication: 2008; five-issue mini-series; Story: Frank Marraffino; Art: Henry Flint; Publisher: Vertigo.

The setting is updated from World War II to Operation Iraqi Freedom Confederate General J.E.B Stuart becomes guardian of a M1 Abrams tank under the command of African American Sergeant Jamal Stuart. This creates conflict with the ghost of Stuart who is now criticized for his views on race and slavery.

3. Comic book (2).

First appearance: *G.I. Combat: The Haunted Tank* #5 (December 2012); Three-part "New 52" story; Publisher: DC Comics.

Jeb Stuart, formerly Tennessee Captain of the U.S. 3D Armored Division is now in retirement. But he learns he still has one final mission to complete when the ghost of J.E.B. Stuart pays him a visit. The Haunted Tank crew rescue Stuart's great grandson Scott from captivity in Afghanistan, thus saving the Stuart family line. But the descendant of one of Jeb Stuart's old Nazi enemies from World War II ruins the family reunion and Jeb Stuart returns to America to be laid to rest at the age of 92.

The Haunting at Stratton Falls [Juvenile book; WW]

Author: Brenda Seabrooke; First publication: New York: Dutton Children's Books, 2000.

December 1944. Eleven-year-old Abby is staying with relatives in Stratton Falls, New York, while her father is declared missing in action in World War Europe. Stories about the house being haunted appear to be confirmed when Abby notices wet footprints in the hallway that lead to the ghost of Felicia Stratton. She tragically drowned while her father fought in the American Civil War. Abby fears the appearance of the ghost may be warning of another death.

The Haunting of Holroyd Hill [Juvenile book; WW]

Author: Brenda Seabrooke; First publication: New York: Cobble Hill Books/Dutton, 1995.

Her family's move from Alexandra to rural Virginia has not made 11-year-old Melinda a happy girl. But her discontent is soon forgotten when Melinda sees a ghost roaming through her new home at night. Together with elder brother Kevin and the neighbor's grandson Dan they maintain a watch on the ghost while encountering two new ghosts. Their research leads them to the Battle of Manassas in the American Civil War.

The Haunting of Marsten Manor (2007) [Film; WW]

Premiere: January 17, 2007; Main Cast: Brianne Davis as Jill, C. Thomas Howell as Captain Williams, Ezra Buzzington as Hank, Janice Knickrehm as Dorothy Marsten, Ken Luckey as Rob, Julie Sapp as Kate Marsten; Producers-Screenplay: Dave Sapp, Julie Sapp; Director: Dave Sapp; 85 min.; Arcadian Pictures; Echo Bridge Home Entertainment; Color.

A blind girl inherits an old mansion and begins to experience strange occurrences connected to the ghost of a dead soldier.

The Haunting of Swain's Fancy [Juvenile book; WW]

Author: Brenda Seabrooke; First publication: New York: Dutton Children's Books, 2003.

Eleven-year-old Taylor isn't entirely happy with her father's new family and home in West Virginia. Not only is Taylor encountering hostility from her step-sister Nicole she has also seen two ghosts on her first night in the house. When Taylor discovers Nicole faked a disembodied head she figures the other ghost was also faked—until Nicole sees it for herself. The two girls decide to get along with each other to investigate the ghosts along with Nicole's brother Peter and her neighbor Cody. They uncover murder involving two brothers on opposite sides during the American Civil War who were both in love with the same woman.

The Haunting of Toby Jugg [Novel; WW]

Author: Dennis Wheatley; First publication: London: Hutchinson & Co., 1948.

Royal Air Force pilot Toby Jugg is confined to a wheelchair after being shot in the back during a bombing raid in Germany, during World War II. During his convalescence in a Welsh castle Jugg begins to see an unearthly shadowy figure of evil. The owner of the castle is a practicing Satanist who may be part of a scheme, devised by Jugg's family, to disinherit him of his fortune before his twenty-first birthday.

See: **The Haunted Airman**

He Walked Around the Horses [Short story; SFW]

Author: H. Beam Piper; First publication: *Astounding Science Fiction Magazine* (April 1948).

November 1809. En route to Hamburg from Vienna government envoy Benjamin Bathurst examines a change of horses for his coach in the yard of an inn in Perleburg, Prussia and is never seen again. Not in this world.

Bathurst finds himself in an alternate timeline where the American Patriots lost their war for independence from the British. Benedict Arnold was shot dead on New Year's Day, 1776 during the storming of Quebec and British General John Burgoyne defeated Horatio Gates at the Battle of Saratoga.

Bathurst's declaration of an alternative history in this new world leads many to believe he is insane. He is imprisoned and shot after attempting to escape.

The Healer's War [Novel; WW]

Author: Elizabeth Ann Scarborough; First publication: New York: Doubleday, 1988.

Inexperienced U.S. Army nurse Lt. Kathleen "Kitty" McCulley encounters overt racism toward the Vietnamese by her colleagues, while on a tour of duty at China Beach. When a dying holy man gives her an amulet Kitty is able to see people's auras. This leads to a hallucinatory journey through the jungle, accompanied by a one-legged Vietnamese boy and a deranged soldier.

The Heap [Comic book character; WW]

First publication: *Air Fighter Comics* #3 (December 1942); Creators: Harry Stein, **Mort Leav**; Publisher: Hillman Periodicals.

World War I, October 12, 1918. Baron Eric von Emmelmann leads his squadron into its final mission. In a dogfight over a "great barren, Polish swamp" his plane is hit and plunges into the swamp. The critically injured Emmelmann is thrown clear. As he clings to life and time passes his body undergoes "an unearthly transformation that has drawn its oxygen food from the vegetation.... A fantastic Heap that is neither animal nor man! It needs oxygen ... it will draw on it in quantity, but especially from the blood vessels of animal or man! The Heap is a supreme master of his primeval domain...."

Heath, Russell (1926–) [Comic book artist]

Born September 29, 1926, in New York City, Russ Heath entered comics at the age of 16, working for Holyoke before moving to Timely Comics in 1946. He soon excelled in the Western genre and gained a reputation for accuracy and realism in his artwork. In 1950 he joined National-DC Comics and proved he had a full range as an artist. But his sphere of excellence was in adventure strips, from sword-and-sorcery to the undersea *Sea Devils* to war. His main contribution to Weird War genre is the **Haunted Tank** strip in *G.I. Combat*.

Hellboy [Comic book character; Film; WW]

1. First appearance: *San Diego Comic-Con Comics* #2 (August 1993); Creator: Mike Mignola; Publisher: Dark Horse Comics.

The demon Hellboy wasn't born but was summoned from Hell by Nazi occultists on December 23, 1944. Although a demon, Hellboy hates the Nazis and actively works against evil forces as a paranormal investigator for the Bureau of Paranormal Research (BRPD).

2. Premiere: April 2, 2004; Main Cast: Ron Perlman as Hellboy, John Hurt as Professor Trevor "Broom" Bruttenholm, Selma Blair as Liz Sherman, Rupert Evans as John Myers, Jeffrey Tambor as Tom Manning, Karel Roden as Grigori Rasputin, Bridget Hodson as Ilsa Haupstein; Doug Jones as Abe Sapien; Executive Producer: Patrick Palmer; Story: Guillermo del Toro, Peter Briggs. Based on the comic book characters created by Mike Mignola; Director: Guillermo del Toro; 122 min.; Dark Horse Entertainment, Starlite Films, Lawrence Gordon Productions, Revolution Studios; Columbia Pictures; Color.

As World War II reaches its conclusion Nazis turn to the occult to defeat the enemy. The demon Hellboy is summoned but is taken by the Allies when they raid the Nazi ritual. Raised by Professor Bruttenholm, Hellboy grows to maturity and joins the Bureau of Paranormal Research where he attempts to rid the world of evil.

See: ***BRPD: 1946***

Hellboy: The Science of Evil [Videogame; WW]

Release date: August 15, 2008; Platforms: PlayStation 3, Xbox 360; Developer: Krome Studios; Publisher: Konami Digital Entertainment.

Hellboy travels through six different settings in his efforts to track down insane Nazi Hermann Von Klempt, clockwork Nazis, cyborg Nazis and zombie Nazis.

Hellsing [Manga: Japan; WW]

First publication: *Young King OURs*, 1997; Creator: Kouta Hirano; Publisher: Shonen Gahosha.

The Hellsing Organization is a British Task Force led by Integra Fairbrook Wingates Hellsing who inherited her role following the death of her father when she was a child. The organization was founded to continue the work of Dr. Abraham Van Helsing who with the help of companions defeated Count Dracula. Members consist of powerful vampire Alucard who now hunts his fellow vampires, Hellsing family butler Walter C. Dornez and former police woman turned vampire Seras Victoria.

Now there is a new threat in the form of neo–

Hellsing: The Dawn [Japan; WW]

1. Manga.

First publication: *Young King OURs*, 2001; Creator: Kouta Hirano; Publisher: Shonen Gahosha.

Set in Nazi-occupied Poland in 1944. Hellsing agent and vampire Alucard is flown to Poland along with the fourteen-year-old Hellsing family butler Walter C. Dornez with a mission to stop the creation of a Nazi vampire army.

2. Animated series.

Air date: July 27, 2011 (Japan); Voice Cast: Jun'ichi Suwabe as Hugh Islands, Nakata Jouji as Alucard, Daisuke Namikawa as Arthur Hellsing, Hiroshi Naka as Doc, Nobuo Tobita as Max Montana, Romi Park as Walter C. Dornez, Nobuo Tobita as The Major; Creator: Kouta Hirano; 3 × 10 min.; Madhouse, Satelight; Color.

Season One: 1:01—*The Dawn: A Supplementary to Hellsing I*; 1:02—*The Dawn: A Supplementary to Hellsing II*; 1:03—*The Dawn: A Supplementary to Hellsing III*

Hellsing Ultimate (2006) [Original video animation; Japan; WW]

Air date: February 10, 2006 (Japan); Voice Cast [U.S.]: K. T. Gray as Seras Victoria, Crispin Freeman as Alucard, Victoria Harwood as Sir Integra Fairbrook Wingates Hellsing, Ralph Lister as Walter C. Dornez, Doug Stones as Sir Hugh Islands, Gildart Jackson as The Major/SS Sturmbannfuhrer Montana Max, J. B. Blanc as Enrico Maxwell, Marcelo Tubert as Doc; Executive Producer: Gen Fukunaga; Screenplay: Hideyuki Kurata, Yousuke Kuroda; Directors: Hiroyuki Tanaka, Tomokazu Tokoro; 10 × 50 min.; Madhouse, Satelight, Studio RF, Inc., Graphicana; Color.

England is plunged into war as Major attacks London with a battalion of 1,000 SS vampires.

Season One: 1:01—*Hellsing I*; 1:02—*Hellsing II*; 1:03—*Hellsing III*; 1:04—*Hellsing IV*; 1:05—*Hellsing V*; 1:06—*Hellsing VI*; 1:07—*Hellsing VII*; 1:08—*Hellsing VIII*; 1:09—*Hellsing IX*; 1:10—*Hellsing X*

Henry Hamilton, Graduate Ghost [Juvenile book; Telefilm; WW]

1. Author: Marilyn Redmond; First publication: Gretna, LA: Pelican, 1982.

Henry Hamilton, a casualty of the Civil War and summa cum laude graduate of Spiritual Specter University eagerly awaits his first ghost assignment. But a computer error has placed him in a modern suburban house occupied by absentminded professor Jean-Paul Landry, his wife and twelve noisy children. Now Henry has the unenviable task of haunting the family.

2. Air date: December 8, 1984; Main Cast: John Lawlor as Paul Landry, Belinda Balaski as Margaret Landry, Steve Nevil as Henry Hamilton, Elizabeth Lyn Fraser as Pam Landry, Christian Jacobs as Kurt Landry, Marissa Mendenhall as Therese Landry, Stu Gilliam as George Sherman, Phyllis Applegate as Evelyn Sherman, Larry Gelman as Curly, Rhonda Bates as Sergeant Broussard, Ronnie Schell as Mr. Shugart, Bill Erwin as Specter Inspector, Johnny Silver as Leon, Ben Kronen as Mr. Scoggins; Executive Producers: Norman Brooks, Fern Field; Teleplay: Jim Carlson, Terrence McDonnell; Based on the book by Marilyn Redmond; Director: Noam Pitlik; 45 min.; Brookfield Productions; American Broadcasting Company (ABC); Color.

This adaptation of Marilyn Redmond's book was broadcast as a segment of the *ABC Weekend Specials* TV series (8:01).

Henry Hamilton in Outer Space [Juvenile book; WW]

Author: Marilyn Redmond; First publication: Gretna, LA: Pelican, 1991.

Civil War ghost Henry Hamilton stows away on the Space Shuttle and haunts the astronauts aboard.

"Henry Horn's Blitz Bomb" [Pulp fiction; SFW]

Author: Dwight V. Swain; First publication: *Amazing Stories* (Vol. 16 #6; June 1942); Publisher: Ziff-Davis Publishing Company.

"Just think how much it would mean to us if our side had the most powerful bomb in the world!"

Professor Joseph Paulsen has retired to a peaceful life raising guinea-pigs. But his companion Henry Horn can't stop himself from inventing. And now Japanese spies have learnt of his latest invention—a super-bomb!

Here and Then [Juvenile book; WW]

Author: George Ella Lyon; First publication: New York: Orchard Books, 1994.

Twelve-year-old Abby maintains a journal for a Civil War nurse named Eliza Hoskins. Abby is portraying Eliza in a reenactment at Camp Robinson, Kentucky. But Abby realizes her hand is being guided in her journal by the "Angel of Camp Robinson" when Eliza asks for blankets and medical supplies for wounded soldiers. Abby is able to deliver the supplies in person when she finds herself back in time in 1861.

Hero [Juvenile book; WW]

Author: Josephine Poole; First publication: London: Hodder Children's, 1997.

When Florry moves to a house in the country with her parents she misses the city life and her friends. But a meeting with the ghost of a World War II pilot gives her life new meaning. Bo has set her a mission so he can finally find peace and move on. But Florry fears losing him if she succeeds.

"Heroes Die Hard" [Pulp fiction; WW]

Author: Henry Gade; First publication: *Fantastic Adventures* (Vol. 5 #10; December 1943); Publisher: Ziff-Davis Publishing Company.

"The Coast Guard cutter *Wallace* had been reported sunk by enemy action. How, then, was she able to aid a sister ship?"

When the *Bertram* comes under attack from a U-boat the *Wallace* intercepts but cannot save the ship from sinking. Captain Wells Arthur is rescued by former *Wallace* Captain Jim Howard. But when Arthur stares at the mirror he sees no reflection of either of them. "Just an empty bunk where he was supposed to be lying."

Heroes vs. Hitler [Comic book; SHW]

"THE APOCALYPSE STONE"

First publication: Summer 2000; Story: Roy Thomas, Bill Schelly; Art: Bill Schelly, Bill Black; Publisher: Hamster Press.

Dr. Weird sends a group of super-heroes back in time to World War II to retrieve the Star of Atlantis. The jewel is sought by Adolf Hitler and Dr. Franz Gruber for its destructive powers that can enable the Nazi domination of the world.

Highlander (1992) [TV series; Canada-France]

Immortal Duncan MacLeod is pursued across time by rival Immortals attempting to destroy him. Main Cast: Adrian Paul as Duncan MacLeod, Elizabeth Gracen as Amanda Darieux, Stan Kirsch as Richard "Richie" Ryan, Jim Byrnes as Joe Dawson, Peter Wingfield as Adam Pierson-Methos; Executive Producers: Christian Charret, Peter S. Davis. Marla Ginsburg, William N. Panzer; 97 × 45 min.; David-Panzer Productions, Filmline International, Gaumont Television; Color.

"THE BLITZ" (4:12) [WW]

Air date: February 5, 1996; Guest Cast: Lisa Howard as Dr. Anne Lindsey, Beverley Elliott as Karen, Alison Moir as Dianne Terrin, Duncan Fraser as Fire Chief; Story: Morrie Ruvinsky; Director: Paolo Barzman.

The present day plight of Dr. Anne Lindsey who is trapped in a collapsed subway station while helping others echoes the predicament of Duncan MacLeod and his girlfriend Dianne Terrin during the blitz in World War II London.

"THE COLONEL" (4:07) [WW]

Air date: November 6, 1995; Guest Cast: Sean Allan as Colonel Simon Killian, Anthony Holland as The General, Sean Campbell as Sgt. Merton, Lisa Butler as Melissa; Producer: Ken Gord; Story: Durnford King; Director: Dennis Berry;

In 1918 France Colonel Simon Killian leads a charge after World War I is over, despite Duncan MacLeod's efforts to stop him. At a court-martial Killian is convicted but avoids execution thanks to MacLeod asking he be committed for life to a criminal asylum. But in the present day the Colonel seeks revenge and kidnaps MacLeod.

"FORGIVE US OUR TRESPASSES" (5:18) [WW]

Air date: May 5, 1997; Guest Cast: Chris Larkin as Steven Keane; Story" Dom Tordjmann; Director: Paolo Barzman.

Immortal Steven Keane seeks revenge on Duncan MacLeod for his role in the killing of the Redcoats at the Battle of Culloden in 1746.

"THE MESSENGER" (5:10) [WW]

Air date: November 26, 1996; Guest Cast: Ron Perlman as The Messenger, Robert Wisden as Col. William Everett Culbraith, Mitch Davies as Capt. Greenwell, Patrick T. Gorman as Sgt. Hickson; Story: David Tynan; Director: James Bruce.

Duncan MacLeod is reminded of the suffering he endured in Andersonville prison during the American Civil War when he comes face-to-face with the Immortal former commander of the prison.

"MORTAL SINS" (3:19) [WW]

Air date: May 8, 1995; Guest Cast: Lisa Howard as Dr. Anne Lindsey, Andrew Woodall as Ernst Daimler, Roger Bret as Father Bernard; Story: Lawrence Shore; Director: Mario Azzopardi.

Paris, 1943. Father Bernard sees Resistance leader Duncan MacLeod die after being shot while ambushing a Nazi courier. He also sees MacLeod return to life and is told the truth of the Immortals by MacLeod. In the present day Father Bernard sees a man he recognizes as a Nazi officer in World War II and realizes he is also an Immortal. He asks for MacLeod's help in putting a stop to his white supremacist group.

"Sins of the Father" (6:03) [WW]
Air date: October 19, 1997; Guest Cast: Ian Richardson as Max Leiner, Dara Tomanovich as Alex Raven, Aaron Swartz as David Leiner. Dean Cook as Young Max Leiner, Charles Daish as Grant Thomas, John Scarborough as George Thomas, Jay Simon as Cameron, Joe Searby as Gerald LeBlanc; Story: James Thorpe; Director: Dennis Berry.

Immortal Alex Raven attempts to make reparation for the murder of her Jewish lover by Nazis by helping his son. But in the process Raven makes matters worse by murdering one of Duncan MacLeod's friends.

"Through a Glass Darkly" (4:18) [WW]
Air Date: May 6, 1996; Guest Cast: Dougray Scott as Warren Goddard/Cochrane, Gresby Nash as Andrew Donnelly, Struan Rodger as Bonnie Prince Charlie; Story: Alan Swayze; Director: Dennis Berry.

Duncan MacLeod is viewed as a traitor by fellow Immortal Warren Cochrane for abandoning Bonnie Prince Charlie in his fight to capture the English throne.

"The Valkyrie" (5:11) [WW]
Air date: January 27, 1997; Guest Cast: Musetta Vander as Ingrid Henning, Martin Evans as Colonel Stauffenburg, L. Harbey Gold as Igor Stefanovich, Patrick Keating as Adolf Hitler, Fulvio Cecere as Alan Wilkinson, Dean Balkwill as German Dissident, Peter Hanlon as Karl Brandt, Jan Triska as Nicolae Breslaw; Story: James Thorpe; Director: Richard Martin.

After failing to kill Adolf Hitler Immortal Ingrid Henning has a mission to assassinate any dictator before they come to power. But Duncan MacLeod stands in her way.

Highlander: The Raven (1998) [Canada-France; TV series]

Highlander spin-off series featuring former cop Nick Wolfe and Immortal Amanda Darieux as they join forces to fight evil Immortals and criminals. Main Cast: Elizabeth Gracen as Amanda Darieux, Paul Johansson as Nick Wolfe, Patricia Gage as Lucy Becker; Executive Producers: Christian Charnet, Peter S. Davis, Marla Ginsburg, William N. Panzer; 22 × 45 min.; Chum Television, Davis-Panser Productions, Gaumont Television, Fireworks Entertainment, Pro 7, M6 Metropole Television; Rysher Entertainment; Color.

"The Unknown Soldier" (1:08) [WW]
Air date: November 14, 1998; Guest Cast: Robert Bockstael as Donald Magus, Walker Boone as Detective Chapman, Michael Copeman as Carl Magnus, Michael Rhoades as John Fielding; Reg Dreger as Col. Benson; Story: James Thorpe; Director: George Mendeluk.

While investigating the death of Carl Magnus Nick Wolfe uncovers clues that lead to Immortal soldier John Fielding, who knew Amanda in World War I and Carl's father Donald Magnus in the Gulf War. The Immortal who killed Carl Magnus is now after Amanda for her role in the deaths of 120 servicemen.

"War and Peace" (1:21) [WW]
Air date: May 15, 1999; Guest Cast: Robert Cavanah as Father Liam Riley, Benedict Bates as Sean, Josephine Butler as Lizzie Tynan, Janet Spencer-Turner as Emma; Story: Catherine Porciuncula; Director: Brian Grant.

An Immortal vows revenge on fellow Immortal Father Liam Riley for the death of his mother in the American War of Independence in 1776.

Highway to Heaven (1984) [TV series]

A probationary angel and a disillusioned former policeman team up to help people in emotional distress. Main Cast: Michael Landon as Jonathan Smith, Victor French as Mark Gordon; Creator-Executive Producer: Michael Landon; Producer: Kent McCray; 111 × 50 min.; Michael Landon Productions; National Broadcasting Company (NBC); Color.

"Another Kind of War, Another Kind of Peace" (3:04) [WW]
Air date: October 15, 1986; Guest Cast: Ernest Borgnine as Guido Liggo, Haunani Minn as Lan Nguyen, Ernie Reyes, Jr., as Michael Nguyen, Conroy Gedeon as Knispel; Story–Director: Dan Gordon.

The father of a son killed in Vietnam has difficulty accepting his late son's relationship with a

Vietnamese woman that resulted in a child. He accepts them into his home but doesn't accept them as family. Jonathan and Mark must intervene.

"Choices" (5:09) [WW]

Air date: June 30, 1989; Guest Cast: Dante Basco as Champ Hopkins, Jusak Bernhard as Dinh "Dinny" Hopkins, Arthur Rosenberg as Howard Hopkins, Michele Marsh as Barbara Hopkins, Haing S. Ngor as Truong Vann Diep, Lang Yuan as Truong Lan Minh; Story: Parke Perine; Director: Michael Landon.

Jonathan and Mark, acting as private investigators, are approached by a Vietnamese couple who were forced to give up their two sons for adoption when they were interred in a Vietnamese death camp. Now, ten years later they have escaped their prison and want to be reunited with their sons. The two young men want to stay in America with their adopted parents, but a promise the older son made to his birth father must be honored.

"Dust Child" (1:11) [WW]

Air date: November 28, 1984; Guest Cast: James Whitmore, Jr., as Richard Gaines, Jenny Sullivan as Susan Gaines, Billy Jacoby as Brad Gaines, Denice Kumagi as Nguyen; Story: Paul W. Cooper; Director: Victor French.

On duty in Saigon, Vietnam, soldier Richard Gaines lives with a Vietnamese woman. They have a daughter, Nguyen. Now years later in America Gaines has married and has a son. When news arrives that Nguyen is coming to live with her father in America the son is emotionally confused. On her arrival Nguyen encounters such hate and prejudice Jonathan is given the task of healing the wounds.

"Hello and Farewell" Parts 1 & 2 (5:01–5:02) [WW]

Air date: December 7, 1988; Guest Cast: David Ackroyd as Commander Matthew Rogers, H. Richard Greene as Sgt. Major Travis Hastings, Shelby Leverington as Annie Hastings, Matthew Perry as David Hastings, Christina Raines-Crowe as Commander Kimberly Michaels; Story: Vince R. Gutierrez; Director: Michael Landon.

An adopted teenage boy entering pilot training learns his mother, who was a nurse in Vietnam, now suffers from Post Traumatic Stress Disorder.

"The Hero" (3:20) [WW]

Air date: February 18, 1987; Guest Cast: James Stacy as Joe Mason, Anne Curry as Kathy Mason, Whitney Rydbeck as Dr. Bonner, Daniel Ziskie as Mel Turner, Joe Unger as Patrick Daley; Story–Director: Michael Landon.

A struggling, disabled veteran discovers the realities of civilian life when his veteran benefits don't include dental work he can't afford.

"The Squeaky Wheel" (5:07) [WW]

Air date: June 16, 1989; Guest Cast: Deborah Benson as Patty Secrest, David Hall as Wayne Secrest, John Milford as Mr. Thatcher; Story: Paul W. Cooper; Director: Michael Landon.

A disabled war veteran has lost both his legs and sense of value to society until Jonathan and Mark make him realize his true worth.

"To Bind the Wounds" (2:18) [WW]

Air date: February 19, 1986; Guest Cast: Eli Wallach as Tim Charles, Meg Wyllie as Miss Foley, Moosie Drier as Tim Charles, Jr., Tony Monaco as Frank Barker, Dennis Redfield as Ted Barker, Richard Muenz as Gary Lee; Story: Dan Gordon; Director: Michael Landon.

Attempts by a father to commemorate his son, who was killed in action in Vietnam, are greeted by indifference. Jonathan and Mark help the community appreciate the sacrifice of the young soldier by recalling how his life affected people.

"The Torch" (2:21) [WW]

Air date: March 12, 1986; Guest Cast: Herschel Bernardi as Everett Solomon, David Kaufman as Joseph Solomon, Mary Ann Chinn as May Baldt, Paul Koslo as John Baldt, Paul-Mark Gosselaar as Rolf Baldt; Story: Lan O'Kun; Director: Michael Landon.

Concentration camp survivor Everett Solomon meets hostile opposition from a local Neo-Nazi group who deny the truth of the Holocaust. Soon the hostility turns to tragedy when Solomon's son David is murdered by Neo-Nazis.

"His Last Appearance" [Pulp fiction; WW]

Author: H. Bedford Jones; First publication: *Weird Tales* (Vol. 36 #12; July 1943); Publisher: Weird Tales.

Six months after the end of the war its ghosts return to a mid–Pacific reef to fight off a Japanese attack. Their renewed sacrifice prompts Rock Gordon to ask for a shipment of Oregon soil to put around their graves. When his request his met with disdain and he is told there is no necessity Gordon responds. "That's the trouble with people like you, from Congress down. When a man's dead there's no necessity of anything. Well I want those two boys reburied in Oregon earth; I want a ton of it brought here and the job done properly, and I'll pay all expenses."

> What makes this country you revere?
> Not trees and earth and citied roar
> And ways of life—but something more;
> Voices that rise from afar and near,
> Voices of those who went before
> And gave their lives by field and shore.

His Majesty's Dragon: A Novel of Temeraire [Novel; WW]

Author: Naomi Novik; First publication: New York: Del Rey Books, 2006.

During the Napoleonic Wars Captain Will Laurence of the HMS Reliant captures a French man-o'-war frigate. The cargo includes a valuable unhatched dragon egg. Captain Laurence finds his future course changed forever when he forms a close bond with the dragon. Changing the sea for the air he joins Britain's dragon-riding Aerial Corps as captain of the dragon Temerairie. Soon he is fighting French dragon riding forces under the leadership of Napoleon Bonaparte as they plan to invade Britain.

This is the first book in the series that features the various adventures of Captain Will Laurence and his noble dragon Temeraire. Each novel continues the story of their fight against Napoleon's forces in Europe. Subsequent volumes include, *Throne of Jade*, *Black Powder War*, *Empire of Ivory*, *Victory of Eagles*, *Tongues of Serpents*, *Crucible of Gold* and *Blood of Tyrants*.

Hitler no Fukkatsu: Top Secret a.k.a. *Bionic Commando* [Videogame; Japan; SFW]

Release date: 1987; Original System: NES; Designers: Hotaru B. Terukun, Junchan, Gamereon, Haihoo K.; Director: Tokuro Fujiwara; Developer-Publisher: Famicom (Japan) Capcom (U.S.).

The player is a bionic soldier whose mission is to stop the Nazi onslaught and the re-animation of Adolf Hitler. The U.S. version replaced Hitler with Master-D and removed all references to Nazis.

Home Again [Novel; WW]

Author: Lenora Nazworth; First publication: New York: Dorchester, 1997.

Jody Calhoun wants to restore the Victorian mansion Spence House but wealthy developer Chase Spence wants to demolish it. When Jody puts herself between the wrecking ball and her beloved mansion she suddenly finds herself thrown back in time to the Civil War. Chase Spence is now her long-lost lover in the past and both have a mission to help a restless ghost find peace.

Horrors of War (2006) [Film; SFW]

Premiere: March 4, 2006; Main Cast: Jon Osbeck as Lt. John Schmidt, Joe Lorenzo as Capt. Joe Russo, Daniel Alan Kiely as Sgt. Stephen Gary, C. Alec Rossel as Capt. Mitchell/Super Soldier; Executive Producer: Tony Kandah; Screenplay: Peter John Ross, John Whitney, Philip R. Garrett, Scott Spears; Directors: Peter John Ross, John Whitney; 99 min.; Sonnyboo Productions, Hollywood Wizard, Arbor Avenue Films; Maverick Entertainment; Color.

The Office of Strategic Services (O.S.S.) aims to discover the source of horrific weapons being used against U.S. forces in Germany. When U.S. soldiers go behind enemy lines they come face-to-face with Hitler's weapon—the super soldier.

The Hotspur [Comic book; UK]

A weekly British publication, aimed at schoolboys, featuring illustrated text stories and comic strips.

"The Destroyer Leads 'Q' Squadron" [SFW]

First publication: #411 (July 12, 1941); 3-page illustrated text story; Publisher: D.C. Thomson.

The "Q" Squadron, led by Captain Dan Blade, fights the Nazis in the skies above the Greek island of Dandros.

"A plane, the type of which the two officers had never seen before, flashed out of the sun at lightning speed. On its gleaming metal body were the British roundels. From its nose protruded a long, sharp ram. Its wings curved to space-like points. Rockets flamed from its tail.

"Straight at the dive-bombers flew the eleventh-hour savior. The leading Junkers swerved too late. The Destroyer, wonder machine of the R.A.F., struck it fair and square with its ram…. The pilot tried to escape, but the Destroyer whipped in, and the ram ripped the bottom out of the Nazi plane."

House (1986) [Film; WW]

Premiere: February 28, 1986; Main Cast: William Katt as Roger Cobb, George Wendt as Harold Gorton, Richard Moll as Big Ben, Kay Lenz as Sandy Sinclair; Executive Producer: Roger Corman; Screenplay: Ethan Wiley; Story: Fred Dekker; Director:

Steve Miner; 93 min.; Sean S. Cunningham Films; New World Pictures; Color.

Author Roger Cobb's experiences as a soldier in Vietnam come back to haunt him in a house that preys on his fears.

The House of Dies Drear [Juvenile book; WW]

Author: Virginia Hamilton; Illustrator: Eros Keith; First publication: New York: Macmillan, 1968.

Thirteen-year-old Thomas is thrilled when his African American family move to a spacious old house in Ohio, with secret tunnels and a connection to the Civil War and the Underground Railroad. Rumors of it being haunted by abolitionist Dies Drear and the two slaves he was hiding add to the air of mystery surrounding the property.

The Human Torch [Comic book character; SFW]

First appearance: *Marvel Comics* #1 (November 1939); Creator: **Carl Burgos**; Publisher: Timely Publications.

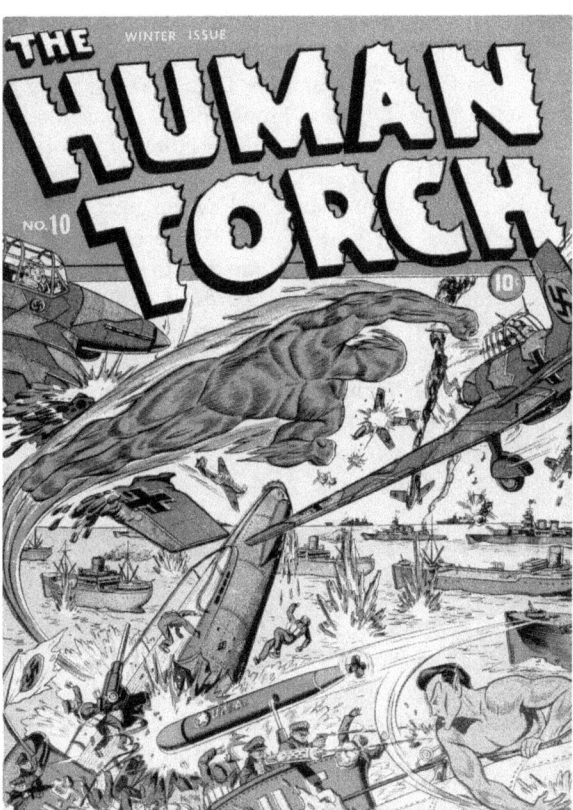

The Human Torch #10 (Winter 1942). Cover art by Alex Schomburg. Published by Timely Comics.

Professor Phineas T. Horton introduces his new creation enclosed in an air-tight glass case, "a synthetic man, an exact replica of a human being.... I call him the Human Torch!" But Horton's creation has one major flaw. "Every time the robot contacts oxygen in the air, he bursts into flame!" An attempt to bury the Human Torch in a steel tube entombed in concrete fails and during his escape a traumatized Human Torch accidentally kills his creator as he struggles to come to terms with his body of fire.

Gradually the Human Torch learns how to control his flames, throw fireballs at his enemies and fly through the air. Adopting a young orphaned sidekick named Toro, who is conveniently immune to his flames, the Human Torch encounters the half human, half-Atlantean **Sub-Mariner** in an epic battle. Soon they forget about their mutual hostility and form an alliance to stop the Japanese and Nazis from completing a tunnel between Siberia and Alaska in *Marvel Mystery* #17 (March 1941).

The Human Torch lost his appeal for readers following the war years with his *Marvel Mystery* strip folding in March 1949. A brief revival in *Young Men* #24 (December 1953) failed to re-ignite interest and in September 1954 the Human Torch made his final bow. He was revived in name only in **Fantastic Four** #1 (November 1961).

The Hunter from the Woods [Short story anthology; WW]

Author: Robert R. McCammon; Illustrator: Vincent Chong; First publication: Burton, MI: Subterranean Press, 2011.

A collection of three short stories and three novellas featuring World War II secret agent and werewolf Michael Gallatin. *The Great White Way*; *The Man From London*; *Sea Chase*; *The Wolf and the Eagle*; *The Room at the Bottom of the Stairs*; *Death of a Hunter*.

From his early life in Russia and recruitment into the British Secret Service to fighting in North Africa and the North Atlantic and a tragic love affair set in the embattled city of Berlin.

See: *The Wolf's Hour*

I Accuse! (1938) [Film; France; WW]

Premiere: January 22, 1938 (France); Main Cast: Victor Francen as Jean Diaz, Lino Noro as

Edith Laurin, Marie Lou as Flo, Marcel Delaitre as Francois Laurin, Jean-Max as Henri Chimay; Producer: Abel Gance; Story-Adaptation: Abel Gance, Steve Passeur; Director: Abel Gance; 104 min; Forrester-Parant Productions; Olive Films; B/W.

Director Abel Gance builds upon the story he first explored in *J'Accuse!* (1919). Jean Diaz renounces war following his traumatic experiences in the trenches of World War I. But now a new war is looming in Europe and once again he summons the spirits of dead soldiers to protest.

I Am Legion [Comic book; WW]

First publication: June 2004; Story: Fabien Nury; Art: John Cassady; Publisher: Les Humanoides Associes, Humanoid Publishing, DC Comics, Devil's Due Productions.

Originally published in France in three volumes between 2004 and 2007, the story takes place during World War II. Romanian resistance fighter Karel Rick plans to assassinate the Nazi officer in charge of "Project: Legion." Nazis want to harness the powers of a 10-year old vampire named Ana. Meanwhile British investigator Stanley Pilgrim uncovers government cover-ups and conspiracies while assigned to a homicide case.

The Iliad [Epic poem; MWW]

This ancient Greek epic poem centered around the Trojan War is attributed to Homer. In its present form the Iliad is dated 760–710 BC, but the oral tradition dates back further and the original pre–Homeric sources of the material are lost in time. It is known to have been recited at the Athenian festival of the Panathenaea in the 6th century B.C. The Alexandrians are responsible for dividing the poems into books.

The prelude to the Trojan War involves Alexander (Paris), son of Priam the King of Troy. When Alexander visits Menelaos, the King of Sparta, he captures the king's wife Helen and takes her back to Troy. The Achaean (Greek) leader Agamemnon, son of Menelaos, goes to war against the Trojans to recover Helen. The siege to Troy has lasted ten years. The goddess of wisdom Athena, the wife of Zeus Hera and sea-god Poseidon aid the Achaeans, while sun-god Apollo, war god Ares and Aphrodite, the mother of Aeneas, favors the Trojans.

Homer's Iliad begins shortly after Agamemnon has claimed the beautiful Chryseis for his own. His refusal to hand her back to her father Chryses, chief priest to the god Apollo, results in Apollo responding to Chryses' prayer to send a plague on the Achaeans. Agamemnon decides to return Chryseis to her father to pacify Apollo, but takes Achilles' concubine Briseis as recompense. An indignant Achilles reacts by laying down arms and refusing to fight in the war.

A reluctant Achilles finally reconciles with Agamemnon when the Trojan Hector kills Patroclus, the warrior and friend who Achilles agreed to replace him in battle. Achilles re-enters the war wearing armor forged by the god Hephaestus and with the help of goddess Athena, slays Hector outside the walls of Troy. After Achilles ties Hector's body to a chariot and drags it into the Achaean camp it remains unburied for eleven days. Achilles agrees to a ransom from Hector's father Priam to return the body to the Trojans where Hector receives a hero's funeral.

Homer tells the post-war story of the Achaean warrior Odysseus (Ulysses), and his ten-year journey returning to Ithaca, in *The Odyssey*.

Ilium [Novel; SFW]

Author: Dan Simmons; First publication: New York: Eos, 2003.

On the planet Mars, the Trojan War is raging at the foot of Olympos Mons, under the guidance of the Greek gods. 20th century Homeric scholar Thomas Hockenberry and other scholars from Earth have been resurrected by the gods to observe the war and note any differences with Homer's account in the *Iliad*. But to his surprise Homer has recorded the words of Achilles and Hector and the other players in the Trojan War with exact accuracy. Meanwhile semi-organic artificial intelligence from Jupiter, known as the moravecs, have been sent to Mars following a disturbance in quantum activity.

See: **Olympos**

"I'll See You Again" [Pulp fiction; SFW]

Author: Duncan Farnsworth; Illustration: Robert Fuqua; First publication: *Amazing Stories* (Vol. 18 #4; September 1944); Publisher: Ziff-Davis Publishing Company.

"No matter what waited over Berlin he promised to come back to her in the springtime, and he did. How is it that he had returned she cared not. The one, important, tinglingly ecstatic thing was he was here. Her face was against the tunic of his uniform, and the silver of his wings was cold against her cheek."

But their reunion would be brief and she would later learn, out of time.

The Illuminatus! Trilogy [Novel; WW]

Authors: Robert Shea, Robert Anton Wilson; First publication (as three separate titles—*The Eye in the Pyramid*; *The Golden Apple*; *Leviathan*): New York: Dell Publishing Co., 1975.

The world is on the brink on nuclear extinction and the institutions mankind has come to trust are not what they seem. Behind these institutions and history itself there is an overreaching power at work. That power is the Illuminati. But is there any real truth to anything? Joe Malik aims to find out.

The multiple-layered surreal trilogy includes a reference to the Nazis. An evil rock band wants to release an all-powerful eternal life energy to, among other characters of doubtful moral integrity, Adolf Hitler. But the energy can only be released through mass human sacrifice. The band members choose Woodstock as the venue, with re-animated Nazi battalions from the bottom of Lake Totenkopf providing the mass slaughter. But the giant goddess Eris has other ideas.

Impact [Comic book]

Anthology title

"Master Race" [WW]

First publication: #1 (April 1955); Art: Bernie Krigstein; Publisher: Entertaining Comics (EC).

Holocaust survivor Carl Reissman is still haunted by memories of his incarceration in Belsen concentration camp. One day while traveling on the subway he sees a man dressed in black. Reissman recognizes him as the same guard who, at the end of World War II vowed, "I'll get you Riessman—if it's the last thing I do."

Now he is seated on the same train. Reissman runs for his life, pursued by the man in black. Reissman runs to the point of exhaustion, before slipping into the path of an oncoming train. The man in black tells everyone the man committed suicide and denies ever seeing him before. "He was a perfect stranger." A case of psychological fear or a former Nazi Belsen death camp guard finally getting his man?

In the Electric Mist with the Confederate Dead [Novel; WW]

Author: James Lee Burke; Publisher: London: Phoenix, 1993.

While tracking a vicious prostitute killer Cajun Detective Dave Robicheaux tries to link the murder to New Orleans mobster "Baby Feet" Balboni who happens to be co-producing a Civil War movie being filmed in New Iberia. When movie star Elrod Sykes talks about a corpse he recently found in local swampland Robicheaux is reminded of the guilt he felt 35 years ago when he witnessed the murder of a chained black man in the marsh and failed to report it. Now Robicheaux is more motivated than ever to connect Balboni to the murders from the past and those in the present. Robicheaux finds himself suffering visions of the Confederate dead and talking to the ghost of General John Bell Hood of the Confederacy as his investigations take on added dimensions.

In the Shadow of Blackbirds [Juvenile book; WW]

Author: Cat Winters; First publication: New York: Abrams; Amulet Books, 2013.

In 1918 San Diego, 16-year-old Mary Shelley Black witnesses grieving relatives of loved ones lost in the Great War or to the deadly outbreak of Spanish influenza, as they try to find comfort in séances and spirit photographers. Her skepticism about the booming business of Spiritualism is tempered when she encounters a ghost after suffering none life threatening electrocution. It is the troubled spirit of her first love, Stephen. She was told he died a heroic death in the trenches, but he tells Mary a different story. "Birdmen" tortured and killed him. His spirit can only find peace when Mary has discovered the truth behind his mysterious death.

In Time of War (*Alex Balfour* book #4) [Novel; SFW]

Author; Allen Appel; First publication: New York: Carroll & Graf, 2003.

Historian and time-traveler Alex Balfour journeys back to the American Civil War in the hope of changing his personal past and future. Balfour's girlfriend Molly Glenn died in his arms in his previous time travel adventure, *Till the End of Time*. Now he finds himself seriously injured on a Civil War battlefield, after witnessing the murder of another soldier. Balfour recuperates in a Washington hospital where he meets Ambrose Bierce and Walt Whitman. Balfour's pregnant, journalist girlfriend, Molly, has also been transported back in time, working as a seer in a brothel. His main desire is to reunite with Molly and bring her back safely with him to the present. But there is also a little matter of an overheard conversation of John Wilkes Booth and an impending assassination of President Lincoln to deal with. Plus finding the truth behind a cold-blooded murder he personally witnessed.

See: *Till the End of Time*

In War Times [Novel; AHW]

Author: Kathleen Ann Goonan; First publication: New York: Tor, 2007.

December 1941. U.S. soldier Sam Dance has a talent for science and the saxophone. While studying physics Sam is seduced by his female instructor Dr. Eliani Hadntz, who also happens to be working on a revolutionary device that she claims will end mankind's desire for war. The following day Sam's elder brother is killed at Pearl Harbor. As the war takes Sam to Europe Sam is determined to construct Eliani's strange device from her plans. Can the machine end war for all time? Sam discovers a connection between jazz music and physics that leads to unusual and unforeseen consequences.

The Incredible Mr. Limpet (1964) [Film; WW]

Premiere: May 28, 1964; Main Cast: Don Knotts as Henry Limpet, Carole Cook as Bessie Limpet, Jack Weston as George Stickle, Andrew Duggan as Harlock, Larry Keating as Admiral P.P. Spewter, Oscar Beregi as Nazi Admiral; Producer: John C. Rose; Screenplay: Jameson Brewer, John C. Rose. Adapted by Joe DiMona from the novel by Theodore Pratt; Director: Arthur Lubin; 99 min.; Warner Bros.; Color.

When bookish Henry Limpet fails his medical to join the U.S. Navy in 1941 he dreams of becoming a fish. Miraculously his dream comes true at Coney Island when he falls in the water and turns into a talking fish with pince-nez spectacles. He is then commissioned by the Navy to locate German U-boats. This light-hearted World War II comedy musical includes animation sequences directed by Bill Tytla, Robert McKimson, Hawley Pratt and Gerry Chiniquy.

See: *Mr. Limpet*

Indiana Jones and the Emperor's Tomb [Videogame; WW]

Release Date: February 17, 2003; Voice Cast: David Esch as Indiana Jones, Vivian Wu as Mei Ying, Keone Young as Marshall Kai/Ch'in Shi-Huang-Ti, Nick Jameson as Von Beck, Kai Wulff as Richter, Matt Lindquist as Kent, Alan Drevin as Wu Han, Kevin Michaela Richardson as Homonculus/Triad Ghoul; Producer: Rick Watters; Story: Brad Santos; Single-player; Original platform: Xbox; Developer: The Collective; Publisher: LucasArts.

A mythical black pearl known as "Heart of the Dragon" grants the owner magical power. Indiana Jones is sent on a mission by Marshall Kai Ti Chan to retrieve the pearl buried in the lost tomb

The Incredible Mr. Limpet (1964), starring Don Knotts as Henry Limpet, Carole Cook as Bessie Limpet, Andrew Duggan as Harlock, Jack Weston as George Stickle, and Larry Keating as Admiral P.P. Spewter (Warner Bros.).

of Qin Shi Huangdi, the first Emperor of China. Pieces of the "Mirror of Dreams" scattered in different locations reveal the whereabouts of the tomb. Jones finds himself in competition with Nazis and their allies the Black Dragon Triad. Betrayed by Kai, Jones disguises himself as a Nazi to reach the Black Dragon fortress where he fights demonic forces. Jones soon discovers the "Heart of the Dragon" has more power than he could ever imagine.

Indiana Jones and the Fate of Atlantis [Comic book; Videogame; WW]

1. First publication: March 1991; Story: William-Loebs, Dan Barry; Art: Dan Barry, Karl Kesel; Publisher: Dark Horse Comics.

2. Release Date: June 1992; Single-player; Original platforms: DOS, Microsoft Windows; Story-Design: Hal Barwood, Noah Falstein; Developer-Publisher: LucasArts.

On the eve of World War II Nazis seek to unleash the secret powers of Atlantis as they pursue Indiana Jones and his psychic assistant Sophia Hapgood in their search for the mythical sunken city.

The player controls Indiana Jones and his psychic colleague Sophia Hapgood as they unravel puzzles, encounter dangerous situations and attempt to vanquish the Reich. An enhanced "talkie" edition was released in May 1993.

Indiana Jones and the Iron Phoenix [Comic book; WW]

First publication: December 1994; 4-issue mini-series; Story: Lee Mars; Art: Leo Duranona; Publisher: Dark Horse Comics.

Post-war Nazis strive to revive the Third Reich in 1947 Berlin. The legendary Philosopher's Stone is said to resurrect the dead and turn lead into gold. Indiana Jones, Soviets and Nazis all seek the Stone, but first they must find the Key of Solomon, a scroll that details the location of the Philosopher's Stone.

Indiana Jones and the Last Crusade (1989) [Film; WW]

Premiere: May 24, 1989; Main Cast: Harrison Ford as Indiana Jones, Sean Connery as Professor Henry Jones, Denholm Elliott as Marcus Brody, Alison Doody as Elsa, River Phoenix as Young Indiana Jones, John Rhys-Davies as Sallah, Julian Glover as Walter Donovan; Executive Producers: George Lucas, Frank Marshall; Story: Menno Meyjes; Screenplay: Jeffrey Boam; Director: Steven Spielberg; 127 min.; Lucasfilm, Paramount Pictures; Color.

Archaeologist Indiana Jones and his father Henry encounter occultist Nazis in their search for the elusive Holy Grail.

Cinefantastique (Vol. 20 #1–2: November 1989) film critic Charles D. Leayman noted: "Christ's holy vessel becomes just one more notch on Indiana's list of cultural acquisitions, and even its healing use on the fatally wounded father seems oddly perfunctory. For all of Spielberg and Lucas' alleged interest in the work of mythologist Joseph Campbell, this most venerable of relics appears as little more than an inconveniently marketed commodity, and Indy's climactic 'leap of faith' a mere calculated bet."

Indiana Jones and the Last Crusade: The Graphic Adventure [Videogame; WW]

Release date: May 1989; Original platforms: DOS, Amiga, Atari ST; Designers: Ron Gilbert, Noah Falstein, David Fox; Developer-Publisher: Lucasfilm Games.

Loosely based on the film of the same name the videogame includes a meeting between Indiana Jones, his father and Adolf Hitler as they attempt to reclaim the Grail Diary.

Indiana Jones and the Spear of Destiny [Comic book; WW]

First publication: April 1995; 4-issue mini-series; Story: Elaine Lee; Art: Will Simpson; Publisher: Dark Horse Comics.

Ireland, 1945. The tip of the Spear of Destiny, which pierced the body of Jesus Christ, has been captured by the Nazis. Indiana and his father Dr. Henry Jones must stop the Nazis from finding the tree rooted from the original thorn and completing the shaft of the Spear.

Indiana Jones and the Staff of Kings [Videogame; WW]

Release date: June 2009; Platforms: Wii, PlayStation 2, Nintendo DS, PlayStation Portable; Developers: Artificial Mind and Movement, Amaze; Publisher: LucasArts.

Indiana Jones' search for the Staff of Moses, that parted the Red Sea, sees him clash with a group of Nazis and their leader Magnus Voller, who is after the same artifact. Along the way Indiana teams up with Irish photographer Maggie O'Mally who is a secret MI6 agent.

Insensible a.k.a. ***Painless*** (2012) [Film; Spain-France-Portugal; WW]
Premiere: September 8, 2012; Main Cast: Alex Brendemuhl as David, Tomas Lemarquis as Berkano, Derek de Lint as Dr. Holzmann, Ramon Fontsere as Dr. Carcedo, Ilias Stothart as Child Beningo, Mot Stothart as Adolescent Benigno; Executive Producers: Manuel Monzon, Isaac Torres; Story: Luiso Berdejo, Juan Carlos Medina; Director: Juan Carlos Medina; 100 min.; Les Films d'Antoine, Tobina Film, Fado Filmes; Color.

During the Spanish Civil War in 1931 Catalonia a group of children who feel no pain are subjected to medical testing. Dr. Holzmann and Dr. Carcedo have conflicting views on how to rehabilitate the children, in particular the gifted child named Benigno. When the hospital is taken over by the military all plans come to nothing.

In the present day David, requiring a bone marrow transplant to survive his lymphoma, learns he was adopted and sets out to find his biological parents. But he uncovers an unpleasant truth. His father was Benigno, the child who suffered no pain. Benigno was taken by the military as an adolescent and renamed Berkano. And now his father inflicts pain on others by torturing his victims.

Insurrection [Board-Miniatures game; WW]
First publication: 2009; Designer: Jim Bailey; Art: David Ausloos, Keith Lowe, Tears of Envy; Publisher: Grindhouse Games.

MI-13 British Commandos and the U.S. Lucky Seventh are in a race against time to shut down the Doomsday Device situated in a dangerous, convoluted labyrinth under Gibraltar. Standing in their way are the monstrous German SWD. A game for two players.

"The Interval" [Short story; WW]
Author: Vincent O'Sullivan; First publication: *The Boston Evening Transcript* (1917).

Mrs. Wilton longs to see and hear her husband again. A soldier who recently died serving in the colonies. But her visits to various "seers" results in silence, until she meets "a little, fat, weary-faced woman about fifty." When her husband Hugh appears to the woman, she tells Mrs. Wilton she will see him again.

Her words come to pass when Mrs. Wilton is mysteriously drawn to enter a church where she notices a man seated in a pew. It is Hugh. But the verger of the church tempers her enthusiasm in a condescending manner. "There's nobody here. Only you and me. Ladies are often taken funny since the war."

A couple of days later her husband appears again in a restaurant in the Bayswater district. Taking her seat at a table she is astonished to see Hugh seated opposite her. That is the final time anybody sees Mrs. Wilton. But her husband makes another appearance standing at the foot of her bed in his military uniform. He picks up her slippers as he departs the bedroom. When they discover Mrs. Wilton's dead body in her bed her slippers cannot be found.

Into the Storm (*Destroyermen*, Book 1) [Novel; AHW]
Author: Taylor Anderson; First publication: New York: Roc, 2008.

World War II destroyer U.S.S. Walker under the command of Lieutenant Commander Matthew Patrick Reddy, sails into a storm trying to evade the Japanese battleship Amagi. But when the ship and crew emerge from the storm they find themselves in an alternate reality where raptor dinosaurs have evolved into the savage Gliks, who are at war with the peace-loving cat-like Lemurians.

Book one of the *Destroyermen* trilogy.
See: ***Crusade***

"Intruders from the Stars" [Pulp fiction: SFW]
Author: Ross Rocklynne; First publication: *Amazing Stories* (Vol. 18 #1; January 1944); Publisher: Ziff-Davis Publishing Company.

So cruel was Bess-Istra's reign that her own world cast her out. Now an exile on Earth, she is thrust into World War II and the fight against Mussolini. Her skills result in the war coming to an end with Hitler defeated. But soon the enemy will come from within as "Earth lay helpless and supine before this lovely, evil woman from beyond the stars. Was there any way to defeat her?"

The Invaders [Comic book characters; SHW]
First appearance: *The Avengers* #71 (December 1969); Creators: Roy Thomas, Sal Buscema; Publisher: Marvel Comics.

Originally introduced in the pages of *The Avengers* comic book, *The Invaders* graduated to their own title beginning with *Giant-Size Invaders*

#1 (June 1975). The original team consisted of World War II versions of **Captain America** and Bucky Barnes, **Human Torch** and Toro and **Sub-Mariner**. They were later joined in their fight against the Axis powers by Union Jack, **Spitfire**, **Miss America**, **Whizzer**, the Blazing Skull and Silver Scorpion among others before the title folded with #41 (September 1979).

Following their reintroduction in *The Avengers* (vol. 3, # 82) in 2004 *The Invaders* returned for a revamped ten-issue run in *The New Invaders* (2004–2005). With the help of the unsuspecting **Thin Man** the new team is formed by the **Red Skull** under the guise of U.S. Secretary of Defense Dell Rusk. Team members include Captain America (John Walker), Blazing Skull (Mark Todd), Union Jack, Thin Man, Human Torch and the Red Skull's spy within the team, the flame throwing Tara.

In 2007 *The Invaders* returned for a third incarnation in a 12-issue ***Avengers/Invaders*** cross-over series that takes place in the present day. Captain America, Bucky, Human Torch, Toro and Sub-Mariner believe they are still fighting Nazis. Eventually, thanks to the Cosmic Cube, they are able to return to the past with an American soldier who traveled into the future with them. But the soldier alters history by saving his dead friends in the past and allowing the Cosmic Cube to be stolen by the Red Skull. *The Invaders* and The Avengers travel to the past only to find history changed. In order to deceive and defeat the Red Skull The Avengers adopt the personas of World War II super-heroes.

Invaders Now! was published in September 2010 as part of a mini-series featuring Captain America (Bucky Barnes), Human Torch, Toro, Sub-Mariner, Captain Steve Rogers and Spitfire. In World War II Arnim Zola creates a pathogen that results in mutated deformation in its victims and a superhuman rage that causes them to infect others. The Vision and Union Jack reassemble *The Invaders* to fight the disease that has mutated through to the present day.

In March 2014 *All-New Invaders* was published over 15-issues by Marvel. This time featuring Captain America, Winter Soldier, Human Torch, Namor the Sub-Mariner and Radiance, the Japanese grand-daughter of Golden Girl. One storyline involved Union Jack, Spitfire and **The Destroyer** fighting a Martian invasion of London in 1917.

See: *The Super Hero Squad Show*.

"Invasion Dust" [Pulp fiction; SFW]

Author: Don Wilcox; Illustrator: Julian Krupa; First publication: *Amazing Stories* (Vol. 18 #5; December 1944); Publisher: Ziff-Davis Publishing Company.

"A man made of iron couldn't have gotten that message through, but a man made of stone could! He wore a strange machine over his heart; this man who leaped from a plane on a D-Day mission."

Invisible Agent (1942) [Film; SFW]

Premiere: August 7, 1942; Main Cast: Jon Hall as Frank Raymond, Ilona Massey as Maria Sorenson, Peter Lorre as Baron Ikito, Cedric Hardwicke as Conrad Stauffer; Producer: Frank Lloyd; Story: Curt Siodmak, based on the H.G. Wells novel "The Invisible Man"; Director: Edwin L. Marin; 81

Invisible Agent (1942), starring (from left) Ilona Massey as Maria Sorenson, Jon Hall as Frank Raymond, Peter Lorre as Baron Ikito (Universal Pictures).

min.; Frank Lloyd Productions; Universal Pictures; B/W.

Frank Raymond, the grandson of the Invisible Man, has maintained a low profile, keeping the formula for invisibility secret. But the bombing of Pearl Harbor makes him realize the formula can be used for good and he agrees to become a spy behind enemy lines in Germany. He finds himself romancing a beautiful double agent as he makes fools of the Nazis with his invisible antics. But it all turns deadly serious when he learns of Hitler's secret plan to attack America.

The Iron Dream [Novel; AHW]

Author: Norman Spinrad; First publication: New York: Avon, 1972.

This alternate history novel-within-a-novel sees Adolf Hitler emigrate to the United States in 1919 after the end of World War I. He becomes a science fiction artist, editor and author, finding fame with his Hugo Award winning novel *Lord of the Swastika* in 1953.

Spinrad highlights Hitler's "pure race" philosophy in his novel where "the High Republic of Heldon" wants to maintain racial purity by killing all the mutants that have been corrupted by the radioactive fallout of a nuclear war. Even within an alternate history timeline Adolf Hitler's literature betrays his racist beliefs.

Iron Sky (2012) [Film; Finland; SFW]

Premiere: January 30, 2012; Main Cast: Udo Kier as Wolfgang Kortzfleisch, Julie Dietze as Renate Richter, Stephanie Paul as President of the United States, Peta Sergeant as Vivian Wagner; Executive Producers: Michael Cowan, San Fu Maltha, Sean O'Kelly, Jason Piette; Screenplay: Michael Kalesniko, Timo Vuorensola; Based on a story by Johanna Sinisalo and original concept by Jarmo Puskala; Director: Timo Vuorensola; 93 min.; 27 Films Production, New Holland Pictures, Blind Spot Pictures Oy; Entertainment One; Color.

Nazis flee to the dark side of the moon at the end of World War II. Setting up base with a fleet of flying saucers the Nazis plan an attack on Earth where the Fourth Reich will rule.

Iron Sky: Invasion [Videogame; SFW]

Release date: December 2012; Platforms: Android, Mac OS X, Microsoft Windows, PlayStation 3, iOS, Xbox 369; Designer: Miroslaw Dymek; Developer: Reality Pump, Mauro; Publisher: TopWare Interactive.

Based on the film *Iron Sky* (2012) the video game continues the fight against a Nazi invasion of Earth from their base on the dark side of the Moon. Players control spaceships with weapons and equipment to counter the Nazi threat and destroy their moon base.

Iron Sky: The Coming Race (2017) [Film; Finland; SFW]

Premiere: August 2017; Main Cast: Tom Green as Donald, Udo Kier as Wolfgang Kortzfleisch, Emily Atack as Tyler, Julia Dietze as Renate Richter, Stephanie Paul as Vril Sarah Pallin, Ho Ping Tang as Vril Genghis Khan, Kari Ketonen as Vril Vladimir Putin, Abbas Shirafkhan as Vril Osama bin Laden, Duta Skhirtladze as Vril Stalin; Story: Dalan Musson, Timo Vuorensola; Director: Timo Vuorensola; 27 Films, Potemkino, Atlas International Film; Color.

Sequel to *Iron Sky* (2012) that takes place twenty years later. Following a nuclear war the former Nazi moonbase has become the last refuge of mankind. But to save humanity the Vril, an ancient shape shifting race of reptiles and their dinosaurs must be defeated.

Iron Wolf a.k.a. *Werewolf of Terror* (2013) [Film; Germany; WW]

Premiere: September 13, 2013 (Germany); Main Cast: Carolina Rath as Jersey, Roland Freitag as Leon, Hannes Sell as Trigger, Dominik Strack as Spike Jones; Producers; Jens Nier, Nico Sentner, Dominic Starck; Story: Jens Nier; Director: David Bruckner; 93 min.; Generation X Group Film-Medienproduktion; IPA Asia Pacific; Color.

When the Russian army destroys a Nazi laboratory after they enter Berlin in 1945 an immortal threat is buried. But in 2012 a punk rock band decides to clean up the lab to play their reunion concert. The Nazi terror is freed in the form of a bloodthirsty werewolf.

Isle of the Dead (1945) [Film; WW]

Premiere: September 1, 1945; Main Cast: Boris Karloff as General Pherides, Ellen Drew as Thea, Katherine Emery as Mary St. Aubyn, Jason Robards (Sr.) as Albrecht, Alan Napier as St. Aubyn, Marc Cramer as Oliver Davis, Helene Thimig as Madame Kyra; Producer: Val Lewton; Screenplay: Joseph Mischel, Ardel Wray; Director: Mark Robson; 72 min.; RKO Radio Pictures; B/W.

"Under conquest and oppression the people of Greece allowed their legends to degenerate into superstition, the Goddess Aphrodite giving way to the *Varvolaka*. This nightmare figure was very

Isle of the Dead (1945), starring Boris Karloff as General Pherides (RKO Radio Pictures).

much alive in the minds of the peasants when Greece fought the victorious war of 1912."

General Pherides is quarantined on a Greek island when a plague breaks out on the battlefield. Superstitious inhabitants of the island are convinced they are under the grip of the demon Vorvolakas. Murders, a woman subject to cataleptic trances and a guest suspected by a local of being a vampire possessed by the spirit of the plague add to the tense atmosphere.

J'Accuse! (1919) [Film; France; WW]
Premiere: April 25, 1919 (France); Main Cast: Romuald Joube as Jean Diaz, Maxime Desjardins as Maria Lazare, Severin Mars as Francois Laurin, Angele Guys as Angele, Maryse Dauvray as Edith Laurin; Producer: Charles Pathe; Story-Director: Abel Gance; 166 min; Pathe Freres; United Artists; B/W.

Jean Diaz and Francois Laurin have one person in common. Edith Laurin. The rugged Francois is her husband and the sensitive poet Jean is in love with her. When World War I is declared the two men's lives are thrown together in the trenches of France. Tragedy awaits with the death of Francois on the battlefield and a shell-shocked and traumatized Jean suffering insanity. In his mind the dead soldiers rise again and accuse the villagers of their sins during the war.

Abel Gance remade his film in 1938 with the addition of sound and an updated screenplay.

See: ***I, Accuse!***

Jack Frost [Comic book character; WW]
First appearance: *U.S.A. Comics* #1 (August 1941); Creators; Stan Lee, Frank Giacoia; Publisher: Timely Comics.

Liberty Legion member Jack Frost can manipulate ice and withstand freezing temperatures. During World War II he protects the United States from Axis powers on American soil.

Jackboot & Ironheel [Comic book; WW]
First publication: August 2006; Story-Art: Max Millgate; Publisher: IDW Publishing.

West Ham United fan Eddie Neale signs up with the British Air Force and is soon bombing Nazi Germany. But when he is captured and imprisoned in a P.O.W. camp in Lungotz Luftzig he faces a new undead enemy.

Jacob's Ladder (1990) [Film; WW]
Premiere: November 2, 1990; Main Cast: Tim Robbins as Jacob Singer, Elizabeth Pena as Jezebel, Danny Aiello as Louis, Matt Craven as Michael, Jason Alexander as Geary, Ving Rhames as George; Executive Producers: Mario Kassar, Andrew Vajna; Story: Bruce Joel Rubin; Director: Adrian Lyne; 113 min.; Carolco Pictures; TriStar Pictures; Color.

Vietnam war veteran Jacob Singer suffers flashbacks to his tour of duty where he was wounded in a bayonet attack. Adding to his problems is a gradual removal from reality involving his dead son, his first marriage and an army conspiracy.

The Jazz Age (1968) [TV series; UK]
Anthology series of plays set in the 1920s.

"Post Mortem" [WW]
Air date: September 17, 1968; Main Cast: Keith Barron as John, Moira Redmond as Monica, Bernard Lee as Sir James, Nora Swinburne as Lady Cavan, Colin Jeavons as Perry, Hazel Hughes as Lady Stagg-Mortimer; Producer: Harry Moore; Playwright: Noel Coward; Director: John MacKenzie; 50 min.; British Broadcasting Corporation (BBC); BBC Two; Color.

Television dramatization of Noel Coward's anti-war play about a soldier who returns as a ghost.

See: ***Post-Mortem***

The Jewel and the Key [Juvenile book; WW]
Author: Louise Spiegler; First publication: New York: Clarion Books, 2011.

Seventeen-year-old Addie McNeal is a talented, but frustrated actress who can't make progress in the school drama group. But when an earthquake and the discovery of an antique pocket mirror combine forces Addie is thrown back in time to 1917 Seattle. Addie immerses herself in the local Jewel Theater and becomes friends with a young man who finds the idea of enlisting in World War I, a great adventure. As Addie travels between past and present her mission is to restore the dilapidated Jewel Theater to its former glory.

Jewels of Time [Novel; WW]
Author: Tess Mallory; First publication: Dorchester Publishing, 1994.

Victoria "Torri" Hamilton receives the gifts of a heirloom necklace and a small diary that both belonged to the first Victoria Hamilton. Her grandfather Nathaniel tells Torri, "You'll understand everything after you've read this. It will tell you how to travel through time." Torri follows the instructions and finds herself in the American Civil War, where she is rescued from death by Confederate Lt. Jake Cameron. But he has suspicions Torri may be a spy.

Joan the Woman (1916) [Film; WW]
Premiere: December 25, 1916; Main Cast: Geraldine Farrar as Jeanne d'Arc, Raymond Hatton as Charles VII, King of France, Wallace Reid as Eric Trent, Hobart Bosworth as General La Hire, Theodore Roberts as Cauchon, Hugo B. Koch as Duke of Burgundy; Producer: Cecil B DeMille; Scenario: Jeanie MacPherson; Director: Cecil B. DeMille; 138 min.; Cardinal Film Corp.; Silent; B/W-color.

In the World War I battlefield trenches of France British officer Eric Trent finds an old, rusted sword in his bunker. When the soldiers are informed about volunteering to destroy "Enemy Trench No. 2" with a hand-held bomb, Trent gives it serious thought. "The man who goes will not come back." That evening, with sword in hand, Trent is visited by the spirit of Joan of Arc. She tells him, "The time has come for thee to expiate thy sin against me."

The story moves back in time to 1429 France where Trent's ancestor is fighting for the cause of the Duke of Burgundy, who supports the English against the weak-willed Charles VII of France. Trent first encounters Joan in the village of Domremy after the Burgundian forces raid the village for cattle. There is a mutual attraction but Joan has a mission, guided by a vision where she is told to save France for the King. Now a warrior for France, Joan is captured by Trent who tells him he has betrayed her. Trent, now the Count of Diermont, is full of remorse and attempts to save her from her grim fate at the stake.

The film moves back to the present in 1916 where Trent awakens, kisses the sword and sacrifices himself for his country by blowing up the trench and the Germans. Joan greets Eric Trent in death.

John Kowalski [Comic book character; WW]
First appearance: *War is Hell* #9 (October 1974); Creators: Tony Isabella, Roy Thomas, Chris Claremont; Publisher: Marvel Comics.

The figure of Death summons deceased Polish soldier John Kowalski to possess the bodies of imminent victims of World War II as an act of penance for his dishonorable actions during his own lifetime.

Johnny and the Bomb (*The Johnny Maxwell Trilogy* book #3) [Juvenile book; SFW]
Author: Terry Pratchett; First publication: London: Doubleday, 1996.

Johnny Maxwell and his friends discover the black bags in homeless woman Mrs. Tachyon's shopping cart allow them to travel in time. With his friends Wobbler, Bigmac, Kirsty and Yo-Less, Johnny goes back in time to his home town of Blackbury in 1941 but end up changing the future.

Johnny and the Bomb [TV series: SFW]
Air date: January 15, 2006; Main Cast: George MacKay as Johnny Maxwell, Lucien Laviscount as Yo-Less, Jazmine Franks as Kirsty, Kyle Herbert as Wobbler, Scott Kay as Bigmac, Anthony Bowers as PC Gallagher, Samantha Seagar as Carol Maxwell, Roy Brandon as Home Guard, Holliday Grainger as Rose Bushell, Frank Finlay as Tom Maxwell, William Beck as Dr. Harris, Paul Copley as Sgt. Bourke; Executive Producer: Jon East; Story: Peter Tabern; Based on the book by Terry Pratchett; Director: Dermot Boyd; 3 × 40 min.; Childsplay Productions, British Broadcasting Corporation (BBC); Color.

Mini-series based on the book by Terry Pratchett.

Episodes: *Mrs. Tachyon and the Bags of Time* (1:01); *The Butterfly Effect* (1:02); *Deja Voodoo* (1:03).

Johnny and the Dead (*The Johnny Maxwell Trilogy* book #2) [Juvenile book; SFW]
Author: Terry Pratchett; First publication: London: Doubleday, 1993.

When developers make plans to bulldoze a local cemetery 12-year-old Johnny Maxwell starts interacting with the spirits of those buried in the cemetery. Johnny and his three friends research the town's history and make a case for preservation. Meanwhile Johnny is drawn to Tommy Atkins, the last surviving member of the Blackbury Pals battalion from World War I.

Pratchett's book has been adapted as a London Weekend Television four-part mini-series (1995) and a play by Stephen Briggs (1996).

Jonah Hex [Comic book character; Film; WW]

1. First appearance: ***All-Star Western*** #10 (February–March 1972); Creators: John Albano, Tony DeZuniga; Publisher: DC comics.

Sold as a slave to the Apache tribe by his alcoholic father, Jonah Woodson Hex received his "mark of the demon" facial scar from an Apache's red-hot tomahawk following a trial of combat with the chief's son who had previously betrayed him. The embittered and disfigured former Confederate officer became a bounty hunter with weapons including a Winchester rifle, Colt Peacemaker .45, Colt Dragoon .44 and Colt Navy .36. His days of bounty hunting caught up with him in old age when he was killed in cold blood by George Barrow in 1904.

Jonah Hex is primarily a Weird Western character, but his Civil War Confederate background is a vital part of his personality and has often been used as a back story to his Old West adventures.

2. Premiere: June 17, 2010; Main Cast: Josh Brolin as Jonah Hex, John Malkovich as Quentin Turnbull, Megan Fox as Lilah, Michael Fassbender as Burke, Will Arnett as Lieutenant Grass, Aidan Quinn as President Grant, Tom Wopat as Colonel Slocum; Producers; Akiva Goldsman, Andrew Lazar; Story: Mark Neveldine, Brian Taylor, William Farmer, John Albano; Director: Jimmy Hayward; 81 min.; Warner Bros; Color.

Disfigured bounty hunter Jonah Hex is on the vengeance trail for the murder of his wife and son by fellow Confederate veteran Quentin Turnbull. Now Turnbull has turned his attention to destroying the Union and Washington with a super-weapon of mass destruction. Hex is offered amnesty and freedom by President Grant in return for helping stop Turnbull and his renegade army.

Based on the DC Comics character, the film re-imagines Hex's disfigurement, replacing Native Americans with the diabolical Turnbull and giving Hex the power to talk to and resurrect the dead. Reviews were mixed. *The New York Times* critic Manohla Dargis (June 17, 2010) was positive. "Though it has bad word of mouth, 'Jonah Hex' is generally better, sprier and more diverting than most of the action flicks playing, 'The A-Team' included." Claudia Puig of *USA Today* (June 19, 2010) was less generous. "The opening frame of Jonah Hex should say: 'Caution: Made expressly for the male teen demographic. Not suitable for anyone of any age who prefers movies with coherence, an original plot or characters they give a hoot about.'"

Audiences stayed away as the opening weekend ranked a disappointing number 8 with earnings of $5.8 million. Given the estimated $47 million budget and a U.S. gross of $11 million *Jonah Hex* was a major disappointment for Warner Bros.

Jonathan Strange & Mr. Norrell (2015) [TV series; UK; WW]

Air date: May 17, 2015; Main Cast: Bertie Carvel as Jonathan Strange, Eddie Marsan as Mr. Norrel, Charlotte Riley as Arabella, Alice Englert as Lady Ple, Samuel West as Sir Walter Pole, Marc Warren as The Gentleman; Producers: Greg Dummett, Nick Hirschkorn; Story: Susanna Clarke, Peter Harness; Director: Toby Haynes; 7 × 60 min.; Far Moor, Screen Yorkshire, Feel Films, Bell Media, BBC America, Cuba Pictures; British Broadcasting Company (BBC); Color.

Two men, of different temperaments and objectives, attempt to restore the lost art of magic to England. Episodes include Jonathan Strange helping the Duke of Wellington win the Battle of Waterloo, with a little magical assistance.

Season One

Chapter One—*The Friends of Magic*; Chapter Two—*How Is Lady Pole?*; Chapter Three—*The Education of a Magician*; Chapter Four—*All Mirrors of the World*; Chapter Five—*Arabella*; Chapter Six—*The Black Tower*; Chapter Seven—*Jonathan Strange and Mr. Norrell*

Jonny Quest (1964) [Animated TV series]

The adventures of research scientist Dr. Benton Quest, his son Jonny, bodyguard Race Bannon, Indian orphan Hadji and Bandit the dog.

"The Devil's Tower" (1:21) [WW]

Air date: February 4, 1965; Voice Cast: Mike Road as Roger "Race" Bannon, Tim Matheson as Jonny

Quest, Don Messick as Dr. Benton Quest, Danny Bravo as Hadji, Henry Corden as Heinrich Von Duffel a.k.a. Kalus; Producers: Joseph Barbera, William Hanna; Story: William Hamilton; Directors: Joseph Barbera, William Hanna; 30 min.; Screen Gems Television, Hanna-Barbera Productions; American Broadcasting Company (ABC); Color.

When the Quest team attempts to retrieve Dr. Quest's weather balloon from the Devil's Escarpment, they encounter a mad Nazi war criminal, his Neanderthal servants and a diamond mine.

JSA: The Liberty Files [Comic book; SHW]

First publication: February 2000; Two-issue miniseries; Story: Dan Jolley; Art: ray Snyder, Tony Harris; Publisher: DC Comics.

World War II, 1942. Covert agents the Bat, Owl and Clock are on a mission to recover a vital package, now in the possession of a crazed albino smuggler. Their mission leads them to the discovery of a Nazi "Super-Man," and encounters with undead assassin the Scarecrow and Adolf Hitler.

Followed by the mini-series, *JSA Liberty Files: The Unholy Three* (2003) and *JSA Liberty Files: The Whistling Skull* (2012).

Jughead's Time Police [Comic book]

The adventures of Jughead Jones and his travels through time.

"Will the Real Colonel Pickens Please Stand Up?" [SFW]

First publication: #5 (March 1991); Story: Rich Margopoulos; Art: Gene Colan, Rudy Lapick; Publisher: Archie Comic Publications, Inc.

Jughead wants to learn more about the puzzling Colonel Pickens who played a major part in a Civil War battle in Riverdale. Jughead decides to experience the Colonel first hand and travels back in time to the Civil War.

Julius Caesar [Stage play; Film; TV] [WW]

First performance: 1599, Globe Theatre; Playwright: William Shakespeare; First printed edition: 1623 Folio "The Tragedy of Julius Caesar."

A dramatization of the events leading up to the assassination of Julius Caesar and its immediate aftermath. Assassin Marcus Brutus forms an uneasy alliance with Caius Cassius and is visited by the ghost of Julius Caesar before the Battle of Philippi.

"How ill this taper burns! Ha! Who comes here?
I think it is the weakness of mine eyes
That shapes this monstrous apparition
It comes upon me. Art thou any thing?
Art thou some god, some angel, or some devil,
That mak'st my blood cold, and my hair to star?
Speak to me what thou art."

Caesar's ghost responds that Brutus will see him again at Philippi. The following day on the battlefield Brutus faces defeat, and tells fellow officer and soldier Volumnius:

"The ghost of Caesar hath appeared to me
Two several times by night—at Sardis once,
And this last night, here in Philippi fields.
I know my hour is come."

Brutus asks Volumnius to: "Hold thou my sword hilts whilst I run on it."

He dies with honor, praised by Mark Antony. Unlike his fellow conspirators he struck his dagger in Caesar not out of envy but as a man looking toward the common good for his people. "This was the noblest Roman of them all."

Shakespeare's play has been adapted to film and television many times. The following is a selection of notable productions: Italy, 1914—Amleto

Julius Caesar: Act IV Scene III by William Shakespeare. Illustration by R. Westall R.A. Published by J & J Boydell (London), 1803.

Novelli as Julius Caesar, Antonio Nazzari as Brutus; Director: Enrico Guazzoni; U.S., 1950—Harold Tasker as Caesar, David Bradley as Brutus, Charlton Heston as Mark Antony; Director: David Bradley; U.S., 1953—Louis Calhern as Julius Caesar, James Mason as Brutus, Marlon Brando as Mark Antony, John Gielgud as Cassius; Director: Joseph L. Mankiewicz; UK, 1970—John Gielgud as Caesar, Jason Robards as Brutus, Charlton Heston as Mark Antony, Richard Johnson as Cassius; Director: Stuart Burge; TV, UK, 1951—*BBC Sunday Night Theatre* (2:08); Walter Hudd as Julius Caesar, Patrick Barras as Marcus Brutus, Clement McCallin as Cassius, Anthony Hawtrey as Marcus Antonius; Director: Leonard Brett; TV, U.S., 1955—*Studio One in Hollywood* (7:46); Theodore Bikel as Caesar, Philip Bourneuf as Brutus, Shepperd Strudwick as Cassius, Alfred Ryder as Mark Antony; Director: Daniel Petrie; CBS; TV, UK, 1979—*BBC Television Shakespeare*; Charles Gray as Caesar, Richard Pasco as Brutus, Keith Michell as Mark Antony; Director: Herbert Wise; TV, UK, 2012—*Royal Shakespeare Company*; Jeffrey Jissoon as Julius Caesar, Paterson Joseph as Brutus, Cyril Nri as Cassius; Director; Gregory Doran; BBC TV.

Justice League (2001) [Animated TV series]

Animated adventures of the DC Comics superhero team.

"The Savage Time" (1:24–1:26) [AHW]
Air dates: November 9, 2002; Voice Cast: Kevin Conroy as **Batman**, Susan Eisenberg as **Wonder Woman**, Maria Canais-Barrera as Hawkgirl, George Newbern as **Superman**, Phil LaMarr as Green Lantern, Michael Rosenbaum as The Flash, Carl Lumbly as J'onn J'onzz, Fred Dryer as Sgt. Rock, Robert Picardo as Blackhawk, Ted Levine as Bulldozer, Patrick Duffy as Steve Trevor, Phil Morris as Vandal Savage, Grant Albrecht as General Hoffman; Story: Stan Berkowitz, Bill Finger; Based on characters created by Joe Shuster, Jerry Siegel, Bob Kane, William Moulton Marston; Directors: Butch Lukic, Dan Riba (pt. 2); 3 × 22 min.; DC Comics, Warner Bros. Animation; Color.

In this three-part adventure the Justice League journey back in time to an alternate World War II. They find the immortal **Vandal Savage** is now the new führer in power, after placing Adolf Hitler in deep freeze. Savage has gone back in time to change history using future warfare technology and the now the Justice League must reverse it. They begin by helping the Allied forces at Normandy and are joined in the air battle by the **Blackhawks**. Meanwhile **Wonder Woman** and Steve Trevor try to foil a planned attack on England and Green Lantern (as John Stewart) joins forces with **Sgt. Rock and Easy Company**.

"Operation Endgame" begins as Wonder Woman and Steve Trevor discover the invasion of England has been abandoned in favor of the airborne invasion of America. John Stewart and Sgt. Rock uncover a secret airbase but Stewart is captured and tortured by Savage in his attempt to sabotage the jet bombers from the future. The remaining Justice League members, the Blackhawks and the U.S. Navy save the day.

Justice Society of America [Comic book characters; SHW]

First appearance: *All Star Comics* #3 (Winter 1940): Creators: Sheldon Mayer, Gardner Fox; Publisher: National Periodical Publications (DC).

Charter members the Flash, Hawkman, the Spectre, Dr. Fate, Hourman, the Atom and Sandman are later joined by Black Canary, Dr. Mid-Nite, Johnny Thunder, Mr. Terrific, Harlequin, Scribbly the Red Tornado, Wildcat, **Superman** and **Batman** as they fight to protect America and help its allies during World War II. **Wonder Woman** becomes a charter member of the JSA and the newly formed Justice Battalion of America, acting chiefly as secretary.

"Justice Society Joins the War on Japan." [SFW]
First publication: *All-Star Comics* #11 (June–July 1942); Story: Gardner Fox; Art: Jack Burnley.

Wonder Woman as nurse Diana Prince is assigned to the Ambulance Corps in the Philippines, ministering to the American wounded. Realizing she can be more effective as Wonder Woman she fights and captures the Japanese troops on the island. Back in America a meeting of high-ranking army commanders gathers members of the Justice Society of America together. The Commanding Officer tells Hawkman he has wired Washington "for permission to make you a special battalion ... to be known as the Justice Battalion of America." Dr. Fate suggests Wonder Woman "ought to be a member too!"

The original JSA went into retirement after their final adventure in *All-Star Comics* #57 (February 1951). In August 1963 Gardner Fox revived the JSA in *Justice League of America* #21. The old wartime heroes now lived on a parallel Earth known as Earth-2.

Kade Mourning Sun [Comic book; WW]

First publication: March 2012; Story: Sean Patrick O'Reilly; Art: Robert Gill; Publisher: Arcana Studios.

When the demon Apollyon ordered all children born under the solar eclipse killed Kade was one of the slaughtered children. But his spirit lives on as an immortal ageless warrior damned to an eternity battling evil. The spirit of vengeance trapped in a long dead body that cannot feel pleasure or pain. In 1941 Kade finds himself among fleeing refugees and a retreating Soviet army escaping a German Panzer division under the command of Lucifer, disguised as a S.S. General. To add to the horrors, the Nazis now have an undead army on the march through Europe.

Kanigher, Robert (1915–2002) [Comic book writer]

Born June 18, 1915, in New York, Robert Kanigher's best known creation remains **Sgt. Rock and Easy Company**. Kanigher began his career writing and directing stage plays and radio shows before concentrating on the medium that made him famous—comic books. Kanigher worked in every genre but his style and personality was particularly suited to war comics. At National-DC Comics he edited *Our Army At War, Our Fighting Forces, All-American Men of War, Star Spangled War Stories, G.I. Combat,* **Tomahawk** and *Enemy Ace* among others. His Weird War creations include **The War That Time Forget** and **The Haunted Tank**.

Robert Kanigher had a reputation for being a taskmaster, who pushed himself as hard as the artists under his editorship. But the key to his long and successful writing career may be summed up in his own words. "Reader's can't be fooled. They don't believe in assembly-line emotion. They recognize in my books one drive, one thought, one mind. The stories bear my stamp."

Robert Kanigher died May 6, 2002, at the age of 86.

The Keep [Novel; Film; WW]

1. Author: F. Paul Wilson; First publication: New York: Morrow, 1981.

An ancient evil awakens in a garrison in Transylvanian Alps. Nazi soldiers are being killed and mutilated one-by-one every night.

2. Premiere: December 16, 1983; Main Cast: Scott Glenn as Glaeken, Alberta Watson as Eva Cuza, Gabriel Byrne as Kaempffer, Jurgen Prochnow as Woermann, Ian McKellen as Dr. Theodore Cuza, Robert Prosky as Father Fonescu; Executive Producer: Colin M. Brewer: Screenplay: Michael Mann. Based on the novel by F. Paul Wilson; Director: Michael Mann; 96 min.; Paramount Pictures; Color.

Romania, 1942. German Commander Woermann and his troop of Nazi soldiers have orders to occupy a medieval fortress known as "The Keep."

But when the explore the fortress in search of treasures the soldiers unleash an evil force that kills them. The Nazis must turn to Jewish antiquarian Dr. Theodore Cuza and his daughter Eva to translate a mysterious message written on the castle walls. But only the lonely ancient gatekeeper Glaeken understands the true danger of the evil presence known as Molasar.

Writing for *Cinefantastique* (Vol. 14 #3: May 1984), Dennis Fischer comments: "For the first half, the film is both effective and mysterious. But the character of Molasar is defined only physically. He gradually takes on the appearance of a skinless man, and ends up resembling the "Swamp Thing" with red eyes and a red glow in his mouth. The film, by this time, has crossed over the boundary of the sublime into the ridiculous. The saddest thing about THE KEEP is that it had the potential and resources to be a very good, very noteworthy film."

Kid Eternity [Comic book character]

"THE MAN WHO CONTROLLED THE PAST" [WW]

First publication: *Kid Eternity* #2 (Summer 1946); Story: Bill Woolfolk; Art: Al Bryant; Publisher: Quality Comics Group.

Mr. Keeper is told by Father Time that somebody on Earth is fooling around with time. Kid Eternity is given a "celestial trouble finder" by Mr. Keeper as he travels to Earth and speaks the word "Eternity!" to become visible to mortal eyes. The Kid locates evil Dr. Marko and his time globe who has plans to destroy America by sabotaging Christopher Columbus and his Santa Maria ship in 1492. But when Kid Eternity foils his plans he locates Marko again in Charlestown, Massachusetts, on April 18, 1775. Marko is leading Paul Revere into an ambush by the British Redcoats. Kid

Eternity arrives in time to warn Revere and tackle the Redcoats himself on Alexander the Great's famous steed horse Bucephalus.

"The Origin of Kid Eternity" [WW]
First publication: *Hit Comics* #25 (December 1942); Art: Sheldon Moldoff; Publisher: Quality Comics Group.

1942. A merchant vessel in the Atlantic, carrying a precious cargo of rubber and crude oil is torpedoed by a Nazi submarine. A youngster referred to as "kid" and his grandpa are killed in the attack and now stand at the pearly gates. When the kid's name isn't listed as ready for arrival Mr. Keeper realizes he has made his first-ever error. The kid wasn't due to die for another 75 years.

The kid returns to Earth in ghostly form with Mr. Keeper in time to see his body being buried at sea. Mr. Keeper takes the kid on a journey through history and tells him he can call on any person in time and enter their body by saying the word "Eternity!" And that same word can make him visible to mortals. Under his new name of Kid Eternity he is told by Mr. Keeper, "Your job is to fight the future, and all its evils!"

The King [Novel; AHW]
Author: Donald Barthelme; First publication: New York: Harper & Row, 1990.

King Arthur and his Knights of the Round Table fight the Nazis in 1940s England, while traitor Lord Haw-Haw spreads false claims Guinevere was captured at Dunkirk. Meanwhile Lancelot is believed to be sleeping with Guinevere and thinks Churchill is "less than competent."

King of the Zombies (1941) [Film; WW]
Premiere: May 14, 1941; Main Cast: Dick Purcell as James McCarthy, Joan Woodbury as Barbara Winslow, Mantan Moreland as Jeff Jackson, Henry Victor as Dr. Sangre, John Archer as Bill Summers; Producer: Lindsley Parsons; Screenplay: Edmond Kelso; Director: Jean Yarbrough; 67 min.; Monogram Pictures; B/W.

A bad storm forces a small plane to crash land on an island off the coasts of Cuba and Puerto Rico. Pilot James McCarthy, Bill Summers and Jeff, his manservant take refuge in a mansion owned by Dr. Sangre. Jeff tries to convince the others that the mansion has zombies roaming its halls. It is only when the trio venture into the cellar and see Dr. Sangre experimenting on zombies that they believe Jeff. The doctor is a spy during World War II acquiring the knowledge of his captors by transferring their thoughts into zombies that he controls.

Kirby, Jack (1917–1994) [Comic book artist-writer]

The son of Austrian immigrants, Jacob Kurtzberg was born August 28, 1917, in New York City. He began his career at the Max Fleischer animation studio, near Times Square, as assistant animator on *Popeye* cartoons. After stints illustrating newspaper-comic strips for the Lincoln Features Syndicate and the Eisner-Iger studio Kirby joined Timely Comics in 1939. One year later the first issue of **Captain America** was published and a new creative team was born with Jack

Kid Eternity #2 (Summer, 1946), "The Man Who Controlled the Past," page 1. Art by Al Bryant. Published by Quality Comics Group.

Kirby and **Joe Simon**. Super-soldier and patriot Captain America would fight Adolf Hitler and the Nazis before America officially entered World War II in the real world. Kirby and Simon's creation was generally well received, but Kirby was also subject to threats from Nazi sympathizers. He recalled, "I once got a letter from a Nazi who told me to pick out any lamppost I wanted on Times Square, because when Hitler arrived, they'd hang me from it."

In 1964 Kirby and editor-writer **Stan Lee** relaunched Captain America for a new audience under the "Marvel Age" of comics banner. Kirby's contribution to comic books which also includes the co-creation of **Boy Commandos**, **Sgt. Fury and His Howling Commandos**, **Fantastic Four**, *The Incredible Hulk*, *The Mighty Thor* and *The Avengers* has received international acclaim. On February 6, 1994, he suffered a fatal heart attack in his kitchen, shortly after taking in his morning paper, *The Los Angeles Times*, to read. He is still fondly remembered today as Jack "King" Kirby, a towering figure in comic book history.

Kishin Corps a.k.a. *Alien Defender Geo Armor: Kishin Corps* [Novel series; OVA; Japan; SFW]

1. Author: Masaki Yamada; Ten volumes; First published: 1990; Publisher: Chokoron-Shinsha.

1941. World War II is raging in Europe, but the Nazis aren't the only enemy. The Axis powers have joined forces with extraterrestrial invaders. To counter the threat the Kishin Corps are formed, using alien technology, to power giant armored robots. The Nazis also have plans to build their own robots—but first they must steal the alien technology from a young man named Taishi.

2. [Original video animation; Japan]
Release: March 24, 1993; Directors: Takaaki Ishiyama, Kazunori Mizuno; 7 × 30 min.; AIC Pioneer LDC, Geneon; Color.

Based on the novel series by Masaki Yamada.
Episodes: 1. *Mission Call for Kishin Thunder*; 2. *Surprise Attack! Battle of the Island Fortress*; 3. *The Battle! Operation Runaway Train*; 4. *Kishin vs. Panzer Knight* (Part 1); 5. *Kishin vs. Panzer Knight* (Part 2); 6. *Storming the Base of the Alien Foe*; 7. *Youth to the Rescue*.

3. [Manga]
First published: *Monthy Shonen Captain* (1994); Three volumes; Story: Masaki Yamada; Art: Shohei Oka; Publisher: Tokuma Shoten.

A continuation of the novel series.

Konpeki no Kantai a.k.a. *Deep Blue Fleet* [Novel series; OVA; Japan; AHW]

1. Author: Yoshio Aramaki; Ten volumes; First published: December 1990; Publisher: Tokyo: Tokuma Shoken.

This alternate history war novel sees Japanese pilot Isoroku Takano shot down and killed when his plane crashes on Bougainville Island in 1943. He awakens to find himself restored to life but displaced in time. It is 1915. Able to live his life again with full knowledge of his previous self, Takano decides this time around Japan will defeat the Americans in World War II. In 1941 he teams up with fellow time traveler Lt. General Yasaburo Otaka and destroys the military base at Pearl Harbor. Continued victories against Allied forces occur, but Nazi Germany is taking note and Heinrich von Hitler declares war on Japan.

2. [Original Video Animation; Japan]
Release: 1993; Story: Yoshio Aramaki, Ryosuke Takahashi; Directors: Takeyuki Kanda, Hiromichi Matano; 32 × 40 min.; J. C. Staff; Color.

Based on the novel series by Yoshio Aramaki.

3. [Videogame]
Release: March 31, 1995; Platform: PC-FX; Developer: MicroCabin; Publisher: NEC International.

Two more strategy games followed on April 21, 1995 (3DO; MicroCabin, Tokuma Shoten) and November 2, 1995 (Super Famicom; Access Co., Angel).

Kubert, Joe (1926–2012) [Comic book artist]

Born Yosaif Kubert in Ozeryany, southern Poland (now Ukraine) on September 18, 1926, his parents emigrated to America when Kubert was two-months old. Settling in Brooklyn, New York, the young Kubert was attracted to newspaper strips, specifically Hal Foster's *Tarzan*. While still a student, Kubert caught the attention of artist Harry "A" Chesler, who offered him the opportunity to learn his craft in a professional studio environment. Kubert's reputation today rests primarily on his 1959 collaboration with writer **Robert Kanigher**. Kubert's gritty artwork was a perfect match for **Sgt. Rock and Easy Company**. That style would later be transferred to numerous war titles, including *G.I. Combat, Our Army At War, Star Spangled War Stories, Our Fighting Forces* and **Weird War Tales**. Outside of his wartime comic book work the award winning Kubert is well known for his critically acclaimed adaptation of Tarzan in the 1970s and his work on *Tor* and *Hawkman* for DC Comics. He founded *The Joe Kubert School of Cartoon and Graphic Design* in 1976. Two of his sons, Adam and Andy Kubert have continued in the family tradition as comic book artists.

Joe Kubert passed away on August 12, 2012, age 86.

Kung Fury (2015) [Short film; Sweden; SFW]

Premiere: May 28, 2015; Main Cast: David Sandberg as Kung Fury, Jorma Taccone as Adolf Hitler, Steven Chew as Dragon, Andreas Cahling as Thor, Per-Henrik Arvidius as Voice of Thor, Leopold Nilsson as Hackerman, Magnus Betner as Colonel Reichstache, Bjorn Gustafsson as Pvt. Lahmstache, Eleni Young as Barbarianna, David Hasselhoff as Hoff 9000 (voice); Producer-Story-Director: David Sandberg; 31 min.; Lampray, Laser Unicorns; Color.

After a friend of Kung Fury is assassinated by kung fu master criminal Kung Fuhrer Hitler in 1985 Kung Fury goes back in time to ask for Thor's help in destroying Adolf Hitler in Nazi Germany.

Lady Lazarus [Novel; WW]

Author: Michele Lang; First publication: New York: Tor, 2010.

Following the death of her mother twenty-year-old Magdalena Lazarus has to come to terms with her Lazarus witch heritage. It is the summer of 1939 and Hitler is about to invade Poland. As the last in line she searches for her family's lost Book of Raziel and its magical text before the demon Asmodel and his minions, who are allied with Hitler, can claim it. In desperation Magdalena summons her family's guardian angel Raziel.

See: **Dark Victory**

The Lamb and the Fuhrer [Graphic novel; WW]

First publication: 2014; Story: Dr. Ravi Zacharias; Art: Jeff Slemons, Geof Isherwood; Publisher: Kingstone Comics.

"Enter with me into Hitler's bunker and listen as the Fuhrer, gun in hand, is about to end his life.... How could people have followed such an evil man? What is the origin of such violence? How does blood recompense for blood? Listen as Jesus, Hitler and Bonnhoeffer engage in a life-and-death discussion."

Lammas Night [Novel; WW]

Author: Katherine Kurtz; First publication: New York: Ballantine Books, 1983.

1940. A group of English witches' covens are united by John Graham, colonel of British Intelligence. Their mission—to stop the black magic about to be unleashed on England by Nazi Germany.

Land of Mist and Snow [Novel; AHW]

Authors: Debra Doyle, James Macdonald; First publication: New York: Eos, 2006.

Union Navy Lieutenant John Nevis is assigned to a unique warship during the Civil War. The USS Nicodemus, constructed in the frozen north, has cannonballs of virgin brass and is powered by an air elemental that allows it to travel without steam or sail. Its mission is to defeat the CSS Alecto, a demon raider operated by an enemy who demands blood sacrifice.

The Land That Time Forgot [Film; WW]

1. Premiere: August 13, 1975; Main Cast: Doug McClure as Bowen Tyler, John McEnery as Capt. Von Schoenvorts, Susan Penhaligon as Lisa Clayton, Keith Barron as Bradley; Executive Producer: David Rinawi; Screenplay: James Cawthorn, Michael Moorcock. Based on the novel by Edgar Rice Burroughs; Director: Kevin Connor; 90 min.; Lion International, Amicus Productions; American International Pictures, British Lion Film Corp.; Color.

World War I, 1916. A German U-boat torpedoes a British ship and takes the survivors on board. Finding themselves lost in the ocean they come across a strange, new land called Caprona. The German and British have to join forces to survive as they encounter dinosaurs, primitive humans and a hostile landscape.

Based on *The Land That Time Forgot* by Edgar Rice Burroughs. First published as three-part serial in *Blue Book Magazine* (September–December 1918).

2. Premiere: June 23, 2009; Main Cast: C. Thomas Howell as Frost Michaels, Anya Benton as Karen Michaels, Timothy Bottoms as Captain Burroughs, Lindsey McKeon as Lindsey Stevens, Darren Dalton as Cole Stevens; Executive Producer: Robert H. Greenberg; Screenplay: Darren Dalton. Based on the novel by Edgar Rice Burroughs; Director: C. Thomas Howell; 88 min.; The Asylum; Color.

This updated version of Edgar Rice Burrough's

The Land That Time Forgot (1975), starring Doug McClure as Bowen Tyler, Susan Penhaligon as Lisa Clayton and John McEnery as Capt. Von Schoenvorts (British Lion, Amicus, American-International).

Lightning Comics Vol. 2 #3 (October 1941) featuring Lash Lightning. Cover art by Jim Mooney. Published by Ace Magazines.

story sees two newlywed couples encountering a violent storm on their Caribbean cruise. When it passes the couples find themselves on the shore of the island Caprona in a different time. Together with the crew of an abandoned German U–Boat they tackle dinosaurs and other dangers on the island.

Lash Lightning [Comic book character; SHW]

First appearance: *Sure-Fire Comics* #1 (June 1940); Publisher: Ace Magazines.

The final issue of *Lightning Comics* (Vol. 3 #1; June 1942) introduced Lightning Girl.

The Teacher has a plan to destroy the American fleet and the U.S. army at Dutch Harbor and to place the blame on Commander Blake and his daughter Isobel. Lash Lightning is captured by the Teacher and receives enough electricity to "tear apart a battleship" rendering his powers useless. Now it is up to the Commander's daughter Isobel to save the day. Lash Lightning sends thousands of volts through her body and Lightning Girl is born. "On your way! Make the fleet change it course!" commands Lash Lightning.

Lightning Girl accomplishes her mission and Lash Lightning's powers return. The Teacher is defeated ... for now. "Our jobs are just beginning," states Lash. "So long as there is injustice and wrongs to be righted, you'll be there, and I'll be with you, fighting always at your side!"

In early stories Lash Lightning is referred to as "Flash" Lightning.

Last Ghost at Gettysburg [Juvenile book; WW]

Author: Paul Ferrante; First publication: White Bear Lake, MN: Melange Books, 2013.

A vacation with Uncle Mike, a Park Ranger at the Gettysburg National Battlefield doesn't excite high school freshman T.J. Jackson until he sees how adopted cousin LouAnne has turned into a beautiful, sexy girl. Add a Confederate ghost whose been frightening visitors to the battlefield, a competitor for LouAnne's attention in the form of T.J's best friend and a murder mystery. T.J. has enough excitement to last all summer.

Leav, Mort (1916–2005) [Comic book artist]

Born July 9, 1916, in New York City, Mort Leav entered the comic book industry in 1941, working for the S.M. Iger studio. Iger supplied strips to various publishers including Fiction House, MLJ, Quality and Hillman. Leav was kept busy providing artwork for **Doll Man** and **Uncle Sam** for Quality, *The Hangman* for MLJ and **The Heap** for *Air Fighters Comics*. When he joined Quality in 1942 as a staff artist Leav worked on **Kid Eternity** and **Blackhawk**. He also provided strips for Timely's post-war **Captain America**. After leaving the comic book industry in 1954 Leav joined Benton and Bowles Advertising Agency. He passed away September 21, 2005, age 89.

Lee, Stan (1922–) [Comic book writer]

Born December 28, 1922, in New York City, Stanley Martin Lieber entered the comic book industry age 17. When **Joe Simon** and **Jack Kirby** left Timely Comics for National-DC in 1942, Lieber took over their editorial duties. Lieber adopted the pen-name Stan Lee when writing for **Captain America** and other Timely wartime strips, including **The Destroyer**, **Jack Frost** and **The Whizzer**. Post-war the comic book industry went into a slump and Lee considered leaving the profession when he was reduced to turning out various monster titles for the Atlas group in the late 1950s.

The 1960s saw a turnaround in his fortunes and the most prolific and successful period of his career to date. He introduced The Marvel Age with titles such as **Fantastic Four**, *Amazing Spider-Man* and *Daredevil* and became a celebrity in his own right. His comic book characters became more human with personal problems readers could identify with. He encouraged feedback from readers and made them feel part of the creative process. He also maintained the link between Timely Comics characters and Marvel by re-introducing Captain America, the **Sub-Mariner** and **Human Torch**, together with vintage Timely artists such as Jack Kirby and **Bill Everett**.

Unlike many of the artists who worked for Marvel, Stan Lee has lived long enough to see his creations become box-office hits, with state-of-the-art digital effects. He's even managed to add acting to his resume with brief cameos in the Marvel films. Stan Lee has arguably had the greatest impact on pop culture of anyone in the comic books industry. There have been detractors who claim he has taken too much credit for the achievements of Marvel Comics, but there is no doubting his talent for self promotion and revitalizing a comics industry that was desperately short of new ideas.

Leviathan [Novel; SFW]

Author: Scott Westerfeld; Art: Keith Thompson; First publication: New York: Simon Pulse, 2009.

June 1914. Deryn Sharp is a teenage girl disguised as an airman with the British Air Service serving on a genetically fabricated biological whale airship known as the Leviathan. She is a Darwinist fighting a war with the machine based Clankers out of Austria, Hungary and Germany. Prince Aleksander, a Clanker, has fled Austria after the assassination of his parents. When the paths of Deryn and Aleksander cross they form a friendship that transcends the hostilities of war.

See: **Behemoth**

Leviathan: Le Patient Zero [Comic book; France; WW]

First publication: January 2015; Story: Carlos G. Campillo; Art: Alfonso Ruiz; Publisher: Wanga Comics.

Using potent sorcery, Himmler and his S.S. scientists have created a super-weapon capable of mass destruction. The Allies elite soldier Mazzara must stop the Nazi weapon, named Leviathan, or risk losing the war.

Liberty Belle [Comic book character; SHW]

First appearance: *Boy Commandos* #1 (December 1942); Creators: Don Cameron, Chuck Winter; Publisher: National Periodical Publications, DC Comics.

Libby Lawrence's ancestor Bess Lynn fought as Miss Liberty during the Revolutionary War. Following the death of her father Major James Lawrence in Nazi occupied Poland Libby adopts the persona of Liberty Belle and becomes a founding member of the **All-Star Squadron**. When the original Liberty Bell is rung by its custodian Tom Revere, a tiny replica of the bell that she wears on her belt, also rings, adrenaline surges through her body and she gains strength and speed. Liberty Belle can also shatter objects thanks to sonic pulses that vibrate from her hands.

The Liberty Legion [Comic book characters; SHW]

First appearance: *Marvel Premiere* #29 (April 1976); Creator: Roy Thomas; Publisher: Marvel Comics Group.

"AMERICA'S HOME FRONT HEROES OF WORLD WAR II."

Fighting the Axis powers and fifth columnists on American soil, the team features: The Patriot, the **Blue Diamond**, **Jack Frost**, **Miss America**, **Red Raven**, the **Thin Man** and the **Whizzer**.

The Life Eaters [Graphic novel; MWW]

First publication: 2003; Story: David Brin; Art: Scott Hampton; Publisher: WildStorm.

In the winter of 1943 Nazis find allies in the Aesir Norse gods. But Loki works against his fellow Norse gods and rescues death camp internees, revealing the source of the Nazi's power to be necromancy. The Nazis extend their alliances to the Japanese Shinto gods and threaten the future of the Earth.

The Light & Darkness War [Comic book; WW]

First publication: October 1988; Six-issue miniseries; Story: Tom Veitch; Art: Cam Kennedy; Publisher: Epic Comics.

Helicopter pilot Lazarus Jones becomes an emotional wreck after he is the only person to survive the loss of his platoon in Vietnam. Twenty years later a severely depressed Jones enters a twilight world where he rejoins his fallen comrades and battles a new war between Light and Darkness.

Light Brigade [Comic book; WW]

First publication: February 2004; 4-issue miniseries; Story: Peter J. Tomasi; Art: Peter Snejbjerg; Publisher: DC Comics.

Chris Stavros and his platoon are given a task by celestial warriors on the battlefield during World War II. They must recover the lost Sword of God to prevent a troop of invulnerable German soldiers from finding it first and storming Heaven's Gate.

Lincoln's Legacy (*Blast From the Past* book #1) [Juvenile book; SFW]

Authors: Stacia Deutsch, Rhody Cohon; Illustrator: David Wenzel; First publication: New York: Aladdin, 2005.

Third graders Abigail, Jacob, Zack and Bo always look forward to Mr. Caruthers's history class. Today he is asking the question, "What if Abraham Lincoln never freed the slaves?" But today this question isn't hypothetical.

After class Mr. Caruthers approaches Abigail and her friends and shows them a device that resembles a handheld video game. But it isn't a game, it's a computer. Mr. Caruthers then takes a square cartridge out of his pocket with a picture of Abraham Lincoln on it. He tells the children, "When you put this into the back of the computer, it will take you to September 22, 1862."

Abigail and her friends must convince President Lincoln not to quit and to deliver the Emancipation Proclamation that will free the slaves. But that will be easier said than done.

See: **Washington's War**

Lincoln's Sword [Novel; AHW]

Authors: Debra Doyle, James Macdonald; First publication: New York, Eos, 2010.

First Lady Mary Todd Lincoln has troubled dreams of a bleak future for the Union. Her friend Mercy interprets Mrs. Lincoln's dreams and fears for the worst. But a mysterious traveler from the future offers hope, and a magical sword, seen by Mrs. Lincoln in her dreams, may be they key to a brighter future.

The Living and the Dead (2007) [Film; Croatia; WW]

Premiere; July 20, 2007 (Croatia); Main Cast: Filip Sovagovic as Tomo/Martin, Velibor Topic as Vijali, Slaven Knezovic as Coro, Marinko Prga as Mali, Borko Peric as Robe, Miro Barnjak as Ivo; Producers: Miro Branjak, Igor Nola, Domagoj Poavic, Marijo Vukadin; Screenplay: Ivan Pavlicic; Based on the book *Zivi I Mrtvi* by Josip Mlakic; Director: Kristijan Milic; 87 min.; Mainframe Productions; VMI Worldwide; Filmed in sepia tones.

1943. Croatian soldiers in Western Bosnia are ambushed by Communist partisans after encountering the supernatural. In 1993, Tomo the grandson of Croatian soldier Martin from 1943 is with his fellow soldiers in the same area of Bosnia. As they journey through the same forests and haunted cemetery hill the soldiers once again encounter the supernatural as they shoot at invisible enemies.

The Locked Spirit [Novel; WW]
Author: Julie F. E. Neil; First publication: Indianapolis, IN: Dog Ear, 2010.

Renny Thomas successfully bids on the Civil War belongings of a Confederate soldier at an antique auction. The soldier, Richard Hollingsworth was killed for shooting his own men. Now he makes contact with Renny to free his spirit.

London Calling [Juvenile book; SFW]
Author: Edward Bloor; First publication: New York: Alfred A. Knopf, 2006.

Martin Conway is an unhappy boy. His alcoholic father has deserted his family and his life lacks excitement. But when Martin's late grandmother leaves him a World War II Philco radio, and he has repeated strange encounters with a boy named Jimmy Harker, his life changes. Suddenly he is transported with Jimmy back to 1940s London during the Blitz. It is only by learning about the past that his life takes on greater meaning.

Look Magazine [Comic strip; SHW]
First publication: February 27, 1940; Story: Jerry Siegel; Art: The Joe Schuster Studio.

Superman made a two-page appearance in the popular weekly pictorial magazine in the early days of World War II. Superman races along the Siegfried Line destroying the concrete Westwall with an invitation to the French troops to "Come and get 'em!" Next stop Germany and Adolf Hitler as Superman grabs the dictator and flies with him to Moscow where he also grabs Josef Stalin. At the League of Nations in Geneva, Switzerland Hitler and Stalin are found guilty of "unprovoked aggression against defenseless countries."

Look Who's Back a.k.a. *Er ist wieder da* (Original German title) [Novel; WW]
Author: Timur Vermes; First publication: Germany: Eichborn Verlag, 2012.

Adolf Hitler awakens from a 66-year sleep in his Berlin bunker to a new world of technology. Confused and disheartened with the multicultural world he sees before him Hitler continues to try and spread his Nazi ideology. The public, believing he is an accomplished Hitler impersonator, make him a star on YouTube and television. Hitler realizes the media of 2011 is the perfect promotional tool as he creates his own political party in the hope of returning to power.

Lorelei: The Witch of the Pacific Ocean (2005) [Film; Japan; AHW]
Premiere: March 5, 2005; Main Cast: Koji Yakusho as Masami Shin'ichi, Satoshi Tsumabuki as Yukito Origasa, Toshiro Yanagiba as Kizaki Toshiro, Shin'ichi Tsutsumi as Asakura Ryokitsu, Yu Kashi as Paula Atsuko Ebner; Producer: Chihiro Kameyama; Screenplay: Satoshi Suzuki; Based on the novel "Shusen No Lorelei" by Harutoshi Fukui; Director: Shinji Higuchi; 128 min.; Fuji Television Network, King Records, Cine Bazar; Toho Company, Protean Image Group, KTV; Color.

July 1945. The Japanese Navy receive an experimental submarine, the *I-507*, from Germany. Its mission, to sink an American ship carrying an atomic bomb to Tinian in the Mariana Islands. On board is a highly sensitive young woman with supernatural abilities who operates the Lorelei system. She tells the captain that the Americans plan to drop a third atomic bomb on Tokyo using a B-29 bomber out of Tinian. But a traitor exists at the Japanese naval headquarters in Tokyo who has placed armed men on the *I-507* to take command and foil attempts to stop the atomic attack on Tokyo.

Lost at Khe Sanh (*Ghosts of War* #2) [Juvenile book; WW]
Author: Steve Watkins; First publication: New York: Scholastic Paperbacks, 2015.

Greg and Julie warn Anderson not to delve into the contents of the strange trunk in his uncle's basement again, but curiosity gets the better of him. Inside is a grenade with a message scratched on it, accompanied by the ghost of a soldier from the Vietnam War who claims it was his lucky grenade. Anderson, Greg and Julie must find out more about the mystery ghost and why he is still earthbound.

See: **AWOL in North Africa**

"Lost City of Burma" [Pulp fiction; WW]
Author: Edmond Hamilton; First publication: *Fantastic Adventures* (Vol. 4 #12; December 1942); Publisher: Ziff-Davis Publishing Company.

Lashio, at the vital junction of the Burma Road, is falling to the Japanese, but not without last-minute resistance from the Chinese, British and Americans. Captain John Terrell of United States

Army Intelligence decides to take the road north out of Lashio, to the consternation of his Burmese companion, Sigri. The road supposedly leads to the fabled land of Yamaya and the legendary Flame of Life, which is said to have the power to make men immortal. Terrell dismisses his superstitious friend and is captured on the road north by the Japanese—who happen to believe the Flame of Life is real and seek its immortal properties.

Lost Horizon [Videogame; Germany; WW]

Release date: August 20, 2010; Voice Cast: Stefan Gunther as Fenton Paddock, Farina Brock as Kim Wuang, Kathrin Simon as Hanna Grafin, Christian Baumann as Richard; Platform: Microsoft Windows; Story: Claudia Kern, Marco Zeugner; Developer: Animation Arts; Publisher: Deep Silver.

Former British soldier Fenton Paddock searches for his friend Richard, who has disappeared in 1930s Tibet. But he encounters soldiers of the Third Reich on their own quest, for the mystical Shambala and occult weapons that will enable them to conquer the world.

The Lost Platoon (1990) [Film: WW]

Premiere: June 30, 1990; Main Cast: William Knight as Hollander, David parry as Jonathan Hancock, Stephen Quadros as Walker, Michael Wayne as Hayden, Sean Heyman as Keeler, Roger Bayless as Vladimir; Producer: Kimberley Casey; Screenplay: David A. Orior, Ted Prior; Director: David A. Prior; 86 min.; Action International Pictures (AIP); Color.

While reporting on the civil war in Nicaragua, an American journalist who served in World War II comes across four veteran soldiers he knew from that war. But they don't appear to have aged. Further digging uncovers the eerie truth. The soldiers are now vampires in a war with the Nicaraguan general who commands his own army of vampires.

Lost Squad [Comic book; WW]

First publication: September 2005; 6-issue miniseries; Story: Chris Kirby; Art: Alan Robinson; Publisher: Devil's Due.

The U.S. Army has a secret unit that deals with the bizarre. When the Nazis continue their march through Europe in 1942 with the help of a mysterious device Codename: Sybil, the Lost Squad are called into action. Soon they are fighting flying commandos, demon soldiers and the Third Reich's latest weapon, the Wulf Spyder tank.

"The Lost Warship" [Pulp fiction; SFW]

Author: Robert Moore Williams; Illustrator: J. Allen St. John; First publication: *Amazing Stories* (Vol. 17 #1; January 1943); Publisher: Ziff-Davis Publishing Company.

The U.S. battleship *Idaho*, part of a Pacific task force that includes a carrier, cruisers and several destroyers, comes under attack from Japanese bombers. But there is something amiss. A sheet of dancing, intensely blue flame, dances around the horizon and suddenly the sun jumps in the sky. The Japanese bombers have disappeared. There is only an eerie silence that is broken by a howling wind. The *Idaho* is alone in strange seas. They have fallen through a space-time fault into an antediluvian world inhabited by gigantic bird-lizards and dinosaurs.

Luft Krieg [RPG; AHW]

First publication: 2001; Designers: Chris Hartford, Gene Marcil, Stephane I. Matis, Pierre Ouellette; Art: Ghislain Barbe, Vankhumi Darhim, Pierre Ouellette, Marc Ouellette, Kieran Yanner; System: Silhouette; Publisher: Dream Pod 9.

This tabletop air combat wargame is set in an alternate world inspired by World War II, where science is greatly advanced. The player controls the air forces of any one of five nations in a battle to save the world.

"Luvium, the Invisible City" [Pulp fiction; SFW]

Author: A.R. McKenzie; First publication: *Amazing Stories* (Vol. 17 #9; September 1943); Publisher: Ziff-Davis Publishing Company.

In the Libyan desert there are rumors of a secret Nazi base. A subterranean hideout under the sands of the Sahara. U.S. pilot Greg Nason discovers the rumors are true. Luvium is "a living nation imprisoned in rock beneath a giant pressure resisting dome." Now the Nazis have discovered Luvium and are harnessing its advanced technology.

The Madmen of Mandoras (1963) [Film; SFW]

Premiere: November 13, 1963; Main Cast: Walter Stocker as Phil Day, Audrey Caire as Kathy Coleman Day, Carlos Rivas as Camino Padua/Teo Padua, John Holland as Professor John Coleman, Marshall Reed as Frank Dvorak, Bill Freed as Adolf Hitler; Executive Producer: Anthony Sanucci; Story: Steve Bennett, Richard Miles; Director: David Bradley;

74 min.; Sans-S; Crown International Pictures; B/W.

The preserved head of Adolf Hitler is smuggled out of Germany to South America at the end of World War II. Hitler and the Nazis plan on world domination with the release of the deadly "G-Gas" and kidnap a scientist to stop him working on the antidote.

An edited version with new footage was released in 1968 under the title *They Saved Hitler's Brain*.

Maelstrom (*Destroyermen*, Book 3) [Novel; AHW]

Author: Taylor Anderson; First publication: New York: Roc, 2009.

In the final book of the *Destroyermen* trilogy Supreme Commander Lt. Cmdr. Matthew Reddy prepares for a showdown between American sailors, the peace-loving native Lemurians and the vicious raptor-like Grik, who now control the Japanese battleship Amagi.

Author Taylor Anderson extended the *Destroyermen* series past its initial trilogy with the publication of *Distant Thunders* (2010), *Rising Tides* (2011), *Firestorm* (2011), *Iron Gray Sea* (2012), *Storm Surge* (2013), *Deadly Shores* (2014) and *Straits of Hell* (2015).

The Magic Face (1951) [Film; AHW]

Premiere: August 13, 1951; Main Cast: Luther Adler as Rudi Janus/Janus the Great/Adolf Hitler, Patricia Knight as Vera Janus, Jaspar von Oertzen as Major Fritz Weinrich, William L. Shirer as Himself, Eric Zuckmann as Heinrich Himmler, Herman Erhardt as Hermann Göring; Producers-Story: Mort Briskin, Robert Smith; Director: Frank Tuttle; 88 min.; Columbia Pictures; B/W.

Following the murder of German leader Adolf Hitler, entertainer Janus the Great successfully impersonates him, ensuring the Allies defeat the Third Reich.

The Magicians of Night (*Sun-Cross* book #2) [Novel; WW]

Author: Barbara Hambly; First publication: New York: Del Rey Books, 1992.

Wizard Rhion emerges from his magical world into World War II Germany. Captured by the Nazis who want to harness the powers of magic for their evil purposes Rhion only wants to escape war-torn Germany.

A sequel to *The Rainbow Abyss* where author Hambly highlights the world of Rhion. A world where wizards and their magic are treated with hostility. The Dark Well acts as a portal to other universes that lack magic but may need his help.

Major Victory [Comic book character; WW]

First appearance: *Dynamic* #1 (October 1941); Creator-Artist: Charles Sultan; Publisher: Publisher: Harry "A" Chesler.

At the U.S. Army post Camp Courage, a lone sentry checks a suspicious light in the arsenal but is too late to defuse a bomb. From the wreckage two ghostly figures bring the guard's lifeless body before the feet of a spirit born in 1776, Father Patriot.

"Now to give him life. Ring the Liberty Bell. You have been spared because of your courage and fearlessness."

The stroke of the Bell revives the guard. Henceforth he will be known as Major Victory. "Go forth Major Victory ... strike and strike hard! When I need you I'll strike the Bell. Only you shall hear it," declares Father Patriot.

Major Victory #3 (Summer, 1945). Cover art by Charles Sultan. Published by Harry "A" Chesler.

Back on Earth Major Victory finds himself atop a mountain. "A wireless shack and an airplane hangar. A perfect hideout." But in the town of Alumino the notorious Baron Von Krumm and his sinister band are planning to destroy the mines and take control of the powerhouse, railroad and communications center. "Then our bombers will go to work!" boasts Von Krumm.

In his mountain retreat Major Victory picks up Von Krumm's radio broadcast declaring Alumino is in the hands of Fifth Columnists and threatening to blow up the mines to stop plane production. Major Victory comes to the rescue in a victorious air battle.

Father Patriot concludes, "Well done Major Victory but our work has only just begun."

Making History [Novel; SFW]

Author: Stephen Fry; First publication: New York: Random House, 1996.

Cambridge University graduate student Michael Young and German physicist Leo Zuckermann devise a plan to stop Adolf Hitler from being born. They send male contraceptive pills back in time to a well that supplies water to Hitler's father to make him sterile. Suddenly Michael Young is a student at Princeton in a different timeline. They have changed history, but for the worse. In place of Hitler another dictator comes to power who is first to develop the atom bomb. Michael Young must change history yet again to redress the balance.

The Man from U.N.C.L.E. (1964) [TV series)

Napoleon Solo and Illya Kuryakin of the United Network Command for Law and Enforcement combat THRUSH and all enemies of peace. Main Cast: Robert Vaughn as Napoleon Solo, David McCallum as Illya Kuryakin, Leo G. Carroll as Alexander Waverly; Creator: Sam Rolfe; Executive Producer: Norman Felton; 50 min.; Arena Productions, MGM Television; National Broadcasting Company (NBC); Color–B/W (season one).

"The Deadly Games Affair" (1:05) [SFW]
Air date: October 20, 1964; Guest Cast: Alexander Scourby as Professor Amadeus, Burt Brinkerhoff as Chuck Bosin, Janine Gray as Angelique, Felix Locher as Major Ernst Neubel, Brooke Bundy as Terry Brent; Story: Dick Nelson; Director: Alvin Ganzer.

Former Nazi scientist Professor Amadeus requires a blood type to match Adolf Hitler so he can restore him to life from suspended animation. Napoleon Solo is a perfect match.

"The Gurnius Affair" (4:11) [SFW]
Air date: November 27, 1967; Guest Cast: George McCready as Zorgon Gurnius, Judy Carne as Terry Cook, Will Kuluva as Dr. Hans Von Etske; Story: Milton S. Gelman; Director: Barry Shear.

An escaped Nazi scientist, a mind-control ray, Washington, D.C., and the President of the USA are all part of a nefarious plot by THRUSH that Solo and Kuryakin must unravel before it is too late.

"The Man Who Cried Werewolf" [Pulp fiction; WW]

Author: P.F. Costello; Illustrator: A.K. Binder; First publication: *Fantastic Adventures* (Vol. 5 #3; March 1943); Publisher: Ziff-Davis Publishing Company.

In this story written under William P. McGivern's pseudonym, P.F. Costello army reject Billy Poindexter takes up demonology to get into another branch of the service.

"I feel that if the army doesn't want me I'm no good to anyone and it doesn't matter what I do with myself. So I'm forsaking this modern life completely."

Poindexter studies werewolves and adopts a large dog. Soon Poindexter disappears and is no longer seen again. Only his dog remains. His friend decides to ship the dog off to the Army Dog Corps. Poindexter has finally been accepted into another branch of the army.

"The Man Who Hated War" [Pulp fiction; SFW]

Author: Emil Petaja; Illustrator: Julian Krupa; First publication: *Amazing Stories* (Vol. 18 #5; December 1944); Publisher: Ziff-Davis Publishing Company.

Sickened by war, Doctor Foster has discovered a means of releasing his mental consciousness from his physical self, transforming it into a higher dimension where all time exists at once. Foster plans to return to his frozen body centuries into the future when he expects mankind would learn to live in peace. But when he returns Foster finds himself at the center of the Science-Religion cult and a deadly new war.

Manticore (2005) [Telefilm; WW]

Premiere: November 26, 2005; Main Cast: Robert Beltran as Sgt. Baker, Jeff Fahey as Major Kramer, Chase Masterson as Ashley Pierce, Heather Donahue as Corporal. Keats; Executive Producer: T.J. Sakajegawa; Story: John Werner; Director: Tripp Reed; 88 min.; Sci-Fi Pictures, Secure Productions,

United Film Organization (UFO); Sci-Fi Channel; Color.

In Iraq, while looting a museum two Iraqis find a sacred amulet. Captured by U.S. soldiers the thieves escape their custody and meet a terrorist who takes them to a cave. He confiscates the amulet for a ceremony that summons an ancient creature that is a mix of a lion, a dragon and a scorpion. Now U.S. soldiers and an embedded female reporter face a new enemy in Iraq—the Manticore.

"The Map of Fate" [Pulp fiction; SFW]

Author: Donald Bern; Illustrator: Brady; First publication: *Amazing Stories* (Vol. 18 #5; December 1944); Publisher: Ziff-Davis Publishing Company.

"It beats me!" Captain Hanely exploded "I can't figure it out! ... none of our men could have known the Japs took over Eagle Peak. Even I didn't know until five minutes ago. Yet someone has already moved a Jap pin over Eagle Peak on the map!"

The following day the Japanese retreat when they have the American troops cornered. They had abandoned the area just as the pin was pulled out of the map. The Japanese were still concentrated in large numbers in Port Naguro. It was time to pull the Japanese pin from Port Naguro on the map.

Marvels [Comic book; Graphic Novel; SHW]

First publication: January 1994; Story: Kurt Busiek; Art: Alex Ross; Publisher: Marvel Comics.

The original mini-series featuring a re-imagining of events from the Marvel Universe was collected into one volume in 2009. The graphic novel includes the World War II era **Human Torch**, **Sub-Mariner** and **Captain America**. The story is based on original material first published in Timely's *Marvel Comics, Marvel Mystery Comics, Captain America Comics, Sub-Mariner* and *Human Torch*. Events include the origin of the Human Torch, the battle between Namor the Sub-Mariner and the Human Torch, Sub-Mariner and Human Torch joining forces against the "Nazi-Jap war machine" and Captain America and Bucky defeating Nazi saboteurs, assassination rings and fifth columnists.

"Matches and Kings" [Pulp fiction; SFW]

Author: John York Cabot; Illustrator: Julian S. Krupa; First publication: *Amazing Stories* (Vol. 18 #4; September 1944); Publisher: Ziff-Davis Publishing Company.

Top turret gunner Fenwick refuses to have his cigarette lit by the same match as his buddies Nolan and Callahan. "It was proved in the last war that every time three guys used the same match, one of 'em got knocked off within twenty-four hours."

Radio gunner Viborg tells the story of Lars Klobar, the Match King and how all three who took the match suffered great misfortune with Klobar rumored to have committed suicide shortly after. After listening to Viborg's account the soldiers need no more convincing.

A Matter of Life and Death a.k.a. *Stairway to Heaven* (1946) [Film; WW]

Premiere (UK): November 1, 1946; Main Cast: David Niven as Squadron Leader Peter David Carter, Kim Hunter as June, Roger Livesey as Dr. Frank Reeves, Marius Goring as Conductor 71, Raymond Massey as Abraham Farlan, Robert Coote as Flying Officer Bob Trubshawe; Screenplay-Producers-Directors: Michael Powell, Emeric Pressburger; 104 min.; Distribution: Eagle-Lion Films, Universal Studios; Production Company: The Archers, J. Arthur Rank; B&W-Technicolor.

May 2, 1945. Night over Europe. With his life hanging in the balance in a doomed Lancaster bomber airman Peter David Carter, with a penchant for quoting poetry, makes radio contact with June from the American Women's Army Corps (WAC) and jumps from his plane without a parachute. The British Royal Air Force pilot miraculously survives the fall and meets and falls in love with June who is riding home across a beach on her bicycle. But he is living on borrowed time and has in fact suffered a critical brain injury and must provide a case for his life before a heavenly tribunal.

Prosecutor Abraham Farlan is an American, the first casualty of the Revolutionary War, killed with a British bullet in 1775. Carter's wartime friend Doctor Reeves who died recently in a motorcycle accident represents Carter. The pros and cons of British and American culture throughout history results in deadlock and it is the power of love between a man and a woman that finally wins the day.

Released as *Stairway to Heaven* in the USA the film received mixed reviews.

C.A. Lejeune from *The Observer* (UK November 3, 1946) commented: "The main trouble with

A Matter of Life and Death a.k.a. *Stairway to Heaven* (1946), starring (from left) Kim Hunter as June, David Niven as Squadron Leader Peter David Carter (J. Arthur Rank).

"A Matter of Life and Death" is that it leaves us in grave doubts whether it is intended to be serious or gay…. When they insist that this bleak, aseptic Heaven, as functional as a labour exchange and as verbose as a debate on some local Housing Bill is the creation of a poet's mind, I reply, but firmly, that they are talking utter rot."

Variety (December 1946) commented: "For the first ten minutes, apart from some pretentious poppycock, the picture looks like living up to its boosting. This is real cinema, then action gives way to talk, some of it flat and dreary. With all their ingenuity, Powell, Pressburger and Alfred Junge could only invent a heaven reminiscent of the Hollywood Bowl and an exclusive celestial nightclub where hostesses dish out wings to dead pilots."

The film was later adapted to television and radio with David Niven reprising his role on *Lux Radio Theatre* in 1955.

See: **Stairway to Heaven**.

Maus: A Survivor's Tale [Graphic novel; WW]

Author-Art: Art Spiegelman; First publication: New York: Pantheon Books-Random House, 1986.

Cartoonist Art Spiegelman, the son of Auschwitz death camp survivor Vladek Spiegelman recalls the life of his parents, and his troubled relationship with his father, in the form of a graphic novel where the Jews are portrayed as mice and the Nazis as cats.

Spiegelman's Jewish parents grow up in wartime Poland, where Vladek becomes a small-time textile salesman. In 1937 he marries into a wealthy Sosnowiec hosiery family. His wife, Anja Zylberberg, and Vladek soon find themselves hiding from the Nazis, before they are captured trying to escape to Hungary. In March 1944 Auschwitz awaits.

Although the book and it's sequel *Maus II: A Survivor's Tale: And Here My Troubles Began* (1991) are primarily anthromorphic cartoon memoirs that show the horrific brutality and sadism of the Jews' Nazi captors, there are sequences that cross over into Weird War territory.

To escape life in a Prisoner-of-War camp, Vladek answers an announcement that reads, "Workers Needed. War Prisoners may volunteer for labor assignments to replace German workers called to the front. Housing and abundant food will be supplied." Despite his fears that it might be a trick

Maus: A Survivor's Tale by Art Spiegelman.

Vladek volunteers. To his surprise accommodation is a big improvement on the tents at the P.O.W. camp. Pleasant wooden houses with beds, sheets, pillows and a stove. But the daily work is grueling. Leveling four-yard high hills with a pick and shovel. Complainers are sent back to the P.O.W. camp.

One restless night Vladek has a dream where he is talking to his dead grandfather. The voice comforts him. "Don't worry my child. You will come out of this place—free! On the day of Parsha's Truma." The next day he tells a Rabbi about his dream and asks him when he is due to read Parsha's Truma again. His answer seems like an eternity. Three months of hard work lay ahead before the reading. But when the day arrives he is released by the Germans. His late grandfather's voice has proven to be true.

Spiegelman's *Maus*, originally published, in part, in *Raw* magazine, has received universal praise. Fellow cartoonist Jules Feiffer stated, "A remarkable book, awesome in its conception and execution ... at one and the same time a novel, a documentary, a memoir, and a comic book. Brilliant, just brilliant." Novelist Umberto Eco commented, "When two of the mice speak of love, you are moved, when they suffer, you weep."

Medal of Honor: Underground [Video game; WW]

Release date: October 2000; Platforms: PlayStation, Game Boy Advance; Developers: PlayStation, DreamWorks Interactive, Game Boy Advance, Rebellion Developments; Publishers: PlayStation, Electronic Arts, Game Boy Advance, Sony Computer Entertainment.

The World War II video game centered around the daring exploits of OSS member Manon Batiste and her undercover missions in Europe and Africa includes the bonus level "Panzerknacker Unleashed" that enters Weird War territory. The player controls Lt. Jimmy Patterson as he infiltrates Wewelsburg Castle on a mission to retrieve the Knife of Abraham. Entering the castle Patterson encounters all manner of strange creatures including dancing dogs armed with machine guns, zombie soldiers, robot soldiers and knights.

The Medusa Amulet [Novel; WW]

Author: Robert Masello; First publication: New York: Bantam Books, 2011.

Renaissance scholar David Franco of Chicago's Newberry Library is offered $1 million to find a mystical amulet created by Benvenuto Cellini using water from the retreat of the Gorgon Medusa. Franco's grasps at the chance to possibly save his sister who is dying from breast cancer. With help of a beautiful Italian tour guide Franco uncovers a link between the amulet and Adolf Hitler who has used its mystical powers to survive into the present day under an alias.

The Men Who Stare at Goats (2009) [Film; WW]

Premiere: September 5, 2009; Main Cast: George Clooney as Lyn Cassady, Ewan McGregor as Bob Wilton, Jeff Bridges as Bill Django, Stephen Land as Brigadier General Dean Hopgood, Robert Patrick as Todd Nixon; Executive Producers: Barbara A. Hall, James Holt, Alison Owen, David M. Thompson; Screenplay: Peter Straughan. Based on the book by Jon Ronson; Director: Grant Heslov; 94 min.; Ruby Films, Smokehouse, BBC Films: Overture Films; Color.

In Iraq journalist Bob Wilton uncovers a story about a secret psychic military unit, the New Earth Army. Lyn Cassady claims his staring "sparkly eyes" can kill a goat at a distance and if required, the military enemy, thus making mind control the latest lethal weapon in warfare.

USA Today film critic Claudia Puig stated (November 8, 2009): "The scenarios posited are just specific and bizarre enough to be convincing, luring the audience into its weirdly tangled web.... *The Men Who Stare at Goats* is irreverent and lighthearted."

Merlin the Magician [Comic book character; WW]

First appearance: *National Comics* #1 (July 1940); Creator: Fred Guardineer; Publisher: Quality Comics Group.

English playboy Jock Kellog is told by his dying uncle that he is a descendant of Merlin, the magician from King Arthur's court. He hands Kellogg a cloak. "That is your inheritance. Keep it, for you are the last Merlin."

When he dons the cloak Kellog discovers he has magical powers. He disappears from the night club scene as war consumes the world and confronts Mars, god of war. Seeking a meaning to the endless destruction from Mars he is greeted with derision. "It is to amuse myself with the sniveling acts of men weak enough to obey me. And no mortal can appear before me and live."

Merlin escapes and comes across a beautiful

girl shackled to a rock. She is Peace who can only be freed if Merlin defeats Mars in battle. Merlin confronts Mars yet again but first he must defeat the personifications of Hunger and Poverty. Merlin is up to the task and finally forces Mars to beg for mercy. On Earth the great statesmen of the world sign a peace treaty. The war is finally over and peace reigns.

When World War II reached the shores of America at Pearl Harbor Merlin's adventures concentrated more on the real-life Nazi and Japanese menace.

The Midnight Guardian: A Millennial Novel [Novel; WW]

Author: Sarah Jane Stratford; First publication: New York: St. Martin's Press, 2009.

1938. London's ancient vampire tribunal send five of their millennial vampires to Berlin to destroy the ambitions of Adolf Hitler and his Third Reich. The vampires aren't motivated by peace but fearful their fresh supply of human blood will become rationed in another world war. But the Nazis have their own army of vampire hunters intent on keeping Hitler's vision alive and purifying the world of vampires.

See: *The Moonlight Brigade: A Millennial Novel*

Midnighter [Comic book]

First publication: January 2007: Five-issue story; Story: Garth Ennis; Art: Chris Sprouse, Karl Story; Publisher: Wildstorm.

"Killing Machine" [WW]

Returning from Afghanistan *Midnighter* is ambushed and given the choice of "kill a mass murderer or die." The Midnighter's secondary heart has been replaced with a time-detonated bomb and unless he kills Corporal Adolf Hitler in the trenches of World War I France the Midnighter will die. Traveling in time through a teleportation portal the Midnighter fails to carry out his mission before he is apprehended by time police from the future. But he manages to crash their time machine, landing in 1945 shortly before Hitler's bunker suicide in Berlin.

El Ministerio del Tiempo (2015) [TV series; Spain]

First broadcast: February 24, 2015; Main Cast: Aura Garrido as Amelia Folch, Cayetana Guillen Cuervo as Irene Larra, Juan Gea as Ernesto Jiminez, Francesca Pinon as Augustias Vazquez, Jaime Blanch as Salvador Marti, Nacho Fresneda as Alonso de Entrerrios; Creators: Javier Olivares, Pablo Olivares; Executive producers: Maite Pisonero, Maria Roy; 21 × 70 min.; Cliffhanger, Onza Partners, Television Espanola (TVE); Color.

The Ministry of Time is a secret Spanish government agency, founded by Queen Isabel I and King Ferdinand, that employs patrols to guard doors that allow time travel. When intruders are detected the patrols travel back into history to prevent anyone from the present or the past from using the doors to change history. The latest patrol consists of 16th century Army of Flanders soldier Alonso de Entrerrios, Amelia Foch, a pioneering female university student from Barcelona in 1880, and present day Samur paramedic Julian Martinez, still recovering from the death of his wife.

"Cambio del Tiempo" (2:13) [SFW]

Air Date: May 23, 2016: Guest Cast: Carlos Hipolito as Philip II of Spain, Marta Nieto as Isabella of Portugal, Victor Dupla as Augustin Arguelles, Carlos Kaniowsky as Mateo Vazquez de Leca; Story: Pablo Lara, Mairena Ruiz Denia; Director: Marc Vigil.

Philip II of Spain travels back in time in an attempt to reverse the defeat of his Spanish Armada. But when he faces opposition from the Ministry he discovers he can also travel forward in time. In 2016 he plans to be King of the world and time itself. When the patrol returns from a mission in 1812 they find history has changed for the worse. Restoring the timeline will not be an easy task.

"Cómo se Reescribe el Tiempo" (1:03) [SFW]

Air Date: March 9, 2015: Guest Cast: David Luque as Heinrich Himmler, Francisco Franco; Story: Javier Olivares, Anais Schaaff; Director: Marc Vigil.

World War II, 1940. When a former member of the Ministry reveals the secrets of the time traveling doors to Heinrich Himmler, he attempts to gain control of one of the doors at the Santa Maria de Montserrat Abbey. Not only must Himmler be stopped from visiting Montserrat, a meeting between Hitler and Franco to negotiate the participation of Spain in World War II has to be avoided.

"El Monasterio del Tiempo" (2:04) [SFW]

Air date: March 7, 2016; Guest Cast: Fernando Cayo as Napoleon Bonaparte, Jordi Martinez as Michel Ney, Ismael Martinez as Rodolfo Suarez, Nadia de Santiago as Rosa del Amo; Story: Javier Olivares, Diana Rojo, Peris Romano, Anais Schaaff; Director: Jorge Dorado.

Christmas, 1808. The death of an abbess at the

Santa Clara de Tordesillas abbey has distorted the timeline. The Time Ministry patrol must stop Napoleonic soldiers from executing three men accused of spying. One of those men is the ancestor of Spanish President Adolfo Suarez. Ministry secretary Augustias must pose as the dead abbess to try and convince Napoleon not to execute the prisoners.

"Tiempo de Gloria" (1:02) [SFW]
Air date: March 2, 2015; Guest Cast: Victor Clavijo as Lope de Vega, Miguel Rellan as Gil Perez; Story: Javier Olivares, Pablo Olivares; Director: Abigail Schaaff.

Julian, Amelia and Alonso travel back in time to 1588 to make certain Lope de Vegas changes ships from the San Esteban to the San Juan. He must avoid dying when the Spanish Armada ship San Esteban is attacked and sunk by the English.

"Tiempo de valientes" (2:07–2:08) [SFW]
Air dates: March 28, April 4, 2016; Guest Cast: Pedro Alonso as Saturnino Martin Cerezo, Paco Marin as Rogelio Vigil de Quinones, Aitor Merino as Antonio Sanchez Menache, Juan Jose Ballesta as Vicente Gonzalez Toca, Monica Estarreado as Asuncion; Story: Carlos de Pando, Javier Olivares; Director: Marc Vigil.

When Julian does a favor for a dying man he becomes trapped in the Siege of Baler. The beleaguered Spanish are fighting for territory that has reverted back to Cuba and the Philippines.

"El Tiempo Es El Que Es" (1:01) [SFW]
Air Date: February 24, 2015; Guest Cast: Hovik Keuchkerian as Juan Martin Diez, "El Empecinado," Josep Linuesa as Thibaud, Ivan Villanueva as Benito; Story: Javier Olivares, Pablo Olivares; Director: Marc Vigil.

A modern-day pistol must be retrieved by the Time Ministry patrol in the year 1808, the prevent the killing of Juan Martin Diez, "El Empecinado."

Diez, an officer in the Peninsular War, was a key player in the retreat of Napoleonic forces from Spain and the defeat of Napoleon.

Minute-Man [Comic book character]
First appearance: *Master Comics* #11 (February 1941); Creator: Charlie Sultan; Publisher: Fawcett Publications.

"His friends and comrades-in-arms call him Jack Weston, buck private of the new citizen Army. The enemies of his country fear him as Minute-Man, the one-man avalanche of destruction that strikes down all who plan the downfall of America!"

In his patriotic stars and stripes costume Minute-Man possesses no super-powers but does encounter occasional Weird War opponents.

"The Hooded Death" [WW]
First publication: *Minute Man* #2 (Winter 1941); Publisher: Fawcett Publications.

Illyria, queen of spies stands before a hooded man who gives her orders to "Get Minute-Man." Meanwhile the army are aware of the nefarious activities of Illyria but fail to see through her disguise as an old woman as she infiltrates the camp. She captures General Milton and reports to the Green Hood who proceeds to set his thug Bismark on both the General and Illyria for failing to capture Minute-Man. The Green Hood has other plans at work to destroy Minute-Man. A new super-weapon—a deadly gas machine-tank that sprays its victims and destroys all obstacles in its path.

"Illyria, Queen of Spies" [WW]
First publication: *Minute Man* #1 (1941); Art: Sheldon Moldoff; Publisher: Fawcett Publications.

Private Jack Weston is transferred to Barracoon

Minute Man #2 (Winter 1941). Cover art by Mac Raboy. Published by Fawcett Publications.

in the Gulf of Mexico. The U.S. government has just purchased the island to be used as a fortified naval base. But on the island Illyria, queen of foreign spies, has plans to start a rebellion among the natives by stirring up voodoo prophecies.

After capturing Minute-Man Illyria tells him, "Your American soldiers are few. These people think their gods can command them to destroy such strangers. It will happen. Then, before more Americans come, my own people will land a strong force here!"

Appearing in a costume to instill fear and awe among the natives Priestess Illyria arms them with guns and commands them to kill the last soldier. Meanwhile Minute-Man escapes a watery death planned by Illyria, battles an alligator and warns the Army Sergeant of the threat by tapping morse code on jungle drums.

"The Miracle at Dunkirk" [Pulp fiction; SFW]

Author: John York Cabot; Illustrator: Robert Fuqua; First publication: *Fantastic Adventures* (Vol. 3 #7; September 1941); Publisher: Ziff-Davis Publishing Company.

"Who was the inspired military genius who held back Nazi mechanized might while the British turned defeat into honor and glory?"

The Miracle at Verdun a.k.a. *Wunder um Verdun* (1930) [Stage play; WW]

First performance: October 1930: Leipzig, Germany; U.S. Premiere: March 16, 1931; Martin Beck Theatre, New York; Main Cast: Edward Arnold as Dr. Paetz/Reich Chancellor Overtuesch, J.W. Austin as Sharpe/Lord Grathford, Jules Epailly as Remusat/Premier Delcampe, Robert Middlemass as Jackson/Clarkson, George Magis as Mazas, Anthony Baker as Schmidt, Jacob B. Leifer as Weber, George Brant as Shroeder; Production: The Theatre Guild; Playwright: Hans von Chlumberg; U.S. Adaptation: Julian Leigh; Staging: Herbert Biberman.

This anti-war play in eight scenes is based on the real-life Battle of Verdun which lasted from March 16, 1916, to December 22, 1916. The French and Germans suffered extensive casualties with approximately 420,000 dead in total.

The play begins at a small military cemetery in Argonne Forest, France in August 1934. A group of tourists visit the graves of those killed in World War I. One of the tourists shows his disrespect for the dead by arguing about the number of graves.

Jackson: Well I'll be damned. Ten thousand killed and two thousand graves—but it costs us two hundred French francs to see them.

Vernier: What's that sir?

Jackson: I mean your company is damned expensive, charging so much and showing so little...

Arguments continue as the English and Americans attempt to belittle the French and Germans.

The dead soldiers are ordered to rise from their graves by a Messenger but are ignored by the Prime Minister of England, Lord Grathford and French Premier Minister Michel Delcampe. The wife of German Reich Chancellor Overtuesch states "He has nothing to do with the dead! He has a hard enough time with the living!"

The heads of nations convene to declare the resurrection of the soldiers is not a miracle and they must return to their graves. In the concluding scene we learn the risen soldiers were all part of a German tourist's dream.

Despite the weak conclusion the play has a powerful message with the prophetic words of playwright Chlumberg. They are given voice though the Messenger who foresees World War II nine years before the event. "... the mad pestilence that brought upon you untimely destruction does not cease to rage on earth. No! The earth will shortly be full of misery again, and desolate...."

Hans von Chlumberg died tragically during the dress rehearsal of the play in Leipzig, Germany in 1930 from injuries sustained when he fell into the orchestra pit.

"The Miracle of Bulldozer Mike" [Pulp fiction; SFW]

Author: Robert Moore Williams; Illustrator: Brady; First publication: *Amazing Stories* (Vol. 19 #4; December 1945); Publisher: Ziff-Davis Publishing Company.

"Something happened on this Pacific Isle that could only be called a miracle—but what it really was, Bulldozer Mike didn't want to say."

Bulldozer Mike appears out of nowhere to build an airfield on a Pacific island surrounded by Japanese. Some time later he defeats a Japanese land attack using only his mysterious knife from Damascus, with its handle of ivory and gold and sides of the blade covered in a scroll of finely crafted figures. To add to his mystique Bulldozer Mike fights of a renewed attack piloting a Thunderbolt plane. And then he disappears, never to be seen again. It later transpires that the airfield was built on the wrong island.

"I wonder if Mike had contrived to have this happen here. For this was certainly the right island, the one right island in the whole Pacific. Maybe our being here was a miracle. Maybe miracles happen."

"The Miracle of Kicker McGuire" [Pulp fiction; WW]

Author: Robert Moore Williams; First publication: *Fantastic Adventures* (Vol. 5 #5; May 1943); Publisher: Ziff-Davis Publishing Company.

"Just kids playing war. But suddenly the toy gun of one spat a weird blue ray—and death came!"

The Mirk and Midnight Hour [Juvenile book; WW]

Author: Jane Nickerson; First publication: New York: Alfred A. Knopf, 2014.

Violet Dancey is living through a time of change. A new step-mother, step-sister and two distant cousins are staying for the summer while her father fights for the South in the Civil War. Violet has already lost her twin brother to the war. So when she discovers a severely wounded Union soldier in an abandoned lodge in the woods she's aware he may be responsible for her brother's death. But Violet likes the soldier named Thomas and is intrigued to find others have been tending to his wounds and keeping him alive. Violet's intrigue turns to fear when she learns of the power of hoodoo and snake worship that soon threatens her family and Thomas.

Misfits (2009) [TV series; UK]

A group of young offenders gain supernatural powers following an electrical storm.

"Episode #3.4" [SFW]

Air date: November 20, 2011; Main Cast: Joseph Gilgun as Rudy Wade, Iwan Rheon as Simon Bellamy, Lauren Socha as Kelly Bailey. Nathan Stewart-Jarrett as Curtis Donovan, Antonia Thomas as Alisha Daniels, Craig Parkinson as Shaun. Matthew McNulty as Seth, Fred Pearson as Friedrich Hirsch, David Barrass as Adolf Hitler, Glenn Spears as Captain Smith; Executive Producers: Murray Ferguson, Petra Fried, Howard Overman; Story: Howard Overman; Directors: Alex Garcia Lopez, Wayne Che Yip; 49 min.; Clarkenwell Films; Color.

When time-traveler Friedrich Hirsch fails in his attempt to kill Adolf Hitler in the 1930s he changes history when the Nazis discover his cell phone and use the technology to win World War II. The United Kingdom is now under Nazi control. Misfit Kelly Bailey must return to the 1930s to recover Hirsch's phone and restore the timeline.

Miss America [Comic book character; SHW]

1. First appearance: *Military Comics* #1 (August 1941); Creator: Elmer Wexler; Publisher: Quality Comics Group.

"Out of the very heart of the spirit that is America comes a new champion of democracy—young Joan Dale, reporter."

In a dream the Statue of Liberty comes to life and grants Joan magical powers. "So that you may give your country, the help it needs." When Joan awakens she tests her powers and to her astonishment makes a tree magically disappear. Her dream is a reality.

In her first heroic deed she rescues a man from a gang of ruffians by changing them into peaceful doves. When the thankful man tells Joan, "Girls like you are the real spirit of America. You're the real Miss America" Joan adopts the name for her new heroic persona.

In issue #4 of *Military Comics* (November 1941) Joan quits her job as reporter for "The Daily Star" to work for the F.B.I. At the El Toro Club she uncovers a Nazi spy ring and a deadly plot to bomb the club with robot controlled planes. Wearing her costume for the first time Miss America makes certain the plot fails.

Unfortunately for Miss America fans her comic strip adventures came to a premature conclusion with issue #7 in 1942.

2. First appearance: *Marvel Mystery* #49 (November 1943); Creators: Otto Binder, Al Gabriele; Publisher: Timely Comics.

Teenage heiress Madeline Joyce is intrigued by a device that supposedly gave a scientist super powers when he was struck by lightning. When she is knocked unconscious during a thunderstorm while holding the device the scientist believes she has died. In a state of panic he destroys the device and then himself. Meanwhile the young heiress recovers and discovers she has the power to levitate, temporary x-ray vision and the "strength of a thousand men."

Going by the name of Miss America and wearing a patriotic costume, she becomes a member of the **All-Winners Squad**, **Liberty Legion** and the **Invaders** during World War II. Madeline Joyce falls in love with Robert Frank alias the **Whizzer** but sadly dies after her second child is stillborn due to radiation poisoning.

Mr. Justice [Comic book character; WW]

First appearance: *Blue Ribbon Mystery Comics* #9 (February 1941); Creators: Joe Blair, Sam Cooper; Publisher: MLJ Magazines.

"Resting on the boundary line between Scotland and England, stands the ancient castle of Solway Firth. Erected in the year 1540, the medieval fortress has withstood countless scores of attacks. Now in the year 1940, a new and terrible enemy hurls down tons of thunderous destruction. But in releasing the rack-loads of death, the invaders are about to release *from* death—the most bewildering, the most incredible, the most mysterious man the earth has ever known!"

In the castle a guide informs tourists of the story of the murder of Prince James, heir to the throne of England. Legend tells of his spirit rising from the dead to strangle the men who murdered him. "His spirit still lives on within these very walls. Someday the castle will be destroyed, and the spirit of Prince James will return to earth once again."

At a meeting of the Home Ministry the decision is made to preserve the castle from attack during World War II by dismantling it brick-by-brick and moving it to a sanctuary in America. But on the journey across the Atlantic the British ship transporting the castle is blown apart by a torpedo attack from a U-boat.

"And as it slowly settles for the death plunge, a mysterious vapor takes form above the ship and the spirit of martyred Prince James returns to the world."

The spirit undergoes a metamorphosis, assuming the shape of a mortal man. But in times of danger he reverts to spirit form. "At last I've found my destiny ... as Mr. Justice!"

"Waltz of the Vampire"

First publication: *Blue Ribbon Mystery Comics* #11 (April 1941); Story: Joe Blair; Art: Sam Cooper.

Carlos Hubbello has been transformed into a vampire by Nazis who plan to use him to sabotage a vital trade agreement "which will leave Nazi Germany out in the cold." Attending the trade meeting in his mortal form he senses the presence of evil and travels with Hubbello to South America to confront the King of Vampires and defeat the Nazi menace as Mr. Justice.

Mr. Justice personally confronted Adolf Hitler, referred to as "The Dictator," in a story that spanned *Blue Ribbon Mystery Comics* #13–#16 (June–September 1941). Issue #13 featured inventive page design by artist Warren King.

Satan adopts human form "to join all evil men together in a great dictatorship, with himself as director." Taking root in Nazi Germany Satan makes certain "the shadows of suppression sweep across the Eastern hemisphere." Mr. Justice takes a stand to stop "the man and his fanatical lieutenants before they destroy civilization."

When Mayor Clark's daughter Pat is kidnapped from her home and transferred to a U-boat Mr. Justice goes into action in his spirit form. Rescuing Pat from the clutches of the Nazis Mr. Justice confronts the Dictator face-to-face and is shown his true identity as Satan.

In Europe Mr. Justice witnesses the secret po-

Mr. Justice (left) and Captain Flag (right) in *Blue Ribbon Comics* #17 (October 1941). Cover art by Sam Cooper. Published by MLJ Magazines Inc.

lice arresting Hans Muller for "divulging secrets of our country." Taken to a concentration camp to be executed Muller is rescued from the firing squad by the spirit of Mr. Justice. But Muller's girlfriend Christine is still held captive. When the Dictator learns of Muller's escape he orders her immediate execution. But Mr. Justice comes to the rescue once again and manages to turn the secret police chief's men against him, resulting in his death.

Mr. Justice now sets out to destroy the Dictator's three remaining right-hand men. The Dictator hands each of his men a rare jewel of King Ming II. "No immortal dares to attack a person who carries one." But Mr. Justice has a plan to turn his men against the Dictator. First is foreign minister Von Fibbenfop.

"So the Dictator warned you of me did he? How much better it would have been had he warned you about himself. Or, the plot of the propaganda minister to kill you."

Next is Field Marshall Boreing. Mr. Justice pays him a visit in his human form and also warns him of a plot against his life by the propaganda minister Gobbels.

His final visit is to Gobbels where he warns him of Von Fibbenfop. "If he sees you again, he may try to kill you!" Gobbels kills Von Fibbenfop first by blowing up the train he is traveling on. Field Marshall Boreing believes he is next and sets a trap for Gobbels who is shot down in a hail of bullets. Boreing's next target is the Dictator and total power for himself. But following a fierce struggle the Dictator spares Boreing's life after he decides he still needs him to fight Mr. Justice.

The Dictator hands Field Marshall Boreing a drink that will make him "invulnerable to all immortals" as they plan to attack the Republic of Kurtey. In human form Mr. Justice warns the President of Kurtey to evacuate the capital city. Boreing orders four hundred heavy bombers to comprise the first wave, followed by one thousand light bombers over the capital.

Mr. Justice captures Boreing and takes him hostage with the warning, "If your bombers carry out their mission, there will be nothing left of the city ... or of you!" But it is too late for Boreing as the planes drop their bombs and Boreing dies.

Satan decides to change tactics, deserting the Dictator in favor of the monstrous Green Ghoul to spread fear and murder in America.

Mr. Liberty [Comic book character; WW]

First appearance: *USA Comics* #1 (August 1941); Creator: Syd Shores; Publisher: Timely Comics.

American History Professor John Liberty is visited by a ghost who clothes him in a costume influenced by the Revolutionary War. John Liberty is now Mr. Liberty. Soon he receives another spectral visitor in the form of Paul Revere, who warns him of impending danger from Nazi saboteurs. Liberty discovers he can also summon other spirits to help him when the ghosts of Ethan Allen and the Green Mountain Boys distract the Nazis from rigging their explosives.

Mr. Limpet [Novel; WW]

Author: Theodore Pratt; Illustrator: Garrett Price; First publication: New York: Alfred A. Knopf, 1942.

Henry and Bessie Limpet visit Coney Island amusement park with their friends George and Clara Stickle. Mr. Limpet is attracted by the school of fish swimming beneath the pier. Some have commented he resembles a fish himself.

Mr. Limpet was a skinny little man whose only marked feature was a prominent, very pointed nose on which eyeglasses were perched precariously. He was slightly pop-eyed....

With an overbearing wife and thoughts of the present war swimming in his mind, Limpet looks over the pier and wishes he was a fish. He gets his wish when he falls (or jumps) into the ocean below. Mr. Stickle attempts to rescue him but is amazed at the sight before him.

Mr. Stickle had the curious impression that the fish was wearing eyeglasses, but this could not be. Oddly, however, it struck him that the fish looked a good deal like Mr. Limpet.

Mr. Limpet is now a fish who wants to serve his country by helping the U.S. Navy locate U-boats. George Stickle convinces the Navy Mr. Limpet is real and can help them. Meanwhile Adolf Hitler learns about Limpet and wants him to work as a spy for the Nazis. Limpet refuses and continues his work for the U.S. Navy, but when the war ends Stickle warns him not trust the ulterior motives of the scientists who claim they can return him to human form. Mr. Limpet, disillusioned with the state of the world, decides to stay a fish and says a final farewell to his wife Bessie before swimming out to sea with his new love, Ladyfish.

See: ***The Incredible Mr. Limpet***

"Mistress of the Dark" [Pulp fiction; WW]

Author: Elroy Arno; Illustrator: Magarian; First publication: *Fantastic Adventures* (Vol. 5 #5; May 1943); Publisher: Ziff-Davis Publishing Company.

"A London cellar gave up a girl and Roger Bacon's secret. Both combined to promise sure defeat for the Axis. In the possession of the girl were the secrets of the ancient alchemists."

Monster Killer (2013) [Film; SFW]

Premiere: May 1, 2013; Main Cast: Phillip gay as Andrew James, Marc Maynon as Mark Roberts, Katelynn Dubow as Katherine, Tammie Smalls as Gloria; Producer: John Paul Rice; Story-Director: Edgar Michael Bravo; 76 min.; No Restrictions Entertainment; Color.

Andrew James, a 155-year-old slave from the American Civil War can travel between parallel universes by taking the life force of serial killers. When he saves the life of 19-year-old Mark Roberts their lives become interlocked.

The Monster Society of Evil [Comic book characters; SHW]

First publication: *Captain Marvel Adventures* #22 (March 1943); Creators: Otto Binder, C.C. Beck; Fawcett Comics.

Founder member Mr. Mind "The World's Wickedest Worm" gathers an evil group to defeat **Captain Marvel** and rule the world. In his quest for world domination he enlists the help of **Captain Nazi**, deranged scientist Dr. Sivana, Black Adam, Herkimer the Crocodile Man, Goat-Man, hypnotic monster Evil Eye, Japanese agent Nippo the Nipponese, Nazi spy Mr. Banjo, Jeepers the bat-monster, King Kull the Beastman, immortal Oggar, IBAC the cursed, atomic robot Mr. Atom and real-life dictators Adolf Hitler, Hideki Tojo and Benito Mussolini.

The Monster Society of Evil, the first super villain team to appear in comic books, appeared in a serialized story lasting 25 issues from March 1943 to May 1945. Over the course of the story *Captain Marvel* defeats Nippo's plans to create a second Pearl Harbor and a plot by Sivana to turn America into an Arctic wasteland. At the conclusion Mr. Mind is sentenced to death for the murder of 186,744 people and his "little worm" body stuffed and placed in a museum.

The team was revived by DC Comics in 1974 and appeared sporadically over the following decades.

Moonbranches [Juvenile book; WW]

Author: Ann Rundle; First publication: New York: Macmillan, 1986.

During World War I, 14-year-old Frances is spending summer at a Scottish mansion where her aunt is the housekeeper. Hallowes has a violent past involving the death of a twin brother. That same twin now visits Frances in spirit form, seeking justice for his death. In the midst of the family intrigue, Frances worries about her father who is fighting in the war.

Moonfisher [Novel; WW]

Author: Victoria Mosley; First publication: London: Quartet, 2011.

Violet, was raised a farm in the Dordogne, but now runs a vintage clothes shop in modern-day London. She also suffers from vivid dreams where she inhabits the mind and body of another woman. Meanwhile a woman named Anouk, who lives in Nazi-occupied France in 1943, works for Winston Churchill's special operations department and has vivid dreams of a girl and her dog, surrounded by huge glass buildings.

The Moonlight Brigade: A Millennial Novel [Novel; WW]

Author: Sarah Jane Stratford; First publication: New York: St. Martin's Griffin, 2011.

British millennial leader Mors' search for a missing member of his team following a fight with Nazi vampire hunters leads him to Rome. Before his rebirth as a vampire Mors was a truly great general in the Roman Republic. Now he sees how far Italy has fallen under Fascism and vows to return it to a republic. But an attraction to beautiful human partisan organizer Giulia and his lust for power threatens his plans as Nazi vampire hunters remain on the prowl.

"A Most Ingenious Paradox" [Pulp fiction; SFW]

Author: George Tashman; Illustrator: Arnold Kohn; First publication: *Amazing Stories* (Vol. 18 #5; December 1944); Publisher: Ziff-Davis Publishing Company.

Lieutenant Ernst Schlagel is ruled by German logic, but when he encounters a wise old man on a Greek island his logic deserts him. Trapped on the island Schlagel discovers he has been talking with Roman Emperor Zeno.

The Mother (1938) [Stage play; Czechoslovakia; WW]

U.S. Premiere: April 25, 1939, Lyceum Theatre, New York, NY; Main Cast: Alla Nazimova as The Mother, Reginald Bach as The Father, Montgomery Clift as Tony, Stephen Ker Appleby as Andrew, Carl Norval as George, Tom Palmer as Peter, Alan Brixey as Christopher, Edward Broadley as The Old Man; Producer: Victor Payne-Jennings in association with Kathleen Robinson; Playwright: Karel Capek; Adaptation: Paul Selver, Miles Malleson; Director: Miles Malleson.

Influenced by the Spanish Civil War, Capek's anti-war play in three acts takes place in the "Father's Room of the Mother's Home." Dolores can communicate with the dead members of her family. She believes her husband and son Ondra threw away their lives fighting in Africa. With the news of the worsening war she sees two of her children in the room and knows they have also died. Only Tony remains alive and Dolores knows he too will go to war.

Mother Russia [Comic book; WW]

First publication: November 2015; Story-Art: Jeff McComsey; Publisher: Fubar Press.

Stalingrad, 1943. The dead have risen and the thunder of war has been replaced with the moans of the undead. A former Russian ballerina is now the Sniper following the death of her entire family at the hands of invading Nazis. When the Sniper spots a two-year-old child walking among the Nazi zombies she comes to his rescue. But their future remains in peril in zombie-infested Stalingrad.

Mysterious Island [Film serial, Film, TV series, Telefilm; SFW]

1. [Film serial] Subtitled "Captain Harding's Fabulous Adventures."

Premiere: September 13, 1951; Main Cast; Richard Crane as Captain Cyrus Harding, Marshall Reed as Jack Pencroft, Karen Randle as Rulu of Mercury, Ralph Hodges as Herbert "Bert" Brown, Leonard Penn as Captain Nemo, Hugh Prosser as Gideon Spilett, Gene Roth as Pirate Captain Shard, Bernard Hamilton as Neb, Rusty Wescoatt as Moley, William Fawcett as Mr. Jackson, Terry Frost as Ayrton, George Robotham as Mercurian; Producer: Sam Katzman; Screenplay: Lewis Clay, Royal K. Cole, George H. Plympton; Based on the story "L'Île mystérieuse," after the novel by Jules Verne; Director: Sydney Bennet; 252 min. total (15 episodes); Columbia Pictures; B/W.

Opening narration: "In March, 1865, the great war between the States raged toward its climax as the Union forces circled and besieged the vital city of Richmond. On the fields and highways of Virginia the armies of north and south locked in mortal combat. The federal web was spun ever closer to the doomed city, planned and executed by the brilliant Officer of the Engineers, Captain Cyrus Harding."

Harding and his small detachment are observed while on a scouting mission by Confederates in an observation balloon. Captured and placed under house arrest, Captain Harding is approached by Gideon Spilett who talks of "escaping through the lines" by the observation balloon. Harding is soon joined by his African American servant Neb, sailor Jack Pencroft and Herbert Brown, the son of Pencroft's skipper.

Under cover of night they escape in the Confederate balloon, along with Top the dog. A freak hurricane strikes, blowing them south westward for five days and nights, before they lose altitude and land on a volcanic island. On the island they see a strange metallic craft land and a beautiful, young woman and her men emerge. It is Rula from the planet Mercury who has plans to conquer Earth. Strange volcanic men and a wild man add to their woes in their new, hostile environment.

Chapter titles: 1. *Lost in Space*; 2. *Sinister Savage*; 3. *Savage Justice*; 4. *Wild Man at Large*; 5. *Trail of the Mystery Man*; 6. *The Pirate Attack*; 7. *Menace of the Mercurians*; 8. *Between Two Fires*; 9. *Shrine of the Silver Bird*; 10. *Fighting Fury*; 11. *Desperate Chance*; 12. *Mystery of the Mine*; 13. *Jungle Downfall*; 14. *Man from Tomorrow*; 15. *The Last of Mysterious Island*.

2. [Film]

Premiere: August 31, 1961; Main Cast: Michael Craig as Captain Cyrus Harding, Joan Greenwood as Lady Mary Fairchild, Beth Rogan as Elena Fairchild, Herbert Lom as Captain Nemo, Gary Merrill as Gideon Spilett, Michael Callan as Herbert Brown, Percy Herbert as Sgt. Pencroft, Dan Jackson as Corporal Neb Nugent; Producer: Charles H. Schneer; Screenplay: John Prebble, Daniel Ullman, Crane Wilbur; Based on the novel by Jules Verne; Director: Cy Endfield; 101 min.; Ameran Films; Columbia Pictures Corp.; Color.

At the Siege of Richmond, Virginia, in 1865 three Union soldiers escape from Libby Military Prison. A Union war journalist for the *New York*

Herald and a Confederate stowaway join the soldiers in their hot air balloon escape. Crash landing off the coast of a South Pacific island the men are joined by shipwrecked castaways Lady Mary Fairchild and her beautiful young niece Elena. Together they must survive on an island inhabited by giant birds, crabs and bees. The person behind the giant fauna and wildlife is none other than Captain Nemo.

3. [TV series; Canada]

Executive Producers: Stephen Alix, Martin Katz, Don Reynolds; 22 × 43; Atlantis Films; Tasman Film and Television, Fremantle Corp, Canwest Global Systems; Color.

"Genesis" (1:01)

Air date: June 15, 1995; Main Cast: Alan Scarfe as Captain Harding, C. David Johnson as Jack Pencroft, Collette Stevenson as Joanna Pencroft, Gordon Michael Woolvett as Herbert Pencroft, Stephen Lovatt as Gideon Spilett, Andy Marshall as Neb Nugent, John Bach as Captain Nemo; Teleplay: Stephen Alix, Glenn Norman; Director: William Fruett.

After escaping from the Confederates in a balloon a Union captain, a freed slave, a journalist and the Pencroft family land on a Pacific island inhabited by giant creatures and fauna.

4. [Telefilm]

Air date: September 17, 2005; Main Cast: Kyle MacLachlan as Captain Cyrus Smith, Patrick Stewart as Captain Nemo, Gabrielle Anwar as Jane, Danielle Calvert as Helen, Omar Gooding as Neb Nugent, Jason Durr as Pencroff; Executive Producers: Robert Halmi, Jr., Larry Levinson; Teleplay: Adam Armus, Nora Kay Foster; Based on the novel by Jules Verne; Director: Russell Mulcahy; 172 min.; Silverstar Ltd, Living Films, Hallmark Entertainment; The Hallmark Channel; Color.

This adaptation of Jules Verne's novel sees Captain Cyrus Smith and his family escaping the terrors of the American Civil War only to find themselves on an island populated by giant, hostile life.

5. [Telefilm] a.k.a. *Jules Verne's Mysterious Island*

Air date: February 11, 2012; Main Cast: Gina Holden as Julia Fogg, Lochlyn Munro as Captain Cyrus Harding, Susie Abromeit as Abby Fogg, Mark Sheppard as Young Captain Nemo, William Morgan Sheppard as Captain Nemo, J.D. Evermore as Bonaventure Pencroft, Edrick Browne as Neb Nugent, Pruitt Taylor Vince as Gideon Spilett; Producers: Matt Keith, George M. Kostuch, Cameron Larson; Teleplay: Cameron Larson; Based on the novel by Jules Verne; Director: Mark Sheppard; 91 min.; K2 Pictures; Syfy Channel; Color.

This production adds a new twist to Jules Verne's classic tale with the introduction of Julie and Abby Fogg who are stranded on the island after passing through the Bermuda Triangle.

Mysterious Stories [Comic book]

1950s anthology title from Premier Magazines.

"Friend to the End" [WW]

First publication: #3 (April 1955).

Al Morgan flees his flaming house but struggles to breathe as his legs buckle and a sharp pain pierces his side. His mind wanders back to Fort Wellington and his army friend Dave Bradley. They are fighting in Korea. Suddenly Morgan receives "a bellyful of shrapnel" saving Bradley's life. Bradley is now in his friend's debt and he expresses it in a note. "This note entitles Al Morgan to one free life-saving from his pal. I.O.U. one life … signed, Dave Bradley."

Bradley is killed five months later but now he has returned to keep his promise. Al Morgan owes his life to his late friend and has been "Paid in Full."

"From Time to Time" [WW]

First publication: #7 (December 1955–January 1956); Art: Hy Fleishman.

Historian Edan Lawrence prefers books to people and now he has a great desire to visit the places he researches. Mr. Hassim helps Lawrence travel through time by concentrating on a newspaper from August 18, 1862. Suddenly he is back in time and part of the Union army preparing to fight the Rebels. But Lawrence's amazing knowledge of the Civil War attracts suspicion and he is arrested for being a spy and prepared for execution by firing squad.

Able to return to 1955 by concentrating on a newspaper that falls out of his jacket Edan Lawrence is convinced it has all been a dream. But he is unable to explain why he is still wearing his Union army uniform.

"Nightmare!" [WW]

First publication: #3 (April 1955); Art: George Woodbridge, Angle Torres.

Dan McGrew makes a pact with two Union army friends from the 7th New York Cavalry to get together after the war on January 1, 1900, to celebrate the new century. Ordered to patrol a valley by their Sergeant, the three men split up and each take a part of the valley. Ambushed by Confederates the comrade soldiers survive and come across a wagon containing a chest full of gold. McGrew is overcome with gold fever and knowingly sends his two friends into a Confederate camp. He rides from the scene with the gold as he hears gunfire that signals the death of his fellow Union soldiers.

Now it is midnight and the new century has arrived. McGrew hears a knock at the door and opens it to find his two friends from the Civil War have kept their appointment—even in death. They escort him to the police station where he confesses his war crimes.

"Smart Soldiers Never Die" [WW]

First publication: #3 (April 1955); Art: Hy Fleischman.

"Alan Taylor's first days in combat were a grim lesson in death for the young recruit. The rest of his men lay killed in action behind enemy lines. Alan had to make his way through ten miles of Communist-infested land before he could reach safety."

Thank goodness for wounded buddy George Randall, his savior in Kwang Tynng, Korea. Randall guides Taylor through enemy territory to safety. Not bad for a soldier who died yesterday!

The Mystery at Fort Thunderbolt (*Pretty Darn Scary Mysteries* #3) [Juvenile book; WW]

Author: Carole Marsh; First publication: Peachtree City, GA: Gallopade International, 2007.

When brother and sister Telly and Tim are told that their doctor parents are in quarantine in Africa for the deadly Ebola virus the children decide to stowaway on a freighter to get to them. As they make travel plans at the historic Revolutionary and Civil War Fort Pulaski they receive the help of two ghosts. But the Savannah Police Barracks aims to stop Telly and Tim from making their dangerous and potentially deadly journey.

Nang-Nak (1999) [Film; Thailand; WW]

Premiere: May 20, 2000; Main Cast: Intira Jaroenpura as Nak, Winai Kraibutr as Mak; Producers: Nonzee Nimibutr, Visute Poolvoralaks; Story: Wisit Sasanatieng; Director: Nonzee Nimibutr; 100 min.; Tai Entertainment: Kino Video; Color.

Prakanong, 1868. While her husband Mak is fighting in the Chiang Toong War his wife Nak dies in childbirth giving birth to their son. When the man returns home to his village he greets his dead wife not knowing she is dead. Meanwhile the villagers who are aware Nak is dead are at the mercy of her wrath. She keeps the villagers from telling her husband the truth of her death by terrorizing them. Her love for Mak is overpowering even to the point of conquering death.

Nanny McPhee and the Big Bang a.k.a. **Nanny McPhee Returns** (2010) [Film; WW]

Premiere: March 8, 2010; Main Cast: Emma Thompson as Nanny McPhee, Ewan McGregor as Mr. Green, Maggie Smith as Mrs. Docherty, Maggie Gyllenhaal as Isabel Green, Asa Butterfield as Norman Green, Rhys Ifans as Phil Green, Oscar Steer as Vincent Green, Lil Woods as Megsie Green, Sam Kelly as Mr. Docherty, Eros Vlahos as Cyril Gray, Rosie Taylor-Ritson as Celia Gray, Daniel Mays as Blenkinsop, Sinead Matthews as Miss Topsey, Katy Brand as Miss Turvey, Ralph Fiennes as Lord Gray; Producers: Liza Chasin, Debra Osborne, Emma Thompson; Story: Emma Thompson; Director: Susanna White; 109 min.; Relativity Media, Working Title Films, StudioCanal, Three Street Angels; Universal Pictures; Color.

In rural England during World War II, magical Nanny McPhee helps a mother of three children cope while her husband is way at war. Isabel Green's already frayed nerves are frayed even further with news her husband has been killed in action. But the eldest child Norman feels the telegram is a ploy by his uncle Phil to force Mrs. Green to sell her farm, to cover his gambling debts.

Nazi Dawn (2014) [Film; WW]

Premiere: February 3, 2014; Main Cast: Veronica Ricci as Agness, Kristen Walterscheid Casner as Dawn, Laura Azevedo as Alex, Kelly Erin Decker as Alyson, Ryan Keely as Janet, Lora McHugh as Eve, Kristian Merrill as Tip, Robert Rhine as SS Colonel Krieger; Producer: David S. Sterling; Story: Karianne Davis, Monte Hunter; Director: Dennis Devine; 85 min.; Tom Cat Films; Color.

An evil force from World War II awaits six sorority girls on a weekend break in the countryside. A séance awakens the spirit of the great-grandfather of legacy pledge Dawn, who also happens to be an evil Nazi killer torturer and killer. With Dawn possessed by her ancestral spirit the sorority girls and their male companions are the Nazi's new targets for torture and murder.

"Nazi Diamond" [Pulp fiction; SFW]
Author: Richard O. Lewis; First publication: *Amazing Stories* (Vol. 16 #11; November 1942); Publisher: Ziff-Davis Publishing Company.

"When a machine pops up that can grow artificial diamonds, that's a matter for the FBI; and the Nazis. And trouble for Jeb Caldwell. Diamonds are vital in the war effort for tool making so there was a reason to value this invention."

The Nazi Occult [RPG book; UK; WW]
Author: Kenneth Hite; First publication: UK: Osprey Publishing, 2013.

Author Hite details the occult practices of Adolf Hitler and the Nazi party in this gaming supplement book that reads like real-life history. The reader learns of the Nazi quests for the Ark of the Covenant, the Holy Grail and the Spear of Destiny and their experimentations with the dark arts. Demons, U.F.O.'s, werewolf saboteurs and attempts to preserve Hitler's brain are recorded, together with period photographs from historical archives.

Nazi Werewolf Zombie Inferno [Graphic novel; UK; WW]
Story: Chris Bradshaw; Art: Karl Jull; Publisher: London: Markosia Enterprises, 2014.

Mercenaries hunting for Nazi gold become trapped in a World War II underground bunker where they encounter an undead horror.

Nazi Werewolves from Outer Space [Comic book; SFW]
First publication: January 2013; Story: Simon Sanchez; Art: Dean Juliette; Two-issue mini-series; Publisher: Trauma Comics.

The Nazis have returned—as alien werewolves. Their leader Adolf Hitler now finds his head attached to a gorilla's body. Their mission—to kill and capture humans for grisly experimentation aboard their spaceships. Jack Lynch is among those captured, but he won't be turned into a zombie or some human-animal hybrid without a fight.

Nazi Zombie Army 2 [Video game; WW]
Release date: October 31, 2013; Developer: Rebellion Developments; Publisher: 505 Games.

Mankind's salvation lies in the sacred artifacts hidden under demon-infested Berlin and the Fuhrerbunker.

Zombie Army Trilogy, released March 2015, includes remastered versions of **Sniper Elite: Nazi Zombie Army** and **Nazi Zombie Army 2**.

Nazis at the Center of the Earth (2012) [Film; SFW]
Premiere: April 22, 2012; Main Cast: Dominique Swain as Dr. Paige Morgan, Jake Busey as Dr. Adrian Riestad, Josh Allen as Dr. Lucas Moss, Christopher K. Johnson as Dr. Joseph Mengele, James Maxwell as Adolf Hitler; Executive Producer: David Rinawi; Story: Paul Bales; Director: Joseph J. Lawson; 89 min.; The Asylum; Color.

Storm troopers abduct researchers in Antarctica and take them to the center of the Earth where the Third Reich is planning a comeback with gruesome zombie-like Nazi soldiers.

Neither Heaven Nor Earth a.k.a. **The Wakhan Front** a.k.a. **Ni le Ciel Ni la Terre** (2015) [Film; France-Belgium; WW]
Premiere: May 16, 2015; Main Cast: Jeremie Renier as Capt. Antares Bonassieu, Swann Arlaud as Jeremie Lemowski, Kevin Azais as William Denis, Marc Robert as Jean-Baptiste Frering, Finnegan Oldfield as Patrick Mercier, Christophe Tek as Stephane, Hamid Reza Javdan as Taliban Sultan; Producer: Jean-Christophe Reymond; Screenplay-Director: Clement Cogitore; 100 min.; Kazak Productions; Wolf Films; Color.

French soldiers, on a mission in Afghanistan, begin to disappear from their posts. Captain Antares Bonassieu investigates by talking to local villagers but the mystery remains. Could supernatural forces be at work?

The New Avengers (1976) [TV Series; UK-Canada-France]
Main Cast: Patrick McNee as John Steed, Joanna Lumley as Purdey, Gareth Hunt as Gambit.

British secret agent John Steed and his colleagues Purdey and Mike Gambit investigate unusual cases.

"THE EAGLE'S NEST" (1:01) [SFW]
Air date: September 22, 1976: Guest Cast: Peter Cushing as Professor Von Claus, Derek Farr as Father Trasker, Frank Gatliff as Karl, Sydney Bromley as Hara, Trevor Baxter as Brown-Fitch, Brian Anthony as Stannard, Peter Porteous as Nazi Corporal, Jerold Wells as Ralph/Barker; Producers: Albert Fennell, Brian Clemens; Story: Brian Clemens; Director: Desmond Davis; 50 min.; Avengers (Film & TV) Enterprises, IDTV TV Productions Paris,

Neilsen-Ferns Toronto; Independent Television (ITV); Color.

A monastery on the remote island of St. Dorca is the secret headquarters of Nazis. A plane crashed on the island in 1945 transporting, "Germany's greatest treasure"—Adolf Hitler. Now a specialist in suspended animation, Professor Von Claus has been abducted and forced to work on reviving Hitler. Steed, Purdey and Gambit infiltrate the headquarters to put an end to Father Trasker's plans to revive Hitler and form a new Reich.

Nick of Time [Juvenile book; SFW]

Author: Ted Bell; First publication: New York: St. Martin's Griffin, 2008.

Channel Islands, England, 1939. Twelve-year-old Nick McIver and his younger sister Kate live in a lighthouse. Their father is working for Winston Churchill, informing him of the Nazi U-boat threat to the islands. But Kate is conducting her own methods to stop the Nazi menace, enlisting the aide of scientific detectives Lord Hawke and Commander Hobbes.

Meanwhile Nick discovers a sea chest on nearby Greybeard Island. The chest originally belonged to one of Nick's ancestors, Captain Nicholas McIver, who served with Admiral Nelson's fleet. When the chest is opened they find a gleaming golden ball—the "Tempus Machina" created four hundred years ago by Leonardo da Vinci. The golden ball opens in two halves, revealing the beauty within.

"Nick had no idea what he'd been expecting to find inside the machine—whirling atoms, perhaps. Actually the device resembled an exquisite piece of jewelry. Delicate scrolled writing surrounded and engraving of the sun and its nine planets on one half, and there was a pyramid with what appeared to be Greek symbols on the other."

Commander Hobbes presses an emerald within the globe and the calendar in the machine advances or retreats through time. Nick decides to go back in time to 1805 to rescue his ancestor and save Admiral Nelson's fleet from the French and the mutinous Captain Blood.

The Night Boat [Novel; WW]

Author: Robert R. McCammon; First publication: New York: Avon Books, 1980.

Salvage diver David Moore comes across a sunken Nazi U-boat buried in the sands under a the deep waters of a Caribbean lagoon. But noises are heard deep within the submarine. The long-dead crew are restless and want revenge.

Author Robert R. McCammon commented, "*The Night Boat* is about the merging of dream and nightmare, confinement and escape, and what I think of as the whirlpool of Fate. David Moore thought he'd escaped that whirlpool, but it was waiting for him, there below the surface of emerald waters, where the monsters doze but never sleep."

Night Gallery a.k.a. *Rod Serling's Night Gallery* (1969) [TV series]

Anthology series hosted by Rod Serling where paintings illustrate various tales of horror and fantasy. Main Cast: Rod Serling (host); Creator: Rod Serling; Producer: Jack Laird; 28 × 50 min.; 15 × 25 min.; Universal Television; National Broadcasting Company (NBC); Color.

"THE DEVIL IS NOT MOCKED" (2:06) [WW]

Air date: October 27, 1971; Guest Cast: Helmut Dantine as General von Grunn, Francis Lederer as The Count, Hank Brandt as Karnaz, Martin Kosleck

Cover of *Nick of Time* by Ted Bell (2000).

as Hugo; Teleplay: Gene R. Kearney; Based on the short story by Manly Wade Wellman; Director: Gene Kearney; 10 min.

The second segment sees a Transylvanian Count welcoming an invading Nazi general to his castle with food and drink. The general talks of defeating the Resistance not realizing they are werewolves and the Count a vampire.

"A QUESTION OF FEAR" (2:06) [WW]

Air date: October 27, 1971; Guest Cast: Leslie Nielsen as Colonel Dennis Malloy, Fritz Weaver as Dr. Mazi, Jack Bannon as Al, Ivan Bonar as Fred; Teleplay: Theodore J. Flicker. Based on the short story by Bryan Lewis; Director: Jack Laird.; 40 min.

In the first segment a colonel and mercenary who fought in the Spanish Civil War and served with British and U.S. forces is bet $15,000 he cannot survive one night in a haunted house.

Colonel Malloy proudly states, "Fear is a disease.... I am incapable of fear." But he discovers the person making the bet is the son of a German prisoner Malloy tortured and burnt during the war. Now his son seeks revenge with fear as the weapon.

Night Wars (1988) [Film; SFW]

Premiere: March 31, 1988; Main Cast: Dan Haggerty as Dr. Miles Campbell, Brian O'Connor as Trent Matthews, Cameron Smith as Jim Lowery, Jill Foor as Susanne Matthews, Steve Horton as McGregor, Chet Hood as Johnny, David Ott as Jack Shane; Executive Producers: David Winters, Marc Winters; Story: David A. Prior, Ted Prior, William Zipp; Director: David A. Prior; 88 min; Action International Pictures (AIP); Color.

Vietnam veterans Trent Matthews and Jim Lowery have been suffering nightmares after leaving their fellow soldier Johnny to die in Vietnam. Matthews' nightmares take him back to Vietnam where he tries to rescue Johnny. But when he awakes Matthews discovers a real-life shrapnel wound in his hand and cuts to his neck. Past and present intermingle as dreams become their own reality along with the horrors of Vietnam.

Nostradamus Ate My Hamster [Novel; SFW]

Author: Robert Rankin; First publication: London: Doubleday, 1996.

Russell Nice is an ordinary guy with extraordinary abilities. He can create holograms of any film star, living or dead and place them in new films. After he learns Adolf Hitler is alive in the present day and wants to regain power by winning the people over with the brainwashing power of film Nice attempts to prevent Hitler's plans with time travel.

NUTS! War Without End: Weird War 2 [Board Game; WW]

First publication: 2011; Designers: John Cunningham, Ed Teixeira; Art: Paul Kime; Publisher: Two Hour Wargames (THW Game Design).

"Start with the inherent weirdness of World War II, add the public fascination with the new science being unleashed around them and top off with the popular pulps and comic books of the day—and you have set the stage for Weird War 2. welcome to the Weird War, a no-holds barred clash of chaos in which combat walkers stride the battlefields, yankee rocketmen blaze through the skies and ray guns reduce tanks to glowing scrap metal."

The players create Weird Science campaigns using their Weird Science unit, vehicles and fantastic technologies. Sample scenarios are fought with players taking opposing sides, solo or working together against the game.

Oasis of the Zombies (1982) [Film; France-Spain; WW]

Premiere: April 21, 1982; Main Cast: Manuel Gelin as Robert Blabert, Eduardo Fajardo as Colonel Kurt Meitzell, France Jordan as Erika, Jeff Montgomery as Ben, Javier Maiza as Captain Blabert, Antonio Mayans as Sheik Mohamed Al-Kafir; Story" Ramon Lido; Screenplay: A.L. Mariaux, (Jesus Franco); Director: A.M. Frank (Jesus Franco); 82 min.; Marte Films, Diasa P.C.; Eurocine; Image Entertainment; Color.

Original title: *La tumba de los Muertos Vivientes*

In the African desert an army of Nazi zombies guards a multi-million dollar hoard of hidden treasure from World War II.

The Objective (2008) [Film; WW]

Premiere: April 18, 2008; Main Cast: Jonas Ball as Benjamin Keynes, Vanessa Johansson as Stacy Keynes, Matthew R. Anderson as Wally Hamer, Chems-Eddine Zinoune as Abdul, Jon Heurtas as Sgt. Vincent Degetau; Executive Producers: Steffen Aumeller, Claus Clausen; Story: Daniel Myrick, Mark A. Patton, Wesley Clark, Jr.; Director: Daniel Myrick; 90 min.; Kasbah-Film Tangier, Jaz Films; IFC Films; Color.

A Special Forces team in Ghazni Province, Afghanistan, on a mission to find an Afghan cleric, experience the supernatural as they venture into the mountainous terrain where the cleric may be hiding.

"An Occurrence at Owl Creek Bridge" [Short story; WW]

1. Author: Ambrose Bierce; First publication: *The San Francisco Examiner*, 1890.

On a railroad bridge in Northern Alabama, well-to-do planter and slave-owner Peyton Farquhar is about to be hanged by Union soldiers. But as he plunges to his death the rope breaks and he falls into the stream below. Farquhar succeeds in freeing his tied hands and releasing the rope from his neck as he forces himself to the surface only to find himself the target of the soldiers on the bridge. Evading the shots Furquhar finally reaches the gate of his home.

"His wife, looking fresh and cool and sweet, steps down from the veranda to greet him…. And how beautiful she is!"

But only darkness and the silence of eternity awaits Furquhar as his lifeless body "swings gently from side to side, beneath the timbers of the Owl Creek bridge."

2. [France; Short film]

Premiere: May 1962; Main Cast: Roger Jaquet as Peyton Farquhar, Anne Cornaly as Mrs. Farquhar, Stephane Frey as Union Officer; Producers: Paul de Roubaix, Marcel Ichac; Adapted by Roberto Enrico from the original story by Ambrose Bierce; Director: Roberto Enrico; 28 min.; Filmartic, Films du Centuare; B/W.

This adaptation of Ambrose Bierce's short story effectively incorporates the sound of bird song and the flowing river beneath Owl Creek bridge as a metaphor for freedom as Peyton Farquhar escapes the hangman's noose. But the love of his wife as she runs to greet him remains out of his grasp as the illusion of freedom is shattered with the snap of his neck. Director Roberto Enrico captures a dream like quality that reinforces the fantasy of Farquhar's experiences and is enhanced by an almost dialogue free soundtrack.

The winner of the Cannes Film Festival, 1962 this adaptation was broadcast as an episode of *The Twilight Zone* in February 1964.

3. [Film]

Premiere: August 25, 2005; Main Cast: Bradley Egen as Peyton Farquhar, Jody Chansuolme as Libbie Farquhar, Aaron Jackson as The Scout; Screenplay: Brian James Egen, based on the short story by Ambrose Bierce; Director: Brian James Egen; 51 min.; Owl Creek Productions; Color.

Low budget film based on Bierce's short story, using Civil War reenactors as Union soldiers.

See: **Alfred Hitchcock Presents**; **Eerie**

"The Odyssey of Battling Bert" [Pulp fiction; SFW]

Authors: Stanton A. Coblentz; Illustrator: Robert Fuqua, James B. Settles; First publication: *Amazing Stories* (Vol. 18 #5; December 1944); Publisher: Ziff-Davis Publishing Company.

"There came a weird thunder, then out of nowhere a salvo of tremendous shells. Giant shells only a battleship could fire—yet there was no ship."

Olympos [Novel; MWW]

Author: Dan Simmons; First publication: New York: Eos, 2005.

On the Plains of Ilium at the foot of Olympos Mons on Mars, resurrected 20th century Homeric scholar Thomas Hockenberry has been observing the Trojan War. But in this version of the war Achilles and his enemy Hector join forces against Zeus and the pantheon of gods. On Earth, creatures from Shakespeare's *The Tempest* are preparing for their own battle.

See: *Ilium*

On Her Majesty's Behalf: The Great Undead War (Book 2) [Novel; WW]

Author: Joseph Nassise; First publication: New York: Harper Voyager, 2014.

In this sequel to ***By the Blood of Heroes*** Michael "Madman" Burke and his company and the undead Red Baron, Manfred von Richthofen are both after the same British Royal Family. Burke has been assigned by the President to rescue them but must face a new enemy. Super-soldiers known as shredders who have the conquest of Britain as their goal.

Once Was a Time [Juvenile book; SFW]

Author: Leila Sales; First publication: San Francisco: Chronicle Books, 2016.

Ten-year-old Charlotte "Lottie" Bromley and her best friend Kitty McLaughlin live in wartime England, under constant threat from Hitler's bombing raids. Lottie's father is working on top secret time travel research under the Official Secrets Act. His research places Lottie's life in danger as the Nazis covet her father's research. When Nazis kidnap Lottie and her friend Kitty, Lottie leaps through a time portal to Wisconsin in 2013. Stranded in America, Lottie adapts to her new life and foster parents but can't forget the best friend she left behind in England. She has to find a way to communicate with Kitty, through time and space.

One Step Beyond (1959) [TV series]

Anthology series featuring dramatized tales of the supernatural based on real-life events. Host: John Newland; Producer: Collier Young; 94x30 min.; Joseph M. Schenck Enterprises, World Television Programming; American Broadcasting Company (ABC); B/W.

"THE AVENGERS" (3:28) [WW]

Air date: April 25, 1961; Guest Cast: Jan Conrad Andre Morrell as General Guenther Hautmann, Lisa Gastoni as Marianne, Walter Gotell as Sergeant; Story Supervisor: Martin Benson; Director: John Newland.

Nazi general Guenther Hautmann holds a macabre party where he invites guests he plans to send to death camps. But his plans are foiled by the ghosts of party guests who suffered a similar fate.

"THE EXECUTIONER" (3:15) [WW]

Air date: January 3, 1961; Guest Cast: Crahan Denton as Colonel Martin, Buzz Martin as Jess Bradley, Jeremy Slate as Capt. Adams, Tom Middleton as Sgt. Evans; Story: Bob Duncan, Wanda Duncan, Merwin Gerard; Director: John Newland.

Confederate soldier Jess Bradley is captured by Union officer Colonel Martin. But when Bradley's dog is killed supernatural events begin to occur. The sadistic Colonel is avenged and Bradley saved from the firing squad.

"THE HAUNTED U-BOAT" (1:17) [WW]

Air date: May 12, 1959; Guest Cast: Werner Klemperer as Herr Bautmann, Eric Feldary as Captain Eric Kreig, Wesley Lau as Lt. Schneider, Kort Falkenberg as Lt. Friedel; Story: Merwin Gerard, Larry Marcus; Director: John Newland.

The crew of a German U–Boat discover the loud banging in their submarine is caused by the ghost of a former construction worker.

"THE MASK" (2:24) [WW]

Air date: March 1, 1960; Guest Cast: Wesley Lau as Lt. Harold Wilenski, Luis Van Rooten as Brimley, Stephen Bekassy as Dr. Beauvais, Joan Elan as Nurse; Story: Russell Beggs, Merwin Gerard, Joseph Petracca; Director: John Newland.

World War II. Air Force Lieutenant Harold Wilenski is rescued after his plane crashes in in the harsh Sahara Desert. But to Wilenski's bewilderment his face now resembles an Egyptian Pharaoh. The spirit of the Egyptian has possessed his body.

"NIGHT OF DECISION" (3:21) [WW]

Air date: February 21, 1961; Guest Cast: Robert Douglas as General George Washington, Richard Carlyle as Colonel Danforth, Donald Buka as Marquis de Lafayette, Richard Hale as Chief Otumcas; Executive Writer: Larry Marcus; Teleplay: Merwin Gerard; Director: John Newland.

General George Washington faces a moral dilemma when his prophetic dreams tell him the American Revolution will be a success but will also lead to a terrible civil war.

"THE PRISONER" (3:29) [WW]

Air date: May 2, 1961; Guest Cast: Anton Diffring as Wilhelm Hessler, Annette Carell as Frieda Hessler, Sandor Eles as Samuel, Catherine Feller as Ruth Goldman, Faith Brook as Nurse; Story: Larry Marcus; Director: John Newland.

Nazi death camp survivor Ruth Goldman murders Wilhelm Hessler—the officer in charge of her sadistic treatment at the death camp. But when a doctor examines Hessler's corpse he states Hessler has been dead for six years.

"THE RETURN" (3:04) [WW]

Air date: October 11, 1960; Guest Cast: Richard Davalos as Corporal Fred Cossage, Charles H. Gray as Sgt. Kirsch, Jack Mullaney as Capt. Youngblood, Chris Winters as Lt. Heinmetz; Story: Larry Marcus; Director: John Newland.

Blinded and wounded Corporal Fred Cossage, is detached from his unit while on a mission in Korea. But he finds his way back to camp using his psychic powers.

"REUNION" (2:10) [WW]

Air date: November 24, 1959; Guest Cast: Betsy von Furstenberg as Helga, Rory Harrity as Hans, Paul Carr as Peter, Page Slattery as Theo; Story: Merwin Gerard, Larry Marcus; Director: John Newland.

A group of German glider enthusiasts must go their separate ways after Adolf Hitler invades Poland in 1939. They decide on a reunion after the war ends but have no idea how strange that reunion will be.

"Signal Received" (3:26) [WW]
Air date: April 4, 1961; Guest Cast: Mark Eden as Johnny Watson, Terry Palmer as George Breed, Richard Gale as Robin Hughes, Viola Keats as Mrs. Breed; Executive Writer: Larry Marcus; Story: Merwin Gerard, Derry Quinn; Director: John Newland.

World War II. Johnny Watson and George Breed hear a radio broadcast stating their ship HMS Hood has been hit and sunk. But they both know their ship is safe and ready to sail. Meanwhile fellow sailor Robin Hughes is told by a fortune teller that he will lead a long life. As the HMS Hood is set to sail Hughes is transferred to another ship. Watson and Breed are lost at sea while Hughes survives into old age.

"The Sorceror" (3:31) [WW]
Air date: May 23, 1961: Guest Cast: Christopher Lee as Wilhelm Reitlinger, Martin Benson as Klaus Karnak, Alfred Burke as Scholl, Gabrielli Licudi as Elsa Bruck, Frederick Jaeger as Johann; Story Dramatization: Derry Quinn; Director: John Newland.

World War I. German officer Wilhelm Reitlinger murders his cheating girlfriend while undergoing an out-of-body experience. When he is found innocent of the crime Reitlinger plans another murder to ensure he receives his just punishment for killing his girlfriend, Elsa.

"To Know the End" (3:07) [WW]
Air date: November 1, 1960; Guest Cast: Ellen Willard as Emily MacDougall, Alex Davion as Harry MacDougall, Sally Fraser as Ann, James Forrest as British Army Sergeant, Noel Drayton as British Army Officer; Story: Merwin Gerard, Larry Marcus; Director: John Newland.

Emily MacDougall has visions of death in World War II England. Those visions include her husband dying in battle.

"The Vision" (1:10) [WW]
Air date: March 24, 1959; Guest Cast: Bruce Gordon as Captain Emil Tremaine, Pernell Roberts as Sgt. Valli, H.M. Wyant as Pvt. Lacoste, Jerry Odo as Pvt. Mollene; Story: Merwin Gerard, Larry Marcus; Director: John Newland.

When four French soldiers desert the battlefield during World War I they talk of a strange light in the sky that controlled their actions.

One Summer at Deer's Leap [Novel; WW]
Author: Elizabeth Elgin; First publication: London: HarperCollins, 1999.

Driving in the Vale of Boland en-route to a fancydress party, Cassie Johns picks up a handsome young man wearing a Royal Air Force uniform. Cassie searches for him at the party, but to no avail. He's disappeared. Trying to discover more about the handsome stranger, Cassie learns of a pilot named Jack Hunter who died when his plane crashed during World War II. Since that day his spirit has been obsessed with the girl he loved at Deer's Leap. Now love from the past takes on a new life.

Only You Can Save Mankind (*The Johnny Maxwell Trilogy* book #1) [Juvenile book; SFW]
Author: Terry Pratchett; First publication: London: Doubleday, 1992.

Twelve-year-old Johnny Maxwell endures an unhappy life at home with his parents on the verge of going their separate ways. The non-stop television coverage of the Gulf War adds to his sense of anxiety. When his friend Wobbler gives him a pirated copy of the video game *Only You Can Save Mankind* Johnny's life changes. The game becomes real as the ScreeWee Empire surrenders to him and he enters the game world in his dreams. Meanwhile all mention of the ScreeWee has mysteriously disappeared in all other existing copies of the game.

The story contrasts the world of the video game with the media coverage of the real-life Gulf War. Both deal in depersonalizing the enemy and delivering their message through monitors.

See: ***Johnny and the Dead***

Operation Darkness [RPG; Japan; WW]
Release Date: October 11, 2007 (Japan); Platform: Xbox 360; Executive Producer: Takato Yoshinari; Story: Ken Ogura; Director: Hisakazu Masubuchi; Developer: Success Corp.; Publishers: Success Corp., Atlus (U.S.).

James Gallant is leader of the Wolf Pack who with his squad of elite soldiers goes into battle against Nazi leader Adolf Hitler, SS head Heinrich Himmler and Nazi vampire soldiers of the Blood Clan led by SS Sturmbannfuhrer Alexander Vlado. The tactical role-playing game also includes Nazi zombie soldiers, werewolves, Jack the Ripper, a descendant of Van Helsing, fire starters, dragons, skeleton warriors and magic.

Operation: Nazi Zombies (2003) [Film; WW]
Premiere: August 13, 2003; Main Cast: Thomas Reilly as General Gibbs, Elissa Mullen as Lieutenant

Meyer, Christopher Connolly as Chaplain Johnson, John Weidemoyer as Major O'Malley; Producers; Joseph DeChristopher Jr., Thomas Reilly, Robert Schiller, Dave Stewart, Jr.; Story-Director: David B. Stewart III; 87 min.; Dapper Cat Pictures, S&H Productions; Brain Damage Films; Color.

An Army Special Forces unit encounters the deadly results of a recreated Nazi experiment performed by the Army Chemical Corps and the CIA.

Operation: Peril [Comic book]

Anthology title.

"The Time Travelers" [SFW]

First publication: #3 (February–March 1951); Art: Jack Katz; Publisher: Standard Comics/Visual Editions.

Hopewell College is threatened with closure. Dr. Tom Redfield must persuade J.P. Frisbee to continue his financial support for the school. But to guarantee Frisbee's support Redfield must prove time travel is a reality by going back to the 6th century and returning with King Arthur's Excalibur sword.

Once back in time Redfield realizes King Arthur's knights will be outnumbered by the Black Teutonic Knights summoned by Morgan Le Fay. Redfield goes forward in time to 1945 where he is U.S. Army Captain Redfield in charge of an allied motor pool in Germany. He orders his men to load armored motor-cycles onto his jet transport which doubles for his time-traveling rocket ship.

Back at King Arthur's court the motor-cycles are manned by Arthur's knights who defeat the Black Knights. Merlin lends Redfield Excalibur to present to J.P. Frisbee in the present. His ten million dollar check saves Hopewell College from closure.

"The Time Travelers" [SFW]

First publication: #12 (August–September 1952); Art: George Wilhelms; Publisher: Standard Comics/Visual Editions.

"The Roman Sixth Legion was one of the greatest armies of all time—never defeated in battle until it attempted the conquest of Britain! And yet at the height of its martial glory the Sixth Legion was virtually wiped out without a single spear or arrow being raised against it. It's up to Dr. Tom Redfield to learn the reason—when his spaceship takes him back to England as it was nineteen centuries ago—during the reign of Queen Boadicea."

The Order of the Black Eagle (1987) [Film; AHW]

Premiere: December 31, 1987; Main Cast: Ian Hunter as Duncan Jax, C.K. Bibby as Star, Jill Donnellan as Tiffany Youngblood, William Hicks as The Baron, Anna Rapagna as Maxie Ryder, Stephan Krayk as Dr. George Brinkman, Shangtai Tuan as Sato, Typhoon as Boon the Baboon; Executive Producers: Betty Stephens, John A. Stephens; Screenplay: Phil Behrens; Director: Worth Keeter; 93 min.; Manson International, Polo Players Ltd., International Film Marketing; Color.

Dr. Brinkman, the leading expert in laser technology, is kidnapped by Neo-Nazis in Geneva, Switzerland. The Neo-Nazis are led by the Baron, a leader in Hitler's youth movement. He has used his family fortune to move to an ancient temple ruin in the jungles of South America. Now he plans to resurrect the cryogenically preserved body of Adolf Hitler on the anniversary of his birth. Agents Duncan Jax and Tiffany Youngblood are assigned to South America to rescue Dr. Brinkman and put a stop to the Neo-Nazi's plans. Aiding Duncan Jax is his companion, Boon—an intelligent and rude baboon.

Out of the Shadows [Comic book]

Anthology title.

"The Sergeant" [WW]

First publication: #10 (October 1953); Art: Jack Katz; Publisher: Standard Comics/Visual Editions.

A group of G.I.'s are trapped and lost near Cassino, Italy in 1944. Their Sergeant guides them through Nazi territory to safety despite being dead for two days.

Outer Limits (1995) [TV series]

Science fiction anthology series.

"Gettysburg" (6:17) [SFW]

Air date: July 28, 2000; Main Cast: Joshua Leonard as Andy, Jonathan Scarfe as Vince, Meatloaf as Colonel Angus Devine, James Lauder as General Lee, Alex Diakun as Nicholas Prentice, Aaron Pearl as Lt. Winters; Executive Producers: Pen Densham, Richard Barton Lewis, Mark Stern, John Watson; Story: Sam Egan; Director: Mario Azzopardi; 44 min.; Atlantis Films, Showtime, CanWest Global, Trilogy, MGM; Color.

Two enthusiasts play Union medic and a Confederate soldier at a Civil War re-enactment at

Gettysburg. But after they pose for a photographer they find themselves thrown back in time to the real-life battle.

"Tribunal" (5:12) [SFW]

Air date: May 14, 1999; Main Cast: Saul Rubinek as Aaron Zgierski, Alex Diakun as Nicholas Prentice, Lindsay Crouse as Gwen Sawyer, Peter Boretski as Leon Zgierski, Roman Danylo as Young Leon Zgierski, Holly Ferguson as Miriam Zgierski, Kyra Azzopardi as Hannah Zgierski, Alex Zahara as Karl Rademacher, Jan Rubes as Robert Greene/older Karl Rademacher; Producer: Brent Karl Clarkson; Story: Sam Egan; Director: Mario Azzopardi; 44 min.; Atlantis Films, Showtime, CanWest Global, Trilogy, MGM; Color.

A time traveler helps a lawyer find evidence to convict a Nazi, now in his eighties, who killed the lawyer's mother in cold blood at Auschwitz concentration camp in 1944.

Outlander (2014) [TV series; SFW]

Premiere: August 9, 2014; Main Cast: Caitriona Balfe as Claire Randall, Sam Heughan as Jamie Frser, Tobias Menzies as Frank Randall/Black Jack Randall; Executive Producer: Ronald D. Moore; 64 min.; Tall Ship Productions, Story Mining & Supply Co., Left Bank productions; Sony Pictures Television; Starz!; Color.

Based on the series of books by Diana Gabaldon, this television series tells the story of English front-line combat nurse Claire Randall. Enjoying a second honeymoon in Scotland after the end of World War II her husband Frank Randall researches his ancestor, 18th century British army officer Black Jack Randall. Meanwhile Claire visits a Druid site and suddenly finds herself thrown back in time to 1743 Scotland. Here she meets and falls in love with a handsome Scottish warrior named Jamie Fraser.

The series includes a storyline where Claire Randall and Jamie Fraser attempt to prevent the Battle of Culloden by infiltrating the Jacobite rebellion led by "Bonnie" Prince Charles Stuart.

Outpost (2007) [Film; UK; WW]

Premiere: December 7, 2007; Main cast: Ray Stevenson as DC, Julian Wadham as Hunt, Richard Brake as Prior, Paul Blair as Jordan, Brett Fancy as Taktarov, Enoch Frost as Cotter; Executive Producers; Graham Begg, Jamie Carmichael, Nigel Thomas; Story: Rae Brunton, Kieran Parker, Steve Barker; Director: Steve Barker; 90 min.; Regent Capital, Black Camel Pictures; Screen Gems, Sony Pictures Entertainment; Color.

An ex-marine and a team of former soldiers play bodyguard to a businessman in war-torn Eastern Europe. Their mission to lead him to a World War II bunker becomes a question of why after they discover the bunker was used for gruesome Nazi experiments on soldiers. And they are now the target of something that has survived in the bunker and has a taste for death.

Outpost: Black Sun (2012) [Film; UK; WW]

Premiere: April 29, 2012; Main Cast: Clive Russell as Marius, Richard Coyle as Wallace, Catherine Steadman as Lena, Michael Byrne as Neurath, David Grant as Klausener; Executive Producers: Jamie Carmichael, Shail Sha, Nigel Thomas, Charlotte Walls; Story: Steve Barker, Rae Brunton; Director: Steve Barker; 101 min.; Black Camel Pictures; Xlrator Media; Color.

In Eastern Europe a battalion of Nazi zombie storm troopers is on the march. War-criminal Klausener first worked on perfecting the undead Nazi army back in the closing days of World War II. Now investigator Helena, Nazi chaser Wallace and a Special Forces Unit go behind enemy lines to track the secret source of the Nazi zombies.

Outpost: Rise of the Spetsnaz (2013) [Film; UK; WW]

Premiere: June 27, 2013 (UK); Main Cast: Bryan Larkin as Dolokhov, Ivan Kamaras as Fyodor, Michael McKell as Strasser, Velibor Topic as Arkadi, Laurence Possa as Osakin; Executive Producers: Jamie Carmichael, Nigel Thomas, Charlotte Walls; Story: Rae Brunton; Director: Kieran Barker; 87 min.; Black Camel Pictures, Savalas Films; Xlrator Media; Color.

The third film in the *Outpost* series sees the Russian Spetsnaz fighting the Nazi zombies.

The Oval Portrait a.k.a. *One Minute Before Death* (1972) [Film; Mexico; WW]

Premiere: 1972; Main Cast: Wanda Hendrix as Genevieve Howard, Barry Coe as Joseph Hudson, Gisele MacKenzie as Mrs. Warren, Maray Ayres as Rebecca Doris Buckinham as Mrs. Buckingham, Pia Shandel as Regina; Producer–Story: Enrique Torres Tudela; Based on the story by Edgar Allan Poe; Director: Rogelio Gonzalez, Jr.; 86 min.; Alternative Cinema; Color.

While visiting an old house to hear the reading of a relative's will Genevieve Howard is fascinated by the portrait of a woman in a painting. Soon

Genevieve feels herself controlled by the painting. The story is set against a backdrop of the American Civil War.

Overseas [Novel; SFW]

Author: Beatriz Williams; First publication: New York: G.P. Putnam's Sons, 2011.

Julian Ashford is a British officer fighting on the Western Front in Amiens, France during World War I. Kate Wilson is a young American who approaches Capt. Ashford in Amiens with vital information about a reconnaissance mission. She appears to know him but he has never seen Kate before. Their paths cross again in 2008. Kate Wilson is now a Wall Street brokerage analyst who meets and falls in love with hedge fund billionaire Julian. He knows Kate from another time but Kate has no recall of him. We learn that Julian has traveled forward in time from 1916 and Kate has traveled to 1916 from 2008.

P-51 Dragon Fighter (2014) [Film; WW]

Premiere: September 5, 2014; Main Cast: Scott Martin as Lt. John Robbins, Stephanie Beran as Rachel McKee, Ross Brooks as Lt. Drake Holdrin, Osman Soykut as Dr. Heinrich Gudrun, Robert Pike Daniel as General Irwin Rommel; Executive Producers: Frank Morehead, Joy Poth-Aleman; Story-Director: Mark Atkins; 85 min.; Rogue State, Archstone Pictures; Color.

1943. The war in North Africa reaches a climax as Nazis unleash their latest weapon—dragons. Only the Allies' expert dragon fighter pilots can save the day.

Pan's Labyrinth a.k.a. *El Laberinto del Fauno* (2006) [Film; Spain-Mexico; WW]

Premiere: January 19, 2007; Main Cast: Ivana Baquero as Ofelia, Sergi Lopez as Captain Vidal, Maribel Verdu as Mercedes, Ariadna Gil as Carmen Vidal, Doug Jones as Faun-Pale Man, Alex Angulo as Dr. Ferreiro; Executive Producers: Belen Atienza, Elena Manrique; Producer-Story-Director: Guillermo del Toro; 118 min.; Sententia Entertainment, Tequila Gang, Esperanto Filmoj, Estudios Picasso; Warner Bros., Picturehouse; Color.

Spain, 1944. Twelve year-old Ofelia and her pregnant mother Carmen travel to the Spanish countryside to live with her sadistic stepfather Vidal, a captain with the Spanish army. Living in an old mill surrounded by woodland that hides a rocky labyrinth Ofelia retreats into a fantasy world as her stepfather and his falangist troops tackle anti-falangist rebels in Franco's new Spain. They young girl imagines she meets a fairy who guides her through a labyrinth to meet a faun. He tells Ofelia she is a princess but must accomplish three dangerous tasks before she can meet her father who died in the Spanish Civil War.

Winner of three Academy Awards, the film was praised by critics. Wesley Morris of the *Boston Globe* (January 12, 2007) commented, "Pan's Labyrinth is a transcendent work of art."

"A Patriot Never Dies" [Pulp fiction; WW]

Author: Frank Patton; Illustrator: A.K. Bilder; First publication: *Amazing Stories* (Vol. 17 #8; August 1943); Publisher: Ziff-Davis Publishing Company.

"Who was John Smith? And what sort of pact made him risk his life without an explanation? Like a ghost he came onto the battlefield. But no ghost fought as this man did! Who-or what-was he?"

Pax Romana [Comic book; SFW]

First publication: December 2007; Four-issue miniseries; Story-Art: Jonathan Hickman; Publisher: Image Comics.

The Vatican has discovered the secret of time travel and plans to right the wrongs of history, thus changing future events. The Church sends modern weaponry and enhanced soldiers back in time to Rome 312 A.D., but the soldiers, led by retired General Nicholas Chase, find their mission compromised when the Cardinal in charge is shot dead.

"Periscope Prey" [Pulp fiction; SFW]

Author: David Wright O'Brien; First publication: *Amazing Stories* (Vol. 17 #14; April 1943); Publisher: Ziff-Davis Publishing Company.

Nazi submarine Commander Rickhart "had the cunning and the patience of a wolf." His U–Boat surfaces as he and his small crew inspect "a listless old sailing vessel" that at first glance has nothing but skeletons aboard. Soon he discovers a yellowed volume that proves to be the log of the ship. Written in German on the cover is the name of the stricken ship, "Sinister." Rickhart reads about the Captain picking up two hundred blacks which he chained in holds. With the ship becalmed and the "blacks in hold beginning to stink" the crew mutinies. After days of fighting aboard only the Captain and Second Mate Stover are left alive.

Stover rages at the Captain, "You shall die and die again for every shackle you seek to fetter the arms and legs of God's children." The Captain smashes Stover's head open with his rifle butt while Stover fires a bullet into the Captain's chest. Both men die. But not before the Captain signs the log, "Captain Wolfgang Rickhart." The man was Commander Rickhart's great grandfather.

He turns as he hears a voice yell, "Enslaver Rickhart!" and sees a hideous specter of a man with one half of his head, "a mess of smashed bone and blood and brain." It is Stover and Rickhart's great grandson is his target.

Persona 2: Innocent Sin [Videogame; Japan; WW]

Release date: June 24, 1999; Platform: PlayStation; Developer-Publisher: Atlus.

Modern day Sumaru City, Japan is invaded by Hitler, who survived World War II. Hitler and his Last Battalion, along with Masked Circle members, are repelled by Seven Sisters senior high school student Tatsuya Suou and his group of friends. The Fuhrer escapes to the alien spaceship Xibalba where Tasuya and the others find Hitler holding the Spear of Destiny. But all the events have been manipulated by Nyarlathotep who has plans on destroying the Earth.

Perversions of Science (1997) [TV series]

Science fiction anthology series hosted by a sexy female robot named Chrome.

"The Exile" (1:04) [SFW]

Air date: June 11, 1997; Main Cast: Jeffrey Combs as 50557, David Warner as Dr. Nordhoff, Ron Perlman as 40139, Jeff Corey as The Judge, Brian Brophy as Investigator, Oscar Dillon as Jailer, Craig Olsen as Lupita, Jae Woo Lee as Coopersmith, Christopher John Fields as Adolf Hitler, Maureen Teefy as voice of Chrome; Producer: Gilbert Adler; Teleplay: David J. Schow; Based on the story in *Weird Fantasy* by William M. Gaines; Director: William Malone; 26 min.; Two Fisted Holdings, Home Box Office (HBO); Color.

Dr. Nordhoff attempts to rehabilitate a chronic psychotic murderer using methods of torture. But 50557 resists as he mocks Nordhoff's failed attempts. "Nothing you ever do is going to change me."

After the prisoner murders his cellmate 40139 he is sentenced to exile. Attempting a futile escape 50557 discovers his prison is on a spaceship. 50557's memory is erased and he finally departs his prison when he exiled to Earth in the year 1927. But Nordhoff has made a major blunder in sending 50557 into exile. He will be better known on Earth as Adolf Hitler.

Peter Panzerfaust [Comic book; WW]

First publication: February 2012; Creators: Kurtis J. Wiebe, Tyler Jenkins; Publisher: Image-Shadowline.

Peter Pan re-imagined as a mysterious American boy helping a group of French orphans in World War II France.

"Peter Pettigrew's Prisoner" [Pulp fiction; SFW]

Author: Nelson S. Bond; Illustrator: Milburn; First publication: *Amazing Stories* (Vol. 16 #7; July 1942); Publisher: Ziff-Davis Publishing Company.

"Pettigrew captured a strange prisoner; one whose methods of sabotage were unique. He had weird dust in a bag...."

The Phantom Goes to War a.k.a. *The Inexorables* [Newspaper strip; WW]

First publication: February 2, 1942–January 9, 1943; 49 weeks; Story: Lee Falk: Art: Ray Moore, Wilson McCoy; Syndicated.

"This is the home of the Bandara, the pygmy poison people—a place feared by all jungle people. This is the home of the Ghost Who Walks—they see for the first time his legendary Skull Cave."

The Phantom, the giver of jungle law and peace speaks. "The warriors of Nippon have invaded the jungle. We will unite. We will fight together until the enemy is destroyed!"

Major Palmer contacts his niece Diana with orders for the Phantom. But when she enters the Bengali jungle with Captain Byron they are captured by a Japanese tank unit. The Phantom vows to fight to the last man, "until all Japs are driven from the sea."

The Philadelphia Experiment [Film; SFW]

1. Premiere: August 3, 1984; Main Cast: Michael Pare as David Herdeg, Nancy Allen as Allison Hayes, Eric Christmas as Dr. James Longstreet, Louise Latham as Pamela, Bobby De Cicco as Jim Parker, Kene Holliday as Major Clark; Executive Producer: John Carpenter; Story: Wallace C. Bennet, Don Jakoby; Screenplay: Michael Janover, William Gray; Director: Stewart Raffill; 102 min.; New World Pictures; Color.

A military experiment to make U.S. warships

invisible to radar in 1943 goes wrong when the Navy destroyer escort U.S.S. Eldridge disappears in Philadelphia harbor and two members of the crew are transported to 1984. The two sailors must locate the scientist responsible for their travel through time—Dr. James Longstreet in the hope he can send them back to 1943.

2. [Telefilm] Premiere: July 28, 2012; Main Cast: Nicholas Lea as Bill Gardner, Emilie Ullerup as Molly Gardner, Michael Pare as Hagan, Ryan Robbins as Richard Faulkner, Malcolm McDowell as Morton Salinger; Executive Producers: Tom Berry, Lisa Hansen, Paul Hertzberg; Story: Andy Briggs; Director: Paul Ziller; 89 min.; CineTel Films, Rainbow Pictures, Movie Central, Reel One Entertainment; Syfy; Color.

Dr. Richard Faulkner has perfected the cloaking device first tested during World War II. But when the device is tested the U.S.S. *Eldridge* appears out of thin air. Only Lt. Bill Gardner survives on the ship, but he is disorientated and flees. Faulkner explains that for the rift in time to be closed Gardner must return to 1943. He enlists the help of original "Philadelphia Experiment" project chief Morton Salinger. But Kathryn Moore has orders to destroy the ship and the cloaking technology.

The TV film suffers from inconsistencies, including the character Morton Salinger. As the original project chief he would be in his 90s in 2012 if he was a young man back in 1943.

Philadelphia Experiment II (1993) [Film: SFW]

Premiere: November 12, 1993; Main Cast: Brad Johnson as David Herdeg. Marjean Holden as Jess, James Greene as Professor Longstreet, John Christian Graas as Benjamin Herdeg, Gerrit Graham as Dr. William Mailer-Fredrich Mahler; Executive Producer: Mark Amin; Story: Kim Steven Ketelsen; Screenplay: Kevin Rock, Nick Paine; Director: Stephen Cornwell; 97 min.; Trimark Pictures; Color.

A stealth bomber from 1993 is sent back in time to Nazi Germany in 1943 and becomes the decisive factor in Germany winning World War II. Meanwhile David Herdeg finds himself in a 1993 where the Nazis rule. Only he can correct history.

Phoenix and Ashes [Novel; WW]

Author: Mercedes Lackey; First publication: New York: DAW Books, 2004.

Reginald Fenyx, an Elemental Master of the Air, is an air ace with the Royal Flying Corps during World War I. But one day he meets his match in aerial combat and crashes to Earth. The emotional torment of being attacked by Elemental Earth creatures as he lies trapped for days results in Fenyx giving up magic.

Picture the Dead [Juvenile book; WW]

Author: Adele Griffin; Illustrator: Lisa Brown; First publication: Naperville, Ill: Sourcebooks Fire, 2010.

Jennie Lovell feels the presence of her twin brother Toby and her fiancé, Will after they are killed in the Civil War. When she attempts to contact them through a photographer's alleged images of the spirit world the ghost of Will provides disturbing clues to the real nature of his death.

The story is made more vivid with the inclusion of a scrapbook that includes family portraits, letters and newspaper clippings.

The Piper [Juvenile book; WW]

Author: Danny Weston; First publication: London: Andersen Press, 2014.

Peter and his younger sister Daisy are part of a mass evacuation from London during World War II called Operation Pied Piper. Billeted to the isolated farm, Sheldon Grange, in mist-covered Romney Marsh, their new home has many secrets. Children dance to eerie flute music at night. One day while visiting the local town, Peter meets Professor Lowell, who tells him about the Sheldon family curse. Daisy is in danger if she stays at Sheldon Grange.

Post-Mortem [Stage play; UK; WW]

Premiere: Prisoner-of-war camp, Austria, 1944; Playwright: Noel Coward.

Originally written in 1930 this one-act anti-war play in eight scenes remained out of production until 1944 when it was first performed at a POW camp in Austria. Apart from a BBC TV production in 1968 the play remained in limbo until October 1992 when it received its professional Fringe Theatre debut at the King's Head Pub in Islington, London.

Inspired by *Journey's End*, a play Coward appeared in, *Post-Mortem* begins with mortally wounded soldier John, in the World War I trenches of France. The time moves forward to 1930 where John is a ghost still dressed in the uniform he died in. As he meets his friends who survived the war he comes to a greater understanding of the futility of war.

See: *The Jazz Age*

"Private Prune Speaking" [Pulp fiction; SFW]

Author: David Wright O'Brien; Illustrator: Herbert McClure; First publication: *Amazing Stories* (Vol. 18 #4; September 1944); Publisher: Ziff-Davis Publishing Company.

Average soldier Private Percival Prune becomes part of a military experiment that takes an unexpected turn when scientists throw the wrong switch.

"The terrible something that had him in its power was, basically, a sort of mocking-bird-itis which made him a perfect, though unwitting, vocal mimic of others. And it was something more than that, too. It was something quite beyond a mere inexplicable mimicry that permitted him to sound like people other than himself. It was something that enabled him to say their words in advance of their actual utterance!"

Professor Supermind and Son [Comic book characters; SHW]

First appearance: *Popular Comics* #60 (February 1941); Creator: Maurice Kashuba; Publisher: R.S. Callender (Dell Publishing).

"In his famous mountaintop laboratory, Professor Warren, known to the world as Supermind, and his equally famous son, Dan, are in a state of great excitement."

The Professor tells Dan about his new invention—the Televisoscope. "The first television machine to receive light reflections out of the air from anywhere or any distance…. The whole globe becomes a constant sending station, operating twenty-four hours a day."

Dan is given super-powers by his father. "This ultra-frequency apparatus will store super-human energies in your body son. Do not misuse it!" With Dan's dynamic super-powers and the Televisoscope to detect danger Dan prepares for his first mission—to destroy a secret enemy submarine base. "The powers stored in me are pulling me like a thousand horses…. I'm off!"

Flying to the base located on a Pacific island—"Dan's dynamic power sends the Orientals flying in all directions … squealing with terror." But Dan's fury has to be checked by his father, Supermind, who through the ethereal power of his "thought voice" tells his son, "Do not destroy needlessly. Return! Your deed is done!"

Project Arbiter (2013), starring Alexis Cassar as Captain Joseph Coburn.

Project Arbiter (2013) [Short film; SFW]

Premiere; February 4, 2014; Main Cast: Alexis Cassar as Captain Joseph Colburn, Jake Lyall as Tom Hardy, Tim Coyne as Dr. Ernst von Reiner, William Charlton as Heinrich, Andrew Dillon as Ulrich, Artem Mishin as Fritz; Producer: Vicki de Mey; Story-Director: Michael Chance; 22 min.; Color.

1943. A small plane flies over the Polish border. The crew's mission to discover the secrets inside a villa operated by Nazis. Special Fields Operative Captain Joseph Colburn parachutes into the grounds of the villa, protected by a skull-faced helmet and prototype suit that makes him invisible to the enemy.

The Proteus Operation [Novel; SFW]

Author: James P. Hogan; First publication: Toronto; New York: Bantam Books, 1985.

In 1974 the Nazis rule America. Agents discover Adolf Hitler won World War II because people from the future went back in time to help the Nazis. Operation Proteus, consisting of commandos, physicists and politicians aims to go back in time to 1939 to correct the timeline and make certain Hitler loses the war.

Puppet Master (1989) [Film; WW]

Premiere: October 12, 1989; Main Cast: William Hickey as Andre Toulon, Paul Le Mat as Alex Whitaker, Irene Miracle as Dana Hadley, Jimmie F. Skaggs as Neil Gallagher, Robin Frates as Megan Gallagher, Matt Roe as Frank Forrester, Kathryn O'Reilly as Carlissa Stamford; Producer: Hope Perello; Screenplay: Joseph G. Collodi; Story: Charles Band, Kenneth J. Hall; Director: David Schmoeller; 90 min.; Empire Pictures; Echo Home Entertainment; Color.

Puppet master Andre Toulon has discovered the ancient Egyptian formula to the "Secret of Life" and given life to his puppets. But when the Nazis seek the formula for their own nefarious purposes Toulon shoots himself rather than divulge the secret. 50 years later a group of psychics find themselves targeted by the puppets after they are reanimated.

Puppet Master: Axis of Evil (2010) [Film; WW]

Premiere: July 27, 2010; Main Cast: Levi Fiehler as Danny Coogan, Erica Shaffer as Elma Coogan, Jerry Hoffman as Uncle Len, Taylor M. Graham as Don, Tom Sandoval as Ben-Max, Ada Chao as Ozu, Aaron Riber as Klaus, Jenna Gallaher as Beth; Executive Producers; Danny Draven, Henry Luk; Story: August White (Dominic Muir); Director: David DeCoteau; 83 min.; ACE Studios; Full Moon Entertainment; Color.

Bodega Bay Inn, 1939. Andre Toulon kills himself before Nazis can discover his secret. A young man named Fiehler finds himself confronting Nazi and Japanese saboteurs in California after he discovers a chest containing Toulon's puppets and his secret formula that brings them to life.

The straight-to-video film is historically inaccurate. In 1939 America wasn't at war with Germany or Japan. It also fails to follow the 1944 timeline of ***Puppet Master III: Toulon's Revenge*** (1991).

Puppet Master: Axis Termination (2016) [Film; WW]

Premiere: 2016; Main Cast: Kip Canyon as Danny Coogan, Jean Louise O'Sullivan as Beth; Producer-Story-Director: Charles Band; Full Moon Features: Color.

Set in Los Angeles in World War II, Toulon's puppets join forces with psychic Allied operatives as they fight evil Axis puppets Bombshell, Weremacht and Blitzkrieg.

Puppet Master III: Toulon's Revenge (1991) [Film; WW]

Premiere: October 17, 1991; Main Cast: Guy Rolfe as Andre Toulon, Richard Lynch as Major Kraus, Ian Abercrombie as Dr. Hess, Sarah Douglas as Elsa Toulon, Kristopher Logan as Lt. Eric Stein; Producers: David DeCoteau, John Schouweiller; Story: C. Courtney Joyner, based on the original idea by Charles Band; Director: David DeCoteau; 86 min.; Full Moon Entertainment; Echo Bridge Home Entertainment; Color.

"The Nazis thought they held the world's strings but Andre Toulon didn't need wires to make death move."

During World War II, the work of master puppeteer Andre Toulon attracts the attention of the Nazi party. They want the secret to re-animation and raid his home searching for his formula. But when Gestapo Commandant Major Krause kills Toulon's wife in front of him Toulon takes revenge with the help of his murderous puppets in the form of Blade, Jester, Pinhead, Tunneler and Leech Woman.

Puppet Master X: Axis Rising (2012) [Film; WW]

Premiere: September 15, 2012; Main Cast: Kip Canyon as Danny Coogan, Jean Louise O'Sullivan as Beth, Scott Anthony King as Commandant Moebius, Paul Thomas Arnold as General Porter, Brad Potts as Sergeant Stone, Kurt Sinclair as Major Collins, Oto Brezina as Freuhoffer, Stephanie Sanditz as Uschi, Terumi Shimazu as Ozu; Producer: Charles Band; Story: Charles Band, Shane Bitterling; Director: Charles Band; 86 min.; Full Moon Entertainment: Full Moon Features; Color.

Synthesizing the life giving puppet formula Commandant Moebius creates a master race of German soldiers during World War II. Meanwhile a deadly group of Nazi puppets have been created and given life. Only Toulon's puppets and a secret weapon can stop the Nazi menace.

Pyroman [Comic book character; SFW]

First publication: *Startling Comics* #18 (December 1942); Publisher: Better Publications.

"Saved from an unjust death in the electric chair, Dick Martin, finds white-hot current stored in his body. Passing as a research student, he uses his crackling energy as Pyroman … the dread of dictators!"

In *Startling Comics* #20 (March 1943), with art by Jack Binder, the story opens at Gestapo headquarters where an officer reports to his superior that Venom has everything prepared in America. From his underground headquarters Venom tells members of the Black Boas to crush America. Pyroman rescues General Blair and Joyce Clark from Venom before revealing him to be nothing more than a radio-controlled dummy. Pyroman concludes, "Just another proof of how blindly the slaves of fascism serve … a voice!"

Pyroman in *Startling Comics* #20 (March 1943). Cover art by Jack Binder. Published by Better Publications Inc.

Quantum Leap (1989) [TV series]

Sam Beckett, trapped in time, leaps between different eras and bodies within his own lifetime. Main Cast: Scott Bakula as Dr. Sam Beckett, Dean Stockwell as Admiral Al Calavicci; Executive Producer-Creator: Donald P. Bellisario; Universal Television; Belisarius Productions; National Broadcasting Company (NBC); Color.

"The Beast Within—November 6, 1972" (5:19) [SFW]

Air date: March 16, 1993; Guest Cast: Mike Jolly as Henry Adams, Sean Gregory Sullivan as Roy Brown, Pat Skipper as Lucas Marlet, Eileen Seeley as Karen Marlet, David Denney as Deputy Curtis; Story: John D'Aquino; Director: Gus Trikonis.

Sam Beckett leaps into the body of Vietnam veteran Henry Adams who lives in the mountains with fellow vet Roy Brown. Adams is mistaken for Bigfoot by the sheriff's young daughter when he attempts to get medication for Brown. Brown suffers from seizures and PTSD following a brain injury received while serving in Vietnam as a "tunnel rat." The local sheriff has his own agenda for preventing Brown from getting the help he needs as he served with Brown and Adams in Vietnam and was partly responsible for the death of a fellow soldier in their platoon.

"The Leap Back—June 15, 1945" (4:01) [SFW]

Air date: September 18, 1991; Guest Cast: Mimi Kuzyk as Dr. Donna Eleese, Amanda Wyss as Suzanne Eksinger, Dean Stockwell/Dean Denton as Capt. Tom Jarrett, Douglas Roberts as Mike, Robert Presott as Clifford White, Candy Ann Brown as Dr. Verbeena Beeks; Story: Donald P. Bellisario; Director: Michael Zinberg.

A lightning bolt strike results in Sam Beckett and Al Calavicci leaping together and exchanging bodies. The leap is within Al's lifetime and not Beckett's. Sam is now back home in 1999, but trapped in the imaging chamber. Al is Captain Tom Jarrett, returning home from the war where he spent three years in a P.O.W. camp. He discovers his girlfriend Suzanne Eksinger is due to marry a guy named Clifford in two days time. She thought Tom died in the war. The person Al has leaped into reflects his own experience of his wife Beth remarrying after she thought he had died in action in Vietnam.

Now that Tom has returned to Crown Point Suzanne wants to ditch Clifford. Newspaper reports from 1945 say Tom and Suzanne committed suicide by driving their car over Lover's Leap. In truth Clifford knocked them both unconscious and pushed the car over the cliff. Sam Beckett must leap into an unconscious Al Calavicci to save them.

"The Leap Between the States—September 20, 1862" (5:20) [SFW]

Air date: March 30, 1993; Guest Cast: Rob Hyland as Capt. John Beckett, Kate McNeil as Olivia Barrett Covington, Geoffrey Lower as Lt. Richard Montgomery, Michael D. Roberts as Isaac King, Neil Giuntoli as Pvt. Ryder; Story: Richard C. Okie; Director: David Hemmings.

Sam Beckett, usually confined to leaps within his lifetime is able to leap into the body of his great-grandfather during the American Civil War because of the blood-relation. As Union Army Captain John Becket he finds himself shot in the arm by Confederates and rescued by black slaves to take shelter in a barn, located in Mansfield County, Virginia. The widowed owner of the farm, Olivia Barrett Covington, takes Beckett prisoner, but Al tells Sam this is the woman John Beckett is destined to marry.

Despite her initial hostility toward Beckett he learns she is sympathetic to her slave Isaac running a stop on the underground railroad for runaway slaves. And Beckett later discovers Isaac will have a famous and very important ancestor.

"THE LEAP HOME: PART 1—NOVEMBER 25, 1969; PART 2—APRIL 7, 1970" (3:01–3:02) [SFW]
Air dates: September 28–October 5, 1990; Guest Cast: David Newsom as Navy Lt. Tom Beckett, Olivia Burnette as Katie Beckett, Adam Affonso as Young Sam Beckett, Andrea Thompson as Maggie Dawson, Ernie Lively as Col. Deke Grimwald; Story: Donald P. Bellisario; Directors: Joe Napolitano (Pt.1) Michael Zinberg (Pt. 2).

In Part 1 Sam Beckett leaps into his younger self to warn his brother Tom about Vietnam. Sam knows his brother will die in battle and wins the high school championship basketball game, hoping Tom will keep his promise to, "crawl into the deepest, thickest, concrete bunker in Vietnam" on April 8.

In Part 2 Beckett finds himself transported to Tom's Navy SEAL squad in Vietnam as soldier Herbert "Magic" Williams. It is April 7, 1970—the day before Tom Beckett dies. But Sam's mission isn't to save his brother's life but to make certain "Operation Lazarus" is a success. Two females will play a key part in the next 24 hours. One will be a traitor leading the squad into an ambush, and another will win a Pulitzer sacrificing her life.

"M.I.A.—APRIL 1, 1969" (2:22) [SFW]
Air date: May 9, 1990; Guest Cast: Jason Beghe as Det. Sgt. Roger Skaggs, Susan Diol as Beth Calavicci, Norman Large as Dirk Simon, Dan Ziskie as Sergeant Riley, Doug Baer as Detective Jake Rawlins; Story: Donald P. Bellisario; Director: Michael Zinberg.

Sam Beckett leaps into the body of Detective Jake Rawlins who is partnered with Sgt. Roger Skaggs. Beckett must stop a woman named Beth from marrying a man she will meet on April 1, 1969. Beth's husband is Missing In Action but still alive in Vietnam after being captured by the Vietcong. But Beth will decide to declare him dead so she can marry again.

Al Calavicci recalls how he was M.I.A. in Vietnam and his wife also left him thinking he was dead. Beckett realizes Beth is the same woman. But he learns the main reason he has leaped is to save the life of Skaggs who is also suffering the after effects of his experiences in Vietnam.

"NOWHERE TO RUN—AUGUST 10, 1968" (5:04) [SFW]
Air date: October 6, 1992; Guest Cast: Jennifer Aniston as Kiki Wilson, Michael Boatman as Sgt. Billy Johnson, Norman Shaw as Commander James Hartig, Gene Lythgow as Holt, Judith Hoag as Julie Miller, Michael Carpenter as Capt. Ron Miller; Story: Tommy Thompson; Director: Alan J. Levi.

Sam Beckett finds himself in a Veterans hospital where he has leapt into the body of a Marine Captain Ron Miller who lost both legs in Vietnam. Miller's paralyzed roommate Sgt. Billy Johnson is depressed to the point of wanting to drown himself in the hospital therapy pool. Meanwhile Miller has personal troubles of his own when his wife Julie announces she has met another man and wants a divorce. And volunteer nurse Kiki Wilson's brother is missing-in-action.

Raiders of the Lost Ark (1981) [Film; WW]

Premiere: June 12, 1981; Main Cast: Harrison Ford as Indiana Jones, Karen Allen as Marion Ravenwood, Paul Freeman as Dr. Rene Belloq, Ronald Lacey as Major Arnold Toht, Alfred Molina as Satipo, Denholm Elliott as Marcus Brody, John Rhys-Davies as Sallah; Executive Producers: George Lucas, Howard Kazanjian; Story: George Lucas, Philip Kaufman; Screenplay: Lawrence Kasdan; Director: Steven Spielberg; 115 min.; Lucasfilm, Paramount Pictures; Color.

Archaeologist-adventurer Indiana Jones is hired by U.S. Army Intelligence agents to stop the Nazis from finding the Lost Ark of the Covenant. Nazis believe in the occult powers of the Ark that contains the shattered tablet remnants of the Ten Commandments—and are convinced it will make their army invincible.

Dan Scapperotti writing for *Cinefantastique* (Vol. 11 #3: September 1981) states: "Harrison Ford is ideal as Jones: intelligent and intrepid. The film has boundless energy. So fast is the action that there is no time to realize the improbability of it all—and it really doesn't matter anyway. They have brought the excitement of the Saturday matinee, given us a hero to cheer for and provided two hours of unadulterated fun."

"Raiders Out of Space" [Pulp fiction; SFW]

Author: Robert Moore Williams; Illustrator: Robert Fuqua; First publication: *Amazing Stories* (Vol. 14 #10; October 1940); Publisher: Ziff-Davis Publishing Company.

"Defeated France was too hot, so Rolf Baden and Danny Walker lit out, bomber and all—on a flight that led into outer space!"

Rebel Angels [Novel; WW]

Author: Michele Lang; First publication: New York: Tor, 2013.

In the conclusion to the *Lady Lazarus* trilogy Magdalena and her husband, the fallen angel Raziel, begin their dangerous quest to find the Heaven Sapphire gem and prevent the Holocaust. They must defeat human and supernatural foes, the demon Asmodel, to claim the magical gem that can destroy either Hitler and his minions or Magdalena.

See: ***Lady Lazarus***

A Rebel in Time [Novel; SFW]

Author: Harry Harrison; First publication: New York: Tom Doherty Associates, 1983.

Colonel McCulloch is a racist who seizes the opportunity to change the outcome of the American Civil War when he's assigned to a time machine project. African American Sergeant Harmon follows him through time to stop his plans but encounters racism in the Confederate deep south.

Rebel Spirits [Juvenile book; WW]

Author: Lois Ruby; First publication: New York: Point, 2013.

Lori Chase reluctantly moves with her parents to Coolspring Inn in Gettysburg, Pennsylvania. She soon discovers that its reputation for being haunted is deserved when she meets handsome but deceased Civil War Union soldier Nathaniel Pierce in her bedroom.

"He shakes his head from side to side, me following those black eyes. He turns all the way around. That's when I see the torn fabric and dried blood of a gaping hole in the middle of his back. As if someone had aimed for his heart."

The ghost tells Lori he didn't die in battle but was murdered. But when Lori's research shows her Pierce was executed after being found guilty of treason she questions his character. She has three days to find out the truth behind his death and charges of treason to put his soul at rest before he disappears forever.

The Reckoning [Novel; WW]

Author: Jeff Long; First publication: New York: Atria Books, 2004.

Photojournalist Molly Drake accompanies a U.S. military search for the remains of an American pilot shot down during the Vietnam War. When bones are discovered Drake breaks her promise not to photograph the remains and is dismissed by the army Captain. Drake, archaeologist Duncan O'Brian and veteran John Kleat, who is seeking his brother's remains, come across the ruins of an ancient city where a U.S. army patrol disappeared decades ago. Soon, they find their survival in peril as the monsoon season approaches in a landscape littered with land mines and the ghostly "dawn people."

Cover of *Rebel Spirits* by Lois Ruby (2013).

Red Dwarf (1988) [TV series; UK]

BBC-TV comedy series featuring the motley crew of Red Dwarf as it travels through interstellar space. Regular Cast: Craig Charles as Dave Lister, Chris Barrie as Arnold Rimmer, Danny John-Jules as Cat, Robert Llewellyn as Kryten, Hattie Hayridge as Holly; Executive Producers: Rob Grant, Doug Naylor; 30 min.; BBC-TV; Color.

"Meltdown" (4:06) [SFW]

Air date: March 21, 1991; Guest Cast: Kenneth Hadley as Adolf Hitler, Tony Hawks as Caligula, Jack Klaff as Abraham Lincoln, Clayton Mark as Elvis Presley,

Pauline Bailey as Marilyn Monroe, Forbes Mason as Stan Laurel, Martin Friend as Albert Einstein, Roger Blake as Noel Coward, Michael Burrell as Pope Gregory, Stephen Tiller as Pythagoras; Story" Rob Grant, Doug Naylor; Director: Ed Bye.

At the android theme park "Waxworld" Dave Lister and Cat are taken prisoner by Adolf Hitler.

"Timeslides" (3:05) [SFW]

Air date: March 12, 1989; Guest Cast: Stephen McKintosh as Fred "Thickie" Holden, Koo Stark as Lady Sabrina Mulholland-Jjones, Ruby Wax as Blaize Falconburger, Robert Addie as Gilbert, Adolf Hitler as Himself; Story: Rob Grant, Doug Naylor; Director: Ed Bye.

Kryten makes a startling discovery while working in the darkroom of the ship. Developing fluid can make photographs come to life. Dave Lister timeslides back in time through a photograph to stand alongside Adolf Hitler. He warns the German crowd to ignore Hitler because he's "a total nutter, and he's only got one testicle."

The Red Panda Adventures (2005) [Radio drama, Podcast; Canada; WW]

First broadcast: August 27, 2005; Creator: Gregg Taylor; Decoder Ring Theatre.

Red Panda aids the war effort as "Canada's One-Man Second Front." Dr. Anna Handbasket, a scientist for the Panda Division, has created Manlonite 990 which gives Red Panda extra strength and speed. Nazi villains include German Von German, commander of an elite team of Nazi Ninjas, Baron Otto Platte, pride of the Luftwaffe, who following his presumed death, is replaced with an army of Nazi android pilots made in his likeness and Professor Friedrich Von Schlick who, after being killed in action, turns into a living oil slick.

The original series, consisting of six episodes, takes place during World War II. Episodes parody the super-heroic patriotic radio dramas of the 1940s together with over-the-top villains. The show changed its timeline to the 1930s for a re-imagined podcast series. Nazi villains have been re-introduced as later season episodes move forward to World War II. Professor Friedrich Von Schlick, is now Professor Friedrich Von Schlitz whose allies include an army of dinosaurs from a bubble universe.

The earlier adventures are explained as taking place on Earth-2.

Episodes: Original Series

1. *Case of the Dynamite Dame*; 2. *Oil Be Home for Christmas*; 3. *Death from Above*; 4. *The Judas Boats*; 5. *The Black Panda*; 6. *A Touch of Grey*.

Red Planet Mars (1952) [Film; SFW]

Premiere: May 15, 1952; Main Cast: Peter Graves as Chris Cronyn, Andrea King as Linda Cronyn, Herbert Berghof as Franz Calder, Walter Sande as Admiral Bill Carey, Willis Bouchey as President, Marvin Miller as Arjenian, Morris Ankrum as Secretary of Defense Sparks, Orley Lindgren as Stewart Cronyn, Bayard Veiller as Roger Cronyn; Producer: Anthony Veiller; Screenplay: John L. Balderston, Anthony Veiller; Based on the play by John L. Balderston and John Hoare; Director: Harry Horner; 87 min.; Melaby Pictures Corporation; United Artists; B/W.

Former Nazi scientist Franz Calder views human beings as "the best guinea pig" when he performs high voltage experiments on the human nervous system. But Calder has also invented the hydrogen valve that allows American scientist Chris Cronyn to attempt communication with Mars. Calder claims Cronyn stole his invention after he discovered his blueprints at Nuremburg.

When Cronyn finally receives replies to his messages to Mars that echo the "Sermon on the Mount" the world undergoes a transformation. But Calder confronts Cronyn and tells him he faked the messages.

"You thought you'd created a new Earth and I destroy it. A new heaven and that I shall destroy. Paradise lost, that's my present to the world. Better to reign in hell than serve in heaven. Lucifer's my hero. God beat him but I'll have beaten God."

But were the messages of peace and love fake or truly from the Martians?

Red Raven [Comic book character; WW]

First appearance: *Red Raven Comics* #1 (August 1940); Creators: Joe Simon, Louis Cazeneuve; Publisher: Timely Comics.

A young red-haired child is traveling with his parents on a passenger plane crossing the Atlantic Ocean, when it encounters heavy clouds and crashes into an island in the sky inhabited by a race of bird people. The young boy, the only survivor, is adopted by the king of the birdmen and grows to maturity. Now twenty-years-old the young man is given his mission in life by the king.

"You are brave as our bravest bird, the Raven! I shall call you the Red Raven! With the aid of your wings we made you, you shall go back to your people to devote your life to eradicating the elements that make for unhappiness in the world!"

On Earth Red Raven joins the **Liberty Legion** during World War II, fighting the **Red Skull** among other Axis foes.

Red Sands (2009) [Film; WW]

Premiere: February 24, 2009; Main Cast: Shane West as Jeff Keller, Leonard Roberts as Marcus Howston, Aldis Hodge as Trevor Anderson, Callum Blue as Gregory Wilcox, Brendan Miller as Chard Davies, Theo Rossi as Tino Hull, Noel G as Jorge Wardell, Mercedes Masohn as Arab Woman; Executive Producer: Sundip Shah; Story: Simon Barrett; Producer-Director: Alex Turnel; 89 min.; Stage 6 Films, Silver Nitrate, Tricky Pictures, Deviant Films; Color.

On patrol in Afghanistan, a group of U.S. soldiers seize control of a road used by the Taliban, but not before one of the soldiers destroys an ancient statue. Unknown to the soldiers a djinn has been released that plays on their psychological fears.

Red Skull [Comic book character; SFW]

First appearance: *Captain America Comics* #1 (March 1941); Creators: **Joe Simon**, **Jack Kirby**, France Herron; Publisher: Timely Comics, Marvel Comics.

George Maxon is the owner of his own aircraft company that supplies planes to the U.S. military. He secretly wants to raise enough money to overthrow the U.S. government by robbing banks wearing a Red Skull mask. Maxon is killed by his own bomb after he mistakenly kidnaps imposters posing as **Captain America** and Bucky.

Captain America #7 (October 1941) reveals Maxon was only a pretend Red Skull. In later issues the reader is told the real Red Skull is Nazi Johann Schmidtt. He is also killed in *Captain America* #61 when he falls from a dam. His next appearance takes a macabre turn in *Captain America's Weird Tales* #74 (October 1949) when we see him in his afterlife in Hades. Captain America is forced to join him by a messenger from "the powers of darkness" after his name is found written in flames in "The Great Volume." A trial by combat follows after Red Skull admits he wrote the name. Captain America defeats the Red Skull and is allowed to return to the "land of mortals."

Red Skull returns to life to fight Captain America in *Young Men* (December 1953). Captain America and Bucky come out of retirement to stop the Red Skull from attacking the U.N. building. But this time the Red Skull is Communist spy Albert Malik.

Red Skull was re-introduced in *Tales of Suspense* #65 (May 1965) in World War II centered stories. In issue #79 (July 1966) he entered the modern era in similar fashion to Captain America—revived from suspended animation. He continued to fight for the Nazi cause, spreading his evil across the world. The Red Skull has survived death and gained a form of immortality through his psionic mind transference and clone technology created by **Arnim Zola** during World War II.

The Red Suitcase [Juvenile book; WW]

Author: Jill Harris; First publication: Eastbourne, New Zealand: Submarine, 2014.

After a suicide bomber disrupts the life of Ruth and her family in Indonesia, they are forced to move back to Takapuna, New Zealand. An emotionally fragile Ruth begins to suffer a series of time-slips to World War II. She finds herself sharing the experiences of the pilot of a bomber. In her grandmother's wardrobe, the contents of a red suitcase are somehow linked to her World War II time-slips. Ruth confides in physics geek Thomas Barnard, who might have some of the answers.

Reign of the Gargoyles (2007) [Telefilm; WW]

Premiere; March 24, 1997; Main Cast: Joe Penny as Gus, Wes Ramsey as Will, Sean Mahon as Deacon, Julia Rose as Sophie, Billy Lush as Chick, John Ashton as Commander Latham, Boris Pankin as Lt. Eyepatch; Executive Producer: TJ Sakasegaawa; Story: Chase Parker; Director: Ayton Davis; 88 min.; Concrete Productions, Sci-Fi Pictures; UFO International Productions; Color.

Gargoyles are brought to life by demonic forces set free by Nazis during World War II. After successfully attacking and destroying Allied bombers in Europe the gargoyles become the prime target of the combined British and American air forces.

The Rest of Heaven Was Blue [Graphic novel; WW]

First publication: 2013; Story: Matthew Wilkins; Art: Emmanuel Xerx Javier; Publisher: Image-Top Cow.

The incessant violence and moral ambiguity of the Vietnam War has a deep psychological effect on one American soldier. Stalked by a phantom figure, twisted visions of death and a real-life platoon sergeant who only adds to his misery, the soldier feels trapped in his hellish environment.

"The Return of the Hun" [Pulp fiction; WW]

Author: William J. Britain; Illustrator: Magarian; First publication: *Fantastic Adventures* (Vol. 4 #7; July 1942); Publisher: Ziff-Davis Publishing Company.

"Two Nazi officers sent their time machine into the future to seek a weapon to win the war—in a future that recorded Nazi defeat!"

Return to Castle Wolfenstein [Videogame; WW]

Release date: November 2001; Original platform: Microsoft Windows; Developers: Grey Matter Interactive, Nerve Software, Splash Damage, Raster Productions; Publisher: ID Software, Activision.

Two agents are imprisoned in Castle Wolfenstein while investigating Heinrich Himmler's SS Paranormal Division. "Operation Resurrection" plans to raise the dead and harness supernatural powers to win World War II.

"Return to Lilliput" [Pulp fiction; WW]

Author: William Brengle; Illustrator: McCanley; First publication: *Fantastic Adventures* (Vol. 5 #5; May 1943); Publisher: Ziff-Davis Publishing Company.

"Five Americans escaped from Japanese-held Java to the modern Lilliput. All was well until two of them turned up missing...."

Return to Never Land (2002) [Animated film; WW]

Premiere: January 1, 2002; Voice Cast: Harriet Owen as Jane/Young Wendy, Blayne Weaver as Peter Pan, Corey Burton as Captain Hook, Kath Soucie as Wendy Darling, Jeff Bennett as Smee, Andrew McDonough as Danny, Roger Rees as Edward; Producers: Cheryl Abood, Christopher Chase, Michelle Pappalardo-Robinson, Dan Rounds; Screenplay: Temple Matthews; Based on the play by J.M. Barrie; Directors: Robin Budd, Donovan Cook; 72 min.; Disney Toon Studios, Walt Disney Pictures, Disney Television Animation; Buena Vista Pictures; Color.

London in 1940 is under attack from German bombers. Wendy Darling tries to instill a sense of hope in her two children during the air raids, but her daughter Jane doesn't believe her mother's fantastic accounts of Peter Pan in Never Land. However her lack of belief is put to the test when Captain Hook mistakes Jane for Wendy and kidnaps her.

Revenge of the Red Baron (1994) [Film; WW]

Premiere: February 16, 1994; Main Cast: Mickey Rooney as Grandpa Spencer, Tobey Maguire as Jimmy Spencer, Larriane Newman as Carol Spencer, Cliff De Young as Richard Spencer, John C. McDonnell as the voice of the Red Baron, Don Stark as Detective Lewis; Executive Producer: Roger Corman; Story: Michael James McDonald; Director: Robert Gordon; 100 min.; Buena Vista Home Entertainment; Color.

Grandpa Spencer, a former World War I ace pilot who shot down the infamous Red Baron, loves to play with radio-controlled toy planes. But his obsession takes a weird turn when the Red Baron returns in the form of an action figure. Grandpa Spencer, his grandson Jimmy and daughter-in-law Carol team up to defeat the legendary World War I combat pilot.

Revenge of the Zombies (1943) [Film: WW]

Premiere: September 17, 1943; Main Cast: John Carradine as Dr. Max Heinrich Von Altermann, Gale Storm as Jennifer Rand, Robert Lowery as Larry Adams, Mauritz Hugo as Scott Warrington, Veda Ann Borg as Lila Von Altermann, Mantan Moreland as Jeff; Producer: Linsley Parsons; Screenplay: Edmond Kelso, Van Norcross; Director: Steve Sekely; 61 min.; Monogram Pictures; B/W.

In their mansion home, deep in the swamps of Louisiana, Nazi scientist Dr. Von Altermann turns his recently deceased wife Lila into a zombie for the Third Reich. But she shows signs of free will and has plans of her own. Meanwhile Lila's brother Scott Warrington and hired detective Larry Adams arrive at the mansion suspecting Dr. Altermann of murder. Wide-eyed manservant Jeff provides the comic relief as the guests remain skeptical of his many encounters with zombies in the swamps.

Revere: Revolution in Silver [Graphic novel; WW]

Author: Ed Lavallee; Illustrator: Grant Bond; Publisher: Fort Lee, NJ: Archaia Studios Press, 2007.

The American Revolution has begun. Silversmith and monster hunter Paul Revere finds himself fighting outlaw Redcoats and killer werewolves terrorizing the townspeople of Boston.

Originally published as a four-issue mini series by Alias Comics.

Revolutionary War on Wednesday (*Magic Tree House* #22) [Juvenile book; WW]

Author: Mary Pope Osborne; Illustrator: Sal Murocca; First publication: New York: Random House–Stepping Stone, 2000.

In Frog Creek, Pennsylvania, eight-year-old Jack and his seven-year-old sister Annie come across a magical tree house filled with books. Those books belong to Morgan le Fay, magical librarian at King Arthur's court in Camelot. The children are given the task of finding four special kind of writings to save Camelot. The tree sends Jack and Annie back in time to Christmas, 1776 where they find themselves in the company of General George Washington as he plans to cross the Delaware River. And the children mustn't forget to collect the second kind of writing, "something to send," for Morgan Le Fay's library.

See: **Civil War on Sunday**

Richard III (Stage play; Film; TV) [WW]

First performance: 1592–1593; Playwright: William Shakespeare; First publication: 1597.

Dramatization of Richard III's quest for the throne of England and his time as King. Act 5, Scene 5 sees King Richard, on the eve of the Battle of Bosworth, encounter the ghosts of those he has slain or murdered. Prince Edward, King Henry VI, Lady Anne, the two young Princes in the Tower, Lord Hastings, Earl Rivers, Lord Gray, Sir Thomas Vaughn, Duke of Clarence, and Duke of Buckingham. The ghost of young Prince Edward is the first to appear to King Richard in a dream.

"Let me sit heavy on thy soul tomorrow,
Prince Edward, son to Henry the Sixth.
Think how thou stabbedst me in my prime of youth
At Tewkesbury. Despair, therefore, and die."

The other ghosts repeat Edward's message to "despair and die" while giving comfort to Henry Earl of Richmond, the future Henry VII. The following day Richard is slain on the battlefield by the Earl of Richmond and King Henry VII ascends the throne of England.

Richard III has been adapted many times to film and television. Notable productions are listed.

(France, U.S., 1912); Frederick Warde as Richard III, Violet Stuart as lady Anne Plantagenet, Carey Lee as Queen Elizabeth; Directors: Andre Calmettes, James Keane.

(UK, 1955); Laurence Olivier as Richard III, John Gielgud as Clarence, Ralph Richardson as Buckingham, Claire Bloom as Lady Anne; Director: Laurence Olivier.

(UK, 1995); Adapted to a modern fascist England setting; Ina McKellen as Richard III, Annette Bening as Queen Elizabeth, Nigel Hawthorne as Duke of Clarence, Kristin Scott Thomas as lady Anne, Maggie Smith as Duchess of York; Director: Richard Loncraine.

(TV, UK, 1983); Ron Cook as Richard III, Michael Byrne as Duke of Buckingham, Peter Benson as King Henry VI; Director: Jane Howell.

Riding with the James Gang: A Luke and Jenny Adventure [Juvenile book; WW]

Author: Gayle Martin; First publication: Chandler, AZ: Five Star Publications, 2007.

Luke and his older sister Jenny spend the final night of their summer vacation camping out on their great-grandmother's Missouri farm. But the ghost of young farm girl Kate takes them back in time to the days of Frank and Jesse James, Cole Younger and his brothers. From their days fighting in the American Civil War to their days as an outlaw gang robbing banks and trains, Luke and Jenny experience it all first-hand.

The Rinaldi Ring [Juvenile book; WW]

Author: Jenny Nimmo; First publication: London: Mammoth, 1999.

Eliot is a troubled young man still grieving for his late mother and unable to get along with his father. While staying with his cousins he is haunted by the violent spirit of Mary-Ellen. Eliot learns she was a prisoner in her room who committed suicide after her lover Orlando Rinaldi died in the trenches during World War I. Orlando's ring was apparently inherited by Orlando's brother, Oliver and then claimed by the menacing Freya Greymark. But Eliot discovers the truth behind Orlando's death, including a baby that was Eliot's grandfather. By uncovering the truth, Eliot not only finds peace for Mary-Ellen's spirit but also heals his own family wounds.

Ring of Red [Videogame; Japan; AHW]

Release date: September 2000; Platform: PlayStation 2; Developer:-Publisher: Konami.

During World War II Nazi Germany create and deploy giant Armored Fighting Walkers (AFWs)—mechanized, walking artillery. But with the defeat of the Nazis they are adopted by the Japanese forces in the Great Asian War between the communist North, supported by the Soviet Union and People's Republic of China and democratic South Japan, supported by the United States and Allied forces.

Rip Hunter: Time Master [Comic book]

Rip Hunter, Jeff Smith, Bonnie Baxter and Corky Baxter travel through time using Hunter's invention the Time Sphere.

"Adolf Hitler's Greatest Secret" [SFW]
First publication: *Rip Hunter: Time Master* #20 (May–June 1964); Story: Jack Miller; Art: Bill Ely; Publisher: DC Comics

When Rip Hunter and his team are trapped in Nazi Germany Adolf Hitler demands Hunter goes back in time to 1815 to return Napoleon Bonaparte to Germany so he can advice Hitler on his Russian campaign.

"George Washington—Enemy Agent" [SFW]
First publication: *Rip Hunter: Time Master* #23 (November–December 1964); Story: Jack Miller; Art: Bill Ely; Publisher: DC Comics

Rip Hunter obeys a request by President Lyndon Johnson to journey back in time to the Revolutionary War. His mission to confirm a note that indicates George Washington was a traitor. But the mission backfires when Hunter is arrested by Washington, accused of being a traitor himself and sentenced to execution by firing squad.

See: ***DC's Legends of Tomorrow***

Ritual of the Stifling Air [Radio drama; UK; WW]
First broadcast: 1977; Story: Paul A. Green; British Broadcasting Company; BBC Radio Three.

A small group of neo–Nazi occultists attempt to contact the spirit of Adolf Hitler in a magical ceremony.

Rocket Ranger [Videogame; Comic book; SFW]

1. Release date: 1988; Original platform: Amiga; Developer-Publisher: Cinemaware.

A single-player game where the player—a U.S. Army scientist from World War II—fights the worldwide Nazi menace with the aid of his rocket pack and radium pistol. Nazis are mining the mineral lunarium on the moon and dropping it as bombs from zeppelins to lower the IQ of males thus making for an easy invasion. The ultimate goal of the game is to collect parts for a rocket ship and lunarium to enable a journey to the moon to destroy the Nazi mines and their alien allies.

2. First publication: 1991; Art: Hector; Publisher: Adventure Comics-Malibu Comics.

Rocket Ranger Tom Cory fights German officer Oberst Leermeister, overseer of the lunarium operation. This B/W comic book adaptation of the videogame ran to five issues before ceasing publication in July 1992.

Rocket Ship Galileo [Juvenile book; SFW]
Author: Robert A. Heinlein; Illustrator: Thomas Voter; First publication: New York: Charles Scribner's Sons, 1947.

Three teenage boys and uncle Dr. Cargraves work on converting a rocket to take them to the Moon. To their horror they discover a secret Nazi base on the Moon after their spaceship is badly damaged by a bomb. Needing the Nazi spaceship to return to Earth Cargraves threatens a captured Nazi with execution unless he instructs him how to pilot the craft.

"Rockets Over Europe" [Pulp fiction; SFW]
Author: Robert Moore Williams; First publication: *Amazing Stories* (Vol. 14 #2; February 1940); Publisher: Ziff-Davis Publishing Company.

"What really happened at Friedrichshafen? Was it an incredible bit of science fiction come true?"

Editorial: "This story is fiction. The editors have no desire to present *Rockets Over Europe* in any other light. Yet in view of the news that has come through the war censorship—the reader may well ask—is this fiction?"

The editors of *Amazing Stories* were referring to the German V2 rockets launched from Germany to bomb London. The fictional story was written before they were public knowledge.

The Rocketeer [Comic book; Film; SFW]
1. First publication: 1983; Story-Art: Dave Stevens; Publisher Pacific Comics-Comico-Eclipse.

April 1938. Pilot Cliff Secord arrives at his rented airplane hangar to find police arresting a couple of crooks attempting to steal his Stubby plane. Wondering why they would want his plane Secord finds an unwrapped bundle in his cockpit, containing a compact, bullet-shaped engine and "Top Secret" papers. When he reads the papers and discovers the engine is a miracle of technology he devises a plan. Contacting his pal Peevy from Bigelow's Air Circus he instructs him to construct a metal helmet.

Side-lined by his discovery Secord arrives late at a scheduled air show, only to find his drunken friend Malcolm struggling in the air. Now is the perfect time to test his rocket engine and rescue Malcolm. The Rocketeer is born.

2. Premiere: June 21, 1991; Main Cast: Bill Campbell as Cliff Secord, Jennifer Connelly as Jenny Blake, Alan Arkin as Peevy, Timothy Dalton as Neville Sinclair, Paul Sorvino as Eddie Valentine, Ed Lauter as Fitch; Producers: Charles Gordon, Lawrence Gordon, Lloyd Levin; Executive Producer: Larry Franco; Story: Danny Bilson, Paul De Meo, William Dear; Based on the comic book series by Dave Stevens; Director: Joe Johnston; 108 min.; Walt Disney Pictures; Buena Vista Pictures; Color.

Cover of *The Rocketeer Adventure Magazine* #1 (July 1988). Published by Comico.

1938. Los Angeles. Pilot Cliff Secord finds a rocket-propelled backpack in an airplane hangar. Designed by Howard Hughes, the propulsion of the rocket enables him to fly at high speeds. He wastes no time in putting it to use when a plane mechanic has an accident during a flight exhibition. With his name making headline news Secord is now firmly in the sights of Nazi spies who want the rocket pack for themselves. Neville Sinclair uses Secord's girlfriend as a pawn when his Nazi spies kidnap her and forces the hand of Secord to come to her rescue as they lay in wait.

Rome Against Rome a.k.a. *Roma contro Roma* a.k.a. *War of the Zombies* (1964) [Film; Italy; WW]

Premiere: February 13, 1964 (Italy); Main Cast: John Drew Barrymore as Aderbal, Susy Andersen as Tullia, Ettore Manni as Gaius, Ida Galli as Rhama, Mino Doro as Lutetius, Ivano Staccioli as Sirion, Philippe Hersent as Azer; Screenplay: Piero Pierotti, Marcello Sartarelli; Director: Giuseppe Vari; 98 min.; Galatea Films; America International Pictures; Color.

High priest Aderbal invokes the power of the one-eyed goddess, daughter of Osiris, to "resurrect our dead enemies from the earth and transform them into mute, invincible allies." To exterminate "our most deadly foe, the Roman legions."

Rosie Goes to War [Juvenile book; SFW]

Author: Alison Knight; First publication: Abercynon, Wales: Accent Press, 2016.

Fifteen-year-old Rosie is searching through junk at her grandmother's house when she discovers a suitcase full of vintage clothes. When a curious Rosie tries them on she travels back in time to wartime London in 1940. Experiencing the harsh life of rationing and the daily grind of factory work she manages to make friends and enjoy the social life, but fears she may be trapped in 1940 unless she can find a way back to the present.

The Royals: Masters of War [Comic book; SFW]

First publication: February 2014; Six issue mini-series; Story: Rob Williams; Art: Simon Coleby; Publisher: Vertigo.

1940. The London blitz. Royalty have special abilities but until now have refused to intervene in the war due to a worldwide truce between those of noble birth. But Prince Henry of England can no longer stay on the sidelines as his country is attacked. He takes part in the Battle of Britain, followed by the Battle of Midway in the Pacific. Prince Arthur and Princess Rose journey to war ravaged Stalingrad to rescue Prince Oscar of the Royal House of Hanover where they encounter something that tests the sanity of Princess Rose.

R–Point a.k.a. *Arpointeu* (2004) [Film; South Korea; WW]

Premiere: July 10, 2005; Main cast: Woo-seong Kam as Lt. Choi Tae-in, Byung-ho Son as Sgt. Jin Chang-rok, Sun-kyun Lee as Sgt. Park, Won-sang Park as Sgt. Cook; Executive Producer: Yun-hyeon Jang; Story: Kong Soo-chang, Yeong-woo Pil; Director: Kong Soo-chang; 107 min.; CJ Entertainment, CN Film; Tartan; Color.

1972, Vietnam. A squad of South Korean soldiers are sent on a mission to rescue a missing platoon from the R–Point. A radio transmission offers hope they are still alive, but they find themselves entering strange territory.

Samurai Commando Mission 1549 (2005) [Film; Japan; SFW]

Premiere: June 11, 2005; Main Cast: Yosuke Eguchi as Yuuke Kashima, Kyoka Suzukii as Rei Kanzaki, Haruki Ayase as Nohime, Masato Ibu as Dohsan Saito, Takeshi Kaga as Tsuyoshi Matoba/Oda Nobugana; Executive Producer: Kazuo Kuroi; Screenplay: Harutoshi Fukui, Yasushi Matsuura, Kiyoto Takeuchi; Based on the novel by Ryo Hanmura; Director: Masaaki Tezuka; 119 min.; Kadokawa Eiga K.K., Japan Film Fund, Nippon Television Network (NTV); Toho Company; Color.

The 3rd Special Experimental Company of Japan's Self-Defense Force accidentally travels 460 years into the past while testing an artificial magnetic shield. They find themselves in 1549, a time when civil wars dominated Japan. Back in the present Japan is experiencing a major disturbance in the space-time continuum. In order to save modern-day Japan the time traveling soldiers must be rescued from the past.

The film is a re-make of *Sengoku jieitai* (1979).

Sanctuary (2008) [TV series; Canada]

Set in Old City, the Sanctuary team track gifted humans and creatures referred to as "Abnormals" to study and protect from harm. First broadcast: October 3, 2008; Main Cast: Amanda Tapping as Dr. Helen Magnus, Robin Dunne as Will Zimmerman, Ryan Robbins as Henry Foss, Agam Darshi as Kate Freelander; Creator: Damian Kindler; Executive Producers: Andrea Gorfolova, Carrie Hall-Mudd, Amanda Tapping, Martin Wood; 45 min.; Bell Broadcast and New Media Fund, Sanctuary 1 Productions, Stage 3 Media; Syfy; Color.

"Normandy" (3:17) [SFW]
Air date: May 23, 2011; Guest Cast: Robin Dunne as Captain Jack Zimmerman, Christopher Heyerdahal as John Druitt, Jonathon Young as Nikola Tesla, Peter Wingfield as Dr. James Watson, Vincent Gale as Nigel Griffin, Douglas O'Keefe as Col. Franz Korba, Erin Lacourciere as Jeanette Adams, Aaron Brooks as Lt. Hallman; Story: Damien Kindler; Director: Martin Wood.

Normandy, France, June 5, 1944. The eve of D-Day. Dr. James Watson must help destroy a weather machine he invented and is now being used by the Nazis to defeat the Allies. Helping him is Dr. Helen Magnus and Nigel Griffin. John Druitt appears to be working for the Nazis, but has been operating undercover. However, the Nazis have discovered Druitt's ability to teleport and have their own "abnormal" in the form a fire elemental. With both Helen Magnus and James Watson captives of the Nazis it is up to Will Zimmerman's ancestor Captain Jack Zimmerman of the U.S. Army to come to the rescue.

Sand Serpents (2009) [Telefilm; Canada; WW]

Premiere: July 11, 2009; Main Cast: Jason Gedrick as Richard Stanley, Tamara Hope as Jan Henle, Elias Toufexis as Pvt. Andrews, Sebastian Knapp as Oscar Kaminsky; Executive Producer: Michael Prupas; Story: Raul Inglis; Director: Jeff Renfroe; 90 min.; Muse Entertainment Enterprises, Media Pro Pictures; RHI Entertainment; Color.

A team of U.S. Marines are taken hostage by the Taliban in the Afghan desert. But the Taliban and the Marines have another enemy at large in the form of giant worms.

The Sarah Jane Adventures (2007); [TV series; UK]

A spin-off series from ***Doctor Who*** featuring former companion and investigative journalist Sarah Jane Smith.

"Lost in Time" (4:23–4:24) [SFW]
Air dates: November 8–9, 2010; Main Cast: Elizabeth Sladen as Sarah Jane Smith, Daniel Anthony as Clyde Langer, Anjli Mohindra as Rani Chandra, Cyril Nri as The Shopkeeper, Amber Beattie as Lady Jane Grey, Fiona Hamilton as Lady Matilda, Gwyn-

neth Keywoth as Emily Morris, Richard Wisker as George Woods, Catherine Bailey as Miss Wyckham, Tom Wlaschiha as Koenig; Executive Producers: Russell T. Davies, Nikki Wilson; Story: Rupert Laight; Director: Joss Agnew; 2 × 30 min.; BBC Cymru, Wales, Children's BBC (CBBC); Color.

Sarah Jane Smith, Rani Chandra and Clyde Langer meet the Shopkeeper who opens a window in time. He sets them the task of finding three pieces of chronosteel before an hourglass runs out. The future of the world is at stake. The three end up in different time zones, with Clyde arriving in Southern England in June 1941, during World War II, as Nazis land on a beach. In a local church Clyde and his friend George Woods notice a piece of the chronosteel in the Nazi's possession. Now he must make a grab for the chronosteel and alert the Home Guard. Meanwhile Rani is sent to July 1553 where he is introduced to Lady Jane Grey in Tudor England and Sarah Jane is ghost hunting in Victorian England in 1889.

Schomburg, Alex (1905–1998) [Comic book artist]

Born Alejandro Schomburg y Rosa on May 10, 1905, in Aguadilla, Puerto Rico, Schomburg moved to New York City as a young man, where he began his career as a commercial artist. He soon found work illustrating pulp magazines and comic books. Freelancing primarily for Timely comics on wartime titles such as **Captain America**, **Sub-Mariner** and **Human Torch**, Schomburg also supplied memorable covers for smaller publishers' wartime super-heroes. With the end of World War II and the decline of the comic book industry in the early 1950s Schomburg abandoned comic books for magazine and book illustration, where he won many awards for his artwork. His extensive work for comics during the war helped define the cover art style of Timely and other publishers.

Alex Schomburg died in Oregon on April 7, 1998, at the age of 92.

Scion Companion [RPG Sourcebook; AHW]

First publication: 2009; Story: Jason Bolte, Ned Coker, Jeff Combos, Jesse Heinig, Joseph Carricker, Jr., Jennifer Lawrence, David Nurenberg, Dean Shomshak, M. Sechin Tower; Publisher: White Wolf Publishing.

Players take on the roles of mortal descendants of the gods in this role-playing game. This sourcebook to *Scion* includes a 72-page full-color guide to "The World at War." The mythologies of the countries taking part in World War II are utilized as a background to the campaign. In this alternate history war Adolf Hitler is granted magical powers by Loki and the Norse gods. Scions of the Yankee and Allied Pantheons include Paul Bunyan, Betsy Ross, Uncle Sam, John Bull, Robin Hood and Britannia.

Second Time Lucky (1984) [Film; New Zealand; WW]

Premiere: October 18, 1984; Main Cast: Diane Franklin as Eve, Roger Wilson as Adam, Robert Morley as God, Robert Helpmann as The Devil, Jon Gadsby as Gabriel; Producers: Brian W. Cook, Antony I. Ginnane; Story: Allan Burns; Director: Michael Anderson; 101 min.; Eadenrock Ltd, Broadbank Investments; Color.

A young couple named Adam and Eve become pawns in a bet between the Devil and God. Traveling through various eras in time beginning with the Garden of Eden, World War I Eve is a nurse in World War I tending to wounded soldiers in France, including Captain Adam Smith. But Eve is a spy for the Germans and is captured by the British and sentenced to execution by firing squad. Eve tells Smith her family is being held hostage by a German General and she must do as he commands. Luckily for Eve, peace is declared just as she is about to be executed.

The Secret History a.k.a. L'Histoire secrète [Graphic novel; France; WW]

First publication: November 2005; Story: Jean-Pierre Pecau; Art: Igor Kordey; Publisher: Delcourt (France); Archaia (U.S.).

Four immortal brothers and sisters travel through time hoping to affect the outcome of history, from ancient Egypt, to the Vatican in Rome, to the Spanish Armada, to Napoleon, to World War I and the Angel of Mons.

The Secret of Midway (Ghosts of War #1) [Juvenile book; WW]

Author: Steve Watkins; First publication: New York: Scholastic Paperbacks, 2014.

Anderson discovers a mysterious trunk in the basement of his uncle's junk shop. Inside he discovers a World War II U.S. Navy pea coat with a letter in a pocket. When Anderson takes the coat and letter home he is visited by the ghost of a sailor with amnesia. Together with his friends

Greg and Julie, Anderson must search for answers about the sailor and his life before his ghost vanishes.

See: *Lost at Khe Sanh*

The Secret of the Nutcracker (2007) [Telefilm; WW]

First broadcast: December 23, 2007; Main Cast: Janelle Jorde as Clara Jenkinson, Tom Carey as Dad, Helene Joy as Mom, Brendan Meyer as Frank, Ryan Grantham as Billy, Ricardo Hoyos as Sasha, Brian Cox as Drosselmeyer, Alberta Ballet; Executive producers: Joe Novak, Matt Gillespie; Writer: John Murrell; Based on the original story by E.T.A. Hoffman; Director: Eric Till; 120 min.; Joe Media Group; Canadian Broadcasting System (CBC); Color.

Christmas Eve in Alberta, Canada, 1943. Anxious about the safety of her father in a Prisoner-of-War camp in Germany 10-year-old Clara picks up a postcard from her father at the local post office and runs home in a state of excitement. But on her journey she encounters Uncle Dross, a strange owl-man and his four crow-like companions he names his "kings." Drosselmeyer meets and enchants Clara's family at Christmas Eve dinner. Joy fills the home, but it is tinged with sadness at the absence of the father.

That night, Clara finds herself transported into a magical world where she confronts her greatest fears and anxieties about her father's Nazi captors.

"We all hate war, but sometimes we must fight in order to live in quietness again. Many things can be put right through tears," states Drosselmeyer to Clara.

Through the magic powers of Uncle Dross Clara meets her father in the German POW camp. His self pity at his situation is tempered when Drosselmeyer makes the father realize the sacrifice his family has made during his captivity. He isn't the only hero.

The Canadian TV movie successfully transforms E.T.A. Hoffman's story and Tchaikovsky's ballet into a World War II setting and demonstrates the power of hope and belief in desperate times.

The Secret Shelter [Juvenile book; SFW]

Author: Sandi LeFaucheur; First publication: Weston, Conn: Brown Barn Books, 2004.

Three London children are exploring an old World War II air-raid shelter when they find themselves sheltering from real-life bombs during the Blitz in World War II. Now they must survive using their wits and find a way back to their own time.

"Secret Unattainable" [Pulp fiction; SFW]

Author; A.E. Van Vogt; Illustrator: Kramer; First publication: *Astounding Science Fiction* (Vol. 29 #5; July 1947); Publisher: Street & Smith Publications.

A German scientist attracts the attention of Nazi Germany when he invents a machine capable of transporting humans or objects to anywhere in the universe. The military uses would surely result in victory for the Nazis. But the scientist has his own agenda. His brother was executed by Nazis and now he seizes the perfect opportunity for revenge.

Secrets of the Third Reich [Board game; AHW]

Release date: 2008; Designers: Jim Bailey, John Bailey; Art: Davis Ausloos, Andy Cooper, Keith Lowe; Publisher: Grindhouse Games; West Wind Productions.

1949. The world is still at war with London and Berlin destroyed by Atom bombs. V-Gas has decimated Northwest Europe and Eastern Russia, with victims of the gas attacks now reanimated as zombies. Despite the carnage small pockets of armed troops still survive as the U.S., British, Russians and Germans continue their battle. But this is a drastically altered world with Super-soldiers with psychic powers, Nazi zombie troopers, vampires, werewolves, Panzer Mecha, Powered Armor and a British Hero Unit that is a reincarnation of King Arthur.

Sengoku jieitai a.k.a. *G. I. Samurai*; *Time Slip* (1979) [Film; Japan; SFW]

Premiere; December 5, 1979; Main Cast: Sonny Chiba as Lt. Yoshiaki Iba, Jun Eto as Nobuhiko Ken, Moeko Ezawa as Widow Yui, Ryo Hayami as Kazumichi Morishita, Isao Natsuyagi as Nagao Kagetora, Hiroshi Tanaka as Takeda Shingen; Executive Producer: Haruki Kadokawa; Story; Toshio Kamata, based on the novel by Ryo Hanmura; Director: Kosei Saito; 139 min.; Kadokawa Haruki Jimusho; Color.

A squadron of Japanese soldiers, suddenly transported 400 years into the past, find themselves in the middle of a war between rival samurai clans. Lieutenant Yoshiaki Iba joins forces with leader Nagao Kagetora who wants to rule Japan.

Meanwhile some of Lt. Iba's men desert him, wanting simply to return home to their time. Those that remain face the forces of Takeda Shingen. But an ally is also plotting against Lt. Iba.

See: **Samurai Commando Mission 1549**

Sgt. Fury and His Howling Commandos [Comic book characters]

Sergeant Nicholas Joseph Fury, a product of Manhattan's Lower East Side, leads his Howling Commandos into battle during World War II. They consist of Irish-American Corporal Timothy "Dum Dum" Dugan, and privates Izzy Cohen, Kentuckian Robert "Reb" Ralston, Italian-American Dino Manelli, Ivy League Jonathan "Junior" Juniper and African American Gabriel "Gabe" Jones.

Following Juniper's death in issue #4 Englishman Percival "Pinky" Pinkerton joined the Howlers in issue #8 and was later joined by disenchanted German Eric Koenig. Most stories deal with conventional war heroics.

"The Death Ray of Dr. Zemo" [SFW]

First publication: *Sgt. Fury and His Howling Commandos* #8 (July 1964); Story: **Stan Lee**; Art: Dick Ayers, George Bell (George Roussos); Publisher: Marvel Comics Group.

Sergeant Nick Fury and his Howling Commandos are on a mission to capture Nazi scientist **Dr. Zemo** and neutralize his death ray.

"What if Sgt. Fury and His Howling Commandos Had Fought World War II in Outer Space?" [SFW]

First publication: *What If?* #14 (April 1979); Story: Don Glut, Gary Friedrich; Art: Herb Trimpe, Pablo Marcos; Publisher: Marvel Comics.

"Keep movin' you lunkheads! Nobody lives forever! So get the lead out and follow me! We got us a space-war to win!"

Sgt. Fury and his commandos fight in space in 1941.

Sgt. Rock and Easy Company [Comic book characters]

First appearance: *Our Army at War* #81 (April 1959); Creator: Robert Kanigher; Publisher: DC Comics.

Creator **Robert Kanigher** partly based his creation Sgt. Frank Rock of Easy Company on the 1st Infantry Division, the Big Red One. In his first story he is described as "Sgt. Rocky—the Rock of Easy Company" as he fights the Nazi Iron Captain.

Initially penciled by Ross Andru, artist **Joe Kubert** later defined the look of *Sgt. Rock* who became DC's most popular and long-running military character. His adventures were mainly straight action-adventure war stories, although they did occasionally cross into Weird War territory.

"Face the Devil" [WW]

First publication: *Our Army at War* #236 (September 1971); Story: Robert "Bob" Kanigher; Art: Russ Heath; Publisher: DC Comics.

Sgt. Rock and Easy Co. are on a mission to take down Satan's Height with new recruit Billy Boy. Suddenly an old wild man with long hair appears out of a blinding fog and hugs Bill Boy, mistaking him for his son. He tells him the legend of the Evil One who brought death and misery upon his village. To put an end to his evil the villagers hid the Evil One's face behind an iron mask and buried him in the graveyard. The old man is the last man standing from those days. But with his story told Easy Company is hit with a barrage of bombs and the old man and Billy Boy are killed.

Lost in the fog Sgt. Fury finds himself fighting a huge man in an iron mask. As he breaks the mask free he reveals a skull with glowing eyes. And as suddenly as the "goon in a mask" appears it vanishes. Sgt. Rock has met the enemy at Satan's Height.

"The Miracle Man of Easy Company" [WW]

First publication: *DC Comics Present* #10 (June 1979); Story: Cary Bates; Art: Joe Staton, Jack Abel; Publisher: DC Comics.

Following a bomb explosion **Superman** is thrown back in time to Paris, France during World War II. Suffering from partial amnesia he decides to wear a U.S. army uniform discarded by a Nazi spy.

Sgt. Rock and Easy Company accept the stranger into their group and slowly Superman's memory returns. Now he can help Sgt. Rock and Easy Co. in secret when they come under attack. Superman allows himself to be captured by the Nazis and destroys their base. He has died a hero and is buried by Sgt. Rock and Easy Co. who have no idea the soldier plans to rise from the dead and return to his own time as Superman.

"The Night Batman Sold His Soul" [WW]

First publication *The Brave and the Bold* #108 (September 1973); Story: Bob Haney; Art: Jim Aparo; Publisher: DC Comics.

Attempting to rescue a young boy from a crazed criminal demanding ransom money, Batman encounters a mysterious man shrouded in a raincoat and hat. The man rescues Batman from drowning in a well after he hears Batman crying out, "I'd give my soul to get out of here. I don't want to die!" The man later reappears with a message for Bruce Wayne. In return for his good deed the man, who knows Wayne is Batman, now owns his soul. An elderly Sgt. Rock intervenes and informs Wayne that the man who claims his soul is none other than Adolf Hitler!

Wayne is unconvinced by Sgt. Rock, even after Rock recalls meeting Hitler after the war ended. Now the hunt is on to find the mysterious stranger and reveal his true identity.

Seven Days (1998) [TV series]

Former Navy SEAL and CIA operative Frank Parker is released from a CIA mental institution to take part in Project Backstep. Chosen for his tolerance for pain Parker travels back in time seven days to change past events.

"For the Children" (2:04) [SFW]

Air date: October 20, 1999; Main Cast: Jonathan LaPaglia as Frank Parker, Don Franklin as Craig Donovan, Justina Vail as Dr. Olga Vukavitch, Nick Searcy as Nathan Ramsay, Alan Scarfe as Dr. Bradley Talmadge, Marc Vann as Sgt. David Korshak, Tim Abell as Sgt. Higgins; Executive Producer: Christopher Crowe; Story: Ann Lewis Hamilton, Director: Don Kurt; 42 min.; Paramount Network Television Productions; United Paramount Network (UPN); Color.

U.S. Army Gulf War veterans suffering from Gulf War Syndrome take 33 Los Angeles Metro train passengers hostage. After their demands for reparations of $300 million are ignored they blow up the train. Parker is only allowed to go back in time to save the hostages after he lies about an important courier being on board the train.

Seventh Sanctuary [Novel; WW]

Author: Daniel Easterman; First publication: New York: Doubleday, 1987.

Archaeologist David Rosen is digging at an ancient site in Syria searching for a lost biblical city. But he finds himself the target of a murder attempt as he uncovers a plot by a mystic to lead descendants of Hitler's Third Reich known as the Valkyrie Brigade to destroy Israel.

The Shadow Children [Juvenile book; WW]

Author: Steven Schnur; Illustrator: Herbert Tauss; First publication: New York: Morrow Junior Books, 1994.

Eleven-year-old Etienne is spending another summer at his grandfather's farm near Mont Brulant. Etienne loves exploring the French countryside but this year he makes a startling discovery. Ragged children hiding in the woods. He slowly comes to realize he is seeing into the past. These are Jewish children who were abandoned by the town, including Etienne's grandfather, and left for the Nazis who took them away on their trains never to be seen again.

Shadows in the Mist [Novel; WW]

Author: Brian Moreland; First publication: New York: Berkley Books, 2008.

Jack Chambers is still haunted by his platoon's massacre in Germany's Hurtgen Forest during World War II. He knows an evil supernatural force was at work and asks his grandson Sean to uncover the truth.

Shadows Over Normandie: Cthulhu Mythos Call One [Board game; WW]

First publication: 2015; Designers: Yann and Clem; Art: Alexander Bonvalot; Publisher: Devil Pig Games, IELLO.

Lost in the woods of Normandy a U.S. Ranger Company confronts the Nazi Cult of the Black Sun and the ancient Deep Ones as they prepare to summon the demonic Cthulhu.

Players control the German Cult of the Black Sun, the ancient Deep Ones or the U.S. Rangers with infantry, tanks, creatures and special heroes and villains units. The mission to thwart Cthulhu or engage him to defeat the enemy.

Shambling Towards Hiroshima [Novel; SFW]

Author: James Morrow; First publication: San Francisco: Tachyon Publications, 2009.

Syms Thorley is a B-movie actor, well known for starring in "monster" films. But now the U.S. Navy has a new role for Thorley, as part of the top-secret Knickerbocker Project. The U.S. has perfected a new biological weapon in the summer of 1945. A breed of gigantic, fire-breathing, mutant iguanas that can destroy Japanese cities. Thorley is told to wear a costume that will transform him into the terrible Gorgantis as he destroys the miniature cities of Japan. It is the hope of the U.S. military that his filmed performance will be so realistic, it will result in the surrender of the Japanese. If he doesn't succeed then the U.S. will be forced to set their real-life monsters on Japanese cities with the subsequent huge loss of life.

She Demons (1958) [Film: SFW]

Premiere: January 1, 1958; Main Cast: Irish McCalla As Jerrie Turner, Tod Griffin as Fred Maklin, Rudolph Anders as Colonel Karl Osler, Leni Tana as Mona Osler, Victor Sen Yung as Sammy Ching; Producer: Arthur A. Jacobs; Story: Richard Cunha, H. E. Barrie; Director: Richard E. Cunha; 77 min.; Screencraft Enterprises; Astor Pictures Corp.; B/W.

Former Nazi Colonel Karl Osler and his army of storm troopers are holding beauty queen winners captive on a tropical island. Osler is restoring his wife's badly disfigured face to its former beauty with a substance extracted from the beauty queens. But more trouble lies ahead with the U.S. Air Force planning an atom bomb test on the island.

Shellshock 2: Blood Trails [Videogame; WW]

Release date: February 2009; Platforms: Microsoft Windows, PlayStation 3, Xbox 360; Developer: Rebellion Developments; Publisher: Eidos Interactive.

This first-person shooter videogame is set during the Vietnam War. Sergeant Caleb "Cal" Walker leads a special operations team into the jungles of Cambodia and comes out alone. Their mission to retrieve cargo known as WhiteKnight has resulted in their infection with a zombie virus. Cal is captured and questioned about White Knight at a U.S. base, but he escapes. Now Cal is the target of VC officer Nguyen Van Trang, while Private Nathaniel "Nate" Walker must stop Trang from killing Cal.

The Shield [Comic book character; SHW]

First appearance: *Pep Comics* #1 (January 1940); Creators: Harry Shorten, Irving Novick; Publisher: MLJ

1916. Lt. Tom Higgins of U.S. Army Intelligence is working on a secret formula that will transform a person into a superhuman. But he has to leave his experiment as he tackles an assignment to stop enemy agents blowing up ammunition barges. Tragically Higgins is killed in the explosion as the barges ignite. The incident is named the Black Tom explosion and Tom Higgins blamed for the failed mission.

Before Higgins dies he tells his son Joe about his S.H.I.E.L.D. formula. After decades of trying to decipher the formula Joe Higgins comes across a medical book that reveals the secret. S.H.I.E.L.D. stands for Sacrum, Heart, Innervation, Eyes, Lungs, Derma. Joe designs a skin tight fibro-metallic suit and lays for 12 hours under fluoroscopic rays that, with the help of the suit, force the chemicals into organs in his body. Now Higgins is bullet and flame-proof and has the power to perform extraordinary feats of physical daring and courage. "He has the speed of a bullet and the strength of Hercules." He can finally bring the ringleader of the German spy ring responsible for the Black Tom explosion to justice and clear his father's name. Only FBI chief J. Edgar Hoover knows Higgins' secret identity as the Shield. Joe Higgins, "G-Man extraordinary" seeks to devote his life to "truth, justice, patriotism and courage"

This patriotic super-hero made his debut four months before **Captain America**, and was joined by Dusty, boy detective in January 1941. He would later share adventures with the Hangman as they fought the criminal underworld and Axis powers through World War II. Readers were asked to buy war bonds or victory stamps in return for membership in the "Young Soldiers of America Club." As Dusty explained, "We need plenty more of these babies to knock the tar outta the Axis! So keep buyin' gang!"

Shining Knight [Comic book character; WW]

First appearance: *Adventure Comics* #66 (September 1941); Creator: Craig Flessel; Publisher: DC Comics.

In 1941 Sir Justin and his winged horse Victory are released from suspended animation. Formerly a member of the Knights of the Round Table with golden, invulnerable shining armor and an enchanted sword, courtesy of Merlin the magician. His invulnerable horse Victory can fly due to Merlin granting him large wings.

Adopting the persona of Justin Arthur, he later joins the ***Seven Soldiers of Victory*** and acts as personal bodyguard to Winston Churchill during World War II.

Shock Waves (1977) [Film; WW]

Premiere: July 15, 1977; Main Cast: Peter Cushing as SS Commander, John Carradine as Capt. Ben

Morris, Brooke Adams as Rose, Fred Buch as Chuck; Producer: Reuben Trane; Screenplay: John Harrison, Ken Wiederhorn; Director: Ken Wiederhorn; 85 min.; Zopix Company; Joseph Brenner Associates; Color.

Shipwrecked passengers on an island check into a hotel run by a former Nazi commander who was in charge of underwater zombies known as the Death Corps. Now they have returned and threaten the lives of everyone on the island.

Silent Storm [Videogame; AHW]

Release date: November 2003; Platform: Microsoft Windows; Developer: Nival Interactive; Publisher: 1C Company, Jo Wood.

A Russian single-player tactical role-playing game where the player commands a team of elite soldiers during World War II. THO (Thor's Hammer Organization) aims at global domination by providing advanced technology to both the Axis and Allied forces. Their intention, to fill the vacuum when both sides destroy each other. The mecha known as Panzerkleins are powered armor suits immune to small arms fire.

Sir Steel [Comic book character; WW]

First appearance: **The Invaders** #7 (July 1976); Creators: Roy Thomas, Frank Robbins; Publisher: Marvel Comics.

Armatage Manor Estate blacksmith Ned Chapel wears the suit of enchanted armor and carries the enchanted sword of Sir Steel as he goes into battle for England during World War I. A member of **Freedom's Five**.

Silver Streak [Comic book character; SHW]

First appearance: *Silver Streak Comics* #3 (March 1940); Creators: Joe Simon, Jack Binder; Publisher: Young Guide Publications (Lev Gleason).

"Just who and what is Silver Streak? A shapeless blur rocketing at an invisible speed across the countryside—a swishing sound that leaves but the breeze against ones face as evidence of his passing presence. This is Silver Streak. The fastest man imaginable. A bolt of lightning embodied in a man!"

A mystical swami hypnotizes a taxicab driver into driving his race car with the words, "You are the Silver Streak—the strongest, bravest, fastest man in the world Do you understand? The swami speaks!"

All of his previous subjects have died crashing their cars after being stung to death by a gigantic fly. The latest driver suffers the same fate but is brought back to life by the "magic" of the swami and the power of hypnotism. Except now the resurrected driver is all-powerful with super speed. His first task is to bring the insane Professor of Zoology, Dr. Katan to justice for his lethal fly attacks. Soon he will fight the Nazi menace as the costumed Silver Streak.

See: ***Daredevil Battles Hitler***

Simon, Joe (1913–2011) [Comic book artist-writer]

Born Hymie Simon, October 11, 1913, in Rochester, New York, Joe Simon is best remembered today for his collaboration with fellow artist-writer **Jack Kirby**. **Captain America** remains his most notable co-creation for Timely Comics. Other wartime creations include **Boy Commandos**, *Newsboy Legion* and the revamped *Manhunter* and *Sandman* for National-DC Comics. Simon commented, "Like so many others, we were ticked off with Hitler and wanted to get our two cents in. We were always looking for that great villain. It was hard to think of a greater villain than Adolf Hitler."

Post World War II Simon and Kirby formed Mainline Comics before Simon and Kirby ended their sixteen-year partnership in 1955. Simon turned to advertising and the creation of further super-heroes for Archie Comics and Harvey.

Joseph "Joe" Simon passed away December 14, 2011, age 98.

1632 [Novel; SFW]

Author: Eric Flint; First publication: Riverdale, NY: Baen, 2000.

The citizens of Grantville, West Virginia, find themselves thrown back in time to 1632 and the Thirty Years War in northern Germany. The Americans from the year 2000 fight to survive in their hostile environment, where food is in short supply and disease is rampant. From out of the chaos and destruction they create a new community.

Eric Flint's twelve volume series spans the years 1632–1636.

'68 [Comic book; WW]

First publication: December 2006; Story: Mark Kidwell; Art: Nat Jones, Tim Vigil, Jay Fotos; Publisher: Image Comics.

February 13, 1968, the day a new undead war began in Vietnam. A five-man U.S. fire team led by Lieutenant Tommy Blake deploys into the dense, humid jungles near the Cambodia border. They discover Viet-Cong guerrillas and the bodies of their dead returned to life.

Originally published as a one-shot comic book this series features stories of undead military horror in a zombie infested Vietnam. The following Weird War comic book titles in the series are all published by Image Comics

'68: Jungle Jim

First publication: November 2011; Four issue mini-series; Story: Mark Kidwell; Art: Nat Jones, Jay Fotos.

Brian Curtiss a.k.a. Jungle Jim searches for the undead remains of Sgt. Jim Asher in war-torn Cambodia.

'68: Last Rites

First publication: July 2015; Four issue mini-series; Story: Mark Kidwell; Art: Jeff Zornow, Jay Fotos.

War-Face and his army of zombies attack Private Kuen Yam and his fellow survivors in Vietnam.

'68: Rule of War

First publication: January 2015; Four issue mini-series; Story: Mark Kidwell; Art: Nat Jones, Jay Fotos.

CIA Special Agent Declan Rule and his dog Nero stalk a neurosurgeon who is experimenting on P.O.W.'s

'68: Scars

First publication: April 2012; Four issue mini-series; Story: Mark Kidwell; Art: Nat Jones, Jay Fotos.

As Saigon goes up in flames a handful of survivors maintain a hold on Ton Son Nhat Airport. Meanwhile, along the Mekong Delta the dead rise.

Slaughterhouse-Five (1972) [Film; SFW]

Premiere: March 15, 1972; Main Cast: Michael Sacks as Billy Pilgrim, Ron Liebman as Paul Lazzaro, Eugene Roche as Edgar Derby; Sharon Gans as Valencia Merble Pilgrim. Valerie Perrine as Montana Wildhack, Perry King as Robert Pilgrim, Frederich von Ledebur as German Leader; Executive Producer: Jennings Lang; Screenplay: Stephen Geller. Based on the original novel by Kurt Vonnegut, Jr.; Director: George Roy Hill; 104 min.; Universal Pictures; Color.

Billie Pilgrim becomes "unstuck in time" and experiences his bewildering life bouncing between different eras. In the past as a young American P.O.W. in World War II where he witnesses the bombing of Dresden, Germany in 1945. In the present Pilgrim is a middle-aged optometrist in upstate New York. And in the future he is an object of display on the planet Tralfamador. Along with his dog and sexy starlet Montana Wildhack, his life is restricted to a glass cage where the natives watch their daily activities with a mixture of curiosity and entertainment.

Slaughterhouse-Five: or, The Children's Crusade, a Duty-Dance with Death [Novel; SFW]

Author: Kurt Vonnegut; First publication: New York: Delacorte Press, 1969.

Billy Pilgrim, chaplain's assistant and German prisoner-of-war in Dresden, travels through time and space contemplating the human condition.

Sledgehammer 44 [Comic book; SFW]

First publication: March 2013; Story: Mike Mignola, John Arcudi; Art: Jason Latour; Publisher: Dark Horse Comics.

August 1944, D'Ebene Chiot, France. Project Epimetheus begins as a bomb named "Sledgehammer" is dropped into Nazi territory. A man in iron armor emerges from the shell of the bomb ready to do battle with the Nazis.

Small Soldiers (1998) [Film; SFW]

Premiere: July 10, 1998; Main Cast: David Cross as Irwin Wayfair, Jay Mohr as Larry Benson, Denis Leary as Gil Mars, Gregory Smith as Alan Abernathy, Kirsten Dunst as Christy Fimple, Phil Hartman as Phil Fimple, Wendy Schaal as Marion Fimple, Jacob Smith as Timmy Fimple, Kevin Dunn as Stuart Abernathy, Ann Magnuson as Irene Abernathy, Robert Ricardo as Ralph, Alexandra Wilson as Ms. Kegel; Voice Cast: Frank Langella As Archer, Ernest Borgnine as Kip Killagin, Jim Brown as Butch Meathook, George Kennedy as Brick Bazooka, Clint Walker as Nick Nitro, Bruce Dern as Link Static, Christopher Guest as Slamfist/Scratch-It, Michael McKean as Insaniac/Freakenstein, Harry Shearer as Punch-It, Sarah Michelle Gellar as Gwendy Doll; Executive Producer: Walter Parkes; Story: Gavin Scott, Adam Rifkin, Ted Elliott, Terry Rossio; Director: Joe Dante; 108 min.: Universal Pictures, Dreamworks Pictures, Amblin Entertainment; Color.

Searching for innovative ideas for his toy company Hartland Play Systems, Gil Mars gives the go-ahead for Larry Benson and Irwin Wayfair to produce a new action-figure line. Major Chip Hazzard is the leader of Commando Elite whose mission is to destroy the alien Gorgonites. Benson orders the Department of Defense's X1000 microchip to give the figures an added boost. What he doesn't realize is the chips are capable of intelligence.

When Alan Abernathy assumes temporary responsibility for his father's toy store he takes a shipment of the action figures and quickly discovers they have a life of their own when Archer, "Emmisary of the Gorgonites" befriends him. Major Chip Hazard and his Commando Elite declare war on the Gorgonites stating, "There will be no mercy." Soon the war spreads through the neighborhood and Alan's "girlfriend" Christy Fimple is held hostage by Hazard and a group of bikini clad Gwendy Doll allies. An electro magnetic pulse is the Commando Elite's only weakness and Alan is the person to put a plan in action.

Sniper Elite: Nazi Zombie Army [Videogame; WW]

Release date: February 28, 2013; Developer: Rebellion; Publishers: Rebellion, Mastertronic.

A stand-alone expansion in the *Sniper Elite* series for 1–4 players. Players assume the role of sniper Karl Fairburne as he fights against occult powers and undead soldiers deployed by Adolf Hitler in the final days of World War II.

See: *Nazi Zombie Army 2*

Snowman 1944 [Comic book; WW]

First publication: October 1996; Creators: Matt Martin, Cameron Enders; Publisher: Entity.

The hostile Native American spirit known as the Snowman can control ice and snow. When fighter pilot Tommy Gunston and his co-pilot are shot down over Germany during World War II they encounter an enemy more fearsome than the Nazis. Cursed Snowman arrowheads owned by the co-pilot and their contact with the Alpine snow bring the Native American spirit back to life. But luckily for the airmen the spirit of the Snowman has a particular hatred for the Nazis.

So Close to You (Book #1) [Juvenile book; SFW]

Author: Rachel Carter; First publication: New York: HarperTeen, 2012.

Seventeen-year-old Lydia Bentley has trouble believing her grandfather's accounts of a wartime government conspiracy named the Montauk Project. People don't just vanish and surely the government wouldn't torture children. But when she searches the abandoned Long Island military base, Camp Hero, she finds herself transported back in time to 1944. Slowly she discovers the reality behind her grandfather's stories of the Montauk Project and the disappearance of her great-grandfather back in 1944.

See: *This Strange and Familiar Place*

Soldiers of the Damned (2015) [Film; UK; WW]

Premiere: August 8, 2015 (UK); Main Cast: Gil Darnell as Major Kurt Fleischer, Miriam Cooke as Prof. Anna Kappel, Lucas Hansen as Major Hinrich Metzger, Tom Sawyer as Lt. Eric Fuchs; Producers: Nigel Horne, Stephen Rigg; Story: Nigel Horne; Director: Mark Nuttall; 99 min.; Blackdog Productions, Viking Film and Television; Safecracker Pictures; Color.

1944. German soldiers are forced to retreat into Romania by advancing Russians. Major Kurt Fleischer is ordered to accompany Professor Anna Kappel into the Romanian forest to retrieve an ancient relic, little realizing the scientist belongs to Himmler's occult forces and danger greater than the Russian soldiers lies ahead.

Son of Vulcan [Comic book character; MWW]

First appearance: *Mysteries of Unexplored Worlds* #45 (May 1965); Story: Pat Masulli; Art: Bill Fraccio, Tony Tallarico; Publisher: Charlton Comics.

Reporter and Korean War veteran Johnny Mann is tired of war. His days of combat have left him with an artificial leg. Now he is on assignment in Cyprete, visiting the great hall of the Olympic god Jupiter. While expressing his anger at the gods for permitting wars, Mann is struck by lightning bolts.

He awakes, surrounded by gods and goddesses. Jupiter is about to slay Mann when Vulcan and his sister Venus ask that his life be spared. But Mars, the god of war agrees that Mann should be put to death. On trial for his life, Vulcan asks that Mann be placed as his ward to fight the war against evil on Earth. Jupiter agrees to his request. Vulcan provides Mann with armor, a sling and the gifts of strength, vitality, flight and the ability to make a weapon materialize in his hand. After making a pledge never to misuse his powers Mann returns to Earth.

"The Second Trojan War"

First publication: *Son of Vulcan* #50 (January 1966); Story: Roy Thomas; Art: Bill Franco, Tony Tallarico; Publisher: Charlton Comics.

World-Wide News reporter Johnny Mann is on assignment in Asia Minor investigating the misfortunes on the film set of "Warrior Against Troy." Director, Mr. Colosso, feels a rival film company is sabotaging his movie. As Colosso talks to Mann a runaway chariot heads toward the actress playing Helen of Troy—Lisa Connors. As the director chases the chariot, Mann transforms into the Son of Vulcan, "the mightiest of mortals, gifted by the gods of ancient Rome, with the power of flight."

He rescues the temperamental actress who storms back to her trailer. Meanwhile the lead actor, Rick Henderson, quits. The Son of Vulcan offers to replace him as Achilles. Watching the events is "the meanest man alive," Dr. Kong, the man behind the misfortunes on set. He plans more havoc when his robot, Adam Klink, kidnaps Lisa Connors. Kong's latest weapon, the anima-ray, gives life to inanimate objects, including the giant Trojan Horse, with Lisa trapped inside.

The Songs of the Kings [Novel; MWW]

Author: Barry Unsworth; First publication: New York: Doubleday, 2003.

The straits of Aulis, 1260 BC The Greek fleet, under Agamemnon en route to the capture of Troy, is halted by harsh northeast winds. A prophecy foretells that only a blood sacrifice to the gods can calm the winds. But when that sacrifice is Iphigeneia, the much loved daughter of Agamemnon the limits of both father and daughter are put to the ultimate test.

Le Souffle du Wendigo [Comic book; France; WW]

First publication: October 2011; Two-issue series; Story: Mathieu Missoffe; Art: Charlie Adlard; Publisher: Soleil.

World War I, July 1917. French and German soldiers declare an uneasy truce on the Front, to combat a supernatural menace. Helping them is Wohati, a Cree Indian from the U.S. Army, who alone knows what awaits them.

A Sound Among the Trees [Novel; WW]

Author: Susan Meissner; First publication: Colorado Springs, CO: Waterbrook Press, 2011.

Susannah Page is said to haunt the antebellum mansion Holly Oak searching for a pardon for her past sins as a spy for the North in the Civil War. But newlywed Marielle Bishop believes the house itself is responsible for the bad luck that women encounter at the mansion.

The Sound of His Horn [Novel; SFW]

Author: Sarban (John William Wall); First publication: London (UK): Peter Davies Ltd., 1952.

British naval Lieutenant Alan Querdillon is taken as a prisoner-of-war during the Battle of Crete in World War II. One morning he awakens to find himself 102 years into the future where Nazis rule the world. Hunted by a "Reichsforester" Querdillon befriends genetically manipulated "undesirables."

Space Western Comics [Comic book; SFW]

First publication: October 1952; Publisher: Charlton-Capitol Stories.

The adventures of Spurs Jackson and his Space Vigilantes as they tackle alien invaders attempting to conquer Earth and the universe. The title was an interesting attempt at crossing the Western, military and science fiction genres and included a bizarre two-issue story involving Spurs Jackson and his Space Vigilantes pursuing Adolf Hitler and his fellow Nazis to Mars and beyond.

"Madman of Mars" (Part One); "Tomorrow the Universe" (Part Two), #44–45 (June–August 1953)

When hydrogen bombs from Mars hit Paris, Moscow, Honolulu, New York City and London, General Carpenter calls Spurs Jackson and his Vigilantes to Washington D. C. where they are assigned to go to Mars to track the source of the bombs. To their amazement Spurs, Strong Bow and Hank Roper come under attack from German Nazis when they arrive on the surface of Mars. They learn that Hitler and nine of his men escaped to Mars at the end of World War II. Hoping to capture Hitler, Spurs is told he escaped in a rocket soon after his arrival. Jackson and the Space Vigilantes track Hitler to an asteroid where one of Hitler's own men turns against Hitler and kills him.

The Spear [Novel; WW]

Author: James Herbert; First publication: London (UK): Hodder & Stoughton, 1991.

Private investigator and former spy Harry Steadman attempts to track down those responsible for the murder of his partner on his front doorstep. His trail leads him to Neo-Nazi cultists involved in re-enacting the story of Parsifal and using the spear of Longinus that stabbed Jesus Christ on the cross as a force for regaining world domination.

Special War Series: Attack! [Comic book]

"The Company of the Dead" [WW]

First publication: #2 (September 1965); Art: Charles Nicholas, Vince Alascia; Publisher: Charlton Comics.

Lieutenant Wardbill's entire company is killed early into the battle, yet they still help him take the hill in Korea.

Spider-Man: The Animated Series (1994) [Animated TV series]

Based on the comic book characters created by **Stan Lee** and Steve Ditko; Executive Producer: Stan Lee; 65 × 21 min.; Marvel Entertainment, Marvel Films Animation, Saban Entertainment; Fox Kids Network; Color.

"Six Forgotten Warriors: Secrets of the Six" (5:04) [SHW]

Air date: October 3, 1997; Voice Cast: Christopher Daniel Barnes as Spider-Man/Peter Parker, Rodney Saulsberry as Robbie Robertson, Majel Barrett as Anna Watson, Julie Bennett as Aunt May Parker, Earl Boen as **Red Skull**, David Hayter as **Captain America**, Dee Bradley Baker as Young **Destroyer**, Paul Winfield as Young Black Marvel, Kathy Garver as **Miss America**, Cain Devore as Young **Whizzer**, Brett King as Young Thunderer, Roscoe Lee Browne as Kingpin; Director: Bob Richardson.

This story spans a five-episode arc which includes this episode that takes place during World War II.

Spider-Man must find the Six Forgotten Warriors and the keys to stop the Doomsday Project. Following the loss of the formula that created Captain America in 1942 five young volunteers undergo new super serum tests that create impermanent powers. A ring turns the powers on and off. The six "American Warriors" comprise of **Destroyer**, **Miss America**, Thunderer, **Whizzer**, Black Marvel and **Captain America**.

When they discover plans for "Project Doomsday"—a deadly weapon created by the **Red Skull** to destroy America **Captain America** sacrifices himself to destabilize the device. The remaining "warriors" are forgotten to time.

Spirit of the Century (RPG; SFW]

Release date: 2006; System: FATE; Designers: Fred Hicks, Bob Donoghue, Leonard Balsera; Publisher: Evil Hat Productions.

A pulp action role-playing game set in the 1920s. Players are known as "Centurions"—pulp heroes with various abilities. The game includes a World War I setting and background to the characters.

Spirit of the Rebellion [Novel; WW]

Author: Debbie Peterson; First publication: Adams Basin, N.Y.: Wild Rose Press, 2012.

Shae Lynn Montgomery accepts a job at Starling Manor translating Civil War documents from Wisconsin's Norwegian regiment. Captain Tristan Jordhal, late of the Union Army was murdered in the manor where Shae now resides with her work. Initially Jordhal tries to scare Shae away but comes to realize she could help him uncover the truth behind his violent death. But an evil spirit stands in their way.

Spitfire [Comic book character; SHW]

First appearance: *The Invaders* #7 (July 1976); Creators: Roy Thomas, Frank Robbins; Publisher: Marvel Comics.

The daughter of Lord Montgomery Falsworth alias Union Jack, costumed hero of World War I. In 1942 Lady Jacqueline Falsworth discovers she has super-powers while recovering in hospital from an attack by vampire and Nazi agent **Baron Blood**. The mix of a life-saving blood transfusion by the **Human Torch** and the deadly bite of Baron Blood results in superhuman strength and speed. Following her recovery she adopts the name of Spitfire, as a tribute to the British fighter planes valiantly winning the battle in the air, and joins the Invaders in their fight against the Nazis in Europe.

Spriggan [Manga; Japan; SFW]

First publication: *Weekly Shonen Sunday*; *Shonen Sunday Super* (1988); Story: Hiroshi Takashige; Art: Ryoji Minagawa; Publisher: Shogakukan.

The eleven volume manga series (1988–1996) centers around mysterious artifacts discovered worldwide by forces that want to use them as weapons of destruction. The ARCAM corporation and their private army employ elite secret agents known as Spriggans to protect the artifacts from falling into the wrong hands. The storyline includes a former Colonel from Nazi Germany named Kutheimer, his assassin Hans Scneider and a split personality Adolf Hitler clone who can heal itself and others.

The Spring Rider [Juvenile book; WW]
Author: John Lawson; First publication: New York: Cromwell, 1968.

The ghost of a Union soldier attracts the attention of a brother and sister when he returns to life with his regiment each spring to relive a battle from the Civil War.

Spy Smasher [Comic book character]
First publication: *Whiz Comics* #2; Creators: Bill Parker, C.C. Beck; Publisher: Fawcett Publications.

"Spy-Smasher. That unknown figure of the shadows. That weird crime fighter of the night whose dauntless battle is to keep alien criminals from American shores."

"Death Over Washington" [WW]
First publication: *Spy Smasher* #5 (June 1942); Art: Emil Gershwin.

"Death itself—dread scythe-rearing figure whose terror is as old as time stalks abroad and pays his personal doom-dealing visits upon high-ranking officers, inventors and military experts. Can the strength and agile mind of mighty Spy Smasher end this frightful, fear-making menace? For if America is to live, Death itself must die!"

Death pays a visit to Washington, D.C., and Admiral Thompson. Alan Armstrong alias Spy Smasher investigates but is sidetracked when the figure of Death leads Spy Smasher to Satan and a visit to Hell.

Death returns to D.C. telling Congress to disband or all will die, with the President first in line. Back in Hell Spy Smasher is tortured to reveal the secret of the gyro-sub, his craft that can travel as fast as light, underwater, on land and in the air. Meanwhile Alan Armstrong's fiancé Eve Corby has become suspicious of the figure of Death and locates Hell in caves under the Capitol. Death is unmasked as Baroness Von Toat, spy for Hitler. The mock Hell was part of Hitler's plan to extort military secrets.

"For Fear of Little Men" [SFW]
First publication: *Spy Smasher* #3 (February 1942).

The cover of this issue features a scientist wearing a Nazi uniform glowering over his miniaturized subjects. In the comic strip Doctor Potz is described as a "spy scientist" who has reduced three men to the size of insects. Their mission—a government official marked for murder. Spy Smasher arrives too late to save the official but before he dies the official warns Spy Smasher of "inch-high men."

The next target for the little men is the secret government papers of Admiral Corby detailing the defense plans for New York. Potz plans to use his enlarging ray on a column of his personal tiny troops to attack New York. Meanwhile Spy Smasher has been reduced in size by Potz and is trapped in a spider's web.

"Spy Smasher and the Jap Devil Dragon" [SFW]
First publication: *Spy Smasher* #7 (October 1942); Art: Emil Gershwin.

Alan Armstrong, Virginia sportsman, encounters two enemy agents on a ship in the Pacific who want to know the secret identity of Spy Smasher. Armstrong jumps ship and launches his gyro-sub toward Australia. But danger awaits Armstrong alias Spy Smasher in the form of the gigantic Japanese Devil Dragon—as it paves a path for the Japanese army and navy.

The Squad (2011) [Film; Colombia; WW]
Premiere: October 7, 2011 (Colombia); Main Cast: Juan Pablo Barragan as Ponce, Alejandro Aguilar as Cortez, Mauricio Navas as Teniente, Juan David Restrepo as Ramos, Andres Castaneda as Sargento; Executive Producer: Steven Grisales; Story: Jaime Osorio Marquez, Diego Vivanco; Director: Jaime Osorio Marquez; 108 min.; Sudesta Films, Rhayuela Films, Alta Films; Color.

A commando unit investigates a remote military base in Colombia that they suspect may have come under a guerrilla attack. They find an empty base except for a lone peasant woman, chained and enclosed in a concrete wall. Who is the enemy and why is the woman chained? Some suspect she might be a witch responsible for the empty camp.

Star Spangled Kid & Stripesy [Comic book character; SFW]
First appearance: *Action Comics* #40 (September 1941); Creators: Jerry Siegel, Hal Sherman; Publisher: National Periodical Publications (DC).

Teenage heir Sylvester Pemberton and former pugilist Pat Dugan break up a protest by Nazis at a patriotic movie. They decide to form a team to "make the flag come alive" after they meet again at Dugan's garage the following day. Together, as the Star Spangled Kid and Stripesy, they set out on their mission to fight the Nazis and fifth columnists. Dugan is hired by Pemberton as the family chauffeur, who customizes the Pemberton limousine into the Star Rocket Racer—a green bubble top vehicle, complete with wings, rockets and the ability to function as a helicopter. The pair later join the Seven Soldiers of Victory.

Star Spangled War Stories [Comic book]
"You Can't Pin a Medal on a Gorilla" [WW]
First publication: #126 (April–May 1966); Story: **Robert Kanigher**; Art: **Joe Kubert**; Publisher: DC Comics.

"Featuring the only non-com who escaped from a zoo to join the Marines—Sgt. Gorilla!"

As he entertains troops in the South Pacific Charlie the Gorilla has ambitions of being a U.S. Marine. When his trainer Sgt. Pinky Donovan is called to action Charlie hitches a ride aboard the assault boat. He soon sees action on a Pacific island and becomes a hero, helping the troops defeat the Japanese and raising the Stars and Stripes. A Marine admits, "That big ape acted like a real Marine!"

Star Trek (1966) [TV series]
Main Cast: William Shatner as Capt. James T. Kirk, Leonard Nimoy as Mr. Spock, DeForest Kelley as Dr. Leonard "Bones" McCoy, James Doohan as Montgomery Scott, Nichelle Nichols as Lt. Uhura, Walter Koenig as Pavel Chekov; Creator-Executive Producer: Gene Roddenberry; 50 min.; Norway Corporation, Paramount Television; National Broadcasting Company (NBC); Color.

Adventures of the crew of the U.S.S. *Enterprise* as it journeys through intergalactic space.

"The City on the Edge of Forever" (1:28) [SFW]
Air date: April 6, 1967; Guest Cast: Joan Collins as Sister Edith Keeler; Story: Harlan Ellison; Director: Joseph Pevney.

Injected with a massive, accidental overdose of a heart stimulant drug, Dr. McCoy flees the U.S.S. *Enterprise* in a mad, wild, frenzy. Captain Kirk and Mr. Spock pursue him to the surface of the planet below and through a time portal, self-described as "the guardian of forever." Arriving in New York City, 1930, Kirk and Spock meet social worker Edith Keeler at the twenty-first street mission. Kirk finds himself falling in love with Keeler, who he views as a woman of unusual insight. Meanwhile Spock has built a computer that can scan through news headlines of the future, where he discovers Keeler is to be killed in a traffic accident in a few days time. But she has another possible future where she leads a peace movement that delays America's entry into World War II. The delay results in Germany developing the A-bomb first and winning the war. Dr. McCoy is the random element who can change time. Kirk and Spock must find McCoy and Kirk must choose between saving the life of the woman he loves or condemning millions in the future to death.

"Patterns of Force" (2:21) [SFW]
Air date: February 16, 1968; Guest cast: Richard Evans as Isak, Valora Noland as Daras, Skip Homeier as Melakon, David Brian as Professor John Gill, Gilbert Green as S.S. Major; Producer-Story: John Meredyth Lewis; Director: Vincent McEveety.

On the planet Ekos, Captain Kirk and Mr. Spock of the U.S.S. Enterprise encounter an alien society patterned after the Earth's 1940s Nazi regime who are at war with neighboring planet Zeon. And the missing Federation cultural observer, Professor John Gill, is now a neo–Nazi Fuhrer. But all is not what it seems when Spock and Kirk, posing as Nazi documentary filmmakers, infiltrate the party headquarters. Gill's original good intentions have been perverted by Melakon, who controls his people using a heavily drugged Gill as a puppet leader.

"The Savage Curtain" (3:22) [SFW]
Air date: March 7, 1969; Guest Cast: Lee Bergere as Abraham Lincoln, Nathan Jung as Ghengis Khan, Barry Atwater as Surak, Phillip Pine as Colonel Green, Carol Daniels DeMent as Zora, Bob Herron as Kahless; Producer: Fred Freiberger; Story: Gene Roddenberry; Teleplay Gene Roddenberry, Arthur Heinemann; Director: Herschel Daugherty.

The concept of good vs. evil is put to the test by a rock creature on the planet Excalbia. Kirk, Spock, Abraham Lincoln and legendary Vulcan Surak must do battle with the notorious Genghis Khan, evil war leader Colonel Green, Zora of Tiburon and Klingon Kahless the Unforgettable. And unless Kirk and Co. win, the *Enterprise* will be destroyed in four hours.

Star Trek: Enterprise (2001) [TV series]
The formative years of Starfleet is explored in this prequel to ***Star Trek***.

"Storm Front" Part 1–2 (4:01–4:02) [SFW]
Air dates: October 8–October 15, 2004; Main Cast: Scott Bakula as Capt. Jonathan Archer, John Billingsley as Dr. Phlox, Jolene Blalock as Sub-Commander T'Pol, Dominic Keating as Lt. Malcolm Reed, Anthony Montgomery as Ensign Travis Mayweather, Linda Park as Ensign Hoshi Sato, Golden Brooks as Alicia Travers, Jack Gwaltney as Vosk, Christopher Neame as German General, Steven R. Schrippa as Carmine, John Fleck as Silik, Matt Winston as Temporal Agent Daniels; Executive Producers: Rick Berman, Brannon Braga, Manny Coto; Story: Manny Coto; Directors: Allan Kroeker (Pt. 1), David Straiton (Pt. 2); 42 min.; Paramount Television; United Paramount Network (UPN); Color.

Shuttlepod One is attacked by P-51 Mustangs and Captain Archer captured by Nazis. The *Enterprise* has arrived at an alternate Earth where Nazi Germany has invaded the United States, aided by extraterrestrials.

Star Trek: Voyager (1995) [TV series]

The adventures of Captain Kathryn Janeway and her crew on the U.S.S. *Voyager*.

"The Killing Game" Part 1–2 (4:18–4:19) [SFW]
Air dates: March 4–March 11, 1998; Main Cast: Kate Mulgrew as Captain Kathryn Janeway/Katrine, Garrett Wang as Ensign Harry Kim, Robert Picardo as The Doctor, Jeri Ryan as Seven of Nine, Tim Russ as Tuvok, Ethan Phillips as Neelix, as Roxann Dawson as Chief Engineer B'Elanna Torres, Robert Beltran as First Officer Chakotay/Captain Miller, Robert Duncan McNeill as Lt. Tom Paris/Lt. Bobby Davis, Danny Goldring as Alpha Hirogen, J. Paul Boehmer as Nazi Hauptmann, David Keith Anderson as Ensign Ashmore, Mark Deakins as Hirogen SS Officer, Paul S. Eckstein as Young Hirogen, Peter Hendrixson as Klingon Hologram, Mark Metcalf as Hirogen Medic; Executive Producers: Rick Berman, Jeri Taylor; Story: Brannon Braga, Joe Menosky; Director: David Livingston.

The Hirogen take control of U.S.S. *Voyager* and its crew by converting the ship into one giant Holodeck. Captain Kathryn Janeway believes she is in the Nazi occupied town of Saint Clare in 1944. She is Katrine, leader of the French Resistance who works behind the cover of a restaurant. Other crew members work for Katrine in the Resistance. Only the Doctor with the help of Ensign Kim and Seven of Nine can restore the memories of the crew. But meanwhile a holographic version of World War II continues to escalate on *Voyager*.

Steel Commando [Comic book character; UK; WW]

First appearance: *Thunder* #1 (October 17, 1970); Creators: Frank S. Pepper, Alex Henderson; Publisher: IPC Magazines.

During World War II, the unimposing figure of Lance Corporal Ernie "Excused-Boots" Bates is put in charge of the "Mark I: Indestructible Robot" constructed by Allied forces to fight the Nazis. The Steel Commando, also known as "Old Ironsides" who only takes orders from Ernie Bates, possesses incredible strength, but has been known to breakdown due to faulty circuitry.

Stir of Echoes: The Homecoming (2007) [Telefilm; WW]

Air Date: August 11, 2007; Main Cast: Rob Lowe as Ted Cogan, Marnie McPhail as Molly Cogan, Ben Lewis as Max Cogan, Vik Sahay as Farzan, Tatiana Maslany as Sammi, Shawn Roberts as Luke, Zachary Bennett as Jake Witzky, Elias Zarov as Iraqi Officer; Producers: Philip Stilman, Claire Welland; Story-Director: Ernie Barbarash; 89 min.; Lions Gate Entertainment, Sci-Fi Channel; Color.

Back home after serving in Iraq, discharged U.S. National Guard captain Ted Cogan suffers from PTSD and visions of a burning ghost. His time in Iraq has left him mentally and physically scarred. Now he must come to terms with past actions and failing relationships at home. And a ghost who possesses him.

Stitched (2011) [Short film; Comic book; WW]

1. Premiere: July 21, 2011; Main Cast: Larry "Tank" Jones as Pruitt, Lauren Alonzo as Cooper, Kate Kugler as Twiggy, Eric Zaragoza as Stitched; Executive Producers: William Christensen, Garth Ennis; Screenplay-Director: Garth Ennis; 18 min.; Spitfire Productions, Mischief Maker Studios; Avatar Press; Color.

In modern day Afghanistan three soldiers battle the harsh environment after their Blackhawk helicopter crashes. But a foe worse than the Taliban emerges when seemingly indestructible near-human creatures attack them.

2. First publication: September 2011; Story-Creator Garth Ennis; Art: Mike Wolfer: Publisher: Avatar Press.

This ongoing comic book is based on the short film by Garth Ennis.

Storming Paradise [Comic book; AHW]

First publication: September 2008; Story: Chuck Dixon; Art: Butch Guice; Publisher: DC Comics.

1945. The Nazis have been defeated. But there is a problem with Japan. The Manhattan Project has failed with the scientists working on the atom bomb dead. Now American forces must invade Japan in Operation Olympus. But the invasion will prove to be bloody and brutal with the total annihilation of Japanese culture at risk.

"The Story Vinton First Heard at Mallorie" [Short story; WW]

Author: Katherine Prescott Moseley; First publication: *Scribner's Magazine* (1918).

"When war broke out there were two beautiful daughters, living most of their time, down there at Mallorie Abbey, and a son went over with the expeditionary force as soon as war was declared. The young man was killed in action, under the most heroic circumstances."

On the anniversary of her brother's death Lady Maurya sees a Zeppelin hovering above and suddenly out of nowhere "without a sound and straight at the Zeppelin" an airplane appears. Without a shot being fired the airplane twists and turns as if capturing the Zeppelin "in some intangible net." The Zeppelin crashes to earth followed by the safe landing of the airplane.

"And there she came face to face with the aeronaut. He wore no helmet, and in this very early light, for it was the first days of the year, he looked as if he stood in a shining black armor. His hair was golden, and the rising son touched it, and he was the most beautiful creature that she had ever seen...."

Intrigued by the young man Lady Maurya asks him how he could have brought the Zeppelin to earth without a single shot being fired.

"Because in me is all the strength of that bright ardor which has led young warriors to die in battle for the right since earth began.... Such souls are the stuff of which are made the angels and archangels and all the heavenly host."

She asks his name but before he answers he is gone. At that moment a great northeaster stops howling. Was he Michael, Gabriel or Raphael?

"When I remember that all the trouble on earth comes in the train of that infernal thing we call the ego it seems to me that heavenly thing must indeed arise from its complete surrender."

Strange Adventures [Comic book]

Science fiction anthology title from DC Comics.

"Gran'pa Fights a Space War!" [SFW]

First publication: *Strange Adventures* #41 (June 1962); Story: Gardner Fox; Art: Sid Greene.

Gran'pa loves to tell the tale of how he met aliens from outer space during World War II. Only his grandson Johnny believes his story and soon Gran'pa's knowledge of how to defeat them is put to the test when the aliens return in the present day.

"The Secret Fate of Adolph [sic] Hitler!" [SFW]

First publication: *Strange Adventures* #3 (December 1950–January 1951); Story: H.L. Gold; Art: Curt Swan, Jon Small.

Arrested and put on trial by Martians, Adolph Hitler is sentenced to permanent exile in space.

A Strange and Familiar Place (Book #2) [Juvenile book; SFW]

Author: Rachel Carter; First publication: New York: HarperTeen, 2013.

Lydia Bentley has traveled back in time to 1944 to discover her grandfather's stories about the Montauk Project on Long Island are true. The government has been conducting rime travel experiments since World War II. Now Lydia has returned to 2012, only to find herself in an altered timeline. When Montauk Project operative Wes appears in 2012 he tells Lydia they must travel to 1989, in the hope of reversing her grandfather's disappearance.

See: ***Find Me Where the Water Ends***

Strange Conflict [Novel; WW]

Author: Dennis Wheatley; First publication: London: Anchor Press, 1941.

London, 1941. The Duke de Richleau must consider the possibility the Nazis are receiving supernatural help from the astral plane to uncover the secret routes of Atlantic convoys. But to fight the enemy the Duke and his followers must stay awake. The astral enemies must be kept at bay until they have enough magical protection to face them and save the world from the combined forces of Nazis and the forces of darkness.

Strike Witches (2007) [Original video animation; Japan; WW]

1. Release: January 1, 2007; Creator; Humikane Shimada; Director: Kunihisa Sugishima; 24 min.; Gonzo; Color.

1939. The alien force known as the Neuroi invade Earth. Young witches gather to counter the alien threat and develop a weapon called the "Striker Unit." With a mixture of magic and weaponry the witches unite as the pilots of the 501st Joint Fighter Wing also known as the Strike Witches. Magic allows the teenage witches to take on the characteristics of military planes. While searching for her missing father Fuso witch Yoshika Miyafuji becomes a Strike Witch, joining the fight against the Neuroi invaders.

2. [Animated Television Series; Japan] Release: July 3, 2008; Story: Tsuyoshi Tamai, Shoji Saeki, Takaaki Suzuki, Tatsuhiko Urahata; 24 × 25 min.; Director: Kazuhiro Takamura; Gonzo, AIC; Madman Entertainment; Chiba TV; Color.

Season One

1:01—*Magical Girl*; 1:02—*That Which I Can Do*; 1:03—*You're Not Alone*; 1:04—*Thanks*; 1:05—*Fast, Big, Soft*; 1:06—*We're the Same*; 1:07—*Nice and Breezy*; 1:08—*I Won't Forget You*; 1:09—*What I Want to Protect*; 1:10—*I Want You to Believe*; 1:11—*Into the Sky*; 1:12—*Strike Witches*

Season Two (Title: *Strike Witches 2*)

1:01—*Into the Sky Once More*; 1:02—*The Legendary Witches*; 1:03—*That Which We Can Do*; 1:04—*Hard, Fast, Amazing!*; 1:05—*My Romagna*; 1:06—*Higher than the Sky*; 1:07—*It's All Creep, Crawly*; 1:08—*Please Grant Me Wings*; 1:09—*The Bridge to Tomorrow*; 1:10—*500 Overs*; 1:11—*To Be Myself*; 1:12—*Beyond the Eternal Skies*

Strike Witches: Operation Victory Arrow (2014) [Original Video Animation; Japan; WW]

Release: September 20, 2014; Story: Takaaki Suzuki; Director: Kazuhiro Takamura; 76 min. total (3 chapters); Silver Link; Color.

The action takes place between the end of Season Two of the animated series and *Strike Witches: The Movie* (2012).

Chapters: 1. *St. Trond's Thunder*; 2. *Goddess of the Aegean Sea*; 3. *Arnhem Bridge*.

Strike Witches: The Movie (2012) [Animated film; Japan; WW]

Premiere: March 17, 2012; Voice Cast: Misato Fukuen as Yoshika Miyafuji, Aya Uchida as Shizuka Hattori, Yumi Hara as Aleksandra Ivanovna Pokryshkin, Ryo Hirohashi as Luciana Mazzei, Saori Seto as Mio Sakamoto, Kairi Nazuka as Lynette Bishop; Screenplay: Huminake Shimada, Kazuhiro Takamura, Kenichi Yatagai, Takaati Suzuki, Tasuhiko Urahata; Director: Kazuhiro Takamura; 94 min.; Anime International Company (AIC); Kodokwa Pictures; Color.

Yoshika Miyafuji has lost her powers and is studying to be a doctor when she is transferred to Europe with Imperial Navy Cadet Shizuka Hattori as her escort. Soon she is helping fellow Strike Witches to defeat a new generation of Neuroi that move in swarms, can jam radios and are capable of movement on the ground as well as the air.

Strikers 1945 [Videogame; Japan; SFW]

Release date: 1995; Platforms: Arcade, Sega Saturn, PlayStation; Developer: Psikyo; Publishers: Psikyo, Atlus, Taito.

This scrolling shooter game is set in 1945. CANY is a secret military organization with plans on conquering the world using military vehicles that transform into gigantic robots. This forces world war enemies to become allies as six pilots from America, Britain, Germany and Japan unite to defeat the common enemy. The planes, which include a Mustang, Spitfire, Lightning, Messerschmitt, Zero and Shinden have three attack modes.

The Sub-Mariner [Comic book character; SHW]

First appearance: *Motion Picture Funnies Weekly* #1 (1939); Creator: **Bill Everett**; Publisher: First Funnies, Inc.; Timely Publications.

Princess Fen of Atlantis is sent by her people to seduce Naval Commander McKenzie who has been destroying their undersea kingdom by using dynamite on icebergs. The Atlanteans plan to attack the American surface fleet to save their kingdom beneath the waves. But when Princess Fen falls in love with McKenzie she compromises the battle plans and feels betrayed by McKenzie when he destroys the Atlantean army.

Giving birth to McKenzie's son, Princess Fin waits until he reaches maturity to tell him, "to avenge the brutal harm done us...." Able to live on land and under the sea Prince Namor, the Sub-Mariner follows his mothers wishes and soon finds a perfect nemesis on land—the **Human Torch**. But after their epic battle that spans *Marvel Mystery Comics* #8–#10 they both realize a greater enemy needs defeating. Nazi Germany and the Axis powers.

The original 8-page comic strip "Here is, the Sub-Mariner" published in *Motion Picture Funnies Weekly* #1 (1939) was expanded to a 12-page strip in *Marvel Comics* #1 (December 1939).

Sub-Mariner Comics #1 (1941). Cover art by Alex Schomburg. Published by Timely Comics.

Sucker Punch (2011) [Film; SFW]

Premiere: February 20, 2011; Main Cast: Emily Browning as Babydoll, Abbie Cornish as Sweet Pea, Jena Malone as Rocket, Vanessa Hudgens as Blondie. Jamie Chung as Amber, Carla Gugino as Dr. Vera Gorski, Oscar Isaac as Blue Jones, Jon Hamm as High Roller/Doctor, Scott Glenn as Wise Man, Malcolm Scott as The Cook, Gerard Plunkett as Stepfather; Producers: Deborah Snyder, Zack Snyder; Screenplay: Zack Snyder, Steve Shibuya; Director: Zack Snyder; 110 min.; Legendary Pictures, Cruel and Unusual, Lennox House Films; Warner Bros.; Color.

A 20-year-old girl seeking to escape from a mental asylum, along with four other inmates, retreats into a world where fantasy and reality is blurred. Among their fantasies is a steam punk World War I scenario known as "The Cathedral" where dead German soldiers are reanimated with a combination of clockworks and steam, triplanes and other worldly Zeppelins.

The backstory is told in the short film *The Trenches* that accompanies the main feature. At the ruins of a church, undead troops gather, but fail to stop four young girls from stealing a map carried by a Courier.

Sunset of the Gods [Novel; MWW]

Author: Steve White; First publication: Riverdale, N.Y.: Baen, 2013.

Jason Thanou and a time traveling expedition of scholars go back to the Battle of Marathon in ancient Greece. But extraterrestrials are posing as Olympian gods. Only Thanou can prevent Pan and his followers from taking over the ancient world and threatening the future of democracy.

See: **Ghosts of Time**

The Super Hero Squad Show (2009) [Animated TV series]

Voice Cast: Tara Strong as Scarlet Witch/Toro, Jim Cummings as Thanos/Human Torch Android, Mark Hamill as Red Skull, Tom Kenny as Captain America/Iron Man, Rod Keller as Bucky, Alimi Ballard as Falcon, Dave Boat as Thor, Steve Blum as Wolverine, Travis Willingham as Hulk, Charlie Adler as Dr. Doom; Executive Producers: **Stan Lee**, Alan Fine, Joe Quesada, Simon Phillips, Eric Rollman; 52 × 23 min.; Film Roman, Ingenious Media, Marvel Animation; Cartoon Network (CN); Color.

Light-hearted animated adventures that parody the Marvel super heroes. Based on the Hasbro action figures.

"WORLD WAR WITCH!" (2:03) [SHW]
Air date: October 30, 2010; Story: Nicole Dubuc; Director: Michael R. Gerard.

Scarlet Witch is captured by the **Red Skull** when she is thrown back in time by Thanos. Tied to a rocket that is ready to launch Scarlet Witch is rescued by **Captain America**, Bucky, **Human Torch** and Toro. In the present members of the *Super Hero Squad* buy a time machine from an **Invaders** comic book and travel back to 1942 to rescue Scarlet Witch and defeat Red Skull's plans to destroy Europe.

"WRATH OF THE RED SKULL" (1:23) [SHW]
Air date: January 30, 2010; Story: Mark Hoffmeir; Directors: Michael R. Gerard, Mitch Schauer.

On Captain America's birthday Dr. Doom thaws the Red Skull from a decades long deep freeze but is upset when Red Skull decides to be the big boss. In black-and-white flashbacks to World War II we see Red Skull fighting Captain America. In the present his "Plan Usb" involves a Uber Skull Bot that will finally defeat Captain America. But the Hulk's deadly singing voice destroys the Skull Bot and the Red Skull ends up frozen by his own freeze ray.

Super Soldier [Comic book character; SHW]

First appearance: *Super Marvel Versus DC* #3 (April 1996); Publisher: Marvel-DC Comics.

Two universes are merged to form the Amalgam universe where new heroes are born. **Superman** and **Captain America** are combined to create Super Soldier, the ultimate hero to defeat the Axis powers during World War II.

Superboy [Comic book]

The adventures of **Superman** as a boy, growing up in Smallville.

"Superboy's Civil War Time Trip!" [SHW]

First publication: #19 (September 1961); Story: Jerry Siegel; Art: George Papp; Publisher: National Periodical Publications, Inc. (DC).

Superboy visits a planet where the American Civil War is still being fought with doubles of people on Earth, including Clark Kent and his adopted parents. But they all have different identities and personalities and on this planet Clark Kent is Clark Brent—Confederate spy, his father General Kane and his mother Nurse Bertha.

Superman [Comic book character]

First appearance: *Action Comics* #1 (1938); Creators: Jerry Siegel, Joe Schuster; Publisher: National Periodical Publications, Inc. (DC).

World War II presented a problem for the writers of the invincible super-hero Superman. He could easily defeat the Nazi and Japanese armed forces by himself and end the war in a day. The problem was solved by having his alter-ego Clark Kent fail his eyesight test by accidentally reading the wrong chart. Instead of going to war Kent reported the war for the Daily Planet newspaper in Metropolis. Meanwhile Superman tackled Axis powers on the home front. "Japanazis" graced the covers of *Action Comics* and *Superman* before America entered the war and the enemy could be specifically named. Superman would finally confront Adolf Hitler face-to-face helping the British allies in Europe.

1. Comic book; Publisher: National Periodical Publications (DC Comics)

"The Conquest of a City" [SHW]

First publication: *Superman* #18 (September–October 1942); Story: Jerry Siegel; Art: The Joe Schuster Studio.

As World War II rages in Europe Clark Kent sees a complacent Metropolis, seemingly unaware of any impending danger. "Everywhere there is a false sense of gaiety—the people have got to wake up," declares Kent. Lawyer Carl Brand suggests a mock Nazi invasion to stir the people. But Brand is a Nazi spy and Superman will have to defend Metropolis from a genuine invasion.

"Meet the Squiffles" [SHW]

First publication: *Superman* #22; Story: Jerry Siegel; Art: Sam Citron.

A dejected Adolf Hitler is visited by hobgoblin type creatures known as the Squiffles. They promise they will help "retard the development of the American aircraft industry" if Hitler's grants them a favor in return. He agrees and soon there are a series of airplane crashes in America. Pilots tell fantastic stories of elves crawling over the planes during flight and causing them to crash.

Superman gets to work with his solution—a counterattack by the Gremlins. The Squiffles retreat but still hold Hitler to his promise. The favor they demand is the possession of his body and soul.

"Suicide Voyage" [SHW]

First publication: *Superman* #24 (September–October 1943); Story: Don Cameron; Art: Ed Dobrotka, George Roussos.

Nazi and Japanese forces in the Arctic protect their aerial routes by attacking American forces locating sites for airfields across the North Pole. Superman comes to their rescue with the aid of a polar bear. "The Russian bear has had you Nazis on the run for quite some time—let's see what an American bear can do," declares Superman to the retreating Nazis.

"The United States Navy" [SHW]

First publication: *Superman* #34; Story: Don Cameron; Art: Pete Riss, George Roussos.

Clark Kent is assigned to the U.S.S. Davey Jones as it leads a destroyer squadron into action in the Pacific. When two Japanese carriers with a Destroyer escort are headed their way the lone U.S. submarine Squamos targets torpedoes at the Japanese but is attacked in return by their Destroyers. Now the American Destroyer is vulnerable to attack. Enter Superman who diverts the Japanese Destroyer leaving it to the U.S. Navy to finish the job.

2. Sunday Newspaper strip

Superman also fought World War II in his syndicated Sunday newspaper comic strip. Artist

Wayne Boring came to define the patriotic Superman in these color strips.

From January 16–March 5, 1944, Superman featured in a story where Judy King can't decide which woman's service to join. She asks Superman to help choose which of her male admirers is doing the best job for his country. Superman agrees and checks out Tom Jones of the U.S. Army as he fights and captures Nazis in Italy. Next is Dick Adams serving on a submarine in the Western Pacific under attack from a Japanese Destroyer. The remaining men, a decorated Marine and Coast Guard are recovering from wounds at a military hospital. Superman tells Judy she must decide for herself. After watching the men in a joint amphibious training exercise Judy learns that teamwork matters the most in the war. Superman never learns who she chooses but tells the reader, "It doesn't matter which branch of the of the service you belong to—belonging is the important thing! This is a woman's war too...."

In the strips published between March 11–25, 1945, Superman is invited to visit Adolf Hitler at a bombproof shelter in his German mountain retreat. Superman is confronted with Hitler and his henchman dressed in Superman costumes. They want Superman to join them and rule the world together. When he refuses they decide to send Superman on his way with their latest super-weapon—the V-72 bomb. Superman survives and Hitler and his cronies are left frustrated.

3. Animated short series

Main Voice Cast: Budd Collyer as Superman/Clark Kent, Joan Alexander as Lois Lane; Based on the comic strip: *Superman* by Joe Shuster and Jerome Siegel; Famous Studios; Paramount Pictures, Inc.; Color.

The Fleischer Studios began production on a series of animated short films featuring Superman in 1941. When Famous Studios took control of production in 1942, war-themed stories became more prevalent.

"Destruction Inc." (1942) [SHW]
Premiere: December 25, 1942; Story: Jay Morton; Animation: Dave Tendlar, Tom Moore; Director: I. Sparber; 9 min.

The watchman at the Metropolis munitions plant is found floating dead in the local swamp, the victim of an organized ring of saboteurs. Working undercover at the plant Lois Lane overhears a plan to blow up the plant with TNT. Unfortunately Lois is spotted and captured by the saboteurs and placed inside the head of a torpedo.

On the torpedo testing range an old boat is targeted for practice with Lois trapped in the torpedo. Superman saves Lois and the munitions plant from being blown up.

"Eleventh Hour" (1942) [SHW]
Premiere: November 20, 1942; Story: Carl Meyer, William Turner; Animation: Willard Bowsky, William Henning; Director: Dan Gordon; 8 min.

Yokohama, Japan. Clark Kent and Lois Lane are under house arrest. But unknown to Lois, Clark Kent is sabotaging the Japanese military installations as Superman. The Japanese issue a warning. "*Superman.* One more act of sabotage and the American girl reporter will be *executed* at once!" Just as Lois Lane is about to face the firing squad Superman saves the day.

"Japoteurs" (1942) [SHW]
Premiere: September 18, 1942; Story: Bill Turner, Carl Meyer; Animation: Myron Waldman, Nicholas Tafuri; Director: Seymour Kneitel; 9 min.

Daily Planet headline: "World's Largest Bombing Plane Finally Completed—Preparations Rushed For Test Flight."

Daily Planet reporter Lois Lane stows away on the maiden flight only to discover Japanese spies onboard have stolen the plane and intend to bomb American targets. Superman comes to the rescue and saves the plane from crash landing in the crowded Metropolis.

"Jungle Drums" (1943) [SHW]
Premiere: March 26, 1943; Story: Robert Little, Jay Morton; Animation: Orestes Calpini, H.C. Ellison; Director: Dan Gordon; 8 min.

A plane is shot down over the jungle and Lois Lane captured by a Nazi spy posing as an African hooded leader. He threatens Lois with death unless she reveals the whereabouts of vital secret papers passed on to her by the dying pilot of the crashed plane.

Lois refuses to cooperate and is tied to a wooden stake to be burnt to death. As the flames begin to envelop her Superman comes to her rescue. Meanwhile the Nazi spy is preparing for a submarine attack after he locates the papers. Lois alerts the U.S. air force who dive bomb the submarines and defeat the Nazi threat.

Superman's Pal, Jimmy Olsen
[Comic book]
Adventures of the *Daily Planet* reporter.

"JIMMY'S D-DAY ADVENTURE!" [SFW]
First appearance: #86 (July 1965); Story: Leo Dorfman; Art: Curt Swan, George Klein; Publisher: DC Comics.

Curious *Daily Planet* reporter Jimmy Olsen is intrigued by newsreel footage of his lookalike, a Nazi standing next to Adolf Hitler. Borrowing Professor Potter's time travel device to journey back in time to World War II and D-Day, Olsen impresses the Nazis with his knowledge of the war. Before he leaves the past behind Olsen poses for newsreel footage—the same footage he watched before his journey in time began.

Supernatural (2005) [TV series]
Brothers Sam and Dean Winchester track supernatural forces and demons across America. Main Cast: Jared Padalecki as Sam Winchester, Jensen Ackles as Dean Winchester.

"EVERYBODY HATES HITLER" (8:13) [WW]
Air date: February 6, 2013; Guest Cast: Hal Linden as Rabbi Isaac Bass, Adam Rose as Aaron Bass, John DeSanti as The Golem; Story: Ben Edlund; Director: Phil Sgriccia; 43 min.; Wonderland Sound & Vision; Warner Bros., CW Television Network; Color.

Vitsyebsk, Belarus, 1944. German soldiers are attacked and killed by a Golem. In the present day Sam and Dean Winchester investigate the circumstances surrounding the spontaneous combustion of Rabbi Bass. They uncover Nazi necromancers and a Golem who belongs to the Rabbi's grandson Aaron.

"THE VESSEL" (11:14) [SFW]
Air date: February 17, 2016; Guest Cast: Misha Collins as Castiel/Lucifer, Mark A. Sheppard as Crowley, Weronika Rosati as Delphine Seydoux; Grant Harvey as Petey Giraldi; Darren Dolynski as Capt. James Dearborn, Richard Stroh as Befehlsleiter Gumprecht; Executive producer: Jeremy Carver; Story: Robert Berens; Director: John Badham; 42 min.; Scrap Metal & Kripke Entertainment Enterprises (KEI); CW Television Network; Color.

Dean Winchester travels back in time to World War II to recover an artefact he hopes will defeat Amara. In 1943 Nazi occupied France, woman of letters Delphine Seydoux steals the Hand of God artefact from Nazi Befehlsleiter Gumprecht. She plans to get it to the safety of a Men of Letters safe house in America via the U.S.S. Bluefin submarine. But Dean knows the submarine is doomed and transports to U.S.S. *Bluefin* to recover the Hand of God before it's attacked and sunk by a German destroyer.

The Supernaturals (1986) [Film; WW]
Premiere: June 30, 1986; Main cast: Matthew Caulfield as Pvt. Ray Ellis, Nichelle Nichols as Sgt. Leona Hawkins, Talia Balsam as Pvt. Angela Lejune, LeVar Burton as Pvt. Michael Osgood, Bradford Bancroft as Pvt. Tom Weir; Executive Producers: Don Levin, Mel Pearl; Story: Joel Soisson, Michael S. Murphy; Director: Armand Mastroianni; 91 min.; Embassy Home Entertainment; Color.

On a training exercise Sergeant Leona Hawkins and her platoon accidentally enter the same territory where Union soldiers slaughtered Confederates. Now those corpses have risen and want revenge.

Tannhauser [Board game; France; WW]
Release date: 2007; Designers: William Grosselin, Didier Poli; Publishers: Fantasy Flight Games, Take On You.

A 35-year war continues into 1949. The Reich's 13th Occult Division are on the verge of a major turning point in the war when they gain access to a portal leading to hell buried within a crypt in Europe. If they summon the Cohorts of Chaos the world will be under their dominion. Only the men and women of the Union's 42nd Alter-Marine Special Forces can stop the demonic threat.

Taskmaster [Comic book]
"THE TOWN WHERE EVERYONE IS HITLER." [WW]
First publication: *Taskmaster* #3 (January 1, 2011); Story: Fred Van Lente; Art: Jefte Palo; Publisher: Marvel Comics.

Deadly assassin Taskmaster, the target of a billion dollar bounty hunt, searches for those who framed him. High in the South American Andes he storms a Bavarian castle and comes across a town where everyone is Adolf Hitler.

Teenape vs. The Monster Nazi Apocalypse (2012) [Film; SFW]
Premiere: February 8, 2013; Main Cast: Jesse Ames as Marge/Kinko, Casey Bowker as Teenape, Nicola Fiore as Thunder Ambrose, Billy Garberina as Deathbone, Josh Suire as Hitler/Leo; Producers: Joe Davis,

Allen Dinning, Joe Fiorello, Rachel Lovinger; Director: Chris Seaver; 78 min.; Low Budget Pictures; Toma Entertainment; Color.

The Paranormal Investigation Agency (P.I.A.) defeat Adolf Hitler's plan to unleash man-made monsters on to the world in 1945. But now in the present day one of Hitler's assistants possesses the DNA to Hitler and his genetic mutations. Teenape and his team must save the day before Hitler lives again and brings about the Fourth Reich.

"The Temple" [Pulp fiction; WW]
Author: H. P. Lovecraft; First publication: *Weird Tales* #24 (September 1925).

World War I, June 17. Submarine U-29 Lieutenant Commander Karl Heinrich Graf von Altberg-Ehrenstein torpedoes the British freighter Victory. One of the dead crew from the Victory is found with a mysterious ivory in his coat pocket "carved to represent a youth's head crowned with laurel." The commander and crew of the German U-boat begin to experience strange occurrences. Fear grips the crew and insanity follows as the Commander resorts to murder to stop an onboard mutiny.

Only the Commander remains alive as the U-boat sinks to the bottom of the ocean amid the ruins of a once-glorious city that he believes to be the lost city of Atlantis. Within the temple ruins he discovers, "The head of the radiant god in the sculptures on the rock temple is the same as that carven bit of ivory which the dead sailor brought from the sea." Death then claims the final soul from U-boat 29.

The Temple and the Crown (*Knights Templar* Book #2) [Novel; AHW]
Authors: Katherine Kurtz, Deborah Turner Harris; First publication: New York: Warner Books, 2001.

England's Edward I wants to defeat the Knights Templar and the Scots, while King Philip IV of France desires the Templar's legendary wealth. But both Edward and Philip are being manipulated by the demonic Order of the Knights of the Black Swan. The Knights of Satan are ready to fight the Knights Templar and the Scots at the Battle of Bannockburn in their quest for the destruction of the Temple and with it the obliteration of Christianity. Loyal knights Arnault de Saint Clair and Torquil Lennox must retrieve sacred relics from the Holy Land and return with them to Scotland to help win the Battle of Bannockburn.

The Temple and the Stone (*Knights Templar* Book #1) [Novel; AHW]
Authors: Katherine Kurtz, Deborah Turner Harris; First publication: New York: Warner Books, 1998.

The Order of the Knights Templar survived the Crusades, but went into hiding—until now. William "Braveheart" Wallace and Robert the Bruce are fighting the English forces of King Edward I in the Anglo-Scottish war. The Knights Templar support the Scottish quest for independence. Knights Arnault de Saint Clair and Torquil Lennox travel to Scotland to establish a Fifth Temple. But to achieve this they must restore magic to the Stone of Destiny, in order to crown the new monarch and provide the cornerstone for the temple. But first they will have to defeat he black magic powers of the Pictish Comyns.

See: *The Temple and the Crown*

Terror at Troy (*Secret in the Attic* series) [Juvenile book; MWW]
Author: L.A. Peacock; Illustrator: Nathan Hale; First publication: New York: Scholastic, 2012.

Twins Jess and Josh discover a time-compass in their family attic that enables them to travel back in time to ancient Greece and the city of Troy. While searching for their mysterious Uncle Harry the twins meet the mighty warrior Achilles.

Tetsujin 28-gou a.k.a. ***Gigantor***; ***Iron Man 28*** [Manga; Animated TV series; Japan; SFW]

1. Manga; First publication: *Shonen Magazine* (July 1956); Creator: Mitsuteru Yokoyama; 24 volumes (1956–1966).

During World War II a.k.a. the Pacific War, Dr. Kaneda develops experimental giant robots for the Japanese Secret Weapon Institute. But the robots are destroyed by U.S. bombers before they can do any harm. Rumors persist some robots survived the bombing—especially the powerful Tetusjin-28. Kaneda's son Shoutarou becomes aware the mob are hunting for the robot and manages, with the help of Professor Shikashima, to locate Tetusjin-28 first. Now the giant robot will be used for keeping the peace rather than promoting war.

2. Animated TV series; Air date: October 20, 1963; Voice Cast: Yuzuru Fujimoto as Narrator, Kazue

Takahashi as Shoutarou Kaneda, Minouri Yada as Professor Shikishima, Kosei Tomita as Police Chief Otsuka; Story: Toshimichi Okawa; 96 × 25 min.; TCJ Animation Center, Eiken; King Records; B/W.

3. Animated TV series; Air date: April 8, 2004; Voice Cast: Motoko Kumai as Shoutarou Kaneda, Yuji Mikimoto as Kenji Murasame, Shigeru Ushiyama as Professor Shikishima; Storyboard: Hidehito Ueda; Key animation: You Yoshinari, Director: Yasuhiro Imagawa; 26 × 22 min.; Genco; Color.

"They Forgot to Remember Pearl Harbor" [Pulp fiction; SFW]

Author: P. F. Costello; First publication: *Amazing Stories* (Vol. 16 #6; June 1942); Publisher: Ziff-Davis Publishing Company.

"The lesson the Japs taught us was futile — America forgot, all except broken, betrayed Ward Blackson. Even a court martial and dishonorable discharge couldn't make Ward Blackson forget Pearl Harbor."

They Saved Hitler's Brain (1968) [Telefilm; SFW]

Premiere: August 18, 1968; Main Cast: Walter Stocker as Phil Day, Audrey Caire as Kathy Coleman Day, Carlos Rivas as Camino Padua/Teo Padua, John Holland as Professor John Coleman, Marshall Reed as Frank Dvorak; Story: Steve Bennett, Richard Miles; Director: David Bradley; 91 min.; Paragon Films, Inc., Sans-S; B/W.

The preserved head of Adolf Hitler is smuggled out of Germany to South America at the end of World War II. Hitler and the Nazis plan on world domination with the release of the deadly "G-Gas" and kidnap a scientist to stop him working on the antidote.

This version is a re-edited version of *The Madmen of Mandoras* (1963) with new footage added.

They Used Dark Forces [Novel; WW]

Author: Dennis Wheatley; First publication: London: Hutchison, 1964.

Secret agent Gregory Sallust parachutes into Germany in June 1943 with a mission to discover more about Hitler's deadly V rockets. His later encounter with Jewish Satanist Ibrahim Mallacou leads to an uneasy partnership as they attempt to destroy Hitler using the occult. But it will come at a dangerous cost to Sallust's spiritual well being.

Thin Air [Novel; SFW]

Authors: George E. Simpson, Neal R. Burger; First publication: New York: Dell, 1977.

Near the end of World War II the crew of the USS Sturman are ordered to the ship's deck and promptly disappear into thin air. 25 years later a man wakes up screaming with vague memories of the Navy. Naval investigator Nicholas Hammond is assigned to investigate the disappearance of the USS Sturman and its crew.

The Thin Man [Comic book character; SFW]

First appearance: *Mystic Comics* #4 (July 1940); Creators: Klaus Nordling, Roy Thomas (retroactive origin); Publisher: Timely Comics.

Scientist Dr. Bruce Dickson encounters the technologically advanced lost civilization of Kalahia on an expedition to the Himalayas. Exposure to a substance developed by the Kahalians allows him to change and stretch his body shape to ultra-thin and flat. The substance also makes him immune to disease and aging.

Originally limited to a one-issue run in 1940, the Thin Man was revived by **Roy Thomas** in *Marvel Premiere* #29 (April 1976) as a founding member of the **Liberty Legion** during World War II.

The Thing! [Comic book]

"Weird Tales of Suspense and Horror!"

"The Creature from Dimension 2-K-31" [SFW]

First publication: *The Thing!* #1 (February 1952); Art: Albert Tyler, Bob Forgione; Publisher: Outstanding Comics (Charlton).

In his laboratory physicist Dr. Eustus Riko attempts to transport an ape to Dimension 2-K-31. But his experiment fails and the ape is lost. Unknown to Dr. Riko the ape did make it to the other dimension but instead of returning to his laboratory was replaced by a hideous creature that is now in the frontline of the Korean war.

"The Marching Dead Men" [WW]

First publication: *The Thing!* #3 (June 1952); Art: Bob Forgione; Publisher: Outstanding Comics (Charlton).

Landing behind Korean lines in Mongolia, U.S. Air Force pilots Tom Kingsley and Sleepy Harlow join a party of marching dead men led by a Shaman. They are all coming home to finally rest-in-peace. But first they must help Kingsley and Harlow defeat the enemy.

"You can only kill the living but you can not harm the dead!"

The Third Section [Novel; WW]
Author: Jasper Kent; First publication: Amherst NY: Pyr, 2011.

In the besieged Crimean city of Sevastopol in 1855 Dimitry Alekseevich Danilov is surrounded by British and French armies. But an even greater enemy lurks beneath the earth. Creatures his father entombed thirty years ago.

See: ***Twelve***

30 Days of Night: Red Snow [Comic book; WW]
First publication: September 2007; Three-issue mini-series; Story-Art: Ben Templesmith; Publisher: IDW Publishing.

Winter 1941. British military attaché Corporal Charlie Keating ensures the Russians receive critical supplies in their continued fight against the Nazis on the Eastern Front. But a greater enemy exists, waiting to attack.

This Boy [Juvenile book; WW]
Author: Pippa Goodheart; Illustrator: Iva Sasheva; First publication: London: Collins Education, 2012.

Young Kerry hates her new school and finds her new house creepy. One day while waiting for her Mum she meets a sad young boy by the old war memorial. But there is something strange about this boy. Joe is a ghost who was killed in World War I.

Thomas, Roy (b.1942) [Comic book writer]
Born November 22, 1942, in Jackson, Missouri. Roy Thomas first attracted attention as the editor of the celebrated fanzine *Alter-Ego*. Following a two week stint at National-DC Comics under editor Mort Weisinger, Thomas moved to Marvel in 1965. His first long-term writing assignment was on **Sgt. Fury and His Howling Commandos**, followed by *The Avengers*. In the 1970s Thomas adapted Robert E. Howard's *Conan the Barbarian*, and effectively initiated the sword-and-sorcery boom in the comic book industry.

His main contributions to the Weird War genre include **The Invaders** and ***All-Star Squadron***, featuring Golden Age comic book heroes in a World War II setting. In 2007 he created the alternate history World War II comic book ***Anthem*** for small press publisher Heroic.

"**Thompson's Time Traveling Theory**" [Pulp fiction: SFW]
Author: Sgt. Mort Weisinger; First publication: *Amazing Stories* (Vol. 18 #2; March 1944); Publisher: Ziff-Davis Publishing Company.

"Young Donald Thompson changes time in 1943."

Thor [Comic book character]
"Thunder Over Troy" [MWW]
First publication: *Thor King-Size Annual* #8 (1979); Story: Roy Thomas; Art: John Buscema, Tony DeZuniga, Mike Esposito; Publisher: Marvel Comics.

Thor and Loki lose their memory as they travel through a crack in time to the Trojan War. Thor meets Aeneas and battles the god Zeus while Loki inadvertently becomes a factor in the creation of the Trojan Horse.

Thor Meets Captain America [Novella; MWW]
Author: David Brin; First publication: *The Magazine of Fantasy and Science Fiction* (July 1986).

Nazi Germany is on the verge of defeat in World War II when an unlikely ally comes to their aid. The Norse gods from Valhalla. Captain Chris Turing and his team are joined by Norse renegade Loki in Operation Ragnarok. When the mission fails Turing is captured and interrogated by Thor to reveal the location of Loki. Turing has no knowledge of his whereabouts but comes to the realization that necromancy has created the Norse gods and fueled the evil of the Nazi death camps.

Three Hearts and Three Lions [Novel; SFW]
Author: Poul Anderson; First publication: Garden City N.Y.; Doubleday; 1961.

Holger Carlson, a Danish engineer working with the Resistance receives a head wound while battling the Nazis on a beach. He awakes in a parallel universe where the forces of Law and Chaos rage in a mythic medieval world of knights, dragons, faeries, trolls, giants and werewolves. In this reality Holger is the Champion of Law. A knight with a mission to defeat Chaos whose outcome will also effect the world where Nazi Germany also threatens to spread chaos.

"**Three Wise Men of Space**" [Pulp fiction; SFW]
Author: Donald Bern; Illustrator: Julian Krupa; First publication: *Amazing Stories* (Vol. 14 #12; Decem-

ber 1940); Publisher: Ziff-Davis Publishing Company.

"Three voyagers from deep in space come to Earth, seeking a place to live—and land amid a hell of Nazi dive bombers!"

"The Throne of Valhalla" [Pulp fiction; MWW]

Author: Arthur T. Harris; Illustrator: Jay Jackson; First publication: *Amazing Stories* (Vol. 15 #9; September 1941); Publisher: Ziff-Davis Publishing Company.

"It was a gentleman's fight—between Nazi leader and Tommy ace. But they didn't expect to fight in Valhalla."

"The Tiger Has a Soul!" [Pulp fiction; WW]

Author: Lester Barclay; Illustrator: Ronald Clyne; First publication: *Fantastic Adventures* (Vol. 7 #3; July 1945); Publisher: Ziff-Davis Publishing Company.

Scotty and Mace Morris have been called to protect Rangoon, Burma with two squadrons out of Mingaladon Airdrome. Mace finds it impossible to shake a Japanese plane on his tail. "It was a model he had never seen before.... Also it's markings were different. Where the others had the usual Rising Sun insignia, this plane was unmarked except for a large black dragon painted on its fuselage."

Although Mace is the leading ace pilot with fourteen planes brought down that one plane remains elusive. Soon that will change when the pilot, Baron Hokadi leaves a note in a bottle challenging Mace to "mortal combat" at dawn. The combat proceeds with Mace believing he's the victor, until, to his astonishment, Hokadi returns to do battle again. Mace is defiant.

"This is it! And this time there'll be no escape; I'll make sure of that."

Their planes become locked in flight and crash to the earth as the two pilots escape unhurt. Now they engage in hand-to hand combat before Mace loses consciousness. When he awakens Hokadi has disappeared, but the body of a tiger lies at his feet. Walking along the river's edge Mace comes across the partly decomposed body of Baron Hokadi.

"A Japanese aviator had flown a plane and dealt out death in the skies ... and had done so while his body lay dead and rotting, in a jungle clearing! And now a tiger lay dead a few yards back in the jungle, the mark of human fingers deep in the fur of its throat ... a tiger, where there should have been a man!"

Till the End of Time [Novel; SFW]

Authors: Allen Appell, Irving Freeman; First publication: New York: Doubleday, 1990.

History professor Alex Balfour can travel back and forth in time. This time he's back in World War II where he travels from Pearl Harbor to the Pacific Islands to report back to Franklin Roosevelt on the latest Japanese atomic research. Along the way he meets Albert Einstein and helps Lieutenant John F. Kennedy and his crew survive the sinking of PT 109. Meanwhile Balfour's girlfriend is Molly Glenn is working a *New York Times* article about Japanese germ warfare performed on American POW's.

Time and Time Again [Novel; SFW]

Author: Ben Elton; First publication: New York: St. Martin's Press, 2015.

Hugh Stanton knows the future because he has already lived it. Now he is in June 1914 and knows the Great War is coming. He also knows he must change history and prevent World War I with a single bullet.

Time Bomb [Graphic Novel; SFW]

First publication: March 2011; Story-Creators: Jimmy Palmiotti, Justin Gray; Art: Paul Gulacy; Publisher: Radical Publishing.

When a group of scientists and archeologists uncover a hidden city beneath the streets of Berlin they accidentally activate a doomsday weapon designed by Adolf Hitler during World War II. To stop the Omega bomb from destroying humanity the scientists must travel 24 hours back in time to deactivate the bomb. But instead of traveling one day back in time they travel 65 years when Hitler is still ruling over his Nazi regime.

Time to Go Back [Juvenile book; SFW]

Author: Mabel Esther Allan; First publication: London: Abelard-Schuman; New York: Criterion Books, 1972.

Rebellious 16-year-old Sarah Farrant returns to Wallasey in the north of England to stay with her grandmother. One day, while walking home Sarah is suddenly transported through time to 1941, where she meets her teenage mother and younger grandmother. Meanwhile her attraction to a boy pulls her loyalties between past and present. She comes away from her experience with a greater appreciation of the past and the struggles her family had to endure during World War II.

Time Riders [Juvenile book; SFW]
Author: Alex Scarrow; First publication: New York: Walker & Co., 2010.

Three teenagers are saved from death in different time eras. Sixteen-year-old Liam O'Connor from death on the Titanic in April 1912. Eighteen-year-old Maddy Carter from death in a plane crash in 2010 and 13-year-old Saleena Vikram from death in a fire in 2026.

They become agents for the Time Rider team who combat any attempt to change history. When someone attempts to alter the outcome of World War II the team must find those responsible by going back to Nazi Germany.

This novel aimed at senior high school readers is the first in the *Time Rider* series.

Time Riders: The Eternal War [Juvenile book; SFW]
Author: Alex Scarrow; First publication: New York: Walker Books, 2013.

When Abraham Lincoln follows Time Rider Liam O'Connor into the present day American history is changed. If the team fail to return Lincoln to his own time America could end up in a permanent state of Civil War.

Time Train to the Blitz [Juvenile book; SFW]
Author: Sophie McKenzie; First publication: London: Usborne, 2010.

Scarlett, Joe and Pippy the dog travel back in time to wartime London in the 1940s, on a ghost train. They have one hour to save the life of youngster Alfie Suggs, who was killed while trying to rescue his grandmother during the Blitz. But the trio find themselves trapped in the grandmother's house with an unexploded bomb and an injured Alfie. The success of their mission hangs in the balance.

The Time Tunnel (1966) [TV series]
Main Cast: James Darren as Dr. Tony Newman, Robert Colbert as Dr. Doug Phillips, Whit Bissell as Lt. General Heywood Kirk, Lee Meriwether as Dr. Ann MacGregor, John Zaremba as Dr. Raymond Swain; Creator-Executive Producer: Irwin Allen; 30 × 50 min.; Irwin Allen Productions, Kent Productions, 20th Century-Fox Television; American Broadcasting System (ABC); Color.

1. Scientists Tony Newman and Doug Philips have been working on the top secret "Project Tic-Toc" for ten years. An impatient senator threatens to cut their funding if he cannot see the "Time Tunnel" in action. Tony Newman accepts the challenge and enters the tunnel, traveling back in time to 1912 on board the S.S. Titanic. When Doug Philips joins him they both become trapped in "the endless corridor of time" and are thrown from one time period to another. Back at the HQ scientists remain in visual communication with the trapped time travelers whilst attempting to repair the time tunnel.

"THE ALAMO" (1:13) [SFW]
Air date: December 9, 1966; Guest Cast: Rhodes Reason as Col. William Barrett Travis, John Lupton as Capt. Reynerson, Elizabeth Rogers as Mrs. Reynerson, Jim Davis as Colonel Jim Bowie, Edward Colmans as Dr. Armandez, Alberto Monte as Sgt. Garcia, Rodolfo Hoyos as Capt. Rodriguez; Story" Bob and Wanda Duncan; Director: Sobey Martin.

March 1836 on the eve of the Battle of Alamo, Doug and Tony are captured and imprisoned as spies by Colonel Travis after he fails to heed their warnings about the battle ahead.

"THE DAY THE SKY FELL IN" (1:04) [SFW]
Air date: September 30, 1966; Guest Cast: Linden Chiles as Tony Newman, Sr., Sam Groom as Jerry, Lew Gallo as Lt. Anderson, Robert Riordan as Admiral Brandt, Caroline Kido as Yuko, Susan Flannery as Louise Neal, Sheldon Golomb as Tony Newman, Jr. (child); Story: Ellis St. Joseph; Director: William Hale.

When Tony Newman and Doug Phillips time travel to Pearl Harbor the day before the Japanese attack Tony tries to warn his father in the hope of saving his life. Meanwhile Jerry, a Time Tunnel technician plans to prevent Pearl Harbor by sending present day military planes and aircraft carriers back to 1941.

"THE DEATH MERCHANT" (1:25) [SFW]
Air date: March 3, 1967; Guest Cast: Malachi Throne as Niccolo Machiavelli/Michaels, John Crawford as Major, Kevin Hagen as Sgt. Maddox, Kevin O'Neal as Corporal Perkins; Story: Bob and Wanda Duncan; Director: Nathan Juran.

Machiavelli attempts to change the outcome of the Battle of Gettysburg after traveling in time from the Renaissance. Doug and Tony must stop him despite finding themselves on opposite sides in the American Civil War battle.

"THE GHOST OF NERO" (1:19) [WW]
Air date: January 20, 1967; Guest Cast: Nino Candido as Benito Mussolini, Eduardo Ciannelli as Count Enrico Galba, Gunnar Hellstrom as Major Neistadt, John Hoyt as Dr. Steinholz, Richard Jaeckel as Sgt. Mueller; Story: Leonard Stadd; Director: Sobey Martin.

While seeking shelter from the bombing of an Italian villa during World War I Doug and Tony encounter the ghost of Roman Emperor Nero. The ghost is seeking revenge on Count Enrico Galba, the owner of the villa and a descendant of one of Nero's enemies.

"INVASION" (1:15) [SFW]
Air date: December 23, 1966; Guest Cast: Lyle Bettger as Major Hoffman, Robert Carricart as Mirabeau, John Wengraf as Dr. Hans Kleinemann, Michael St. Clair as Duchamps, Joey Tata as Verlaine, Francis De Sales as Dr. Shumate; Story: Bob and Wanda Duncan; Director: Sobey Martin.

Doug is brainwashed by Gestapo Dr. Hans Kleinemann and ordered to kill Tony Newman, two days before D-Day, June 4, 1944.

"KILL TWO BY TWO" (1:17) [SFW]
Air date: January 6, 1967; Guest Cast: Mako as Lt. Nakamura, Kam Tong as Sgt. Itsugi, Philip Ahn as Dr. Nakamura, Vince Howard as Medic; Story: Bob and Wanda Duncan; Director: Herschel Daugherty.

Doug and Tony become the prey of Japanese Lieutenant Nakamura on a Pacific island on the eve of the attack of Iwo-Jima.

"THE LAST PATROL" (1:05) [SFW]
Air date: October 7, 1966; Guest Cast: Carroll O'Connor as General/Colonel Southall, Michael Pate as Capt. Hotchkiss, John Napier as Capt. Jenkins, David Watson as Lt. Rynerson; Story: Bob and Wanda Duncan: Director: Sobey Martin.

The War of 1812. Doug and Tony arrive in New Orleans on the eve of a decisive battle in 1815 and are captured by Colonel "The Butcher" Southall of the British Seventh Royal Regiment. Charged as spies they are sentenced to be executed by firing squad.

"MASSACRE" (1:08) [SFW]
Air date: October 28, 1966; Guest Cast: Joe Marcos as General George Armstrong Custer, Christopher Dark as Crazy Horse, Paul Comi as Capt. Frederick Benteen, George Mitchell as Sitting Bull, Lawrence Montaigne as Yellow Elk, Bruce Mars as Tom Custer, Perry Lopez as Dr. Charles Whitebird, Jim Halferty as Trooper Tim McGinnis; Story: Carey Wilber; Director: Murray Golden.

Doug and Tony are transported to Montana in 1876 during the Great Sioux Wars. It is the eve of the Battle of the Little Bighorn and the massacre of General Custer and his 7th Cavalry Regiment.

"RAIDERS FROM OUTER SPACE" (1:29) [SFW]
Air date: March 31, 1967; Guest Cast: John Crawford as Henderson, Kevin Hagen as Alien leader Prince; Story: Bob and Wanda Duncan; Director: Nathan Juran.

On the eve of the Battle of Khartoum in November 1883, Doug and Tony discover a planned invasion by extraterrestrials that also includes an attack on the Time Tunnel headquarters.

"REVENGE OF THE GODS" (1:07) [SFW]
Air date: October 21, 1966; Guest Cast: John Doucette as Ulysses, Dee Hartford as Helen of Troy, Paul Carr as Paris, Joseph Ruskin as Sardis, Abraham Sofaer as Epeios; Story: Allan Balter, William Read Woodfield; Directors: Nathan Juran, Sobey Martin.

Doug and Tony are mistaken for gods when they land in the middle of the Trojan War. Tony plans to enter Troy in the Trojan Horse and rescue the captive Doug and Helen of Troy.

2. [Comic book]

"THE CONQUERORS" [SFW]
First publication: *The Time Tunnel* #2 (July 1967); Story: Paul S. Newman; Art: Tom Gill; Publisher: Gold Key/Western Publishing.

"D-Day 1944. The Nazis get a second chance — this time with weapons from the future!"

Timecop 2: The Berlin Decision (2003) [Film; SFW]

Premiere: September 30, 2003; Main Cast: Jason Scott Lee as Ryan Chan, Thomas Ian Griffith as Brandon Miller, Mary Page Keller as Doc, John Beck as O'Rourke, Tava Smiley as Tyler Jeffers, Tricia Barry as Sasha Miller; Executive Producer: Christopher Taylor; Story: Gary Scott Thompson; Director: Stephen Boyum; 78 min.; Capital Arts Entertainment, TE Encore Films; Universal Home Entertainment Productions; Color.

Time Enforcement Commission Agency (TEC) agent Ryan Chan is tracking a time criminal in World War II Germany when fellow time cop Brandon Miller becomes obsessed with the idea of killing Adolf Hitler. Knowing the consequences of changing time Chan stops Miller but in the process Miller's wife Sasha dies. Miller now wants revenge and vows to erase Chan's ancestors thus ensuring the death of present day Ryan Chan.

Timeless (2016) [TV series]
Main Cast; Abigail Spencer as Lucy Preston, Goran Visnjic as Garcia Flynn, Matt Lanter as Wyatt Logan, Malcolm Barrett as Rufus Carlin, Sakina Jaffrey as Agent Denise Christopher; Creators: Shawn Ryan, Eric Kripke; Executive Producers: John Davis, John Fox, Marney Hochman, Eric Kripke, Neil Marshall, Shawn Ryan; 45 min; Davis Entertainment, Kripke Enterprises, MiddKid Productions, Universal Television, Sony Pictures Television; National Broadcasting Company (NBC); Color.

"The Alamo" (1:05) [SFW]
Air date: October 31, 2016; Guest Cast: David Chisum as William Barret Travis, Alex Fernandez as General Antonio Lopez de Santa Anna, Chris Browning as Jim Bowie, Jeff Kober as Davy Crockett, Susanna Thompson as Carol Preston, Hector Hugo as Patrick Ramsey; Story: Anne Cofell Saunders; Director: John Terlesky.

The team finds themselves trapped inside the fort at the Alamo in March 1836, surrounded by Mexican soldiers.

"The Assassination of Abraham Lincoln" (1:02) [SFW]
Air date: October 10, 2016; Guest Cast: Neal Blesdoe as Robert Todd Lincoln, Kelly Blatz as John Wilkes Booth, Michael Krebs as President Abraham Lincoln, Mike Wade as Nicholas Biddle; Story: Tom Smuts; Director: Neil Marshall.

After Garcia Flynn is seen kidnapping the time team's project leader Anthony Bruhl, the team follows them into the past where they are greeted with fireworks celebrating the end of the Civil War. It is April 14, 1865, the night of President Lincoln's assassination. Lucy Preston, posing as actress Juliet Shakesman, forms a friendship with President Lincoln's son, Robert Todd Lincoln who invites her to Ford's Theatre. Meanwhile she fears Flynn is planning to kill Vice President Johnson, Secretary of State Stewart and General Grant to cripple the Union and revive the Confederacy. Lucy comments, "America as we know it would be unrecognizable." But Flynn claims he is trying to save America.

"Party at Castle Varlar" (1:04) [SFW]
Air date: October 24, 2016; Guest Cast: Sean Maguire as Ian Fleming, Christian Oliver as Werner Von Braun, Matt Frewer as Anthony Bruhl; Story: Jim Barnes; Director: Billy Gierhart.

The team travel to Nazi Germany, December 9, 1944, to stop Garcia Flynn from abducting Werner Von Braun and changing the course of the American space program.

They are aided in their efforts by future James Bond author Ian Fleming, who is working for the Allied Resistance, posing as a Nazi.

"Pilot" (1:01) [SFW]
Air date: October 3, 2016; Guest Cast: Bailey Noble as Amy Preston, Shantel VanSanten as Kate Drummond, Susanna Thompson as Carol Preston, Kurt Max Runte as Commander Rosendahl, Noel Johansen as Captain Max Pruss; Story: Eric Kripke, Shawn Ryan; Director: Neil Marshall.

Fugitive Garcia Flynn steals a state-of-the-art time machine, with the purpose of changing history and destroying America in the process. Scientist Rufus Carlin, soldier Wyatt Logan and history professor Lucy Preston use the time machine's prototype to track Flynn to 1937 and the Hindenburg disaster. But they discover avoiding the disaster would change history, the outcome of World War II and result in Lucy Preston's sister never being born.

Timeline (2003) [Film; SFW]
Premiere: November 26, 2003; Main Cast: Paul Walker as Chris Johnston, Billy Connolly as Professor Johnston, Frances O'Connor as Kate Ericson, Gerard Butler as Andre Marek, David Thewliss as Robert Doniger, Anna Friel as Lady Claire, Neal McDonough as Frank Gordon, Lambert Wilson as Lord Arnault; Executive producers: Don Granger, Gary Levinsohn, Michael Ovitz; Screenplay: Jeff Maguire, George Nolfi; Based on the novel by Michael Crichton; Director: Richard Donner; 116 min.; Paramount Pictures; Color.

Chris Johnston is puzzled after finding a modern-day bifocal lens along with a message from his father Professor Johnston with the date 1357 and the location Castlegard, France. On a visit to International Technology Corp. (ITC) in New Mexico Chris and his companions are told about experimentations in time travel via a wormhole. To rescue his father Chris and his companions must travel through time to France in 1357 and the Hundred Years War. But in the process they may affect the course of history.

"Tink Fights the Gremlins" [Pulp fiction; WW]
Author: William P. McGivern; First publication: *Fantastic Adventures* (Vol. 5 #9; October 1943); Publisher: Ziff-Davis Publishing Company.

When the campaign in Africa is menaced by

gremlins, Irish leprechauns Tink and Nastee and beautiful elfin sprite Jing step in to stop the gremlins from fighting on the wrong side.

"Tink Takes Command" [Pulp fiction; WW]

Author: William P. McGivern; First publication: *Fantastic Adventures* (Vol. 4 #2; August 1942); Publisher: Ziff-Davis Publishing Company.

"American soldiers were in Ireland, homesick and unhappy. Tink and Jing, little leprechaun fairy creatures, decided to do something to cheer them up. But Nastee threw a monkey wrench into things."

Tom Strong [Comic book character; SHW]

The physical and mental perfection of Tom Strong has been aided by his upbringing on the island of Attabar Teru where the natives gave him a root that also drastically reduced his natural aging process. Born at the start of the 20th century Tom Strong is still alive and vigorously active in the 21st century.

"SWASTIKA GIRLS" [SFW]

First publication: *Tom Strong #4*; Story: Alan Moore; Art: Art Adams, Chris Sprouse; Publisher: America's Best Comics.

In the last days of World War II in Berlin, Germany Tom Strong finds himself captive of the Nazi superwoman Heidi Weiss.

Tomahawk [Comic book; WW]

First appearance: *Star-Spangled Comics* #69 (June 1947); Creators: Joe Samachson, Edmund Good; Publisher: National Periodical Publications-DC Comics.

Indian-raised white man Tom Hawk works as a frontier scout in the American Revolutionary War with young sidekick Dan Hunter. He was promoted to his own title in September–October 1950. The stories took on a weird quality from the late 1950s until the late 1960s when *Tomahawk* encountered "The Valley of the Giant Warriors" (#46–February 1957), "The Lost Tribe of Tiny Warriors" (#54–February 1958), "The Frontier Dinosaur" (#58–September–October 1958), "King Cobweb and His Killer Insects" (#99–July–August 1965), "Frontier Frankenstein" (#103–March–April 1966) plus various aliens, sorcerers, cavemen, golden warriors, giant gorillas and giant robots. Tomahawk even briefly gained super-strength and invulnerability when an Indian potion transformed him into "The Frontier Superman" (#68–May–June 1960).

In the time-traveling story "The Coward Who Lived Forever" (#120–January–February 1969) Tomahawk travels forward in time where he discovers the ancestors of a new spineless Ranger have all been cowards in the major wars. From the Civil War battlefield of Gettysburg to World Wars I and II.

Tomorrow I'll Wake Up and Scald Myself with Tea (1977) [Film; Czechoslovakia; SFW]

Premiere: August 1, 1977; Main Cast: Petr Kostka as Jan Bures/Karel Bures, Jiri Ovak as Klaus Abard, Vladimir Mensik as Rolf Kraus, Marie Rosulkova as Shirley White, Otto Simanek as Patrick White, Valerie Chmelova as Helena; Producer: Jan Suster; Screenplay: Milos Macourek, Jindrich Polak; Story: Josef Nesvadba; Director: Jindrich Polak; 93 min.; Filmove Studio Barrandov; Color.

A plot to travel back in time to Germany in 1944 to give Hitler an hydrogen boom backfires when the time traveling pilot dies. The pilot's twin brother takes his place but proves to be incompetent when he loses the bomb and lands back in time in 1941.

The Tomorrow People (1973) [TV series; UK]

Main Cast: Nicholas Young as John, Misako Koba as Hsui Tai, Michael Holloway as Mike, Philip Gilbert as the voice of Tim the computer; Creator: Roger Price; 68 × 25 min.; Thames Television, ITV; Color.

A group of teenagers known as the Tomorrow People, have powers of telepathy, telekinesis and teleportation a.k.a. jaunting.

"HITLER'S LAST STAND: MEN LIKE RATS" (6:03) [SFW]; "HITLER'S LAST STAND: SEEDS OF DESTRUCTION" (6:04) [SFW]

Air dates: June 5–12, 1978; Guest Cast: Michael Sheard as Hitler, Richard Warner as Professor Friedl, Nicholas Lyndhurst as Karl Brandt, Earl Rhodes as Will Frisch, Ray Burdis as Blitz, Leon Eagles as Major Hughes, Charles Skinner as Wolfgang Crass; Producer: Vic Hughes; Story: Roger Price; Director: Leon Thau; 25 min.; Thames Television; Color.

In this two-part story a teenage boy in a S.S. uniform dies after being run over in present day Germany. *The Tomorrow People* link the teenage boy with Hitler's wartime experiments in cryonic suspension after they see the boy in film footage from 1944.

Now Adolf Hitler has been revived from cryonic suspension and plans to brainwash today's youth. But in a twist to the tale the Tomorrow People discover Hitler is a shape-shifting extraterrestrial after they raid his bunker.

Torchwood (2006) [TV series; UK-Canada]

The Torchwood Institute and its members protect Earth from alien threats from their secret base in Cardiff, Wales.

"Captain Jack Harkness" (1:12) [SFW]

Air date: January 1, 2007; Main Cast: John Barrowman as Capt. Jack Harkness, Eve Myles as Gwen Cooper, Burn Gorman as Owen Harper, Naoko Mori as Toshiko Sato, Gareth David-Lloyd as Ianto Jones, Matt Rippy as The Captain, Murray Melvin as Bilis Manger; Executive Producer: Julie Gardner; Story: Catherine Tregenna; Director: Ashley Way; 50 min.; BBC Wales, Canadian Broadcasting Corporation (CBC); Color.

While investigating music coming from an abandoned music hall Jack Harkness and Toshiko Sato become stranded in 1941. Events take an even weirder turn when Harkness meets his namesake, an American RAF pilot.

In the present Gwen Cooper, Ianto Jones and Owen Harper must rescue Harkness and Toshiko from the past.

Touched by an Angel (1994) [TV series]

Main Cast: Roma Downey as Monica, Della Reese as Tess, John Dye as Andrew, Valerie Bertinelli as Gloria; Creator: John Masius; Executive producer: Martha Williamson; 211 × 45 min.; CBS Productions, Caroline Productions, Moon Water Productions; Columbia Broadcasting System (CBS); Color.

Heavenly angel Monica and her supervisor Tess provide guidance, support and hope for troubled souls on earth.

"The Compass" (6:02) [WW]

Air date: October 3, 1999; Guest Cast: Christian Leffler as Pvt. Joe Faraday, Steve Martini as Nick, Esteban Powell as Homer, Matthew Glave as Sgt. Walker, Amy Locane as Stella, Andrew Kavovitas as Eddie Rourke; Story: Martha Williamson, Glenn Berenbeim; Director: Peter H. Hunt.

Monica is assigned Private Joe Faraday, one month after D-Day in July 1944. Her job is to help Faraday become a hero by retrieving the final letters of his fallen comrades and composing his own, before his death.

"Dear God" (2:19) [WW]

Air date: March 9, 1996; Guest Cast: Elliot Gould as Max, Kelsey Mulrooney as Tanya Brenner, Willie Garson as Eddie Brenner, Mel Winkler as Pete, Patricia Belcher as Miss Raphael; Story: Glenn Berenbeim; Director: Tim Van Batten.

Holocaust survivor Max has lost his personal faith in God, but his duties at the Post Office include answering letters addressed to God. Monica helps Max restore his faith through a child who has lost his father.

"God And Country" (4:19) [WW]

Air date: March 15, 1998; Guest Cast: Edward James Olmos as Colonel Victor Wallis, Alexis Cruz as Rafael, Vincent Loresca as Tomas Parades, Rose Portillo as Maria Parades, Michael Cudlitz as Chug Landau; Story: R. J. Colleary, Glenn Berenbeim; Director: Bethany Rooney.

A base commander takes out his personal problems on his troops and his remaining son when his favorite son is declared Missing-In-Action. The angels pose as military recruits to help ease the tension between the commander and his surviving son.

"Here I Am" (6:17) [WW]

Air date: February 27, 2000; Guest Cast: Edward Asner as Bud, Giancarlo Esposito as Antonio Gaudi, April Grace as Constance, Robert Bailey, Jr., as Morgan; Story: Ken Lazebnik; Director: Joel J. Feigenbaum.

Vietnam veteran Bud is on his final day as security guard at a New York art museum. Haunted by a painting of a little girl holding flowers, Monica helps him resolve his personal conflict that harks back to a tragedy in Vietnam.

"Made in the U.S.A." (5:21) [WW]

Air date: April 11, 1999; Guest Cast: Eric Roberts as Nick Stratton, Jennifer Paz as Am-Nhac Nguyen, Toshi Toda as Cadao Nguyen, Kiev Chinh as Lang, John Colella as Del, Joshua Keaton as Young Nick; Story: Christine Pettit, Rosanne Welch; Director: Bethany Rooney.

Vietnam veteran and owner of Stratton Apparel, Nick Stratton, fires his underpaid and abused Vietnam refugee staff when he experiences tax problems. Feeling trapped by his situation Stratton decides to blow up his factory—until Monica appears to put him on the right path.

"Missing in Action" (3:23) [WW]

Air date: April 13, 1997; Guest Cast: Darren McGavin as George Zarko, Gwen Verdon as Lorraine

McCully, Christina Pickles as Stephanie Hancock; Story: Rosanne Welch, Christine Pettit; Director: Tim Van Patten.

World War II and Korean War veteran George Zarko has grown into a cynical old man. Monica is assigned to lift his spirits and transform his personality by joining him, disguised as an elderly woman, in his retirement home. But things get complicated when George falls for Monica.

"**The Traitor**" [Pulp fiction; WW]
Author: Arthur T. Harris; First publication: *Fantastic Adventures* (Vol. 4 #7; July 1942); Publisher: Ziff-Davis Publishing Company.

When a Nazi invites a Field Marshal to travel into the future to see the fate of Germany the Field Marshal becomes resigned to the futility of the war. The Nazi knows his actions have sowed the seeds of defeat through the Fatherland and sacrifices his life over the English Channel. A lone Luftwaffe pilot offering no resistance.

"**Trophy**" [Pulp fiction; SFW]
Author: Scott Morgan; First publication: *Thrilling Wonder Stories* (Vol. 25 #2; Winter 1942); Publisher: Standard Magazines, Inc.

Sadistic Japanese surgeon Major Satura captures a U.S. soldier after his plane crashes on a Pacific island. Satura notes the American plane had been followed by "an aircraft of some strange type—it resembled a stubby torpedo. It roared down over the island like a bellowing thunderbolt, raising a hurricane of blasting wind that caught the heeling Yank plane and cracked it up in the surf, a crumpled, hopeless wreck."

On the jungle trail Satura and the captured American come across a pile of English gold sovereigns that suddenly vanishes, to be replaced by "a girl, tall, slim, with a form like Aphrodite of the Shell, her whole body a symphony of smooth flowing lines that were graceful and attractive almost beyond earthly allure. But her eyes were not human."

The beautiful apparition from another world was their introduction to the Hunter and his trophies.

"**Trouble in Avalon**" [Pulp fiction; SFW]
Author: Russell Storm; Illustrator: Julian Krupa; First publication: *Fantastic Adventures* (Vol. 2 #6; June 1940); Publisher: Ziff-Davis Publishing Company.

"There ain't no such thing as a ghost," roared Sergeant Buttle. But when he led his patrol into No Man's Land that night things happened. Ghostly knights went down in heaps beneath the ruthless Nazi fire."

Private John Spaulding and Leo Terry are about to enter Avalon where they will meet King Arthur and Merlin.

Troy [Juvenile book; MWW]
Author: Adele Garas; First publication: San Diego: Harcourt, 2001.

The final weeks of the Trojan War are told from the perspective of the Trojan women, when the gods and goddesses are still finding ways to create more conflict and trouble.

"**Truk Island**" [Pulp fiction; WW]
Author: Berkeley Livingston; Illustrator: Robert Fuqua; First publication: *Amazing Stories* (Vol. 18 #5; December 1944); Publisher: Ziff-Davis Publishing Company.

"Long before Pearl Harbor, the Japs held Truk—but they didn't know what lay beneath their fortified island—in Lemuris."

Tuman (2010) [TV mini-series; Russia; SFW]
Air date: May 9, 2010 (Russia); Main Cast: Artur Enikeev as Podpolkovnik Aksyuta, Anastasiya Bezborodova as Katya, Aleksey Markov as Rybak, Ilya Glinnikov as Babnik, Rodion Galyuchenko as Mukha, Ivan Lapin as Mikhnovets; Producers: Rezo Gigineishvili, Vyacheslav Murugov; Story: Leonid Kuprido; Directors: Ivan Shurkhovetskiy, Artem Aksenenko; VVP-Alyans; Color.

Young Russian soldiers in the present day experience the reality of war when they emerge from a strange fog into the heat of battle in World War II.

TV Action [Comic book; UK]
The weekly UK comic book from Polystyle Publications featured a ***Doctor Who*** comic strip. A few included Weird War adventures featuring the third Doctor.

"THE GLEN OF SLEEPING"
First publication: *TV Action* #107–111 (March 3–March 31, 1973); Story: Dick O'Neill; Art: Gerry Haylock.

Red Angus and his Scottish clansmen are summoned from their centuries-long sleep by the Master, who plans to capture a nuclear submarine. But the Doctor has discovered their sleep was the result of an alien time-trap device and now he sends himself, the Master and the clansmen back to 1745. But the Doctor finds himself the target of British Redcoats.

"Who Is the Stranger?"
First publication: *TV Action* #104 (February 10, 1973); Story: Dennis Hopper; Art: Gerry Haylock.

The Doctor is captured by the Gestapo on Nazi occupied Paris. Professor Schmidt's plans to test a truth serum drug on the Doctor are foiled when the Doctor forces him to take it. He learns there is a Nazi spy among the Reynard Resistance Group, but first he must earn their trust.

TV Comic [Comic book; UK]

The long-running weekly UK comic book from Polystyle Publications featured a **Doctor Who** comic strip from 1964–1970 and 1973–1979.

"The Amateur"
First publication: *TV Comic* # 1148–1154 (December 15, 1973–January 26, 1974); Art: Gerry Haylock.

The third Doctor lands on the battlefield during World War I. His companions include scientist Tobias Philby who escaped his castle after villagers, believing his work to be that of the Devil, set fire to the castle. But now the Doctor, Philby and his servant find themselves prisoners of the Germans, accused of being British spies. Escaping their captors only leads to further trouble as the British believe they are German spies and don't take the threat of an imminent attack by German forces seriously.

"Treasure Trail"
First publication: *TV Comic* #1266–1272 (March 20, 1976–May 1, 1976).

The fourth Doctor and his companion Sarah are sent by the Time Lords to Borosini, Italy in 1944. Hermann Göring's Nazis are searching the village church for art treasures. To keep the art safe the Time Lords send the art treasures, the Doctor and Sarah to 1948, after the Nazis lost World War II.

Twelve [Novel; WW]

Author: Jasper Kent; First publication: Amherst NY: Pyr, 2010.

Russian Captain Aleski Ivanovich Danilov is facing defeat by the Grand Army of Napoleon Bonaparte in the autumn of 1812. At a tavern in Moscow a Russian officer named Dimitry tells Captain Danilov he has enlisted the aid of the Oprichniki. Twelve mercenaries who claim they can defeat Napoleon also have a deadly secret. They are vampires who feed on the French and Russians alike.

See: *The Third Section*

The Twelve: Spearhead [Comic book; SFW]

First publication: March 2010; Story: Chris Weston; Art: Chris Weston, Gary Erskine; Publisher: Marvel Comics.

In the final days of World War II the Phantom Reporter wants to join **Captain America** as he leads a mission to destroy the Nazi missile program.

The 25th Reich (2012) [Film; Australia; SFW]

Premiere: May 10, 2012; Main Cast: Jim Knobeloch as Cpt. Donald O'Brian, Serge De Nardo as Sgt. Carl Weaver, Angelo Salamanca as Roberto Barelli; Executive Producers: Stephen Amis, Mark Kimonides, Stevie Kimonides; Screenplay: Stephen Amis, Serge De Nardo, David Richardson. Based on the novella "50,000 Years Until Tomorrow" by J.J. Solomon; 85 min.; Revolution Pictures, KikGroup, Acme Film Co.; Moonstar Studios; Color.

A time travel story featuring a team of U.S. soldiers from 1943 selected by the O.S.S. to stop Hitler's despotic 25th Reich from reigning in the future.

Twice Upon a Time [Novel; AHW]

Author: Allen Appel; First publication: New York: Carroll & Graf, 1988.

Historian Alex Balfour has a unique genetic condition that allows him to travel back in time. At the Philadelphia Exposition of 1876 Balfour meets Mark Twain. Releasing two captured American Indians from the exhibit, Balfour, Twain, the Indians and an emancipated black slave travel West. Meanwhile, in the present day, Balfour's girlfriend, New York Times reporter Molly Glenn, is kidnapped by a young Sioux who believes he is a descendant of Crazy Horse. Past and present converge as Balfour arrives at the Little Big Horn, site of the Indian massacre of Custer's 7th Cavalry, in the hope of changing history.

The Twilight Zone (1959) [TV Series]

1. Science fiction anthology series hosted by Rod Serling. Seasons 1–3, 5 (25 minutes), Season 4 (50

minutes); Cayuga Productions; CBS Television; B/W.

"Deaths-Head Revisited" (3:09)

First broadcast: November 10, 1961; Main Cast: Joseph Schildkraut as Becker, Oscar Beregi as S.S. Capt. Lutze, Chuck Fox as Dachau victim, Ben Wright as Doctor, Karen Verne as Innkeeper; Producer: Buck Houghton: Story: Rod Serling; Director: Don Medford.

Former S.S. Captain Gunther Lutze who now calls himself Mr. Schmidt revisits the concentration at Dachau in Bavaria. But his feelings of nostalgia are soon replaced with horror when he is forced to experience the pain he cruelly inflicted on the inmates during World War II.

A powerful episode that doesn't flinch from the grim details of Dachau. Becker, the caretaker of Dachau who is the ghost of an inmate tells Capt. Lutze, "You burned them in furnaces. You shoveled them into the earth. You tore up their bodies in rage. And now you come back to your scenes of horror, and you wonder that the misery that you planted has lived after you."

Rod Serling's closing monologue is a moving account of the need to preserve the past, lest we forget the inhumanity of man.

"And the moment we forget this, the moment we cease to be haunted by its remembrance, then we become the gravediggers."

"The Encounter" (5:31)

First broadcast: May 1, 1964; Main Cast: Neville Brand as Fenton, George Takei as Taro-Arthur; Producer: William Froug: Story: Martin M. Goldsmith; Director: Robert Butler.

Cleaning his attic veteran Fenton comes across a samurai sword he saved as a souvenir from World War II. But when a Japanese American he's invited to join him in his attic picks up the sword he feels compelled to kill Fenton. Both men have been hiding secrets about their pasts. Fenton killed a Japanese soldier with the sword after he surrendered and Japanese American Taro's father was a traitor at Pearl Harbor. Now their guilt will be wiped clean with two final acts of redemption.

"He's Alive" (4:04)

First broadcast: January 24, 1963; Main Cast: Dennis Hopper as Peter Vollmer, Ludwig Donath as Ernerst Ganz, Curt Conway as Adolf Hitler; Producer: Herbert Hirschman; Story: Rod Serling; Director: Stuart Rosenberg.

The ghost of Adolf Hitler acts as mentor to American neo–Nazi Peter Vollmer as he preaches his ideology of hate, bigotry and intolerance.

Hitler tells Vollmer, "How do you move a mob? When you speak to them, speak as though you are a member of the mob. Speak to them in their language. Make their hate your hate."

Vollmer's descent into self destruction begins when Hitler orders him to kill his Jewish friend Gantz to create a martyr. To blame his death on agitators and spread hatred and the desire for revenge among the mob.

"The Howling Man" (2:05)

First broadcast: November 4, 1960; Main Cast: H.M. Wynant as David Ellington, John Carradine as Brother Jerome, Robin Hughes as Howling Man, Frederic Ledebur as Brother Christophorus, Ezelle Poule as Housekeeper; Producer: Buck Houghton; Story: Charles Beaumont; Director: Douglas Heyes.

On a walking trip through Europe, in the days following the Great War, an American named David Ellington is lost in a storm and seeks refuge in a hermitage. Brother Jerome tells him to leave, but Ellington is intrigued by a howling noise and a prisoner being held in the castle. "It is the devil himself," warns Jerome, but Ellington thinks the old man is mad and releases the prisoner.

Ellington should have believed Jerome for now the devil is let loose once again. Ellington becomes obsessed with capturing him, but it is only after the horrors of World War II, the Korean War and nuclear weapons that he succeeds. Locked in a cell Ellington tells his maid never to release him. But the temptation proves too great for her and the devil is let loose once again.

"In Praise of Pip" (5:01)

First broadcast: September 27, 1963; Main Cast: Jack Klugman as Max Phillips, Billy Mumy as young Pip, Bob Diamond as Pvt. Pip Phillips; Producer: Bert Granet; Story: Rod Serling: Director: Joseph M. Newman.

Private Pip Phillips is dying of multiple shrapnel wounds in Vietnam. His father Max, a heavy drinking bookie, learns of his son's condition by phone before being stabbed in an altercation over money. With his life unraveling before him Max sees his son at the local amusement park. Pip is 10-years-old again with a youngster's enthusiasm for the attractions of the amusement park and the love of his father. Max is realizing the importance of love too late in life and asks God to exchange his life for his son Pip's.

"Judgment Night" (1:10)
First broadcast: December 4, 1959; Main Cast: Nehemiah Persoff as Carl Lanser. Patrick MacNee as First Officer, James Franciscus as Lt. Mueller; Producer: Buck Houghton; Story: Rod Serling; Director: John Brahm.

1942. The S.S *Queen of Glasgow* sails out of Liverpool, England on its journey to New York. On board is Carl Lanser, a German who is faintly aware he's been here before, but has no memory of boarding the ship. Lanser can't shake a feeling of impending doom and his worst fears are realized when a U–Boat surfaces and sinks the freighter, killing everyone on board, including himself. But before he dies Lanser comes face-to-face with himself, Kapitan Lieutenant Lanser, Navy of the Third Reich—doomed to relive this moment for eternity.

"King Nine Will Not Return" (2:01)
First broadcast: September 30, 1960; Main Cast: Bob Cummings as Capt. James Embry, Paul Lambert as Doctor, Gene Lyons as Psychiatrist; Producer: Buck Houghton; Story: Rod Serling; Director: Buzz Kulik.

Africa, 1943. The B-25 bomber "King Nine" of the Twelfth Air Force crashes in the desert en route from Tunisia to southern Italy. Captain Embrey recovers consciousness to find his crew missing. But did Embry crash with his crew in 1943 or miss the flight and survive?

"Odd how the real consorts with the shadows, how the present fuses with the past"—Rod Serling.

This episode was based on true story of the B-24 bomber "Lady Be Good" that crashed in 1943 with no trace of the nine man crew on board.

"The Last Flight" (1:18)
First broadcast: February 5, 1960: Main Cast: Kenneth Haigh as Flight Lt. William Decker, Simon Scott as Major Wilson, Alexander Scourby as General Harper, Robert Warwick as Air Marshal MacKaye; Producer: Buck Houghton; Story: Richard Matheson; Director: William Claxton.

Flight Lieutenant William Terence Decker of the Royal Flying Corps has a panic attack when he finds himself surrounded by German planes during World War I. Abandoning his best friend, Decker flees the scene and enters a mysterious white cloud. The British fighter pilot lands his Nieuport biplane at the American Lafayette Air Base in Reims, France only to discover he has been transported through time and space from 1917 to 1959. Decker is told Air Vice-Marshal Alexander MacKaye is on route to visit the base for a tour of inspection. But Decker knows when he deserted his squadron in 1917 MacKaye or "Old Leadbottom" died. He must go back in time to rejoin his squadron and save MacKaye's life.

"The Man in the Bottle" (2:02)
First broadcast: October 7, 1960; Main Cast: Luther Adler as Arthur Castle, Vivi Janiss as Edna Castle, Joseph Ruskin as Genie, Olan Soule as IRS tax collector, Lisa Golm as Mrs. Gumley; Producer: Buck Houghton; Story; Rod Sterling; Director: Don Medford.

On the verge of bankruptcy, antique store owner Arthur Castle is offered an "heirloom" by Mrs. Gumley. Feeling sorry for his customer he pays her $1.00 for the basic wine mug. Suddenly a genie appears out of the bottle and offers Mr. and Mrs. Castle four wishes—but once the wish is fulfilled it can only be altered by another wish. The first wish aims to prove if the genie is genuine. Repair the shattered glass in a display cabinet. But then greed takes hold and Arthur Castle wishes for a million dollars—forgetting about the tax he will owe.

Left with less than he began with Mr. Castle now wants power and wishes to be a leader of a foreign country where he can't be voted out of office. To his dismay he finds himself in a bunker at the end of World War II as Adolf Hitler. His fourth wish sees Castle back in the present with his wife at his side. He realizes his life isn't as bad as he thought it was.

"No Time Like the Past" (4:10)
First broadcast: March 7, 1963; Main Cast: Dana Andrews as Paul Driscoll, Abigail Sloan as Patricia Breslin, Robert F. Simon as Harvey, Malcolm Atterbury as Professor Elliot; Producer: Herbert Hirschman; Story: Rod Serling: Director: Jus Addis.

Paul Driscoll has an intense dislike of the 20th century and journeys back in time in the hope of changing the future.

August 1945. First stop Hiroshima, Japan where he fails to convince authorities of the impending atomic bomb attack. Next stop, August 1939 and a failed attempt to so assassinate Adolf Hitler. Third stop is 1915 and the R.M.S. Lusitania. The captain refuses to change course and avoid being torpedoed.

Driscoll retreats to Homeville, Indiana, in July

1881, but discovers in trying to change history he has become the cause of a county school fire.

"Leave the yesterdays alone. Do something about the tomorrows."

"An Occurrence at Owl Creek Bridge" (5:22)

This episode featured a French adaptation of the short story by Ambrose Bierce set in the American Civil War.

See: **An Occurrence at Owl Creek Bridge**

"The Passersby" (3:04)

First broadcast; October 6, 1961; Main Cast: James Gregory as Sergeant, Joan Linville as Lavinia, Austin Green as Abraham Lincoln, Rex Holman as Charlie, David Garcia as Lieutenant, Warren Kemmerling as Jud; Producer: Buck Houghton; Story: Rod Serling; Director: Elliot Silverstein.

April 1965. A Confederate sergeant meets Lavinia Godwin in front of her burnt out mansion. Her hatred of Union soldiers is so intense she shoots at a blinded Union soldier. But the bullet has no effect for they are all dead. A fact confirmed by Lavinia's dead husband Jud and Abraham Lincoln who are all traveling on the same dirt road in the twilight zone.

"The Purple Testament" (1:19)

First broadcast: February 12, 1960: Main Cast: William Reynolds as Lt. William Fitzgerald, Dick York as Capt. Riker, Barney Phillips as Capt. Gunther, Warren Oates as Jeep driver; Producer: Buck Houghton; Story: Rod Serling; Director: Richard L. Bare.

First platoon "A" Company, Philippine Islands 1945. Lieutenant Fitzgerald has a special gift that is more like a curse. Before going into battle he sees a strange light on the faces of those who are about to die in action.

On February 12, 1960, the day the episode premiered on CBS, director Richard L. Bare and actor William Reynolds almost drowned when their plane Grumman Goose crashed into the Caribbean. The fact didn't escape Bare who jokingly told Reynolds, "Please don't look at me!" as they swam to shore and safety.

"A Quality of Mercy" (3:16)

First broadcast: December 29, 1961; Main Cast: Dean Stockwell as Lt. Katell—Lt. Yamuri, Albert Salmi as Sgt. Causarano, Jerry Fujikawa as Japanese Captain, Leonard Nimoy as Hansen; Producer: Buck Houghton: Story: Rod Serling, based on an idea by Sam Rolfe; Director: Buzz Kulik.

August 1945. The Philippine Islands. Lieutenant Katell orders his platoon to attack a group of Japanese soldiers gathered in a cave. Despite pleas from Sgt. Causarano, Lt. Katell wants the soldiers dead. Suddenly Katell changes bodies. Now he is Lt. Yamuri pleading with his Japanese captain not to attack a group of American soldiers holed up in a cave. But his pleas fall on deaf ears.

Katell is thrown back into his own body and orders his platoon to fall back after hearing news that an atomic bomb has been dropped on Japan. Having experienced the front line from the perspective of two nationalities Katell has a personal sense of the futility of war.

"The 7th Is Made Up of Phantoms" (5:10)

First broadcast: December 6, 1963; Main Cast: Ron Foster as Sgt. Connors, Randy Boone as Pfc. McCluskey, Warren Oates as Cpl. Langsford, Robert Bray as Captain; Producer: Bert Granet; Story: Rod Serling; Director: Alan Crosland, Jr.

Three National Guardsmen on maneuvers near Little Big Horn hear gunfire, come across a teepee and a U.S. 7th Cavalry canteen in almost new condition. The date should be June 25, 1963, but instead they find themselves transported to June 25, 1876, and under attack by a Sioux war party.

"Still Valley" (3:11)

First broadcast: November 24, 1961; Main Cast: Garry Merrill as Joseph Paradine, Vaughn Taylor as Old Man, Ben Cooper as Dauger; Producer: Buck Houghton: Story: Rod Serling, based on the short story "The Valley Was Still" by Mardy Wade Wellman; Director: James Sheldon.

1963, Virginia. Joseph Paradine of the Confederate Cavalry wanders into a town where all the Union soldiers are under the spell of black magic. Time has stopped for them. An old man gives his book of magic to Paradine, telling him to use it wisely to win the Civil War. Paradine's plans for freezing the entire Union army in time are halted when he learns he has to make a deal with the Devil to achieve his wishes. The war continues without the Devil's magic as Paradine journeys to Gettysburg.

"The Thirty Fathom Grave" (4:02)

First broadcast: January 10, 1963; Main Cast: Simon Oakland as Capt. Beecham, Mike Kellin as Chief Bell. John Considine as McClure, Bill Bixby as O.O.D., David Sheiner as Doc; Producer: Herbert Hirschman; Story: Rod Serling; Director: Patrick Lafferty.

The South Pacific Ocean, 1962. A Unites States naval destroyer picks up the sound of tapping on metal. Diver McClure is sent down to check out the noise and discovers a submarine sunk in action during the first battle of the Solomons, August 7, 1942. On board the destroyer Chief Bosun's mate Bell sees visions of his dead crew mates motioning him to follow them. Meanwhile McClure has found Bell's dog tags on the deck of the submarine where he served as signalman. Bell blames himself for the death of his crew mates and is suffering from survivor's guilt with tragic consequences.

The Twilight Zone (1985) [TV Series]

2. Science fiction anthology series. Narrator: Charles Aidman (1985–87); Robin Ward (1988–89); 45 min.; Persistence of Vision Films, Atlantis Films, London Film Productions, CBS Entertainment. Packaged in syndication as one three-season series, the third season featured a new production team and was produced separately from the previous two seasons.

"Nightcrawlers" (1:04)

First broadcast: October 18, 1985; Main Cast: Scott Paulin as Price, James Whitmore, Jr., as Sheriff Dennis Wells, Robert Swan as Bob, Exene Cervenka as Waitress; Producer; Harvey Frand; Story: Philip De Guere, Robert R. McCammon; Director: William Friedkin.

A state trooper and a family sheltering from the wind and rain in a diner encounter a Vietnam veteran, traumatized by the war. He still suffers guilt from abandoning his patrol, the Nightcrawlers, and leaving them to die under enemy fire. But his nightmares of the battlefield become reality when the diner comes under attack by his dead patrol.

"Paladin of the Lost" (1:07)

First broadcast: November 8, 1985. Main Cast: Danny Kaye as Gaspar, Glynn Turman as Billy Kinetta; Executive Producer: Philip De Guere; Producer: Harvey Frand; Story: Harlan Ellison based on his short story "Paladin"; Director Alan Smithee (Gilbert Cates).

While visiting the grave of his wife, the elderly Gaspar is rescued from a mugging by a young black man named Billy. The two form a friendship and discuss their fears. Gaspar is scared of death and leaving the memory of his beloved wife behind. Billy has been traumatized by his experiences in Vietnam, in particular a soldier who was blown apart saving his life. As he relives the event Billy screams in anguish, "There's pieces of him floating on the water." His big regret is never having the chance to say thank you before the soldier was gone.

On their final visit to the cemetery Gaspar tells Billy of his magical pocket watch. The time is 11 o'clock and it must never strike 12 or the universe will cease to exist—to be replaced by infinite emptiness. The watch must be passed to a new owner to stop it ticking, but before Gaspar dies and Billy takes the watch he is granted one minute by the watch to relive his experience in Vietnam and thank the soldier who has haunted his memories.

This moving and thoughtful Writer's Guild award winning episode by Harlan Ellison featured the penultimate screen performance of Danny Kaye as the man who passes on the memory of his wife to the young man and in doing so keeps her spirit alive.

"The Road Less Travelled" (2:07)

First broadcast: December 18, 1986; Main Cast: Cliff De Young as Jeff McDowell, Margaret Klenck as Denise McDowell, Jaclyn-Rose Lester as Megan McDowell; Producer: Harvey Frand; Story: George R.R. Martin; Director: Wes Craven.

A Vietnam draft dodger experiences flashbacks of being in battle in an alternate reality where he fought in the war. He eventually confronts his alternate self who lost his legs after hitting a land mine in Vietnam.

"Shelter Kelter" (2:09)

First broadcast: May 21, 1987; Main Cast: Joe Mantegna as Harry Dobbs, Joan Allen as Sally Dobbs, John Gries as Nick Gatlin; Producer: Harvey Frand; Teleplay: Ron Cobb, Robin Love; Director: Martha Coolidge.

The fallout shelter is a family secret. Harry Dobbs welcomes the idea of a nuclear war and a purified world free from pimps, cowards, pornographers and degenerate rock stars. One drunken night Harry tells his best friend Nick about the shelter and then the bomb drops. Paranoia takes hold as Harry and Nick survive alone in the shelter that will become their tomb.

"A Small Talent for War" (1:15)

First broadcast; January 24, 1986; Main Cast: John Glover as Alien Ambassador, Peter Michael Goetz as American Ambassador Fraser, Stefan Gierasch as Russian diplomat, Fran Bennett as U.N. Chairman; Executive Producer: Philip De Guere; Producer: Harvey Frand; Story: Carter Scholz, Alan Brennert; Director: Claudia Weill.

An alien ambassador from a distant galaxy addresses the United Nations with an ultimatum. The U.N. has 24 hours to prove humans deserve to live. The 15 members of the Security Council declare worldwide peace and unilateral disarmament for the first time. But to their dismay the alien is disappointed. On their planet they breed warriors. It is their lack of warfare skills that has condemned the humans. "You have too small a talent for war."

The Twilight Zone (2002) [TV series]

3. Science fiction anthology series. Host: Forest Whitaker. 43 min.; New Line Television, Spirit Dance Entertainment, Trilogy Entertainment, United Paramount Network (UPN)

"CRADLE OF DARKNESS" (1:05)

First broadcast: October 2, 2002; Main Cast: Katherine Heigl as Andrea Collins, James Remar as Alois Hitler, Nancy Sivak as Klara Hitler, Jillian Fargey as Kristina; Executive Producers: Brent V. Friedman, John Peter Kousakis; Story: Kamran Pasha; Director: Jeande Segonzac.

Andrea Collins travels back in time and faces the moral dilemma of saving millions of lives by sacrificing the life of a baby named Adolf Hitler. Andrea discovers she cannot bring herself to kill the baby and tells Klara to leave her anti–Semitic husband Alois Hitler. When this fails to work Andrea decides to kidnap the baby and jump into the river. But even this fails to work as the baby is replaced by another by the housekeeper Kristina. He will grow up to be the notorious Adolf Hitler of history.

"HOMECOMING" (1:42)

First broadcast: May 7, 2003; Main Cast: Gil Bellows as Major Rob Malone, Dallas Blake as Capt. Michael Beckett, Rebecca Jenkins as Mrs. Malone, Penn Badgley as Trace Malone, Jason Gaffney as Cpl. Rosey, Benjamin Rogers as lance; Executive Producers: Ira Steven Behr, Jim Rosenthal; Story: Bradley Thompson, David Weddle; Teleplay: Michael Angeli; Director: Risa Bramon Garcia.

Major Rob Malone, missing in action in Iraq, is followed by a ghostly platoon when he returns home to his family.

The Twilight Zone [Comic book]

1. Anthology title, officially based on Rod Serling's television series, published by Western Publishing/Gold Key/Whitman.

"THE CAPTIVE TOWN" [WW]
First publication: #28 (March 1969); Art: Luis Dominguez.
"A celebration becomes a nightmare when a mock Civil War turns into a grim reality!"

"CAPTIVES OF THE MIRAGE" [WW]
First publication: #6 (February 1964); Story: Dick Wood; Art: George Tuska, Don Heck.
"Across the trackless desert, a downed bomber crew follows a magic amulet to treachery in a strange oasis!"

"THE GREMLINS" [WW]
First publication: #11 (May 1965); Story: Dick Wood; Art: Mel Crawford.
"A fighter pilot battles an enemy only he can see!"

"SOLDIER OF DEATH" [WW]
First publication: #91 (June 1979); Art: Mike Roy.
"How many times can a soldier kill the same man?"

Cover of *The Twilight Zone* #6 (February 1964). Published by Gold Key.

2. Anthology title published by Dynamite Entertainment.

First publication: *The Twilight Zone* #10 (December 2014); Story: J. Michael Straczynski; Art: Guiu Vilanova.

Jaded and disillusioned private investigator Ben Chambers tackles one final case. The murder of an Iraq War veteran killed after an anti-war rally. But his investigation enters the twilight zone when he literally travels back in time to the scene of the murder.

The Twilight Zone—Radio Dramas (2002)

Main Cast: Stacy Keach as the Host; Producers: Carl Amari, Roger Wolski; Directors: Carl Amari, JoBe Cerny; 40 min.; Falcon Picture Group, CBS Enterprises.

Nationally syndicated radio show adaptations of episodes from the original ***Twilight Zone*** television series. The adaptations by Dennis Etchison, M.J. Elliott and Chas Holloway among others have been approved by the Rod Serling Estate.

"Deaths-Head Revisited" Cast: H. M. Wynant; Vol. 8.

"The Encounter" Cast: Stacy Keach, Byron Mann; Vol. 13.

"He's Alive" Cast: Marshall Allman; Vol. 11.

"In Praise of Pip" Cast: Fred Willard; Vol. 11.

"Judgment Night" Cast: Chelcie Ross; Vol. 12.

"King Nine Will Not Return" Cast: Adam Baldwin; Vol. 4.

"The Last Flight" Cast: Charles Shaughnessy; Vol. 12.

"No Time Like the Past" Cast: Jason Alexander; Vol. 4.

"An Occurrence at Owl Creek Bridge" Cast: Christian Stolte; Vol. 16.

"The Passersby" Cast: Morgan Brittany; Vol. 3.

"The Purple Testament" Cast: Michael Rooker; Vol. 9.

"A Quality of Mercy" Cast: Robert Knepper; Vol. 10.

"The 7th Is Made Up of Phantoms" Cast: Richard Grieco; Vol. 5.

"Still Valley" Cast: Adam West; Vol. 4.

"The Thirty Fathom Grave" Cast: Blair Underwood; Vol. 1.

Twilight Zone: The Movie (1983)

Premiere; June 24, 1983; Main Cast (segment #1 "Time Out"): Vic Morrow as Bill Connor, Doug McGrath as Larry, Charles Hallahan as Ray; Executive Producer: Frank Marshall; Story-Director: John Landis; 101 min.; Amblin Entertainment, Warner Bros.; Color.

Racist bigot Bill Connor assumes the identities of the same ethnicities he expresses hatred for. As a Jew in Nazi occupied France, an African American about to be lynched by the Klu Klux Klan, a Vietnamese man during the Vietnam War and finally as a captor of the Nazis on his way to a death camp.

The Vic Morrow segment was marked by tragedy during the filming of a scene where Morrow's character is rescuing two young Vietnamese orphans from a U.S. helicopter attack. The helicopter crashed, instantly killing Morrow and two children (Myca Dinh Le and Renee Chen) age 6 and 7. Director John Landis, associate producer George Folsey, Jr., unit production manager Dan Allingham, special effects coordinator Paul Stewart and helicopter pilot Dorcey Wingo were charged with involuntary manslaughter and child endangerment. Five years later all defendants were acquitted. Landis, Folsey, Allingham and Warner Bros. also circumvented the State of California's child labor laws by hiring the two children illegally and placing them in danger. They were each fined the maximum $5,000 and Landis reprimanded by the Director's Guild.

Uber [Comic book; SFW]

First publication: April 2013; Story: Kieron Gillen; Art: Canaan White; Publisher: Avatar Press.

The German Reich is in its death throes as Berlin prepares to surrender near the end of World War II. But unknown to the Allies General Sankt has been in charge of the Ubermensch program perfecting weaponized humans who are ready to extend the war.

UberSoldier [Videogame; Russia; WW]

Release date: March 2006; First person-shooter; Platform: Microsoft Windows; Developer: Burut Creative Team; Publisher: CDV.

Originally killed in action, German soldier Karl Stolz has returned to life as a super-soldier with supernatural powers. But now he works for the German Resistance against his former masters the Nazis.

U-Man a.k.a. Meranno [Comic book character; SFW]

First appearance: *The Invaders* #3 (November 1975); Creators: Roy Thomas, Frank Robbins; Publisher: Marvel Comics.

Meranno's hatred for Namor, the **Sub-Mariner** takes on added weight when Meranno joins forces with Nazi Germany and reveals the location of Atlantis. Adopting the persona of *U-Man* he subjects himself to Nazi surgery to give him superhuman strength and stamina. *U-Man* later joins the Super-Axis team formed by Japanese spy Lady Lotus, who exerts mental control over *U-Man*.

The Unborn (2009) (Film; WW]

Premiere: January 9, 2009; Main Cast: Odette Yustman as Casey Beldon, Gary Oldman as Rabbi Sendak, Cam Gigandet as Mark, Meagan Good as Romy, Idris Elba as Arthur Wyndham, Jane Alexander as Sofi Kozma, James Remar as Gordon Beldon, Braden Moran as Joseph Mengele; Executive Producers: Jessika Borsiczky Goyer, William Beasley; Story-Director: David S. Goyer; 88 min.; Relativity Media, Rogue Picture, Platinum Dunes; Color.

Casey Beldon keeps seeing a mysterious boy and the message, "Jumby wants to be born now." She discovers she's a twin and her unborn brother died when his umbilical cord became twisted around his throat in the womb. As a result Casey's mother became clinically depressed and took her own life. The family history becomes even darker when Casey visits her grandmother Sofi. She is told Sofi's twin brother Bartok died in 1944 in Auschwitz concentration camp after the Nazi doctor became fascinated with the mysteries of genetics. His experiments blurred the line between science and the occult and Sofi became aware something else was inhabiting her brother's body. The soul of a dead person barred from entering heaven seeks another twin to inhabit. That entity is known as a dybbuk. Before she dies Sofi tells Casey, "Be careful, the dybbuk feeds on fear. It is you that it most desires."

Uncle Sam [Comic book character; WW]

First appearance: *National Comics* #1 (July 1940): Creators: Will Eisner, Lou Fine; Publisher: Quality Comics.

A new spirit was born in 1776 as a new flag was raised. Uncle Sam was born. He carried the flag in the Civil War and when the states were united again. In the trenches of World War I he fought to preserve democracy. Now his spirit is present again to fight new evils and injustice in World War II with his young friend Buddy at his side. Uncle Sam can leap great distances, possesses superstrength and cannot be photographed. His pow-

Uncle Sam Quarterly #7 (Summer 1943). Cover art by Al Bryant. Published by Quality Comics.

ers, which come from the belief of the American people, are diminished when that belief is lost.

Inspired by James Montgomery Flagg's World War I "I Want You!" recruiting poster and the illustrated cover of *Liberty Magazine* (January 19, 1935).

"Undersea Guardians" (Pulp fiction; WW)

Author: Ray Bradbury; Illustrator: Arnold Kohn; First publication: *Amazing Stories* (Vol. 18 #5; December 1944); Publisher: Ziff-Davis Publishing Company.

The torpedoed and submerged cargo ship U.S.S. *Atlantic* is guarded by its undead naked crew with the purpose of preventing more victims of German submarines. "A thousand people died when the Atlantic went down, but twenty of us came out, half-dead because we have somebody to guard."

But a U-boat has its torpedoes targeted on a convoy of destroyers, cruisers, corvettes and cargo ships. A convoy carrying the former lovers and sons of the undead undersea guardians.

The Unholy (2007) [Film; SFW]

Premiere: September 4, 2007; Main Cast: Adrienne Barbeau as Martha, Nicholas Brendon as Lucas, Siri Baruc as Hope; Executive Producer: Josh Blumenfeld; Story: Sam Freeman, Daryl Goldberg; Director: Daryl Goldberg; 90 min.; Catfish Studios, Sky Whisper Productions; Anchor Bay Entertainment; Color.

When a widow named Martha is unable to stop her daughter from shooting herself in their home she uncovers a local conspiracy involving Nazis experimenting in the occult and the top secret Philadelphia Experiment. "Many believe to this day the experiments continue to exist."

Unknown Soldier a.k.a. ***Soldato ignoto*** (1995) [Film; Italy; WW]

Premiere: 1995; Main Cast: Martin Balsam, Giovanni Guidelli, Stephen Joseph Nalewicki, Angelo Orlando; Producer-Story-Director: Marcello Aliprandi; 95 min.; Movietone Surf Film, MIBAC; Color.

Italian and Allied soldiers have to come to terms with their fate in 1943. Believing themselves trapped in a villa they discover the grim truth that they all died in battle. They feel cheated of life and want to return to the land of the living.

The Unknown Soldier [Comic book characters; SFW]

1. First appearance: *Our Flag Comics* #1 (August 1941); Publisher: Ace Magazines.

"Equipped with a nitro gun which shoots explosive pellets instead of bullets, plus amazing strength and the power to whiz through the air at blinding speed, the Unknown Soldier is more than a match for whole armies. He is the might and courage of a man fighting for the right. Masked and uniformed, his true identity remains a mystery. He is spoken only as the Unknown Soldier."

2. First appearance: *Our Army at War* #168 (June 1966); Creators: **Robert Kanigher**, **Joe Kubert**; Publisher: DC Comics.

The Unknown Soldier enlists in the U.S. Army with his brother Harry shortly before the Japanese attack on Pearl Harbor. When America becomes involved in World War II, Harry and his brother are assigned to the Philippines where Harry dies, saving his brother from a hand grenade. But the blast disfigures the surviving brother's face so badly his facial features are destroyed. From that point on he dedicates himself to working as an intelligence operative codenamed "The Unknown Soldier." A master of disguise, skilled in making life-like masks and assuming the identity of his enemies to infiltrate their ranks, he often operates with his face covered in bandages.

In the final story "A Farewell to War" (*The Unknown Soldier* #268; October 1982) the Unknown Soldier is sent to Berlin in the final days of the war to stop the Nazi vampiric super-weapon "Nosferatu." During his mission the Unknown Soldier uses his master-of-disguise skills to pose as Adolf Hitler after he kills him and set up Hitler's death as a cowardly suicide. Later, he apparently

The Unknown Soldier featured in *Our Flag Comics* #1 (August 1941). Published by Ace Magazines.

sacrifices his life saving the life of a girl from a bomb blast. But the reader is left with the question, "Did he survive?" after a Sergeant is seen scratching his face, suggesting his latest disguise is making his face itch in typical Unknown Soldier fashion.

The Unknown Soldier's subsequent comic book incarnations have been post–World War II with a strong emphasis on revisionism. As such they don't qualify as Weird War titles.

The Unseen [Comic book]

Supernatural anthology title.

"THE GHOSTS IN BLUE" [WW]

First publication: #7 (November 1952); Art: Art Saaf; Publisher: Standard Comics.

In this one-page strip a young woman encounters ghosts of Union soldiers who appear on the anniversary of a Civil War battle still looking for their regiment.

Unusual Tales [Comic book]

Supernatural-fantasy anthology title.

"THE CONFEDERATE GIRL" [WW]

First publication: #25 (December 1960); Story: Joe Gill; Art: Steve Ditko; Publisher: Charlton Comics.

In the Georgian backwoods, Hiram White, Civil War writer and debunker of myths and fables encounters ghosts who talk of setting free Miss Belle Herbert—a Southern spy captured by Major Joshua White.

White then sees the ghost of Belle Herbert—or is it? White knows his great-great grandfather fell in love with Belle, promising to marry her when he returned from war. But he never saw her again and now Hiram White has returned to fall in love with a young woman who looks exactly like Belle.

The ghost seated on his horse looks on as White embraces the young woman. "We can rest now Satan, Miss Belle is in safe hands!"

Urda a.k.a. **URDA: Third Reich** (2002) [Original net animation; Japan; SFW]

Premiere: May 2002; Story-Director: Romanov Higa; Voice Cast (U.S.): Cindy Robinson as Erna Kurtz, Mona Marshall as Grimhild Kurtz, Mami Maynard as Janet Hunter, Rebecca Forstadt as Chris, Joshua Kern as Alan, Steve Kramer as Baltram, Dan Woren as Pilot/Soldier, Steve Schatzberg as Officer; 5 × 5 min.; Romanov Films; Color.

World War II, 1943. Nazis discover a spaceship that can travel through time and initiate the URDA project. Allied spy Erna Kurtz encounters URDA's project commander Glimhild Kurtz as she tries to rescue a Nazi test subject, a young girl from the future. But Erna finds herself facing her own past and future.

The Vampire Diaries (2009) [TV series]

Brothers Damon and Stefan Salvatore are eternal youths living in the 21st century who cannot age since they became vampires in Mystic Falls, Virginia, in 1864.

Unusual Tales # 25 (December 1960), "The Confederate Girl," page 1. Art by Steve Ditko. Published by Charlton Comics.

"Hell Is Other People" (7:10) [WW]
Air date: January 29, 2016; Main cast: Paul Wesley as Stefan Salvatore, Ian Somerhalder as Damon Salvatore, Kat Graham as Bonnie Bennett, Todd Lasance as Julian; Producer: Trish Stanard; Story; Holly Brix, Neil Reynolds; Director: Deborah Chow; 41 min.; Outerbanks Entertainment, Alloy Entertainment, CBS Television Studios, Warner Bros. Television; The CW Television Network; Color.

Damon's soul is trapped inside the Phoenix stone where he is repeatedly confronted by his traumatic experiences from the American Civil War. Bonnie Bennett must free him before the stone overpowers him.

Vampirella vs. Lady Death [Comic book; SFW]

First publication: #23 (May 2000); Story: David Conway; Art: Dorian Cleavenger; Four-part story; Publisher: Harris Comics.

Despite her evil intentions towards Vampirella Lady Death teams up with Vampirella and Pantha to defeat the Nazis.

Vandal Savage [Comic book character; SFW]

First appearance: *Green Lantern* #10 (December 1943); Creators: Alfred Bester, Martin Nodell; Publisher: DC Comics.

An immortal, superhuman villain involved in numerous wars throughout history. The origins of Savage's journey through time begins with Vandar Adg, leader of the Cro-Magnon Blood Tribe. Vandar achieves immortality when he discovers a strange meteorite that saturates him in radiation. Savage has adopted numerous personas in his quest for power including Alexander the Great, Julius Caesar, Genghis Khan and Vlad the Impaler. He has also worked in close collaboration with William the Conqueror, Napoleon Bonaparte, Otto von Bismark and Adolf Hitler.

See: *DC's Legends of Tomorrow*

"Vengeance in Her Bones" [Pulp fiction; WW]

Author: Malcolm Jameson; First publication: *Weird Tales* (Vol. 36 #5; May 1942); Publisher:

Old Captain Tolliver is brought out of retirement to command the "rogue" ship *Sadie Saxon*. The messenger informs Tolliver, "They're putting her back in commission, but she won't leave port. They need ships now that America is at war. Every ship. That's why they need you."

The ship has a mind of its own and only Captain Tolliver understands her. As he takes control and they head for Bermuda the *Sadie Saxon* begins to steer herself and crashes into "something under the fore-foot and along the keel." She has run down a Nazi submarine. Undergoing repairs to her damaged bow in Bermuda, Tolliver and his crew once again take to the sea, and one again the ship neutralizes a U-boat under her own power.

Tolliver tells the story of the ship. In 1914 she was brand new and named the *Koenigen Von Sachsen*—out of the Vulcan Works at Stettin. But the years of abuse by the Germans instilled in her a hatred of them. "In those days our Secret Service wasn't as good as it is now, and a saboteur got aboard. He gummed up things pretty bad. So bad that we caught afire and almost sank in mid-ocean. Well that was the end of her patience. She went hog-wild. After that, no matter whether she was in convoy or not, whenever anything that was German was around—sub, torpedo, raider or what not—she went after it."

"Victory from the Void" [Pulp fiction; SFW]

Authors: William P. McGivern, David Wright O'Brien; Illustrator: Jay Jackson; First publication: *Amazing Stories* (Vol. 17 #3; March 1943).

"Out there in space was a new body, an asteroid from nowhere, but the Nazis were there, using it as a base."

Viking Commando [Comic book character; MWW]

Creators: **Robert Kanigher**, George Evans; First appearance: *All-Out War* (October 1979); Publisher: DC Comics.

Valoric, a 5th century Viking, is near to death after battling the Huns. The Valkyrie Frey accompanies him to Valhalla, and at the command of Odin, onward to Europe in 1944, where he joins the Allies to fight the Germans.

The Violent Century [Novel; SFW]

Author: Lavie Tidhar; First publication: New York: Thomas Dunne/St. Martin's Press, 2013.

Germany, 1933. Scientist Dr. Joachim Vomacht creates a machine that changes the physical structure of human beings, giving some the ability to control fire, water, the weather or time. The Vomacht Wave affects not only Germans, but anyone caught in its path. Ubermenschen become a powerful Nazi weapon as World War II approaches.

Elsewhere in the world the Axis powers create their own supermen. America prefers costumed super-heroes whilst the British have created a network of invisible spies run by a figure simply known as the Old Man. Spies Oblivion and Fogg are trained at the Farm and assigned to various war-torn locations, including Minsk, Leningrad, Paris and Transylvania. But it is in Berlin that Oblivion and Fogg have to come to terms with a secret that splits them apart.

Voodoo [Comic book]

Horror anthology title.

"Corpses of the Jury"
First publication: #5 (January 1953); Story-Art: The Iger Studio; Publisher: Ajax-Farrell.

A Nazi concentration camp, 1945. Colonel Karl Bucher saves a beautiful girl from the gas chamber for his own pleasure. But when she refuses his advances the young woman strikes the officer for killing her father. With that blow she seals her fate and is thrown alive onto the corpse pit and left to die.

When the war ends Bucher escapes to New York under his new name Karl Miller. He has one ambition—to create a revived Nazi party with himself as the leader. But out of the shadows of his apartment emerges the specters of hundreds of his victims from the corpse pit. The girl who was dumped into the pit has come to reclaim Bucher's gloves, made of the skin from her hands. Her revenge is complete as Bucher is skinned alive. "On the wall is left a grisly, red dripping thing!"

Voyage to the Bottom of the Sea (1964) [TV series]

Main Cast: Richard Basehart as Admiral Harriman Nelson, David Hedison as Capt. Lee B. Crane; 110 × 60 min; Creator-Producer: Irwin Allen; Cambridge Productions; Irwin Allen Productions; Twentieth Century–Fox Television; American Broadcasting Company (ABC); B/W (season one); Color.

The adventures of the crew of the U.S. nuclear submarine Seaview, "dedicated to the fight against the forces of the cataclysmic upheavals of nature which threaten whole populations, and to the purpose of thwarting Cold War aggression by the enemy's military forces."

"Death from the Past" (3:16) [SFW]
Premiere: January 8, 1967; Guest Cast: John Van Dreelen as Admiral the Baron Gustave Von Neuberg, Jan Merlin as Lt. Froelich; Story: Charles Bennett, Sidney Marshall; Director: Justus Addiss.

The Seaview comes across a large seaweed covered mound and the sound of heartbeats. When Captain Crane and Kowalski investigate they discover a Nazi Admiral and Lieutenant in a weapons laboratory. They have recovered from suspended animation and mistakenly think they are still at war in 1945. The Seaview and its crew are in their sights as they prepare to launch their weapons of mass destruction aimed at Paris, London, Moscow and Washington, D.C.

"No Way Back" (4:26) [SFW]
Premiere: March 31, 1968; Guest Cast: Henry Jones as Mr. Pem, Barry Atwater as Major General Benedict Arnold, William Beckley as Major John Andre; Story: William Welch; Director: Robert Sparr.

In this final episode of the series the Seaview is destroyed by a bomb and all the crew on board killed. Mr. Pem is asked by Admiral Nelson who wasn't on board, to use his time device to travel back in time to prevent the tragedy. Pem agrees and they board the Seaview 24 hours before the explosion. But Pem has other plans and after perfecting his time device he takes the Seaview and her crew back in time to September 22, 1780.

Major General Benedict Arnold and Mr. Pem take control of the Seaview, with Major Jon Andre joining them. Pem aims to change the course of the Revolutionary War by attacking and destroying West Point with Seaview's missiles.

"The Phantom Returns" (2:26) [WW]
Premiere: March 20, 1966; Guest Cast: Alfred Ryder as Capt. Gerhardt Kreuger, Vitina Marcus as Lani; Story: William Welch; Director: Sutton Roley.

This sequel to episode to "The Phantom Strikes" sees Captain Kreuger return to the Seaview where he finally possesses the body of Captain Crane. Escaping in the Flying Sub, Crane-Krueger travels to an island where he wants to restore his deceased former love Lani to life.

"The Phantom Strikes" (2:17) [WW]
Premiere: January 16, 1966; Guest Cast: Alfred Ryder as Capt. Gerhardt Kreuger; Story: William Welch; Director: Sutton Roley.

When a German named Captain Gerhardt Kreuger comes aboard the Seaview he claims to be the survivor of the S.S. Edelweiss out of Hamburg whose ship was rammed by a German U-boat. But he is the ghost Captain of a World War

I German U-boat recently discovered by the Seaview on the ocean floor. His mission is to possess the body of Captain Crane so he can live again.

"TIME LOCK" (4:08) [SFW]
Premiere: November 12, 1967; Guest Cast: John Crawford as Alpha; Story: William Welch: Director: Jerry Hopper.

Admiral Nelson is captured by two beings on the Seaview who transport him into the future. He is greeted by Alpha, a man who collects military officers from the past for his private collection. Admiral Nelson is the latest addition to his "hobby" but first he must reduce him to an automaton like the other military figures. Alpha has a hidden agenda with his collection as he intends to use them in preparation for starting his own war.

War (Watchers book #4) [Juvenile book; WW]

Author: Peter Lerangis; First publication: New York: Scholastic, 1999.

Teenage Civil War history buff Jake Branford is intrigued when he comes across a secret film and a mysterious director and his crew shooting a Civil War movie. But Jake soon discovers the set is a little too real for comfort as he finds himself living his fantasy of fighting for the Union.

The War at Troy [Novel; MWW]

Author: Lindsay Clarke; First publication: New York: Thomas Dunne, 2004.

Phemius the bard of Ithaca introduces the reader to a mix of myth and history surrounding the Trojan War. "The people who lived in those days were closer to gods than we are, and great deeds and marvels were commoner then, which is why stories we have from them are nobler and richer than our own. So that these stories should not pass from the earth, I have decided to set down everything I know of the stories of the war at Troy."

"War Criminal of Renault Island" [Pulp fiction; SFW]

Author: C.A. Baldwin; Illustrator: Julian Krupa; First publication: *Amazing Stories* (Vol. 18 #5; December 1944); Publisher: Ziff-Davis Publishing Company.

Hitler and Hirohito are no longer in exile on Renault Island. Both are now on Mars, and have been for the past two years. With their help the Martians are planning an invasion of Earth. Princess Jonice, a strikingly attractive female from Uranus, informs Captain Chris Lester, late of the U.S. Air Corps and invites him to be military Commander of Uranus. He accepts and travels to Uranus to prevent the Martians from gathering the ore Stulite required for making a super weapon. On the journey their spacecraft is surrounded and attacked by a Martian fleet under the command of Hirohito, who boards the craft.

"... the door was thrown open and in walked the scrawny, yellow Jap—dressed in the uniform of Mars and wearing a chest of medals. I had all I could do to keep myself from smashing that grinning mouth."

Hirohito gives the ultimatum to allow a small army of occupation while they remove the Stulite or Uranus will be destroyed. Commander Lester has his own ideas of how to deal with Hirohito. Soon he faces as great a threat on Mars when he comes face-to-face with Adolf Hitler and realizes somebody on Uranus has betrayed him and his fighting companions.

War of the Dead [Film: WW]

1. [Canada] Premiere: February 7, 2006; Main Cast: Camille Djokoto as Special Agent Kelly Conda, Myer Gordon as Vincent, Lauren Kurtz as Tracy, Colin Nash as Zombie Gotz, Mihkel Ranniste as Zombie Fritz, Sean Cisterna as Zombie Klaus; Executive Producers: Alessandro Fracassi, Robbie Little; Story:; Director: Sean Cisterna; 88 min.; Kaboom! Entertainment; Color.

Low budget Canadian production about World War II veterans being hunted by three Nazi zombies. Only Vanguards special agent Kelly Conda can save the last remaining World War II veteran from a fate worse than death.

2. Premiere: January 1, 2011; Main Cast: Andrew Tiernan as Capt. Martin Stone, Juoko Ahola as Capt. Niemi, Samuel Vauramo as Kolya, Mikko Leppilampi as Lt. Laasko; Producers: Barr B. Potter, Ramunas Skikas; Screenplay-Director: Marko Makilaakso; 86 min.; Media One Entertainment, Rialto International, Accelerator Films; Entertainment One; Color.

"The deadliest enemy is one that won't die." 1941. A platoon of soldiers are on a secret mission in Russian territory to take out a bunker held by Germans during World War II. But before they reach the bunker the platoon is almost wiped out by what appear to be zombie German soldiers. The surviving American and Finnish soldiers will soon discover the bunker holds the secret to the undead Germans.

War Picture Library [Comic book; UK]
"Ghost Platoon" [WW]
First publication: #269 (December 1964); Publisher: Fleetway.

A shepherd warns the British Eighth Platoon of a deadly premonition as they prepare for an assault on Chateau de Ruhl. He tells them only one of them will survive. Second Lieutenant Mark Nichols has already lost the confidence of his platoon with his cowardly actions during an artillery barrage. Now he has a second chance to prove himself by volunteering to go behind enemy lines to get help for the platoon. At the conclusion of the story the shepherd's premonition appears to have come true as he watches the ghosts of British troops marching toward the front.

The War That Time Forgot [Comic book feature; SFW]
1. First publication: *Star Spangled War Stories* #90 (May 1960); Creators: **Robert Kanigher**, Ross Andru; Publisher: DC Comics.

Investigating the disappearance of two patrols in the Pacific during World War II, a U.S. patrol becomes stranded on the Island of Armored Giants. It soon becomes evident that living, breathing dinosaurs are responsible and now the latest patrol to visit the island is in mortal danger.

This blend of war and science fiction originally ran for eight years in the pages of DC's *Star Spangled War Stories* until February–March 1968. It has been revived since in **Weird War Tales**, *Guns of the Dragon* and DC: *The New Frontier* and the 12 part-series *The Land That Time Forgot* (see below).

2. [Comic book; SFW]
First publication: May 2008; 12 issue-series; Story: Bruce Jones; Art: Jimmy Palmiotti, Jared K. Fletcher; Publisher: DC Comics.

Heroes of past and future find themselves stranded on a mysterious island populated by dinosaurs. Lieutenant Carson from World War II and Akisha, female soldier from the future are joined by **Tomahawk**, Firehair, Viking Prince, **G.I. Robot**, Golden Gladiator and Hans Von Hammer, World War I Enemy Ace.

"War Worker 17" [Pulp fiction; WW]
Author: Frank Patton; First publication: *Amazing Stories* (Vol. 17 #9; September 1943); Publisher: Ziff-Davis Publishing Company.

"My name is Mary Sweeney. I work in a war plant; help make planes, motors, guns. We are engaged in a war. We use guns to fight the war.... Gas masks to keep us from dying in gas attacks...."

The tall man spoke. "You are a very clever girl. And we are more than surprised at the advanced civilization from which you come—and extremely shocked to discover you use that civilization to wage war.... Perhaps we can do something to remedy the situation.... We have no desire to harm you. We only delve into other universes as a matter of learning more about the things we know exist outside of our own particular vibratory sphere."

Warbirds (2008) [Telefilm; SFW]
Air date: April 19, 2008; Main Cast: Jamie Elle Mann as Maxine West, Brian Krause as Colonel Jack Toller, Tohoru Masamune as Captain Ozu, Shauna Rappold as Betsy Quigley, Lucy Faust as Hoodsie Smith; Executive Producer: William R. Greenblatt; Story; Kevin Gendreau, Christian McIntire, John Terlesky, Scott Wheeler; Director: Kevin Gendreau; 85 min.; New Symphony Pictures, Clockwork Planet, Curmudgeon Films; Sci-Fi Channel; Color.

During the final days of World War II the Women's Air Service Corps (WASPS) are enlisted on a secret mission. When a storm forces them to land in enemy territory they soon discover the enemy isn't the Japanese but giant Pterodons.

Warfront: Tales of Combat [Comic book]
"The Spirit of '52" [WW]
First publication: #27 (October 1955); No credits; Publisher: Harvey Picture Magazines, Inc.

The ghost of "The Spirit of '76" succeeds in raising the morale of an American soldier fighting in Korea.

"Warrior Queen of Lolarth" [Pulp fiction; SFW]
Author: Ross Rocklynne; Illustrator: Robert Fuqua; First publication: *Amazing Stories* (Vol. 17 #5; May 1943); Publisher: Ziff-Davis Publishing Company.

"Captain Burke Donlevy thought he at last knew what hell was. He had missed Dunkirk and the first Dieppe invasion, but he was certain they could not have been worse than weird Lolarth. The queen of another world has a weapon that would make Hitler eat dirt."

Warrior Rising [Novel; MWW]
Author: P. C. Cast; First publication: New York: Berkley Sensation, 2008.

Goddesses, Hera, Athena and Venus summon Kat and Jackie, two females from the University of Tulsa. Their mission, to go back in time and distract Achilles and his cousin Patroklos from fighting the Trojan War. Kat is transformed into a Trojan princess to win the heart of Achilles. But, while Patroklos falls in love with Jackie, Kat has a harder time convincing Achilles to stop fighting and must also try to pacify Achilles foe, King Agamemnon.

Warrior Woman [Comic book character; SFW]
First appearance: *The Invaders* #16 (May 1977); Creators: Roy Thomas, Frank Robbins; Publisher: Marvel Comics.

Nazi spy Julia Koenig interrogates an American soldier in the hope of obtaining the secret of the Super-Soldier serum that created **Captain America**. When she attempts to replicate the unstable formula on herself Kloenig is transformed into *Warrior Woman*. Hitler's plans to join *Warrior Woman* and fellow Nazi super warrior *Master Man* in marriage are defeated by **The Invaders**.

Warrior Woman and *Master Man* resurfaced in December 1990 in the pages of *Namor, the* **Sub-Mariner**. They were placed in suspended animation near the end of World War II in the hope of reviving them and Nazi rule at a later date. When they are discovered in the secret laboratory Master Man is revived but *Warrior Woman* requires a blood transfusion from the original **Human Torch** and Toro's widow Ann Raymond.

The Wars of Other Men (2014) [Short film; SFW]
Premiere: April 4, 2014; Main Cast: Scott Newman as The Lieutenant, Jonny Victor as Corporal MacCrae, Tommy Beardmore as Private Kilpatrick, Jonathan West as Captain Dougherty, Mitchell Koory as Private Eiger, Stevie Robinson as Private Cavanaugh, Pauline Ann Johnson as Lt. Col. Farben, Steve Gualtieri as Dr. Adam Weishaupt; Producers: Michael Einheuser, Connie Mangilin; Story-Director: Mike Zawacki; 25 min.; Paradise Valley Media; Color.

In an alternate reality resembling the 1920s a chemical super weapon known as the Fog is turning the tide of the world war. The Lieutenant is ordered to capture the scientist responsible for the weapon, but in doing so will face his own moral dilemma.

Wartime (1987) [Short film; UK; WW]
Release: 1987; Main Cast: John Levene as Warrant Officer John Benton, Michael Wisher as Father, Mary Greenhalgh as Mother, Peter Greenhalgh as Chris Benton, Steven Stanley as Johnnie Benton, Peter Noad as Private Willis, Paul Flanagan as Man, Nicholas Briggs as Soldier, Nicholas Courtney as Voice of Brigadier Lethbridge-Stewart; Screenplay: Andy Lane, Helen Stirling; Producer-Director: Keith Barnfather; 35 min.; Reeltime Pictures; Color.

On a mission to deliver valuable radioactive material to United Nations Intelligence Taskforce (UNIT) headquarters, Warrant Officer John Benton has the desire to visit the grave of his brother Chris. This marks the beginning of the ghostly apparitions that take John Benton back in time to World War II to relive traumatic experiences from his past. These include the death of Chris, falling among stone ruins while playing a game of soldiers and his father's death at Normandy in 1944. Benton is still tormented with guilt over the death of his brother. All he wants is his father's approval that his death was just an accident.

This film features characters first introduced in the **Doctor Who** television series.

Washington's War (*Blast From the Past* book #7) [Juvenile book; SFW]
Authors: Stacia Deutsch, Rhody Cohon; Illustrator: Guy Francis; First publication: New York: Aladdin, 2007.

Babs Magee is traveling through time trying to discourage famous historical figures so she can change history and become famous herself. Youngsters Abigail, Jacob, Zack and Bo, members of the school History Club, chase her through time, thanks to Mr. Caruthers' time-travel computer. They must convince George Washington to remain at Valley Forge and not go back to Mount Vernon. The future outcome of the Revolutionary War depends on their powers of persuasion.

See: **Lincoln's Legacy**

Weapons of Choice [Novel; SFW]
Author: John Birmingham; First publication: New York: Del Rey-Ballantine Books, 2004.

In the first book of the *Axis of Time* trilogy World War II is dramatically altered when a multinational military experiment in 2021 results in the naval task force being sent back in time to

1942 and the Battle of Midway. 21st century technology and warfare has been transplanted to World War II and history changed forever.

See: **Designated Targets**

Web of Mystery [Comic book]

Fantasy-mystery anthology title.

"True Tales of Unexplained Mystery #9" [WW]

First publication: #5 (October 1951); Art: Sy Grudko; Publisher: Ace Magazines.

"The story of a Lieutenant and his platoon of French soldiers is one of the strangest to come out of World War I."

The Lieutenant is critically injured charging the enemy but the next morning the French soldiers take the ridge under the leadership of the Lieutenant, only to discover he died the previous night.

"His spirit did not rest until victory."

Weird Fantasy [Comic book]

Science fiction and horror anthology title.

"The Exile" [SFW]

First publication: *Weird Fantasy* #14 (July–August 1952); Story: Al Feldstein; Art: Wally Wood; Publisher: Entertaining Comics (EC).

The latest prisoner on the penal planet named Earth is Adolf Hitler.

See: **Perversions of Science**

Weird Horrors [Comic book]

Supernatural-fantasy anthology title.

"The Phantom Bowmen" [WW]

First publication: #5 (December 1952); Art: Andre LeBlanc; Publisher: St. John Publishing Co.

World War I. A group of thirty British soldiers are trapped in a trench, cut off from their men and held down by enemy fire. The soldiers decide they have no choice but to charge the Huns, even if it means death. But to their amazement they are joined by an army of phantom bowmen leading them through enemy lines. The Huns retreat but the mystery of the bowmen remains.

See: "**The Bowmen**"

Weird Terror [Comic book]

Supernatural-fantasy anthology title.

"Hitler's Head" [WW]

First publication: #1 (September 1952); Art: Don Heck; Publisher: Comic Media.

Former Gestapo general Eric Hausner and his fellow Nazis have escaped to the jungles of South America after the end of the war. But Hausner is still haunted by the final days of Adolf Hitler when he promised Hausner he would revenge his "chicken-hearted squeamishness." One fateful night Hausner sees Hitler in his bedroom. "It is your Fuhrer, Hausner. Did you think you could really escape me? I came back from Hell for you!"

Weird Thrillers [Comic book]

Supernatural-fantasy anthology title.

"Letter in Black" [WW]

First publication: #3 (January–March 1952); Story: Ed Silverman; Art: Everett Raymond Kinstler; Publisher: Approved Comics (Ziff-Davis).

On the night of June 27–28, 1914, a restless Monseigneur Joseph De Lanyi, Bishop of Grosswarden, enters his study to find a letter bordered in black on his table. But when he asks his butler Charles about the letter it has disappeared and Charles claims to have never seen it. The Bishop writes down the contents of the letter before it fades from memory and to prove it wasn't an hallucination.

The following morning he receives the news that Archduke Ferdinand has been assassinated and war has been declared. The Bishop reads the contents of his mysterious letter he received the night before: "Your Eminence, my wife and I have been victims of a political crime. We commend ourselves to your prayers. Franz Ferdinand, Srajevo, June 28, 1914. 4:00 a.m."

Weird War Tales [Comic book; WW]

First publication: September–October 1971; Publisher: DC Comics.

Anthology title featuring fantasy, supernatural and science fiction war stories hosted by the skeletal figure of Death dressed in different military garb each issue. He was introduced on the cover of the first issue in Nazi uniform attacking U.S. troops. The title had originally been slated for two issues of reprints in *Super DC Giant*, but when that comic book was canceled *Weird War Tales* was given its own bi-monthly title, under the editorship of **Joe Kubert** and Joe Orlando. The initial reprints from DC's various war titles, including *All-American Men Of War* and *G.I. Combat* were soon replaced with new material beginning with issue #5.

Weird War Tales introduced recurring characters including **G.I. Robot, Creature Commandos** and the return of the *Star Spangled War Stories* series **The War That Time Forgot**. The title's final issue was #124 (June 1983).

Issue #100 (June 1981) featured a splash page by Joe Kubert where a skeletal soldier carrying a scythe is surrounded by the helmets of his victims from various wars across time. "You know my name—I am Death, the ultimate equalizer—and nowhere is my kingdom greater than here—in the Weird War. Come! Take my hand and join me here—if you dare!"

Weird War Tales was briefly revived in June 1997 for a four issue mini-series from DC-Vertigo. A one-issue "Special" was published in April 2000 followed by a *Weird War Tales* "One-Shot" from DC in November 2010.

Sample stories include:

"Black Magic—White Death" (#25; May 1974; Story: George Kashdan; Art: Alfredo P. Alcala); Emperor Napoleon's army encounters voodoo in Haiti.

"Corporal Kelly's Private War" (#23; March 1974; Story: George Kashdan; Art: Alex Nino); While manning a radar station on an island in the Pacific during World War II, a corporal in the U.S. Army is transported to another planet and an alien war.

"Deliver Me from D-Day" (#64; June 1978; Story: Wyatt Gwyon; Art: Frank Miller, Danny Bulanadi); A G.I. makes a deal with the Devil to survive D-Day.

"The Die-Hards" (#13; April 1973; Story: Jack Oleck; Art: Nestor Redondo); Nazis are overcome by vampires in a village in Eastern Europe.

"Hand of Hell" (#12; March 1973; Story: **Robert Kanigher**; Art: Tony DeZuniga); "Desert Fox" General Rommel and his men suffer the wrath of Dinna, sacred priestess of fox god Anubis, in the burning sands of Egypt.

"The Invisible Enemy" (#24; April 1974); Story: Jack Oleck; Art: Ernie Chua); An Oberlieutenant orders the execution of a gypsy woman and her young child during World War II. Before her death she swears revenge from beyond the grave. Soon the Nazi begins to have nightmares of a tiger stalking him. As the war comes to an end he is trapped in a constant battle with a spectral tiger—and his conscience!

"It Takes Brains to be a Killer" (#81; November 1979; Story: George Kashdan: Art: Gerry Talaoc); Korea, 1951. Chinese troops attack an American weather station and capture Major Walter Reilly. He is subjected to a grotesque experiment where his functioning brain is removed from his body. Using Reilly's brain as part of a network of brains in a "Brain Machine" the Chinese launch a nuclear attack. But the brains send it off course to explode harmlessly. Their combined goal is peace—not war.

"Oct. 30, 1947—Nurenberg Prison" (#11; February 1973; Story: Sheldon Mayer; Art: Alex Nino); General Von Krauss escapes execution when he injects himself with a serum contained in the insignia of his ring. Suddenly he is transported from 1947 to Christmas, 2047 where he finds himself in the middle of another world war between the under-grounders and the over-grounders.

"One Hour to Kill" (#21; January 1974; Story: Jack Oleck; Art: Frank Robbins); A U.S. army captain travels back in time to kill Leonardo Da Vinci and prevent the invention of guns and future wars. But he finds himself unable to kill Da Vinci and leaves his .45 automatic gun behind in the 15th century when he returns to the present.

"An Outbreak of Peace" (#82; December 1979; Story: George Kashdan; Art: Don Newton, Dave Hunt); During World War II a Navy frogman is sucked through a watery vortex and finds himself in the peaceful, underwater world of Atlantis.

"The Primate Patrol" (#89: Story: George Kashdan; Art: Ken Landgraf, Dave Simons); Armed Nazi gorillas fight in World War II Africa.

"Thou Shalt Not Kill" (#10; November 1973; Art: Neal Adams, Steve Harper); Prague, 1943. Persecuted Jews call to the Golem for help against the rampaging Nazis.

"The Warrior and the Witch Doctors" (#12; Story: Arnold Drake; Art: Don Perlin); The part-savage painted tribesmen of Britain turn to their Druid gods to defeat the invading Romans.

"The Unseen Warriors" (#25; May 1974; Story: George Kashdan; Art: Alex Nino); A German soldier, covered in bandages, discovers he is invisible and targets U.S. soldiers as Berlin falls.

Weird Wars: Tour of Darkness [RPG; Sourcebook; WW]

First publication: October 2004; System: Savage Worlds; d20; Design: Shane Lacy Hensley, Simon Lucas, Dr. Rob Musk; Story: Teller; Art: Niklas

Brandt, Gil Formosa, Richard Pollard, Zeke Sparks, Cheyenne Wright; Publisher: Pinnacle Entertainment.

The G.I. must swiftly adapt to the dangers lurking in the jungles of Vietnam. And if he gets drafted into the Phoenix Program he'll learn about the secret cults of the high mountains and the Plain of Jars.

Weird Wars: Rome [RPG; Setting book; WW]

First publication: September 2013; Story: Paul "Wiggy" Wade-Williams; Art: Aaron Acevedo; Publisher: Pinnacle Entertainment.

The legions of Rome battle their enemies and strange creatures in the Roman Empire, spreading across the Celtic wilderness to the forests of Germania and the deserts of Aegyptus.

Weird Wars Rome: Nox Germanica [Adventure book; WW]

First publication: August 2014; Story: Teller; Art: Aaron Acevedo; System: Savage Worlds; Publisher: Pinnacle Entertainment.

This 32-page adventure sees Roman legionaries on watch over the mysterious, eerie forests of Germanica. The barbarians resists Roman rule and may have sinister allies lurking deep within the dark heart of the forests.

Weird Wars Rome: The Half-Set Sun [Adventure book; WW]

First publication: November 2013; Story: Teller; Art: Aaron Acevedo; System: Savage Worlds; Publisher: Pinnacle Entertainment.

In the mysterious ancient land of Aegyptus Alexandria receives news that the Nubians have sieged the frontier city of Swenett and its fortress at Elephantine. Now the heroes must retake the fortresses and villages and discover the uncanny source behind the Nubians' thirst for war.

Weird Wars Rome: Wellspring [Adventure book; WW]

First publication: November 2013; Story: John Beattie; Art: Aaron Acevedo; System: Savage Worlds; Publisher: Pinnacle Entertainment.

The Picts are on the attack in Britannia and the Roman legions have been pushed back to Hadrian's Wall. Magic is at work in the disappearance of legionaries. The source of the Picts strength and bewitching warfare must be found and destroyed before it is too late.

Weird Wars: Weird War I [RPG; Player's Guide; War Master's Handbook; WW]

First publication: 2016; System: Savage Worlds; Story: James Cambias, Teller; Art: Tomek Towrek; Publisher: Pinnacle Entertainment.

The war to end all wars where soldiers, sailors, airmen and civilians suffer the horrors of World War I on the battlefields of France. "Things not of this earth crawl through the corpse-choked mud of Flanders. Shapes beyond imagining shamble in the murky chlorine clouds that drift across the Ypres battlefield. Scaled things crawl from the dark waters of the Pripet marshes."

Weird Wars: Weird War II [RPG; WW]

First publication: 2001; Systems: d20, Savage Worlds; Story: Shane Hensley, Mike Montesa; Art: Cheyenne Wright, Jordan Peacock; Publisher: Pinnacle Entertainment.

The Weird War II setting spans Southeast Asia where Japanese await in the jungles, the South Pacific where aircraft carriers do battle, North Africa where tanks cross the desert, England where planes duel overhead and mainland Europe where Nazis continue their blitzkrieg. Fighting alongside the Axis forces are the creatures of nightmares.

Weird Wars: Weird War II: Afrika Korpse [Sourcebook; WW]

First publication: July 2004; System: d20; Story: Peter Schweighofer; Publisher: Pinnacle Entertainment.

This 114-page book details the Weird War in Africa. "Rommel's Desert Rats lurk somewhere out there. Somewhere in the dunes. Rumor is he has a new tank—the dreaded Tiger. Patrols are out but have not yet returned. Have they been captured by the Germans? There's blood in the sand and death in the dunes, and those shapes you see shambling toward you might not be a mirage."

Weird Wars: Weird War II: Blood on the Rhine [RPG; WW]

First publication: 2001; System: d20; Story: John R. Hopler, Shane Lacy Hensley; Publisher: Pinnacle Entertainment.

Players represent Allied forces as they fight mutant Nazis and haunted vehicles. Membership of the Office of Supernatural Investigations (OSI) is available to heroes who confront the supernatural. Access to Divine and Arcane Magic is granted to those who take the OSI Chaplain and Adept Prestige Classes. Nazi foes include Blood

Mages who have the power to harness the evil of death camps and battlefields.

Weird Wars: Weird War II: Dead From Above [Core rulebook; WW]

First publication: 2001; System: d20; Story: John R. Hopler, Aaron Rosenberg; Publisher: Pinnacle Entertainment.

Rules for bombing, strafing runs and dogfights with statistics for major Allied and Axis fighters and bombers on the Western Front. Allied bombers have more than Messerschmitts to contend with in the Weird War skies. Includes the adventure "Memphis Hell" about a ghostly B-17 Flying Fortress.

Weird Wars: Weird War II: Hell Freezes Over—The Russian Front [War Master's Handbook; WW]

First publication: 2004; System: d20; Story: David Niecikowski, Edward Niecikowski; John Niecikowski; Publisher: Pinnacle Entertainment.

Play Weird Wars on the Eastern Front with this complete history of the Weird War in Russia. The player fights for Mother Russia from the Volga to Stalingrad to tank battles on the frozen steppes. A setting for the *Weird Wars: Weird War II* roleplaying game.

Weird Wars: Weird War II: Hell in the Hedgerows [Adventure book; WW]

First publication: 2002; System: d20; Story: Otto Cargill, Shane Lacy Hensley, Mark Metzner, Gareth Michael Skarka; Publisher: Pinnacle Entertainment.

Four sagas of Weird Wars terror that start in Normandy and the hedgerows of France and conclude in Germany. This supplement to *Weird War II: Blood on the Rhine* can be played as stand-alone adventures or as a short campaign.

Weird Wars: Weird War II: Horrors of Weird War Two [Game Master's Handbook; WW]

First publication: July 2004; System: d20; Publisher: Pinnacle Entertainment.

Over 100 new creatures containing an adventure seed that can be worked into the player's campaign. Includes the adventure "The Secret of the Caves."

Weird Wars: Weird War II: Island of Dreams [Adventure book; WW]

First publication: February 2011; System: Savage Worlds; Story: Darryl Nichols; Art: Richard Clark; Publisher: Pinnacle Entertainment.

37-page journey that goes from tropical paradise to tropical nightmare in the World War II Pacific Theater.

Weird Wars: Weird War II: Land of the Rising Dead [Sourcebook; WW]

First publication: July 2004; System: d20; Publisher: Pinnacle Entertainment.

Sourcebook for the Pacific Theatre and a setting for Weird Wars: Weird War II where the enemy has kamikaze dive bombers, suicidal troops and the islands of Okinawa, Midway, Iwo Jima and Corredigor in the South Pacific crawling with monsters.

Wendigo Tales: A Tale of the Weird Wars: Hellfighter [Novella; WW]

First publication: October 2013; Story: Ed Wetterman; Art: Cheyenne Wright; Publisher: Pinnacle Entertainment.

On the French front during World War I the African American "Harlem Hellfighters" of the 369th Infantry Regiment under the command of Sgt. Buck Henry encounter more than they bargained for.

Wendigo Tales: A Tale of the Weird Wars: Los! [Novella; WW]

First publication: October 2013; Story: Timothy Brian Brown; Art: Thomas Denmark; Publisher: Pinnacle Entertainment.

In this "Tale of Weird War One" the crew of U-Boat 532 and the SS officers on board hear mysterious sounds coming from the latest weapon—a torpedo.

Wendigo Tales: A Tale of the Weird Wars: No Man's Land [Novella; WW]

First publication: October 2013; Story: Kevin Andrew Murphy; Art: Thomas Denmark; Publisher: Pinnacle Entertainment.

Conrad Von Helmond has avoided the front lines of World War I thanks to the influence of his great aunt. She wants to him to concentrate his efforts providing proof of the existence of fairies.

Wendigo Tales: A Tale of the Weird Wars: Raid on Fort Douaumont [Adventure book; WW]

First publication: 20016; Systems: Savage Worlds; Story: Eddy Webb, Teller; Publisher: Pinnacle Entertainment.

This 32-page PDF adventure is a mix of action,

warfare and ancient evils. French infantrymen meet Sir Arthur Conan Doyle and enter the battered remains of Fort Douaumont.

Wendigo Tales: A Tale of the Weird Wars: Teufelshunde [Novella; WW]

First publication: October 2013; Story: John R. Hopler; Art: Thomas Denmark, Cheyenne Wright; Publisher: Pinnacle Entertainment.

World War I. Herbert Lansing is a coward who is forced to fight a war he has no stomach for. But in Belleau Woods his cowardice may risk him losing his soul.

Wendigo Tales: A Tale of the Weird Wars: With Utmost Dispatch [Novella; WW]

First publication: August 2013; Story: Aaron Rosenberg; Art: Thomas Denmark; Publisher: Pinnacle Entertainment.

When Legionary Titus Aetius is ordered to track down his best friend and fellow Roman soldier for desertion he encounters unknown horrors in the forests of Gaul.

Wendigo Tales: A Tale of the Weird Wars: Without Fear [Novella; WW]

First publication: August 2013; Story: Shane Lacy Hensley; Art: Thomas Denmark; Publisher: Pinnacle Entertainment.

Thracian gladiator and slave Magnus Bos is a man without fear after battling the strange gray beast of Aegyptus. But when Bos is bought by a strange cabal and transported to a cursed village on a faraway island his lack of fear is put to the test.

Wendigo Tales: A Tale of the Weird Wars: Wunderwaffe [Novella; WW]

First publication: October 2013; Story: Timothy Brian Brown; Art: Thomas Denmark; Publisher: Pinnacle Entertainment.

During World War I Luftwaffe pilot Karl Schmidt wears a strange amulet during each flight accompanied by an eerie passenger.

Werewolf Women of the S.S. [Film trailer; WW]

Premiere: April 6, 2007; Main Cast: Nicholas Cage as Dr. Fu Manchu, Udo Kier as Commandant Franz Hess, Sheri Moon as Eva Krupp, Tom Towles as Lt. Boorman, Sybil Danning as Gretchen Krupp, Bill Moseley as Dr. Heinrich von Strasser, Andrew Martin, Vladimir Kozlov as Nazi boxers, Olja Hrustic, Meriah Nelson, Lorelle New as Werewolf Women; Director: Rod Zombie; 1:45; 4:59 (extended version); Troublemaker Studios, Dimension Films; Color.

Eva and Gretchen Krupp—the She-Devils of Balzac—lead a group of Nazis in the final days of World War II, intent on creating an army of super-werewolves. This "fake" trailer was one of three exploitation trailers seen in the double-feature *Grindhouse* (2007).

The Werewolf's Tale [Novel; WW]

Author: Richard Jaccoma; First publication: New York: Ballantine Books, 1988.

Manhattan private detective Jimmy Underhill has returned from the Spanish Civil War to tackle cases involving vampirism, demons, witchcraft and the occult. His latest client, an attractive Jewish vampire leads to a female werewolf who transforms Underhill with one bite. Fighting the beast within, Underhill tracks the beasts hidden among the streets of New York. Nazis engaging in the occult to raise the undead and gather the forces of evil to empower the master beast at work in Europe.

Where Dead Soldiers Walk [Novel; WW]

Author: Lloyd Biggle, Jr.; First publication: New York: St. Martin's Press, 1994.

Private detective J. Pletcher investigates a series of murders in Napoleon Corners, Georgia, that appear to involve monks, a witch, a grandfather who thinks he's a Confederate General and the ghosts of Union soldiers.

"The White Battalion" [Short story; WW]

Author: Frances Gilchrist Wood; First publication: *The Bookman* (May 1918).

"It began with the great retreat of 1914 ... when the Germans were driving us back toward Paris.... We faced annihilation! In the years of struggle that came after the retreat, our women of France have taken the places of men behind the lines while our soldiers hold the Front."

The "flame of common inspiration" touches the widows of the fallen soldiers as they petition to be entered and drilled as the Battalion of Avengers. After many objections from the military the women are accepted and trained. They will attempt to retake the ground "held to the death by their men" on the Front.

At the Front, ready to attack, the women are

stopped in their advance by Huns holding hundreds of little children above their heads.

"God! Men—they knew! The devil tells them! They knew this section was held by women! For us to hold the Front—our share of the Front—these mothers must bayonet their way through crying, helpless babies!"

But the women have their own saviors—"a battalion of marching shadows in a blur of the old red and blue" outstrips the Avengers' advance as they sweep "over the untouched children into the trench." The fallen battalion has returned to save their women. A White Battalion—"a crowding host killed in battle—the red life of gallant youth given so gloriously that it cannot die!"

White Tiger (2012) [Film; Russia; WW]
Premiere: May 3, 2012 (Russia); Main Cast: Aleksey Vertkov as Sergeant Ivan Naydenov, Vitaliy Kishchenko as Fedotov, Valeriy Grishko as Zhukov, Dmitriy Bykovskiy as Smirnov; Producers: Galina Shadur, Karen Shakhnazarov; Screenplay: Aleksandr Borodyanskiy, Karen Shakhnazarov; Based on the novel *Tankist, Ili Belyy Tigr* by Ilya Boyashov; Director: Karen Shakhnazarov; 104 min.; Channel One, Russia, Mosfilm; Aya Pro; Color.

Wounded Soviet tank commander Naydenov believes he can communicate with tanks. A rumor about an invincible Nazi tank that appears out of thin air begins to circulate. Nicknamed the White Tiger, Naydenov is convinced the tank is responsible for his wounds and the destruction of his tank. His quest to find and destroy the White Tiger becomes an obsession.

The Whizzer [Comic book character; SHW]
First appearance: *USA Comics* #1 (August 1941); Creators: Al Avison, Al Gabriele; Publisher: Timely Comics.

In the African jungle Dr. Emil Frank's son Robert is dying from a fever. Suddenly a mongoose darts out of the dense foliage with lightning speed and kills a snake that is ready to lunge at Robert. A grateful Dr. Frank thanks the mongoose and decides to inject the blood of the mongoose into his son. Dr. Emil Frank's health declines over the next weeks but before he dies he tells his son, "You're to be different than other men!"

True to his father's word, Robert Frank discovers he now possesses the speed of a mongoose. "My arm, it's really whizzing…. Dad was right—I'm a whizzer!"

The Whizzer becomes a member of the **Liberty Legion** and the **All-Winners Squad**, fighting the **Red Skull** during World War II.

The Wild, Wild West (1965) [TV series]
Premiere: September 17, 1965; Main Cast: Robert Conrad as James T. West, Ross Martin as Artemus Gordon; Creator: Michael Garrison; Executive Producers: Philip Leacock, Michael Garrison; 104 × 60 min, 2 × 90 min.; CBS; B/W (Season One), Color.

A blend of James Bond, steampunk and science fiction set in the Old West of the 1870s, *The Wild Wild West* was an inventive series created by Michael Garrison. Robert Conrad starred as James T. West, a secret agent working for President Ulysses S. Grant. His companion was master of disguise, Artemus Gordon, played by Ross Martin. Occasional episodes featured American Civil War themes.

"The Night of the Kraken" (4:06) [WW]
Air date: November 1, 1968; Story: Stephen Kandel; Director: Michael Caffey.

When West and Gordon investigate a series of deaths by sea monsters, they discover a sinister plot to sink America's latest battleship.

"The Night of the Lord of the Limbo" (2:15) [SFW]
Air date: December 30, 1966; Guest Star: Ricardo Montalban as Noel Bartley Vautrain; Story: Henry Sharp; Director: Jesse Hibbs.

Crippled Confederate colonel Vautrain travels back in time with West and Gordon to restore his legs and change the outcome of the Civil War by murdering General Grant.

"The Night of the Returning Dead" (2:05) [WW]
Air date: October 14, 1966; Guest Stars: Sammy Davis, Jr., as Jeremiah; Peter Lawford as Carl Jackson; Story: John Kneubuhl; Director: Richard Donner.

When West and Gordon confront a mysterious Confederate ghost rider, their bullets have no effect. The mysterious Jeremiah, a stable boy, claims to have power over animals and holds the key to the secret of the ghost rider.

"The Night of the Spanish Curse" (4:14) [WW]
Air date: January 3, 1969; Guest Star: Thayer David as Cortez; Story: Robert E. Kent; Director: Paul Stanley.

The townspeople of Soledad, New Mexico, are

convinced they are being haunted by the ghosts of Cortez and his Conquistadors.

"THE NIGHT OF THE STEEL ASSASSIN" (1:16) [SFW]

Air Date: January 7, 1966; Guest Star: John Dehner as Iron Man Torres; Story: Calvin Clements; Director: Lee H. Katzin.

Following an explosion that left him crippled, Civil War officer Colonel "Iron Man" Torres has reconstructed his body with steel. With superhuman strength, Torres seeks revenge on those who wronged him, including President Grant.

The Wild, Wild West Revisited (1979) [Telefilm; SFW]

Premiere: May 9, 1979; Main Cast: Robert Conrad as James West, Ross Martin as Artemus Gordon, Paul Williams as Dr. Michelito Loveless, Jr., Rene Auberjonois as Capt. Sir David Edney, Harry Morgan as Robert T. Malone, Jo Ann Harris as Carmelita, Trisha Noble as Penelope; Executive Producer: Jay Bernstein; Story: William Bowers; Director: Burt Kennedy; 96 min; CBS Television; Color.

James West and Artemus Gordon are called out of retirement to track down Dr. Michelito Loveless, Jr., before he replaces President Grover Cleveland and leaders of England, Spain and Russia with doubles in his quest for world domination.

Window of Time [Juvenile book; WW]

Author: Karen Weinberg; First publication: Shippensburg, Pa: White Mane Publishing, 1991.

Ben Leeds and his family have moved to a condominium in Westminster, Maryland. The former owner, Professor Henderson taught history at the same college where Ben's father works as a music professor. While cleaning the basement Ben discovers some old boots and clothes. Removing the wood from a boarded up window Ben climbs through the broken glass. But on the other side of the window it is June 28, 1863. When he attempts to climb back though the window he is chased away by a vicious dog who lived in the house in 1863. Ben makes friends with nine-year-old Joseph Harner. The older brother Andrew is a Union soldier, who will soon be fighting in the Battle of Gettysburg. Ben must return to the present or risk being trapped in the time of the Civil War.

Wings to the Kingdom [Novel; WW]

Author: Cherie Priest; First publication: New York: Tor, 2006.

Sightings of Old Green Eyes, guardian of the Confederate and Union dead are frequent at the Civil War battlefield at Chickamauga, Georgia. But recently the ghosts have started to point into the distance. Eden Moore, the girl who can see ghosts, checks out the scene with two classmates who attempt to capture the ghosts on photographs and on tape. When someone begins shooting at battlefield visitors and celebrity ghost hunters arrive chaos breaks loose. But Eden concentrates on her task of uncovering the mystery of what or who the ghosts are pointing towards.

Reluctant ghost hunter Eden Moore was first introduced to readers in Cherie Priest's *Four and Twenty Blackbirds* (2005).

Witchblade (2001) [TV series]

First broadcast: June 12, 2001; Creators: Marc Silvestri, Michael Turner; Main Cast: Yancy Butler as Detective Sara Pezzini, David Chokachi as Detective Jake McCartey, Anthony Cistaro as Kenneth Irons, Will Yun Lee as Detective Danny Woo, Eric Etebari as Ian Nottingham, Nestor Serrano as Capt. Bruno Dante; 44 min.; Halsted Pictures, Tip Cow Productions, Blade TV Productions, Mythic Films; Turner Television Network (TNT); Color.

"You're from a line going back through time and into the future. A part of a wave, a force, a warrior bloodline." New York detective Sara "Pez" Pezzini fights crime using her natural skills and the magic of the Witchblade. The series has a Weird War backstory that is highlighted in various episodes.

"DESTINY" (2:02)

Air date: June 17, 2002; Guest Cast: Kathryn Winslow as Vicky Po, Bill McDonald as Jerry Orlinsky, Johnie Chase as Sgt. Turnbull, Lazar Rockwood as Lazar; Story: Jorge Zamacona, William J. McDonald; Director: David Carson.

Another twist to the history of the Witchblade is revealed in this episode when Joan of Arc is seen wearing the Witchblade in a painting.

"LEGION" (1:05) [WW]

Air date: July 10, 2001; Guest Cast: Roger Daltrey as Father Del Toro, Paul Robbins as Edward Nolan, David Hemblen as Father Joe Bellamy, Sandrine Holt as Sandrine Malraux; Story: Richard C. Okie, Ralph Hemecker; Director: Neal Fearnley.

Sara Pezzinni learns the Witchblade was owned by the Vatican for 500 years before Adolf Hitler obtained it.

"Sacrifice" (1:04) [WW]
Air date: July 3, 2001: Guest Cast: John Hensley as Gabriel Bowman, Kim De Lury as Conchobar; Story: Richard C. Okie, Ralph Hemecker; Director: David S. Jackson.

In this episode we learn that Elizabeth Bronte, the previous owner of the Witchblade, was given the object by her lover, an S.S. Lieutenant who stole it from Adolf Hitler's personal collection.

Witchfinder General (1968) [Film; UK; WW]

Premiere: May 15, 1968; Main Cast: Vincent Price as Matthew Hopkins, Ian Ogilvy as Richard Marshall, Rupert Davies as John Lowes, Hilary Dwyer as Sara, Robert Russell as John Stearne, Nicky Henson as Swallow, Tony Selby as Salter; Executive Producers: Tony Tenser, Samuel Z. Arkoff; Screenplay: Tom Baker, Michael Reeves; Based on the novel by Ronald Bassett; Director: Michael Reeves; 86 min.; Tigon British-American International Productions; American International Pictures; Color.

During the English Civil War in 1645, Matthew Hopkins and his cohort Richard Stearne exploit fear and superstition traveling from village to village in East Anglia, torturing and executing witches and preachers who they claim carry the "Devil's Mark" on their bodies. Roundhead Richard Marshall is in love with Sara, niece of local preacher John Lowes. When Lowes is captured, tortured and executed by Hopkins and Sara is attacked and raped by Stearne, Marshall vows revenge on those responsible.

The Witching Hour [Comic book]

Supernatural anthology title.

"The Diggers (Or, Dig, They Must!)" [WW]
First publication: #18 (December 1971–January 1972); Story: Bob Haney; Art: Bob Brown, Frank Giacoia; Publisher: DC Comics.

Left to die in a trench during World War I, the soldier haunts the man, Achilles Moreau, responsible for his death.

The Witness Tree and the Shadow of the Noose [Juvenile book; WW]

Author: K.E.M. Johnston; First publication: Shippensburg, PA: White Mane Kids, 2009.

Sixth-grader Jake Salmon moves with his family to an old, spooky house located near the Civil War battlefield of Manassas, Virginia. Jake is puzzled when he sees a Civil War soldier carrying an axe running across his lawn but leaving no footprints in the snow. Is this the ghost of Confederate soldier Thomas Garnet? Jake investigates with the help of his younger brother and friend.

Wolfenstein [Videogame; WW]

Release date: August 2009; Original platforms: Microsoft Windows, PlayStation 3, Xbox 360; Developers: Raven Software, Endrant Studios; Publisher: id Software.

In this sequel to **Return to Castle Wolfenstein** "Office of Secret Actions" (OSA) operative BJ Blazkowicz is sent to the Nazi occupied town of Isenstadt. The Germans are excavating Nachtsonne crystals containing supernatural powers that can gain access to the "Black Sun" dimension.

Wolfenstein: Enemy Territory [Videogame; WW]

Release date: May 2003; Original platform: Microsoft Windows; Developer: Splash Damage, Raster Productions; Publisher: Activision.

An expanded edition of **Return to Castle Wolfenstein**.

Wolfenstein: The New Order [Videogame; AHW]

Release date: May 2014; Voice Cast: Brian Bloom as William "BJ" Blazkowicz, Kaspar Eichel as Wilhelm "Deathshead" Strasse, Alicja Bachleda as Anya Oliwa; Directors: Jerk Gustafsson, Jens Matthies; Multiple platforms; First-person shooter; Developer: MachineGames; Publisher: Bethesda Softworks.

An alternate history reboot of the **Wolfenstein** franchise set in 1946. The Nazis rule the world and OSA agent BJ Blazkowicz's mission to assassinate General Deathshead results in total failure. During his escape from Nazi forces he is critically injured and enters a deep coma that lasts until 1960. Blaszkowicz escapes his Nazi captors and fights to overthrow them with the help of The Resistance.

Wolfenstein: The Old Blood [Videogame; AHW]

Release date: May 2015; Multiple platforms; Developer: MachineGames; Publisher: Bethesda Softworks.

With a storyline that has strong similarities to **Return to Castle Wolfenstein** this game serves as a prequel to **Wolfenstein: The New Order**.

Agent One is captured and killed by Nazi troopers after he infiltrates Castle Wolfenstein with fel-

Wolfenstein: The Old Blood videogame. Copyright 2015 Bethesda Softworks LLC. All rights reserved.

low agent BJ Blazkowicz. A top secret document stating the location of General Deathshead has been moved from the castle. After escaping from Castle Wolfenstein Blazkowicz tracks the document to the village of Paderborn and Nazi neurologist Helga Von Schabbs. But his trail also leads to supernatural events and Helga's quest a vault containing knowledge of the occult.

The Wolf's Hour [Novel; WW]
Author: Robert R. McCammon; First publication: New York: Pocket Books, 1989.

1944. British secret agent Michael Gallatin is assigned to occupied France where he must uncover the Nazi secret plan known as Iron Fist. Gallatin has his own secret. He is the victim of an ancient curse that transforms him into a werewolf and makes him a formidable foe for the Nazis.

See: *The Hunter from the Woods*

Wolverine [Comic book character; SFW]
First appearance: *The Incredible Hulk* #180 (October 1974); Creators: Len Wein, John Romita, Jr.; Herb Trimpe, Publisher: Marvel Comics.

Born in Alberta, Canada in the late 1800s and raised in a giant mansion, sickly James Howlett's latent mutant powers are unleashed after seeing his father murdered by groundskeeper Thomas Logan. Howlett now possesses acute senses of sight, hearing and smell, enhanced physical strength, razor sharp bone claws (later fused with the metal adamantium) that spring from his fists and the power of self healing that reduces his aging process. Howlett kills Logan and flees into Yukon Territory with his close friend Rose who later dies while trying to protect him from the groundkeeper's vengeful son Dog. Adopting the name of Logan, James Howlett serves in World War I, fighting the Germans in Belgium and defeating the angel of death Lazaer in a battle for Logan's soul.

In 1937 Logan fights alongside Ernest Hemingway in the Spanish Civil War and joins **Captain America** and Sergeant Nick Fury in Operation: Blueboy during World War II before parting company with Captain America on unfriendly terms, despite saving his life. Logan suffers internment in a Nazi death camp in Poland before mentally breaking camp leader Major Bauman. Near the conclusion of the war Logan finds himself in a POW camp near Hiroshima, Japan and is witness to the atom bomb dropped on the city.

The Wolverine (2013) [Film; SFW]
Premiere: July 26, 2013; Main Cast: Hugh Jackman as Logan-Wolverine, Tao Okamoto as Manko, Rila Fukushima as Yukio. Hiroyuki Sanada as Shingen, Haruhiko Yamanouchi as Yashida, Svetlana Khodchenkova as Viper, Famke Janssen as Jean Grey, Brian Tee as Noburo; Executive Producers: Joe Caracciolo, Jr., **Stan Lee**; Screenplay: Mark Bomback, Scott Frank; Director: James Mangold; 126 min.; Twentieth Century–Fox, Marvel Entertainment, The Donners' Company; 3-D; Color.

1945. Nagasaki, Japan. As the atom bomb is about to drop Logan saves the life of Japanese soldier Yashida by sheltering in a bunker. Years later in Japan a dying Yashida contacts Logan through his granddaughter Yukio. Logan decides to pay his respects and is offered mortality by Yashida but Logan refuses. He soon comes into conflict with Yashida's doctor, Viper and Yashida himself and his adamantium suit of armor that preserves his life.

Wonder Woman [Comic book character]
1. First appearance: *All-Star* #8 (December 1941); Creator: William Moulton Marston; Publisher:

All-American; National Periodical Publications (DC).

Amazon Princess Diana leaves her all-female Paradise Island for the love of U.S. army intelligence officer, Captain Steve Trevor. "And so Diana, the Wonder Woman gives up her heritage to take the man she loves to America—the land she learns to love and protect, adopts as her own."

Soon Wonder Woman is fighting the Japanese with the aid of her invisible plane, truth compelling lasso and metal bracelets that repel bullets. She helps American forces secure the Philippines and is inducted into the "Justice Battalion of America" with fellow **Justice Society** members.

"Adventure of the Pilotless Plane" [SFW]
First publication: *Sensation Comics* #24 (December 1943); Story: William Moulton Marston; Art: H.G. Peter.

On Paradise Island Princess Diana listens to her mother's warning. The Japanese have created a new weapon. The Magic Sphere reveals the Japanese army commander reporting to the female Premier, "Her highness, our chemical research chief, has found means to keep all American planes from flying."

Wonder Woman seeks the guidance of Aphrodite, goddess of love and beauty. But thousands of miles away a poison gas explosion at a U.S. airfield on the Chinese front leaves American planes unable to fly. The Japanese are preparing to bomb U.S. troops. Inspired by Aphrodite Wonder Woman has decided to control her invisible plane by mental radio. The enemy cannot fight a plane they cannot see and soon the Japanese air fleet is decimated.

"The Invasion of Paradise Island" [SFW]
First publication: *Sensation Comics* #37 (January 1945); Story: William Moulton Marston; Art: H.G. Peter.

Two abused children run away from their orphanage and hide in a big wooden trunk that is loaded on to Wonder Woman's invisible plane. Landing on Paradise Island the stowaways quickly make friends with the children on the island. Meanwhile the power plant is undergoing repairs leaving the island temporarily vulnerable to attack. With the protective current disabled a U-boat is hurled toward Paradise Island by its release from centripetal force. The armed Nazi crew land ashore and take the children and Wonder Woman prisoner. Using her mental radio Wonder Woman sends a message to Mala who comes to the rescue with her fellow Amazons, protected from Nazi gunfire with their magic bracelets.

"The Spirit of War" [WW]
First publication: *Wonder Woman* #2 (Fall 1942); Story: William Moulton Marston; Art: H.G. Peter.

"Wonder Woman is helping America win the war and if America win, peace will return—the world will be ruled happily by the love and beauty of Aphrodite." Mars, the god of war, wants Wonder Woman captured and calls upon his assistants the Duke of Deception, the Earl of Greed and the Count of Conquest to bring Wonder Woman before him in chains. Meanwhile Wonder Woman is stopping an attack on America by the Gestapo, while the Earl of Greed, in his astral body, whispers in Hitler's ear that raiding America's treasury, buried in underground vaults, will double his private fortune. Wonder Woman and Etta Candy uncover a plot by Holliday College President Hezekiah Deacon to aid the Nazis in transporting their stolen gold shipment to Mars.

"Wanted by Hitler, Dead or Alive" [WW]
First publication: *Comic Cavalcade* #2 (Spring 1943); Story: William Moulton Marston; Art: Frank Godwin.

When a reporter asks Lieutenant Diana Prince and Steve Rogers questions about Wonder Woman's "mental radio" that picks up thought waves Diana fears she may be an Axis spy. Her hunch is correct. Rora Blank from the Daily Tab is Fausta Grables, Gestapo agent. Wanting to discover the secret of the mental radio Steve Rogers is kidnapped and threatened with torture, but Wonder woman comes to the rescue. Agent Fausta is humiliated and told by her Axis chiefs to succeed in capturing Wonder Woman next time, or face the consequences.

Fausta stars in her own "Masked Marvel" strong woman act and reveals herself to the audience as Wonder Woman. In the audience Diane Prince is confused and in disguise challenges the imposter to a wrestling match. The stolen Wonder Woman costume has given Fausta super-strength and Diane underestimates her when she gains control of her magic lasso. The real Wonder Woman is bundled into a trunk with Germany as her final destination.

2. [TV series; SFW]
Premiere: November 7, 1975; Main Cast: Lynda Carter as Wonder Woman/Diana Prince, Lyle Wag-

goner as Steve Trevor, John Randolph as General Blankenship (pilot), Richard Eastham as General Blankenship (telefilms, season one), Beatrice Colen as Etta Candy (telefilms, season one); Executive Producer: Douglas S. Cramer; Based on characters created by William M. Marston; Developed by Stanley Ralph Ross; 58 × 50 min.; Bruce Lansbury Productions, Douglas S. Cramer Company, Warner Bros. Television; American Broadcasting Company (ABC), Columbia Broadcasting System (CBS); Color.

World War II episodes:

"Anschluss '77" (2:02)

Air date: September 23, 1977; Story: Dallas L. Barnes; Director: Alan Crosland.

In Season Two the series moved forward in time to 1977 and moved from the ABC network to CBS. Inter Agency Defense Command agent Diana Prince (Wonder Woman) is partnered with the son of Steve Trevor. The season featured two World War II related episodes.

IADC agents Diana Prince and Steve Trevor investigate Neo-Nazis in South America who plan to clone Adolf Hitler and restore the Third Reich.

"Beauty on Parade" (1:04)

Air date: October 13, 1976; Story: Ron Friedman; Director: Richard Kinon.

After one pilot and two TV specials **Wonder Woman** premiered as a weekly series. Diana Prince seeks out saboteurs by entering a beauty pageant.

"The Bushwackers" (1:13)

Air date: January 29, 1977; Story: Skip Webster; Director: Stuart Margolin.

Nazi cattle rustlers in Texas are sabotaging the war effort. Steve Trevor and Wonder Woman attempt to rectify the situation by helping cattle rancher J.P. Hadley (Roy Rogers). But when Wonder Woman is imprisoned by the Nazis and her magic belt stolen Hadley's adopted children rescue her.

"Fausta, the Nazi Wonder Woman" (1:03)

Air date: April 28, 1976; Story: Bruce Shelley, David Ketcham; Director: Barry Crane.

Fausta (Lynda Day George), a Nazi operative, poses as Wonder Woman to lure her into a trap. Steve Trevor follows Fausta and the real Wonder Woman to Germany but is captured himself. Meanwhile Wonder Woman escapes her captor but now has to rescue Steve Trevor.

"The Feminine Mystique" (1:05–1:06)

Air dates: November 6, November 8, 1976; Story: Barbara Avedon, Barbara Corday; Teleplay: Jimmy Sangster; Director: Herb Wallerson.

In this two-part adventure Wonder Woman's younger sister, Drusilla (Debra Winger) has been told by the Queen to bring Diana back to Paradise Island. But Diana refuses and states her case for remaining in America to fight the Nazis. Soon Drusilla discovers why the Nazi threat has to be defeated when she is held hostage by them. They want the secret of her bullet-proof bracelets and plan an attack on Paradise Island after Drusilla accidentally reveals the secret location of the island to her captors. Wonder Woman must save the day.

"Formula 407" (1:12)

Air date: January 22, 1977; Story: Elroy Schwartz; Director: Herb Wallerstein.

In Buenos Aires Diana Prince and Steve Trevor discover a formula for making rubber tires as strong as steel. The Nazis have their own plans for the formula.

"Judgement from Outer Space" (1:10–1:11)

Air date: January 15, January 17, 1977; Story: Steve Kandel; Director: Alan Crosland.

While attempting to rescue an alien named Andros (Tim O'Connor), Wonder Woman and Steve Trevor are captured in Nazi Germany. A two-part episode that sees threats from both the Nazis and the inter-galactic council of planets who declare Earth must be sterilized.

"The Last of the $2 Bills" (1:09)

Air date: January 8, 1977; Story: Paul Dubov, Gwen Bagni; Director: Stuart Margolin.

The U.S. economy is threatened when Nazis circulate counterfeit $2 bills.

"The Man Who Could Move the World" (2:03)

Air date: September 30, 1977; Story: Judy Burns; Director: Bob Kelljan.

A Japanese man blames Wonder Woman for the death of his brother during World War II.

"The New Original Wonder Woman" (1:01)

Air date: November 7, 1975; Story: Stanley Ralph Ross; Director: Leonard Horn; 90 min.

The premise of the series is set up in the 90-minute pilot. After U.S. Air Corp Major Steve Trevor is shot down by a German plane he finds himself on Paradise Island, home to immortal female Amazons. A contest is held to decide who should return to America with Steve Trevor and help defeat the Nazi threat. The Queen's daughter Diana is forbidden to enter but disguises herself and wins the contest. In America she disguises herself as Diana Prince serving with the U.S. Navy. But when she dons her costume, armed with her magic lasso she battles the Nazis.

"THE PLUTO FILE" (1:08)
Air date: December 25, 1976; Story: Herbert Bermann; Director: Herb Wallerstein.

Washington, D.C., is under threat of destruction by a person who can create earthquakes.

"WONDER WOMAN IN HOLLYWOOD" (1:14)
Air date: February 16, 1977; Story: Jimmy Sangster; Director: Bruce Bilson.

Drusilla alias Wonder Girl (Debra Winger) journeys to Hollywood at the request of the Queen. In an effort to increase soldier morale a film is being made using real-life war heroes. But when Nazis kidnap the heroes, Wonder Woman must save them from being executed in Germany.

"WONDER WOMAN MEETS BARONESS VON GUNTHER" (1:02)
Air Date: April 21, 1976; Story: Margaret Armen; Director: Barry Crane.

Wonder Woman attempts to clear Steve Trevor of espionage claims by proving a prisoner and former leader of a Nazi spy ring, Baroness Von Gunther (Christine Belford), is the culprit.

"WONDER WOMAN VS. GARGANTUA" (1:07)
Air date: December 18, 1976; Story: David Ketchum, Tony DiMarco; Director: Charles R. Rondeau.

Wonder Woman's life is threatened by an unlikely enemy—a gorilla trained by Nazis to destroy her.

World War Cthulhu [RPG game; UK; WW]

Release date: 2013; Setting: Call of Cthulu; Story: Dominic McDowall, Gareth Ryder-Hanrahan, Jason Durall, Stuart Boon, Martin Dougherty, Ken Spencer; Art: Jon Hodgson, Paul Bourne, Scott Neill, Scott Purdy, Steffon Worthington; Publisher: Cubicle 7 Entertainment, Swindon, UK.

"The forces of fascism have overwhelmed Europe. In forgotten corners, darkness stirs. The cycles of ancient god-things are measured in millennia, but those who serve them plot to take advantage of the chaos of conflict to advance their own schemes."

A World War II setting for the Call of Cthulhu roleplaying game. Players representing the British Secret Intelligence Service fight against the dual threat from Axis forces and ancient evils out of time.

World War Cthulhu: A Collection of Lovecraftian War Stories [Short story anthology; WW]

Editors: Brian M. Sammons, Glynn Owen Barrass; Art: M. Wayne Miller; First publication: Portland, Oregon: Dark Regions Press, 2014.

Authors share a collection of short war stories that span history based on H.P. Lovecraft's Cthulhu mythos. From Roman Britain to the American Civil War, World War II, Vietnam, the Cold War and the future. Each of the 22 stories is accompanied by full-color artwork by W. Wayne Miller.

Worldwar: In the Balance [Novel; SFW]

Author: Harry Turtledove; First publication: New York: Ballantine Books, 1994.

In May 1942 World War II comes to a sudden halt when former enemies face a new, common foe from outer space known as "The Race." Washington, D.C., is destroyed and Europe and the Soviet Union ravaged by the alien invaders. Now Roosevelt, Churchill, Hitler, Stalin and Hirohito must unite to save the Earth.

The first in the four-book *Worldwar* series from Harry Turtledove. The story continues in *Tilting the Balance* (1995), *Upsetting the Balance* (1996) and *Striking the Balance* (1996).

Wunderwaffen [Comic book; France; AHW]

First publication: March 2012; Nine volumes; Story: Richard D. Nolane; Art: Maza, Milorad Vicanovic; Publisher: Soleil.

In summer 1946 the Japanese were defeated but World War II continues in Europe after the failure of the "Disaster Day" landings. Miracle weapons, commonly known as Wunderwaffen protect Germany. The revolutionary jet aircraft is piloted by the decorated Major Walter Murnau. But Murnau soon becomes aware he is being used by Himmler in a play for power within the S.S. for control of the Reich.

Wunderwaffen Présente Space Reich [Graphic novel; France; AHW]

First publication: January 2015; Story: Richard D. Nolane; Art: Maza, Marko Nikolic; Publisher: Soleil.

1945. The Third Reich now extends from the

Atlantic to Vladivostok in Russia. The United States is now the target of Nazi rocket scientist Werner von Braun and Adolf Hitler who wants to beat America into space and install a Nazi base on the moon.

Wunderwaffen Présente Zeppelin's War [Comic book; France; AHW]

First publication: June 2014; Story: Richard D. Nolane; Art: Vicenc Villagrasa Jovensa; Publisher: Soleil.

German Zeppelin airships piloted by Adolf Hitler and Hermann Göring attack Paris, France in 1916 as World War I continues. But laying in wait is the Russian Empire and Rasputin.

X-Men: Magneto Testament [Comic book; SFW]

First publication: November 2008; Story: Greg Pak; Art: Carmine Di Giandomenico; Publisher: Marvel Comics.

Schoolboy Max Eisenhardt and his father facing persecution as Jews in Nazi Germany escape to Poland but are captured. When Max faces the firing squad he miraculously survives but finds himself transported by train to the death camp Auschwitz-Birkenau.

The origin story of the mutant known as Magneto.

X-Men Origins: Wolverine (2009) [Film; SFW]

Premiere: May 1, 2009; Main Cast: Hugh Jackman as Logan/Wolverine, Liev Shreiber as Victor Creed, Danny Huston as Major William Stryker, Will. i. Am as John Wraith, Lynn Collins as Kayla Silverfox, Kevin Durand as Fred Dukes, Ryan Reynolds as Wade Wilson, Taylor Kitsch as Remy Le Beau, Dominic Monaghan as Bradley; Executive Producers: **Stan Lee**, Richard Donner; Screenplay: David Benioff, Skip Woods; Director: Gavin Hood; 107 min.; Twentieth Century–Fox, Dune Entertainment III, TCF Hungary Film; Color.

Logan seeks revenge against Victor Creed after he murders his girlfriend Kayla Silverfox. As part of Stryker's Team X project Logan undergoes a physical transformation when he is bonded with an adamantium exoskeleton. But when Logan overhears Stryker ordering his memory erased Logan flees the facility. Later, Logan learns that Stryker and Creed are working together experimenting on mutants. Stryker has become involved in his own personal war against mutants after his mutant son killed Stryker's wife. Stryker has created the ultimate mutant—Weapon XI. Adding to Logan's woes is Kayla Silverfox, who still lives after faking her own death.

The first eight minutes of the film recounts Wolverine's childhood origin story in the Northwest Territories, Canada in 1845 and footage of Logan and his brother Victor Creed fighting side-by-side in the American Civil War, World War I, World War II and the Vietnam War. The origin story differs from the Marvel comic book origin with an earlier childhood at a time when the Northwest Territories in Canada didn't exist. Added to the problems of the screenplay is the fact Logan and Creed, both Canadian citizens, are seen fighting in the various wars in American uniform.

The Yank and the Rebel [Comic book characters; SFW]

First appearance: *The Flame* #7 (October 1941); Creator: Larry Antonette (as Dix Mason); Publisher: Fox Feature Syndicate.

"1863 ... Gettysburg.... Overhead a shell bursts. The terrific explosion opens a fissure in the earth. Locked in each others arms, the two soldiers lie unconscious, in a cavern bathed in a radioactive pool. Kept in a state of suspended animation the Yank and the Rebel lie as in combat, as the years parade by and fade into the curtain of the past."

1941. The cavern roof is dislodged in cannon fire as the Yank and the Rebel are revived by the fresh air. Unaware of the passage of time the Union and Confederate soldier resume their fighting, until passing troops bring them to the surface and confront them with the reality of their situation. Soon they are working together to stop Nazi spies and helping to defuse a deadly bomb.

Yankee Doodle Jones [Comic book character; SFW]

First appearance: *Yankee Comics* #1 (September 1941); Creator: George Sultan; Publisher: Harry "A" Chesler.

A strange group of crippled war veterans gather at the home of an eminent surgeon. "You men of different faiths gladly gave your services for Uncle Sam in the last war. Are you ready now to give up your lives?"

The veterans reply in unison, "Willingly, so that from us a protector of the American doctrines shall rise!"

The surgeon transplants living organisms to

produce an "invincibility" serum. The test subject, Yankee Doodle Jones, is waiting to be injected. "The strength of the army lies in this fluid.... You'll be the greatest living thing the world has ever seen."

The surgeon's young son Dandy, watches from across the room as his father is shot by Nazi spies lying in wait. As Yankee Doodle Jones fights the Nazi intruders Dandy injects himself with the remaining serum. "Now to avenge my father!"

Dandy's dying father utters his final words. "And from now on let it be Yankee Doodle and Dandy. Uncle Sam will honor your deeds to preserve his freedom!"

Yellow Blue Tibia [Novel; SFW]

Author: Adam Roberts; First publication: London: Gollanz, 2009.

Soviet science fiction author Konstantin Skvorecky and five of his peers are ordered by Stalin to concoct a story about aliens poised to invade Earth that is so believable the population of the whole world will be fooled. Then unexpectedly after months of work Stalin has a change of heart and the writers go their separate ways. The years pass, but the story the writers created decades ago appears to be coming true in the wake of Chernobyl.

The Yesterday Machine (1963) [Film; SFW]

Premiere: 1963; Main Cast: Tim Holt as Police Lieutenant Partane, James Britton as Jim Crandall, Jack Herman as Professor Ernest Von Hauser, Ann Pellegrino as Sandy De Mar, Jay Ramsay as Howie Ellison, Linda Jenkins as Marjie De Mar, Robert Kelly as Detective Lasky; Executive Producer: Don Holloway; Story-Director: Russ Marker; 79 min.; Carter Film Productions; B/W.

When their car breaks down honor student Howie Ellison and band majorette Margie De Mar search for a farm and encounter two hostile Confederate soldiers. Ellison recovers in hospital from his gunshot wound but Margie disappears out of sight. Police lieutenant Parlane suspects a link to Dr. Ernest Von Hauser and his time travel experiments in Nazi death camps in 1945. Jim Crandall and Margie DeMar's sister Sandy investigate and find themselves instantly transported to Von Hauser's laboratory. They learn he is holding Margie prisoner and using her as a test subject perfecting his "Super Spectronic Relativity" machine. He plans to use his time machine to restore Adolf Hitler and the Third Reich to power again.

Police lieutenant Parlane concludes, "Yesterday should be left alone because today the world has enough problems just making sure we have a tomorrow."

Young Allies [Comic book; SHW]

First publication: Summer 1941; Creators: **Jack Kirby**, **Joe Simon**, Otto Binder, C. Wostkoski; Publisher: Timely Comics.

The young sidekicks of **Captain America** and the **Human Torch** compete to lead a group of four kids against various adversaries, including the Nazi **Red Skull**. Percival O'Toole, known as Knuckles, is from New York's Lower East Side. Henry Tinkle is the overweight kid known as Tubby. Jeff Sandervilt is simply referred to as Jeff and Whitewash Jones is the black stereotype.

The Young Indiana Jones Chronicles (1992) [TV series]

Executive Producer: George Lucas; 22 × 45 min.; Lucasfilm, Amblin Entertainment, Paramount Television; American Broadcasting Company (ABC); Color.

The early adventures of Indiana Jones as a 10-year-old boy and later as a teenager, fighting in World War I.

"Transylvania—January, 1918" (2:22) [WW]
Air date: August 21, 1993; Main Cast: Sean Patrick Flannery as Indiana Jones, George Hall as Old Indy, Bob Peck as General Targo, Keith Szarabajka, Simone Bendix as Maria, Paul Klyman as Nicholas Hunyadi, Sam Kelly as Dr. Franz Heinzer/Captain Adolf Schmidt, Alan Polonsky as Agent McCall, Steven Hartley as Agent Picard, William Armstrong as The Major; Producer: Rick McCallum; Story: Jonathan Hensleigh; Director: Dick Maas.

Old Indy recalls a spooky mission he undertook as a youth in 1918, to three children trick or treating on Halloween. Deep in Transylvania Romanian General Targo has been raiding a German P.O.W. camp. Indiana Jones and his fellow agents have to find out why. To their amazement they discover Targo is a vampire who plans to create a conquering vampire army.

Youth Without Youth (2007) [Film; WW]

Premiere: October 27, 2007; Main Cast: Tim Roth as Dominic Matei, Alexandra Maria Lara as Veronica/Laura, Bruno Ganz as Professor Roman Stanciulescu, Andre Hennicke as Dr. Josef Rudolf; Based on the novella by Mircea Eliade; Producer-Story-

Director: Francis Ford Coppola; 124 min.; American Zoetrope; Sony Pictures Classics; Color.

Aging Professor Dominic Matei's plans to commit suicide are interrupted when he is struck by lightning and to his astonishment grows younger. But in World War II Europe he is targeted by Nazis who want to discover the secret of his powers. The professor then meets and falls in love with a young woman who has undergone a similar path after being struck by lightning.

Zipang [Manga; Animated TV series; Japan; SFW]

1. First publication: *Weekly Morning* (2000); Story-Art: Kaji Kawaguchi; Publisher: Kodansha.

2. Premiere: October 7, 2004; Story: Kazuhiro Furuhashi, Yuichiro Takeda; Director: Kazuhiro Furuhashi; 26 × 24 min.; Studio Deen; Tokyo Broadcasting System (TBS); Color.

Based on the manga by Kaji Kawaguchi, the animated series begins as the Japanese Destroyer Mirai is headed to Pearl Harbor for a training exercise with the U.S. Navy. Near Midway Island the Mirai loses contact with the other ships in the Japanese Maritime Self Defense Force when they encounter an unusual electrical storm. Suddenly the Mirai sees the Imperial Navy battleship Yamato straight ahead. The ship and her crew have traveled back in time to the night before the Battle of Midway in 1942. The crew must decide between changing history or remaining neutral while avoiding the Allied forces.

Season One

1:01—*The Mirai Sets Sail*; 1:02—*Midway*; 1:03—*Person Adrift*; 1:04—*Mirai's Battle*; 1:05—*Kusaka's Choice*; 1:06—*Order of Attack*; 1:07—*Malay Railway*; 1:08—*The Pursuer*; 1:09—*Deadline*; 1:10—*Interchange*; 1:11—*Guadalcanal Island*; 1:12—*The Arrow of Sagittarius*; 1:13—*The Land of Gold*; 1:14—*Collision!*; 1:15—*The Living and the Dead*; 1:16—*The Will of Lieutenant Okamura*; 1:17—*Zipang Initiation*; 1:18—*The Reunion*; 1:19—*The Other Staff Headquarters*; 1:20—*Submarine I-21*; 1:21—*One Versus Forty*; 1:22—*Warning*; 1:23—*Sinking the Wasp*; 1:24—*The Dead and the Alive*; 1:25—*Coming Home*; 1:26—*The Place of Return*

ZMD: Zombies of Mass Destruction [Comic book; WW]

First publication: July 2008; Six-issue mini-series; Story: Kevin Grevioux; Art: Gerald Parel, Geraldo Borges; Publisher: Red 5 Comics.

The U.S. has developed a new biologic weapon of mass destruction as zombies are dropped into the battle zone. But when a U.S. military zombie goes missing in Lebanon and the military zombie experiment goes rogue, Colonel Matthew Drake is sent into the heart of the Middle East zombie zone.

Zombie Lake (1981) [Film; France-Spain; WW]

Premiere: September 1985; Main Cast: Howard Vernon as The Mayor, Anouchka as Helena, Pierre Escourrou as German Soldier; Producers: Marius Lesouer, Daniel White; Story: Julius Valery, A. L. Mariaux a.k.a. Marius Lesouer; Director: J. A. Laser; 90 min.; J.E. Films, Eurocine; Image Entertainment; Color.

During World War II members of the French Resistance kill occupying Germans in a French village. But the same German soldiers rise from the lake that has been their grave for the last ten years and attack the locals. Now the Nazi undead must be destroyed with the help of Helena, the daughter of a union between a local woman and a Nazi soldier during the war.

The film was directed by the combined efforts of Jean Rollin and Julian de Laserna under the pseudonym J.A. Lazer.

Original title: *Le Lac des morts vivants*

Zombie War [Comic book; WW]

First publication: 1992; Story: Kevin Brook Eastman, Tom Skulan; Art: Kevin Brook Eastman, Eric Talbot; Publisher: Fantaco-Tundra.

The only survivor of a dead alien race seeks revenge on humans who he blames for the destruction of his planet. Dead soldiers of the world arise from military cemeteries to destroy the Earth. Fighter pilot and military detective Jina joins forces with the alien to stop the zombies after the alien has a change of heart after seeing the death and destruction being caused by the zombie soldiers in Washington, D.C., and New York City.

Originally published in black-and-white the two issue series was reprinted in color by IDW Publishing in 2013.

Zombies vs. Nazis: A Lost History of the Walking Dead [Novel; WW]

Author: Scott Kenemore; Illustrator: Adam Wallenta; First publication: New York: Skyhorse, 2011.

When the Nazi Sicherheitsdienst attempt to control Haitian Voodoo for military purposes they discover zombies are only motivated by a taste for human flesh. And that flesh is just as tasty if it's Nazi flavored.

Zone Troopers (1985) [Film; SFW]

Premiere: October 1, 1985; Main Cast: Tim Thomerson as The Sarge, Timothy Van Patten as PFC Joey Verona, Art La Fleur as "Mittens" Makinsky, Biff Manard as Charlie Dolan, Max Turilli as SS Sgt. Zeller, William Paulson as The Alien, Alviero Martin as The Fuhrer, Joshua McDonald as Zone Trooper Captain; Executive Producer: Charles Band; Story: Danny Bilson, Paul De Meo, Director: Danny Bilson; 86 min.; Altar Productions; Empire Pictures; Color.

Somewhere in Italy, 1944. Caught behind enemy lines and under attack from Nazi troops a depleted U.S. squad, consisting of the "Iron Sarge," pulp fiction fan, PFC Joey Verona, "Mittens" Makinsky, and war correspondent Charlie Dolan retreat to the cover of woodland. In a clearing they discover a mysterious crash-landed craft. Joey speculates to the Sarge that it might be a spaceship. Meanwhile Dolan and Mittens have been captured by Nazis, who are also holding an alien creature captive. Adolf Hitler pays a visit to the camp to view the bug-eyed, hairy creature, but ends up with a bloody nose, courtesy of Mittens.

Joey and the Sarge manage to free Dolan, Mittens and the alien from their captors. The alien shows the ability to vaporize objects, including Nazi tanks, but cannot save Joey when he is killed-in-action. As he dies he asks Dolan to write his story, "Joey Verona met the men from space." When the Sarge sacrifices his life, only two men remain. Mittens and Dolan come under Nazi attack, but are rescued by the aliens, before they leave for home.

Dalton keeps his promise to Joey and sells his "Zone Troopers" story to Joey's favorite pulp magazine, "Fantastic Fiction."

Appendix: Weird War Stories by Medium

Animated Film
Dragon Ball Z: Fusion Reborn
First Squad: The Moment of Truth
Fullmetal Alchemist: Conqueror of Shambala
Return to Never Land
Strike Witches: The Movie

Animated Short
Superman

Animated Television Series [Weird War titles]
Big X
Cybersix
Gunparade March: The New March
Gunparade Orchestra
Hellsing: The Dawn
Strike Witches
Zipang

Animated Television Series [featuring WW episodes]
Back to the Future
Captain America
Family Guy
Futurama
Jonny Quest
Justice League
Spider-Man: The Animated Series
The Super Hero Squad Show
Tetsujin 28-gou

Animated Television Special
Futatsu no Kurumi

Audio Drama
Bernice Summerfield: Just War
Bernice Summerfield: Secret Origins
Bernice Summerfield: The Oracle of the Delphi
Doctor Who: Colditz
Doctor Who: Daleks Among Us
Doctor Who: Dark Convoy
Doctor Who: Persuasion
Doctor Who: Resistance
Doctor Who: The Churchill Years: Hounded
Doctor Who: The Churchill Years: Living History
Doctor Who: The Churchill Years: The Oncoming Storm
Doctor Who: The Nemonite Invasion
Doctor Who: The Scapegoat

Board Game
Dust Tactics
Insurrection
NUTS! War Without End—Weird War 2
Secrets of the Third Reich
Shadows Over Normandie: Cthulhu Mythos Call One
Tannhauser

Comic Book [Weird War titles]
Age of Bronze: The Story of the Trojan War
Airboy (2015)
Airboy 1942: Best of Enemies
All-Star Squadron
Anthem
Arrowsmith
Atomic Robo and the Dogs of War
Battle Hymn
Breath of Bones: A Tale of the Golem
Bring the Thunder
B.R.P.D. 1946
Bulletproof Monk
Captain Confederacy
Captain Fearless
Chrononauts
Chronos Commandos
Common Foe
Cry Havoc
Cybersix
Daredevil Battles Hitler
Dark Axis—Secret Battles of World War II: Rise of the Overmen
DC Comics: Bombshells
Dead Soldier
Dessous: La Montagne des Morts
Les Divisions de Fer
Dust Wars
Fiends of the Eastern Front
Fiends of the Eastern Front: Stalingrad
Fighting Yank
Flash Gordon: Zeitgeist
Fubar: American History Z
Fubar: By the Sword
Fubar: Declassified
Fubar: Empire of the Rising Dead
Fubar: European Theater of Blood
Graveyard of Empires
Great American Comics Present: The Secret Voice
Grunts
Half Past Danger
The Haunted Tank

215

Appendix

Heroes vs. Hitler
Homer's Iliad
I Am Legion
The Iliad
Indiana Jones and the Fate of Atlantis
Indiana Jones and the Iron Phoenix
Indiana Jones and the Spear of Destiny
The Invaders
Jackboot & Ironheel
JSA: The Liberty Files
Kade Mourning Sun
Leviathan: Le Patient Zero
The Light & Darkness War
Light Brigade
Lost Squad
Marvels
Mother Russia
Nazi Werewolves from Outer Space
Pax Romana
Peter Panzerfaust
Rocket Ranger
The Rocketeer
The Royals: Masters of War
'68
'68: Jungle Jim
'68: Last Rites
'68: Rules of Law
'68: Scars
Sledge-Hammer 44
Snowman 1944
Le Souffle du Wendigo
Stitched
Storming Paradise
Taskmaster
30 Days of Night: Red Snow
Trojan War
The Twelve: Spearhead
Uber
Vampirella vs. Lady Death
The War That Time Forgot
Weird War Tales
Wunderwaffen
Wunderwaffen Présente Zeppelin's War
X Men: Magneto Testament
Young Allies
ZMD: Zombies of Mass Destruction
Zombie War

Comic Book [titles featuring WW stories]

Action Comics
Adventure Comics
Adventures into Darkness
Adventures into the Unknown
The Adventures of Bob Hope
Adventures of the Outsiders
Amazing Adult Fantasy
American Vampire
Baffling Mysteries
Batman
The Beyond
Chamber of Chills
Countdown
Creepy
Dark Mysteries
Dark Shadows
The Demon
Doctor Who
Doctor Who Adventures
Doctor Who Magazine
Eerie
Fantastic Four
Forbidden Worlds
Ghost Stories
Ghostly Tales
Ghosts
The Hotspur
Impact
Jughead's Time Police
Midnighter
Mysterious Stories
Operation: Peril
Out of the Shadows
Rip Hunter: Time Master
Rover
Rover and Wizard
Sgt. Fury and His Howling Commandos
Sgt. Rock and Easy Company
Space Western Comics
Special War Series: Attack!
Star Spangled War Stories
Strange Adventures
Superboy
Superman
Superman's Pal Jimmy Olsen
The Thing!
Thor
The Time Tunnel
Tomahawk
TV Action
TV Comic
The Twilight Zone
The Unseen
Unusual Tales
Voodoo
War Picture Library
Warfront: Tales of Combat
Web of Mystery
Weird Fantasy
Weird Horrors
Weird Terror
Weird Thrillers
The Witching Hour

Comic Book Artist

Burgos, Carl
Everett, Bill
Heath, Russell
Kirby, Jack
Kubert, Joe
Leav, Mort
Schomburg, Alex
Simon, Joe

Comic Book Character(s)

Airboy
All-Winners Squad
Amazing Man
The American Crusader
The American Eagle
Arnim Zola
Athena Voltaire
Atomic Knight
Baron Blitzkrieg
Baron Blood
Baron Heinrich Zemo
Battler Britton
The Black Beetle
Black Max
The Black Terror
The Blackhawks
Blazing Glory
The Blue Diamond
The Blue Tracer
Bombshell, Son of War
Braddock
Brainiape
Bulletman
Captain America
Captain Battle
Captain Hurricane

Captain Marvel
Captain Marvel, Jr.
Captain Midnight
Captain Nazi
Captain Wonder
The Claw
Commander Steel
The Conqueror
The Creature Commandos
The Destroyer
Doctor Manhattan
Doll Man
Dynaman
The Escapist
Firebrand
The Flag
The Flame
Freedom Fighters
Freedom's Five
The Gay Ghost
Ghost Patrol
G.I. Robot
G.I. Zombie
The Hate-Monger
The Heap
The Human Torch
The Invaders
Jack Frost
John Kowalski
Jonah Hex
Justice Society of America
Kid Eternity
Lash Lightning
Liberty Belle
The Liberty Legion
Major Victory
Merlin the Magician
Minute-Man
Miss America
Mr. Justice
Mr. Liberty
The Monster Society of Evil
Professor Supermind and Son
Pyroman
Red Raven
Red Skull
Sgt. Fury and His Howling Commandos
Sgt. Rock and Easy Company
The Shield
Shining Knight
Silver Streak
Sir Steel
Son of Vulcan

Spitfire
Spy Smasher
Star Spangled Kid & Stripesy
Steel Commando
The Sub-Mariner
Superman
Super Soldier
The Thin Man
Tom Strong
U-Man
Uncle Sam
The Unknown Soldier
Vandal Savage
Viking Commando
Warrior Woman
The Whizzer
Wolverine
Wonder Woman
The Yank and the Rebel
Yankee Doodle Jones

Comic Book Writer

Burgos, Carl
Everett, Bill
Kanigher, Robert
Kirby, Jack
Lee, Stan
Simon, Joe
Thomas, Roy

Epic Poem

The Aeneid
The Iliad

Film

Abraham Lincoln, Vampire Hunter
Abraham Lincoln vs. Zombies
Army of Frankensteins
Backtrack: Nazi Regression
Bedknobs and Broomsticks
Below
Biggles, Adventures in Time
Blood Creek
Bloodrayne: The Third Reich
Blubberella
El Bose
The Boys from Brazil
Bulletproof Monk
The Bunker
Cannibal Apocalypse
Captain America
Captain America: The First Avenger

Captain Battle: Legacy of War
Code Red
Creature with the Atom Brain
Crusade in Jeans
Dead Birds
Dead of Night
Dead Snow
Dead Snow 2: Red vs. Dead
Dead Walkers: Rise of the 4th Reich
Death Ship
Deathwatch
The Devil's Backbone
Devils of War
The Devil's Rock
The Devil's Tomb
Djinns
Elves
The Enemy
Exit Humanity
The Extraordinary Seaman
FDR: American Badass!
A Field in England
The Final Countdown
The Flesh Eaters
Flesh Feast
Flight World War II
Frankenstein's Army
From a Whisper to a Scream
Frostbitten
The Frozen Dead
Gamma 693
Ghost Fever
Gojira
Grey Knight
Gun of the Black Sun
A Guy Named Joe
Hanussen
Hard Rock Zombies
The Haunting of Marsten Manor
Hellboy
Horrors of War
House
I Accuse!
The Incredible Mr. Limpet
Indiana Jones and the Last Crusade
Insensible
Invisible Agent
Iron Sky
Iron Sky: The Coming Race
Iron Wolf
Isle of the Dead
J'Accuse!

Appendix

Jacob's Ladder
Joan the Woman
Jonah Hex
Julius Caesar
The Keep
King of the Zombies
The Land That Time Forgot
The Living and the Dead
A Matter of Life and Death
Lorelei: The Witch of the Pacific Ocean
The Lost Platoon
The Madmen of Madoras
The Magic Face
A Matter of Life and Death
The Men Who Stare at Goats
Monster Killer
Mysterious Island
Nang Nak
Nanny McPhee and the Big Bang
Nazi Dawn
Nazis at the Center of the Earth
Neither Heaven Nor Earth
Night Wars
Oasis of the Zombies
The Objective
The Order of the Black Eagle
Outpost
Outpost: Black Sun
Outpost: Rise of the Spetsnaz
The Oval Portrait
P-51 Dragon Fighter
Pan's Labyrinth
The Philadelphia Experiment
Philadelphia Experiment II
Puppetmaster
Puppet Master: Axis of Evil
Puppet Master: Axis Termination
Puppetmaster III: Toulon's Revenge
Puppet Master X: Axis Rising
Raiders of the Lost Ark
Red Planet Mars
Red Sands
Revenge of the Red Baron
Revenge of the Zombies
Richard III
The Rocketeer
Rome Against Rome
R–Point
Samurai Commando Mission 1549
Second Time Lucky
Sengoku Jieitai
She Demons
Shock Waves
Slaughterhouse Five
Small Soldiers
Soldiers of the Damned
The Squad
Sucker Punch
The Supernaturals
Teenape vs. The Monster Nazi Apocalypse
Timecop 2: The Berlin Decision
Timeline
Tomorrow I'll Wake Up and Scald Myself with Tea
The 25th Reich
Twilight Zone: The Movie
The Unborn
The Unholy
War of the Dead
White Tiger
Witchfinder General
The Wolverine
X-Men Origins: Wolverine
The Yesterday Machine
Youth Without Youth
Zombie Lake
Zone Troopers

Film Serial

Batman
Mysterious Island

Film Trailer

Werewolf Women of the S.S.

Graphic Novel

Andie and the Alien
General Leonardo
The Lamb and the Fuhrer
The Life Eaters
Marvels
Maus: A Survivor's Tale
Maus II: And Here My Troubles Began
Nazi Werewolf Zombie Inferno
The Rest of Heaven Was Blue
Revere: Revolution in Silver
The Secret History
Time Bomb
Wunderwaffen Présente Space Reich

Juvenile Book

Abe Lincoln at Last!
An Angel for May
Are You Afraid of the Dark?— The Tale of the Zero Hero
At the Firefly Gate
AWOL in North Africa
The Backyard Ghost
Beware of the Haunted Toilet
Blitzed
The Case of the Soldier's Ghost
Charlotte Sometimes
Civil War on Sunday
A Coming Evil
Confederates Don't Wear Couture
Danger in the Darkest Hour
Day of the Assassins
The Deepest Night
The Demon Assassin
The Discovery
Escape from Ghost Hotel
Fallen in Fredericksburg
Find Me Where the Water Ends
Friends Forever: The Mystery Tour
George Washington's Socks
Ghost Cadet
Ghost of the Great River Inn
Ghost Soldier
The Ghost Wore Gray
The Ghosts of Iron Bottom Sound
Ghosts of the Civil War
Ghostscape
Gingersnap
The Haunting at Stratton Falls
The Haunting of Holroyd Hill
The Haunting of Swain's Fancy
Henry Hamilton, Graduate Ghost
Henry Hamilton in Outer Space
Here and Then
Hero
The House of Dies Drear
In the Shadow of Blackbirds
The Jewel and the Key
Johnny and the Bomb
Johnny and the Dead
Last Ghost at Gettysburg
Lincoln's Legacy
London Calling
Lost at Khe Sanh
The Mirk and Midnight Hour
Moonbranches
The Mystery at Fort Thunderbolt
Nick of Time
Once Was a Time
Only You Can Save Mankind
Picture the Dead

The Piper
The Red Suitcase
Rebel Spirits
Revolutionary War on Wednesday
Riding with the James Gang
The Rinaldi Ring
Rocket Ship Galileo
Rosie Goes to War
The Secret of Midway
The Secret Shelter
The Shadow Children
So Close to You
The Spring Rider
A Strange and Familiar Place
This Boy
Time Riders
Time Riders: The Eternal War
Time to Go Back
Time Train to the Blitz
Troy
War
Washington's War
Window of Time: A Story
The Witness Tree and the Shadow of the Noose

Manga

Big X
Gunparade March
Hellsing
Hellsing: The Dawn
Samurai Commando: Mission 1549
Spriggan
Tetsujin 28-gou
Zipang

Newspaper-Magazine Strip

Look Magazine
The Phantom Goes to War
Superman

Novel

Abraham Lincoln: Vampire Hunter
Achilles
After Dachau: A Novel
After the Downfall
Against the Tide of Years
All Clear
All Evil Shed Away
Andersonville

Baltimore, or, The Steadfast Tin Soldier and the Vampire
The Bargain
Behemoth
Bitter Seeds
Blackout
Blood Red Roses
Bloody Awful
Bloody Good
The Bloody Red Baron
Bloody Right
Blue Devil Island
Bride of the Night
Bring the Jubilee
By the Blood of Heroes: The Great Undead War
The Castle in the Forest
Catch Me Once, Catch Me Twice
Crusade
Dark Victory
Declare
Designated Targets
Devils of D-Day
Doctor Who and the Crusaders
Doctor Who: Atom Bomb Blues
Doctor Who: Autumn Mist
Doctor Who: Illegal Alien
Doctor Who: Just War
Doctor Who: The Shadow in the Glass
Doctor Who: Timewyrm: Exodus
The Dragon in the Sword
The Dragon Waiting: A Masque of History
The Dreamthief's Daughter: A Tale of the Albino
Druid's Sword
The Enchanted Life of Adam Hope
Fiends of the Eastern Front: Blood Red Army
Fiends of the Eastern Front: Fiends of the Rising Sun
Fiends of the Eastern Front: Operation Vampyr
Fiends of the Eastern Front: Twilight of the Dead
The Final Impact
The Firebrand
'48
From Time to Time
The Gate of Time
Gene
Germania

Ghost Talkers
Ghosts of Time
Goliath
The Guns of the South
The Haunting of Toby Jugg
The Healer's War
His Majesty's Dragon: A Novel of Temeraire
Home Again
Ilium
The Illuminatus! Trilogy
In the Electric Mist with the Confederate Dead
In Time of War
In War Times
Into the Storm
The Iron Dream
Island in the Sea of Time
Jewels of Time
The Keep
The King
Kishin Corps
Konkepi no Kantai
Lady Lazarus
Lammas Night
The Land That Time Forgot
Land of Mist and Snow
Leviathan
Lincoln's Sword
The Locked Spirit
Look Who's Back
Maelstrom
The Magicians of Night
Making History
The Medusa Amulet
The Midnight Guardian
Moonfisher
The Moonlight Brigade
Mr. Limpet
The Night Boat
Nostradamus Ate My Hamster
Olympos
On Her Majesty's Behalf: The Great Undead War
On the Oceans of Eternity
One Summer at Deer's Leap
Overseas
Phoenix and Ashes
The Proteus Operation
Rebel Angels
A Rebel in Time
The Reckoning
Seventh Sanctuary
Shadows in the Mist

Appendix

Shambling Towards Hiroshima
1632
Slaughterhouse Five: or, The Children's Crusade, a Duty Dance with Death
The Songs of the Kings
A Sound Among the Trees
The Spear
Spirit of the Century
Spirit of the Rebellion
Strange Conflict
Sunset of the Gods
The Temple and the Crown
The Temple and the Stone
They Used Dark Forces
Thin Air
The Third Section
Three Hearts and Two Lions
Till the End of Time
Time and Time Again
Twelve
Twice Upon a Time
The Violent Century
The War at Troy
Warrior Rising
Weapons of Choice
The Werewolf's Tale
Where Dead Soldiers Walk
Wings to the Kingdom
The Wolf's Hour
Worldwar: In the Balance
Yellow Blue Tibia
Zombies vs. Nazis: A Lost History of the Walking Dead

Novella

The Forest of Time
Thor Meets Captain America
Wendigo Tales: A Tale of Weird Wars: Hellfighters
Wendigo Tales: A Tale of Weird Wars: Los!
Wendigo Tales: A Tale of Weird Wars: No Man's Land
Wendigo Tales: A Tale of Weird Wars: Raid on Fort Douaumont
Wendigo Tales: A Tale of Weird Wars: Teufelshunde
Wendigo Tales: A Tale of Weird Wars: With Utmost Dispatch
Wendigo Tales: A Tale of Weird Wars: Without Fear
Wendigo Tales: A Tale of Weird Wars: Wunderwaffe

Original Net Animation (ONA)

Urda

Original Video Animation (OVA)

Hellsing: Ultimate
Kishin Corps
Konkepi no Kantai
Strike Witches
Strike Witches: Operation Victory

Pulp Fiction

"Adam Link Fights a War"
"Adam Link Saves the World"
"The Avengers"
"Baby Face"
"The Battle of Manetong"
"Blitz Against Japan"
"Blitzkrieg in the Past"
"Cave City of Hel"
"Change for the Bitter"
"The Curse of El Dorado"
"Dagon"
"The Daughter of Thor"
"Direct Wire"
"Dr. Loudon's Armageddon"
"Dragons Behind Us"
"Fifth Column of Mars"
"For the Love of Barbra Allen"
"From the House of the Rat Catcher"
"From Out of the Dark Water"
"Fugitives from Earth"
"Gallery of Glacial Doom"
"The Ghost That Haunted Hitler"
"Gods of the Jungle"
"Henry Horn's Blitz Bomb"
"Heroes Die Hard"
"His Last Appearance"
"I'll See You Again"
"Intruders from the Stars"
"Invasion Dust"
"Lost City of Burma"
"The Lost Warship"
"Luvium, the Invisible City"
"The Man Who Cried Werewolf"
"The Man Who Hated War"
"The Map of Fate"
"Matches and Kings"
"The Miracle at Dunkirk"
"The Miracle of Bulldozer Mike"
"The Miracle of Kicker McGuire"
"Mistress of the Dark"
"A Most Ingenious Paradox"
"Nazi Diamond"
"The Odyssey of Battling Bert"
"A Patriot Never Dies"
"Periscope Prey"
"Peter Pettigrew's Prisoner"
"Private Prune Speaking"
"Raiders Out of Space"
"The Return of the Hun"
"Return to Lilliput"
"Rockets Over Europe"
"Secret Unattainable"
"The Temple"
"They Forgot to Remember Pearl Harbor"
"Thompson's Time-Traveling Theory"
"Three Wise Men of Space"
"The Throne of Valhalla"
"The Tiger Has a Soul"
"Tink Fights the Gremlins"
"Tink Takes Command"
"The Traitor"
"Trophy"
"Trouble in Avalon"
"Truk Island"
"The Undersea Guardians"
"Vengeance in Her Bones"
"Victory from the Void"
"War Criminal of Renault Island"
"War Worker 17"
"Warrior Queen of Lolarth"

Radio—Podcast Drama

The Red Panda Adventures
Ritual of the Stifling Air
The Twilight Zone—Radio Dramas

RPG Book

Achtung! Cthulhu: Dark Tales from the Secret War
Achtung! Cthulhu: Heroes of the Sea
Achtung! Cthulhu: Interface 19.40

Achtung! Cthulhu: Kontamination
Achtung! Cthulhu: Shadows of Atlantis
Achtung! Cthulhu: Terrors of the Secret War
Achtung! Cthulu: The Crystal Void—The Seraph Chronicles Book Two
Achtung! Cthulu: Three Kings
Achtung! Cthulu: Tomb of the Aeons—The Seraph Chronicles Book Three
Achtung! Cthulhu: Trellborg Monstrosities
Dust Adventures Core Book
Dust Adventures: Operation Apocalypse
GURPS Weird War II: Secret Weapons and Twisted History
GURPS Weird War II: The Secret of the Gneisenau
The Nazi Occult
Scion Companion
Weird Wars: Rome: Nox Germanica
Weird Wars: Rome: The Half-Set Sun
Weird Wars: Rome: Wellspring
Weird Wars: Tour of Darkness
Weird Wars: Weird Wars II: Afrika Korpse
Weird Wars: Weird Wars II: Blood on the Rhine
Weird Wars: Weird Wars II: Dead From Above
Weird Wars: Weird Wars II: Hell Freezes Over
Weird Wars: Weird Wars II: Hell in the Hedgerows
Weird Wars: Weird Wars II: Horrors of Weird War II
Weird Wars: Weird Wars II: Island of Dreams
Weird Wars: Weird Wars II: Land of the Rising Dead

RPG Game

Achtung! Cthulhu
Achtung! Cthulhu: Elder Godlike
Achtung! Cthulhu: Secrets of the Dust
Cold City
Gear Krieg
Gear Krieg: African Theater
Godlike: Superhero Roleplaying in a World on Fire, 1936–1946
GURPS World War II: Weird War II
Luft Krieg
Operation Darkness
Spirit of the Century
Weird Wars: Rome
Weird Wars: Weird War I
Weird Wars: Weird Wars II
World War Cthulhu

Short Film

Blackadder Back & Forth
Death of a Shadow
The Devil with Hitler
Kung Fury
An Occurrence at Owl Creek Bridge
Project Arbiter
Stitched
The Wars of Other Men
Wartime

Short Story

"The Bowmen"
"Cain's Atonement"
"Delenda Est"
"La Dernière mobilization"
"Extra Men"
"The Flying Teuton"
"He Walked Around the Horses"
"The Interval"
"An Occurrence at Owl Creek Bridge"
"The Story Vinton First Heard at Mallorie"
"The White Battalion"

Short Story Anthology

Doctor Who: More Short Trips
Doctor Who: Short Trips: The Ghosts of Christmas
Fantastic World War II
The Hunter from the Woods
World War Cthulhu: A Collection of Lovecraftian War Stories

Stage Play—Theater

Bury the Dead
Julius Caesar
The Miracle at Verdun
The Mother
Post-Mortem
Richard III

Telefilm

An Angel for May
Camel Spiders
A Carol for Another Christmas
The Devil's Arithmetic
S.S. Doomtrooper
Ghost Boat
The Haunted Airman
Henry Hamilton, Graduate Ghost
Manticore
Mysterious Island
The Philadelphia Experiment
Reign of the Gargoyles
Sand Serpents
The Secret of the Nutcracker
Stir of Echoes: The Homecoming
They Saved Hitler's Brain
Warbirds
The Wild, Wild West Revisited

Television Series [featuring Weird War episodes or themes]

Alfred Hitchcock Presents
Amazing Stories
Angel
Are You Afraid of the Dark?
The Burning Zone
Circle of Fear
Danger 5
Darkroom
DC's Legends of Tomorrow
Doctor Who
Fantasy Island
Galactica 1980
Ghost Whisperer
Goodnight Sweetheart
Highlander
Highlander: The Raven
Highway to Heaven
The Jazz Age
Johnny and the Bomb
Jonathan Strange & Mr. Norrell
The Man from U.N.C.L.E.

Appendix

El Ministerio del Tiempo
Misfits
Mysterious Island
The New Avengers
Night Gallery
One Step Beyond
Outer Limits
Outlander
Perversions of Science
Quantum Leap
Red Dwarf
Sanctuary
The Sarah Jane Adventures
Seven Days
Star Trek
Star Trek: Enterprise
Star Trek: Voyager
Supernatural
The Time Tunnel
Timeless
The Tomorrow People
Torchwood
Touched by an Angel
Tuman
The Twilight Zone
The Vampire Diaries
Voyage to the Bottom of the Sea
The Wild, Wild West
Witchblade
Wonder Woman
The Young Indiana Jones Chronicles

Video Game

Assassin's Creed
Black Dahlia
BloodRayne
Call of Cthulhu: The Wasted Land
Call of Duty: World at War: Zombies
Captain America: Super Soldier
Clive Barker's Jericho
Command & Conquer: Red Alert
Command & Conquer: Red Alert 2
Command & Conquer: Red Alert 3
Command & Conquer: Red Alert 3: Uprising
Command & Conquer: Yuri's Revenge
Gunparade March
Hellboy: The Science of Evil
Hitler no Fukkatsu: Top Secret
Indiana Jones and the Emperor's Tomb
Indiana Jones and the Fate of Atlantis
Indiana Jones and the Last Crusade: The Graphic Adventure
Indiana Jones and the Staff of Kings
Iron Sky: Invasion
Konkepi no Kantai
Medal of Honor: Underground
Nazi Zombie Army 2
Persona 2: Innocent Sin
Return to Castle Wolfenstein
Ring of Red
Rocket Ranger
Shellshock 2: Blood Trails
Silent Storm
Sniper Elite: Nazi Zombie Army
Strikers 1945
Ubersoldier
Wolfenstein
Wolfenstein: Enemy Territory
Wolfenstein: The New Order
Wolfenstein: The Old Blood

Bibliography

Books and Periodicals

Cabarga, Leslie. *The Fleischer Story*. New York: Da Capo Press, 1976.

Conroy, Mike. *500 Great Comic Book Action Heroes*. New York: Chrysalis Impact, 2002.

Crawford, Hubert H. *Crawford's Encyclopedia of Comic Books*. Middle Village, NY: Jonathan David, 1978.

Di Paolo, Marc. *War, Politics and Superheroes*. Jefferson, NC: McFarland, 2011.

Gerani, Gary, and Paul H. Schulman. *Fantastic Television*. Godalming, Surrey, England: LSP Books, 1977.

Gifford, Denis. *The International Book of Comics*. London: Deans International Publishing (Hamlyn) for W.H. Smith, 1984.

Gilbert, Laura (ed.) *DC Comics Year by Year: A Visual Chronicle*. New York: DK Publishing, 2010.

Gunden, Kenneth Von, and Stuart H. Stock. *Twenty All-Time Great Science Fiction Films*. New York: Arlington House, 1982.

Gunn, James. *Alternate Worlds—The Illustrated History of Science Fiction*. Englewood Hills, NJ: Prentice-Hall, 1975.

Hopkins, Robert Thurston, and Forbes Alexander Phillips. *War and the Weird*. London: Simpkin, Marshall, Hamilton, Kent & Co., 1916.

Horn, Maurice (ed.) *The World Encyclopedia of Comics*. New York: Chelsea House Publishers, 1076.

Lupoff, Dick, and Don Thompson (ed.). *All in Color for a Dime*. New York: Ace Books, 1970.

McEwan, Cameron K. *The Who's Who of Doctor Who*. New York: Race Point Publishing, 2014.

Miller, Cynthia J., and A. Bowdoin Van Ripper (ed.) *The Horrors of War: The Undead on the Battlefield*. Lanham, MD: Rowman & Littlefield, 2015.

Rigelsford, Adrian. *The Doctors 30 Years of Time Travel*. London: Boxtree, 1994.

Rogers, Dave. *The Avengers Anew*. London: Michael Joseph, 1985.

Steranko, James. *The Steranko History of Comics—Volume One*. Reading, PA: Supergraphics, 1970.

Steranko, James. *The Steranko History of Comics—Volume Two*. Reading, PA: Supergraphics, 1972.

Thomas, John Rhett. *Captain America 75th Anniversary Magazine*. New York: Marvel Worldwide Inc., June 2016.

Thomas, Roy. *Batman: The War Years, 1939–1945*. New York: Chartwell Books, 2015.

Thomas, Roy. *Superman: The War Years 1938–1945*. New York: Chartwell Books, 2015.

Thomas, Roy. *Wonder Woman: The War Years, 1941–1945*. New York: Chartwell Books, 2015.

Wright, Nicky. *The Classic Era of American Comics*. London: Prion Books (Carlton), 2000.

Zicree, Marc Scott. *The Twilight Zone Companion—Second Edition*. Los Angeles: Silman-James Press, 1992.

Internet Sources

Amazon https://www.amazon.com

Anime News Network http://animenewsnetwork.com

Board Game Geek https://boardgamegeek.com

Comic Book Plus http://comicbookplus.com

DC Comics Database http://dc.wikia.com

Doctor Who Guide http://www.drwhoguide.com

Don Markstein's Toonopedia www.toonopedia.com

DriveThru RPG http://drivethrurpg.com

Good Reads http://www.goodreads.com

Grand Comic Book Database http://www.comics.org

Heritage Auctions www.ha.com

Internet Movie Pro Database https://pro-labs.imdb.com

Newspapers.com http://www.newspapers.com

The Online Books Page http://onlinebooks.library/open.edu

Playbill http://static.playbill.com

The Powell & Pressburger Pages http://www.powell-pressburger.org

The Pulp Magazine Project www.pulpmags.com

Bibliography

Project Gutenberg www.gutenberg.org
RPG Geek https://rpggeek.com
SparkNotes http://www.sparknotes.com
Spartacus Educational http://spartacus-educational.com
Tardis Data Core http://tardis.wikia.com
TCM: Turner Classic Movies http://www.tcm.com
Variety http://variety.com
Wikipedia www.wikipedia.org
WorldCat www.worldcat.org
YouTube www.youtube.com

Index

Numbers in **_bold italics_** indicate pages with photographs.

Abe Lincoln at Last! 7
Abraham Lincoln, Vampire Hunter 7, **_8_**, 9
Abraham Lincoln vs. Zombies **_8_**, 9
Achilles 9
Achilles 3, 9, 12, 57, 96, 135, 163, 174, 198, 206
Action Comics 165–166, 171
Achtung! Cthulhu 9
Achtung! Cthulhu: Dark Tales from the Secret War 9
Achtung! Cthulhu: Elder Godlike 9
Achtung! Cthulhu: Heroes of the Sea 9
Achtung! Cthulhu: Interface 19.40 9
Achtung! Cthulhu: Kontamination 9
Achtung! Cthulhu: Secrets of the Dust 9
Achtung! Cthulhu: Shadows of Atlantis 9
Achtung! Cthulhu: Terrors of the Secret War 9–10
Achtung! Cthulu: The Crystal Void—The Seraph Chronicles Book Two 10
Achtung! Cthulhu: Three Kings 10
Achtung! Cthulu: Tomb of the Aeons—The Seraph Chronicles Book Three 10
Achtung! Cthulhu: Trellborg Monstrosities 10
"Adam Link Fights a War" 10
"Adam Link Saves the World" 10
Adventure Comics 10, 152, 159
Adventures into Darkness 10
Adventures into the Unknown 10–11
The Adventures of Bob Hope 11
Adventures of the Outsiders 11
Aeneas 3, 11–12, 96, 176
The Aeneid 3, 11–12
Afghanistan 1, 6, 33, 35, 47, 75, 84, 88, 122, 132, 134, 149, 167
After Dachau: A Novel 12
After the Downfall 12
Against the Tide of Years 12
Agamemnon 12, 57, 96, 163, 198
Age of Bronze: The Story of the Trojan War 12
Air Fighters Comics 12, **_13_**, 113
Airboy 12, **_13_**
Airboy (2015) 13
Airboy 1942: Best of Enemies 13
The Alamo 15, 178, 180
Alfred Hitchcock Presents 13, 135

All Clear 13–14
All Evil Shed Away 14
All-Star Squadron 14, 20, 45, 63, 70, 113, 176
All-Winners Squad 14, 125, 204
Allen, Irwin 5, 178, 195
Amazing Adult Fantasy 14
The Amazing Adventures of Kavalier and Clay 14
Amazing Man 14, 65
Amazing Stories (TV) 14–15
Amazing Stories (pulp) 4, 10, 19, 27, 42, 55–56, 69, 75–76, 83, 90, 96, 101, 116, 118–119, 124, 128, 132, 135, 140–141, 143, 146, 152, 175–177, 183, 191, 194, 196–197
American Civil War 1, 3, 13–14, 17, 19, 24, 43, 51, 55, 64–65, 77–78, 83, 88, 91, 97, 104, 128, 130, 140, 145, 147, 171, 178, 182, 194, 204, 210–211
The American Crusader **_15_**
The American Eagle **_15_**
American Vampire 16
America's Best Comics **_15_**, 181
Andersonville 16
Andie and the Alien 16
Angel 16
An Angel for May 16–17
angel(s) 1, 3, 16, 30–31, 43, 46, 50, 57, 91–92, 111, 147, 155, 168, 182, 207
"Angels of Mons" 3, 30–31
Anthem 17, 176
Are You Afraid of the Dark? 17
Are You Afraid of the Dark?—The Tale of the Zero Hero 17
Ark of the Covenant 132, 146
Army of Frankensteins 17
Arnim Zola 18, 101, 149
Arpointeu 154
Arrowsmith 18
Assassin's Creed 18
At the Firefly Gate 18
Athena Voltaire 18
Atlantis 9, 21, 45, 50, 99, 169, 174, 191, 200
Atomic Knight 18
Atomic Robo and the Dogs of War 19
"The Avengers" 19
AWOL in North Africa 19
Axis powers 5, 14, 21–22, 26, 39, 45, 49, 53, 62, 71, 73, 101, 103, 110, 114, 159, 169, 171, 195

"Baby Face" 19
Back to the Future 19
Backtrack: Nazi Regression 19–20
The Backyard Ghost 20
Baffling Mysteries 20
Baltimore, or, The Steadfast Tin Soldier and the Vampire 20
The Bargain 20
Baron Blitzkrieg 20, 45
Baron Blood 20–21, 74, 164
Baron Heinrich Zemo 21, 37
Batman 5, 21, **_22_**, 107, 157–158
Battle Hymn 22
Battle of Bosworth Field 3, 62, 151
Battle of Britain 154
Battle of Culloden 91, 139
Battle of Flodden Field 10
Battle of Gettysburg 5, 8, 32–33, 42, 112–113, 138–139, **_147_**, 178, 181, 187, 205, 211
Battle of Khartoum 179
Battle of Manassas 88
"The Battle of Manetong" 22
Battle of Marathon 170
Battle of Midway 154–156, 199, 202, 213
Battle of Philippi 3, 106
Battle of the Bulge 45, 58
Battle of the Little Bighorn 179, 184
Battle of the Somme 78–79
Battle of Waterloo 26, 105
Battler Britton 22–23
Bedknobs and Broomsticks 23
Behemoth 23
Behind the Red Mist 23
Below 23
Bengal Revolt 46–47
Berlin 12, 14, 32–33, 43, 58, 68, 77, 87, 95–96, 99, 102, 115, 112. 132, 156, 177, 179, 181, 190, 192, 195, 200
Bernice Summerfield: Just War 23
Bernice Summerfield: Secret Origins 24
Bernice Summerfield: The Oracle of the Delphi 24
Beware of the Haunted Toilet 23
The Beyond 24
Bierce, Ambrose 13, 64, 97, 115, 135, 187
Big X 24
Biggles, Adventures in Time 24–25
Binder, Otto 10, 40, 125, 128, 212
Biro, Charles 12, **_13_**, 48, **_49_**

225

Index

Bitter Seeds 25
The Black Beetle 25
Black Dahlia 25
Black Max 25
The Black Terror 25
Blackadder Back & Forth 25–26
The Blackhawks **26**, 107
Blackout 26, **27**
Blazing Glory 26–27
"Blitz Against Japan" 27
Blitzed 27
"Blitzkrieg in the Past" 27
Blood Creek 27
Blood Red Roses 27–28
BloodRayne 28
Bloodrayne: The Third Reich 28
Bloody Awful 28
Bloody Good 28
The Bloody Red Baron 28
Bloody Right 28
Blubberella 29
Blue Devil Island 29
The Blue Diamond 29, 114
The Blue Tracer 29
Bombshell, Son of War 29–30
El Bose 30
"The Bowmen" **30**, 31
Boy Commandos 31, 110, 113, 160
The Boys from Brazil 31, **32**
Braddock 32
Brainiape 32
Breath of Bones: A Tale of the Golem 32
Bride of the Night 32
Bring the Jubilee 32–33
Bring the Thunder 33
B.R.P.D. 1946 33
Bulletman 33, 40
Bulletproof Monk 33
The Bunker 33–34
Bureau of Paranormal Research and Defense 33, 89
Burgos, Carl 34, 95
The Burning Zone 34
Bury the Dead 34
By the Blood of Heroes: The Great Undead War 34

Cabot, John York 27, 119, 124
"Cain's Atonement" 34–35
Call of Cthulhu: The Wasted Land 35
Call of Duty: World at War: Zombies 35
Camel Spiders 35
Cannibal Apocalypse 35
Captain America 35–37, 101, 109–110, 113, 119, 149, 155, 159–160, 164, 170–171, 176, 184, 198, 207, 212
Captain America: Super Soldier 37
Captain America: The First Avenger **37**, 38
Captain Battle 5, 38
Captain Battle: Legacy of War 38
Captain Confederacy 38
Captain Fearless 5, 38
Captain Hurricane 38, **39**
Captain Marvel 39–40, 128
Captain Marvel, Jr. 39–40

Captain Midnight 39–40
Captain Nazi 39–40, 128
Captain Wonder 40
A Carol for Another Christmas 40–41
The Case of the Soldier's Ghost 41
The Castle in the Forest 41
Catch Me Once, Catch Me Twice 41–42
"Cave City of Hel" 42
Chamber of Chills 42
"Change for the Bitter" 42
Charlotte Sometimes 42
Chrononauts 42
Chronos Commandos 42
Churchill, Winston 6, 28, 45, 49, 53, 58, 60, 109, 128, 133, 159, 210
Circle of Fear 42–43
Civil War on Sunday 43
The Claw 43, 49
Clive Barker's Jericho 43
Code Red 43
Cold City 43
A Coming Evil 43–44
Command & Conquer: Red Alert 44
Command & Conquer: Red Alert 2 44
Command & Conquer: Red Alert 3 44
Command & Conquer: Red Alert 3: Uprising 44
Command & Conquer: Yuri's Revenge 44–45
Commander Steel 14, 45, 51
Common Foe 45
Concentration camp 20–21, 23, 33, 49, 54, 64, 79, 93, 97, 127, 139, 191, 195
Confederates Don't Wear Couture 45
The Conqueror 45
Corydon and the Siege of Troy 45–46
Countdown 46
The Creature Commandos 46, 200
Creature with the Atom Brain 46
Creepy 5, 46–47
Crusade 47
Crusade in Jeans 47
The Crusades 1, 18, 47, 174
Cry Havoc 47
"The Curse of El Dorado" 47
Cybersix 47–48

"Dagon" 48
Danger 5 48
Danger in the Darkest Hour 48
Daredevil Battles Hitler 48, **49**
Dark Axis—Secret Battles of World War II: Rise of the Overmen 49
Dark Mysteries 49
Dark Shadows 49–50
Dark Victory 50
Darkroom 50
"The Daughter of Thor" 50
Day of the Assassins 50
DC Comics: Bombshells 50
DC's Legends of Tomorrow 50–51
D-Day 6, 34, 55, 101, 173, 179, 182, 200
Dead Birds 51
Dead of Night 51–52
Dead Snow 52
Dead Soldier 52

Dead Walkers: Rise of the 4th Reich 52
Death of a Shadow 52
Death Ship 52
Deathwatch 52–53
Declare 53
Deep Blue Fleet 110
The Deepest Night 53
"Delenda Est" 53
The Demon 53
The Demon Assassin 53
Demons 1, 9, 16, 25, 33, 41, 50–51, 53, 55, 59, 64, 89, 99, 103, 105, 108, 111, 116, 118, 132, 147, 149, 158–159, 173–174, 203
"La Dernière Mobilization" 53
Designated Targets 53
Dessous: La Montagne des Morts 53–54
The Destroyer 54, 101, 113
Destroyermen 100, 117
The Devil with Hitler 54
The Devil's Arithmetic 54
The Devil's Backbone 54
Devils of D-Day 54–55
Devils of War 55
The Devil's Rock 55
The Devil's Tomb 55
Dinosaurs 36, 42, 83, 86, 100, 102, 111–112, 116, 148, 197
"Direct Wire" 55
The Discovery 55
Les Divisions de Fer 55–56
Djinns 6, 56
"Dr. Loudon's Armageddon" 61
Doctor Manhattan 56
Doctor Who 46, 56–58, 183–184, 198
Doctor Who Adventures 58
Doctor Who and the Crusaders 58
Doctor Who: Atom Bomb Blues 58
Doctor Who: Autumn Mist 58
Doctor Who: Casualties of War 58
Doctor Who: Colditz 58–59
Doctor Who: Daleks Among Us 59
Doctor Who: Dark Convoy 59
Doctor Who: Illegal Alien 59
Doctor Who: Just War 59
Doctor Who Magazine 59
Doctor Who: More Short Trips 59–60
Doctor Who: Persuasion 60
Doctor Who: Resistance 60
Doctor Who: Short Trips: The Ghosts of Christmas 60
Doctor Who: The Churchill Years: Hounded 60
Doctor Who: The Churchill Years: Living History 60
Doctor Who: The Churchill Years: The Oncoming Storm 60
Doctor Who: The Nemonite Invasion 60–61
Doctor Who: The Scapegoat 61
Doctor Who: The Shadow in the Glass 61
Doctor Who: Timewyrm: Exodus 61
Doll Man 61
S.S. Doomtrooper 61
Dragon Ball Z: Fusion Reborn 61
The Dragon in the Sword 61–62
The Dragon Waiting: A Masque of History 62

"Dragons Behind Us" 62
The Dreamthief's Daughter: A Tale of the Albino 62
Druid's Sword 62
Dunne, Irene 86
Dust Adventures Core Book 62
Dust Adventures: Operation Apocalypse 62
Dust Tactics 62–63
Dust Wars 63
Dynaman 63

Eerie 5, 63–64
Einstein, Albert 16, 44–45, 51, 68, 148, 177
Elves 64
The Enchanted Life of Adam Hope 64
The Enemy 64–65
English Civil War 1, 68, 206
Escape from Ghost Hotel 65
The Escapist 14, 65
Everett, Bill 14, 45, 65, 113, 169
Exit Humanity 65
"Extra Men" 65–66
The Extraordinary Seaman 66

Fallen in Fredericksburg 66
Family Guy 66
Fantastic Adventures 22, 42, 47, 50, 62, 79, 91, 115–116, 118, 124–125, 128, 150, 177, 180–181, 183
Fantastic Four 66, 87, 95, 110, 113
Fantastic World War II 67
Fantasy Island 67–68
FDR: American Badass! 68
A Field in England 68
Fiends of the Eastern Front 68
Fiends of the Eastern Front: Fiends of the Rising Sun 68
Fiends of the Eastern Front: Operation Vampyr 68
Fiends of the Eastern Front: Stalingrad 68
Fiends of the Eastern Front: The Blood Red Army 69
Fiends of the Eastern Front: Twilight of the Dead 69
"Fifth Column of Mars" 69
Fifth columnists 38, 114, 118–119, 166
Fighting Yank 69, 70
The Final Countdown 70
The Final Impact 70
Find Me Where the Water Ends 70
Firebrand 70
The Firebrand 70
First Squad: The Moment of Truth 70–71
The Flag 71
The Flame 71
Flash Gordon: Zeitgeist 71–72
The Flesh Eaters 72
Flesh Feast 72
Flight World War II
"The Flying Teuton" 72
"For the Love of Barbra Allen" 72
Forbidden Worlds 73
The Forest of Time 73
'48 73
Frankenstein 73

Frankenstein's Army 73
Freedom Fighters 73
Freedom's Five 74
French resistance 48, 60–51, 67, 167, 213
Friends Forever: The Mystery Tour 74
From a Whisper to a Scream 74
"From Out of the Dark Water" 74
"From the House of the Rat Catcher" 74
From Time to Time 74
Frostbitten 74
The Frozen Dead 74–75
Fubar: American History Z 75
Fubar: By the Sword 75
Fubar: Declassified 75
Fubar: Empire of the Rising Dead 75
Fubar: European Theater of Blood 75
"Fugitives from Earth" 75
Fullmetal Alchemist: Conqueror of Shambala 75
Futatsu no Kurumi 75
Futurama 75–76

Galactica 1980 76
"Gallery of Glacial Doom" 76
Gamma 693 76
The Gate of Time 76
The Gay Ghost 76
Gear Krieg 76
Gear Krieg: African Theater 76–77
Gene 77
General Grant 180, 204
General Lee 83, 85, 138
General Leonardo 77
Genghis Khan 75, 102, 166, 194
George Washington's Socks 77
Germania 77
Ghost Boat 77
Ghost Cadet 77
Ghost Fever 77
Ghost of the Great River Inn 77–78
Ghost Patrol 78
Ghost Soldier 78–79
Ghost Stories 79
Ghost Talkers 79
"The Ghost That Haunted Hitler" 79, 80
Ghost Whisperer 80
The Ghost Wore Gray 80
Ghostly Tales 80, 81, 82
Ghosts 82
Ghosts 1, 3, 11, 17, 19–20, 60, 66, 73, 77–83, 86, 88, 93, 115, 127, 131, 136, 151, 155, 170, 193, 197, 203, 205
The Ghosts of Iron Bottom Sound 82
Ghosts of the Civil War 82–83
Ghosts of Time 83
Ghostscape 80
G.I. Robot 83, 197, 200
G.I. Samurai 156
G.I. Zombie 83
Gibson, Charles Dana 4
Gigantor 174–175
Gingersnap 83
Godlike: Superhero Roleplaying in a World on Fire, 1936–1946 83
"Gods of the Jungle" 83

Godzilla 83–84
Göring, Hermann 42, 62, 77, 117, 184, 211
Gojira 83–84
Golem 32, 173, 200
Goliath 84
Goodnight Sweetheart 84
Goodwin, Archie 63–64
Graveyard of Empires 84
Great American Comics Present: The Secret Voice 84
Great Sioux Wars 179
Grey Knight 84
Grunts 84
Gulf War 38, 92, 137, 158
Gun of the Black Sun 84–85
Gunparade March 85
Gunparade March: The New March 85
Gunparade Orchestra 85
The Guns of the South 85
GURPS Weird War II: Secret Weapons and Twisted History 85
GURPS Weird War II: The Secret of the Gneisenau 86
GURPS World War II: Weird War II 86
A Guy Named Joe 86

Half Past Danger 86
Hanussen 86–87
Hard Rock Zombies 87
The Hate-Monger 87
The Haunted Airman 87
The Haunted Tank 87–89, 108
The Haunting at Stratton Falls 88
The Haunting of Holroyd Hill 88
The Haunting of Marsten Manor 88
The Haunting of Swain's Fancy 88
The Haunting of Toby Jugg 88
"He Walked Around the Horses" 88–89
The Healer's War 89
The Heap 89
Heath, Russell 89
Hector 3, 9, 11, 96, 135
Hellboy 89
Hellboy: The Science of Evil 89–90
Hellsing: The Dawn 90
Hellsing: Ultimate 90
Henry Hamilton, Graduate Ghost 90
Henry Hamilton in Outer Space 90
"Henry Horn's Blitz Bomb" 90
Here and Then 90–91
Hero 91
"Heroes Die Hard" 91
Heroes vs. Hitler 91
Highlander 91–92
Highlander: The Raven 92
Highway to Heaven 92–93
Himmler, Heinrich 38, 77, 85, 113, 117, 122, 137, 150, 162, 210
Hirohito 22, 42, 68, 196, 210
Hiroshima 41, 84, 186, 207
"His Last Appearance" 93–94
His Majesty's Dragon: A Novel of Temeraire 94
Hitler, Adolf 4, 6, 11–12, 17–21, 25, 27–29, 31–32, 35–36, 38–41, 43–46, 48, 49, 50, 54–55, 57–58, 61–

Index

64, 66, 68–69, 72–73, 75–80, 86–87, 91–92, 94, 97, 99, 102, 106–107, 110–111, 115–118, 121–122, 125–128, 132–138, 141, 143, 147–148, 152, 155, 158, 160, 162–163, 165, 168, 171–175, 177, 179, 181–182, 184–186, 189, 192, 194, 196–199, 205–206, 208–212, 214
Hitler no Fukkatsu: Top Secret 94
The Holocaust 6, 75, 93, 97, **120**, 121, 147, 182
Holy Grail 62, 99, 132
Home Again 94
Homer's Iliad 94
Horrors of War 94
The Hotspur 94
House 94–95
The House of Dies Drear 95
The Human Torch 5, 14, 20, 34, 65–66, **95**, 101, 113, 119, 155, 164, 169–170, 198, 212
Hundred Years War 180
Hunter, Kim 119, **120**
The Hunter from the Woods 95

I Accuse! 95–96
I Am Legion 96
The Iliad 3, 12, 96
Ilium 96–97
"I'll See You Again" 97
The Illuminatus! Trilogy 97
Impact 97
In the Electric Mist with the Confederate Dead 97
In the Shadow of Blackbirds 97
In Time of War 97–98
In War Times 98
The Incredible Mr. Limpet **98**
Indiana Jones and the Emperor's Tomb 98–99
Indiana Jones and the Fate of Atlantis 99
Indiana Jones and the Iron Phoenix 99
Indiana Jones and the Last Crusade 99
Indiana Jones and the Last Crusade: The Graphic Adventure 99
Indiana Jones and the Spear of Destiny 99
Indiana Jones and the Staff of Kings 99
The Inexorables 141
Insensible 100
Insurrection 100
"The Interval" 100
Into the Storm 100
"Intruders from the Stars" 100
The Invaders 54, 66, 74, 100–101, 126, 160, 164, 176, 190, 198
"Invasion Dust" 101
Invisible Agent **101**, 102
Iraq 1, 6, 38, 80, 87, 119, 121, 167, 189–190
The Iron Dream 102
Iron Man 28 174–175
Iron Sky 102
Iron Sky: Invasion 102
Iron Sky: The Coming Race 102
Iron Wolf 102
Island in the Sea of Time 12

Isle of the Dead 102, **103**
Iwo-Jima 179, 202

J'Accuse! 96, 103
Jack Frost 103, 113–114
Jackboot & Ironheel 103
Jacob's Ladder 103
The Jazz Age 103
The Jewel and the Key 103–104
Jewels of Time 104
Jews 6, 44, 64, 120–121, 200, 211
Joan the Woman 104
John Kowalski 104
Johnny and the Bomb 104
Johnny and the Dead 104–105
Jonah Hex 105
Jonathan Strange & Mr. Norrell 105
Jonny Quest 105–106
JSA: The Liberty Files 106
Jughead's Time Police 106
Julius Caesar 3, **106**, 107
Justice League 107
Justice League of America 14, 73, 108
Justice Society of America 14, 51, 63, 73, 107–108

Kade Mourning Sun 108
Kanigher, Robert 83, 87, 108, 110, 157, 166, 192, 194, 197, 200
Karloff, Boris 102, **103**
The Keep 103
Kid Eternity 108, **109**, 113
The Killing Box 84
The King 109
King of the Zombies 109
Kirby, Jack 5, 18, 21, 31, 36–38, 87, 109–110, 113, 149, 160, 212
Kishin Corps 110
Knights Templar 18, 44, 174
Knotts, Don 6, **98**
Konkepi no Kantai 110
Korean War 1, 162, 175, 183, 185
Kubert, Joe 110–111, 157, 166, 192, 199, 200
Kung Fury 111

Lady Lazarus 111
The Lamb and the Fuhrer 111
Lammas Night 111
Land of Mist and Snow 111
The Land That Time Forgot 111, **112**
Lash Lightning **112**
Last Ghost at Gettysburg 112–113
Leav, Mort 89, 113
Lee, Stan 5, 14, 21, 36, 54, 87, 113, 157, 164, 170, 207, 211
Leviathan 113
Leviathan: Le Patient Zero 113
Liberty Belle 14, 113–114
The Liberty Legion 29, 103, 114, 125, 149, 175, 204
Life 4
The Life Eaters 114
The Light & Darkness War 114
Light Brigade 114
Lightning Comics 112
Lincoln, Abraham 7, **8**, 9, 68, 82–83, 114, 147–148, 166, 178, 180, 187
Lincoln's Legacy 114

Lincoln's Sword 114
The Living and the Dead 114–115
The Locked Spirit 115
London Blitz 13–14, 26, 50, 53, 57, 59, 62, 74, 80, 91, 115, 178
London Calling 115
Look Magazine 115
Look Who's Back 115
Lorelei: The Witch of the Pacific Ocean 115
Lost at Khe Sanh 116
"Lost City of Burma" 115–116
The Lost Platoon 116
Lost Squad 116
"The Lost Warship" 116
Lovecraft, H.P. 9, 35, 48, 174, 210
Luft Krieg 116
Luftwaffe 62, 148, 183, 203
"Luvium, the Invisible City" 116

Machen, Arthur 3, **30**, 31
The Madmen of Madoras 116–117
Maelstrom 117
Magic 1, 7, 11–12, 18, 23, 25, 35, 43, 48, 50, 53, 57, 62–63, 74, 77, 98, 105, 111, 114, 117, 121, 125, 131, 137, 142, 146–147, 151–152, 155–156, 159–160, 168–169, 174, 187–189, 200–201, 205, 208–210
The Magic Face 117
The Magicians of Night 117
Major Victory **117**, 118
Making History 118
The Man from U.N.C.L.E. 118
"The Man Who Cried Werewolf" 118
"The Man Who Hated War" 118
Manticore 118
"The Map of Fate" 119
Marvels 119
"Matches and Kings" 119
A Matter of Life and Death 119, **120**
Maus: A Survivor's Tale **120**, 121
Maus II: And Here My Troubles Began 120
McGivern, William P. 19, 22, **79**, 80, 180–181, 194
Medal of Honor: Underground 121
The Medusa Amulet 121
The Men Who Stare at Goats 121
Mengele, Dr. Josef 31, **32**, 132, 191
Merlin the Magician 121–122
The Midnight Guardian 122
Midnighter 122
El Ministerio del Tiempo 122–123
Minute-Man **123**, 124
"The Miracle at Dunkirk" 124
The Miracle at Verdun 124
"The Miracle of Bulldozer Mike" 124–125
"The Miracle of Kicker McGuire" 125
The Mirk and Midnight Hour 125
Misfits 125
Miss America 14, 63, 101, 114, 125–126, 164
Mr. Justice **126**, 127
Mr. Liberty 127
Mr. Limpet 127
"Mistress of the Dark" 128

Monster Killer 128
The *Monster Society of Evil* 128
Moonbranches 128
Moonfisher 128
The Moonlight Brigade 128
"A Most Ingenious Paradox" 128
The Mother 129
Mother Russia 129
Mujahideen 6, 56
Mussolini, Benito 37, 54–55, 68, 100, 128, 179
Mysterious Island 129–131
Mysterious Stories 131
The Mystery at Fort Thunderbolt 131

Nagasaki 84, 207
Nang Nak 131
Nanny McPhee and the Big Bang 131
Napoleonic Wars 1, 10, 20, 25–26, 94, 122–123, 152, 155, 184, 194, 200
Nazi Dawn 131
"Nazi Diamond" 132
The Nazi Occult 132
Nazi occultists 18, 33, 52. 71, 89, 132, 152
Nazi Werewolf Zombie Inferno 132
Nazi Werewolves from Outer Space 132
Nazi Zombie Army 2 132
Nazis at the Center of the Earth 132
Neither Heaven Nor Earth 132
The New Avengers 132–133
Newland, John 136–137
Nick of Time **133**
The Night Boat 133
Night Gallery 133–134
Night Wars 134
Niven, David 5, 66, 119, **120**
Nostradamus Ate My Hamster 134
NUTS! War Without End—Weird War 2 134

Oasis of the Zombies 134
The Objective 134–135
"An Occurrence at Owl Creek Bridge" 13, 64, 135, 187, 190
"The Odyssey of Battling Bert" 135
Olivier, Laurence 31, **32**, 151
Olympos 135
On Her Majesty's Behalf: The Great Undead War 135
On the Oceans of Eternity 135
Once Was a Time 135–136
One Minute Before Death 139–140
One Step Beyond 136–137
One Summer at Deer's Leap 137
Only You Can Save Mankind 137
Operation Darkness 137
Operation: Nazi Zombies 137–138
Operation: Peril 138
The Order of the Black Eagle 138
Out of the Shadows 138
Outer Limits 138–139
Outlander 139
Outpost 139
Outpost: Black Sun 139
Outpost: Rise of the Spetsnaz 139
The Oval Portrait 139–140
Overseas 140

P-51 Dragon Fighter 140
Painless 100
Pan's Labyrinth 140
"A Patriot Never Dies" 140
Pax Romana 140
Pearl Harbor 4, 6, 14, 27, 70, 98, 102, 110, 122, 128, 175, 177–178, 183, 185, 192, 213
Peck, Gregory 31, **32**
"Periscope Prey" 140–141
Persona 2: Innocent Sin 141
Perversions of Science 141
Peter Panzerfaust 141
"Peter Pettigrew's Prisoner" 141
The Phantom Goes to War 141
The Philadelphia Experiment 141–142
Philadelphia Experiment II 142
Phoenix and Ashes 142
Picture the Dead 142
The Piper 142
Post-Mortem 142
"Private Prune Speaking" 143
Professor Supermind and Son 143
Project Arbiter **143**
The Proteus Operation 143
Puppet Master: Axis of Evil 144
Puppet Master: Axis Termination 144
Puppet Master X: Axis Rising 144
Puppetmaster 143–144
Puppetmaster III: Toulon's Revenge 144
Pyroman **15**, 144, **145**

Quantum Leap 145–146

R-Point 154
Raiders of the Lost Ark 146–147
"Raiders Out of Space" 147
Rebel Angels 147
A Rebel in Time 147
Rebel Spirits **147**
The Reckoning 147
Red Baron 28, 63, 135, 150
Red Dwarf 147–148
The Red Panda Adventures 148
Red Planet Mars 148
Red Raven 114, 148–149
Red Sands 149
Red Skull 35–37, 101, 149, 164, 170, 204, 212
The Red Suitcase 149
Reign of the Gargoyles 149
The Rest of Heaven Was Blue 149–150
"The Return of the Hun" 150
Return to Castle Wolfenstein 150
"Return to Lilliput" 150
Return to Never Land 150
Revenge of the Red Baron 150
Revenge of the Zombies 150
Revere, Paul 10, 108–109, 127, 150
Revere: Revolution in Silver 150
Revolutionary War 1, 10, 17, 63, 82, 113, 119, 127, 151–152, 181, 185, 198
Revolutionary War on Wednesday 151
Richard the Lionheart 56, 58
Richard III 3, 62, 151
Riding with the James Gang 151
The Rinaldi Ring 151
Ring of Red 151–152

Rip Hunter: Time Master 152
Ritual of the Stifling Air 152
Rocket Ranger 152
Rocket Ship Galileo 152
"Rockets Over Europe" 152
The Rocketeer 152, **153**
Rome 3, 11–12, 53, 62, 67, 77, 128, 140, 153, 155, 163, 201
Rome Against Rome 153
Roosevelt, Eleanor 68, 76
Roosevelt, Franklin D. 14, 40, 48, 68, 177, 210
Rosie Goes to War 153
Rover 32
Rover and Wizard 32
The Royals: Masters of War 153–154

Samurai Commando Mission 1549 154
Sanctuary 154
Sand Serpents 154
The Sarah Jane Adventures 154–155
Schomburg, Alex **15**, **69**, **95**, 155, **170**
Scion Companion 155
Second Punic War 53
Second Time Lucky 155
The Secret History 155
The Secret of Midway 155–156
The Secret of the Nutcracker 156
The Secret Shelter 156
"Secret Unattainable" 156
Secrets of the Third Reich 156
Sengoku Jieitai 156–157
Sgt. Fury and His Howling Commandos 110, 157, 176
Sgt. Rock and Easy Company 107–108, 110, 157–158
Serling, Rod 5, 41, 133, 184–187, **189**, 190
Seven Days 158
Seventh Sanctuary 158
The Shadow Children 158
Shadows in the Mist 158
Shadows Over Normandie: Cthulhu Mythos Call One 158
Shakespeare, William 3, 25–26, **106**, 107, 135, 151
Shambling Towards Hiroshima 158–159
She Demons 159
Shellshock 2: Blood Trails 159
The Shield 159
Shining Knight 14, 18, 159
Shock Waves 159–160
Silent Storm 160
Silver Streak 49, 160
Simon, Joe 31, 35, 37, 110, 130, 148–149, 160, 212
Sir Steel 74, 160
1632 160
'68 160–161
'68: Jungle Jim 161
'68: Last Rites 161
'68: Rules of Law 161
'68: Scars 161
Slaughterhouse Five: or, The Children's Crusade, a Duty Dance with Death 161
Sledge-Hammer 44 161

Small Soldiers 161–162
Sniper Elite: Nazi Zombie Army 162
Snowman 1944 162
So Close to You 162
Soldiers of the Damned 162
Son of Vulcan 162–163
The Songs of the Kings 163
Le Souffle du Wendigo 163
A Sound Among the Trees 163
Soviet Union 44, 53, 62, 70, 152, 210
Space Western Comics 163
Spanish Civil War 1, 25, 30, 54, 100, 129, 134, 140, 203, 207
The Spear 163–164
Special War Series: Attack! 164
Spider-Man: The Animated Series 164
Spirit of the Century 164
Spirit of the Rebellion 164
Spitfire 20, 54, 101, 164
Spriggan 164–165
The Spring Rider 165
Spy Smasher 165
The Squad 165
Stairway to Heaven 119, **120**
Stalin, Josef 43–44, 115, 210, 212
Stalingrad 68, 129, 154, 202
Star Spangled Kid & Stripesy 165–166
Star Spangled War Stories 166
Star Trek 166
Star Trek: Enterprise 166–167
Star Trek: Voyager 167
Steel Commando 167
Stir of Echoes: The Homecoming 167
Stitched 167
Stone of Destiny 174
Storming Paradise 167–168
"The Story Vinton First Heard at Mallorie" 168
Strange Adventures 18, 168
A Strange and Familiar Place 168
Strange Conflict 168
Strike Witches 168–169
Strike Witches: Operation Victory 169
Strike Witches: The Movie 169
Strikers 1945 169
The Sub-Mariner 5, 14, 20–21, 36, 65, 95, 101, 113, 119, 155, 169, **170**, 191, 198
Sucker Punch 170
Sunset of the Gods 170
The Super Hero Squad Show 170
Super Natural Acts 28
Super Soldier 171
Super soldier(s) 4, 36–37, 54–55, 61, 94, 110, 135, 156, 176, 190, 198
Superboy 10, 171
Superman 5, 107, 115, 157, 171–173, 181
Superman's Pal Jimmy Olsen 173
Supernatural 173
Supernatural 1, 3–6, 10, 14, 16, 20, 24–25, 28, 31, 33–34, 42–43, 45, 50, 53, 56, 62–64, 71, 79–80, 82, 87, 114–115, 125, 132, 135–136, 147, 150, 158, 163, 173, 190, 193, 199, 201, 206–207
The Supernaturals 173
Syria 6, 158

The Tale of the Zero Hero 173
Taliban 6, 35, 84, 132, 149, 154, 167
Tannhauser 173
Taskmaster 173
Teenape vs. The Monster Nazi Apocalypse 173–174
Telepathy 1, 181
"The Temple" 174
The Temple and the Crown 174
The Temple and the Stone 174
Tetsujin 28-gou 174–175
"They Forgot to Remember Pearl Harbor" 175
They Saved Hitler's Brain 175
They Used Dark Forces 175
Thin Air 175
The Thin Man 114, 175
The Thing! 175
Third Reich 12, 16, 18, 27–19, 34, 38, 54, 59, 77, 79, 90, 99, 116–117, 122, 186, 193, 209–210, 212
The Third Section 176
30 Days of Night: Red Snow 176
Thirty Years War 160
This Boy 176
Thomas, Roy 14, 17, 20, 54, 66, 70, 74, 91, 100, 101, 114, 160, 163–164, 174–176, 190, 198
"Thompson's Time-Traveling Theory" 176
Thor 176
Thor Meets Captain America 176
Three Hearts and Two Lions 176
"Three Wise Men of Space" 176–177
"The Throne of Valhalla" 177
Thule Society 25, 75
"The Tiger Has a Soul" 177
Till the End of Time 177
Time and Time Again 177
Time Bomb 177
Time Riders 178
Time Riders: The Eternal War 178
Time Slip 156
Time to Go Back 177–178
Time Train to the Blitz 178
Time travel 2, 4–5, 7, 13–14, 24, 26, 42, 53, 57–59, 73, 83, 85, 97, 110, 122, 125, 134–135, 138–140, 154, 170, 173, 176, 178, 180–181, 184, 198, 212
The Time Tunnel 178–179
Timecop 2: The Berlin Decision 179
Timeless 180
Timeline 180
"Tink Fights the Gremlins" 180–181
"Tink Takes Command" 181
Tom Strong 181
Tomahawk 108, 181, 197
Tomorrow I'll Wake Up and Scald Myself with Tea 181
The Tomorrow People 181–182
Torchwood 182
Touched by an Angel 182–183
Tracy, Spencer **86**
"The Traitor" 183
Trojan Horse 3, 57, 163, 176, 179
Trojan War 1–3, 12, 57, 77, 96, 135, 163, 176, 179, 183, 196, 198
"Trophy" 183

"Trouble in Avalon" 183
Troy 183
"Truk Island" 183
Tuman 183
TV Action 183–184
TV Comic 184
Twelve 184
The Twelve: Spearhead 184
The 25th Reich 184
Twice Upon a Time 184
The Twilight Zone 184–189, **190**
The Twilight Zone—Radio Dramas 190
Twilight Zone: The Movie 190

U-Man 190–191
Uber 190
Ubersoldier 190
The Unborn 191
Uncle Sam 73, 113, **191**
Undead 1, 20, 24, 29, 34–35, 46, 52, 61, 65, 68, 73, 75, 83–84, 103, 106, 108, 129, 132, 135, 139, 160–162, 170, 191, 197, 203, 213
Underground Railroad 65, 80, 95, 146
"The Undersea Guardians" 191
The Unholy 192
The Unknown Soldier **192**, 193
The Unseen 193
Unusual Tales **193**
Urda 193

Vampire 1, 4, 7–9, 16, 18, 20, 28–29, 32, 38, 47, 49–50, 62, 68, 74, 89–90, 96, 103, 116, 122, 126, 128, 134, 137, 156, 164, 184, 193–194, 200, 203, 212
The Vampire Diaries 193–194
Vampirella vs. Lady Death 194
Vandal Savage 51, 107, 194
"Vengeance in Her Bones" 194
"Victory from the Void" 194
Vietnam War 1, 5–6, 23, 35, 41–43, 46, 50, 52, 56, 80–82, 89, 92–95, 103, 114–115, 134, 145–147, 149–150, 154, 159–161, 182, 185, 188, 190, 201, 210–211
Viking Commando 194
The Violent Century 194–195
Voodoo 195
Voodoo 55, 104, 124, 200, 213
Voyage to the Bottom of the Sea 195–196

War 196
The War at Troy 196
"War Criminal of Renault Island" 196
War of the Dead 196–197
War Picture Library 197
The War That Time Forgot 197
"War Worker 17" 197
Warbirds 197
Warfront: Tales of Combat 197
Warren, James 5, 46–47
"Warrior Queen of Lolarth" 197
Warrior Rising 198
Warrior Woman 198
The Wars of Other Men 198

Index

Wars of the Roses 62
Wartime 198
Washington, George 10–11, 71, 77, 136, 151–152, 198
Washington's War 198
Weapons of Choice 198–199
Web of Mystery 199
Weird Fantasy 199
Weird Horrors 199
Weird Terror 199
Weird Thrillers 199
Weird War Tales 199–200
Weird Wars: Rome 201
Weird Wars: Rome: Nox Germanica 201
Weird Wars: Rome: The Half- Set Sun 201
Weird Wars: Rome: Wellspring 201
Weird Wars: Tour of Darkness 200–201
Weird Wars: Weird War I 201
Weird Wars: Weird Wars II 201
Weird Wars: Weird Wars II: Afrika Korpse 201
Weird Wars: Weird Wars II: Blood on the Rhine 201–202
Weird Wars: Weird Wars II: Dead from Above 202
Weird Wars: Weird Wars II: Hell Freezes Over 202
Weird Wars: Weird Wars II: Hell in the Hedgerows 202
Weird Wars: Weird Wars II: Horrors of Weird War II 202
Weird Wars: Weird Wars II: Island of Dreams 202
Weird Wars: Weird Wars II: Land of the Rising Dead 202
Wendigo Tales: A Tale of Weird Wars: Hellfighters 202
Wendigo Tales: A Tale of Weird Wars: Los! 202
Wendigo Tales: A Tale of Weird Wars: No Man's Land 202
Wendigo Tales: A Tale of Weird Wars: Raid on Fort Douaumont 202–203
Wendigo Tales: A Tale of Weird Wars: Teufelshunde 203
Wendigo Tales: A Tale of Weird Wars: With Utmost Dispatch 203
Wendigo Tales: A Tale of Weird Wars: Without Fear 203
Wendigo Tales: A Tale of Weird Wars: Wunderwaffe 203
Werewolf of Terror 102
Werewolf Women of the S.S. 203
The Werewolf's Tale 203
Werewolves 1, 11, 46, 68, 85, 87, 95, 102, 118, 132, 134, 137, 150, 156, 176, 203, 207
Where Dead Soldiers Walk 203
"The White Battalion" 203–204
White Tiger 204
The Whizzer 14, 113–114, 126, 204
The Wild, Wild West 204–205
The Wild, Wild West Revisited 205
Window of Time: A Story 205
Wings Comics **78**
Wings to the Kingdom 205
Witchblade 205–206
Witchfinder General 206
The Witching Hour 206
The Witness Tree and the Shadow of the Noose 206
Wolfenstein 206
Wolfenstein: Enemy Territory 206
Wolfenstein: The New Order 206
Wolfenstein: The Old Blood 206, **207**
The Wolf's Hour 206
Wolverine 170, 207, 211
The Wolverine 207
Wonder Woman 5, 20, 50, 107, 207–210
World War Cthulhu 210
World War Cthulhu: A Collection of Lovecraftian War Stories 210
World War I 1–2, **4**, 11, 18, 20, 25, 28, 30–31, 34–35, 40, 42, 46, 48, 52–54, 57–58, 64, 66–67, 73–74, 78–82, 84, 88, 91–92, 96, 102–105, 111, 122–123, 128, 137, 140, 142, 150–151, 155, 160, 163–164, 170, 174, 176–177, 179, 184, 186, 191, 197, 199
World War II 1–2, 5–6, 9–10, 12–14, 16–25, 27–33, 35–43, 46–50, 52–54, 56, 58–68, 70–77, 80–89, 91–92, 96–104, 106–107, 109–110, 114–117, 119, 121–126, 131–132, 134, 136–137, 139, 141–144, 148–152, 155–164, 166–168, 170–181, 183–186, 190–194, 196–200
Worldwar: In the Balance 210
Wunderwaffen 210
Wunderwaffen Présente Space Reich 210–211
Wunderwaffen Présente Zeppelin's War 211

X Men: Magneto Testament 211
X-Men Origins: Wolverine 211

The Yank and the Rebel 211
Yankee Doodle Jones 211–212
Yellow Blue Tibia 212
The Yesterday Machine 212
Young Allies 212
The Young Indiana Jones Chronicles 212
Youth Without Youth 212–213

Zipang 213
ZMD: Zombies of Mass Destruction 213
Zombie Lake 213
Zombie War 213
Zombies vs. Nazis: A Lost History of the Walking Dead 213–214
Zone Troopers 214

www.ingramcontent.com/pod-product-compliance
Lightning Source LLC
Chambersburg PA
CBHW081552300426
44116CB00015B/2852